**Progress in Probability and Statistics**
**Vol. 2**

**Edited by**
**P. Huber and**
**M. Rosenblatt**

Birkhäuser
Boston · Basel · Stuttgart

Harry Kesten

# Percolation Theory for Mathematicians

1982

Birkhäuser
Boston • Basel • Stuttgart

Author:

Harry Kesten
Department of Mathematics
Cornell University
Ithaca, NY 14853

Library of Congress Cataloging in Publication Data

Kesten, Harry, 1931-
Percolation theory for mathematicians.

(Progress in probability and statistics ; v. 2)
Bibliography: p.
Includes index.
1. Percolation (Statistical physics) I. Title.
II. Series.
QC174.85.P45K47 1982 530.1'3 82-19746
ISBN 3-7643-3107-0 (Switzerland)

CIP-Kurztitelaufnahme der Deutschen Bibliothek

Kesten, Harry:
Percolation theory for mathematicians / Harry Kesten. - Boston ; Basel ; Stuttgart : Birkhauser, 1982.
(Progress in probability and statistics ; Vol. 2)
ISBN 3-7643-3107-0

NE: GT



ISBN 3-7643-3107-0

Printed in USA

# PREFACE

Quite apart from the fact that percolation theory had its origin in an honest applied problem (see Hammersley and Welsh (1980)), it is a source of fascinating problems of the best kind a mathematician can wish for: problems which are easy to state with a minimum of preparation, but whose solutions are (apparently) difficult and require new methods. At the same time many of the problems are of interest to or proposed by statistical physicists and not dreamt up merely to demonstrate ingenuity.

Progress in the field has been slow. Relatively few results have been established rigorously, despite the rapidly growing literature with variations and extensions of the basic model, conjectures, plausibility arguments and results of simulations. It is my aim to treat here some basic results with rigorous proofs. This is in the first place a research monograph, but there are few prerequisites; one term of any standard graduate course in probability should be more than enough. Much of the material is quite recent or new, and many of the proofs are still clumsy. Especially the attempt to give proofs valid for as many graphs as possible led to more complications than expected. I hope that the Applications and Examples provide justification for going to this level of generality. I taught a graduate course on this material at Cornell University in Spring 1981, but the beginning of the monograph was a set of notes for a series of lectures at Kyoto University, Japan, which I visited in summer 1981 on a Fellowship of the Japan Society for the Promotion of Science.

I am indebted to a large number of people for helpful discussions. I especially value various suggestions made by J.T. Cox, R. Durrett, G.R. Grimmett and S. Kotani. I also wish to thank members of the Department of Mathematics at Kyoto University, and in particular my host, Professor S. Watanabe, for their hospitality and for giving me the opportunity to try out a first version of these notes in their seminar. Last but not least, I am grateful to the National Science

Foundation and the Japan Society for the Promotion of Science for their financial support during my work on this monograph.

The reader should be aware of the fact that some standard notation is defined only in the Index of Symbols at the end.

Ithaca, New York, July 1982

TABLE OF CONTENTS

## 1. INTRODUCTION AND SUMMARY.

The earliest example of percolation was discussed in Broadbent (1954) and Broadbent and Hammersley (1957) as a model for the spread of fluid or gas through a random medium. The fluid, say, spreads through channels; fluid will move through a channel if and only if the channel is wide enough. There is therefore no randomness in the motion of the fluid itself, such as in a diffusion process, but only in the medium, i.e., in the system of channels. Broadbent and Hammersley modeled this as follows. The channels are the edges or bonds between adjacent sites on the integer lattice in the plane, $\mathbb{Z}^2$. Each bond is passable (blocked) with probability $p(q = 1 - p)$, and all bonds are independent of each other. Let $P_p$ denote the corresponding probability measure for the total configuration of all the bonds. One is now interested in probabilistic properties of the configuration of passable bonds, and, especially in the dependence on the basic parameter $p$ of these properties. Broadbent and Hammersley began with the question whether fluid from outside a large region, say outside $|x| < N$, can reach the origin. This is of course equivalent to asking for the probability of a passable path[1)] from the origin to $|x| \geq N$. For $v \in \mathbb{Z}^2$, let $W(v)$ be the union of all edges which belong to a passable path starting at $v$. This is the set of all points which can be reached by fluid from $v$. It is called the open component or cluster of $v$. $W(v)$ is empty iff the four edges incident on $v$ are blocked. If we write $W$ for $W(0)$, then the above question asks for the behavior for large $N$ of

$$P_p \{ W \cap \{|x| \geq N\} \neq \emptyset\} . \tag{1.1}$$

---

1) This is a path made up of passable edges between neighbors of $\mathbb{Z}^2$. Two successive edges of the path must have a vertex of $\mathbb{Z}^2$ in common. Precise definitions are given in later chapters.

The limit of (1.1) as $N \to \infty$ equals

(1.2) $$\theta(p) := P_p\{\# W = \infty\} ,$$

where $\#W$ denotes the number of edges in $W$. It is immediate that $\theta(0) = 0$, $\theta(1) = 1$ and that $p \to \theta(p)$ is non-decreasing. Therefore the so called critical probability

(1.3) $$p_H := \sup\{p : \theta(p) = 0\}$$

is such that $\theta(p) = 0$ for $p < p_H$, and $\theta(p) > 0$ for $p > p_H$. Broadbent and Hammersley (1957), Hammersley (1957), and Hammersley (1959) made the remarkable discovery that $p_H$ lies strictly between 0 and 1, and in fact

(1.4) $$\frac{1}{\lambda} \le p_H \le 1 - \frac{1}{\lambda} ,$$

where $\lambda$ is the so-called connectivity constant of $\mathbb{Z}^2$. The exact value of $\lambda$ is unknown, but one trivially has $\lambda \le 3$. Thus, there are two regions for the parameter $p$ with drastically different behavior of the system. For $p < p_H$ no infinite clusters are formed. For $p > p_H$ there is a positive probability of an infinite cluster. In fact, Harris (1960) proved that with probability one there is a unique infinite cluster, when $p > p_H$ (see also Fisher (1961)). The existence of a threshold value such as $p_H$ was well known in many models of statistical mechanics, in particular in the Ising model for magnetism. Moreover the proof of (1.4) involved a Peierls argument - i.e., a counting of certain paths and contours - quite familiar to students of critical phenomena. As a consequence much of the work on percolation theory has and is being done by people in statistical mechanics, in the hope that the percolation model is simple enough to allow explicit computation of many quantities which are hard to deal with in various other models for critical phenomena. Despite the considerable activity in the field, as witnessed by the recent survey articles of Stauffer (1979), Essam (1980), Hammersley and Welsh (1980), Wierman (1982a), few mathematically rigorous results have been obtained. In this monograph we want to present those results which can be proved rigorously. As our title indicates we expect that the stress on rigour will appeal more to the mathematician than the physicist. Even mathematicians will surely become impatient with the unpleasant details of many a proof; it often happened to the author while writing the proofs. What is worse though, there are quite a few phenomena about which we cannot (yet?) say much, if anything, rigorously. This monograph will therefore not go as far as physicists would like.

We stressed above the interest for statistical mechanics of percolation theory, because that seems the most important area of application for percolation theory. There are, however, other interpretations and applications of percolation theory such as the spread of disease in an orchard; the reader is referred to Frisch and Hammersley (1963) for a list of some of these.

In the remaining part of this introduction we want to summarize the results and questions which are treated here. Much of the early work dealt with the determination of the critical probability $p_H$ defined above. Harris (1960) improved the lower bound in (1.4) to $p_H \geq \frac{1}{2}$. Sykes and Essam (1964) gave an ingenious, but incomplete, argument that $p_H$ should equal $\frac{1}{2}$. No progress on this problem seems to have been made between 1964 and the two independent articles Seymour and Welsh (1978) and Russo (1978). These articles introduced two further critical probabilities:

(1.5) $$p_T = \sup \{p : E_p\{\#W\} < \infty \}$$

and [1)]

(1.6) $$p_S = \sup \{p : \lim \tau_0((n,n),1,p) = 0\} \quad ,$$

where

(1.7) $$\tau_0((n,n),1,p) = P_p \{ \exists \text{ passable path in } [o,n] \times [o,3n] \text{ connecting the left and right edge of this rectangle} \} .$$

1) $p_S$ appears explicitly only in Seymour and Welsh (1978) and is defined slightly differently from (1.6). However, it turns out that under certain symmetry conditions the two definitions lead to the same $p_S$. For our treatment (1.6) is the more useful definition.

$p_T$ separates the p-values where the expected size of the cluster of the origin is finite and infinite, respectively. $p_S$ concerns the possibility of crossing large rectangles. For $p < p_S$ the probability of a passable horizontal crosssing of a rectangle of size $n \times 3n$ tends to zero, while such crossings occur with a probability bounded away from zero - at least along a subsequence of n's - if $p > p_S$. Seymour and Welsh and Russo proved various relations between $p_H$, $p_T$ and $p_S$ which finally enabled Kesten (1980a) to prove $p_H = p_T = p_S = \frac{1}{2}$. This will be a special case of the main theorem in Ch. 3 .

The problem discussed so far is called the bond-percolation problem for $\mathbb{Z}^2$. To describe the contents of Theorems 3.1 and 3.2 somewhat more, we observe first that one can easily replace $\mathbb{Z}^2$ by any infinite graph $\mathcal{G}$ . One obtains bond-percolation on $\mathcal{G}$, by choosing the edges of $\mathcal{G}$ independently of each other as passable or blocked. In this case the clusters $W(v)$ can be defined as above. Another variant of the model is site-percolation on $\mathcal{G}$. One now divides the sites, rather than the bonds into two classes. Usually these are named "occupied" and "vacant". Again the classifications of the sites are random and independent of each other. The occupied cluster of v, W(v), will now be defined as the union of all edges and vertices, which can be reached from v by a path on $\mathcal{G}$ which passes only through occupied sites. In both bond- and site-percolation one often allows different probabilities for different bonds to be passable, or sites to be occupied. Normally, one only allows a finite number of parameters; the graph and the pattern of probabilities assigned to the bonds or edges are taken periodic. For instance, Sykes and Essam (1964) considered the bond-problem on $\mathbb{Z}^2$ in which each horizontal (vertical) bond is passable with probability $p_{hor}$ ($p_{vert.}$). In all cases the first question is when percolation occurs, i.e., for which values of the parameters do infinite clusters arise? In only very few cases has one been able to determine this "percolative region" in the parameter space explicitly. These were all derived heuristically already by Sykes and Essam (1964). Theorem 3.1 contains a rigourous confirmation of most of the Sykes and Essam work. This includes the triangular site problem (with one parameter; the critical probability equals $\frac{1}{2}$), the two parameter bond-problem on $\mathbb{Z}^2$ mentioned above (percolation occurs iff $p_{hor} + p_{vert} > 1$) and a two parameter bond-problem on the triangular and hexagonal lattice. (Wierman (1981) gave the first rigorous treatment of the one-parameter case; Sykes and Essam allow three different probabilities for different bonds, but our method requires too much symmetry to be applicable to the original three parameter problem).

Theorems 3.1 and 3.2 only apply to so called matching pairs of graphs $\mathcal{G}$ and $\mathcal{G}^*$ in the plane with one of the coordinate-axes as symmetry axis and certain relations between $\mathcal{G}$ and $\mathcal{G}^*$. Moreover these theorems only yield explicit answers in the few examples mentioned above. In other cases the best one can obtain from the theorems is some generalized form of the result

$$p_H = p_T = p_S \quad , \tag{1.8}$$

and even this often requires extra work. We generalize Russo (1981) in demonstrating (1.8) for a two-parameter site-problem on $\mathbb{Z}^2$, and a one-parameter site-problem on the diced lattice.

The emphasis in the recent physics literature has shifted to power laws or scaling laws. In one-parameter problems, many quantities show some kind of singular behavior in their dependence on the basic parameter $p$, as $p$ approaches $p_H$. Many people believe, and numerical evidence supports them, that the singular behavior will be like that of powers of $|p-p_H|$ (see Stauffer (1979), Essam (1980)). More specifically, one expects that (see p.422 for $E_p$)

$$\theta(p) \sim C(p-p_H)^{\beta} \quad , p \downarrow p_H , \tag{1.9}$$

$$E_p\{\#W; \#W < \infty\} \sim C_{\pm} |p-p_H|^{-\gamma\pm} , p \to p_H , \tag{1.10}$$

for some positive constants $C, C_{\pm}, \beta, \gamma\pm$, where the plus (minus) in (1.10) refers to the approach of $p-p_H$ to zero from the positive (negative) side. The meaning of (1.9) or (1.10) is still somewhat vague. It may mean that the ratio of the left and right hand side tends to one, but its meaning may be as weak as convergence of the ratio of the logarithms of the left and right hand side to one. In addition there is the belief that the exponents $\beta$ and $\gamma$ are universal, that is, that their values depend only on the dimension of the graph $\mathcal{G}$, but are (practically) the same for a large class of graphs. The numerical evidence presently available does not seem to rule this out (see Essam (1980), Appendix 1). We still seem to be far removed from proving any power law. The best results known to us are presented in Ch. 8.

There we prove power estimates of the form

$$(1.11) \qquad C_1(p-p_H)^{\beta_1} \le \theta(p) \le C_2(p-p_H)^{\beta_2}, \quad p \ge p_H,$$

$$(1.12) \qquad C_3\,|p-p_H|^{-\gamma_1} \le E_p\{\#W;\ \#W < \infty\} \le C_4\,|p-p_H|^{-\gamma_2}$$

for some positive $C_i$, $\beta_i$ and $\gamma_i$, for bond- or site-percolation on $\mathbb{Z}^2$.

Another function which is expected to have a power law is the second derivative of $\Delta(p)$, where $\Delta(p)$ is the average number of clusters per site under $P_p$ (see Ch. 9 for a precise definition). The arguments of Sykes and Essam (1964) for determining $p_H$ referred to above were based on this function $\Delta(p)$. On the basis of analogy with statistical mechanics they assumed that $p \to \Delta(p)$ has only one singularity and that it is located at $p = p_H$. In Sect. 9.3 we show that for bond- and site-percolation $\Delta(.)$ is twice continuously differentiable on $[0,1]$, including at $p_H$ and that it is analytic for $p \neq p_H$. However, we have been unable to show that $\Delta(.)$ has a singularity at $p_H$.

The values for $\beta_1$ and $\beta_2$, or $\gamma_1$ and $\gamma_2$, in (1.11) and (1.12) obtained from our proof are still very far apart. The difficulty lies in part in finding good estimates for

$$(1.13) \qquad P_p\{n \le \#W < \infty\}$$

for large $n$ and $p < p_H$, but close to $p_H$. This problem is treated (in a multiparameter setting) in Ch. 5, where it is shown that for $p < p_T$ (1.13) decreases exponentially in $n$, i.e., that (1.13) is bounded by

$$(1.14) \qquad C_1(p)\exp - C_2(p)\,n \quad .$$

This estimate works for all graphs, but unfortunately only up to $p_T$. Only for those graphs for which we know that $p_T = p_H$ can this estimate be used for deriving power laws, and even then, it leads to poor estimates of $\beta_i$ and $\gamma_i$, because the estimate for $C_2(p)$ in Ch. 5 is a very rough one.

Some results on the behavior of (1.13) for $p > p_H$ and the continuity of $\theta(.)$ are in Sect. 5.2 and 5.3.

In Ch. 10 we prove that

$$(1.15) \qquad p_H(\mathcal{H}) > p_H(\mathcal{G})$$

for certain graphs $\mathcal{G}$, $\mathcal{H}$, with $\mathcal{H}$ a subgraph of $\mathcal{G}$. Here $p_H(\mathcal{G})$ is the critical probability $p_H$ for site-percolation on $\mathcal{G}$.

A different class of problems is treated in Ch. 11, which deals with random electrical networks. For simplicity we restrict discussion here to a bond-problem on $\mathbb{Z}^d$. Assume each bond between two vertices of $\mathbb{Z}^d$ is a resistor of 1 ohm with probability $p$, and removed from the graph with probability $q = 1 - p$ (equivalently we can make it an insulator with infinite resistance with probability $q$). Let $B_n$ be the cube

$$B_n = \{x = (x(1),\dots,x(d)): 0 \leq x(i) \leq n, 1 \leq i \leq d\}$$

and

$$A_n^0 = \{x : x \in B_n, x(1) = 0\} \quad \text{and}$$

$$A_n^1 = \{x: x \in B_n, x(1) = n\}$$

its left and right face respectively. Finally, let $R_n$ be the electrical resistance of the random network in $B_n$, between $A_n^0$ and $A_n^1$. We are interested in the behavior of $n^{d-2}R_n$ as $n \to \infty$ for various $p$. (see Ch. 11 for the motivation of the power of $n$). This leads to the introduction of a further critical probability $p_R$. Various definitions are possible; we expect that they all lead to the same value of $p_R$. Here we only mention

$$(1.16) \qquad p_R = \inf\{p : P_p\{\limsup n^{d-2}R_n < \infty\} = 1\} .$$

It is immediate from the definitions that $R_n = \infty$ infinitely often a.s. $[P_p]$ when $p < p_S$ (and in fact for all $d$ we show that $R_n = \infty$ eventually a.s. $[P_p]$ when $p < p_S$). We also show $p_R \leq \frac{1}{2}$ so that

$$(1.17) \qquad p_S \leq p_R \leq \frac{1}{2} \quad \text{for all} \quad d \geq 2 .$$

For $d = 2$ we show that actually

$$p_H = p_T = p_S = p_R = \frac{1}{2}, \tag{1.18}$$

so that there still is only one critical probability. The last equality in (1.18) is obtained from the existence of a constant $C > 0$ such that for $p > \frac{1}{2}$ one has

(1.19) $P_p\{$for all large $n$ there exist $Cn$ disjoint passable paths in $[0,n]\times[0,3n]$ connecting the left and right edge of this rectangle$\} = 1$.

When we compare (1.19) with the definition (1.6) of $p_S$ we see that for bond-percolation on $\mathbb{Z}^2$, not only is $\frac{1}{2}$ the separation point between the p-values for which there does not or does exist a single passable crossing of a large rectangle, but once $p$ gets above this separation point, there are necessarily very many disjoint passable crossings.

We conclude this monograph with a list of some unsolved problems in Ch. 12.

For the expert we briefly point out which parts of this monograph have not appeared in print before; we also list some of the important topics which have been omitted. New are the determination in Ch. 3 of the percolative region in some multiparameter percolation problems, an improved lower bound for the cluster size distribution in the percolative region in Sect. 5.2, the strict inequalities in Sect. 10.2 (even though a special case of this has been proven recently by Higuchi (1982)) and the treatment of random electric networks in Ch. 11. As for restrictions and omissions, we are dealing only with Bernoulli percolation on the sites or bonds of an undirected graph. Thus we do not discuss mixed bond- site problems (about which little is known so far), but also omit "directed percolation problems" for which Durrett and Griffeath (1983) recently have obtained many new results, and we also omit any discussion of models in which the bonds or sites are not independent. Thus there is no mention of the Ising model, even though Kasteleyn and Fortuin (1969) proved an exact relation between the Ising model and percolation. As far as we are aware this relationship has enhanced people's intuitive understanding of both models, but it has not helped in proving new results about either model. Another area that is essentially untouched is percolation in dimension $\geq 3$. Except in Ch. 5 the methods are strictly two-dimensional. Recently Aizenman (1982) and Aizenman and Fröhlich (1982) have dealt with random surfaces. These may be the proper dual for bond percolation on $\mathbb{Z}^3$ and may lead to a treatment of percolation problems in dimension three.

We have also left out the central limit theorems for various percolation-theoretical functions of Brånvall (1980), Cox and Grimmett (1981), Newman (1980) and Newman and Wright (1981).

Finally, we mention a new and highly original proof of Russo (1982) for the equality $p_H = p_S$, which is known to imply $p_H = \frac{1}{2}$ for bond-percolation on $\mathbb{Z}^2$. Russo's proof uses less geometry than ours and may be useful for problems in higher dimensions. We stuck with the more geometric proof of Theorems 3.1 and 3.2 because so far it is the only method of proof which we know how to jack up to obtain the power estimates (1.11) and (1.12). Also the geometric method of proof seems to be the only suitable one for obtaining the strict inequalities of Sect. 10.2.

## 2. WHICH GRAPHS DO WE CONSIDER?

This chapter discusses the graphs with which we shall work, as well as several graph-theoretical tools. Except for the basic definitions in Sect. 2.1-2.3 the reader should skip the remaining parts of this chapter until the need for them arises.

### 2.1 Periodic graphs.

Throughout this monograph we consider only graphs which are imbedded in $\mathbb{R}^d$ for some $d < \infty$. Only when strictly necessary shall we make a distinction between a graph and its image under the imbedding. Usually we denote the graph by $\mathcal{G}$, a generic vertex of $\mathcal{G}$ by u, v or w (with or without subscripts), and a generic edge of $\mathcal{G}$ by e, f or g (with or without subscripts). "Site" will be synonymous with "vertex", and "bond" will be synonymous with "edge". The collection of vertices of $\mathcal{G}$ will always be a countable subset of $\mathbb{R}^d$. The collection of edges of $\mathcal{G}$ will also be countable, and each edge will be a simple arc - that is, a homeomorphic image of the interval $[0,1]$ - in $\mathbb{R}^d$, with two vertices as endpoints but no vertices of $\mathcal{G}$ in its interior. In particular we take an edge to be closed, i.e., we include the endpoints in the edge. If e is an edge, then we denote its interior, i.e., e minus its endpoints, by $\mathring{e}$. We shall say that e is <u>incident to</u> v if v is an endpoint of e. We only allow graphs in which the endpoints of each edge are distinct; thus we assume

(2.1) $\mathcal{G}$ contains no loops.

We shall, however, allow several edges between the same pair of distinct vertices.

The notation

$$v_1 \mathcal{G} v_2 \text{ or equivalently } v_2 \mathcal{G} v_1$$

will be used to denote that $v_1$ and $v_2$ are <u>adjacent</u> or <u>neighbors</u> on $\mathcal{G}$. This means that there exists an edge of $\mathcal{G}$ with endpoints $v_1$ and $v_2$.

A path on $\mathcal{G}$ will be a sequence $r = (v_0, e_1, \dots, e_\nu, v_\nu)$ with $v_0, \dots, v_\nu$ vertices of $\mathcal{G}$ and $e_1, \dots, e_\nu$ edges of $\mathcal{G}$ such that $e_{i+1}$ is an edge with endpoints $v_i$ and $v_{i+1}$. We call $v_0$ $(v_\nu)$ the first or initial (last or final) vertex of $r$ and say that $r$ is a path from $v_0$ to $v_\nu$. The path $r$ is called self-avoiding if all its vertices are distinct. Unless otherwise stated all paths are tacitly taken to be self-avoiding. In the few cases where we have to deal with paths which are not necessarily self-avoiding we shall call them paths with possible double points. If $\mathcal{G}$ is any graph then we can always turn a path with possible double points $r = (v_0, e_1, \dots, e_\nu, v_\nu)$ into a self-avoiding sub-path $\tilde{r}$ with the same initial and final vertex as $r$. This is done by the process of loop-removal which works as follows: Let $\rho_1$ be the smallest index for which there exists a $\tau_1 > \rho_1$ with $v_{\tau_1} = v_{\rho_1}$. From the possible $\tau_1$ with this property choose the largest one. Form the path $r_1 = (v_0, e_1, \dots, v_{\rho_1} = v_{\tau_1}, e_{\tau_1+1}, v_{\tau_1+1}, \dots, e_\nu, v_\nu)$ by removal of the "loop" $(v_{\rho_1}, e_{\rho_1+1}, v_{\rho_1+1}, \dots, e_{\tau_1})$. The piece $(v_0, \dots, v_{\rho_1})$ of $r$ is free of double-points and, by the maximality of $\tau_1$, it is not hit again by the remaining piece $(e_{\tau_1+1}, \dots, e_\nu, v_\nu)$ of $r_1$. Thus, if $r_1$ still has a double point there have to exist $\tau_1 < \rho_2 < \tau_2$ with $v_{\rho_2} = v_{\tau_2}$. Again we choose the smallest such $\rho_2$ and then the largest $\tau_2$ for that $\rho_2$, and remove from $r_1$ the piece $(v_{\rho_2}, e_{\rho_2+1}, \dots, e_{\tau_2})$ to obtain another subpath $r_2$ of $r_1$. We continue in this way until we arrive at a path $\tilde{r}$ without double points. One easily verifies that removal of a loop neither changes the first nor the last vertex of a path.

In addition to (2.1) we shall almost always impose the conditions (2.2)-(2.5) below on our graphs:

(2.2) $\mathcal{G}$ is imbedded in $\mathbb{R}^d$ in such a way that each coordinate vector of $\mathbb{R}^d$ is a period for the image.

By (2.2) we mean that $v \in \mathbb{R}^d$ is a vertex of (the image of) $\mathcal{G}$ iff $v + \sum_1^d k_i \xi_i$ is a vertex of $\mathcal{G}$ for all $k_i \in \mathbb{Z}$, where $\xi_i$ denotes the ith coordinate vector of $\mathbb{R}^d$. Also, $e \subset \mathbb{R}^d$ is an edge of (the image of) $\mathcal{G}$ iff $e + \sum_1^d k_i \xi_i$ is an edge for all $k_i \in \mathbb{Z}$.

(2.3) There exists a $z < \infty$ such that there are at most $z$ edges of $\mathcal{G}$ incident to any vertex of $\mathcal{G}$.

(2.4) All edges of $\mathcal{G}$ have finite diameter. Every compact set of $\mathbb{R}^d$ intersects only finitely many edges of $\mathcal{G}$.

(2.5) $\mathcal{G}$ is connected.

Of course (2.5) means that for every pair of vertices $v_1$, $v_2$ of $\mathcal{G}$ there exists a path on $\mathcal{G}$ from $v_1$ to $v_2$.

Def. 1. A periodic graph $\mathcal{G}$ is a graph which is imbedded in some $\mathbb{R}^d$, $d < \infty$, such that (2.1)-(2.5) hold. ///

The name "periodic graph" is a bit of a misnomer. It is really the imbedding which is periodic. It will be obvious from Ch. 3 that our percolation problems depend only on the abstract structure of the graph $\mathcal{G}$, and not on its imbedding. For the proofs it is often advantageous to change the imbedding from a standard one, by mapping $\mathbb{R}^d$ onto itself by an affine isomorphism. As stated, this does not effect the percolation theory problems. We illustrate with some standard examples.

Examples.

(i) One of the most familiar graphs is the simple quadratic lattice. It is imbedded in $\mathbb{R}^2$; its vertex set is $\mathbb{Z}^2$, and the edges are the straight-line segments between $(i_1,i_2)$ and $(i_1 \pm 1, i_2)$ and between $(i_1,i_2)$ and $(i_1,i_2 \pm 1)$, $i_1,i_2 \in \mathbb{Z}$. Thus, two vertices $(i_1,i_2)$ and $(j_1,j_2)$ $(i_r,j_r \in \mathbb{Z})$ are neighbors iff

$$|i_1-j_1| + |i_2-j_2| = 1. \tag{2.6}$$

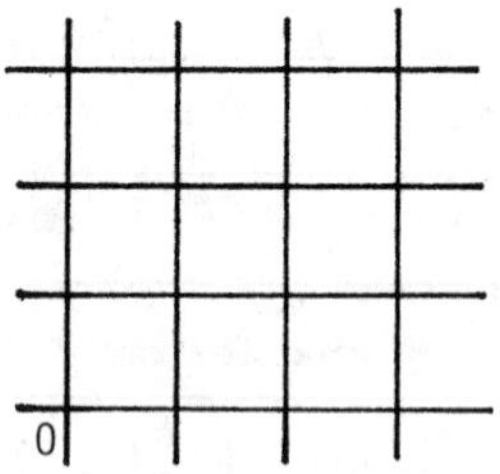


Figure 2.1 $\mathcal{G}_0$

This is a periodic graph, and we denote it by $\mathcal{G}_0$ throughout this monograph.

(ii) For bond-percolation on $\mathbb{Z}^2$ one wants to use the graph which is obtained by adding diagonals to alternating squares in $\mathcal{G}_0$.

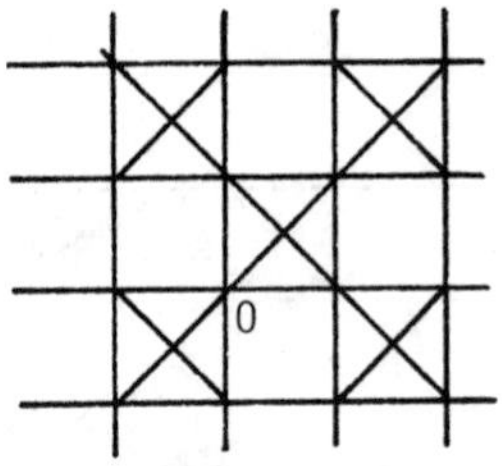

Figure 2.2

The formal description for this imbedding in $\mathbb{R}^2$ is that the vertex set is $\mathbb{Z}^2$, and two vertices $v = (i_1, i_2)$ and $w = (j_1, j_2)$ $(i_r, j_r \in \mathbb{Z})$ are neighbors iff (2.6), or (2.7) below holds.

(2.7) $\quad |i_1 - j_1| = |i_2 - j_2| = 1$ and $i_1 + i_2$ is odd or $i_1 - i_2$ is even.

Under this imbedding we do not have a periodic graph, because the periods are only $2\xi_1$ and $2\xi_2$, where $\xi_1 = (1,0)$, $\xi_2 = (0,1)$ are the coordinate vectors of $\mathbb{R}^2$. For our purposes the preferred imbedding, which does give us a periodic graph, is obtained by translating the coordinate system in Fig. 2.2 by the vector $(\frac{1}{2}, \frac{1}{2})$, rotating it over 45° and changing the scale by a factor $\sqrt{2}$. This gives us the periodic graph which we shall call $\mathcal{G}_1$, and which is drawn in Fig. 2.3.

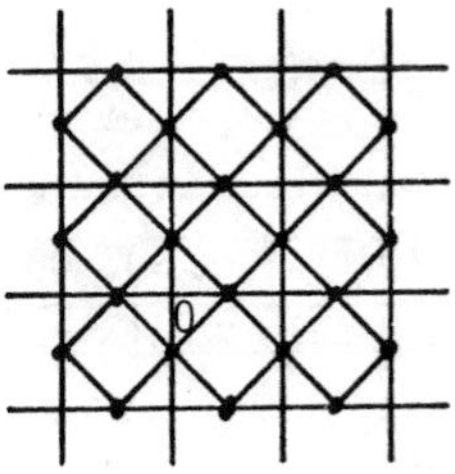

Figure 2.3 $\mathcal{G}_1$

The vertices of $\mathcal{G}_1$ are located at the points $(i_1+\frac{1}{2},i_2)$ and $(i_1,i_2+\frac{1}{2})$, $i_1,i_2 \in \mathbb{Z}$. Two vertices $v = (v(1),v(2))$ and $w = (w(1),w(2))$ are adjacent iff

(2.8) $$v(1) = w(1) \in \mathbb{Z}, v(2),w(2) \in \mathbb{Z}+\frac{1}{2} \text{ and } |v(2)-w(2)| = 1$$

or

(2.9) $$v(2) = w(2) \in \mathbb{Z}, v(1),w(1) \in \mathbb{Z}+\frac{1}{2} \text{ and } |v(1)-w(1)| = 1$$

or

(2.10) $$|v(1)-w(1)| = |v(2)-w(2)| = \frac{1}{2}.$$

(iii) Another familiar example is the socalled triangular lattice: Divide $\mathbb{R}^2$ into equilateral triangles by means of the horizontal lines $x(2) = \frac{k}{2}\sqrt{3}$, $k \in \mathbb{Z}$, and lines under an angle of 60° or 120° with the first coordinate-axis through the points $(k,0)$, $k \in \mathbb{Z}$, see Fig. 2.4.

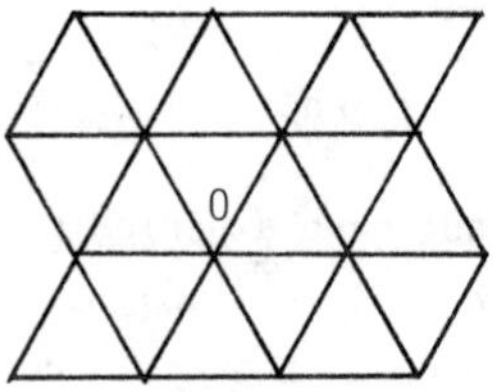


Figure 2.4

The vertices of the graph are the vertices of the equilateral triangles, and two such vertices are adjacent iff they are vertices of one and the same triangle. Even though the vector $(1,0)$ is a period for this imbedding, the vector $(0,1)$ is not. However, if we change the vertical scale by a factor $1/\sqrt{3}$ we obtain a periodic graph in $\mathbb{R}^2$. We denote it by $\mathcal{J}$. Its vertices are located at all points of the form $(i_1,i_2)$ or $(i_1+\frac{1}{2},i_2+\frac{1}{2})$, $i_1,i_2 \in \mathbb{Z}$; each vertex has six neighbors. The six neighbors of the vertex $v$ are

(2.11) $$v+(1,0),\ v+(\tfrac{1}{2},\tfrac{1}{2}),\ v+(-\tfrac{1}{2},\tfrac{1}{2}),$$
$$v+(-1,0),\ v+(-\tfrac{1}{2},-\tfrac{1}{2}), v+(\tfrac{1}{2},-\tfrac{1}{2}).$$

An amusing imbedding for the same graph - which we shall not use - is illustrated in Fig. 2.5. It shows that we can view $\mathcal{G}_0$ of ex. (i) as a subgraph of $\mathcal{T}$

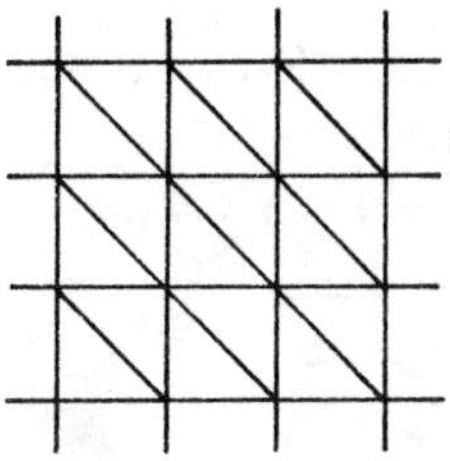

Figure 2.5

(iv) Another graph which we shall use for occasional illustrations is the hexagonal or honeycomb lattice. The usual way to imbed the hexagonal lattice is such that its faces are regular hexagons as illustrated in Fig. 2.6. The vertices are at the points

$$((k_1 + \frac{\ell}{2})\sqrt{3} + \cos(\frac{\pi}{6} + \frac{2\pi j}{6}), 3(k_2 + \frac{\ell}{2}) + \sin(\frac{\pi}{6} + \frac{2\pi j}{6})),$$

$$k_1, k_2 \in \mathbb{Z}, \ \ell = 0,1, \ 0 \leq j \leq 5.$$

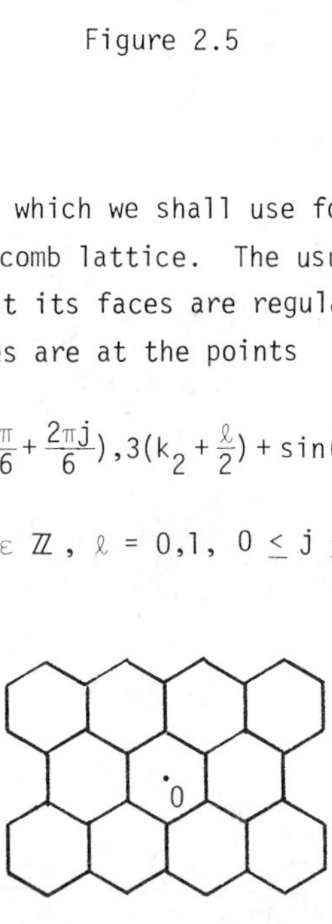


Figure 2.6 Hexagonal or honeycomb lattice

The origin is in the center of one of the hexagons and the periods are $(\sqrt{3},0)$ and $(0,3)$. We shall usually refer to this imbedding of the hexagonal lattice, even though it does not satisfy (2.2). We leave it to the reader to change scale so that (2.2) does become true.

(v) Our final example is the diced lattice, which is somewhat less familiar. We obtain it from the hexagonal lattice with vertices as in the last example by adding for each $k_1, k_2, \ell$ a vertex at $((k_1 + \frac{\ell}{2})\sqrt{3}, 3(k_2 + \frac{1}{2}\ell))$ (the center of one of the regular hexagons in Fig. 2.6) and connecting it to the three vertices

$$((k_1 + \tfrac{\ell}{2})\sqrt{3} + \cos(\tfrac{\pi}{6} + \tfrac{2\pi j}{6}), 3(k_2 + \tfrac{\ell}{2}) + \sin(\tfrac{\pi}{6} + \tfrac{2\pi j}{6})), \quad j = 1,3,5.$$

This is illustrated in Fig. 2.7. The periods of this imbedding are again $(\sqrt{3},0)$ and $(0,3)$.

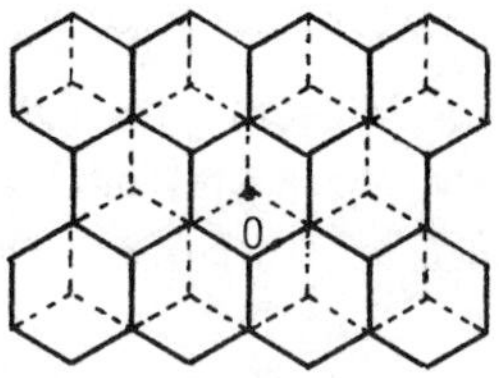


Figure 2.7 The diced lattice. It is obtained from the hexagonal lattice (solid lines) by adding the dashed edges.

## 2.2 Matching pairs.

With the exception of Ch. 5 we shall restrict ourselves to a special class of graphs imbedded in the plane. This class was introduced by Sykes and Essam (1964) and will be described in this section.

Def. 2. A mosaic $\mathcal{M}$ is a graph imbedded in $\mathbb{R}^2$ such that (2.1) and (2.4) hold, such that any two edges of $\mathcal{M}$ are either disjoint or have only one or two endpoints in common (these common endpoints are necessarily vertices of $\mathcal{M}$), and such that each component of $\mathbb{R}^2 \setminus \mathcal{M}$ is bounded by a Jordan curve made up of a finite number of edges of $\mathcal{M}$.

Comments.

(i) A graph which can be imbedded in $\mathbb{R}^2$ such that any two edges can have only endpoints in common is called planar. Thus, any mosaic is a planar graph. If a planar graph $\mathcal{M}$ is imbedded in such a way, then one calls each component of $\mathbb{R}^2 \backslash \mathcal{M}$ a face of $\mathcal{M}$.

(ii) The precise meaning of a "curve made up of edges of $\mathcal{M}$" is as follows: Let $e_1,\dots,e_\nu$ be edges of $\mathcal{M}$ given by the homeomorphisms $\phi_i: [0,1] \to \mathbb{R}^d$, and such that

$$\phi_i(1) = \phi_{i+1}(0), \tag{2.12}$$

i.e., the final point of $e_i$ equals the initial point of $e_{i+1}$. A curve J made up from $e_1,\dots,e_\nu$, or obtained by (successively) traversing a piece of $e_1,e_2,\dots,e_{\nu-1}$, and a piece of $e_\nu$ is a curve which can be represented by a map $\psi:[0,1] \to \mathbb{R}^d$ of the following form: for some $0 \le a < 1$, $0 < b \le 1$:

$$\psi(t) = \begin{cases} \phi_1(a+\nu(1-a)t), & 0 \le t \le \frac{1}{\nu}, \\ \phi_{i+1}\left(\nu(t-\frac{i}{\nu})\right), & \frac{i}{\nu} \le t \le \frac{i+1}{\nu}, \ 1 \le i \le \nu-2, \\ \phi_\nu\left(\nu b(t-\frac{\nu-1}{\nu})\right), & \frac{\nu-1}{\nu} \le t \le 1. \end{cases}$$

The last requirement of Def. 2 is that for each face F of $\mathcal{M}$ there exist edges $e_1,\dots,e_\nu$ satisfying (2.12) and with the final point of $e_\nu$ equal to the initial point of $e_1$, and such that the curve J made up of all of $e_1,e_2,\dots,e_{\nu-1}$ and all of $e_\nu$ is a Jordan curve with $F = \text{int}(J)$[1)]. In this case we call J the perimeter of F and the endpoints of the $e_i$ the vertices on the perimeter of F. In particular each face of a mosaic is bounded.

Def. 3. Let F be a face of a mosaic $\mathcal{M}$. Close-packing F means adding an edge to $\mathcal{M}$ between any pair of vertices on the perimeter on F which are not yet adjacent.

Comment.

(iii) Without loss of generality we shall choose the interiors of new edges in the imbedding inside F when we close-pack a face F. We shall actually construct them even more carefully in Comments 2.3 (i),

1) If J is a Jordan curve in $\mathbb{R}^2$ then $\mathbb{R}^2 \backslash J$ consists of a bounded component denoted by int(J) and an unbounded component denoted by ext(J).

(iii), (v) and 2.4 (iii) when we imbed $\mathcal{G}_{p\ell}$ .

Def. 4. Let $\mathcal{M}$ be a mosaic and $\mathcal{F}$ a subset of its collection of faces. The matching pair $(\mathcal{G},\mathcal{G}^*)$ of graphs based on $(\mathcal{M},\mathcal{F})$ is the following pair of graphs: $\mathcal{G}$ is the graph obtained from $\mathcal{M}$ by close-packing all faces in $\mathcal{F}$. $\mathcal{G}^*$ is the graph obtained from $\mathcal{M}$ by close packing all faces not in $\mathcal{F}$.

Comments.

(iv) If $(\mathcal{G},\mathcal{G}^*)$ is a matching pair based on $(\mathcal{M},\mathcal{F})$ then $\mathcal{M}$, $\mathcal{G}$ and $\mathcal{G}^*$ all have the same vertex set.

(v) If $(\mathcal{G},\mathcal{G}^*)$ is based on $(\mathcal{M},\mathcal{F})$, then $(\mathcal{G}^*,\mathcal{G})$ is a matching pair based on $(\mathcal{M},\mathcal{F}^*)$, where $\mathcal{F}^*$ is the collection of faces of $\mathcal{M}$ which are not in $\mathcal{F}$. Thus we can think of $\mathcal{G}$ as $(\mathcal{G}^*)^*$.

(vi) $\mathcal{F} = \emptyset$ or $\mathcal{F}$ = collection of all faces of $\mathcal{M}$ are allowed in Def. 2. Therefore any mosaic $\mathcal{M}$ equals the first graph of some matching pair - the one based on $(\mathcal{M},\emptyset)$. Compare Ex. (i) below.

(vii) In a matching pair usually at least one of the graphs $\mathcal{G}$ or $\mathcal{G}^*$ is not planar. However, if we add the edges to $\mathcal{M}$ in conformity with Comment (iii), then an edge e of $\mathcal{G}$ and an edge $e^*$ of $\mathcal{G}^*$ can intersect only at endpoints of these edges which are necessarily vertices of $\mathcal{M}$ (unless e and $e^*$ coincide). Two edges $e_1$ and $e_2$ of $\mathcal{G}$ can have an intersection which is not an end-point of both of them only if $e_1$ and $e_2$ are edges whose interiors lie in the same face F of $\mathcal{M}$, which is close-packed in $\mathcal{G}$. In this situation any pair of the endpoints of $e_1$ and $e_2$ are neighbors on $\mathcal{G}$ (because F is close-packed). The same comment applies to two edges $e_1^*$ and $e_2^*$ of $\mathcal{G}^*$.

Examples.

(i) Let $\mathcal{M} = \mathcal{G}_0$, as defined in Ex. 2.1 (i). If we take $\mathcal{F} = \emptyset$, then the complementary collection of faces, $\mathcal{F}^*$, consists of all squares into which the plane is divided by the lines $x(1)=k$ and $x(2)=\ell$ $(k,\ell \in \mathbb{Z})$. The matching pair $(\mathcal{G},\mathcal{G}^*)$ based on $(\mathcal{M},\mathcal{F})$ in this case is described by $\mathcal{G} = \mathcal{G}_0 = \mathcal{M}$ and $\mathcal{G}^*$ is the graph with vertex set $\mathbb{Z}^2$ while $(i_1,i_2)$ and $(j_1,j_2)$ are adjacent on $\mathcal{G}^*$ iff (2.6) holds or

$$|i_1-j_1| = |i_2-j_2| = 1. \tag{2.13}$$

The graphs $\mathcal{G}$ and $\mathcal{G}^*$ are illustrated in Fig. 2.8. $\mathcal{G}^*$ is obtained by adding all "diagonals" to $\mathcal{G}_0$.

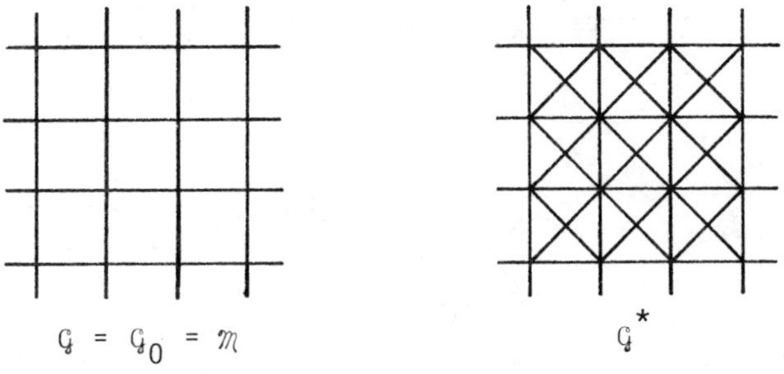


Figure 2.8

(ii) Again take $\mathcal{M} = \mathcal{G}_0$ as above, but this time take $\mathcal{F}$ to be the collection of unit squares $(i_1, i_1+1) \times (i_2, i_2+1)$ with $i_1+i_2$ even. $\mathcal{F}^*$ will consist of the unit squares $(i_1, i_1+1) \times (i_2, i_2+1)$ with $i_1+i_2$ odd. $\mathcal{G}$ will be the graph of Fig. 2.2. $\mathcal{G}^*$ will be a similar graph but now with the diagonals in the set of unit squares which is empty in $\mathcal{G}$. (The formal description is as for $\mathcal{G}$ in Ex. 2.1 (ii) but with odd and even interchanged in (2.7).) Fig. 2.9 shows a picture of the matching pair $(\mathcal{G}, \mathcal{G}^*)$ in this example.

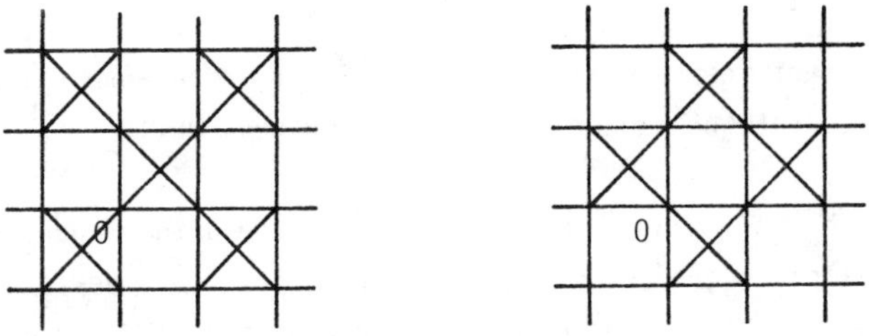


$\mathcal{G}$ Figure 2.9 $\mathcal{G}^*$

Clearly $\mathcal{G}$ and $\mathcal{G}^*$ are isomorphic as graphs. Such a pair is called <u>self-matching</u>.

(iii) Any triangular face is already close-packed. Thus if $\mathcal{M}$ has only triangular faces, then for every choice of $\mathcal{F}$ the matching pair based on $(\mathcal{M}, \mathcal{F})$ is $\mathcal{G} = \mathcal{M}$, $\mathcal{G}^* = \mathcal{M}$. Such a pair is again self-matching. An example of this situation is $\mathcal{M} = \mathcal{T}$, the triangular lattice of ex. 2.1 (iii). Another example for such an $\mathcal{M}$ is the centered quadratic lattice. Its vertex set is $\mathbb{Z}^2 \cup \{(i_1+\frac{1}{2}, i_2+\frac{1}{2}): i_1, i_2 \in \mathbb{Z}\}$.

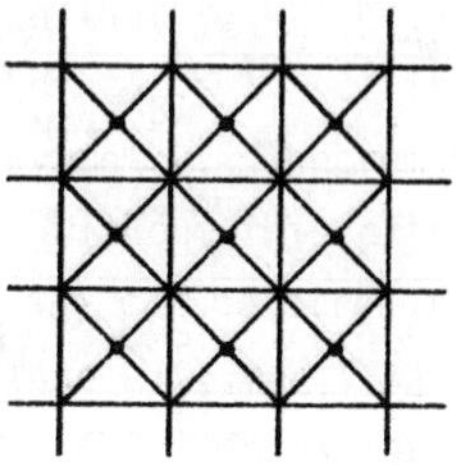

Figure 2.10 The centered quadratic lattice

Two vertices $(i_1, i_2)$, $(j_1, j_2)$ with $i_r, j_r \in \mathbb{Z}$ are adjacent iff (2.6) holds; $(i_1, i_2)$ and $(j_1+\frac{1}{2}, j_2+\frac{1}{2})$ are adjacent iff

(2.14) $\quad i_1 = j_1$ or $j_1+1$ and $i_2 = j_2$ or $j_2+1$.

This graph is not the same as $\mathcal{G}^*$ in Ex. 2.2 (i) because the present $\mathcal{M}$ has vertices at the centers of all the squares, while $\mathcal{G}^*$ of Ex. 2.2 (i) does not.

(iv) The following example illustrates the gain of generality of allowing multiple edges between the same vertices. The vertex set is $\mathbb{Z}^2 \cup \{i_1+\frac{1}{2}, i_2\}$ (i.e., we increase the vertex set $\mathbb{Z}^2$ by adding a vertex in the middle of each horizontal link). The following will be the edges in $\mathcal{M}$: any vertical link between $(i_1, i_2)$ and $(i_1, 1_2+1)$; the horizontal links between $(i_1, i_2)$ and $(i_1 \pm \frac{1}{2}, i_2)$; and two extra edges between $(i_1, i_2)$ and $(i_1+1, i_2)$, one running in each of the squares above and below the line $x(2) = i_2$ (see Fig. 2.11). The vertices $(i_1+\frac{1}{2}, i_2)$ belong to two triangular faces. If we take for $\mathcal{F}$ the collection of all other faces, i.e., the quadrilaterals, then $\mathcal{G}^* = \mathcal{M}$, while $\mathcal{G}$ gains the diagonals in each of the quadrilaterals. If we remove one of the edges from $(i_1, i_2)$ to $(i_1+1, i_2)$ from $\mathcal{G}$, to obtain a graph without multiple edges, then the resulting graph, $\mathcal{G}'$ say, contains the configurations of Fig. 2.12.

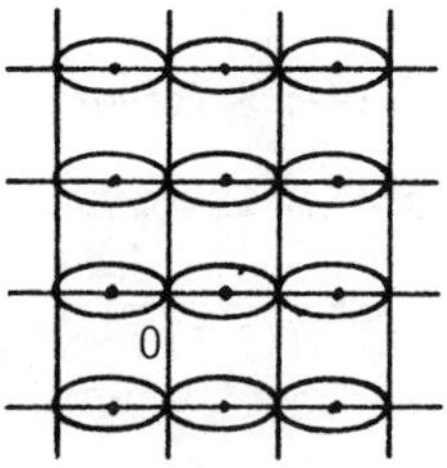

Figure 2.11 Illustration of multiple edges. $\mathscr{M}$

Figure 2.12

Two edges intersect in their interior, but they do not seem to belong to a close-packed face of a mosaic. Thus it seems impossible to view $\mathcal{G}'$ as one of a matching pair. Nevertheless, for the site-percolation problem $\mathcal{G}'$ is equivalent to $\mathcal{G}$ (see Ch. 3). It therefore seems of some use to allow multiple edges.

## 2.3 Planar modifications of matching pairs.

For many proofs it is a great convenience to work with planar graphs. The main advantage is that a self-avoiding path $r = (v_0, e_1, \dots, e_\nu, v_\nu)$ on a planar graph truly has no self intersections. I.e., even though "r is self-avoiding" in our terminology only means that all $v_i$ are different, on a planar graph this also implies that $e_i$ cannot intersect $e_j$ for $j > i$ unless $j = i+1$, and then $e_i \cap e_j = \{ v_i \}$ = the common endpoint of $e_i$ and $e_j$. This is obvious from the fact that on a planar graph two distinct edges can only intersect in a common endpoint. In view of these considerations we introduce planar modifications $\mathcal{G}_{p\ell}$ and $\mathcal{G}^*_{p\ell}$ of a matching pair $\mathcal{G}$ and $\mathcal{G}^*$, as well as planar modification $\mathcal{M}_{p\ell}$ of a mosaic $\mathcal{M}$. For our purposes $\mathcal{G}$ and $\mathcal{G}_{p\ell}$ (as well as $\mathcal{G}^*$ and $\mathcal{G}^*_{p\ell}$) will be practically interchangeable (see Lemma 2.1). Let $(\mathcal{G},\mathcal{G}^*)$ be a matching pair based on $(\mathcal{M},\mathcal{F})$. We then construct $\mathcal{G}_{p\ell}$ as follows: Its vertex set is the vertex set of $\mathcal{G}$ plus one additional vertex in each face $F$ of $\mathcal{F}$. The added vertex inside $F$ will be called the <u>central vertex</u> of $F$. Two vertices $v$ and $w$ of $\mathcal{G}_{p\ell}$ will be adjacent on $\mathcal{G}_{p\ell}$ iff $v$ and $w$ are adjacent on $\mathcal{M}$, or if one of them is the central vertex of some $F \in \mathcal{F}$ and the other is on the perimeter of the same face $F$. The edge set of $\mathcal{G}_{p\ell}$ therefore consists of the edge set of $\mathcal{M}$ plus, for each $F \in \mathcal{F}$, edges between the central vertex of $F$ and all the vertices on the perimeter of $\mathcal{F}$.

<u>Comments</u>.

(i) In order to show that $\mathcal{G}_{p\ell}$ is indeed planar we give an imbedding in $\mathbb{R}^2$ "explicitly". Let $F \in \mathcal{F}$ be a face with perimeter $J$. There then exists a homeomorphism $\psi$ from $\bar{F} := F \cup J$ onto the closed unit disc (by Theorem VI.17.1 of Newman (1951) or by the Riemann mapping theorem, Hille (1962), Theorem 17.5.3). Let $v_i$, $1 \le i \le \nu$ be the vertices of $\mathcal{G}$ (or $\mathcal{M}$) on $J$ and $w_i = \psi(v_i)$, $1 \le i \le \nu$ their images on the unit circle. Then place the central vertex of $F$ at $\psi^{-1}(0)$, and take for the edge from the central vertex to $v_i$ the inverse image under $\psi$ of the ray from 0 to $w_i$. We can use this construction at the same time to obtain a pleasant imbedding for $\mathcal{G}$ itself. We merely take for the edge between $v_i$ and $v_j$, two non-adjacent vertices on $J$, the inverse image of the line segment from $w_i$ to $w_j$. This gives us a simultaneous imbedding of $\mathcal{G}$ and $\mathcal{G}_{p\ell}$ such that the edge of $\mathcal{G}$ from $v_i$ to $v_j$ intersects the edges of $\mathcal{G}_{p\ell}$ from $v_i$ and $v_j$ to the central vertex only in $v_i$ and $v_j$. Also if $e_1$ and $e_2$ are two edges of $\mathcal{G}$ in the face $F$, with endpoints $v_1$, $v_2$ and $v_3$, $v_4$, respectively, then $e_1$ can intersect $e_2$ in a point different from $v_3$, $v_4$ only if the four points $v_1$-$v_4$ are distinct, and $v_1$, $v_2$ separate $v_3$, $v_4$ on $J$. In other words, each of the two arcs of $J$ between $v_3$ and $v_4$ must contain one of $v_1$ and $v_2$.

(ii) Note that we inserted a central vertex in <u>every</u> face $F \in \mathcal{F}$, even if $F$ is a triangle, i.e., bounded by three edges, or a "lens", i.e., bounded by two different edges with the same pair of endpoints. Such faces contain no extra edges in $\mathcal{G}$ when compared to $\mathcal{M}$, but these faces become different after close-packing (compare Ex.2.3 (iii) below).///

$\mathcal{G}^*_{p\ell}$ is defined and constructed in exactly the same way as $\mathcal{G}_{p\ell}$ above; we merely have to replace $\mathcal{G}$ by $\mathcal{G}^*$ and $\mathcal{F}$ by $\mathcal{F}^*$ throughout. In particular $\mathcal{G}^*_{p\ell}$ has only central vertices in faces of $\mathcal{F}^*$, but not in faces of $\mathcal{F}$. A more explicit notation would be $(\mathcal{G}^*)_{p\ell}$. This is not the same as $(\mathcal{G}_{p\ell})^*$, the latter being the second graph of the matching pair $(\mathcal{G}_{p\ell},(\mathcal{G}_{p\ell})^*)$ based on $(\mathcal{G}_{p\ell},\emptyset)$. In these notes we shall never use $(\mathcal{G}_{p\ell})^*$ and $\mathcal{G}^*_{p\ell}$ will always stand for $(\mathcal{G}^*)_{p\ell}$.

$\mathcal{M}_{p\ell}$ is the graph whose vertex (edge) sets is the union of the vertex (edge) sets of $\mathcal{G}_{p\ell}$ and $\mathcal{G}^*_{p\ell}$. Thus $\mathcal{M}_{p\ell}$ has a central vertex added in each face of $\mathcal{M}$.

Comments.

(iii) If $\mathcal{G}$ is periodic, we want to take $\mathcal{G}_{p\ell}$ also periodic. To see that this can be done observe first that if $F$ is any face of $\mathcal{M}$ and $x \in \mathbb{R}^2$ a point in $F$ then $x+k_1e_1+k_2e_2 \notin F$ if $k_1,k_2 \in \mathbb{Z}$, not both zero. For, otherwise, there would exist a continuous path from $x$ to $x+k_1e_1+k_2e_2$ which does not intersect any edge of $\mathcal{M}$. Extending this path periodically would give an unbounded path in $F$, so that the face $F$ of $\mathcal{M}$ would have to be unbounded. But all faces of $\mathcal{M}$ are the interiors of Jordan curves, and hence bounded. This proves the observation. It follows that for any face $F \in \mathcal{F}$, all the faces $F+k_1e_1+k_2e_2$, $k_1,k_2 \in \mathbb{Z}$, are pairwise disjoint. Since $\mathcal{G}$ is periodic, $F \in \mathcal{F}$ implies that this whole class belongs to $\mathcal{F}$. As a result $\mathcal{F}$ can be written as a disjoint union of classes $\mathcal{F}_i$, each $\mathcal{F}_i$ of the form $\{F_i+k_1e_1+k_2e_2: k_1,k_2 \in \mathbb{Z}\}$ and all faces in one $\mathcal{F}_i$ disjoint from each other. If we now add a central vertex in $F_i$, and edges from this central vertex to the vertices on the perimeter of $F_i$, then we can repeat this construction periodically in every face $F_i+k_1e_1+k_2e_2$. Since all these faces are disjoint these constructons do not interfere with each other and the resulting $\mathcal{G}_{p\ell}$ is periodic.

(iv) Two central vertices are never adjacent. This holds on $\mathcal{G}_{p\ell}$, $\mathcal{G}^*_{p\ell}$ and $\mathcal{M}_{p\ell}$.

(v) The imbedding of Comments (i) and (iii) can be extended to give a simultaneous imbedding of $\mathcal{G}_{p\ell}$, $\mathcal{G}^*_{p\ell}$ and $\mathcal{M}_{p\ell}$. An edge $e$ of $\mathcal{G}_{p\ell}$ and an edge $e^*$ of $\mathcal{G}^*_{p\ell}$ can intersect only in a common endpoint, which is necessarily a vertex of $\mathcal{M}$, unless $e$ and $e^*$ coincide (compare Comment 2.2 (vii)). We can even imbed $\mathcal{G}$, $\mathcal{G}^*$, $\mathcal{G}_{p\ell}$, $\mathcal{G}^*_{p\ell}$ and $\mathcal{M}_{p\ell}$ simultaneously. In this case any edge $e$ of $\mathcal{G}$ belongs to the closure $\overline{F}$ of some face $F$ of $\mathcal{F}$. (See Comment 2.2 (iii).) On the other hand, any edge $e^*$ of $\mathcal{G}_{p\ell}$ will either be also an edge of $\mathcal{G}$ or $\overset{\circ}{e}^* \subset F^*$ for some face $F^* \notin \mathcal{F}$. Therefore an edge $e$ of $\mathcal{G}$ and an edge $e^*$ of $\mathcal{G}_{p\ell}$ which do not coincide can again intersect only in a common endpoint which is a vertex of $\mathcal{M}$.

(vi) Any face $F \in \mathcal{F}$ of $\mathcal{M}$ becomes triangulated in $\mathcal{G}_{p\ell}$. Similarly for $F \in \mathcal{F}^*$ in $\mathcal{G}^*_{p\ell}$. All faces of $\mathcal{M}_{p\ell}$ are "triangles", i.e., are bounded by a Jordan curve made up from three edges of $\mathcal{M}_{p\ell}$.

Examples.

(i) Let $(\mathcal{M},\mathcal{F}) = (\mathcal{G}_0,\emptyset)$ and $(\mathcal{G},\mathcal{G}^*)$ the matching pair based on this as in Ex. 2.2 (i). Then $\mathcal{G}_{p\ell} = \mathcal{G} = \mathcal{G}_0 = \mathcal{M}$ while $\mathcal{G}^*_{p\ell} = \mathcal{M}_{p\ell}$ is the centered quadratic lattice of Ex. 2.2 (iii).

(ii) For $\mathcal{M}$, $\mathcal{F}$, $\mathcal{G}$, $\mathcal{G}^*$ as in Ex. 2.2 (ii) $\mathcal{G}_{p\ell}$ and $\mathcal{G}^*_{p\ell}$ are obtained by adding a vertex to $\mathcal{M}$ at each point $(i_1+\frac{1}{2}, i_2+\frac{1}{2})$ with $i_1+i_2$ = even and odd, respectively, and connecting it by an edge to the vertices $(i_1,i_2)$, $(i_1+1,i_2)$, $(i_1+1,i_2+1)$, $(i_1,i_2+1)$.

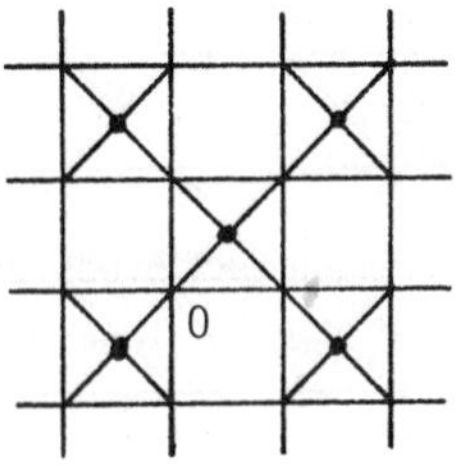


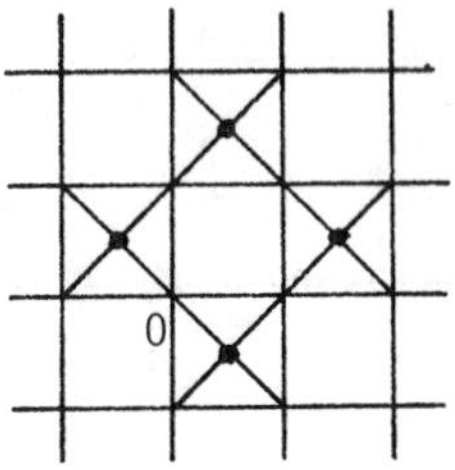


Figure 2.13

(iii) If $\mathcal{M} = \mathcal{J}$ (see Ex. 2.1 (iii)), the triangular lattice, and $\mathcal{F} = \emptyset$, then $\mathcal{G}_{p\ell} = \mathcal{G} = \mathcal{J}$, but $\mathcal{G}^*_{p\ell} = \mathcal{M}_{p\ell}$ has a central vertex placed in each triangle, and this is connected by an edge to each of the three vertices of the triangle. ///

We must now turn to the relationship between $\mathcal{G}$ and $\mathcal{G}_{p\ell}$ - as well as $\mathcal{G}^*$ and $\mathcal{G}^*_{p\ell}$ - in the context of percolation. For reasons to be explained in Sect. 3.1 we restrict ourselves to site percolation. <u>In the remainder of this section</u> $(\mathcal{G},\mathcal{G}^*)$ <u>is a matching pair, based on</u> $(\mathcal{M},\mathcal{F})$.

<u>Def. 5</u>. An <u>occupancy configuration</u> for $\mathcal{M}$ or $\mathcal{G}$ or $\mathcal{G}^*$ is a map $\omega$ from their common vertex set into $\{-1,+1\}$. ///

Usually we call a vertex $v$ with $\omega(v) = +1$ occupied, and with $\omega(v) = -1$ vacant. Thus, an occupancy configuration is merely a partition of the vertices into occupied and vacant ones. We shall always extend such a configuration to an occupancy configuration for $\mathcal{M}_{p\ell}$ or $\mathcal{G}_{p\ell}$ or $\mathcal{G}^*_{p\ell}$ (in obvious terminology) by setting

(2.15) $\omega(v) = +1$ for every central vertex $v$ of an $F \varepsilon \mathcal{F}$,

(2.16) $\omega(v) = -1$ for every central vertex $v$ of an $F \varepsilon \mathcal{F}^*$.

Thus, we always take central vertices of $\mathcal{G}_{p\ell}$ occupied and of $\mathcal{G}^*_{p\ell}$ vacant. (We only make an exception to this rule in Sect. 10.2 and 3, where the exception will be explicitly pointed out.)

Definitions 6 and 7 below refer to a fixed occupancy configuration $\omega$, but usually we suppress the dependence on $\omega$ from the notation.

Def. 6. An occupied path on $\mathcal{G}(\mathcal{G}_{p\ell})$ is a path on $\mathcal{G}(\mathcal{G}_{p\ell})$ all of whose vertices are occupied. A vacant path on $\mathcal{G}^*$ $(\mathcal{G}^*_{p\ell})$ is a path on $\mathcal{G}^*(\mathcal{G}^*_{p\ell})$ all of whose vertices are vacant. ///

The following lemma will allow us to go back and forth between paths on $\mathcal{G}$ and $\mathcal{G}_{p\ell}$ (or $\mathcal{G}^*$ and $\mathcal{G}^*_{p\ell}$).

Lemma 2.1a. Let $r = (v_0, e_1, v_1, \dots, e_\nu, v_\nu)$ be an occupied path on $\mathcal{G}_{p\ell}$. Then there exists an occupied path $\tilde{r}$ on $\mathcal{G}$ whose vertices are exactly the non-central vertices of $r$, and they occur in the same order in $\tilde{r}$ as in $r$. Moreover, if

(2.17) diameter $(e) \leq \Lambda$ for all edges $e$ of $\mathcal{G}$ and $\mathcal{G}_{p\ell}$

then

(2.18) for each point $x$ of $\tilde{r}$ there exists a vertex $y$ of $r$ with $|x-y| \leq \Lambda$ .

Lemma 2.1b. Let $\tilde{r} = (\tilde{v}_0, \tilde{e}_1, \dots, \tilde{e}_\rho, \tilde{v}_\rho)$ be an occupied path on $\mathcal{G}$. Then there exists an occupied path $r$ on $\mathcal{G}_{p\ell}$ (as well as on $\mathcal{M}_{p\ell}$) from $\tilde{v}_0$ to $\tilde{v}_\rho$. The non-central vertices of $r$ form a subset of the vertices of $\tilde{r}$, and occur in the same order in $r$ as in $\tilde{r}$. Moreover if (2.17) holds, then

(2.19) for each point $y$ of $r$ there exists a vertex $x$ of $\tilde{r}$ such that $|x-y| \leq \Lambda$ .

Proof of Lemma 2.1a. Let $v_{i_0}, v_{i_1}, \ldots, v_{i_\rho}$ with $i_0 < i_1 < \ldots < i_\rho$ be all the vertices of $r$ which are not central vertices of $\mathcal{G}_{p\ell}$. Since by construction $\mathcal{G}_{p\ell}$ has no edges between two central vertices, there cannot be two successive central vertices in $r$ (cf. Comment 2.3 (iv)). Consequently, $i_0 \le 1$, $i_{j+1} - i_j \le 2$ and $i_\rho \ge \nu - 1$. If $i_{j+1} = i_j + 1$ then we simply connect $v_{i_j}$ and $v_{i_{j+1}} = v_{i_j+1}$ by the edge $e_{i_j+1}$ from $r$. In this case we take $\tilde{e}_{j+1} = e_{i_j+1}$. If $i_{j+1} = i_j + 2$, then $v_{i_j+1}$ is a central vertex of some face $F$ of $\mathcal{M}$ and $v_{i_j}$ and $v_{i_j+2}$ are both vertices of $\mathcal{G}$ on the perimeter of $F$. Moreover the face $F$ must be close-packed in $\mathcal{G}$, so that there is an edge $\tilde{e}_{j+1}$ of $\mathcal{G}$ contained in the closure of $F$ which connects $v_{i_j}$ and $v_{i_{j+1}} = v_{i_j+2}$. We define $\tilde{v}_j = v_{i_j}$ and take $r = (\tilde{v}_0, \tilde{e}_1, \ldots, \tilde{e}_\rho, \tilde{v}_\rho)$. It is easy to see that $\tilde{r}$ satisfies the requirements of the lemma. We merely remark that $\tilde{r}$ is self-avoiding (recall our convention that a path should be self-avoiding). To see this note that the $\tilde{v}_j$ form a subset of the vertices of the self-avoiding path $r$, and therefore are distinct. The vertices of $\tilde{r}$ are the non-central vertices of $r$, in their original order. $\tilde{r}$ is automatically occupied, since all its vertices are also vertices of the occupied path $r$. Finally, (2.17) implies (2.18) because any point $x$ of $\tilde{r}$ lies on some edge $\tilde{e}_i$ of $\tilde{r}$, and by virtue of (2.17) lies within $\Lambda$ from $\tilde{v}_i$, which is also a vertex of $r$.

Proof of Lemma 2.1b. This proof is almost the reverse of that of Lemma 2.1a. We now insert central vertices whenever necessary. More precisely, if $\tilde{e}_i$ is an edge of $\mathcal{G}$, but not of $\mathcal{G}_{p\ell}$, then its interior must lie in a close-packed face $F$ and its endpoints $\tilde{v}_{i-1}$ and $\tilde{v}_i$ must lie on the perimeter of $F$. Let $c$ be the central vertex of $F$ and $e'$, $e''$ the edges of $\mathcal{G}_{p\ell}$ between $\tilde{v}_{i-1}$ and $c$, and between $c$ and $\tilde{v}_i$, respectively. We now replace the edge $\tilde{e}_i$ by $e'$, $c$, $e''$. If $\tilde{e}_i$ is already an edge of $\mathcal{G}_{p\ell}$, then of course it need not be replaced. We make all the necessary replacements for $i = 1, \ldots, \rho$, and denote the resulting sequence of vertices and edges of $\mathcal{G}_{p\ell}$ by $r = (v_0, e_1, \ldots, e_\nu, v_\nu)$. The $v_j$ consists of the $\tilde{v}_i$ in their original order, with some central vertices of $\mathcal{G}_{p\ell}$ interpolated and $v_0 = \tilde{v}_0$, $v_\nu = \tilde{v}_\rho$. All $v_i$ are automatically occupied by virtue of (2.15) and the fact that $\tilde{r}$ was an occupied path. If $r$ itself is not self-avoiding we make it self-avoiding by loop-removal without changing its first or last point, as described in Sect. 2.1. The resulting path satisfies all requirements.

For (2.19), observe that each edge in the final path has at least one endpoint which is not a central vertex, and hence also belongs to $\tilde{r}$. □

Def. 7. $W(v) = W(v,\omega)$, the occupied cluster or occupied component of $v$ on $\mathcal{G}$ is the union of all edges and vertices of $\mathcal{G}$ which belong to an occupied path on $\mathcal{G}$ with initial point $v$. ///

$v$ is assumed to be a vertex of $\mathcal{G}$ in Def. 7. If $v$ is vacant $W(v) = \phi$. If $v$ is occupied, but all its neighbors are vacant, then $W(v) = \{v\}$.

We define the occupied cluster $W_{p\ell}(v) = W_{p\ell}(v,\omega)$ of $v$ on $\mathcal{G}_{p\ell}$ by replacing $\mathcal{G}$ by $\mathcal{G}_{p\ell}$ in the above definition. No confusion with the occupied cluster of $v$ on $\mathcal{M}_{p\ell}$ can arise because the latter equals $W_{p\ell}(v)$. In fact, by virtue of (2.16), an occupied path on $\mathcal{M}_{p\ell}$ cannot contain any central vertices of $\mathcal{G}^*_{p\ell}$, and therefore is an occupied path on $\mathcal{G}_{p\ell}$ itself. Lemma 2.1 therefore has the following corollary.

Corollary 2.1. For any vertex $v$ of $\mathcal{G}$

(2.20) $W_{p\ell}(v) = W(v) \cup \{$all edges of $\mathcal{G}_{p\ell}$ from a central vertex of $\mathcal{G}_{p\ell}$ to some vertex $w \in W(v)\}$.

Consequently, if (2.17) holds, then

(2.21) $W \subset W_{p\ell} \subset \{x: |x-w| \leq \Lambda$ for some $w \in W\}$.

Proof: If $w$ is a non-central vertex of $\mathcal{G}_{p\ell}$ which can be connected to $v$ by an occupied path on $\mathcal{G}_{p\ell}$, then it is also connected to $v$ by an occupied path on $\mathcal{G}$, and vice versa, by virtue of Lemma 2.1a and 2.1b, respectively. Thus the non-central vertices of $W_{p\ell}$ are precisely the vertices of $W$. Since central vertices only have non-central neighbors on $\mathcal{G}_{p\ell}$ (see Comment 2.3 (iv)) one easily sees that the central vertices of $W_{p\ell}$ are precisely those vertices which are adjacent to some (non-central) vertex of $W$ (recall that $v$ is a vertex of $\mathcal{G}$, hence non-central) (2.20) is immediate from this, while (2.21) follows from (2.17) and (2.20). □

Remark.

One can define a planar modification for certain graphs $\mathcal{G}$ which are not necessarily one of a matching pair. It seems that many percolation results will go through for such graphs. Specifically, let $\mathcal{M}$ be a mosaic and $F$ a face of $\mathcal{M}$ with perimeter $J$. Let $G_1,\ldots,G_k$ be pairwise disjoint sets of vertices on $J$, such that no two vertices of $G_i$ separate two of $G_j$ on $J$, when $i \neq j$. Assume that $\mathcal{G}$ is formed by adding an edge in $\bar{F}$ between any pair of vertices which belong to the same $G_i$, and that these edges are added such that an edge between two vertices of $G_i$ does not intersect an edge between two vertices of $G_j$ for $i \neq j$. For example if $F$ is an octagon as in Fig. 2.14a, then $G_1$ $(G_2)$ might be the top (bottom) four vertices, and $\mathcal{G}$ would have

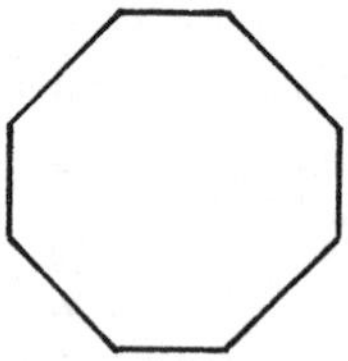

Figure 2.14a $\mathcal{M}$

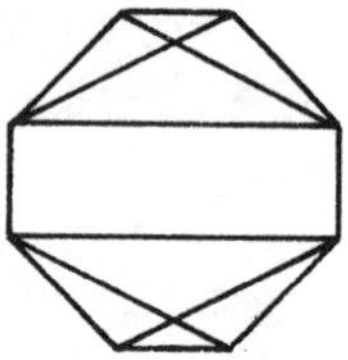

Figure 2.14b $\mathcal{G}$

edges in $\bar{F}$ as indicated in Fig. 2.14b. Such edges could be added in many faces. To form a planar modification - call it $\mathcal{G}_{p\ell}$ again - one would now insert one central vertex $v_i$ in $F$ for each $G_i$. In $\mathcal{G}_{p\ell}$ $v_i$ would be connected by an edge to each vertex in $G_i$ but to no other vertices. For the situation illustrated in Fig. 2.14a and b we would end up with the situation of Fig. 2.14c. If we take all central vertices

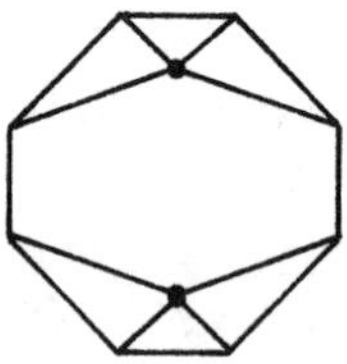

Figure 2.14c $\mathcal{G}_{p\ell}$ corresponding to the $\mathcal{G}$ of Figure 2.14b.

occupied as in (2.15), then Lemmas 2.1a and b and Cor. 2.1 remain valid (with only trivial changes in their proofs). As in the case when $\mathcal{G}$ is one of a matching pair this will allow us to reduce site-percolation problems on $\mathcal{G}$ to equivalent ones on $\mathcal{G}_{p\ell}$. Even though there is no obvious analogue of $\mathcal{G}^*$ for the more general graphs of this remark, we can apply much of the succeeding directly to $\mathcal{G}_{p\ell}$. Indeed $\mathcal{G}_{p\ell}$ is planar, and a mosaic. Thus $\mathcal{G}_{p\ell}$ is one of a pair of matching graphs, based on $(\mathcal{G}_{p\ell},\phi)$ (see Comment 2.2 (vi)). Moreover, if we view $\mathcal{G}_{p\ell}$ as based on $(\mathcal{G}_{p\ell},\phi)$, then $(\mathcal{G}_{p\ell})_{p\ell} = \mathcal{G}_{p\ell}$. Thus results for one of a matching pair of graphs apply to $\mathcal{G}_{p\ell}$.

## 2.4 Separation theorems and related point-set topological results.

In this section we formulate some purely graph-theoretical, or point-set topological nature which will play a fundamental rôle. Their contents are easily acceptable intuitively, but their proofs are somewhat involved. For this reason we postpone the proof of Prop. 2.1-2.3 to the Appendix. In this section $(\mathcal{G},\mathcal{G}^*)$ is again a matching pair of graphs, based on $(\mathcal{M},\mathcal{F})$. First we need the definition of the boundary of a set on a graph.

Def. 8. Let $A$ be a subset of a graph $\mathcal{H}$. Its boundary on $\mathcal{H}$ is the set

$$\partial A = \{v\colon v \text{ a vertex of } \mathcal{H} \text{ outside } A, \text{ but there exists a vertex } w \in A \text{ such that } v \overset{\mathcal{H}}{\sim} w\}.$$

The notation $\partial A$ does not indicate any dependence on $\mathcal{H}$. However, if $\mathcal{H}_1$ and $\mathcal{H}_2$ are two graphs such that $A$ can be viewed as a subset of both of them then the boundary of $A$ may be different on $\mathcal{H}_1$ and on $\mathcal{H}_2$. If necessary we shall indicate on which graph the boundary is to be taken. Often it will be clear from knowing the set $A$ which boundary is intended. E.g. $W(v)$ is defined as a cluster on $\mathcal{G}$, and correspondingly $\partial W$ will always mean the boundary of $W$ on $\mathcal{G}$. On the other hand $\partial W_{p\ell}$ means the boundary of $W_{p\ell}$ on $\mathcal{M}_{p\ell}$, and not on $\mathcal{G}_{p\ell}$, in Prop. 1.

Def. 9. Let $\mathcal{H}$ be a graph imbedded in $\mathbb{R}^2$ and $A \subset \mathbb{R}^2$. A circuit on $\mathcal{H}$ surrounding $A$ is a Jordan curve on $\mathcal{H}$ made up of edges of $\mathcal{H}$ which contains $A$ in its interior (cf. Comment 2.2(ii)). We call the circuit occupied (vacant) if all vertices of $\mathcal{H}$ on the circuit are occupied (vacant).

The following proposition is a version of Theorem 4 in Whitney (1933); it is of fundamental importance in the development of percolation theory.

Proposition 2.1. Let $\partial W_{p\ell}(v)$ be the boundary of $W_{p\ell}(v)$ on $\mathcal{M}_{p\ell}$. If

$W_{p\ell}(v)$ is non-empty and bounded and (2.3)-(2.5) hold with $\mathcal{G}$ replaced by $\mathcal{M}$, then there exists a vacant circuit $J_{p\ell}$ on $\mathcal{M}_{p\ell}$ surrounding $W_{p\ell}(v)$ and such that all vertices of $\mathcal{M}_{p\ell}$ on $J_{p\ell}$ belong to $\partial W_{p\ell}(v)$.

Corollary 2.2. If $W(v)$ is non-empty and bounded and (2.3)-(2.5) hold, then there exists a vacant circuit $J$ on $\mathcal{G}^*$ surrounding $W(v)$.

The proof of this corollary is also in the appendix. We stress that $W(v)$ is a subset of $\mathcal{G}$ while the surrounding circuit is on $\mathcal{G}^*$. It is easy to see that there does not have to exist a circuit on $\mathcal{G}$ itself surrounding $W$. E.g., if $(\mathcal{G},\mathcal{G}^*)$ is the matching pair of ex.2.2(i) and

$$\omega(v) = \begin{cases} +1 & \text{if } v(1) = v(2) \ (v = (v(1),v(2))) \\ -1 & \text{otherwise,} \end{cases}$$

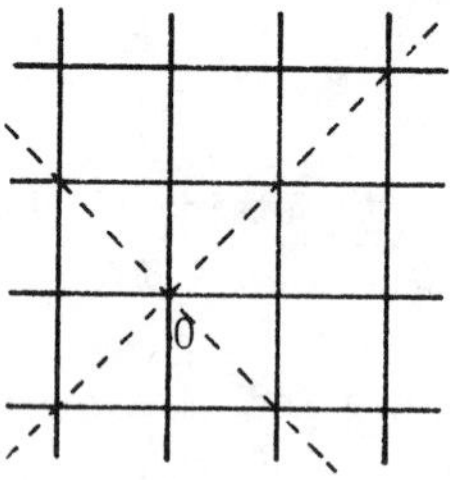


Figure 2.15 $v$ is occupied iff $v$ lies on one of the dashed 45° lines.

then $W(0) = \{0\}$, but no vacant path on $\mathcal{G}$ surrounds the origin.

Proposition 2.2. Let $J$ be a Jordan curve on $\mathcal{M}$ (and hence also on $\mathcal{G}$ and on $\mathcal{G}^*$) which consists of four closed arcs $A_1,A_2,A_3,A_4$ with disjoint interiors, and such that $A_1$ and $A_3$ each contain at least one vertex of $\mathcal{M}$. Assume that one meets these arcs in the order $A_1,A_2,A_3,A_4$ as one traverses $J$ in one direction. Then there exists a path $r$ on $\mathcal{G}$ inside $\bar{J} := J \cup \text{int}(J_1)$ from a vertex on $A_1$ to a vertex on $A_3$, and with all vertices of $r$ in $J\backslash A_1 \cup A_3$ occupied, if and only if there does not exist a vacant path $r^*$ on $\mathcal{G}^*$ inside $J\backslash A_1 \cup A_3$ from

<u>a vertex of $\mathring{A}_2$ to a vertex of $\mathring{A}_4$.</u>[1)]

The next proposition is a cornerstone of the development in these notes. Some form of it has been used by many authors. In its simplest form it says that among all occupied paths connecting the left and right edge of a rectangle there exists a unique lowest one. This has often been taken for granted. Harris (1960) quotes a general theorem from topology to prove this for bond-percolation on $\mathbb{Z}^2$. We do, however, need a more general result, and this is not valid on all graphs. We therefore give a proof of Prop. 2.3 in the Appendix, which closely follows Lemma 1 of Kesten (1980a). An examination of the proof will show that it is crucial that $\mathcal{G}_{p\ell}$ is planar.

Some preparation concerning symmetry axes of a graph, and a partial ordering of paths is needed first.

<u>Def. 10</u>. Let $\mathcal{H}$ be a graph imbedded in $\mathbb{R}^2$. The line $L: x(1) = a$ is an <u>axis of symmetry</u> for $\mathcal{H}$ if $\mathcal{H}$ is invariant under the reflection of $L$ which takes $y = (y(1),y(2))$ to $(2a-y(1),y(2))$. Similarly if $L$ is a vertical line of the form $x(2) = a$.

<u>Comments</u>.

(i) $L$ is an axis of symmetry for $\mathcal{H}$ iff the image under the imbedding of each vertex and edge of $\mathcal{H}$ goes over into the image under the imbedding of a vertex and edge, respectively, under reflection in $L$. It would therefore be more accurate, but also more cumbersome to call $L$ an axis of symmetry for the imbedding of $\mathcal{H}$, rather than for $\mathcal{H}$.

As we pointed out after Def. 2.1 of a periodic graph, percolation problems depend only on the abstract structure of the graphs, and not on their imbedding. Just as one can sometimes change an imbedding to obtain a periodic one, one can sometimes change an imbedding to make one of the coordinate-axes an axis of symmetry. E.g. neither of the coordinate-axes is an axis of symmetry for the imbedding of Fig. 2.5 for the triangular lattice, while both of them are for the imbedding of Fig. 2.4. Even though we require in several theorems that the graph is imbedded periodically and with a coordinate axis as symmetry axis, what really counts is that the graph <u>can be</u> imbedded such that it has these properties.

(ii) Assume $L$ is an axis of symmetry for $\mathcal{G}_{p\ell}$ and $e$ an edge

---

1) When $A$ is an arc we use $\mathring{A}$ to denote $A$ minus its endpoints.

of $\mathcal{G}_{p\ell}$ which intersects $L$ in a point $m$. Denote by $\tilde{e}$ the reflection of $e$ in $L$. Then $\tilde{e}$ is also an edge of $\mathcal{G}_{p\ell}$ which intersects $L$ in $m$. We shall show that exactly one of the four following cases must obtain:

(a) $e$ lies on $L$,

(b) $e$ has both endpoints, but no other points on $L$, and these points on $L$ are the only common points of $e$ and $\tilde{e}$,

(c) $e$ has exactly one endpoint, but no other points on $L$, and this point on $L$ is the only common point of $e$ and $\tilde{e}$,

(d) $e$ intersects $L$ only in one point $m$ which is not an endpoint, $e$ is symmetric with respect to $L$, i.e., $e$ coincides with $\tilde{e}$, and $m$ is the midpoint of $e$.

To see this assume first that $e$ intersects $L$ also in another point $m' \neq m$. Then $e$ intersects $\tilde{e}$ in $m$ and $m' \neq m$. Then either $m$ and $m'$ are common endpoints of $e$ and $\tilde{e}$ and they have no further points in common (case (b)) or $e$ and $\tilde{e}$ also have an interior point in common, in which case they coincide and case (a) obtains (recall that $\mathcal{G}_{p\ell}$ is planar and $e$ is a simple arc). Next consider the situation where $e$ intersects $L$ only in $m$. If $m$ is an endpoint of $e$ then we are in case (c), because $e$ and $\tilde{e}$ must lie on opposite sides of $L$. Finally if the common point $m$ of $e$ and $\tilde{e}$ is an interior point of either one of them then they must again coincide, and case (d) obtains.

A good illustration of this situation is provided by the triangular lattice of Fig. 2.4. The lines $x(1) = k$, $k \in \mathbb{Z}$ are axes of symmetry; half the horizontal edges are in case (d), while the other half and all non-horizontal edges are in case (c).

(iii) In most of our theorems we shall deal with a matching pair of periodic graphs $(\mathcal{G},\mathcal{G}^*)$ based on $(\mathcal{M},\mathcal{F})$ for which $x(1) = 0$ and/or $x(2) = 0$ is an axis of symmetry. In the proofs we shall work with the planar modifications $\mathcal{G}_{p\ell}$ and $\mathcal{G}^*_{p\ell}$, and it will be necessary that these graphs too have $x(1) = 0$ and/or $x(2) = 0$ as axis of symmetry, in addition to the properties of Comments 2.3(i),(iii) and (v). This can be achieved as follows. If $L_1$: $x(1) = 0$ is an axis of symmetry and $F \in \mathcal{F}$ is a face of $\mathcal{M}$ which intersects $L_1$, then $\bar{F}$ is symmetric with respect to $L_1$. We then choose the homeomorphism $\psi$ on $F$ of Comment 2.3 (i) such that $\psi(\tilde{x}) = \widetilde{\psi(x)}$, where $\tilde{x}$ is the reflection of $x$ in $L_1$. A map $\psi$ with this symmetry property obviously exists; simply construct $\psi$ on $\bar{F} \cap \{x(1) \geq 0\}$ such that $\bar{F} \cap \{x(1) = 0\}$ is mapped into

$\{x(1) = 0\}$ and then reflect in $L_1$ (see Newman (1951), ex. VI.18.2. Alternatively one can use the Schwarz reflection principle, Rudin (1966), Theorem 11.17. We can then extend the construction for $F$ periodically to faces $F+k_1e_1+k_2e_2$ as in Comment 2.3 (iii). This method will take care of the faces in any class $\mathcal{F}_i$ of Comment 2.3 (iii) which contains an $F$ which intersects $L_1$. If none of the faces in $\mathcal{F}_i$ intersect $L_1$, then $\mathcal{F}_i$ contains a face $F$ in $\{0 < x(1) < 1\}$ and we can choose $\psi$ symmetric with respect to $x(1) = \frac{1}{2}$ on $\overline{F} \cup \{\tilde{\overline{F}} + \xi_1\}$. This can then again be extended periodically to $\overline{F}+k_1e_1+k_2e_2$ and to $\tilde{\overline{F}}+\ell_1e_1+\ell_2e_2$, $k_i$, $\ell_j \in \mathbb{Z}$. The same method works if $L_2$: $x(2) = 0$ is an axis of symmetry. It even works if both $L_1$ and $L_2$ are axes of symmetry. In this last case $\psi$ also has to satisfy $\psi(\tilde{x}) = \widetilde{\psi(x)}$ as well as $\psi(\tilde{\tilde{x}}) = \widetilde{\widetilde{\psi(x)}}$, where $\tilde{\tilde{x}}$ is the reflection of $x$ in $L_2$. If $F$ intersects $L_1$ and $L_2$ we can construct such a homeomorphism $\psi$ on $F$ by first constructing $\psi$ on $\overline{F} \cap \{x(1) \geq 0, x(2) \geq 0\}$ and then reflecting first in $L_2$ and then in $L_1$.

From now on we shall assume that if $(\mathcal{G},\mathcal{G}^*)$ are periodic and symmetric with respect to $L_1$ and/or $L_2$, then the same holds for $\mathcal{G}_{p\ell}$, $\mathcal{G}^*_{p\ell}$. In addition we can and shall assume the properties of Comments 2.2 (vii), 2.3 (i) and (v). ///

Now assume that $L_i$: $x(1) = a_i$, $i = 1,2$ are two vertical axes of symmetry for $\mathcal{G}_{p\ell}$ with $a_1 < a_2$. Let $J$ be a Jordan curve in $\mathbb{R}^2$ consisting of four closed non-empty arcs $B_1,A,B_2,C$ with disjoint interiors and occurring in this order as $J$ is traversed in one direction. Also assume that

(2.22) For $i = 1,2$, $B_i$ is a curve made up from edges of $\mathcal{M}_{p\ell}$, or $B_i$ lies on $L_i$ and $J$ lies in the half plane $(-1)^i(x(1)-a_i) \leq 0$.

(A typical case will be that $J$ is the perimeter of a rectangle with its left edge $B_1$ and right edge $B_2$ on an axis of symmetry.) We shall consider paths $r = (v_0,e_1,\dots,e_\nu,v_\nu)$ on $\mathcal{G}_{p\ell}$ which satisfy the conditions (2.23)-(2.25) below.

(2.23) $$(v_1,e_2,\dots,e_{\nu-1},v_{\nu-1}) \subset \text{int}(J).$$

(2.24) $e_1$ has exactly one point in common with $J$. This lies in $B_1$ and is either $v_0$, or in case $B_1 \subset L_1$, it may be the midpoint of $e_1$.

(2.25) $e_\nu$ has exactly one point in common with $J$. This lies in $B_2$ and is either $v_\nu$, or in case $B_2 \subset L_2$, it may be the midpoint of $e_\nu$.

Note that if $B_1 \subset L_1$, then (2.24) implies that $e_1$ has to be in case (c) or case (d) of Comment 2.4 (ii). If case (d) occurs then $v_0 \in \text{ext}(J)$, because $v_1 \in \text{int}(J)$ lies to the right of $L_1$ and $v_0$ must be the reflection of $v_1$ in $L_1$. A similar comment applies to $v_\nu$.

In several applications it will be necessary to restrict the location of $r$ further. If $S$ is a subset of $\mathbb{R}^2$, then $r \subset S$ will mean that all edges and vertices of $r$ lie in $S$. To avoid (mild) complications we shall only consider situations with

$$B_1 \cap B_2 \cap S = \emptyset. \tag{2.26}$$

For an $r$ satisfying (2.23)-(2.25) we write $m_0$ for the unique point of $e_1$ on $J$; $m_0$ is either the initial point $v_0$ of $r$ or the midpoint of $e_1$. We shall also write $e_1'$ for the closed segment of $e_1$ from $m_0$ to $v_1$. We define $m_\nu$ and $e_\nu'$ similarly, and put $r' = (m_0, e_1', v_1, \dots, v_{\nu-1}, e_\nu', m_\nu)$. $r'$ may not be an honest path on $\mathcal{G}_{p\ell}$, because $e_1'$ and/or $e_\nu'$ may only be half an edge, while $m_0$ and/or $m_\nu$ may not be a vertex of $\mathcal{G}_{p\ell}$. Nevertheless, in an obvious sense, $r'$ has no double points (see the beginning of Sect. 2.3), and the curve on $\mathcal{G}_{p\ell}$ made up from $e_1', e_2, \dots, e_{\nu-1}, e_\nu'$ is a simple arc in $\text{int}(J)$, except for its endpoints $m_0$ and $m_\nu$ which lie in $B_1$ and $B_2$, respectively. Thus $r'$ divides $\text{int}(J)$ into two components (Newman (1951), Theorem V.11.8). On various occasions we shall use $r$ (or $r'$) to denote a path as well as to denote the curve made up from the edges of $r$ (or $r'$). This abuse of notation is not likely to lead to confusion. For instance the components of $\text{int}(J)$ mentioned above will be called the components of $\text{int}(J) \backslash r'$. In this notation we have

$$\text{int}(J) \backslash r = \text{int}(J) \backslash r'$$

since $r$ differs from $r'$ by the piece of $e_1$ from $v_0$ to $m_0$, excluding $m_0$, and the piece of $e_\nu$ from $m_\nu$ to $v_\nu$, excluding $m_\nu$. These pieces of $e_1$ and $e_\nu$ are either empty or lie to the left of $L_1$ and right of $L_2$, respectively. In either case they are contained in $\text{ext}(J)$.

<u>Def. 11</u>. Let $J, B_1, A, B_2$ and $C$ be as above and let $r$ be a path on $\mathcal{G}_{p\ell}$ satisfying (2.23)-(2.25). Then $J^-(r)$ denotes the component of

$\text{int}(J)\backslash r$ which has $A$ in its boundary, and $J^+(r)$ the component of $\text{int}(J)\backslash r$ which has $C$ in its boundary.

To be even more explicit, $J^-(r)$ $(J^+(r))$ is the interior of the Jordan curve consisting of $r'$ followed by the arc of $J$ from $m_\nu$ to $m_0$ which contains $A(C)$.

Def. 12. If $J, B_1, A, B_2$ and $C$ are as above and $r_1$, $r_2$ are two paths on $\mathcal{G}_{p\ell}$ satisfying (2.23)-(2.25) then we say that $r_1$ *precedes* $r_2$, and denote this by $r_1 \prec r_2$, iff $J^-(r_1) \subset J^-(r_2)$.

Proposition 2.3. *Assume that (2.3)-(2.5) hold with $\mathcal{G}$ replaced by $\mathcal{M}$ and that $L_i$: $x(1) = a_i$, $i = 1,2$ are axes of symmetry for $\mathcal{G}_{p\ell}$, with $a_1 < a_2$. Let $J$ be a Jordan curve consisting of four closed non-empty arcs $B_1, A, B_2$ and $C$ as above satisfying (2.22). Let $S$ be any subset of $\mathbb{R}^2$ such that (2.26) holds. Denote by $\mathcal{R} = \mathcal{R}(S,\omega)$ the collection of all occupied paths $r$ on $\mathcal{G}_{p\ell}$ which satisfy (2.23)-(2.25) and $r \subset S$. If $\mathcal{R} \neq \emptyset$ then it has a unique element $R = R(S,\omega)$ which precedes all others. Any occupied path $r$ on $\mathcal{G}_{p\ell}$ which satisfies (2.23)-(2.25) and $r \subset S$ also satisfies*

$$r \cap \bar{J} \subset \bar{J}^+(R) \quad \text{and} \quad R \cap \bar{J} \subset \bar{J}^-(r). \tag{2.27}$$

*Finally, let $r_0$ be a fixed path on $\mathcal{G}_{p\ell}$ satisfying (2.23)-(2.25) and $r_0 \subset S$ (no reference to its occupancy is made here). Then, whether $R = r_0$ or not depends only on the occupancies of the vertices of $\mathcal{G}_{p\ell}$ in the set*

$$(\bar{J}^-(r_0) \cup V_1 \cup V_2) \cap S, \tag{2.28}$$

*where $V_i = \emptyset$ if $B_i$ is made up from edges of $\mathcal{M}_{p\ell}$, while*

$V_i = \{v$: $v$ a vertex of $\mathcal{G}_{p\ell}$ such that its reflection $\tilde{v}$ in $L_i$ belongs to $\bar{J}^-(r_0)$ and such that $e \cap \bar{J} \subset \bar{J}^-(r_0) \cap S$ for some edge $e$ of $\mathcal{G}_{p\ell}$ between $v$ and $\tilde{v}\}$, $i = 1,2$,

*in case $B_i$ lies in $L_i$ but is not made up from edges of $\mathcal{M}_{p\ell}$.*

Another way to express the last conclusion is that for fixed $r_0$, the function of $\omega$

$$I[R(\omega) \text{ exists and equals } r_0] \tag{2.29}$$

depends only on the values of $\omega(v)$ for $v$ a vertex of $\mathcal{G}_{p\ell}$ in the set (2.28). In many applications of this proposition $S$ will be all of $\mathbb{R}^2$, and the restriction $r \subset S$ will be vacuous in such applications. However (2.26) requires that $B_1$ and $B_2$ be disjoint for the choice $S = \mathbb{R}^2$.

## 2.5 Covering graphs.

Fisher (1961) and Fisher and Essam (1961) observed that a bond-percolation problem on a graph $\mathcal{G}$ is equivalent to a site-percolation problem on another graph, the socalled covering graph $\tilde{\mathcal{G}}$ of $\mathcal{G}$. We can only make this precise after the introduction of the relevant probability measures in Sect. 3.1. Here we only give the purely graph theoretical relation between $\mathcal{G}$ and $\tilde{\mathcal{G}}$.

Def. 13. Let $\mathcal{G}$ be any graph. The vertex set of the covering graph $\tilde{\mathcal{G}}$ is in a 1-1 correspondence with the edge set of $\mathcal{G}$. If $\tilde{v}_1 \neq \tilde{v}_2$ are two vertices of $\tilde{\mathcal{G}}$ corresponding to the edges $e_1$ and $e_2$ of $\mathcal{G}$ respectively, then there is one (no, two) edge of $\tilde{\mathcal{G}}$ between $\tilde{v}_1$ and $\tilde{v}_2$, if and only if $e_1$ and $e_2$ have one (no, two) endpoints in common.

Comments.

(i) Some people use the term line graph instead of covering graph.

(ii) If $\mathcal{G}$ is imbedded in $\mathbb{R}^d$ and $e$ is an edge of $\mathcal{G}$, viewed as an arc in $\mathbb{R}^d$, then we can choose the vertex $\tilde{v}$ of $\tilde{\mathcal{G}}$ corresponding to $e$ as a point of $e$. In explicit examples there is often a special choice of $\tilde{v}$ - such as the midpoint of $e$ - and choice of edges between neighbors on $\tilde{\mathcal{G}}$ - such as line segments - which lead to a nice embedding of $\tilde{\mathcal{G}}$ (cf. Ex. 2.5 (i) below).

(iii) Let $r = (v_0, e_1, \dots, e_\nu, v_\nu)$ be a path on $\mathcal{G}$ with possible double points and let $\tilde{v}_i$ be the vertex of $\tilde{\mathcal{G}}$ corresponding to $e_i$. Then there exists an edge $\tilde{e}_i$ of $\tilde{\mathcal{G}}$ between $\tilde{v}_{i-1}$ and $\tilde{v}_i$, because $e_{i-1}$ and $e_i$ have the endpoint $v_i$ in common. Therefore $\tilde{r} = (\tilde{v}_1, \tilde{e}_2, \dots, \tilde{e}_\nu, \tilde{v}_\nu)$ is a path with possible double points on $\tilde{\mathcal{G}}$. If the $\tilde{v}_i$ are chosen as points on $e_i$, as in Comment 2.5 (i) above, then $\tilde{r}$ runs from a point of $e_1$ to a point at $e_\nu$. Conversely if $\tilde{r} = (\tilde{v}_0, \tilde{e}_1, \dots, \tilde{e}_\nu, \tilde{v}_\nu)$ is a path on $\tilde{\mathcal{G}}$, with possible double points, and $e_i$ the edge of $\mathcal{G}$ corresponding to $\tilde{v}_i$, then $e_i$ and $e_{i+1}$ have a common endpoint, $v_i$ say, on $\mathcal{G}$. Then for a suitable choice of the endpoints $v_0$ and $v_\nu$ of $e_1$ and $e_\nu$, respectively, $(v_0, e_1, \dots, e_\nu, v_\nu)$ is a path with possible double points on $\mathcal{G}$. If $\tilde{v}_i$ is a point of $e_i$

as in Comment 2.5 (i), then $r$ is a path from an endpoint of $\tilde{e}_1$ to an endpoint of $e_\nu$. This relation between paths on $\mathcal{G}$ and $\tilde{\mathcal{G}}$ is the basis for the equivalence of bond-percolation on $\mathcal{G}$ and site-percolation on $\tilde{\mathcal{G}}$ (see Prop. 3.1).

Examples.

(i) Let $\mathcal{G}$ be the hexagonal or honeycomb lattice, imbedded in $\mathbb{R}^2$ as described in ex. 2.1 (iv) (see Fig. 2.6). If we place the vertices of $\tilde{\mathcal{G}}$ at the midpoints of the edges of $\mathcal{G}$, and connect neighbors on $\tilde{\mathcal{G}}$ by straight line segments for the edges, then we see that $\tilde{\mathcal{G}}$ is the Kagomé lattice. See Fig. 2.16.

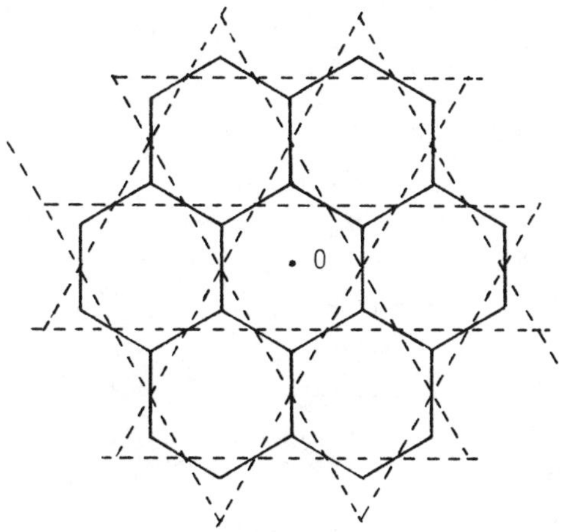


Figure 2.16 —— = hexagonal lattice, $\mathcal{G}$ ,
--- = Kagome lattice, $\tilde{\mathcal{G}}$ .

The faces of $\tilde{\mathcal{G}}$ are regular hexagons and equilateral triangles interspersed between them.

(ii) The covering graph of the graph $\mathcal{G}_0$ in Ex. 2.1 (i) is the graph $\mathcal{G}_1$ of Ex. 2.1 (ii) (see Fig. 2.3).

## 2.6 Dual graphs.

Hammersley (1959), Harris (1960) and Fisher (1961) made heavy use of the socalled dual graphs in their treatment of some bond problems. The role of the dual graph is taken over by the second graph in a matching pair in our treatment, so that we shall be very brief on dual graphs. Assume that $\mathcal{G}$ is a mosaic. We then take the vertex set of the dual graph, $\mathcal{G}_d$, in 1-1 correspondence with the collection of faces of $\mathcal{G}$. In an imbedding of $\mathcal{G}$ each such face $F$ is a Jordan domain and we place the corresponding vertex $v^*$ of $\mathcal{G}_d$ somewhere inside $F$. The edge set of $\mathcal{G}_d$ is in 1-1 correspondence with the edge set of $\mathcal{G}$. Each edge of $\mathcal{G}$ lies in the perimeter of exactly two faces of $\mathcal{G}$. If $e$ lies in the perimeter of $F_1$ and $F_2$, and $v_1^*$ and $v_2^*$ are the vertices of $\mathcal{G}_d$ corresponding to $F_1$ and $F_2$, respectively, then there is an edge of $\mathcal{G}_d$ between $v_1$ and $v_2$ associated to $e$. If the perimeters of $F_1$ and $F_2$ have $\nu$ edges in common, then there will be $\nu$ distinct edges between $v_1^*$ and $v_2^*$. $\mathcal{G}_d$ has no other edges, so that $v_1^*$ and $v_2^*$ are neighbors if and only if they lie in adjacent faces of $\mathcal{G}$ (i.e., faces whose perimeters have an edge in common). In an imbedding of $\mathcal{G}$ we shall draw the edges of $\mathcal{G}_d$ such that an edge $e^*$ of $\mathcal{G}_d$ intersects the unique edge $e$ of $\mathcal{G}$ with which it is associated but no other edges of $\mathcal{G}$. One can show that if $\mathcal{G}$ is a mosaic with dual $\mathcal{G}_d$, then the covering graphs $\tilde{\mathcal{G}}$ and $\tilde{\mathcal{G}}_d$ of $\mathcal{G}$ and $\mathcal{G}_d$, respectively, form a matching pair. We shall not prove this, but it is easily verified for the few instances where we use dual graphs.

## Examples.

(i) Take for $\mathcal{G}$ the simple quadratic lattice $\mathcal{G}_0$ of Ex. 2.1 (i). For its dual $\mathcal{G}_d$ choose a vertex at the center of each square face of $\mathcal{G}$; for the edges of $\mathcal{G}_d$ choose the line segments between the centers of adjacent square faces of $\mathcal{G}_0$ (see Fig. 2.17). $\mathcal{G}_d$ is clearly isomorphic with $\mathcal{G}_0$, in fact it is obtained by translating $\mathcal{G}_0$ by the vector $(\frac{1}{2}, \frac{1}{2})$. We say that $\mathcal{G}_0$ is self-dual.

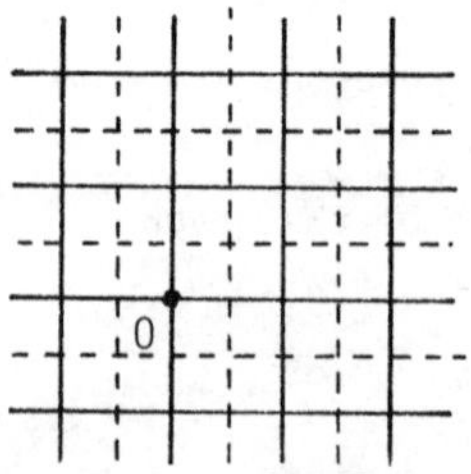


Figure 2.17 —— $= \mathcal{G} = \mathcal{G}_0$ , --- $= \mathcal{G}_d$

(ii) Let $\mathcal{G}$ be the triangular lattice imbedded in $\mathbb{R}^2$ such that each face is an equilateral triangle, as in Fig. 2.4, Ex. 2.1 (iii). Choose the vertex of $\mathcal{G}_d$ corresponding to such an equilateral triangle at its center of gravity, i.e., the intersection of the bisectors of the sides of the triangle. For the edges of $\mathcal{G}_d$ take line segments along these same bisectors, and connecting the centers of gravity of adjacent triangles. $\mathcal{G}_d$ is now a copy of the hexagonal lattice of Ex. 2.1 (iv).

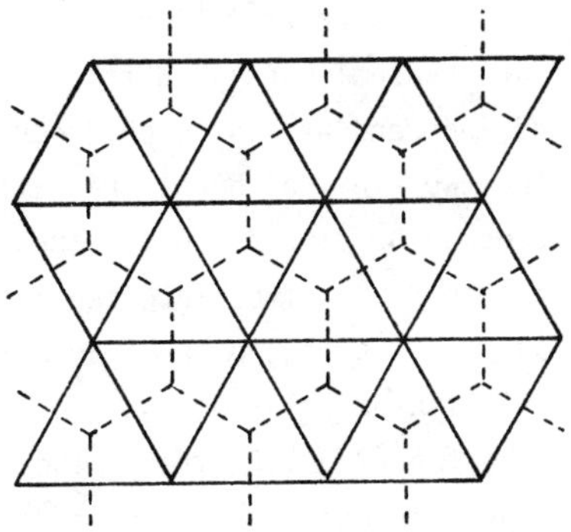

Figure 2.18 —— = $\mathcal{G}$ , the triangular lattice,
- - - = $\mathcal{G}_d$, the hexagonal lattice.

# 3. PERIODIC PERCOLATION PROBLEMS.

## 3.1. Introduction of probability. Site vs bond problems.

Let $\mathcal{G}$ be a graph satisfying (2.1)-(2.5) with vertex set $\mathcal{V}$ and edge set $\mathcal{E}$. The most classical percolation model is the one in which all bonds of $\mathcal{G}$ are randomly assigned to one of two classes, all bonds being assigned independently of each other. This is called bond-percolation, and the two kinds of bonds are called the passable or open bonds and the blocked or closed bonds. Instead of partitioning the bonds one often partitions the sites into two classes. Again all sites are assigned to one class or the other independently of each other. One now speaks of site-percolation and uses occupied and vacant sites to denote the two kinds of sites. The crucial requirement in both models is the independence of the bonds or sites, respectively. This makes the states of the bonds or sites into a family of independent two-valued random variables. Accordingly the above models are called Bernoulli-percolation models.

Formally one describes the models as follows. One denotes the possible configurations of the bonds (sites) by $+1$ and $-1$ with $+1$ standing for passable (occupied) and $-1$ for blocked (vacant). The configuration space for the whole system is then

$$\text{(3.1)} \qquad \Omega_{\mathcal{E}} = \prod_{\mathcal{E}}\{-1,+1\} \quad \text{or} \quad \Omega_{\mathcal{V}} = \prod_{\mathcal{V}}\{-1,+1\}$$

A generic point of $\Omega_{\mathcal{E}}$ is denoted by $\omega = \{\omega(e)\}_{e \in \mathcal{E}}$ and for the $\sigma$-field $\mathcal{B}_{\mathcal{E}}$ in $\Omega_{\mathcal{E}}$ we take $\sigma$-field generated by the cylinder sets of $\Omega_{\mathcal{E}}$, i.e. the sets of the form

$$\text{(3.2)} \qquad \{\omega\colon \omega(e_1) = \varepsilon_1, \dots, \omega(e_n) = \varepsilon_n\}, \ e_i \in \mathcal{E}, \ \varepsilon_i = \pm 1.$$

For the probability measure on $\mathcal{B}_{\mathcal{E}}$ we choose a product measure

$$\text{(3.3)} \qquad P_{\mathcal{E}} = \prod_{e \in \mathcal{E}} \mu_e ,$$

where $\mu_e$ is defined by

(3.4) $\mu_e\{\omega(e) = +1\} = 1 - \mu_e\{\omega(e) = -1\} = p(e)$

for some $0 \le p(e) \le 1$. One defines $\mathcal{B}_{\mathcal{V}}$ and $P_{\mathcal{V}}$ by replacing $\mathcal{E}$ and $e$ by $\mathcal{V}$ and $v$, respectively, in (3.2) - (3.4).

Let $\omega \in \Omega_{\mathcal{E}}$. The open cluster $W(e) = W(e,\omega)$ of an edge $e$ is the union of all edges and vertices which belong to some path $r = (v_0, e_1 = e, \dots, e_\nu, v_\nu)$ on $\mathcal{G}$, with $e_1 = e$ and all $e_i$ passable. (We lose nothing by taking the $r$ self-avoiding.)
For the site problem and $\omega \in \Omega_{\mathcal{V}}$ we defined the occupied cluster $W(v) = W(v,\omega)$ of a vertex $v$ in Def. 2.7. We can of course use this same definition with "occupied" replaced by "open" to define $W(v)$ in the bond-problem. This is what we used in the introduction, but for the comparison of bond and site-problems it is convenient to have $W(e)$ available. Of course for the bond-problem

(3.5) $$W(v) = \bigcup_{\substack{e \text{ incident} \\ \text{to } v}} W(e)$$

so that there is a close relation between $W(e)$ and $W(v)$. We shall use

(3.6) $\#W(e)$ and $\#W(v)$

to denote the number of edges in $W(e)$ and the number of vertices in $W(v)$. The principal questions in percolation theory concern the distribution of $\#W$, in particular the dependence of this distribution on the parameters $p(e)$ and $p(v)$ of $P_{\mathcal{E}}$ and $P_{\mathcal{V}}$. Of special interest are the percolation probabilities

$$\theta_{\mathcal{E}}(e) := P_{\mathcal{E}}\{\#W(e) = \infty\} \quad \text{and}$$

$$\theta_{\mathcal{V}}(v) := P_{\mathcal{V}}\{\#W(v) = \infty\}.$$

The description in this section nowhere refers to the embedding of $\mathcal{G}$ in $\mathbb{R}^d$. It is therefore clear that the distribution of $\#W$ and all related quantities in percolation theory depend only on the abstract structure of $\mathcal{G}$, i.e., on $\mathcal{V}$ and $\mathcal{E}$ and the adjacency relationship. The embedding merely helps us to visualize the situation and to give economical proofs.

Before narrowing down the model further we show that a bond-percolation problem on $\mathcal{G}$ is equivalent to a site-percolation problem on $\tilde{\mathcal{G}}$, the covering graph of $\mathcal{G}$ (see Def. 2.13). For instance the distribution of $\# W(e)$ for an edge $e$ of the simple quadratic lattice $\mathcal{G}_0$ of Ex. 2.1 (i) will be the same as that of $\# W(\tilde{v})$

when $\tilde{v}$ is the vertex of the graph $\mathcal{G}_1$ of Ex. 2.1 (ii) which corresponds to $e$ $(\mathcal{G}_1 = \tilde{\mathcal{G}}_0)$, and when the probability measures on $\mathcal{G}_0$ and $\mathcal{G}_1$ are suitably related. In general, let $\mathcal{G}$ be a graph with covering graph $\tilde{\mathcal{G}}$. Temporarily write a tilde over the entitities introduced above to denote the corresponding entity for $\tilde{\mathcal{G}}$. (e.g. $\tilde{\Omega}_{\tilde{\mathcal{V}}}$, $\tilde{P}_{\tilde{\mathcal{V}}}$). Denote by $\tilde{v}(e)$ the vertex of $\tilde{\mathcal{G}}$ associated to the edge $e$ of $\mathcal{G}$ (see Def. 2.13). We then have the following proposition.

<u>Proposition 3.1. Let</u> $\mathcal{G}$ <u>be a graph with covering graph</u> $\tilde{\mathcal{G}}$. <u>Define the map</u> $\phi : \Omega_{\mathcal{E}} \to \tilde{\Omega}_{\tilde{\mathcal{V}}}$ <u>by</u>

(3.7) $$\phi(\omega)(\tilde{v}(e)) = \omega(e) \quad , \quad e \in \mathcal{E} .$$

<u>Then</u> $\phi$ <u>is</u> 1-1 <u>onto</u> $\tilde{\Omega}_{\tilde{\mathcal{V}}}$, <u>and for any</u> $e \in \mathcal{E}$, $\omega \in \Omega_{\mathcal{E}}$,

(3.8) $$f \in W(e,\omega) \text{ if and only if } \tilde{v}(f) \in \tilde{W}(\tilde{v}(e) , \phi(\omega)).$$

<u>Moreover, if</u> $\tilde{P}_{\tilde{\mathcal{V}}}$ <u>is defined by</u>

(3.9) $$\tilde{P}_{\tilde{\mathcal{V}}} = \prod_{\tilde{v} \in \tilde{\mathcal{V}}} \mu_{\tilde{v}}$$

<u>with</u>

(3.10) $$\tilde{\mu}_{\tilde{v}}\{\tilde{\omega}(\tilde{v}) = +1\} = \mu_e\{\omega(e) = 1\} = p(e)$$

<u>whenever</u> $\tilde{v} = \tilde{v}(e)$, <u>then for all</u> $n \leq \infty$

(3.11) $$\tilde{P}_{\tilde{\mathcal{V}}}\{\#\tilde{W}(\tilde{v}(e)) = n\} = P_{\mathcal{E}}\{\#W(e) = n\}.$$

<u>Proof:</u> $f \in W(e,\omega)$ iff there exists a path $r = (v_0, e_1, \ldots, e_\nu, v_\nu)$ on $\mathcal{G}$ with $\omega(e_i) = 1$ and $e_1 = e$, $e_\nu = f$. For any such $r$ let $\tilde{r} = (\tilde{v}_1, \tilde{e}_1, \ldots, \tilde{v}_\nu)$ be a path with possible double points with $\tilde{v}_i = \tilde{v}(e_i)$ associated to $r$ as in Comment 2.5(iii). Then, by (3.7) $\phi(\omega)(\tilde{v}_i) = \phi(\omega)(\tilde{v}(e_i)) = 1$ so that $f \in W(e,\omega)$ implies

$$\tilde{v}_\nu = \tilde{v}(e_\nu) = \tilde{v}(f) \in \tilde{W}(\tilde{v}_1, \phi(\omega)) = \tilde{W}(\tilde{v}(e), \phi(\omega)) .$$

The other direction of (3.8) is proved in the same way.

Now let $C$ be a fixed union of $n$ distinct edges of $\mathcal{G}$ containing $e$ and such that for each edge $f \in C$ there exists a path $r = (v_0, e_1, \ldots, e_\nu, v_\nu)$ with possible double points on $\mathcal{G}$ with $e_1 = e$, $e_\nu = f$. Then $W(e,\omega) = C$ occurs iff

(3.12) $\omega(f) = 1$ for all $f \in C$, but $\omega(g) = -1$ for all edges $g$ of $\mathcal{G}$ with one endpoint in $C$, but $g$ not belonging to $C$.

Indeed the first requirement of (3.12) says that each edge in $C$ belongs to $W(e,\omega)$ , while the second requirement says that no other edges $f$ belong to $W(e,\omega)$ , for any path from $e$ to an edge outside $C$ has to contain an edge outside $C$ with one endpoint in $C$. Next let $\tilde{C}$ be the union of all vertices $\tilde{v}(f)$, $f \in C$ , and all edges of $\tilde{\mathcal{G}}$ between any two such vertices . $\tilde{C}$ is contained in $\tilde{\mathcal{G}}$ and contains exactly the $n$ distinct vertices $\tilde{v}(f)$ , $f \in C$ , including of course $\tilde{v}(e)$. Moreover $\tilde{W}(\tilde{v}(e), \tilde{\omega}) = \tilde{C}$ iff

(3.13) $\tilde{\omega}(\tilde{w}) = 1$ for all $\tilde{w} \in \tilde{C}$ , but $\tilde{\omega}(\tilde{u}) = -1$ for all vertices $\tilde{u}$ of $\tilde{\mathcal{G}}$ adjacent to a vertex in $\tilde{C}$ , but not belonging to $\tilde{C}$

One easily sees that $g$ has an endpoint in $C$ but does not belong to $C$ iff $\tilde{v}(g)$ is adjacent to some vertex of $\tilde{C}$ , but $\tilde{v}(g) \notin \tilde{C}$ . From this it is easy to see that

$$P_{\mathcal{E}} \{W(e) = C\} = \tilde{P}_{\tilde{\mathcal{V}}} \{\tilde{W}(\tilde{v}(e)) = \tilde{C}\} \tag{3.14}$$

if one takes $\tilde{P}_{\tilde{\mathcal{V}}}$ as in (3.9), (3.10) . But

$$\{\#W(e) = n\} = \bigcup_{\#C=n} \{W(e) = C\} \tag{3.15}$$

with the union in the right hand side of (3.15) being over all $C$ of the type considered above and containing $n$ edges. Similarly

$$\{\#\tilde{W}(\tilde{v}(e)) = n\} = \bigcup_{\#\tilde{C}=n} \{\tilde{W}(\tilde{v}(e)) = \tilde{C}\} \tag{3.16}$$

and each $\tilde{C}$ in the right hand side of (3.16) is the image of a unique $C$ in the right hand side of (3.15). The last statement is easily verified by means of Comment 2.5(iii). (3.11) now follows from (3.14)-(3.16). □

Because of Prop. 3.1 we shall restrict ourselves henceforth to site-percolation. The subscripts $\mathcal{V}$ used in this section therefore become superfluous and will be dropped from now on. We remark that we cannot use a similar procedure to translate a site-percolation problem on every graph $\mathcal{G}$ to a bond-percolation problem on another graph, because $\mathcal{G}$ may not be a covering graph of any other graph. (If $\mathcal{G} = \tilde{\mathcal{H}}$ for some graph $\mathcal{H}$ , and $\mathcal{H}$ has any vertex with three distinct edges $e_1, e_2, e_3$ incident to it, then $\tilde{v}(e_1)$, $\tilde{v}(e_2)$ and $\tilde{v}(e_3)$ are the vertices of a "triangle" in $\mathcal{G}$. Thus the graph $\mathcal{G}_0$ of Ex. 2.1 (i) - which has no triangles - is not a covering graph.) On the other hand, there seems to be no way to go from site-percolation on $\mathcal{G}$ to bond-percolation on $\tilde{\mathcal{G}}$ .

### 3.2. Periodic site-percolation.

Let $\mathcal{G}$ be a periodic graph, imbedded in $\mathbb{R}^d$, with vertex set $\mathcal{V}$ (see Def. 2.1). We consider a periodic partition of $\mathcal{V}$ into $\lambda$ sets $\mathcal{V}_1,\dots,\mathcal{V}_\lambda$, i.e., we assume

$$(3.17)\qquad \mathcal{V}_i \cap \mathcal{V}_j = \phi\ ,\ i \neq j\ ,\quad \mathcal{V} = \bigcup_{i=1}^{\lambda} \mathcal{V}_i\ ,$$

and (with $\xi_1,\dots,\xi_d$ the coordinate vectors of $\mathbb{R}^d$)

$$(3.18)\qquad v \in \mathcal{V}_i \quad \text{iff} \quad v + \sum_{j=1}^{d} k_j\xi_j \in \mathcal{V}_i\ ,$$

$$1 \leq i \leq \lambda\ ,\ k_j \in \mathbb{Z}\ .$$

(In typical examples the $\mathcal{V}_i$ will only have periods which are multiples of $\xi_1,\dots,\xi_d$ and one has to change scale to obtain (3.18); see Ex. 3.2(i) below). We take, as in Sect 3.1

$$(3.19)\qquad \Omega = \prod_{\mathcal{V}}\{-1,+1\}$$

and $\mathcal{B}$ the $\sigma$-field generated by the cylinder sets in $\Omega$. We shall restrict ourselves to probability measures on $\mathcal{B}$ which are specified by $\lambda$ parameters as follows: Let

$$(3.20)\qquad \mathcal{P}_\lambda = [0,1]^\lambda$$

and

$$(3.21)\qquad p = (p(1),\dots,p(\lambda)) \in \mathcal{P}_\lambda$$

Then take

$$(3.22)\qquad P_p = \prod_{v\in\mathcal{V}} \mu_v\ ,$$

where

$$(3.23)\quad \mu_v\{\omega(v)=1\} = 1-\mu_v\{\omega(v)=-1\} = p(i) \quad \text{if} \quad v \in \mathcal{V}_i,\ i\leq i\leq\lambda\ .$$

<u>A probability measure of this form will be called a ($\lambda$-parameter) periodic probability measure. Henceforth we shall consider only periodic probability measures on periodic graphs.</u> $E_p$ will denote expectation with respect to $P_p$.

<u>Examples.</u>

(i) Let $\mathcal{G}_0$ be the periodic graph of Ex. 2.1(i), the simple quadratic lattice. Take $\lambda = 2$, $\mathcal{V}_1 = \{(i_1,i_2): i_1+i_2 \text{ is even}\}$, $\mathcal{V}_2 = \{(i_1,i_2): i_1+i_2 \text{ is odd}\}$. As it stands, this does not satisfy (3.18). However, we only have to make a change of scale to put the example in periodic form. We change the imbedding so that the vertex originally at $(i_1,i_2)$ is now at $(\frac{i_1}{2}\ ,\ \frac{i_2}{2})$, and similarly "multiply the edges by a factor $\frac{1}{2}$". $(\frac{i_1}{2}, \frac{i_2}{2})$ and $(\frac{j_1}{2}, \frac{j_2}{2})$ are neighbors iff (2.6) holds. $\mathcal{V}_1$ now becomes $\{(\frac{i_1}{2}, \frac{i_2}{2}) : i_1+i_2$ is even$\}$ and similarly for $\mathcal{V}_2$.

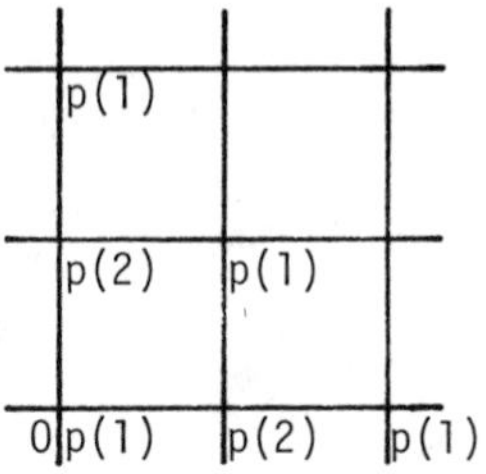


Figure 3.1 Two-parameter site-percolation on $\mathbb{Z}^2$. The p-value next to a vertex gives the probability of being occupied for that vertex.

(ii) We describe this example as a bond-problem, because the transcription to a site-problem on the covering graph is more complicated. In this example we allow three parameters. For $\mathcal{G}$ we take the triangular lattice of Ex. 2.1(iii). We now consider the partition of its <u>bonds</u> into the three sets

(3.24) $\quad \mathcal{E}_j$ = {bonds along the lines under an angle $(j-1)\frac{2\pi}{3}$ with the first coordinate axis}, $j=1,2,3$,

and take each bond in $\mathcal{E}_j$ open with probability $p(j)$. The description in (3.24) presupposes that $\mathcal{G}$ is imbedded in $\mathbb{R}^2$ as in Fig. 2.4

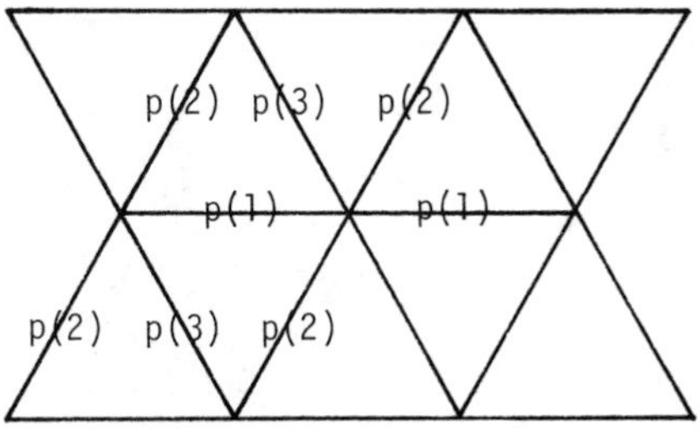


Figure 3.2 The p-value next to an edge gives the probability of that edge being passable.

To transcribe this to a periodic site-problem, we have to assign probability $p(j)$ of being occupied to a vertex of $\tilde{\mathcal{G}}$ corresponding to an edge $e$ in $\mathcal{E}_j$. We also have to change scale as in the description of $\mathcal{T}$ in Ex. 2.1 (iii) to obtain a periodic problem. ///

Define $W(v) = W(v,\omega)$ as in Def. 2.7 with "v occupied" being interpreted as "$\omega(v) = +1$", and set

(3.25) $$\theta(p,v) = P_p\{\#W(v) = \infty\} .$$

The $\lambda$ parameter periodic site-percolation problem is to determine the <u>percolative region</u> in $\mathcal{P}_\lambda$, i.e., to determine the set

(3.26) $$\{p \in \mathcal{P}_\lambda : \theta(p,v) > 0 \ \text{ for some } \ v\} .$$

If $p(i) > 0$ for $i \le i \le \lambda$ then $\theta(p,v) > 0$ for some $v$ iff $\theta(p,v) > 0$ for all $v$ by the FKG inequality (see Broadbent and Hammersley (1957) and Sect. 4.1. below). Therefore the intersection of the set (3.26) with $\{p: p(i) > 0 \ \text{ for } \ 1 \le i \le \lambda\}$ is independent of $v$; it equals the set

(3.27) $$\{p \in \mathcal{P}_\lambda : p(i) > 0 \quad \text{for} \quad 1 \le i \le \lambda \quad \text{and} \quad \theta(p,v) > 0 \ \text{ for all } \ v\}.$$

In the next section we formulate our principal result describing the percolative region, while Sect. 3.4 applies this theorem to give explicit answers in a number of examples. These answers had all been conjectured already in Sykes and Essam (1964).

## 3.3. Crossing probabilities and the principal theorem on percolative regions.

Let $\mathcal{G}$ be a graph imbedded in $\mathbb{R}^d$ which satisfies (2.1)-(2.5). We consider blocks $B$ in $\mathbb{R}^d$ of the form

(3.28) $$B = \prod_1^d [a_i,b_i] = \{x=(x(1),\dots,x(d)): a_i \le x(i) \le b_i, 1 \le i \le d\}$$

<u>Def. 1</u>. An <u>i-crossing</u> (on $\mathcal{G}$) of $B$ is a path $(v_0,e_1,\dots,e_\nu,v_\nu)$ (on $\mathcal{G}$) which satisfies[1)]

(3.29) $$(v_1,e_2,\dots,e_{\nu-1},v_{\nu-1}) \text{ is contained in } \mathring{B} = (a_1,b_1) \times \dots \times (a_d,b_d)$$

---

1) We use standard interval notation for segments of edges. E.g. in (3.30) $(\zeta_1,v_1]$ denotes the piece of $e_1$ between $\zeta_1$ and $v_1$ excluding $\zeta_1$ but including $v_1$. Similarly for the segment $[v_{\nu-1},\zeta_\nu)$ of $e_\nu$ in (3.31).

(3.30) $e_1$ intersects the face $\{x(i) = a_i\} \cap B =$

$[a_1,b_1]\times\ldots\times[a_{i-1},b_{i-1}]\times\{a_i\}\times[a_{i+1},b_{i+1}]\times\ldots\times[a_d,b_d]$

of $B$ in some point $\zeta_1$ such that $(\zeta_1,v_1] \subset \mathring{B}$ .

and

(3.31) $e_\nu$ intersects the face $\{x(i) = b_i\} \cap B$ of $B$ in some point $\zeta_\nu$ such that $[v_{\nu-1},\zeta_\nu) \subset \mathring{B}$ .

Comments .

(i) Note that (3.29)-(3.31) require all but the first and final edge of an i-crossing $(v_0,e_1,\ldots,e_\nu,v_\nu)$ of $B$, as well as the segments $(\zeta_1,v_1]$ and $[v_{\nu-1},\zeta_\nu)$ of the first and final edge to lie in the interior of $B$. When $d = 2$ , i.e. $B$ is a rectangle in the plane, then we shall call a 1-crossing (2-crossing) a <u>horizontal (vertical) crossing</u> of $B$. In this case the continuous curve made up from $[\zeta_1,v_1]$ , $e_2,\ldots,e_{\nu-1}$ and $[v_{\nu-1},\zeta_{\nu-1}]$ is a crosscut of $\mathring{B}$ (in the terminology of Newman (1951), Ch. V.11.). Finally note that the initial and final point $v_0$ and $v_\nu$ of a crossing of $B$ can lie in $\mathring{B}$ or in Fr $(B)$ or outside $B$.

(ii) An i-crossing $r$ of $B$ is minimal in the sense that no subpath of the crossing with fewer edges than $r$ is still an i-crossing. One does, however, have the following obvious monotonicity property. If $[a_i',b_i'] \subset [a_i,b_i]$ but $[a_j,b_j] \subset [a_j',b_j']$ for $j \neq i$ , then an i-crossing $(v_0,e_1,\ldots,e_\nu,v_\nu)$ of $B = \Pi[a_j,b_j]$ contains a subpath $(v_\alpha,e_{\alpha+1},\ldots,e_\beta,v_\beta)$ which is an i-crossing of $B' = \Pi[a_j',b_j']$.

<u>Def. 2</u>. An i-crossing $(v_0,e_1,\ldots,e_\nu,v_\nu)$ of $B$ is called an <u>occupied (vacant) i-crossing</u> if all its vertices are occupied (vacant).

Comments .

(iii) When we shall use vacant crossings we shall usually be dealing with a matching pair of graphs $\mathcal{G}$ and $\mathcal{G}^*$. We shall then be interested in occupied crossings on $\mathcal{G}$ and vacant crossings on $\mathcal{G}^*$ . ///

Now let $P_p$ be a $\lambda$-parameter periodic probability measure, as in Sect. 3.2. Especially important for us will be the probability that there exists an i-crossing of a block with the "lower left" corner at the origin. Formally we define these as follows.

<u>Def. 3</u>. The <u>crossing probability in the i-th direction of</u> $[0,n_1] \times \ldots \times [0,n_d]$ (on $\mathcal{G}$) is

(3.32) $\sigma(\bar{n};i,p) = \sigma(\bar{n};i,p,\mathcal{G}) = P_p\{\exists$ an occupied i-crossing on $\mathcal{G}$ of $[0,n_1] \times \dots \times [0,n_d]\}$ .

The analogous quantity for vacant crossings on $\mathcal{G}^*$ will be written as

(3.33) $\sigma^*(\bar{n};i,p) = \sigma^*(\bar{n};i,p,\mathcal{G}) = \sigma(\bar{n};i,\bar{1}-p,\mathcal{G}^*) = P_p\{\exists$ a vacant i-crossing on $\mathcal{G}^*$ of $[0,n_1] \times \dots \times [0,n_d]\}$

($\bar{n}$ here stands for $(n_1,\dots,n_d)$.)

Comments .

(iv) In (3.33) $\bar{1}-p$ stands for the $\lambda$-vector $(1-p(1),1-p(2),\dots,1-p(\lambda))$ , while $(\mathcal{G},\mathcal{G}^*)$ is a matching pair, based on $(\mathcal{M},\mathcal{F})$ say. Recall that $\mathcal{M},\mathcal{G}$ and $\mathcal{G}^*$ have the same vertex set in this case (Comment 2.2 (iv)). Thus $P_p$ as defined by (3.21)-(3.23) is simultaneously a probability measure on the occupancy configurations on $\mathcal{G}_1$, on $\mathcal{G}^*$ and on $\mathcal{M}$ . The second equality in (3.33) is immediate from

(3.34) $P_p\{v$ is vacant$\} = 1-p(i) = P_{\bar{1}-p}\{v$ is occupied$\}$ , $v \in \mathcal{V}_i$.

(see (3.22), (3.23)).

(v) It is immediate from Def. 3.1, 3.2 and Comment 3.3(ii) that $\sigma(\bar{n};i,p)$ is decreasing in $n_i$ but increasing in each $n_j$ with $j \neq i$ . ///

The remainder of this section gives the formulation of our principal theorems on the percolative region. These deal only with graphs imbedded in the plane. $(\mathcal{G}, \mathcal{G}^*)$ will be a matching pair of periodic graphs imbedded in $\mathbb{R}^2$ , and $P_p$ will be a $\lambda$-parameter probability measure. $W^*(v) = W^*(v,\omega)$ will denote the vacant cluster of $v$ on $\mathcal{G}$ , i.e.,the union of all edges and vertices of $\mathcal{G}^*$ which belong to a vacant path on $\mathcal{G}^*$ with initial point v. The following conditions A and B will be used. They are viewed as conditions on the parameter point $p_0$ for fixed $\mathcal{G}$, $\mathcal{G}^*$ and $\mathcal{V}_1,\dots, \mathcal{V}_\lambda$ . Condition A relates the probabilities of an occupied crossing on $\mathcal{G}$ with those of a vacant crossing on $\mathcal{G}^*$ . Condition B is a relation between horizontal crossings (i.e., crossings in the 1-direction) with vertical crossings (i.e., crossings in the 2-direction).

Condition A. There exists a $0 < \delta \leq \frac{1}{2}$ , an integer $n_0$ and vectors[1] $\bar{\rho} = (\rho_1, \rho_2), \bar{\rho}^* = (\rho_1^*, \rho_2^*)$ such that for $i = 1$ or $i = 2$

(3.35) $\sigma(\bar{n}; i, p_0) \geq \frac{1}{2}$ implies $\sigma^*(\bar{n}-\bar{\rho}; i, p_0) \geq \delta$ ,

whenever $n_1, n_2 \geq n_0$ ,

and also for $j=1$ or $j=2$

(3.36) $\sigma^*(\bar{n}; j, p_0) \geq \frac{1}{2}$ implies $\sigma(\bar{n}-\bar{\rho}^*; j, p_0) \geq \delta$

whenever $n_1, n_2 \geq n_0$ .

Condition B. There exist numbers $\delta > 0$, $0 < a_j, b_j < \infty$, $j = 1,2$ , and sequences $\{\bar{n}_\ell = (n_{\ell 1}, n_{\ell 2})\}_{\ell \geq 1}, \{\bar{m}_\ell = (m_{\ell 1}, m_{\ell 2})\}_{\ell \geq 1}$ such that

(3.37) $n_{\ell j} \to \infty$ , $m_{\ell j} \to \infty$ as $\ell \to \infty$ , $j = 1,2$

and

(3.38) $\sigma(\bar{n}_\ell; 1, p_0) \geq \delta$ , $\sigma((a_1 n_{\ell 1}, a_2 n_{\ell 2}); 2, p_0) \geq \delta$

(3.39) $\sigma^*(\bar{m}_\ell; 1, p_0) \geq \delta$ , $\sigma^*((b_1 m_{\ell 1}, b_2 m_{\ell 2}); 2, p_0) \geq \delta$ .

One more definition and a bit of notation.

Def. 4 We call the line $L : x(1) = a$ or $x(2) = a$ an axis of symmetry for the partition $\mathcal{V}_1, \ldots, \mathcal{V}_\lambda$ of the vertices of $\mathcal{G}$ if each $\mathcal{V}_i$ is invariant under reflection in the line $L$.

Comment.

(vi) If $P_p$ is given by (3.22), (3.23) and $x(1) = a$ is an axis of symmetry for $\mathcal{G}$ and for $\mathcal{V}_1, \ldots, \mathcal{V}_\lambda$ then for $v = (v(1), v(2))$

(3.40) $P_p\{v = (v(1), v(2))$ is occupied$\} = P_p\{(2a - v(1), v(2))$ is occupied$\}$

for any $p \in \mathcal{P}_\lambda$ . Similarly if $x(2) = a$ is an axis of symmetry for $\mathcal{G}$ and $\mathcal{V}_1, \ldots, \mathcal{V}_\lambda$. ///

When dealing with $\lambda$-parameter problems $\bar{0}(\bar{1})$ will denote the $\lambda$-vector all of whose components equal zero (one). For $p \in \mathcal{P}_\lambda$, and real $t$, $tp$ has components $tp(1), \ldots, tp(\lambda)$. Also, for $p', p'' \in \mathcal{P}_\lambda$

(3.41) $p' << p''$ means $p'(i) < p''(i)$ , $i \leq i \leq \lambda$ .

Unfortunately the following two theorems have a forbidding appearance. Nevertheless they allow the determination of the percolative

1) The $\rho_i$ and $\rho_i^*$ can take negative values.

region in several examples, as we demonstrate in the next section.

Theorem 3.1. Let $(\mathcal{G},\mathcal{G}^*)$ be a matching pair of periodic graphs imbedded in $\mathbb{R}^2$ and $\mathcal{V}_1,\dots,\mathcal{V}_\lambda$ a periodic partition of the vertices of $\mathcal{G}$ such that one of the coordinate axis is an axis of symmetry for $\mathcal{G}$, $\mathcal{G}^*$ and the partition $\mathcal{V}_1,\dots,\mathcal{V}_\lambda$. Let $p_0 \in \mathcal{P}_\lambda$ be such that

$$(3.42)\qquad \overline{0} << p_0 << \overline{1}$$

and such that Condition A or Condition B is satisfied. Then

(i) for all vertices $v$ of $\mathcal{G}$ (and hence of $\mathcal{G}^*$)

$$(3.43)\qquad P_{p_0}\{\#W(v) = \infty\} = P_{p_0}\{\#W^*(v) = \infty\} = 0$$

but

$$(3.44)\qquad E_{p_0}\{\#W(v)\} = E_{p_0}\{\#W^*(v)\} = \infty \ .$$

Also, for every square $S_N = \{(x_1,x_2) : |x_1| \le N, |x_2| \le N\}$

$$(3.45)\qquad P_{p_0}\{\exists \text{ an occupied circuit on } \mathcal{G} \text{ surrounding } S_N \text{ and } \exists \text{ a vacant circuit on } \mathcal{G}^* \text{ surrounding } S_N\} = 1 \ .$$

(ii) for any $p' << p_0$

$$(3.46)\qquad P_{p'}\{\#W(v) = \infty\} = 0 \ , \ P_{p'}\{\#W^*(v) = \infty\} > 0$$

and

$$(3.47)\qquad P_{p'}\{\exists \text{ exactly one infinite vacant cluster on } \mathcal{G}^*\} = 1$$

and

$$(3.48)\qquad E_{p'}\{\#W(v)\} < \infty \ .$$

(iii) for any $p'' >> p_0$

$$(3.49)\qquad P_{p''}\{\#W(v) = \infty\} > 0 \ , \ P_{p''}\{\#W^*(v) = \infty\} = 0$$

and

$$(3.50)\qquad P_{p''}\{\exists \text{ exactly one infinite occupied cluster on } \mathcal{G}\} = 1$$

and

$$(3.51)\qquad E_{p''}\{\#W^*(v)\} < \infty \ .$$

Theorem 3.2. Let $\mathcal{G}$, $\mathcal{G}^*$ and $\mathcal{V}_1,\dots,\mathcal{V}_\lambda$ be as in Theorem 3.1. Assume there exist constants $0 < a_j,\dots,d_j < \infty$, $j = 1,2,3$, and for each $p \in \mathcal{P}_\lambda$ with $\overline{0} << p << \overline{1}$ a function $h : (0,1] \to (0,1]$ and an $n_0$ ($h$ and $n_0$ may depend on $p$) such that for $n \ge n_0$ and $0 < x \le 1$

(3.52) $\sigma((n,a_1n);1,p) \geq x$ implies $\sigma((a_2n,a_3n);2,p) \geq h(x) > 0$

(3.53) $\sigma((n,b_1n);2,p) \geq x$ implies $\sigma((b_2n,b_3n);1,p) \geq h(x) > 0$ ,

(3.54) $\sigma^*((n,c_1n);1,p) \geq x$ implies $\sigma^*((c_2n,c_3n);2,p) \geq h(x) > 0$ ,

and

(3.55) $\sigma^*((n,d_1n);2,p) \geq x$ implies $\sigma^*((d_2n,d_3n);1,p) \geq h(x) > 0$ .

For $p_1 \in \mathcal{P}_\lambda$ choose

(3.56) $$t_0 = \inf\{t \geq 0: tp_1 \in \mathcal{P}_\lambda \text{ , } \limsup \sigma((n,a_1n);1,tp_1) > 0 \text{ or } \limsup_{n\to\infty} \sigma((n,b_1n); 2,tp_1) > 0\}$$

provided the set in the right hand side of (3.56) is nonempty. If

$$\bar{0} << p_0 := t_0p_1 << \bar{1} \text{ ,}$$

then condition B holds for $p_0$ , and consequently also (3.43) - (3.51) .

The proof of these theorems will be given in Ch. 7 after the necessary machinery has been developed.

In all examples of the next section the following corollary applies. Let $\mathcal{G}$, $\mathcal{G}^*$ and $\mathcal{V}_1,\ldots, \mathcal{V}_\lambda$ be as in Theorem 3.1. Set

(3.57) $$\mathcal{S} = \{p_0 \in \mathcal{P}_\lambda : \bar{0} << p_0 << \bar{1} \text{ and Condition A or Condition B holds for } p_0\}$$

and

(3.58) $$\mathcal{P}_- = \{p' \in \mathcal{P}_\lambda: p' << p_0 \text{ for some } p_0 \in \mathcal{S}\} \text{ ,}$$

$$\mathcal{P}_+ = \{p'' \in \mathcal{P}_\lambda: p'' >> p_0 \text{ for some } p_0 \in \mathcal{S}\} \text{ .}$$

Corollary 3.1. Let $(\mathcal{G}, \mathcal{G}^*)$ and $\mathcal{V}_1,\ldots, \mathcal{V}_\lambda$ be as in Theorem 3.1. If

(3.59) $$(0,1)^\lambda \subset \mathcal{P}_- \cup \mathcal{S} \cup \mathcal{P}_+$$

then the percolative regions for $\mathcal{G}$ and $\mathcal{G}^*$ in $(0,1)^\lambda$ are $\mathcal{P}_+$ and $\mathcal{P}_-$ , respectively (i.e., for $\bar{0} << p << \bar{1}$ infinite occupied clusters on $\mathcal{G}$ (infinite vacant clusters on $\mathcal{G}^*$) occur iff $p \in \mathcal{P}_+(\mathcal{P}_-)$ .

It is reasonable to call $\mathcal{S}$ the critical surface in the cases where Cor. 1 applies.

## 3.4 Critical probabilities. Applications of the principal theorems.

The FKG inequality implies (see Sect. 4.1) that if $\mathcal{G}$ is connected, and if

(3.60) $P_p\{v$ is occupied$\} > 0$ for all vertices of $\mathcal{G}$ ,

then $\theta(p,v) > 0$ for some v iff $\theta(p,v) > 0$ for all v. Also $E_p\{\#W(v)\} = \infty$ for some v iff this holds for all v (see Sect. 4.1). For one-parameter problems with

(3.61) $P_p\{v$ is occupied$\} = \mu_v\{\omega(v) = 1\} = p$

for all vertices v of a connected graph $\mathcal{G}$ we can therefore define the <u>critical probabilities</u>

(3.62) $p_H = p_H(\mathcal{G}) = \sup\{p \in [0,1] : \theta(p,v) = 0\}$ ,

(3.63) $p_T = p_T(\mathcal{G}) = \sup\{p \in [0,1] : E_p\{\#W(v)\} < \infty\}$ ,

and these numbers are independent of the choice of v. By definition

$$E_p\{\#W(v)\} \geq \theta(p,v) \cdot \infty$$

so that $E_p\{\#W(v)\} = \infty$ for $p > p_H$ . Therefore one always has

(3.64) $$p_T \leq p_H \cdot$$

For periodic graphs $\mathcal{G}$ imbedded in $\mathbb{R}^d$ we define a third critical probability which is a slight modification of one introduced by Seymour and Welsh (1978); see also Russo (1978).

(3.65) $$p_S := \sup\{p \in [0,1] : \lim_{n\to\infty} \sigma((3n,3n,\dots 3n,n,3n,\dots 3n);i,p) = 0 \quad , \quad 1 \leq i \leq d\} .$$

where the one component equal to n in $\sigma((3n,\dots,n,\dots,3n);i,p)$ in (3.65) is the i-th component. It will be a consequence of Theorem 5.1 that for any periodic graph $\mathcal{G}$ imbedded in $\mathbb{R}^d$

(3.66) $$p_T = p_S \cdot$$

In some cases Corollary 3.1 can be used to show that

$$p_T = p_S = p_H \quad ,$$

and in a small class of examples one can even calculate the common value of these critical probabilities. This is demonstrated in the applications below. Again all these applications are for graphs imbedded in the plane.

<u>Applications</u>.

(i) <u>Triangulated graphs</u>. Let $\mathcal{G}$ be a periodic graph imbedded in $\mathbb{R}^2$ such that one of the coordinate axes is a symmetry axis and such that all faces of $\mathcal{G}$ are triangles. Let $P_p$ be the one-parameter probability measure defined by (3.22) and (3.61). In each problem of this form

(3.67) $$p_T = p_S = p_H = \frac{1}{2} .$$

This applies for instance in the site-problem on the triangular lattice of Ex. 2.1(iii) or the centered quadratic lattice of Ex. 2.2 (iii).

It is interesting to observe that one may "decorate" the faces of $\mathcal{G}$ almost arbitrarily without affecting (3.67). That is, if $F$ is a face of $\mathcal{G}$ we may add a number of vertices and edges inside $F$. The addition of these vertices and edges does not increase $\theta(p,v)$. Indeed, any occupied path entering and leaving $\bar{F}$ has to do so at two vertices $v_1$ and $v_2$ on the perimeter of $F$. But then $v_1$ and $v_2$ are occupied and connected by an edge of $\mathcal{G}$, and hence the piece of the path in $\bar{F}$ between $v_1$ and $v_2$ can be replaced by the edge between $v_1$ and $v_2$. We can make such a change in every face; the decorations of different faces don't have to have any relation to each other, and the resulting graph does not have to be periodic or planar. Nevertheless it will have the same value of $\theta(p,v)$ for $v \in \mathcal{G}$ and hence also $p_H = \frac{1}{2}$. If the number of added vertices in any face is uniformly bounded, then a slight extension of the above argument shows that also $p_T = p_S = \frac{1}{2}$ remains true for the decorated graph.

Van den Berg (1981), Fig. 1, shows an interesting example of a graph $\mathcal{G}$ which has all the properties required above, except for the periodicity, but with $p_T = p_H = 1$. This illustrates how crucial periodicity is.

Proof of (3.67): $\mathcal{G}$ is a periodic mosaic and since all faces are already close-packed, we can take $\mathcal{G}^* = \mathcal{G}$. $(\mathcal{G}, \mathcal{G}^*)$ is the matching pair based on $(\mathcal{G}, \emptyset)$; see Ex. 2.2 (iii). $\mathcal{G}$ is self-matching and Condition A holds trivially for $p_0 = \frac{1}{2}$. Indeed

$$P_{\frac{1}{2}}\{v \text{ is occupied}\} = P_{\frac{1}{2}}\{v \text{ is vacant}\} = \frac{1}{2} ,$$

and since $\mathcal{G} = \mathcal{G}^*$ this gives

(3.68) $$\sigma^*(\bar{n};i,\tfrac{1}{2}) = \sigma(\bar{n};i,1-\tfrac{1}{2},\mathcal{G}^*) = \sigma(\bar{n};i,\tfrac{1}{2},\mathcal{G}) .$$

Clearly (3.68) implies (3.35) and (3.36). Thus, by (3.43), (3.46) and (3.49) percolation occurs under $P_p$ iff $p > \frac{1}{2}$. Also,

$E_p\{\#W(v)\} < \infty$ iff $p < \frac{1}{2}$. Thus $p_H = p_T = \frac{1}{2}$ and (3.67) now follows from (3.66).

(ii) Bond percolation on $\mathbb{Z}^2$ and further self-matching problems. In the first application we considered a one-parameter problem with $\mathcal{G} = \mathcal{G}^*$. Here we consider a two-parameter problem for a matching pair of periodic graphs $(\mathcal{G}, \mathcal{G}^*)$ with $\mathcal{G}^*$ a translate of $\mathcal{G}$. Assume that

$$(3.69) \qquad \mathcal{G}^* = \mathcal{G} + \gamma$$

for some vector $\gamma = (\gamma(1),\gamma(2))$. In other words, $\mathcal{G}$ and $\mathcal{G}^*$ are imbedded in $\mathbb{R}^2$ such that $v(e)$ is a vertex (edge) of $\mathcal{G}$ iff $v + \gamma$ $(e + \gamma)$ is a vertex (edge) of $\mathcal{G}^*$. Assume also that the vertex set $\mathcal{V}$ is partitioned into two periodic classes $\mathcal{V}_1$, $\mathcal{V}_2$ which satisfy

$$(3.70) \qquad \mathcal{V}_2 = \mathcal{V}_1 + \gamma ,$$

and that one of the coordinate axes is an axis of symmetry for $\mathcal{G}$, $\mathcal{G}^*$ and $\mathcal{V}_1$, $\mathcal{V}_2$. If $p = (p(1),p(2))$ satisfies

$$(3.71) \qquad p(1) + p(2) = 1 \quad , \quad 0 < p(i) < 1 ,$$

then it is again easy to verify Condition A (see below). Hence (3.71) gives the critical surface in this situation, and percolation occurs on $\mathcal{G}$ under $P_p$ with $p << 1$ iff $p(1) + p(2) > 1$. The restriction of $p$ to the line $p(1) = p(2)$ gives the one-parameter problem, and we see from (3.71) that the critical probabilities are again given by (3.67) in a one-parameter problem on a $\mathcal{G}$ which satisfies (3.69) ((3.70) will not even be needed for the one-parameter problem, since (3.72) below automatically holds at $p = (\frac{1}{2},\frac{1}{2})$ .).

The most classical example of this kind is bond-percolation on $\mathbb{Z}^2$ with

$$P\{e \text{ is passable}\} = \begin{cases} p(1) & \text{if } e \text{ is a horizontal edge} \\ p(2) & \text{if } e \text{ is a vertical edge.} \end{cases}$$

By Prop. 3.1 this is equivalent to site-percolation on the graph $\mathcal{G}_1$ of Ex. 2.1 (ii) with (page 19)

$$\mathcal{V}_1 = \{(i_1 + \tfrac{1}{2}, i_2) : i_1,i_2 \in \mathbb{Z}\} ,$$

$$\mathcal{V}_2 = \{(i_1,i_2 + \tfrac{1}{2}) : i_1,i_2 \in \mathbb{Z}\} .$$

(See also Ex. 2.5 (ii).) To see that this fits in the above framework we take for $\mathcal{M}_1$ the mosaic with vertex set $\mathcal{V}_1 \cup \mathcal{V}_2$ and an edge between the vertices $v = (v(1),v(2))$ and $w = (w(1),w(2))$ iff (2.10) holds. For $\mathcal{F}_1$ we take the faces of $\mathcal{M}_1$ (which are tilted squares, see Fig. 3.3 below) which contain a point $(i_1,i_2)$, with integral $i_1$, $i_2$. $\mathcal{F}_1^*$ will consist of those faces which do not contain a point $(i_1,i_2)$ with integral $i_1,i_2$. Finally $\mathcal{G}_1^*$ is the graph with vertex set $\mathcal{V}_1 \cup \mathcal{V}_2$ and $v = (v(1),v(2))$, $w = (w(1),w(2))$ adjacent iff either (2.10) holds or

$$v(1) = w(1) \in \mathbb{Z} + \frac{1}{2}\ ,\ v(2),w(2) \in \mathbb{Z}\ ,\ |v(2)-w(2)| = 1$$

or

$$v(1),w(1) \in \mathbb{Z}\ , |v(1)-w(1)| = 1,\ v(2) = w(2) \in \mathbb{Z} + \frac{1}{2}\ .$$

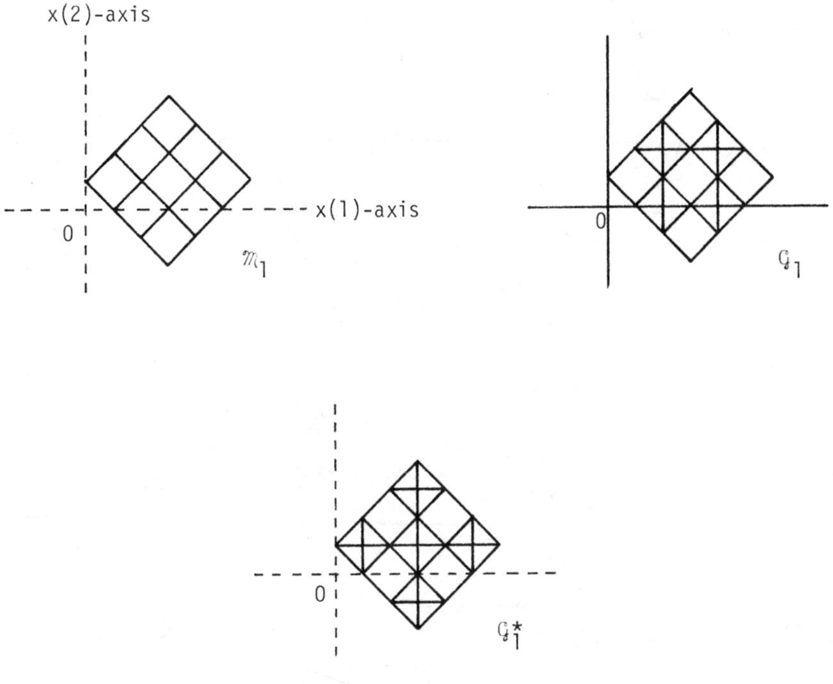


Figure 3.3

One easily checks that $(\mathcal{G}_1, \mathcal{G}_1^*)$ is the matching pair based on $(\mathcal{M}_1, \mathcal{F}_1)$ and that

$$\mathcal{G}_1^* = \mathcal{G}_1 + (\tfrac{1}{2}, \tfrac{1}{2}), \quad \mathcal{V}_2 = \mathcal{V}_1 + (\tfrac{1}{2}, \tfrac{1}{2}).$$

Thus (3.69) and (3.70) hold in this example and (3.71) is the critical surface. A generalization of this result for a mixed percolation model in which bond, sites and faces are random is given by Wierman (1982b).

Another example is $\mathcal{G} = \mathcal{G}^* = \mathcal{T}$, the triangular lattice $\mathcal{T}$ of Ex. 2.1 (iii) with

$$\mathcal{V}_1 = \{(i_1, i_2): i_1, i_2 \in \mathbb{Z}\},$$

$$\mathcal{V}_2 = \{(i_1 + \tfrac{1}{2}, i_2 + \tfrac{1}{2}): i_1, i_2 \in \mathbb{Z}\}.$$

Again (3.69) and (3.70) hold with $\gamma = (\tfrac{1}{2}, \tfrac{1}{2})$, and the critical surface is given by (3.71).

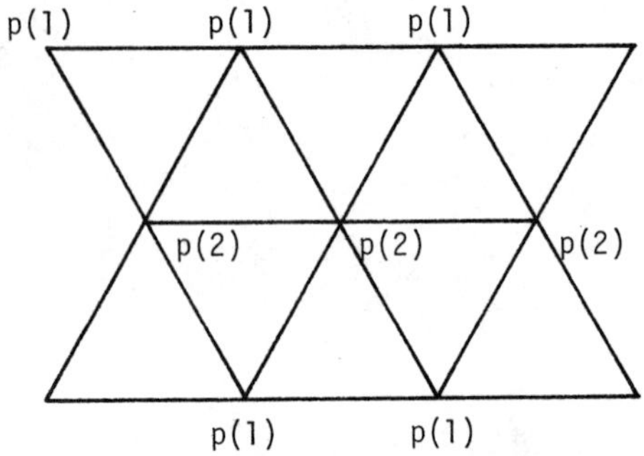


Figure 3.4 The p-value next to a vertex gives the probability of being occupied for that vertex.

Verification of Condition A. Since $\mathcal{G}$ and $\mathcal{G}^*$ have the same vertex set (Comment 2.2 (iv)).

$$\mathcal{V}_1 \cup \mathcal{V}_2 = \mathcal{V} = \text{vertex set of } \mathcal{G}^* = \mathcal{V} + \gamma = (\mathcal{V}_1 + \gamma) \cup (\mathcal{V}_2 + \gamma)$$

$$= \mathcal{V}_2 \cup (\mathcal{V}_2 + \gamma)$$

by (3.69) and (3.70). But $\mathcal{V}_1+\gamma$ and $\mathcal{V}_2+\gamma$ are disjoint, and the same holds for $\mathcal{V}_1$ and $\mathcal{V}_2$ (see (3.17)). Thus, in addition to (3.70)

$$\mathcal{V}_1 = \mathcal{V}_2 + \gamma \quad .$$

Therefore, if $v \in \mathcal{V}_1$, $v+\gamma \in \mathcal{V}_2$ and for $p_0$ satisfying (3.71)

$$P_{p_0}\{v+\gamma \text{ is vacant}\} = 1 - P_{p_0}\{v+\gamma \text{ is occupied}\} = 1 - p_0(2)$$
$$= p_0(1) = P_{p_0}\{v \text{ is occupied}\}.$$

Similarly for $v \in \mathcal{V}_2$, so that for all $v$

(3.72) $$P_{p_0}\{v \text{ is occupied}\} = P_{p_0}\{v+\gamma \text{ is vacant}\}, \text{ and}$$

$$P_{p_0}\{v \text{ is vacant}\} = P_{p_0}\{v+\gamma \text{ is occupied}\}.$$

Consequently the distribution of the set of occupied vertices of $\mathcal{G}$ equals the distribution of the set of vacant vertices on $\mathcal{G}+\gamma = \mathcal{G}^*$. Therefore

(3.73) $$\sigma^*(\bar{n}-\bar{\rho};1,p_0) = P_{p_0}\{\exists \text{ vacant horizontal crossing on } \mathcal{G}^* \text{ of } [0,n_1-\rho_1]\times[0,n_2-\rho_2]\}$$

$$= P_{p_0}\{\exists \text{ occupied horizontal crossing on } \mathcal{G} \text{ of } [-\gamma_1,n_1-\rho_1-\gamma_1]\times[-\gamma_2,n_2-\rho_2-\gamma_2]\} \quad .$$

By means of the monotonicity properties of $\sigma$ given in Comment 3.3 (v) we see that for

(3.74) $$\rho_1 \geq 1 \quad , \quad \rho_2 \leq -1$$

the last member of (3.73) is at least[1)]

$$P_{p_0}\{\exists \text{ occupied horizontal crossing on } \mathcal{G} \text{ of } [-\gamma_1+\lceil\gamma_1\rceil,n_1-\rho_1-\gamma_1+\lceil\gamma_1\rceil]\times[-\gamma_2+\lfloor\gamma_2\rfloor,n_2-\rho_2-\gamma_2+\lfloor\gamma_2\rfloor]\}$$
$$\geq \sigma(\bar{n};1,p_0).$$

1) $\lfloor\gamma\rfloor$ denotes the largest integer $\leq \gamma$ and $\lceil\gamma\rceil$ the smallest integer $\geq \gamma$.

Thus, for any $\rho$ which satisfies (3.74), (3.35) holds with $\delta = \frac{1}{2}$. Similarly for (3.36).

(iii) Bond-percolation on the triangular and the hexagonal lattice. In this application we take $\mathcal{G}$ = the triangular lattice and $\mathcal{G}_d$ = the hexagonal lattice, imbedded as in Ex. 2.6 (ii). Thus the vertices of $\mathcal{G}$ are at the points $(i_1, i_2\sqrt{3})$ and $(j_1 + \frac{1}{2}, (j_2 + \frac{1}{2})\sqrt{3}), i_1, i_2, j_1, j_2 \in \mathbb{Z}$. The faces of $\mathcal{G}$ are equilateral triangles and its edges are under an angle $0$, $\pi/3$ or $2\pi/3$ with the first coordinate axis. The faces of $\mathcal{G}_d$ are regular hexagons and its edges are under angles $\frac{\pi}{2}, \frac{\pi}{2} + \frac{\pi}{3}, \frac{\pi}{2} + \frac{2\pi}{3}$ with the first coordinate axis. Strictly speaking, this is not a periodic imbedding, but as pointed out in Sect. 2.1 one merely has to change the vertical scale to make it periodic. In addition we shall describe this application in terms of bond-percolation. This is simpler than its equivalent formulation as a site-problem which can be obtained by going over to the covering graphs, as discussed in Sect. 2.5. Since $\mathcal{G}$ and $\mathcal{G}_d$ are a dual pair, their covering graphs form a matching pair. (See Sect. 2.6, especially Ex. 2.6 (ii).) One can verify this easily explicitly, but the covering graphs are more complicated than $\mathcal{G}$ and $\mathcal{G}_d$ themselves.

As we shall see below, for the one-parameter bond-problem on these graphs the critical probabilities are given by

$$(3.75) \qquad p_T(\mathcal{G};\text{bond}) = p_S(\mathcal{G};\text{bond}) = p_H(\mathcal{G};\text{bond}) = 2 \sin \frac{\pi}{18},$$

$$(3.76) \qquad p_T(\mathcal{G}_d;\text{bond}) = p_S(\mathcal{G}_d;\text{bond}) = p_H(\mathcal{G}_d;\text{bond}) = 1 - 2 \sin \frac{\pi}{18}.$$

Before we come to this result we describe first the 3-parameter problem of Sykes and Essam (1964). The edge set $\mathcal{E}$ of $\mathcal{G}$ is divided into the three classes

$$\mathcal{E}_i = \{\text{edges of } \mathcal{G} \text{ making an angle of } (i-1)\frac{\pi}{3}$$
$$\text{with first coordinate axis}\},\ i = 1,2,3.$$

An edge of $\mathcal{E}_i$ is passable with probability $p(i)$. Each edge of $\mathcal{G}_d$ intersects exactly one edge of $\mathcal{G}$ and vice versa. In the covering graphs a pair of intersecting edges of $\mathcal{G}$ and $\mathcal{G}_d$ would correspond to one common vertex of the covering graphs. In accordance with this fact we take an edge of $\mathcal{G}_d$ as passable iff the edge of $\mathcal{G}$ which it intersects is passable. Thus, any configuration of passable and blocked edges in $\mathcal{G}$ is viewed at the same time as a configuration of passable and blocked edges on $\mathcal{G}_d$. The analogues of $\sigma$ and $\sigma^*$ in the bond version become

$$\sigma(\bar{n};i,p,\mathcal{G}) = P_p\{\exists \text{ crossing in the i-direction of } [0,n_1]\times[0,n_2] \text{ on } \mathcal{G} \text{ with all its edges passable}\},$$

$$\sigma^*(\bar{n};i,p,\mathcal{G}) = P_p\{\exists \text{ crossing in the i-direction of } [0,n_1]\times[0,n_2] \text{ on } \mathcal{G}^* \text{ with all its edges blocked}\}.$$

To verify condition A with this interpretation of $\sigma$ and $\sigma^*$ we follow Sykes and Essam's ingenious use of the star-triangle transformation. Instead of considering crossing probabilities on $\mathcal{G}_d$ itself, we consider crossing probabilities on a translate of $\mathcal{G}_d$, namely

$$\mathcal{H} := \mathcal{G}_d - (\tfrac{1}{2}, \tfrac{1}{2\sqrt{3}}). \tag{3.77}$$

Of course we take the probability of an edge $e$ of $\mathcal{H}$ being passable equal to the probability that the translated edge $e+(\frac{1}{2},\frac{1}{2\sqrt{3}})$ of $\mathcal{G}_d$ is passable. These probabilities are $p(1)$, $p(2)$ and $p(3)$ for the edges which make an angle of $\frac{\pi}{2}$, $\frac{\pi}{2}+\frac{\pi}{3}$ and $\frac{\pi}{2}+\frac{2\pi}{3}$ with the first coordinate axis, respectively. The vertex set of $\mathcal{H}$ coincides with that of $\mathcal{G}$ and each "up-triangle" of $\mathcal{G}$ (i.e., the closure of a triangular face $F$ of $\mathcal{G}$ with vertices at $(i_1,i_2\sqrt{3})$, $(i_1+1,i_2\sqrt{3})$ and $(i_1+\frac{1}{2},(i_2+\frac{1}{2})\sqrt{3})$ for some $i_1,i_2 \in \mathbb{Z}$) contains a "star" of three edges of $\mathcal{H}$, one through each vertex on the perimeter of $F$ (see Fig. 3.5).

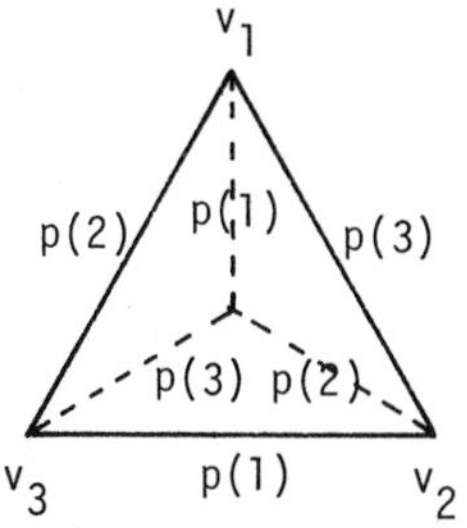


Figure 3.5 An up-triangle of $\mathcal{G}$ with a star of $\mathcal{H}$. —— = edges of $\mathcal{G}$, --- = edges of $\mathcal{H}$. The p-value next to an edge gives the probability for that edge to be passable.

It turns out that the connectivity properties on $\mathcal{G}$ and $\mathcal{H}$ can be made identical by a suitable matching of certain probabilities in each up-triangle separately. Note that it is not so much the full configuration of passable edges in each up-triangle that is important, as the pairs of vertices which are connected in each up-triangle. Here we make the convention that two vertices $v_1$ and $v_2$ on the perimeter of F are connected in $\bar{F}$ on $\mathcal{G}(\mathcal{H})$ if one can go along passable edges of $\mathcal{G}$ (blocked edges of $\mathcal{H}$) in $\bar{F}$ from $v_1$ to $v_2$. If one has a sequence $v_0,\dots,v_\nu$ of distinct vertices of $\mathcal{G}$ (or $\mathcal{H}$) such that $v_{j-1}$ and $v_j$ are connected in the unique up-triangle to which they both belong, $j = 1,\dots,\nu$, then there exists a passable path $(w_0,e_1,\dots,e_\tau,w_\tau)$ on $\mathcal{G}$ (or a path on $\mathcal{H}$ with all its edges blocked) with endpoints $w_0 = v_0$, $w_\tau = v_\nu$ and which contains the vertices $v_0,\dots,v_\nu$ but only enters up-triangles which have one of the $v_i$ as vertices. Since the diameter of any up-triangle equals one, this together with (3.77) implies

$$\begin{aligned}(3.78)\quad \sigma^*(\bar{n}-\bar{\rho};1,p,\mathcal{G}) &= P_p\{\exists \text{ a horizontal crossing of } [-\tfrac{1}{2},n_1-\rho_1-\tfrac{1}{2}]\times[-\tfrac{1}{2\sqrt{3}},n_2-\rho_2-\tfrac{1}{2\sqrt{3}}] \text{ on } \mathcal{H} \text{ all of whose edges are blocked}\}\\ &\geq P_p\{\exists \text{ a sequence of vertices } v_0,\dots,v_\nu \text{ such that } v_{j-1} \text{ and } v_j \text{ are connected on } \mathcal{H},\ 1\leq j\leq\nu, \text{ and}\\ &\qquad v_s\in[-\tfrac{3}{2},n_1-\rho_1+\tfrac{1}{2}]\times[-\tfrac{1}{2\sqrt{3}}+1,n_2-\rho_2-\tfrac{1}{2\sqrt{3}}-1],\ 1\leq s\leq\nu-1,\\ &\qquad \text{while } v_0(1)<-\tfrac{3}{2},\ v_\nu(1)>n_1-\rho_1+\tfrac{1}{2}\}\ .\end{aligned}$$

If the event in the last member of (3.78) occurs and $r = (w_0,e_1,\dots,e_\tau,w_\tau)$ is the path on $\mathcal{H}$ through $v_0,\dots,v_\nu$ as above, then $r$ contains a horizontal crossing of

$$[-\tfrac{1}{2},n_1-\rho_1-\tfrac{1}{2}]\times[-\tfrac{1}{2\sqrt{3}},n_2-\rho_2-\tfrac{1}{2\sqrt{3}}]$$

with all edges blocked. Assume now that $p_0$ is such that for an up-triangle F with vertices $v_1,v_2,v_3$ and any subset $\Gamma$ of $\{1,2,3\}$

(3.79) $P_{p_0}\{$the pairs of vertices connected in $\overline{F}$ on $\mathcal{G}$ are exactly the pairs $v_i, v_j$ with $i,j \in \Gamma\}$

$= P_{p_0}\{$the pairs of vertices connected in $\overline{F}$ on $\mathcal{H}$ are exactly the pairs $v_i, v_j$ with $i,j \in \Gamma\}$ .

Then the right hand side of (3.78) remains unchanged for $p = p_0$ if $\mathcal{H}$ is replaced by $\mathcal{G}$, because distinct up-triangles have no edges in common, and have consequently independent edge configurations. (This holds on $\mathcal{H}$ as well as on $\mathcal{G}$.) However, when $\mathcal{H}$ is replaced by $\mathcal{G}$ the last member of (3.78) is at least equal to

$$P_p\{\exists \text{ a passable horizontal crossing of } [-\tfrac{1}{2}, n_1-\rho_1-\tfrac{1}{2}] \times [-\tfrac{1}{2\sqrt{3}}\, n_2-\rho_2-\tfrac{1}{2\sqrt{3}}] \text{ on } \mathcal{G}\}$$

$$\geq \sigma((n_1-\rho_1+1, n_2-1-\rho_2), 1, p).$$

Therefore (3.35) holds when $\rho_1 \leq 1$, $\rho_2 \geq -1$ for any $p_0$ which satisfies (3.79). Similarly for (3.36), and consequently Condition A is implied by (3.79).

We shall now verify that (3.79) holds for all $p_0 \in \mathcal{S}$, where

(3.80) $$\mathcal{S} = \{p \in \mathcal{P}_3 : 0 << p << 1, p(1)+p(2)+p(3)-p(1)p(2)p(3) = 1\}.$$

The only possibilities for $\Gamma$ are $\phi$, $\{1,2,3\}$ and the three subsets of $\{1,2,3\}$ consisting of exactly one pair. These last three subsets and their probabilities can be obtained from each other by cyclical permutations of the indices, so that it suffices to consider $\Gamma = \phi$, $\Gamma = \{1,2\}$ and $\Gamma = \{1,2,3\}$. For $\Gamma = \phi$, the left and right hand side of (3.79) are, respectively,

(3.81) $$(1-p(1))(1-p(2))(1-p(3))$$

and

(3.82) $$p(1)p(2)p(3) + p(1)p(2)(1-p(3)) + p(1)(1-p(2))p(3) + (1-p(1))p(2)p(3)$$

(recall that on $\mathcal{H}$ we are looking for paths with <u>blocked</u> edges). It is simple algebra to check that (3.81) and (3.82) are equal for $p \in \mathcal{S}$. Equation (3.79) for $\Gamma = \{1,2,3\}$ again reduces to the equality of

(3.81) and (3.82). Finally, if $\Gamma = \{1,2\}$ and the vertices are numbered as in Fig. 3.5, then both sides of (3.79) equal

$$p(3)(1-p(1))(1-p(2)).$$

The above shows that in this example Condition A holds whenever $p_0 \in \mathcal{S}$. Unfortunately, neither of the coordinate axes is an axis of symmetry for the sets $\mathcal{E}_2$ and $\mathcal{E}_3$ and therefore Theorem 1 cannot be used for this 3-parameter problem. To obtain the required amount of symmetry we have to restrict ourselves to the two-parameter problem with $p(2) = p(3)$. In this case Theorem 1 applies, and for this problem the critical surface in $\mathcal{P}_2$ is obtained by taking $p(2) = p(3)$ in (3.80). Thus, if we take

$$P_p\{e \text{ is passable}\} = \begin{cases} p(1) & \text{if } e \in \mathcal{E}_1 \\ p(2) & \text{if } e \in \mathcal{E}_2 \cup \mathcal{E}_3 , \end{cases}$$

then there are infinite passable clusters on the trianglar lattice $\mathcal{G}$ under $P_p$ with $0 < p(1), p(2) < 1$ iff

$$(3.83) \qquad p(1) + 2p(2) - p(1)p(2)^2 > 1.$$

When restricted further to the one-parameter problem with $p(1) = p(2) = p(3)$ we find for the triangular lattice the critical probabilities given in (3.75) since $2 \sin \frac{\pi}{18}$ is the unique root in $(0,1)$ of $3p-p^3 = 1$. This value was conjectured by Sykes and Essam (1964) and first rigorously confirmed by Wierman (1981). By interchanging the role of "passable" and "blocked" one finds for the one-parameter problem on the hexagonal lattice the critical values given in (3.76). Of course, by obvious isomorphisms these results determine the percolative region also when we take $p(1) = p(2)$ or $p(1) = p(3)$ instead of $p(2) = p(3)$.

So far we have been unable to prove the full conjecture of Sykes and Essam (1964) that $\mathcal{S}$ is the critical surface for the three-parameter problem. There are, however, many indications that the conjecture is correct, in addition to the above verification for the two-parameter problem. First, one can prove that no percolation can occur on $\mathcal{G}$ if

$$p(1) + p(2) + p(3) - p(1)p(2)p(3) \leq 1.$$

Thus, the percolative region is contained in $\mathcal{P}_+$ (see (3.58) for notation), and its intersection with the plane $\{p(2) = p(3)\}$ is the same as the intersection of $\mathcal{P}_+$ with this plane. Also, if we take $p(3) = 0$, then the bond-problem on $\mathcal{G}$ reduces to the bond-problem on $\mathbb{Z}^2$ with probabilities $p(1)$ and $p(2)$ for horizontal and vertical edges to be passable. This is evident if we imbed the triangular lattice as in Fig. 2.5 in Ex. 2.1 (iii). However, by Application (ii) above we know that the critical surface for this bond-problem on $\mathbb{Z}^2$ is given by (3.71), which is precisely the restriction of (3.80) to $p(3) = 0$, (if we ignore the requirement $p(3) > 0$). Last, we can modify the three parameter problem slightly so that the first coordinate axis becomes an axis of symmetry. To do this we interchange the role of $p(2)$ and $p(3)$ in every second row of up-triangles. To be precise we leave $\mathcal{E}_1$ as before but replace $\mathcal{E}_2$ and $\mathcal{E}_3$ by

(3.84) $\mathcal{E}_2' = \{e\colon e$ an edge between $(i_1, i_2\sqrt{3})$ and $(i_1 + \frac{1}{2}, (i_2 + \frac{1}{2})\sqrt{3})$ or between $(i_1, i_2\sqrt{3})$ and $(i_1 + \frac{1}{2}, (i_2 - \frac{1}{2})\sqrt{3})$ for some $i_1, i_2 \in \mathbb{Z}\}$

(3.85) $\mathcal{E}_3' = \{e\colon e$ an edge between $(i_1, i_2\sqrt{3})$ and $(i_1 - \frac{1}{2}, (i_2 + \frac{1}{2})\sqrt{3})$ or between $(i_1, i_2\sqrt{3})$ and $(i_1 - \frac{1}{2}, (i_2 - \frac{1}{2})\sqrt{3})$ for some $i_1, i_2 \in \mathbb{Z}\}$

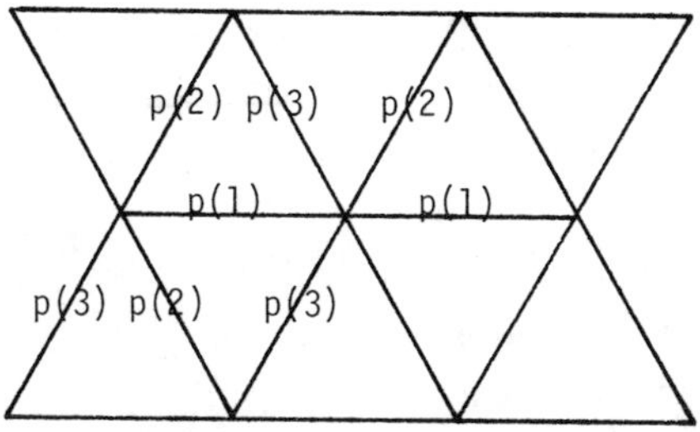


Figure 3.6 A modified 3-parameter bond-problem on the triangular lattice. The p-value next to an edge gives the probability for that edge to be passable.

The assignment of probabilities becomes as indicated in Fig. 3.6. We can define $\mathcal{H}$ as before, but the probabilities of an edge of $\mathcal{H}$ being passable have to be modified in accordance with (3.84) and (3.85). Each up-triangle will have an assignment of probabilities as in Fig. 3.5 or with $p(2)$ and $p(3)$ interchanged. However, the remainder of the argument showing that Condition A holds whenever $p_0 \in \mathcal{S}$ remains unchanged. Since this new example has the first-coordinate axis as axis of symmetry for $\mathcal{G}$, as well as for the edge classes $\mathcal{E}_1, \mathcal{E}_2', \mathcal{E}_3'$, Theorem 1 and Cor. 1 applies. Thus, $\mathcal{S}$ is the critical surface for the modified 3-parameter problem.

(iv) Site-percolation on $\mathbb{Z}^2$. In this example we shall verify Condition B. It will, however, not lead to an explicit determination of the percolative region. For our graph $\mathcal{G}$ we take the quadratic lattice $\mathcal{G}_0$ of Ex. 2.1 (i). We consider the two-parameter site-percolation problem corresponding to

$$\mathcal{V}_1 = \{(i_1,i_2)\colon i_1+i_2 \text{ is even}\} \quad ,$$

$$\mathcal{V}_2 = \{(i_1,i_2)\colon i_1+i_2 \text{ is odd}\} \quad .$$

A trivial change of scale by a factor $\frac{1}{2}$ in both the horizontal and vertical direction is required to bring this problem in the periodic form (3.18), but this will not change the fact that $\mathcal{G}, \mathcal{G}^*, \mathcal{V}_1$ and $\mathcal{V}_2$ are unchanged by reflection in a coordinate axis or in the 45° line $x(1) = x(2)$ (see Fig. 3.1). Thus, both coordinate axes are axes of symmetry while (3.52)-(3.55) hold trivially when all $a_j - d_j$ are equal to one and $h(x) = x$, because the probability of an occupied horizontal crossing of $[0,n]\times[0,m]$ on $\mathcal{G}$ is the same as the probability of an occupied vertical crossing of $[0,m]\times[0,n]$. Similarly for vacant crossings on $\mathcal{G}^*$. Thus, Theorem 3.2 and Cor. 3.1 apply, and the critical surface $\mathcal{S}$ is given in this example by

$$(3.86) \quad \mathcal{S} = \{p_0 = (p_0(1),p_0(2))\colon 0 \ll p_0 \ll 1,\ p_0 = t_0(p_1)p_1$$
$$\text{for } p_1 \text{ of the form } (1,p) \text{ or } (p,1), \text{ with } 0 < p \le 1\} ,$$

where

$$(3.87) \quad t_0(p_1) = \inf\{t \ge 0\colon tp_1 \in \mathcal{P}_2,\ \limsup \sigma((n,n);1,tp_1) > 0\} .$$

Infinite occupied clusters on $\mathcal{G}$ can occur only for $p \in \mathcal{P}_+$ (see (3.58) with $\lambda = 2$), while for $p \in \mathcal{P}_-$

(3.88) $$E_p\{\#W(v)\} < \infty .$$

When restricted to the one-parameter problem $p(1) = p(2)$ Theorem 3.2 (together with (3.66)) implies (see Ex. 2.2 (i) for $\mathcal{G}_0^*$)

(3.89) $$p_T(\mathcal{G}_0) = p_S(\mathcal{G}_0) = p_H(\mathcal{G}_0) = 1-p_T(\mathcal{G}_0^*) = 1-p_S(\mathcal{G}_0^*) = 1-p_H(\mathcal{G}_0^*).$$

This result was recently proved by Russo (1981).

It is also interesting to see how $\mathcal{S}$ behaves near the edges $p(1) = 1$ and $p(2) = 1$ of $\mathcal{P}_2$. For $p(1) = 1$, the occupancy of a path is determined only by the vertices from $\mathcal{V}_2$ on the path. From this it follows that the questions whether $\theta(p,v) > 0$ or $E_p\{\#W(v)\} < \infty$ reduce to the same questions in a one-parameter problem with $p = p(2)$ on the graph $\mathcal{H}$ with vertex set $\mathcal{V}_2$ and with $(i_1,i_2) \in \mathcal{V}_2$ adjacent to $(j_1,j_2) \in \mathcal{V}_2$ on $\mathcal{H}$ iff

$$|i_1-j_1| = 1 \text{ and } |i_2-j_2| = 1$$

or

$$i_1 = j_1, \ |i_2-j_2| = 2$$

or

$$|i_1-j_1| = 2, \ i_2 = j_2 .$$

This graph is drawn in Fig. 3.7, together with $\mathcal{G}_0$ .

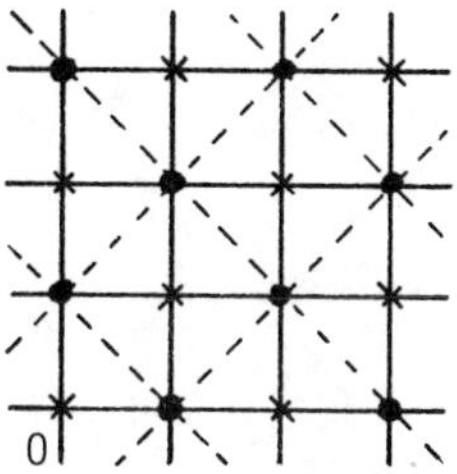


Figure 3.7 $\mathcal{H}$ has vertices at the circles only; its edges are the solid as well as the dashed segments; $\mathcal{G}_0$ has vertices at the circles and at the stars; its edges are the solid segments only.

Clearly $\mathcal{H}$ is isomorphic to $\mathcal{G}_0^*$ (see Ex. 2.2 (i)) and therefore on $p(1) = 1$, infinite occupied clusters occur if and only if $p(2) > p_H(\mathcal{G}_0^*)$; moreover $E_p\{\#W(v)\} < \infty$ for $p(2) < p_H(\mathcal{G}_0^*)$. Simple Peierls arguments (i.e., counting arguments such as in Broadbent and Hammersley (1957), Theorem 7 and Hammersley (1959), Theorem 1) establish that

$$0 < p_H(\mathcal{G}_0^*) < 1 .$$

Thus, for any $0 < p(2) < p_H(\mathcal{G}_0^*)$ and $p = (1,p(2))$ (3.88) holds. Moreover, as we shall see in the proof of Lemma 5.4, $p >> 0$ and (3.88) imply that $\sigma((n,n);i,p) \to 0$. Since (3.88) for any $p$ implies that (3.88) is also valid for any $p'$ with $p'(i) \le p(i)$, $i = 1,2$ (see Lemma 4.1), it follows that $\mathcal{S}$ cannot have any accumulation points in $\{1\} \times [0,p_H(\mathcal{G}_0^*))$. Interchanging the role of $p(1)$ and $p(2)$ we see that $\mathcal{S}$ has no accumulation points in $[0,p_H(\mathcal{G}_0^*)) \times \{1\}$ either. Furthermore, it will be shown in Ch. 10 (see Ex. 10.2 (i)) that in the interior of $\mathcal{P}_2$ $\mathcal{S}$ lies strictly above the line $p(1) + p(2) = 1$. Thus, $\mathcal{S}$, $\mathcal{P}_+$ and $\mathcal{P}_-$ should look more or less as indicated in Fig. 3.8.

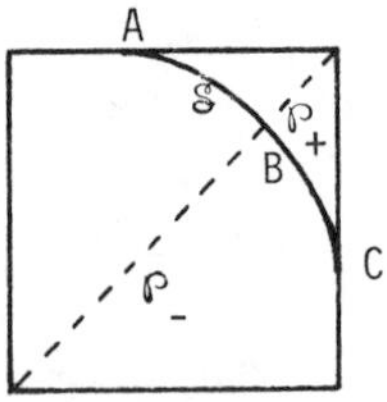


Figure 3.8 $A = (P_H(\mathcal{G}_0^*),1)$, $B = (P_H(\mathcal{G}_0),P_H(\mathcal{G}_0))$, $C = (1,P_H(\mathcal{G}_0^*))$

The points $A = (p_H(\mathcal{G}_0^*),1)$ and $C = (1,p_H(\mathcal{G}_0^*))$ are the points on the boundary of $\mathcal{P}_2$ in the closure of $\mathcal{S}$, while $\mathcal{S}$ intersects the diagonal $p(1) = p(2)$ in $B = (p_H(\mathcal{G}_0),\ p_H(\mathcal{G}_0)) = (1-p_H(\mathcal{G}_0^*),1-p_H(\mathcal{G}_0^*))$.

(v) For a last application we consider <u>one-parameter site-percolation on the diced lattice</u> of Ex. 2.1 (v). We shall show that this graph satisfies (3.52)-(3.55) so that Theorem 3.2 applies. For $p_1$ we can take any number in $(0,1)$. We then find from (3.43)-(3.51) and the definition (3.56)

$$p_0 = \inf\{p \geq 0: \limsup_{n\to\infty} \sigma((n,a_1 n);1,p) > 0 \text{ or } \limsup_{n\to\infty} \sigma((n,b_1 n);2,p) > 0\}$$

$$= p_H \text{ (diced lattice)} = p_T \text{ (diced lattice)}$$

$$= 1-p_H \text{ (matching graph of diced lattice)}$$

$$= 1-p_T \text{ (matching graph of diced lattice)} .$$

Note that the diced lattice is itself a mosaic, $\mathcal{D}$ say. Therefore, the diced lattice $\mathcal{D}$ is the first graph of the matching pair $(\mathcal{D},\mathcal{D}^*)$ based on $(\mathcal{D},\emptyset)$ (Comment 2.2 (vi)). In the imbedding of Ex. 2.1 (v) the diced lattice is clearly invariant under a rotation over 120°, and this will also be true for $\mathcal{D}^*$, where $\mathcal{D}^*$ is obtained by inserting the "diagonal edges" in each face of $\mathcal{D}$. From this property it is easy to derive (3.52)-(3.55) with $h(x) = x$. We content ourselves with demonstrating (3.52). Note that any horizontal crossing on $\mathcal{D}$ of $B = [0,n] \times [0,\frac{1}{4}n]$ contains a continuous curve $\psi$ inside $B$ and connecting the left and right edge of $B$. When $B$ is rotated around the origin over 120° it goes over into the rectangle $\tilde{B}$ with vertices $0$, $P_1 := (-\frac{n}{2},\frac{n}{2}\sqrt{3})$, $P_2 := (-\frac{n}{2}-\frac{n}{8}\sqrt{3}, \frac{n}{2}\sqrt{3}-\frac{n}{8})$, $P_3 := (-\frac{n}{8}\sqrt{3}, -\frac{n}{8})$. $\psi$ goes

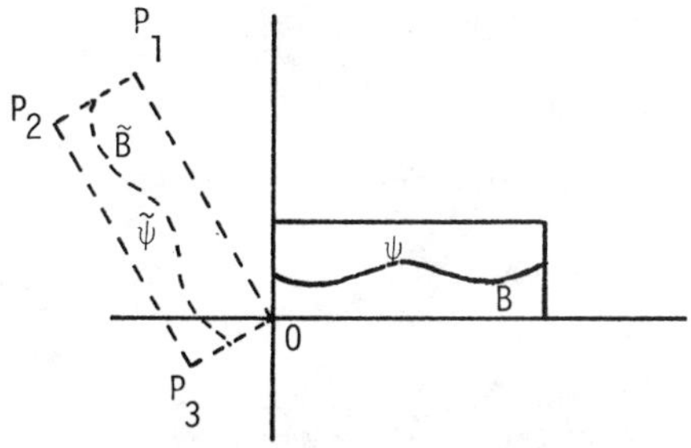


Figure 3.9

over into a continuous curve on $\mathcal{D}$ inside $B$ and connecting the segment from $0$ to $P_3$ with the segment from $P_1$ to $P_2$. In particular $\psi$ begins below the first coordinate-axis $(x(2) = 0)$ and ends above the horizontal line through $P_2$, $x(2) = \frac{n}{2}\sqrt{3} - \frac{n}{8}$ . Also $\psi$ is contained between the vertical lines through $P_2$, $x(1) = -\frac{n}{2} - \frac{n}{8}\sqrt{3}$, and the vertical line through 0, $x(1) = 0$. In particular, $\tilde{\psi}$ contains a vertical crossing of

$$[-\frac{n}{2} - \frac{n}{8}\sqrt{3} - 1, 1] \times [\Lambda, \frac{n}{2}\sqrt{3} - \frac{n}{8} - \Lambda] \quad ,$$

if $\Lambda \geq$ length of any edge of $\mathcal{D}$. By the invariance of $\mathcal{D}$ and $P_p$ under the rotation over 120° we therefore have

(3.90) $\quad P_p\{\exists$ occupied vertical crossing of

$$[-\frac{n}{2} - \frac{n}{8}\sqrt{3} - 1, 1] \times [\Lambda, \frac{n}{2}\sqrt{3} - \Lambda]\}$$

$\geq P_p\{\exists$ continuous curve $\tilde{\psi}$ in $\tilde{B}$ on $\mathcal{D}$ connecting the segment from 0 to $P_3$ with the segment from $P_1$ to $P_2$ and with all vertices on $\psi$ occupied$\}$

$\geq P_p\{\exists$ occupied horizontal crossing of $[0,n] \times [0, \frac{n}{4}]\}$.

This is essentially (3.52), since by the periodicity of $\mathcal{D}$ with periods $(\sqrt{3},0)$, $(0,3)$ the left hand side of (3.90) is at most

(3.91) $\quad P_p\{\exists$ occupied vertical crossing of

$$[0, n(\frac{1}{2} + \frac{\sqrt{3}}{8}) + 2 + \sqrt{3}] \times [0, \frac{n}{2}\sqrt{3} - \frac{n}{8} - 2\Lambda - 3]\}$$

$\leq P_p\{\exists$ occupied vertical crossing of $[0,n] \times [0, \frac{n}{2}]\}$

for large $n$ (use Comment 3.3 (v)). For the imbedding of $\mathcal{D}$ of Ex.2.1 (v) this would say

$$\sigma((n, \tfrac{n}{2}); 2, p, \mathcal{D}) \geq \sigma((n, \tfrac{n}{4}); 1, p, \mathcal{D}). \tag{3.92}$$

This is actually not the inequality which we can use, because we first have to change scale in order to make $\mathcal{D}$ periodic with periods (1,0) and (0,1). This, however, does not change the form of the inequality (3.92), and hence (3.52) follows for some $a_1$-$a_3$ and $h(x) = x$.

## 4. INCREASING EVENTS.

This chapter contains the well known FKG inequality and a formula of Russo's for the derivative of $P_p\{E\}$ with respect to $p$ for an increasing event $E$. No periodicity assumptions are necessary in this chapter, so that we shall take as our probability space the triple $(\Omega_{\mathcal{V}}, \mathcal{B}_{\mathcal{V}}, P_{\mathcal{V}})$ as defined in Sect. 3.1. $E_{\mathcal{V}}$ will denote expectation with respect to $P_{\mathcal{V}}$.

Def. 1 A $\mathcal{B}_{\mathcal{V}}$-measurable function $f:\Omega_{\mathcal{V}} \to \mathbb{R}$ is called increasing (decreasing) if it is[1] increasing (decreasing) in each $\omega(v)$, $v \in \mathcal{V}$. An event $E \in \mathcal{B}_{\mathcal{V}}$ is called increasing (decreasing) if its indicator function is increasing (decreasing).

### Examples

(i) $\{\#W(v)\}$ is an increasing function, since making more sites occupied can only increase $W(v)$.

(ii) $E_1 = \{\#W(v) = \infty\}$ for fixed $v$ is an increasing event; if $E_1$ occurs in the configuration $\omega'$, and every site which is occupied in $\omega'$ is also occupied in $\omega''$ - and possibly more sites are occupied in $\omega''$ - then $E_1$ also occurs in configuration $\omega''$.

(iii) $E_2 = \{\exists$ an occupied path on $\mathcal{G}$ from $v_1$ to $v_2\}$ for fixed vertices $v_1$ and $v_2$ is increasing for the same reasons as $E_1$ in ex. (ii).

(iv) The most important example of an increasing event for our purposes is the existence of an occupied crosscut of a certain Jordan domain in $\mathbb{R}^2$. More precisely we shall be interested in pair of matching graphs $(\mathcal{G},\mathcal{G}^*)$ in $\mathbb{R}^2$ based on $(\mathcal{M},\mathcal{F})$, $\mathcal{G}_{p\ell}$, $\mathcal{G}_{p\ell}^*$ and $\mathcal{M}_{p\ell}$ will be the planar modifications of $\mathcal{G}$, $\mathcal{G}^*$ and $\mathcal{M}$ respectively (see Sect. 2.2 and 2.3). Let $J$ be a Jordan curve on $\mathcal{M}_{p\ell}$

---

1) We use "increasing" and "strictly increasing" instead of "non-decreasing" and "increasing".

consisting of four closed areas $B_1$, $A_1$, $B_2$ and C with disjoint interiors. Then

$$E_3 := \{\, \exists \text{ occupied path } r \text{ on } \mathcal{G}_{p\ell} \text{ with initial (final) point on } B_1(B_2) \text{ and such that } r \text{ minus its endpoints is contained in } \operatorname{int}(J)\} \quad .$$

is an increasing event. For further details see Ex. (iii) in the next section. ///

Before treating the principal results of this chapter we prove a simple lemma, stating that the expectation of an increasing function goes up when the probability that a site is occupied goes up. Inequality (4.2) gives an upper bound for this effect, though. The lemma will be useful later.

Lemma 4.1. If $f:\Omega_{\mathcal{V}} \to [0,\infty)$ is an increasing non-negative function and

$$P_{\mathcal{V}} = \prod_{v \in \mathcal{V}} \mu_v \quad , \quad P'_{\mathcal{V}} = \prod_{v \in \mathcal{V}} \mu'_v$$

are two product measure on $\Omega_{\mathcal{V}}$ which satisfy

$$\mu'_v\,\{\omega(v) = 1\} \geq \mu_v\{\omega(v) = 1\} \quad , \quad v \in \mathcal{V} \quad ,$$

then (with $E_{\mathcal{V}}$ $(E'_{\mathcal{V}})$ denoting expectation with respect to $P_{\mathcal{V}}$ $(P'_{\mathcal{V}})$)

$$(4.1) \qquad E'_{\mathcal{V}}\, f \geq E_{\mathcal{V}}\, f \quad .$$

If $f \geq 0$ depends only on the $\omega(v)$ for $v$ in a subset $\mathcal{W}$ of $\mathcal{V}$ with cardinality $m = \#\mathcal{W}$, then .

$$(4.2) \qquad E'_{\mathcal{V}}\, f \leq \left( \max_{v \in \mathcal{W}} \frac{\mu'_v\{\omega(v) = 1\}}{\mu_v\{\omega(v) = 1\}} \right)^m E_{\mathcal{V}}\, f \;.$$

For a decreasing non-negative function $f$ the inequality in (4.1) is reversed, while (4.2) is to be replaced by

$$E_{\mathcal{V}}\, f \leq \left( \max_{v \in \mathcal{W}} \frac{\mu_v\{\omega(v) = -1\}}{\mu'_v\{\omega(v) = -1\}} \right)^m E'_{\mathcal{V}}\, f$$

Proof: The lemma is proved by "coupling". We construct a measure

P on $(\Omega_{\mathcal{V}} \times \Omega_{\mathcal{V}}, \mathcal{B}_{\mathcal{V}} \times \mathcal{B}_{\mathcal{V}})$ such that its marginal distribution on the first (second) factor is $P_{\mathcal{V}}(P'_{\mathcal{V}})$ and with the following properties:

(4.3) $\qquad P$ is a product measure $\prod_{v \in \mathcal{V}}$ ,

where $\nu_v$ is a measure on $\{-1,1\} \times \{-1,1\}$. Thus if we write a generic point of $\Omega_{\mathcal{V}} \times \Omega_{\mathcal{V}}$ as $\{(\omega(v),\omega'(v)): v \in \mathcal{V}\}$ , then the random variables $(\omega(v),\omega'(v))$, $v \in \mathcal{V}$, are independent under P. Moreover we will have

$$P\{\omega(v) = 1 \mid \omega'(v) = 1\} = \frac{\mu\{\omega(v) = 1\}}{\mu'\{\omega(v) = 1\}} \tag{4.4}$$

and

$$P\{(\omega,\omega') \in \Omega_{\mathcal{V}} \times \Omega_{\mathcal{V}}: \omega(v) \le \omega'(v) \text{ for all } v\} = 1. \tag{4.5}$$

To construct such a product measure we merely have to choose the $\nu_v$ suitably. We take

$$\nu_v\{\omega(v) = -1, \ \omega'(v) = -1\} = \mu'_v\{\omega(v) = -1\} ,$$

$$\nu_v\{\omega(v) = -1, \ \omega'(v) = 1\} = \mu'_v\{\omega(v) = 1\} - \mu_v\{\omega(v) = 1\} ,$$

$$\nu_v\{\omega(v) = 1, \ \omega'(v) = -1\} = 0 ,$$

$$\nu_v\{\omega(v) = 1, \ \omega'(v) = 1\} = \mu\{\omega(v) = 1\} .$$

(4.4) and (4.5) obviously hold for these $\nu_v$, and one easily checks that P has the prescribed marginal distributions. Now, for any increasing $f \ge 0$, by (4.5)

$$E'_{\mathcal{V}} f = \int_{\Omega_{\mathcal{V}}} f(\omega')\, dP'_{\mathcal{V}}(\omega') = \int_{\Omega_{\mathcal{V}} \times \Omega_{\mathcal{V}}} f(\omega')\, dP(\omega,\omega')$$
$$\ge \int_{\Omega_{\mathcal{V}} \times \Omega_{\mathcal{V}}} f(\omega)\, dP(\omega,\omega') = E_{\mathcal{V}} f .$$

This proves (4.1).

To prove (4.2) note that (4.4) implies

$$P\{\omega(v) \geq \omega'(v) \text{ for all } v \in \mathfrak{b} \mid \omega'\}$$

$$= \prod_{\substack{v \in \mathfrak{b} \\ \omega'(v) = 1}} P\{\omega(v) = 1 \mid \omega'(v) = 1\} \geq \left( \min_{v \in \mathfrak{b}} \frac{\mu\{\omega(v) = 1\}}{\mu'\{\omega(v) = 1\}} \right)^m .$$

For an increasing $f \geq 0$ which depends only on the occupancies in $\mathfrak{b}$ we now have

$$E_{\mathfrak{V}} f = \int_{\Omega_{\mathfrak{V}} \times \Omega_{\mathfrak{V}}} f(\omega)\, dP(\omega,\omega')$$

$$\geq \int_{\substack{\Omega_{\mathfrak{V}} \times \Omega_{\mathfrak{V}} \\ \omega(v) \geq \omega'(v) \text{ on } \mathfrak{b}}} f(\omega')\, dP(\omega,\omega')$$

$$= \int_{\Omega} f(\omega')\, P\{\omega(v) \geq \omega'(v) \text{ for all } v \in \mathfrak{b} | \omega')\, dP(\omega')$$

$$\geq \left( \min_{v \in \mathfrak{b}} \frac{\mu\{\omega(v) = 1\}}{\mu'\{\omega(v) = 1\}} \right)^m E'_{\mathfrak{V}} f .$$

This is equivalent to (4.2). We leave it to the reader to derive the analogues of (4.1) and (4.2) for decreasing $f$, by interchanging the roles of $E_{\mathfrak{V}}$ and $E'_{\mathfrak{V}}$. □

4.1. The FKG inequality.

We only discuss the very special case of the FKG inequality which we need in these notes. This special case already appeared in Harris (1960). For more general versions the reader can consult the original article of Fortuin, Kasteleyn and Ginibre (1971) or the recent article by Batty and Bollman (1980) and its references.

Proposition 4.1. *If $f$ and $g$ are two bounded functions on $\Omega_{\mathfrak{V}}$ which depend on finitely many coordinates of $\omega$ only and which are both increasing or both decreasing functions, then*

$$(4.6) \qquad E_{\mathfrak{V}}\{f(\omega)\, g(\omega)\} \geq E_{\mathfrak{V}}\{f(\omega)\}\, E_{\mathfrak{V}}\{g(\omega)\} .$$

*In particular, if $E$ and $F$ are two increasing events, or two decreasing events, which depend on finitely many coordinates of $\omega$ only, then*

(4.7) $$P_{\mathcal{V}}\{E \cap F\} \geq P_{\mathcal{V}}\{E\} \,.\, P_{\mathcal{V}}\{F\} \quad .$$

Proof: For (4.6) it suffices to take $f$ and $g$ increasing. The decreasing case follows by applying (4.6) to $-f$ and $-g$. Order the elements of $\mathcal{V}$ in some arbitrary way as $v_1, v_2, \dots,$ and write $\omega_i$ for $\omega(v_i)$. Without loss of generality assume that $f(\omega)$ and $g(\omega)$ depend on $\omega_1, \dots, \omega_n$ only. If $n = 1$, then (4.6) follows from the fact that for each $\omega_1, \omega_1'$,

$$\{f(\omega_1) - f(\omega_1')\}\{g(\omega_1) - g(\omega_1')\} \geq 0$$

(check the cases $\omega_1 \geq \omega_1'$ and $\omega_1 \leq \omega_1'$). Thus

$$0 \leq \iint \{f(\omega_1) - f(\omega_1')\}\{g(\omega_1) - g(\omega_1')\} \; P_{\mathcal{V}}(d\omega) \; P_{\mathcal{V}}(d\omega')$$

$$= 2\, E_{\mathcal{V}}\{fg\} - 2\, E_{\mathcal{V}}\{f\}\, E_{\mathcal{V}}\{g\} \,.$$

The general case of (4.6) follows by induction on $n$ since

$$E_{\mathcal{V}}\{fg\} = E_{\mathcal{V}}\{E_{\mathcal{V}}\{fg|\omega_2, \dots, {}_n\}\} \quad ,$$

$$\geq E_{\mathcal{V}}\{E_{\mathcal{V}}\{f|\omega_2,\dots,\omega_n\}\, E_{\mathcal{V}}\{g|\omega_2,\dots,\omega_n\}\}$$

(since for fixed $\omega_2,\dots,\omega_n$, $f(\omega)$ and $g(\omega)$ are increasing functions of $\omega_1$ only)

$$\geq E_{\mathcal{V}}\{E_{\mathcal{V}}\{f|\omega_2,\dots,\omega_n\}\}\, E_{\mathcal{V}}\{E_{\mathcal{V}}\{g|\omega_2,\dots,\omega_n\}\}$$

(since $E_{\mathcal{V}}\{f|\omega_2,\dots,\omega_n\}$ is an increasing function of $\omega_2,\dots,\omega_n$ and similarly for $g$, plus the induction hypotheses) $= E_{\mathcal{V}}\{f\}\, E_{\mathcal{V}}\{g\}$ .

This proves (4.6) and (4.7) is the special case with $f = I_E$, $g = I_F$. □

## Application.

For a simple application of the FKG inequality let $v_1, v_2$ be two vertices of a connected graph $\mathcal{G}$. Then if there is an occupied path from $v_1$ to $v_2$ the occupied clusters of $v_1$ and $v_2$ are identical. Therefore, by (4.7) and Ex. 4(i) and 4(iii).

(4.8) $$P_{\mathcal{V}}\{\#W(v_1) \geq n\} \geq P_{\mathcal{V}}\{\exists \text{ occupied path from } v_1 \text{ to } v_2 \text{ and } \#W(v_2) \geq n\} \geq P_{\mathcal{V}}\{\exists \text{ occupied path from } v_1 \text{ to } v_2\} P_{\mathcal{V}}\{\#W(v_2) \geq n\} .$$

If $\mathcal{G}$ is connected and $P_{\mathcal{V}}\{v$ is occupied$\} > 0$ for all $v$, then also

$$P_{\mathcal{V}}\{\exists \text{ occupied path from } v_1 \text{ to } v_2\} > 0 \quad .$$

Therefore

$$\theta(v_2) > 0 \text{ implies } \theta(v_1) > 0 \text{ and}$$

$$E\{\#W(v_2)\} = \infty \text{ implies } E\{\#W(v_1)\} = \infty \quad .$$

This justifies our statement in Sect. 3.4, that $P_H$ and $P_T$ are independent of the choice of $v$.

## 4.2. Pivotal sites and Russo's formula.

Def. 2. Let $E \in \mathcal{B}_{\mathcal{V}}$ be an event and $\omega \in \Omega_{\mathcal{V}}$ an occupancy configuration. A site $v \in \mathcal{V}$ is called **pivotal for $(E,\omega)$** (or for $E$ for short) iff

$$I_E(\omega) \neq I_E(T_v\omega) \quad ,$$

where $T_v\omega \in \Omega$ is determined by

(4.9) $$T_v\omega(w) = \begin{cases} \omega(w) & \text{for } w \in \mathcal{V} \text{ but } w \neq v \\ -\omega(v) & \text{for } w = v \quad . \end{cases}$$

In other words, $v$ is pivotal, if changing the occupancy of $v$ only changes the occupancy configuration from one where $E$ occurs to one where $E$ does not occur, or vice versa.

Examples.

(i) Let $E_1$ be as in Ex. 4(ii) and take

$$F_1 = \{\omega : \#W(w,\omega) = \infty \quad \text{for some neighbor } w \text{ of } v\}$$

Then $v$ is pivotal for $(E_1,\omega)$ iff $\omega \in F_1$. Indeed for $\omega \in F_1$, $E_1$ occurs iff $v$ itself is occupied (recall that $W(v) = \emptyset$ if $v$ is vacant), and hence $I_{E_1}(\omega)$ will change with $\omega(v)$ for $\omega \in F_1$. On the other hand, if $\omega \notin F_1$, then $\#W(v,\omega) < \infty$, no matter what $\omega(v)$ is.

(ii) Let $E_2$ be as in Ex. 4(iii) and take

$$F_2 = E_2 \cap \{\omega : \text{ all occupied paths from } v_1 \text{ to } v_2 \text{ contain the vertex } v\}.$$

Then

$$I_{E_2}(\omega) = 1 \quad \text{and} \quad \omega(v) = 1 \quad \text{for} \quad \omega \in F_2$$

But in $T_v\omega$, $v$ is vacant and there are no longer any occupied paths from $v_1$ to $v_2$, since on $F_2$ all these paths had to go through $v$, and $v$ has now been made vacant. Thus $v$ is pivotal for $(E_2,\omega)$ whenever $\omega \in F_2$.

(iii) This example plays a fundamental role in the later development. Let $(\mathcal{G},\mathcal{G}^*)$ be a periodic matching pair of graphs in $\mathbb{R}^2$, based on $(\mathcal{M},\mathcal{F})$ and let $\mathcal{G}_{p\ell}$, $\mathcal{G}^*_{p\ell}$ and $\mathcal{M}_{p\ell}$ be the planar modifications defined in Sect. 2.3. This time we take $\mathcal{V}$ = vertex set of $\mathcal{G}_{p\ell}$ and define $\Omega_{\mathcal{V}}$, $\mathcal{B}_{\mathcal{V}}$ accordingly. We are interested in the existence of "occupied crosscuts of Jordan domains". More precisely, let $J$ be a Jordan curve on $\mathcal{M}_{p\ell}$, consisting of four closed arcs, $B_1$, $A$, $B_2$ and $C$, with disjoint interiors and occuring in this order as $J$ is traversed in one direction. $\bar{J} = \text{int}(J) \cup J$. We consider paths $r = (v_0,e_1,\dots,e_\nu, v_\nu)$ on $\mathcal{G}_{p\ell}$ which satisfy

$$(4.10) \qquad (e_1 \setminus \{v_0\}, v_1, e_2,\dots, e_{\nu-1}, v_{\nu-1}, e_\nu \setminus \{v_\nu\}) \subset \text{int}(J),$$

and

$$(4.11) \qquad v_0 \in B_1, \; v_\nu \in B_2 .$$

(4.10) and (4.11) are just the conditions (2.23) - (2.25) in the present setup, since an edge of $\mathcal{G}_{p\ell} \subset \mathcal{M}_{p\ell}$ can intersect the curve J on $\mathcal{M}_{p\ell}$ in a vertex of $\mathcal{M}_{p\ell}$ only, by virtue of the planarity of $\mathcal{M}_{p\ell}$. We call any path $r$ on $\mathcal{G}_{p\ell}$ which satisfies (4.10) and (4.11) a crosscut of int(J). We can now define $J^-(r)$ and $J^+(r)$ as in Def. 2.11 and order $r_1$ and $r_2$ as in Def. 2.12, whenever $r, r_1, r_2$ satisfy (4.10) and (4.11). We take

(4.12) $$E_3 = \{\omega: \exists \text{ at least one occupied crosscut of } \operatorname{int}(J)\},$$

and we want to find the pivotal sites for $(E_3,\omega)$ when $\omega \in E_3$. By Prop. 2.3, if $E_3$ occurs, then there exists a unique lowest crosscut of int(J) on $\mathcal{G}_{p\ell}$, which we denote by $R(\omega)$. Now let $\omega \in E_3$, so $R(\omega)$ exists and $v$ a vertex which is not on $R$. Then changing the occupancy of $v$ leaves the crosscut $R$ intact and such a site $v$ is therefore not pivotal for $(E_3,\omega)$. Next consider a $v$ on $R \cap \operatorname{int}(J)$ which has a vacant connection to $\mathring{C}$. By this we mean that there exists a path $s^* = (v_0^*, e_1^*, \dots, e_\rho^*, v_\rho^*)$ on $\mathcal{G}_{p\ell}^*$ satisfying the following conditions (4.13) - (4.16):

(4.13) there exists an edge $e$ of $\mathcal{M}_{p\ell}$ between $v$ and $v_0$ such that $\mathring{e} \subset J^+(R)$ (in particular $v \; \mathcal{M}_{p\ell} \; v_0$),

(4.14) $$v_\rho^* \in \mathring{C},$$

(4.15) $$(v_0^*, e_1^*, \dots, v_{\rho-1}^*, e_\rho^* \setminus \{v_\rho^*\}) \subset J^+(R),$$

(4.16) all vertices of $s^*$ are vacant.

We allow here the possibility $\rho = 0$ in which case $s^*$ reduces to the single vertex $v_0^* = v_\rho^*$, and we make the convention that (4.15) is automatically fulfilled in this case. We claim that any $v \in R \cap \operatorname{int}(J)$ with such a vacant connection to $\mathring{C}$ is pivotal for $(E_3,\omega)$ whenever $\omega \in E_3$. To prove this claim note that $v$ is on $R(\omega)$, hence is occupied in $\omega$, and therefore vacant in $T_v\omega$. If there would exist an occupied crosscut $r$ of int(J) in $T_v\omega$, then $r$ could not contain $v$, which is vacant in $T_v\omega$. Thus $r$ would also be occupied in $\omega$ and by Prop. 2.3 (see (2.27)) we would have

(4.17) $$r \in \overline{J}^+(R).$$

Now, if $R = (v_0, e_1, \dots, e_\nu, v_\nu)$, then the boundary of $J^+(R)$ consists of $R$, the segment of $B_2$ from $v_\nu$ to the intersection of $B_2$

with C(call this segment $B_2^+$) , C, and the segment of $B_1$ from the intersection of $B_1$ with C to $v_0$(call this segment $B_1^+$) ; see Fig. 4.1. This boundary is, in fact, a Jordan curve.

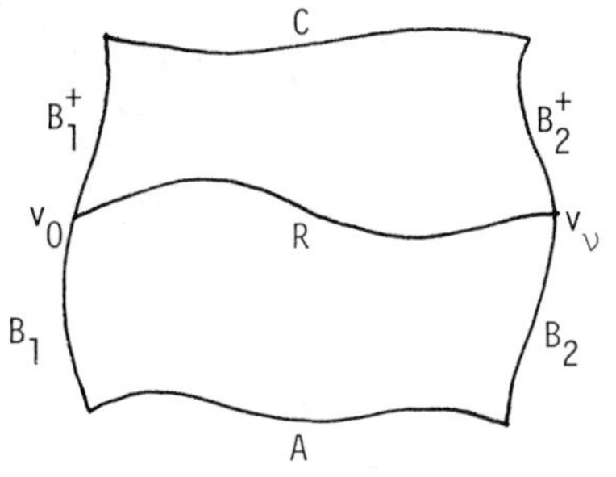


Figure 4.1

Since r would begin on $B_1$ and end on $B_2$ and satisfy (4.17) it would in fact connect a point on $B_1^+$ with a point on $B_2^+$ inside $\bar{J}^+(R)$. Next consider, the path $\tilde{s}$: = $(v,e,v_0^*, e_1^*, \ldots, e_\nu^*, v_\nu^*)$, where e is as in (4.13). From the requirements $\mathring{e} \subset J^+(R)$ , (4.14) and (4.15) it follows that $\tilde{s}$ is a crosscut of $J^+(R)$. Moreover, its endpoints - v on $R \cap \text{int}(J)$ and $v_\rho^*$ on $\mathring{C}$ - separate the endpoints of r on $B_1^+$ and $B_2^+$. Thus r would have to intersect $\tilde{s}$. This, however, is impossible. Indeed, the paths r and $\tilde{s}$ on $\mathcal{M}_{p\ell}$ would have to intersect in a vertex of $\mathcal{M}_{p\ell}$ (recall that $\mathcal{M}_{p\ell}$ is planar) which would have to be occupied - being a vertex of r - as well as vacant - being also a vertex on $\tilde{s}$. (Note that the $v_i^*$ are vacant in $\omega$ , hence in $T_v\omega$ , and v became vacant in $T_v\,\omega$). Thus no occupied crosscut r of int(J) can exist in $T_v\omega$ , i.e., $T_v\omega \notin E_3$, which proves our claim.

We remark (without proof) that a certain converse of the above holds. Assume that $A \cap B_i$ as well as $C \cap B_i$ is a vertex of $\mathcal{M}_{p\ell}$ , i = 1,2. Then under the convention (2.15), (2.16) the only pivotal sites on $R \cap \text{int}(J)$ for $(E_3,\omega)$ are vertices which have a vacant connection to C. (We call $s^*$ a vacant connection to C if (4.13) (4.15) and (4.16) hold but (4.14) is replaced by $v_\rho^* \in C$). This can be derived from a variant of Prop. 2.2. We shall, however, not need this fact.

<u>Proposition 4.2</u> (<u>Russo's formula</u>) <u>Let</u> $E \in \mathcal{B}_\mathcal{V}$ <u>be an increasing event and</u> $P_\mathcal{V}$ <u>as in</u> (3.3), (3.4) <u>with</u> $\mathcal{E}$ <u>replaced by</u> $\mathcal{V}$ .

Then

$$(4.18) \qquad \frac{\partial}{\partial p(v)} P_{\mathcal{V}}\{E\} = P_{\mathcal{V}}\{v \text{ is pivotal for } (E,\omega)\} .$$

Let $p'$ and $p''$ be any two functions from $\mathcal{V}$ into $[0,1]$ and set

$$(4.19) \qquad \mu_{vt}\{\omega(v) = 1\} = 1-\mu_{vt}\{\omega(v) = -1\}$$

$$= (1-t)p'(v) + tp''(v), \ v \in \mathcal{V}, \ 0 \leq t \leq 1,$$

$$(4.20) \qquad P_{\mathcal{V}t} = \prod_{v \in \mathcal{V}} \mu_{vt} .$$

If

$$(4.21) \qquad p'(v) \leq p''(v) \text{ for all } v \in \mathcal{V} ,$$

and $E$ is an increasing event which depends on the occupancy of finitely many vertices only, then for any subset $\mathcal{W}$ of $\mathcal{V}$, then

$$(4.22) \qquad \frac{d}{dt} P_{\mathcal{V}t}\{E\}$$

$$= \sum_{v \in \mathcal{V}} \{p''(v) - p'(v)\} P_{\mathcal{V}t}\{v \text{ is pivotal for } E\}$$

$$\geq \inf_{v \in \mathcal{W}} \{p''(v) - p'(v)\} E_{\mathcal{V}t}\{ \# \text{ of pivotal sites for } E \text{ in } \mathcal{W} \}.$$

(Of course $E_{\mathcal{V}t}$ denotes expectation with respect to $P_{\mathcal{V}t}$)

Proof: (Russo (1981)). To prove (4.18) write

$$(4.23) \qquad P_{\mathcal{V}}\{E\} = E_{\mathcal{V}}\{I_E\} = p(v) E_{\mathcal{V}}\{I_E \mid v \text{ is occupied}\}$$

$$+ (1-p(v)) E_{\mathcal{V}}\{I_E \mid v \text{ is vacant}\} .$$

Since $\omega(v)$ is independent of all other sites, the conditional expectations in the right hand side of (4.23) are integrals with respect to $\prod_{w \neq v} \mu_w$ and are independent of $p(v)$. Therefore

$$(4.24) \qquad \frac{\partial}{\partial\, p(v)} P_{\mathcal{V}}\{E\} = E_{\mathcal{V}}\{I_E \mid v \text{ is occupied}\} - E_{\mathcal{V}}\{I_E \mid v \text{ is vacant}\}.$$

Next set

$$J = J(\omega) = J(\omega;E,v) = \begin{cases} 1 & \text{if } v \text{ is pivotal for } (E,\omega) \\ 0 & \text{if } v \text{ is not pivotal for } (E,\omega). \end{cases}$$

Then, from (4.24)

$$(4.25) \quad \frac{\partial}{\partial\, p(v)} P_{\mathcal{V}}\{E\} = E_{\mathcal{V}}\{I_E J \mid v \text{ is occupied}\} + E_{\mathcal{V}}\{I_E(1-J)|v \text{ is occupied}\} - E_{\mathcal{V}}\{I_E J|v \text{ is vacant}\} - E_{\mathcal{V}}\{I_E(1-J)|v \text{ is vacant}\}.$$

Now the function $I_E(\omega)(1-J(\omega))$ can take only the values 0 and 1. $I_E(\omega)(1-J(\omega)) = 1$ only if $E$ occurs and $v$ is not pivotal for $(E,\omega)$, i.e., $E$ occurs in $\omega$, and also if $\omega(v)$ is changed to $-\omega(v)$. Clearly $I_E(\omega)\,(1-J(\omega)) = 1$ is a condition on $\omega(w)$, $w \neq v$, only, so that $I_E(\omega)(1-J(\omega))$ is independent of $\omega(v)$. Therefore the second and fourth term in the right hand side of (4.25) cancel. Also, if $v$ is pivotal for $(E,\omega)$ and $E$ is increasing, then $E$ must occur if $\omega(v) = 1$ and cannot occur if $\omega(v) = -1$. Therefore the third term in the right hand side of (4.25) vanishes. This leaves us with

$$(4.26) \qquad \frac{\partial}{\partial\, p(v)} P_{\mathcal{V}}\{E\} = \frac{E_{\mathcal{V}}\{I_E(\omega)J(\omega)I[\omega(v) = +1]\}}{P_{\mathcal{V}}\{\omega(v) = 1\}}.$$

But, by the argument just given, $E$ must occur if $J(\omega)I[\omega(v) = 1] = 1$, so that we can drop the factor $I_E$ in the numerator on the right of (4.26). Finally $J(\omega)$ is again independent of $\omega(v)$, since $J(\omega) = 1$ means $\omega(w)$, $w \neq v$, is such that $E$ occurs when $\omega(v) = 1$ and does not occur when $\omega(v) = -1$. Thus, the right hand side of (4.26) equals

$$E_{\mathcal{V}}\{J(\omega)\} = P_{\mathcal{V}}\{v \text{ is pivotal for } E\}.$$

This proves (4.18). (4.22) follows now from the chain rule and

(4.21). (Note that $v$ can be pivotal for $E$ only if $I_E$ depends on $\omega(v)$; hence the sum in the middle of (4.22) has only finitely many non-zero terms). □

## 5. BOUNDS FOR THE DISTRIBUTION OF # W .

The principal result of this chapter is that

$$(5.1) \qquad P_p\{\#W(v) \geq n\}$$

decreases exponentially in n, provided certain crossing probabilities are sufficiently small. This is almost the only theorem which works for a general periodic percolation problem in any dimension. No axes of symmetry are required, nor does the graph have to be one of a matching pair. When Theorem 5.1 is restricted to one-parameter problems, then it shows that (5.1) decreases exponentially for $p < p_T$ and that in general $p_T = p_S$ (see (3.62)-(3.65) for definition). In Sect. 5.2 we discuss lower bounds for

$$(5.2) \qquad P_p\{\#W(v) = n\}$$

when $p$ is so large that percolation occurs. In the one-parameter case this is the interval $p_H < p \leq 1$. It turns out that (5.2), and hence (5.1) does not decrease exponentially in this domain. We have no estimates for (5.1) for p-values at which

$$(5.3) \qquad E_p\{\#W(v)\} = \infty, \text{ but } \quad \theta(p,v) = P_p\{\#W(v) = \infty\} = 0 \text{ ,}$$

except in the special cases of $\mathcal{G}_0$ and $\mathcal{G}_1$ (see Theorem 8.2). Of course if Theorem 3.1 and Cor. 3.1 apply then (5.3) can happen only on the critical surface, and one may conjecture that in general the set of p-values at which (5.3) holds has an empty interior. In one-parameter problems this amounts to the conjecture that $p_T = p_H$ in all periodic percolation problems. If one goes still further one might conjecture that (5.1) decreases only as a power of $n$ whenever (5.3) holds. For bond- or site-percolation on $\mathbb{Z}^2$, Theorem 8.2 indeed gives a lower bound of the form $n^{-\gamma}$ for (5.1) at $p = p_H$.

In Sect. 5.3 we discuss a result of Russo (1981) which is more or less dual to Theorem 5.1. If in dimension two certain crossing probabilities are large enough, then percolation does occur. Sect. 5.2 and 5.3 are not needed for later chapters.

Throughout this chapter $\mathcal{G}$ will be a periodic graph imbedded in $\mathbb{R}^d$ which satisfies (2.2)-(2.5). We deal with a periodic[1] $\lambda$-parameter site problem and take $(\Omega, \mathcal{B}, P_p)$ as in (3.19)-(3.23). We also use the following special notation: For $\bar{n} = (n_1,\dots,n_d)$ we set

(5.4) $$T(\bar{n};i) = \{x = (x(1),\dots,x(d)): 0 \le x(j) \le 3n_j, j \ne i, 0 \le x(i) \le n_i\}$$
$$= [0,3n_1] \times \dots \times [0,3n_{i-1}] \times [0,n_i] \times [0,3n_{i+1}] \times \dots \times [0,3n_d]$$

The block $T(\bar{n};i)$ is "short" in the i-th direction, as illustrated in Fig. 5.1 for d = 2 and $\bar{n} = (1,1)$.

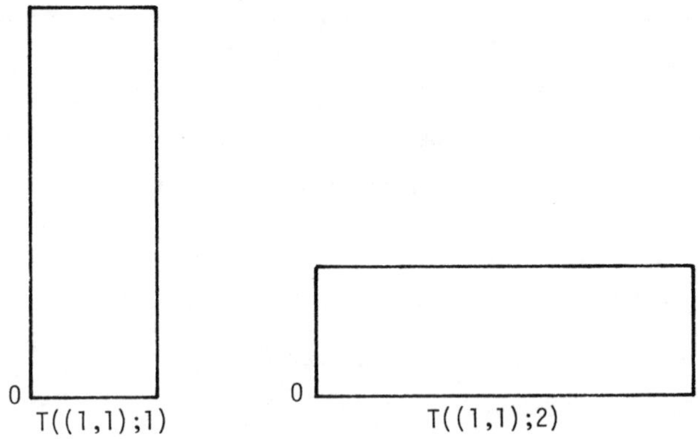


Figure 5.1

The corresponding crossing probabilities are defined as

(5.5) $$\tau(\bar{n};i,p) = \tau(\bar{n};i,p,\mathcal{G}) = \sigma((3n_1,\dots,3n_{i-1},n_i,3n_{i+1},\dots,3n_d);i,p,\mathcal{G})$$
$$= P_p\{\exists \text{ an occupied } i\text{-crossing on } \mathcal{G} \text{ of } T(\bar{n};i)\}$$

1) Actually one does not need periodicity for most results of this chapter, but it simplifies the formulation of the results.

and

(5.6) $\tau^*(\bar{n};i,p) = \tau(\bar{n};i,p,\mathcal{G}) = \tau(n;i,\bar{1}-p,\mathcal{G}^*) = \sigma((3n_1,\ldots,3n_{i-1},n_i,$
$3n_{i+1},\ldots,3n_d;i,\bar{1}-p,\ \mathcal{G}^*) = P_p\{\ \exists$ a vacant i-crossing on $\mathcal{G}^*$
of $T(\bar{n};i)\}$.

5.1 Exponential fall off of $P\{\#W \geq n\}$.

We need the following constants:

(5.7) $\mu$ = number of vertices $v = (v_1,\ldots,v_d)$ of $\mathcal{G}$ with
$0 \leq v_i < 1,\ 1 \leq i \leq d$ .

(5.8) $\Lambda$ is any number such that $|v-w| \leq \Lambda$ for all adjacent pairs of vertices $v,w$ of $\mathcal{G}$.

(5.9) $\kappa = \kappa(d) = \frac{1}{2d}(2e\ 5^d)^{-11^d}$ .

Furthermore, $z_0$ is some fixed vertex of $\mathcal{G}$ and

$$W = W(z_0).$$

*Theorem 5.1. If for some* $\bar{N} = (N_1,\ldots,N_d)$ *with* $N_i \geq \Lambda,\ 1 \leq i \leq d$, *one has*

(5.10) $\tau(\bar{N};i,p) \leq \kappa,\ 1 \leq i \leq d,$

*then there exist constants* $0 < C_1,\ C_2 < \infty$ *such that*

(5.11) $P_p\{\#W \geq n\} \leq C_1 e^{-C_2 n},\ n \geq 0$ .

(*The values of* $C_1$, $C_2$ *are given in (5.40)-(5.42)*). *If*

(5.12) $p(v) > 0$ for all $v$

*and*

(5.13) $E_p\ \{\#W\} < \infty$

*then*

(5.14) $\tau((n,\ldots,n);\ i,p) \to 0$ as $n \to \infty$

*and consequently (5.11) holds*.

Corollary 5.1. The set

(5.15) $\{p \in \mathcal{P}_\lambda : p >> 0 \text{ and } E_p\{\#W\} < \infty\}$

is open in $\mathcal{P}_\lambda$.

Special Case. In the one-parameter problem with $p(v)$ independent of $p$ the implication (5.10) $\Rightarrow$ (5.11) shows that if $p < p_S$, and hence (5.14), then (5.11) holds, and consequently $p < p_T$ (see (3.63),(3.65)). Conversely $p < p_T$ means (5.13) and this implies (5.14), i.e., $p < p_S$. Thus, in any periodic one-parameter percolation problem

(5.16) $$p_T = p_S \leq p_H .$$

(The last inequality is just (3.64)). From the fact that $E_p\{\#W\} = \infty$ immediately to the right of $p_T$ and Cor. 5.1 it further follows that

(5.17) $$E_{p_T}\{\#W\} = \infty$$

is any periodic one-parameter problem. ///

Kunz and Souillard (1978) already proved (5.11) when $p(v) < (z-1)^{-1}$ for all $v$, where $z$ is as in (2.3). The present proof, which is taken from Kesten (1981) is a reduction to the case of small $p(v)$ by a block approach. The blocks $T(\bar{N};i)$ and suitable translates of them are viewed as the vertices of an auxiliary graph $\mathcal{L}$ with vertex set $\mathbb{Z}^d$. A vertex $\bar{\ell}$ of $\mathcal{L}$ is taken as occupied iff there is an occupied crossing of some associated block of $\mathcal{G}$, and this will have a small probability. Therefore, the distribution of the size of the occupied cluster of a vertex on $\mathcal{L}$ will have an exponentially bounded tail. This, in turn, will imply (5.11) via Lemma 5.2, which relates $\#W$ to the size of an occupied cluster on $\mathcal{L}$.

The proof will be broken down into a number of lemmas. As in Kunz and Souillard (1978) we bring in the numbers

(5.18) $$a(0,\ell) := \delta_{1,\ell} ,$$

and for $n \geq 1$

(5.19) $a(n,\ell) = a(n,\ell;z_0,\mathcal{G})$ = number of connected sets $C$ of vertices of $\mathcal{G}$, containing $z_0$, with $\#C = n$, $\#\partial C = \ell$ .

Here, analogously to (3.6), $\#C$ denotes the number of vertices in the set $C$, $\partial C$ is the boundary of $C$ on $\mathcal{G}$ as in Def. 2.8, and $C$ is connected if any two vertices in $C$ are connected by a path on $\mathcal{G}$ all of whose vertices belong to $C$.

Lemma 5.1. For any $0 \le p \le 1$, $q = 1-p$

(5.20) $$\sum_{n=0}^{\infty} \sum_{\ell \ge 0} a(n,\ell) p^n q^\ell = 1-\theta(p,z_0) \le 1 .$$

Consequently

(5.21) $$a(n,\ell) \le \left(\frac{n+\ell}{n}\right)^n \left(\frac{n+\ell}{\ell}\right)^\ell .$$

Also

(5.22) $$\sum_{\ell \ge 0} a(n,\ell) \le \{(z+1)^{z+1} z^{-z}\}^n$$

and for some universal constant $\varepsilon_0 > 0$ and $0 \le x \le \varepsilon_0$, $0 \le p \le 1$, $q = 1-p$ and $n \ge 1$

(5.23) $$\sum_{\substack{\ell \text{ with} \\ |p\ell - qn| \ge xnpq}} a(n,\ell) p^n q^\ell \le nz \exp(-\tfrac{1}{3} x^2 p^2 qn).$$

Proof: The relation (5.20) is well known, and is hardly more than the definition of the percolation probability. It is immediate from

(5.24) $$P_p\{W = C\} = p^n q^\ell$$

for any connected set $C$ of vertices containing $v_0$ and with $\#C = n$, $\#\partial C = \ell$. In fact $\{W = C\}$ occurs iff all vertices of $C$ are occupied, but all vertices adjacent to $C$ but not in $C$ are vacant. The left hand side of (5.20) is simply the sum of (5.24) over all possible finite $C$. (5.21) follows from (5.20) by taking $p = n/(n+\ell)$, $q = \ell/(n+\ell)$. For (5.22) observe that, by (2.3) and $\partial C \ne \phi$.

(5.25) $$1 \le \#\partial C \le z.\#C \quad \text{when} \quad \#C \ge 1 ,$$

so that the sums in (5.20) and (5.22) can be restricted to $1 \le \ell \le n$. when $n \ge 1$. Thus, with $p = (z+1)^{-1}$, $q = z(z+1)^{-1}$ (5.20) yields for $n \ge 1$

$$\sum_{\ell=1}^{n} a(n,\ell) \leq (z+1)^n \left(\frac{z+1}{z}\right)^{zn} \sum_{\ell=1}^{n} a(n,\ell)p^n q^\ell \leq 1,$$

while for $n = 0$ (5.22) is true by definition of $a(0,\ell)$. Finally, by virtue of (5.25) and (5.21) the left hand side of (5.23) is bounded by

$$(5.26) \qquad \sum_{|p\ell-qn| \geq xnpq} a(n,\ell) \left\{\frac{(n+\ell)p}{n}\right\}^n \left\{\frac{(n+\ell)q}{\ell}\right\}^\ell \left(\frac{n}{n+\ell}\right)^n \left(\frac{\ell}{n+\ell}\right)^\ell$$

$$\leq nz \max \left\{\frac{(n+\ell)p}{n}\right\}^n \left\{\frac{(n+\ell)q}{\ell}\right\}^\ell ,$$

where the maximum in (5.26) is over all $1 \leq \ell \leq zn$ with $|p\ell - qn| \geq xnpq$. Now fix $n$ and $p$ and consider

$$(5.27) \qquad f(\ell) := n \log \frac{(n+\ell)p}{n} + \ell \log \frac{(n+\ell)q}{\ell}$$

as a function of a continuous variable $\ell$ on $(0,\infty)$. One easily sees that $f(.)$ is increasing if $(n+\ell)q/\ell \geq 1$ or $p\ell - qn \leq 0$, and decreasing for $p\ell - qn \geq 0$. Thus, the maximum of $f$ over $|p\ell - qn| \geq xnpq$ is taken on when $p\ell - qn = xnpq$ or $p\ell - qn = -xnpq$. For such a choice

$$\ell = \frac{q}{p} n(1 \pm xp), \quad \frac{(n+\ell)p}{n} = 1 \pm xpq, \quad \frac{(n+\ell)q}{\ell} = \frac{1 \pm xpq}{1 \pm xp} .$$

A simple expansion of the logarithms in (5.27) now shows that for small $x$ and $p\ell - qn = \pm xnpq$

$$f(\ell) = -\frac{1}{2} n x^2 p^2 q \{1 + O(x)\} ,$$

with $|x^{-1} O(x)|$ bounded uniformly in $n,\ell,p$. (5.23) follows. □

We now define the auxiliary graph $\mathcal{L}$, and derive a relation between $W$ and a certain occupied component on $\mathcal{L}$. The vertex set of $\mathcal{L}$ is $\mathbb{Z}^d$. The vertices $\bar{k} = (k(1),\dots,k(d))$ and $\bar{\ell} = (\ell(1),\dots,\ell(d))$ are adjacent on $\mathcal{L}$ iff

$$|k(i) - \ell(i)| \leq 2, \ 1 \leq i \leq d .$$

We associate with an occupancy configuration on $\mathcal{G}$ an occupancy configuration on $\mathcal{L}$ in the following manner: We take $\bar{k} \in \mathcal{L}$ occupied iff there exists an occupied path $r = (w_0,e_1,\dots,e_\tau,w_\tau)$ on $\mathcal{G}$ whose initial point satisfies

(5.28) $$k(j)N_j \le w_0(j) < (k(j)+1)N_j,\ 1 \le j \le d,$$

and whose final point $w_\tau$ satisfies

(5.29) $$w_\tau(i) \le (k(i)-1)N_i \quad \text{or} \quad w_\tau(i) \ge (k(i)+2)N_i$$

$$\text{for some } 1 \le i \le d .$$

We shall now prove the estimate

(5.30) $$P_p\{\overline{k} \text{ is occupied}\} \le 2\sum_{i=1}^{d} \tau(\overline{N};i,p) ,$$

which is basic for our proof. To see (5.30) observe that if there exists an occupied path $r$ for which (5.28) and (5.29) hold, then there is a smallest index $b$ for which there exists an $i$ such that $e_b$ intersects one of the hyperplanes

$$H_i^- : \{x : x(i) = (k(i)-1)N_i\} \quad \text{or}$$
$$H_i^+ : \{x : x(i) = (k(i)+2)N_i\} .$$

$e_b$ may intersect $H_i^- \cup H_i^+$ for several $i$. For each such $i$, let $\zeta_{bi}$ be the first intersection of $w_b$ with $H_i^- \cup H_i^+$ and let $i_0$ be an index such that $\zeta_{bi_0}$ precedes all the other $\zeta_{bi}$ which exist. Then

(5.31) $e_\ell$ (including its endpoints $w_{\ell-1}$ and $w_\ell$) lies strictly between $H_j^-$ and $H_j^+$ for all $1 \le \ell < b$ and $1 \le j \le d$; the same is true for the segment $[w_{b-1}, \zeta_{bi_0})$.

For the sake of argument assume $e_b$ intersects $H_{i_0}^+$ so that $\zeta_{bi_0} \in H_{i_0}^+$. Then take $a$ as the largest index less than $b$ for which $e_a$ intersects the hyperplane $x(i_0) = (k(i_0)+1)N_{i_0}$. Such an $a$ exists by (5.28). Also take $\zeta_{ai_0}$ as the last intersection of $w_a$ with the hyperplane $x(i_0) = (k(i_0)+1)N_{i_0}$. Then

(5.32) $e_\ell$(including its endpoints $w_{\ell-1}$ and $w_\ell$) lies strictly between the hyperplanes $x(i_0) = (k(i_0)+1)N_i$ and $H_{i_0}^+$ for all $a < \ell < b$; the same is true for the segment $(\zeta_{ai_0}, w_{a+1}]$.

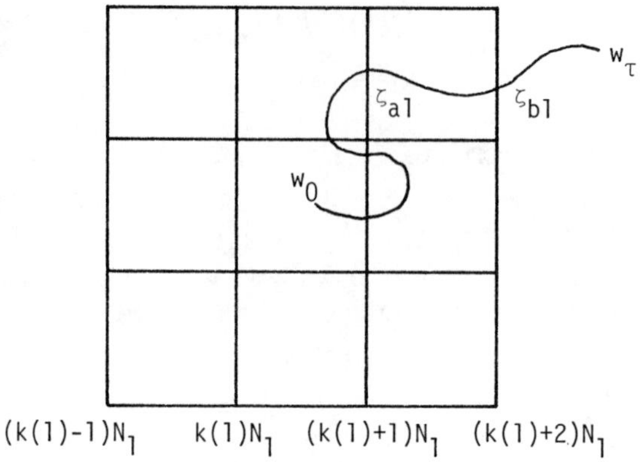


Figure 5.2

(5.31) and (5.32) say that $(w_a, e_{a+1}, \dots, e_b, w_b)$ is an $i_0$-crossing of the block with sides

$$[(k(j) - 1)N_j, (k(j) + 2)N_j] \quad \text{for} \quad j \neq i$$

and

$$[(k(i_0) + 1)N_{i_0}, (k(i_0) + 2)N_{i_0}] \quad \text{for} \quad j = i_0 .$$

This is precisely the block

$$T(\overline{N};i_0) + \sum_{j=1}^{d} (k(j) - 1)N_j\xi_j + 2k(i_0)N_{i_0}\xi_{i_0} , \tag{5.33}$$

where, as before, $\xi_j$ is the $j$-th coordinate vector in $\mathbb{R}^d$. Moreover, since $r$ is occupied $(w_a, e_{a+1}, \dots, e_b, w_b)$ is occupied. By periodicity, the probability that an occupied $i_0$-crossing of (5.33) exists is at most $\tau(\overline{N};i_0,p)$. The same estimate holds when $w_b$ intersects $H_{i_0}^-$ instead of $H_{i_0}^+$ . (5.30) now follows by summing over all possible $i_0$.

We next define $\overline{\nu}$ by

$$\nu_j N_j \leq z_0(j) < (\nu_j + 1)N_j , \quad 1 \leq j \leq d , \tag{5.34}$$

where $z_0$ is the vertex which we singled out in $W = W(z_0)$. $\tilde{W}(\overline{\ell})$ will denote the occupied component of $\overline{\ell}$ on $\mathcal{L}$ . Finally we remind the reader that $\bar{k} \mathcal{L} \bar{\ell}$ means that $\bar{k}$ and $\bar{\ell}$ are adjacent on $\mathcal{L}$.

Lemma 5.2. Assume $W$ contains a vertex $w = (w(1),\ldots,w(d))$ with

(5.35) $$k(j)N_j \le w(j) < (k(j)+1)N_j,\ 1 \le j \le d,$$

for some $\bar{k}$ with

(5.36) $$|k(m) - \nu(m)| \ge 2 \quad \text{for some } 1 \le m \le d.$$

Then there exists an occupied path $(\bar{k}_0, \bar{e}_1, \ldots, \bar{e}_\rho, \bar{k}_\rho)$ on $\mathcal{L}$ with $\bar{k}_0 = \bar{k}$ and

(5.37) $$|k_\rho(j) - \nu(j)| \le 3,\ 1 \le j \le d.$$

($\bar{e}_j$ denotes an edge of $\mathcal{L}$). Furthermore

(5.38) $$\max \ \#\tilde{W}(\ell) \ge \frac{\{\#W - \mu 4^d \prod_{j=1}^{d} N_j\}}{\mu 7^d \prod_{j=1}^{d} N_j},$$

where the max in (5.38) is over those $\bar{\ell}$ with

(5.39) $$|\ell(j) - \nu(j)| \le 3,\ 1 \le j \le d.$$

Proof: Assume $w \in W$ satisfies (5.35) and (5.36). Then there exists an occupied path $(w_0 = w, e_1, \ldots, e_\tau, w_\tau = z_0)$ on $\mathcal{G}$ from $w$ to $z_0$. By (5.36) and the definition of $\bar{\nu}$, $w_\tau = z_0$ satisfies (5.29). Since also $w_0$ satisfies (5.28) (see (5.35)) the vertex $\bar{k}$ of $\mathcal{L}$ is occupied, and there exists a smallest index $b$ with $w_b(i) \le (k(i) - 1)N_i$ or $w_b(i) \ge (k(i) + 2)N_i$ for some $i$. We take $\bar{k}_0 = \bar{k}$ and $\bar{k}_1$ such that

$$k_1(j)N_j \le w_b(j) < (k_1(j)+1)N_j,\ 1 \le j \le d.$$

This $\bar{k}_1$ is uniquely determined, and by virtue of the minimality of $b$, and $N_j \ge \Lambda$,

$$|k_0(j) - k_1(j)| \le 2,\ 1 \le j \le d.$$

(Compare (5.31) and Fig. 5.2.) Thus $\bar{k}_0 \mathcal{L} \bar{k}_1$.

We now repeat the procedure with $w_b$ and $\bar{k}_1$ in the place of $w_0$ and $\bar{k}_0$. If the analogue of (5.36) still holds for $\bar{k}_1$, i.e., if

$|k_1(m) - \nu(m)| \geq 2$ for some $m$, then $\bar{k}_1$ is occupied and we find a neighbor $\bar{k}_2$ of $\bar{k}_1$ on $\mathcal{L}$, and so on. We continue this process as long as possible. It stops when we have obtained a sequence $\bar{k}_0,\dots,\bar{k}_\rho$ of occupied points on $\mathcal{L}$ and a $\bar{k}_{\rho+1} \in \mathcal{L}$ such that

$$\bar{k}_t \; \mathcal{L} \; \bar{k}_{t+1}, \; 0 \leq t \leq \rho ,$$

while the analogue of (5.36) fails for $\bar{k}_{\rho+1}$, i.e.,

$$|k_{\rho+1}(j) - \nu(j)| \leq 1, \; 1 \leq j \leq d .$$

Since $\bar{k}_\rho \; \mathcal{L} \; \bar{k}_{\rho+1}$ this implies that (5.37) holds. Thus there exists an occupied path $(\bar{k}_0 = \bar{k}, \bar{e}_1, \dots, \bar{e}_\rho, \bar{k}_\rho)$ as claimed in the first part of the lemma. (Note that we may have to apply the loop-removal procedure of Sect. 2.1 to make the path self-avoiding.)

The inequality (5.38) now follows easily from the first part of the lemma. Each vertex $w \in W$ with $|w(m) - z_0(m)| \geq 2N_m$ for some $m$ satisfies (5.35) and (5.36) for some $\bar{k}$. There are at least

$$\#W - \mu \prod_{j=1}^{d} (4N_j).$$

such vertices $w$. Each such $w$ leads to an occupied path of the above type on $\mathcal{L}$ starting at some $\bar{k}_0$ and ending at a $\bar{k}_\rho$ satisfying (5.37). A fixed $\bar{k}_0$ can arise as starting point for such a path only for a $w$ with

$$k_0(j)N_j \leq w(j) < (k_0(j) + 1)N_j$$

(see (5.35)). Since there are at most $\mu \prod N_j$ such vertices $w$ on $\mathcal{G}$, at least

$$\{\mu \prod_{j=1}^{d} N_j\}^{-1} \{\#W - \mu \prod_{j=1}^{d} (4N_j)\} \tag{5.40}$$

distinct vertices $\bar{k}_0$ arise as the initial point of an occupied path on $\mathcal{L}$ which ends at some $\bar{k}_\rho$ satisfying (5.37). Since there are at most $7^d$ points $\bar{k}_\rho$ which satisfy (5.37), (5.38) now follows from (5.40). □

Lemma 5.3. (5.10) implies (5.11) with

$$A = 7^{-d}(\mu N_1 \dots, N_d)^{-1} , \tag{5.41}$$

$$(5.42)\qquad C_1 = (\tfrac{7}{5})^d e^{-1} \{2 \sum_{i=1}^{d} \tau(N;i,p)\}^{-11^{-d}}$$

$$[1 - e5^d \{2 \sum_{i=1}^{d} \tau(N;i,p)\}^{11^{-d}}]^{-1}$$

$$\leq (\tfrac{7}{5})^d \{2 \sum_{i=1}^{d} \tau(N;i,p)\}^{-11^{-d}} ,$$

$$(5.43)\qquad e^{-C_2} = (e\, 5^d)^A \{2 \sum_{i=1}^{d} \tau(\overline{N};i,p)\}^{A11^{-d}} \leq 2^{-A} .$$

Proof: By (5.38)

$$(5.44)\qquad P_p\{\#W \geq n\} \leq \sum_{\substack{\overline{\ell}\text{ satisfying}\\(5.39)}} P_p\{\#\tilde{W}(\overline{\ell}) \geq An - 1\} .$$

Set, for any $\overline{\ell} \in \mathcal{L}$

$\tilde{b}(m)$ = number of connected sets on $\mathcal{L}$ of $m$ vertices and containing $\overline{\ell}$ .

Note that $\tilde{b}(m)$ does not depend on $\overline{\ell}$ by the periodicity of $\mathcal{L}$. Recall also that at most $7^d$ points $\overline{\ell}$ satisfy (5.39). Therefore, (compare (3.15) and the proof of (5.20)) the right hand side of (5.44) is bounded by

$$(5.45)\qquad 7^d \sum_{m \geq An-1} \tilde{b}(m) \max_{\#\tilde{C} = m} P_p \{\text{all vertices in } \tilde{C} \text{ are occupied}\}$$

where $\tilde{C}$ in (5.45) runs over the connected sets of vertices of $\mathcal{L}$ with cardinality $m$. To estimate the probability appearing in (5.45) we observe that we are not dealing with a percolation problem on $\mathcal{L}$ because the occupancies of the vertices of $\mathcal{L}$ are not independent. However, the occupancy of a vertex $\overline{\ell}$ of $\mathcal{L}$ depends only on the occupancies of the vertices $v$ of $\mathcal{G}$ with

$$(\ell(j)-2)N_j \leq (\ell(j)-1)N_j-\Lambda \leq v(j) \leq (\ell(j)+2)N_j+\Lambda \leq (\ell(j)+3)N_j, 1 \leq j \leq d.$$

Thus, if $\overline{\ell}_1,\dots,\overline{\ell}_t$ are vertices of $\mathcal{L}$ such that for each $r \neq s$ there exists an $i$ with $|\ell_r(i) - \ell_s(i)| \geq 6$, then the occupancies of $\overline{\ell}_1,\dots,\overline{\ell}_t$ are independent (because they depend on disjoint sets of vertices of $\mathcal{G}$). Now given $\tilde{C}$ with $\#\tilde{C} = m$ we can choose $\overline{\ell}_1,\dots,\overline{\ell}_t \in \tilde{C}$ with the above property for some $t \geq 11^{-d}m$. With $\overline{\ell}_1,\dots,\overline{\ell}_t$ chosen in this way we have by virtue of (5.30)

$$P_p\{\text{all vertices in } \tilde{C} \text{ are occupied}\}$$
$$\le P_p\{\bar{\ell}_1,\dots,\bar{\ell}_t \text{ are occupied}\} \le \{2\sum_{i=1}^{d} \tau(\bar{N};p,i)\}^t .$$

Substitution of this estimate with $t = 11^{-d}m$ into (5.45) yields

$$(5.46)\quad P_p\{\#W \ge n\} \le 7^d \sum_{m \ge An-1} \tilde{b}(m)\{2\sum_{i=1}^{d} \tau(N;p,i)\}^{11^{-d}m} .$$

Finally, (5.22) applied to the graph $\mathcal{L}$ with $5^d - 1$ for $z$ shows

$$\tilde{b}(m) \le \{(z+1)(\tfrac{z+1}{z})^z\}^m \le (e\, 5^d)^m .$$

This together with (5.46) implies (5.11) with the values (5.42) and (5.43) of $C_1$, $C_2$. □

Lemma 5.4. (5.12) and (5.13) imply (5.14).

Proof: This lemma basically proves that the diameter of $W$ has an exponentially decreasing distribution under (5.13). This fact was first proved by Hammersley (1957), Theorem 2. We make the following definition for positive integers $m,M$ and $u$ a vertex of $\mathcal{G}$

$$S_0 = S_0(u,M) = \{w \text{ a vertex of } \mathcal{G}: |w(j) - u(j)| \le M,\ 1 \le j \le d\} ,$$

$$S_1 = S_0 \cup \partial S_0 = \{w \text{ a vertex of } \mathcal{G}: w \in S_0$$
$$\text{or } w \text{ adjacent to a vertex in } S_0\},$$

$$(5.47)\quad A(u,m) = \{\exists \text{ an occupied path on } \mathcal{G} \text{ from a neighbor of } u \text{ to a } w \text{ with } w(1) \ge m\} ,$$

$$g(u,w,M) = P_p\{\exists \text{ occupied path } (w_0,e_1,\dots,e_\rho,w_\rho) \text{ on } \mathcal{G} \text{ with } w_0 \,\mathcal{G}\, u,\ w_\rho \notin S_0(u,M) \text{ and one of the } w_i \text{ equal to } w\}.$$

We claim that if $u(1) < m - M$ then

$$(5.48)\qquad P_p\{A(u,m)\} \le \sum_{w \in S_1(u,M)} g(u,w,M)P_p\{A(w,m)\} .$$

To prove (5.48) assume that $A(u,m)$ occurs. Then there exists an occupied path $r = (v_0 = u,e_1,\dots,e_\nu,v_\nu)$ on $\mathcal{G}$ with $v_0 = u$ and $v_\nu(1) \ge m > v_0(1) + M$. Therefore $v_\nu \in S_0$ and there exists a smallest index $a$, $1 \le a \le \nu$ with $v_a \notin S_0$. Now set

$$R = \{w \in S_1 : \ \exists \text{ occupied path } (w_0, e_1, \dots, e_\rho, w_\rho) \text{ on } \mathcal{G} \text{ with } w_0 \mathcal{G} u,\ w_\rho \notin S_0 \text{ but } w_t \in S_0 \text{ for } t < \rho \text{ and one of the } w_i \text{ equal to } w\}.$$

$R$ is the random set of vertices in $S_1$ through which there exists an occupied path from a neighbor of $u$ to the complement of $S_0$, which except for its final point contains only vertices in $S_0$. By choice of $a$, $v_a \in R$. Let $b \geq a$ be the last index with $v_b \in R$. Now consider the occupied path $(v_{b+1}, e_{b+2}, \dots, e_\nu, v_\nu)$. All its vertices lie outside $R$, its initial point is adjacent to $v_b \in R$ and its final point $v_\nu$ satisfies $v_\nu(1) \geq m$. Thus $A(v_b, m)$ occurs. Summing over all possibilities for $v_b$ and $R$ gives the inequality

$$(5.49) \quad P_p\{A(u,m)\} \leq \sum_{w \in S_1} P_p\{w \in R \text{ and } \exists \text{ an occupied path } (w_0, f_1, \dots, f_\rho, w_\rho) \text{ on } \mathcal{G} \text{ with } w_0 \mathcal{G} w,\ w_\rho(1) \geq m \text{ and } w_i \notin R \text{ for } 0 \leq i \leq \rho\} = \sum_{w \in S_1} \sum_{\substack{C \subset S_1 \\ w \in C}} P_p\{R = C \text{ and } \exists \text{ an occupied path } (w_0, f_1, \dots, f_\rho, w_\rho) \text{ on } \mathcal{G} \text{ with } w_0 \mathcal{G} w,\ w_\rho(1) \geq m \text{ and } w_i \notin C \text{ for } 0 \leq i \leq \rho\}.$$

We now fix $w$ and a subset $C$ of $S$, containing $w$ and estimate the last probability in (5.49). Observe that $R = C$ iff both the following two events occur:

$\mathcal{C}_1$ = {For every vertex $x \in C$ there exists an occupied path $(u_0, g_1, \dots, g_\tau, u_\tau)$ on $\mathcal{G}$ with $u_0 \mathcal{G} u$, $u_\tau \notin S_0$, but $u_\tau \in S_0$ for $t < \tau$, $u_i \in C$ for $0 \leq i \leq \tau$ and $x$ equals one of the $u_i$} ,

$\mathcal{C}_2$ = {any path $(u_0, g_1, \dots, g_\tau, u_\tau)$ on $\mathcal{G}$ with $u_0 \mathcal{G} u$, $u_\tau \notin S_0$, but $u_\tau \in S_0$ for $t < \tau$ and not all $u_i \in C$ contains at least one vacant $u_j \notin C$}.

All vertices on the paths $(u_0, g_1, \dots, u_\tau)$ in the description of $\mathcal{C}_1$ must belong to $C$, because whenever such a path satisfies $u_0 \mathcal{G} u$, $u_\tau \notin S_0$

$u_\tau \in S_0$ for $t < \tau$ and all $u_i$ occupied, then all its $u_i$ automatically belong to R. Not all sets $C \subset S_1$ are such that $\mathcal{C}_1$ can occur; e.g., C can only have components which contain a neighbor of u. But in any case $I_{\mathcal{C}_1}(\omega)$ is a function of the occupancies of the vertices in C only. If $\mathcal{C}_1$ can occur, then

$$\mathcal{C}_1 = \{\text{all vertices of } C \text{ are occupied}\} .$$

Also $I_{\mathcal{C}_2}(\omega)$ is a function of the $\omega(y)$ with $y \notin C$ and it is a decreasing function. On the other hand

$$J(\omega) = J(w,\omega) := I[\ \exists \text{ an occupied path } (w_0, f_1, \dots, f_\rho, w_\rho) \text{ on } \mathcal{G} \text{ with } w_0 \mathcal{G} w,\ w_\rho(1) \geq m \text{ and } w_i \notin C \text{ for } 0 \leq i \leq \rho\} \tag{5.50}$$

is an increasing function of the occupancies of the $\omega(v)$, $y \notin C$. By the independence of the $\omega(y)$ with $y \in C$ and with $y \notin C$ the last probability in (5.49) can be written as

$$E_p\{I_{\mathcal{C}_1} I_{\mathcal{C}_2} J\} = E_p\{I_{\mathcal{C}_1}\}\, E_p\{I_{\mathcal{C}_2} J\} .$$

Next it follows immediately from the FKG inequality (apply Prop. 4.1 to $I_{\mathcal{C}_2}$ and 1-J for instance) that

$$E_p\{I_{\mathcal{C}_2} J\} \leq E_p\{I_{\mathcal{C}_2}\}\, E_p\{J\} .$$

Substituting this into (5.49) and using the independence of $\mathcal{C}_1$ and $\mathcal{C}_2$ once more, as well as the simple inequality $J(w,\omega) \leq I[A(w,m)]$ we obtain

$$P_p\{A(u,m)\} \leq \sum_{w \in S_1} \sum_{\substack{C \subset S_1 \\ w \in C}} E_p\{I_{\mathcal{C}_1}\}\, E_p\{I_{\mathcal{C}_2}\}\, E_p\{J\}$$

$$= \sum_{w \in S_1} \sum_{\substack{C \subset S_1 \\ w \in C}} E_p\{I_{\mathcal{C}_1} I_{\mathcal{C}_2}\} E_p\{J\}$$

$$\leq \sum_{w \in S_1} \sum_{\substack{C \subset S_1 \\ w \in C}} P_p\{R = C\}\, P_p\{A(w,m)\}$$

$$= \sum_{w \in S_1} P_p\{w \in R\}\, P_p\{A(w,m)\} \leq \sum_{w \in S_1} g(u,w,M)\, P_p\{A(w,m)\}.$$

This proves (5.48). We next show that we can choose $M$ such that

$$(5.51) \qquad \sum_{w \in S_1(u,M)} g(u,w,M) \le \frac{3}{4} \quad \text{for all} \quad u \in \mathcal{G} \quad .$$

This is easy, because any path from a neighbor of $u$ to the complement of $S_0(u,M)$ has diameter $\ge M-\Lambda$ and therefore contains at least $M/\Lambda$ vertices. Consequently

$$g(u,w,M) \le P_p\{w \in W(x) \text{ and } \#W(x) \ge M/\Lambda$$
$$\text{for some neighbor } x \text{ of } u\}$$

and, by virtue of (4.8)

$$(5.52) \qquad \sum_{w \in S_1(u,M)} g(u,w,M) \le \sum_{\substack{x \text{ such that} \\ x \mathcal{G} u}} E_p\{\#W(x); \#W(x) \ge \frac{M}{\Lambda}\}$$

$$\le \sum_{x \mathcal{G} u} [P_p\{x \text{ and } u \text{ are occupied}\}]^{-1} E_p\{\#W(u); \#W(u) \ge \frac{M}{\Lambda}\} .$$

Under (5.12) and (5.13) the right hand side of (5.52) tends to zero as $M \to \infty$ when $u = z_0$. But, by the Application in Sect. 4.1 (5.12) and (5.13) imply

$$E_p \{\#W(u)\} < \infty \quad \text{for all} \quad u \in \mathcal{G}$$

Consequently the right and left hand side of (5.52) tend to zero as $M \to \infty$ for any vertex $u$. In particular

$$(5.53) \qquad \lim_{M \to \infty} \sum_{w \in S_1(u,M)} g(u,w,M) = 0$$

uniformly for the finitely many $u$ in $[0,1)^d$. By periodicity,

$$\sum_{w \in S_1(u,M)} g(u,w,M)$$

is unchaged if $u$ is replaced by $u + \sum k_j \xi_j$ , so that (5.53) holds uniformly in $u$.

The above shows that (5.51) holds for large enough $M$. Pick such an $M$. Then, it follows from (5.48) and the fact that

$$w(1) \leq u(1) + M + \Lambda \quad \text{for} \quad w \in S_1(u,M) ,$$

that for $r < m-M$

$$\sup_{u(1) \leq r} P_p\{A(u,m)\}$$

$$\leq \sum_{w \in S_1(u,M)} g(u,w,M) \sup_{u(1) < r+M+\Lambda} P_p\{A(u,m)\}$$

$$\leq \frac{3}{4} \sup_{u(1) \leq r+M+\Lambda} P_p\{A(u,m)\} .$$

It follows immediately that

$$(5.54) \qquad \sup_{u(1) \leq 0} P_p\{A(u,m)\} \leq (\tfrac{3}{4})^{\lfloor (m-M)/(M+\Lambda) \rfloor} .$$

(5.54) says that the probability that $W(u)$ extends $m$ units in the 1-direction decreases exponentially in $m$. $\tau((n,\dots,n);1,p)$ is the probability that there exists an occupied 1-crossing $(v_0,e_1,\dots,e_\nu,v_\nu)$ on $\mathcal{G}$ of $T((n,\dots,n);1)$. By Def. 3.1 (cf. (3.30) and (3.31)) such a crossing must satisfy $v_\nu(1) - v_0(1) \geq n-2\Lambda$ and the initial point $v_0$ has to lie in

$$[-\Lambda,\Lambda] \times [-\Lambda,3n+\Lambda] \times \dots \times [-\Lambda,3n+\Lambda]$$

(see (3.29), (3.30), (5.8 ) ). By periodicity and (5.7) there are at most

$$\mu(2\Lambda+1)\ (3n+2\Lambda+1)^{d-1}$$

such vertices $v_0$. Therefore, by periodicity

$$(5.55) \quad \tau((n,\dots,n);1,p) \leq \mu(2\Lambda+1)(3n+2\Lambda+1)^{d-1} \sup_{u(1) \leq 0} P_p\{A(u,n-3\Lambda)\},$$

so that $\tau((n,\dots,n);1,p)$ tends to zero exponentialy as $n \to \infty$, by virtue of (5.54). The same holds for $\tau((n,\dots,n);i,p)$ for any $1 \leq i \leq d$. This proves the lemma. □

Theorem 5.1 is now just a combination of Lemmas 5.3 and 5.4.

Proof of Cor. 5.1: Assume

$$E_{p_0}\{\#W\} < \infty \quad \text{and} \quad p_0 >> 0$$

for some $p_0 \in \mathcal{P}_\lambda$. By (5.14) we can then find an $n \geq \Lambda$ such that $\tau((n,\dots,n);i,p_0) < \kappa$ for all $1 \leq i \leq d$. Since $\tau((n,\dots,n);i,p)$ is a continuous function of $p$ for fixed $n$ - it only involves the occupancies of a finite number of vertices - it follows that

$$\tau((n,\dots,n);i,p) < \kappa \ , \ 1 \leq i \leq d \ ,$$

holds for $p$ in some neighborhood of $p_0$. For any $p$ in this neighborhood (5.11) holds, and consequently also (5.13). □

5.2. Estimates above the percolation threshold.

Let $\mathcal{G}$ be a periodic graph imbedded in $\mathbb{R}^d$ and $P_p$ a periodic probability measure. Assume that $p$ is such that percolation occurs, i.e., that

(5.56) $$\theta(p,v_0) > 0 \quad \text{for some} \quad v_0 \in \mathcal{G} \ .$$

Aizenman, Delyon and Souillard, (1980) proved that in this case (5.2) does not decrease exponentially. In fact they showed that

(5.57) $$P_p\{\#W=n\} \geq C_3\{p \wedge (1-p)\}^{C_4\Theta^{-2}n^{\frac{d-1}{d}}}$$

for all $n$, where

(5.58) $$p \wedge (1-p) = \min_{v \in [0,1)^d} \{P\{v \text{ is occupied}\} \wedge P\{v \text{ is vacant}\}\},$$

(5.59) $$\Theta = \sum_{v \in [0,1)^d} \theta(p,v).$$

$C_3$ is a constant depending only on $\Theta$ and $d$, and $C_4$ is a constant depending only on $\mathcal{G}$ and $d$. Aizenman et al. (1980), Remark 2.2, pointed out that (5.57) does not give the right behavior near the critical surface, i.e., when $\Theta$ becomes small. Indeed one expects $\Theta$ to tend to zero as $p$ approaches the critical surface, and for $\Theta \to 0$ the exponent in the right hand side of (5.57) blows up. On the other hand, on the basis of Theorem 8.2 (dealing with one-parameter problems on $\mathcal{G}_0$ and $\mathcal{G}_1$) we expect (5.2) to decrease only polynomially in $n$ when $p$ is on the critical surface. Theorem 5.2 gives a lower bound for (5.2) with an exponent containing $\Theta$ to a positive power. Even though this improvement meets the above objection, we have to pay a price. Our estimate is not valid for all $n$, and we do not have much control over the domain of $n$-values for which the estimate holds. It should also be said that Aizenman et al. prove their estimate (5.57) in much more general models than our independent site-percolation models. To avoid uninteresting combinatorial complications we restrict ourselves in Theorem 5.2 to site-percolation on $\mathbb{Z}^d$. The proof should, however, go through for most periodic percolation problems.

Theorem 5.2. Let $P$ be a probability measure on the occupancy configurations on $\mathbb{Z}^d$ which satisfies

(5.60) $$P\{v \text{ is occupied}\} = P\{v+k_0\xi_i \text{ is occupied}\}$$

for some integer $k_0$ and $1 \leq i \leq d$[1]. Let

(5.61) $$\pi := \min_v \{P\{v \text{ is occupied}\} \wedge P\{v \text{ is vacant}\}\} > 0$$

and

(5.62) $$\Theta := \sum_{v \in [0,k_0)^d} P\{\#W(v) = \infty\} > 0 .$$

Then for $d \geq 3$ there exists a $C_3 = C_3(d)$, depending on $d$ only, and an $N_0$, such that for $n \geq N_0$ and all $w \in \mathbb{Z}^d$ one has

(5.63) $$P\{\#W(w) = n\} \geq \pi^{C_3 k_0^{2d-1} \Theta^{1/d} n^{(d-1)/d}} .$$

The estimate (5.63) remains valid for $d = 2$ if (5.61) holds and (5.62) is strengthened[2] to

(5.64) $$E\{\#W^*(v)\} < \infty \quad \text{for some } v,$$

where $W^*(v)$ is the vacant component of $v$ on $(\mathbb{Z}^2)^* = \mathcal{G}_0^*$ (see Ex. 2.2(i) for $\mathcal{G}_0^*$).

---

1) As usual $\xi_i$ is the i-th coordinate vector. For simplicity of notation we required (5.60) instead of our usual periodicity condition (3.18) which corresponds to $k_0 = 1$. To obtain (3.18) one has to replace $\mathbb{Z}^d$ by $k_0^{-1}$ times $\mathbb{Z}^d$.

2) (5.64) and (5.61) imply (5.62) by Lemma 7.3.

Remark.

(i) By Theorem 3.2 (see also Application 3.4(iv)) (5.64) and hence (5.63), hold as soon as (5.61) and (5.62) hold, provided the probability measure $P$ has enough symmetry properties. In particular (5.63) holds for the two-parameter site-percolation problem on $\mathbb{Z}^2$ of Application 3.4(iv) anywhere in the restriction of the percolative region to the interior of $\mathcal{P}_2$, i.e., whenever the parameters $p(1)$, $p(2)$ satisfy $0 < p(1) < 1$, $p(1) + p(2) > 1$. ///

Kunz and Souillard (1978) also prove for $\max_v P\{v \text{ is vacant}\}$ sufficiently small that there exists a constant $D$ for which

$$P\{\#W(w) = n\} \leq \exp -Dn^{(d-1)/d} .$$

To give a proof of this estimate for general $d$ would require too much topological groundwork. We shall therefore only prove this result for $d = 2$ and $\mathcal{G}$ one of a matching pair.

Theorem 5.3. Let $(\mathcal{G},\mathcal{G}^*)$ be a matching pair of periodic graphs in $\mathbb{R}^2$. Denote by $P_p$ a $\lambda$-parameter periodic probability measure defined by means of a periodic partition $\mathcal{V}_1,\ldots,\mathcal{V}_\lambda$ of the vertices of $\mathcal{G}$ as in (3.17)-(3.23). Assume that $p_0 \in \mathcal{P}_\lambda$ satisfies

(5.65) $$0 \ll p_0 \ll 1 \quad \text{and} \quad E_{p_0}\{\#W^*(z_0)\} < \infty ,$$

where $W^*(z_0)$ is the vacant cluster of $z_0$ on $\mathcal{G}^*$. Then there exist constants $0 < D_i = D_i(p_0,\mathcal{G}) < \infty$ such that

(5.66) $$P_p\{n \leq \#W(z_0) < \infty\} \leq D_1 e^{-D_2 n^{1/2}} \qquad \text{for all}$$

$$p = (p(1),\ldots,p(\lambda)) \in \mathcal{P}_\lambda \quad \text{with} \quad p(i) \geq p_0(i),\ 1 \leq i \leq \lambda .$$

Remarks.

(ii) In particular (5.66) holds for any $(\mathcal{G},\mathcal{G}^*)$ to which Cor. 3.1 applies if we take $p \in \mathcal{P}_\lambda^+$, $0 \ll p \ll 1$. I.e., (5.66) holds in the whole percolative region of $(0,1)^\lambda$ (cf. (3.51)). In some two-dimensional examples (such as the two-parameter site-percolation problem on $\mathbb{Z}^2$ of Application 3.4 (iv)) both (5.66) and (5.63) hold, when percolation occurs. For such examples one obtains in the percolative region

$$0 < \liminf -\frac{1}{\sqrt{n}} \log P_p\{\#W(z_0) = n\}$$

$$\leq \limsup -\frac{1}{\sqrt{n}} \log P_p\{\#W(z_0) = n\} < \infty .$$

(iii) Russo (1978) uses estimates of the form (5.66) in one-parameter problems to show that for various graphs $\mathcal{G}$, which are one of a pair of matching periodic graphs, the functions

$$p \to \theta(p,z_0) \quad \text{and} \quad p \to E_p\{\#W(z_0);\ \#W(z_0) < \infty\}$$

are infinitely often differentiable on $(p_H,(\mathcal{G}),1]$. The same argument works for $p \to E_p\{\pi(\#W(z_0));\ \#W(z_0) < \infty\}$ for any polynomial $\pi$.

(iv) Delyon (1980) shows that for most periodic graphs $\mathcal{G}$ the $a(n,\ell)$ of (5.19) satisfy

$$\text{(5.67)} \qquad \lim_{\substack{n \to \infty \\ \frac{\ell}{n} \to \gamma}} \{a(n,\ell)\}^{\frac{1}{n}} = (1+\gamma)^{1+\gamma}\ \gamma^{-\gamma}$$

whenever

$$\gamma < \frac{1 - p_H(\mathcal{G})}{p_H(\mathcal{G})} .$$

The remarkable part of this result is that the limit in (5.67) is independent of $\mathcal{G}$; only the range of $\gamma$'s for which the limit relation (5.67) holds depends on $\mathcal{G}$. One only needs some aperiodicity assumptions on the relation between #C and #∂C for connected sets C of vertices on $\mathcal{G}$ to obtain (5.67). The proof rests on subadditivity arguments such as in Lemma 5.9 below, an estimate like (5.23) and the fact that $P_p\{\#W(z_0) = n\}$ does not decrease exponentially for $p > p_H(\mathcal{G})$. ///

We turn to the proof of Theorem 5.2. Until further notice we deal with the set up of Theorem 5.2 and all its hypotheses are in force. As in Aizenman et al. (1980) the main estimate will be obtained by connecting a number of vertices inside a large cube by occupied paths, and making several vertices in the boundary of the cube vacant. The latter change disconnects a cluster inside the cube from the outside; this allows us to control (from above) the size of a cluster which we constructed inside the cube. Nevertheless the size of this cluster is not fixed, and this method only yields a lower bound for $P\{\#W = n\}$ along a subsequence of $n$'s. The general $n$ is then handled by Lemma 5.9, which shows how lower bounds for various $n$'s can be combined.

$C_i, K_i$ will denote various constants; the $C_i$ depend on $d$ only, while the $K_i$ depend the probability distribution $P$ as well. It is understood that $0 < C_i, K_i < \infty$. In addition we shall use the following sets and events:

$$S(v,M) = [v(1) - M, v(1) + M] \times \ldots \times [v(d) - M, v(d) + M]$$

(a cube of size 2M centered at $v = (v(1),\ldots,v(d))$),

$\Delta S(v,M) = \mathrm{Fr}(S(v,M))$ = topological boundary of $S(v,M)$.

$B(v,M) = \{\exists$ an occupied path on $\mathbb{Z}^d$ inside $S(v,M)$ which connects $v$ with a point in $\Delta S(v,M)\}$,

$B_k(v,M,j,\pm) = \{$at least $k$ vertices on the face $[v(1)-M, v(1)+M] \times \ldots \times [v(j-1)-M, v(j-1)+M] \times \{v(j) \pm M\} \times \ldots \times [v(d)-M, v(d)+M]$ of $S(v,M)$ are connected by an occupied path on $\mathbb{Z}^d$ inside $S(v,M)$ to $v\}$.

Finally

$$\theta(v) = P\{\#W(v) = \infty\}.$$

<u>Lemma 5.5</u>. <u>There exist constants</u> $M_0$ <u>and</u> $K_i$ <u>such that for each set</u> $A$ <u>of vertices of</u> $\mathbb{Z}^d$

$$P\{B(v,M_0) \text{ occurs for more than } 2\sum_{w\in A}\theta(w) \text{ vertices } v \text{ in } A\} \le K_1 \exp - K_2(\#A). \tag{5.68}$$

<u>In addition, for each</u> $k$ <u>there exists an</u> $M_k$ <u>such that for all</u> $v \in \mathbb{Z}^d$ <u>and</u> $M \ge M_k$

$$P\{B_k(v,M,j,\varepsilon)\} \ge \frac{\theta(v)}{4d} \tag{5.69}$$

for some $j, \varepsilon$, which may depend on $v,k,M$.

<u>Proof:</u> First note that by (4.8) (with $n = \infty$) we have for any two vertices $v_1$ and $v_2$ of $\mathbb{Z}^d$ in $[0,k_0)^d$

$$\theta(v_1) \geq P\{\exists \text{ occupied path from } v_1 \text{ to } v_2\}\,\theta(v_2)$$
$$\geq \pi^{C_4 k_0}\,\theta(v_2).$$

If we write $K_3$ for $\pi^{C_4 k_0}$, then this can be written as

$$\theta(v_1) \geq K_3\theta(v_2), \tag{5.70}$$

By virtue of the periodicity assumption (5.60), $\theta(.)$ is periodic with periods $k_0\xi_i$, $1 \leq i \leq d$, and hence (5.70) holds for any pair of vertices $v_1$, $v_2$. Moreover (5.70) implies for any vertex $w$

$$\theta(w) \geq \frac{K_3}{k_0^d} \sum_{v \in [0,k_0)^d} \theta(v) = \frac{K_3}{k_0^d}\,\Theta > 0 \tag{5.71}$$

(see (5.62)). Next observe that the events $B(v,M)$ decrease to $\{\#W(v) = \infty\}$ as $M \uparrow \infty$. Consequently we can find an $M_0$ such that

$$P\,\{B(v,M_0)\} \leq \frac{3}{2}\,\theta(v)\ , \tag{5.72}$$

and by the periodicity assumption (5.60) we can choose $M_0$ independent of $v$. Now if $A$ is any set of vertices of $\mathbb{Z}^d$ we can write $A$ as a union of at most $(2M_0+1)^d$ disjoint sets $A_i$ such that for each pair of vertices $v$ and $w$ in a single $A_i$ one has $|v(j)-w(j)| > 2M_0$ for some $1 \leq j \leq d$. For any such pair of vertices $v$ and $w$ $S(v,M_0)$ and $S(w,M_0)$ are disjoint. Consequently the events $\{B(v,M_0): v \in A_i\}$ are independent for fixed $i$. It follows from standard exponential bounds for independent bounded variables (see Renyi (1970), Ch. VII.4 or Freedman (1973, Theorem (4)) that for all $\lambda \geq 0$

(5.73) $\quad P\{B(v,M_0)$ occurs for more than $2\sum_{w\in A} \theta(w)$ vertices in $A\}$

$\leq \sum_i P\{B(v,M_0)$ occurs for more than $\frac{3}{2}\sum_{w\in A_i} \theta(w) + \frac{1}{2}(2M_0+1)^{-d} \sum_{w\in A}\theta(w)$ vertices in $A_i\}$

$$\leq \sum_i \exp\Big(-\frac{\lambda}{2(2M_0+1)^d}\sum_{w\varepsilon A}\theta(w) - \frac{3\lambda}{2}\sum_{w\varepsilon A_i}\theta(w)\Big)$$

$$\cdot \prod_{w\varepsilon A_i}\{1 + P\{B(w,M_0)\}\,(e^{\lambda} - 1)\}$$

$$\leq \sum_i \exp\{-\frac{\lambda}{2(2M_0+1)^d}\sum_{w\varepsilon A}\theta(w) + \sum_{w\varepsilon A_i}\theta(w)(\tfrac{3}{2}(e^{\lambda}-1) - \tfrac{3}{2}\lambda)\}$$

(use (5.72)). Now pick $\lambda > 0$ such that

$$\frac{3}{2}(e^{\lambda} - 1) - \frac{3}{2}\lambda < \frac{\lambda}{4(2M_0+1)^d} .$$

For such a $\lambda$ the last member of (5.73) is at most

$$\sum_i \exp - \frac{\lambda}{4(2M_0+1)^d}\sum_{w\varepsilon A}\theta(w) .$$

This, together with (5.71) implies (5.68).

Now for the proof of (5.69). Let $\mathfrak{F}(M) = \mathfrak{F}(v,M)$ be the $\sigma$-field generated by $\{\omega(w):w \varepsilon S(v,M)\}$. By the martingale convergence theorem (see Breiman (1968), Cor. 5.22)

$$P\{\#W(v) = \infty|\mathfrak{F}(v,M)\} \to I[\#W(v) = \infty]\ (M \to \infty)$$

with probability one. As pointed out above

(5.74) $$I[B(v,M] \downarrow I[\#W(v) = \infty]\ (M \to \infty),$$

so that

(5.75) $$P\{\#W(v) = \infty|\mathfrak{F}(M)\} - I[B(v,M)] \to 0 \quad (M \to \infty)$$

with probability one. Now define

$W_M(v)$ = collection of edges and vertices of $\mathbb{Z}^d$ which are connected to $v$ by an occupied path in $S(v,M)$

and

$\Gamma_M = \Gamma_M(v)$ = number of vertices in $\Delta S(v,M)$ which are connected by an occupied path in $S(v,M)$ to $v$.

$\Gamma_M$ is just the number of vertices of $W_M(v)$ in $\Delta S(v,M)$. $\#W(v)$ will be finite if all neighbors outside $B(v,M)$ of the $\Gamma_M(v)$ vertices of $W_M(v) \cap \Delta S(v,M)$ are vacant. Indeed, if this occurs no occupied path starting at $v$ can leave $S(v,M)$. Since any vertex has 2d neighbors it follows that

$$(5.76) \qquad P\{\#W(v) = \infty | \mathfrak{F}(M)\} \leq 1 - \pi^{2d\Gamma_M}$$

(see (5.61) for $\pi$ ). (5.61) and (5.74) - (5.76) imply that for each fixed $k$

$$P\{B(v,M) \text{ occurs, but } \Gamma_M \leq 2dk\} \to 0 \ (M \to \infty),$$

and hence

$$P\{B(v,M) \text{ occurs and } \Gamma_M > 2dk\} \to \theta(v)$$

But, by the definition of $\Gamma_M$ and $B_k(.)$

$$\{B(v,M) \text{ and } \Gamma_M > 2dk\} \subset \bigcup_{\substack{j=1,\dots,d \\ \varepsilon = \pm}} B_k(v,M,j,\varepsilon).$$

Consequently, for each $k$ there exists an $M_k$ such that

$$\sum_{\substack{j=1,\dots,d \\ \varepsilon = \pm}} P\{B_k(v,M,j,\varepsilon) \geq \frac{1}{2}\theta(v)$$

for all $M \geq M_k$ . Again by the periodicity assumption (5.60) we can choose $M$ independent of $v$. (5.69) is now immediate. □

Without loss of generality we shall assume that the origin has been chosen such that

$$(5.77) \qquad \theta(0) = \max_v \theta(v)$$

and consequently (see (5.62))

$$(5.78) \qquad 0 \leq \Theta \leq k_0^{\,d}\,\theta(0) .$$

We next define for $v \in S(0,M)$

$W_M(v,0)$ = collection of edges and vertices of $\mathbb{Z}^d$ which are connected to $v$ by an occupied path in $S(0,M)$, and for $m \geq M_k$ choose a $j=j(k,m)$ and an $\varepsilon = \varepsilon(k,m)$ such that

$$P\{B_k(0,m,j,\varepsilon)\} \geq \frac{\theta(0)}{4d}. \tag{5.79}$$

Note that $W_M(v,0) \subset S(0,M)$. A face of $S(0,M)$ is a set of the form

$$\{x \in S(0,M): x(j) = \varepsilon M\}, \quad \varepsilon = +1 \text{ or } -1$$

Any face of $S(0,M)$ is contained in $\Delta S(0,M)$, and in fact, $\Delta S(0,M)$ is the union of all faces of $S(0,M)$.

Lemma 5.6. Assume the origin is chosen such that (5.77) holds. Then there exists a constant $C_5 > 0$ and for all $k \geq 1$ an $\tilde{M}_k$ such that for $M \geq \tilde{M}_k$

$$\begin{aligned} P\{ &\exists \text{ set of vertices } D \text{ in some face of } S(0,M) \text{ with} \\ &\#D \leq 3^d k^{-1} \theta(0) M^{d-1} \text{ and } C_5\theta(0)(M/k_0)^d \leq \#(\bigcup_{w\in D} W_M(w,0)) \\ &\leq 3^{d+1} \theta(0)M^d \text{ and } \#\{\bigcup_{w\in D} W_M(w,0) \cap \Delta S(0,M)\} \leq 4d\theta(0)(3M)^{d-1}\} \\ &\geq \frac{1}{2} C_5(3k_0)^{-d} \theta(0). \end{aligned} \tag{5.80}$$

Proof: Fix $k$ and let $M \geq 4M_k + 8M_0 + 20k_0$. For $m \geq M_k$ we take $j(k,m)$ and $\varepsilon(k,m)$ such that (5.79) holds. For some $j_0, \varepsilon_0$ there exist at least

$$\frac{1}{2d} \left\lfloor \frac{M}{4k_0} \right\rfloor \geq \frac{M}{10d\, k_0}$$

integers $m$ satisfying

$$M_k+2M_0 \leq m \leq \frac{M}{2}, \quad k_0 \text{ divides } M-m \text{ and } j(k,m) = j_0, \varepsilon(k,m) = \varepsilon_0. \tag{5.81}$$

Without loss of generality we assume that $j_0 = 1$, $\varepsilon_0 = -$. For the corresponding $m$ we then have $j(k,m)$, $\varepsilon(k,m) = (j_0,\varepsilon_0) = (1,-)$ and by (5.79) and the periodicity assumption (5.60)

$$P\{B_k(v,m,1,-)\} \geq \frac{\theta(0)}{4d} \tag{5.82}$$

for each vertex $v = (v(1),\dots,v(d))$ with $v(i)$ divisible by $k_0$ for each $i$. We put

$$F_M = \{-M\} \times [-M,M]\times\dots\times[-M,M]$$

$F_M$ is the "left face" of $S(0,M)$. Now let $v$ be such that

(5.83) $v(1) = -M + m$ for some $m$ which satisfies (5.81) and $|v(i)| \le \frac{M}{2}$, $v(i)$ divisible by $k_0$ for $i=2,\dots,d$.

If $B_k(v,M - |v(1)|, 1,-)$ occurs for such a $v$, then $v$ is connected inside $S(v,M-|v(1)|)$ to at least $k$ vertices in

$$\{v(1) - M + |v(1)|\} \times [v(2) - M + |v(1)|, v(2) + M -|v(1)|] \times\dots\times [v(d) - M + |v(1)|, v(d) + M -|v(1)|] \subset F_M$$

Moreover, $S(v,M - |v(1)|) \subset S(0,M)$. Thus, if we define

$$\Gamma_M(v,0) := \text{number of vertices of } W_M(v,0) \text{ in } F_M = \#(W_M(v,0) \cap F_M),$$

then for a $v$ satisfying (5.83) $B_k(v,M - |v(1)|,1,-)$ implies $\Gamma_M(v,0) \ge k$. In addition for any $v$ satisfying (5.83), $k_0$ divides $v(i)$, $1 \le i \le d$, (use (5.81) for $i=1$) and by (5.82)

$$P\{B_k(v,M-|v(1)|, 1,-) = P\{B_k(v,m,1,-) \ge \frac{\theta(0)}{4d}$$

It follows that for $M \ge 4M_k + 8M_0 + 20k_0$

(5.84) $E$ {number of $v$ in $S(0,M)$ which satisfy (5.83) with $\Gamma_M(v,0) \ge k\} \ge \frac{\theta(0)}{4d}$ {number of $v$ satisfying (5.83)}
$\ge 2C_5 \quad (0)\ (M/k_0)^d$

for some $C_5$. Since the total number of $v$ in $S(0,M)$ is $(2M+1)^d$, the left hand side of (5.84) is at most

$$P\{(\text{number of } v \in S(0,M) \text{ which satisfy (5.83) and with } \Gamma_M(v,0) \ge k) \text{ is at least } C_5\theta(0)(M/k_0)^d\} \ (2M+1)^d + C_5\ \theta(0)(M/k_0)^d .$$

It follows from this and (5.84) that

(5.85) $P\{$there are at least $C_5\theta(0)(M/k_0)^d$ vertices $v$ in $S(0,M)$ which satisfy (5.83) and with $\Gamma_M(v,0) \ge k\}$
$\ge C_5(3k_0)^{-d}\ \theta(0)$ .

Now consider the collection of $w$ in $F_M$ which belong to some $W_M(v,0)$ for a $v$ satisfying (5.83) and $\Gamma_M(v,0) \geq k$. Call two vertices $w_1$ and $w_2$ of this kind equivalent if they belong to the same $W_M(v,0)$ with $v$ satisfying (5.83) and $\Gamma_M(v,0) \geq k$. From each equivalence class pick one representative and denote by $D$ the collection of representatives chosen in this way. Note that $D \subset F_M$ and that by definition each equivalence class contains at least $k$ elements. Consequently

$$\#D \leq k^{-1} \text{ (number of vertices in } F_M \text{ which belong to some } W_M(v,0) \text{ with } v \text{ satisfying (5.83))}.$$

Now if $w \in W_M(v,0)$, then $v \in W_M(w,0)$, and if $w(1) = -M$, $v(1) \geq -M + 2M_0$ then $B(w_0,2M_0)$ must occur. Consequently, by (5.68) and (5.77).

$$\#D \leq k^{-1} \text{ (number of } w \in F_M \text{ for which } B(w,2M_0) \text{ occurs)} \leq 2\frac{\theta(0)}{k}\ \#F_M = 2\frac{\theta(0)}{k}\ (2M+1)^{d-1} \tag{5.86}$$

outside a set of probability at most

$$K_1 \exp - K_2(2M+1)^{d-1} \quad .$$

Also, by our choice of $D$

$$\bigcup_{w \in D} W_M(w,0) = \bigcup W_M(v,0) \ , \tag{5.87}$$

where the union in the right hand side is over all $v$ which satisfy (5.83) and have $\Gamma_M(v,0) \geq k$. If the event in braces in (5.85) occurs then this union contains at least $C_5\theta(0)(M/k_0)^d$ vertices. On the other hand, the union in (5.87) is contained in the set

$$\{u \in S(0,M) : B(u,M_0) \text{ occurs}\} \quad .$$

To see this note that if $u \in W_M(w,0)$ for some $w \in D$, then $W_M(u,0) = W_M(w,0) = W_M(v,0)$ for some $v$ satisfying $|v(1)-w(1)| \geq 2M_0$ (by (5.81)) and hence $|u(1)-v(1)| \geq M_0$ or $|u(1)-w(1)| \geq M_0$. In any case, such a $u$ is connected by an occupied path to $\Delta S(u,M_0)$ and $B(u,M_0)$ occurs. The number of vertices in the union in (5.87) is therefore for large $M$ at most

$$\#\{u \varepsilon S(0,M): B(u,M_0) \text{ occurs}\} \le 2\theta(0)\ \#S(0,M) \le 3^{d+1}\ \theta(0)M^d , \tag{5.88}$$

outside a set of probability at most

$$K_1 \exp - K_2(2M+1)^d .$$

(again by (5.68) and (5.77)). For the same reasons

$$\#\{(\bigcup_{w \varepsilon D} W(w,0)) \cap \Delta S(0,M)\} \le 2\theta(0)\ \#\Delta S(0,M) \le 4d\theta(0)\ (3M)^{d-1} \tag{5.89}$$

outside a set of probability at most

$$K_1 \exp - K_2 2d\ (2M+1)^{d-1} .$$

Thus, if the event in braces in (5.85) occurs, and if the estimates (5.86), (5.88) and (5.89) are valid, then the event in braces in (5.80) also occurs. In view of (5.85) and the above estimates this shows that the left hand side of (5.80) is at least

$$C_5(3k_0)^{-d}\ \theta(0) - 2K_1 \exp - K_2(2M+1)^{d-1} - K_1 \exp - K_2(2M+1)^d ,$$

from which (5.80) follows for large $M$. □

Lemma 5.7. Assume (5.77). For $d \ge 3$ there exist constants $C_6$, $C_7$ and $\tilde{M}$ such that for all $M \ge \tilde{M}$ the interval

$$[C_5 k_0^{-d}\ \theta(0)M^d\ ,\ 3^{d+2}\ \theta(0)M^d] \tag{5.90}$$

contains an integer $m$ with

$$P\{\#W(v) = m\} \ge \pi^{C_6\theta(0)M^{d-1}} \ge \pi^{C_7 k_0^{d-1}(\theta(0))^{1/d}\ m^{(d-1)/d}} \tag{5.91}$$

for some $v \in [0,k_0)^d$.

Proof: We take

$$k = \{\theta(0)\}^{-1/(d-2)}.$$

Fix an $\omega$ for which the event in braces in (5.80) occurs. Note that this event depends only on the occupancies in $S(0,M)$, and is therefore independent of all $\omega(u)$ with $u \notin S(0,M)$. We want to show that the $W_M(w,0)$ with $w \in D$ can be connected by paths on $\mathbb{Z}^d$ which (apart from their endpoints in D) lie outside $S(0,M)$ and which contain at most $C_8\theta(0)M^{d-1}$ vertices. To do this fix D such that it satisfies the requirements in (5.80). For the sake of argument assume again that D lies in the face $F_M = \{-M\} \times [-M,M]\times\ldots\times[-M,M]$. Take $D' = D - 2\xi_1$. D' is the translate by $(-2,0,\ldots,0)$ of D so that $\#D' = \#D$. Also each vertex v in D can be connected to $v - 2\xi_1 \in D'$ via a straight line segment of length two containing only the vertex $v-\xi_1$ outside $D \cup D'$. Moreover

$$D' \subset F'_M := F_M - 2\xi_1$$

and $F'_M$ lies outside $S(0,M)$. The paths connecting the vertices in D will consist of all the line segments from $v \in D$ to $v-2\xi_1 \in D'$ plus a number of paths in $F'_M$ connecting all vertices of D'. Hence, they will indeed contain only vertices outside $S(0,M)$ plus endpoints in D, as desired. To construct paths in $F'_M$ connecting all vertices of D' consider the collection of vertices $w = (w(1),\ldots,w(d)) \in F'_M$ of the following form:

(5.92) $w(1) = -M-2$, $w(r)$ is a multiple of $\rho$ for $2 \le r \le d$, $r \ne s$,

and $-M \le w(i) \le M$, $2 \le i \le d$,

where

$$\rho = \lceil\{\frac{k}{\theta(0)}\}^{1/(d-1)}\rceil \sim \{\theta(0)\}^{-1/(d-2)}$$

and s is anyone of the indices $2,\ldots,d$. There are at most $(d-1) \times \rho^{2-d}(2M+\rho)^{d-1}$ such vertices. When $d \ge 3$ all the vertices satisfying (5.92) are connected by line segments in $F'_M$, containing only vertices of the form (5.92). Also, each vertex $v \in F'_M$ can be connected to one of these vertices by a straight line segment in $F'_M$ containing at most

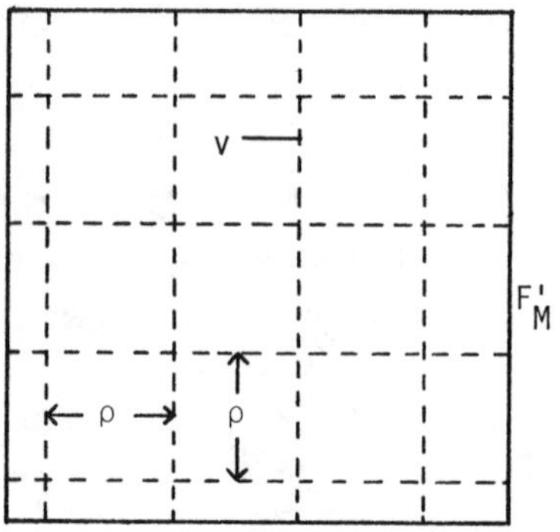


Figure 5.3 The vertices satisfying (5.92) are connected by the dashed lines in $F'_M$. These lines are distance $\rho$ apart. The solid line from $v$ shows how to connect $v$ to this system of lines.

$(d-2)\rho$ vertices for $d \geq 3$. (see Fig. 5.3). Choose such a segment for each vertex $v \in D'$. Let $E$ be the set of all vertices which satisfy (5.92), the vertices on the segments in $F'_M$ which connect vertices of $D'$ to one of the vertices which satisfy (5.92), as well as the vertices in $D-\xi_1$. It follows from the above that any pair of vertices of $D$ can be connected by a path on $\mathbb{Z}^d$ which, apart from its endpoints in $D$, contains only vertices from $E$. By construction $E$ lies outside $S(0,M)$ and for $M \geq \rho$

$$\#E \leq (d-1)\rho^{2-d}(2M+\rho)^{d-1} + ((d-2)\rho+1)\#D \leq C_8\theta(0)M^{d-1} \quad .$$

(the last inequality follows from the upper bound on #D in (5.80)). Moreover, if all vertices in $E$ are occupied, then

$$(5.93) \qquad \bigcup_{w \in D} W_M(w,0) \cup E$$

forms a connected occupied set. When the event in braces in (5.80) occurs and $M$ is sufficiently large, then the number of vertices in the set (5.93) lies in the interval (5.90). Thus $E$ has all the desired properties for connecting the $W_M(w,0)$ with $w \in D$. In addition - because $E$ is disjoint from $S(0,M)$ - the conditional probability that all vertices in $E$ are occupied, given any information about the occupancies in $S(0,M)$, is at least $\pi^{\#E}$. This almost proves our lemma. We merely have to make sure that (5.93) is a maximal occupied component when all of $E$ is occupied, i.e., that it is not part of a bigger occupied component (whose cardinality may lie outside the interval (5.90)). We claim that (5.93) will indeed be a maximal occupied component if all vertices in the following set $G$ are vacant.

$$G := \{\text{all vertices outside } S(0,M) \cup E \text{ which are adjacent to a vertex in } \bigcup_{w \in D} W_M(w,0) \cup E\}.$$

To see this, note that all vertices inside $S(0,M)$ adjacent to the set (5.93), but not belonging to (5.93) itself, are already vacant. This is so because the $W_M(w,0)$ are already maximal occupied components inside $S(0,M)$, so that their neighbors in $S(0,M)$ are vacant. The only vertices of

$$S(0,M) \cap \partial(\bigcup_{w \in D} W_M(w,0) \cup E)$$

which might be occupied would have to lie in $S(0,M) \cap \partial E$. But by our choice of $E$ no such vertices exist, because $S(0,M) \cap \partial E = D$, and this is part of the set (5.93). This proves that if all vertices in $G$ are vacant, then all vertices in

$$\partial(\bigcup_{w \in D} W_M(w,0) \cup E)$$

are vacant. It therefore justifies our claim and thereby shows

$$\begin{aligned} (5.94) \qquad & P\{\exists \text{ a maximal occupied cluster in } [-M-2,M] \times [-M,M]^{d-1} \\ & \qquad \text{with cardinality in the interval (5.90)}\} \\ & \geq P\,\{\text{the event in braces in (5.80) occurs, all vertices in} \\ & \qquad E \text{ are occupied and all vertices in } G \text{ are vacant}\} \\ & \geq E\,\{\pi^{\#E + \#G}; \text{ the event in braces in (5.80) occurs}\}. \end{aligned}$$

It remains to estimate $\#G$. But by definition

$$G \subset \partial E \cup \partial(\bigcup_{w \in D} W_M(w,0) \cap \Delta S(0,M)),$$

so that

$$\#G \leq 2d\,\{\#E + 4d\theta(0)(3M)^{d-1}\}$$

by the bound on $\#\{\bigcup_{w\in D} W_M(w,0) \cap \Delta S(0,M)\}$ in (5.80). Therefore the last member of (5.94) is at least

$$E\,\{\exp(\log\pi)\,\{(2d+1)\#E + 8d^2\theta(0)(3M)^{d-1}\,;$$
$$\text{the event in braces in (5.80) occurs}\}$$
$$\geq \exp\{C_9\theta(0)M^{d-1}\log\pi\}.\ P\{\text{the event in braces in (5.80) occurs}\}$$
$$\geq \exp\{C_9\theta(0)M^{d-1}\log\pi\}\ .\ \tfrac{1}{2}C_5(3k_0)^{-d}\,\theta(0).$$

The lemma follows easily from this lower bound for the first member of (5.94), because any maximal occupied cluster which lies entirely in $[-M-2,M]\times[-M,M]^{d-1}$ equals $W(v)$ for one of the $(2M+3)(2M+1)^{d-1}$ vertices $v$ in this box. In addition the interval (5.90) contains at most $3^{d+2}\theta(0)M^d$ integers, so that

$$\max P\{\#W(v) = m\} \geq (2M+3)^{-d}\,(3^{d+2}\theta(0)M^d)^{-1}$$
$$\tfrac{1}{2}C_5(3k_0)^{-d}\theta(0)\,\exp\{C_9\theta(0)M^{d-1}\log\pi\}\quad .$$

where the max is over all $v$, and over all $m$ in the interval (5.90). We may restrict $v$ to $[0,k_0)^d$ by the periodicity assumption (5.60). This gives the first inequality in (5.91) for large $M$ (since $\pi<1$). The second inequality follows from the fact that $m$ lies in the interval (5.90). □

The proof of the preceding lemma breaks down for $d=2$, because the collection of vertices satisfying (5.92) is no longer connected; it consists merely of the vertices $(-M-2,\ell\rho)$, $|\ell| \leq M/\rho$. Nevertheless the conclusion of Lemma 5.7 remains valid.

Lemma 5.8. Assume (5.77). If $d=2$ and the conditions (5.60), (5.61) and (5.64) hold, then there exists an $\tilde{M}$ such that for each $M \geq \tilde{M}$ the interval

$$\text{(5.95)}\qquad [\,\tfrac{1}{2}C_5\,k_0^{-2}\,\theta(0)M^2,\ 3^4\,\theta(0)M^2\,]$$

contains an integer $m$ for which (5.91) with $d=2$ holds.

Proof: We do not give a detailed proof for $d=2$ here. We shall rely in part on a simple result from Ch. 7. This result shows that for $d=2$ there exists with high probability an occupied path in $S(0,M)$

which connects most occupied clusters in $S(0,M)$. We therefore automatically obtain a large cluster $W_M(v,0)$ in $S(0,M)$, even without the use of any such set as $E$ outside $S(0,M)$, as in the preceding lemma. Specifically we shall prove

$$(5.96) \qquad P\{\ \exists \text{ a vertex } v \text{ in } S(0,M) \text{ for which } \#W_M(v,0) \text{ lies in the interval (5.95) and } \#W_M(v,0) \cap \Delta S(0,M) \le 20\,\theta(0)M\} \ge 2^{-6}\, C_5(3k_0)^{-2}\ \theta(0)\ .$$

This estimate will take the place of the construction of $E$ in Lemma 5.7. For any $\omega$ for which the event in braces in (5.96) occurs choose a $v$ in $S(0,M)$ for which $\#W_M(v,0)$ lies in the interval (5.95) and define $G$ as

$$G := \{\text{all vertices outside } S(0,M) \text{ which are adjacent to } W_M(v,0)\}\ .$$

From here on the proof is practically the same as in Lemma 5.7. When all vertices in $G$ are vacant, then $W_M(v,0)$ is a maximal occupied component, i.e., it equals $W(v)$. Thus

$$P\{\ \exists \text{ a vertex } v \text{ in } S(0,M) \text{ with } \#W(v) \text{ in the interval (5.95)}\} \ge E\{\pi^{\#G}\ ;\ \text{event in braces in (5.96) occurs}\}\ ,$$

and we can estimate this as before. We shall therefore restrict ourselves to proving (5.96) and leave further details to the reader.

The proof of (5.96) relies on Lemma 5.6 which does hold for $d=2$. It is a trivial consequence of (5.80) for $d=2$, that for some face $F_M$ of $S(0,M)$

$$(5.97) \qquad P\{\ \#\bigcup_{w\in F_M} W_M(w,0) \ge C_5\theta(0)(M/k_0)^2\ \} \ge \tfrac{1}{8}C_5(3k_0)^{-2}\ \theta(0)\ .$$

Again without loss of generality we assume that (5.97) holds with $F_M = \{-M\} \times [-M,M]$, the left side of the square $S(0,M)$. Now note that $\mathbb{Z}^2$ is just the graph $\mathcal{G}_0$ of Ex. 2.1. (i). Under the periodicity assumption (5.60), (5.61) and the extra hypothesis (5.64) for $d=2$ we can apply (7.15) as well as Theorem 5.1. (7.15) together with periodicity gives

(5.98) $$P\{\exists \text{ occupied vertical crossing on } \mathcal{G}_0 \text{ of } [-M,-M + C\log M] \times [-M,M]\} \geq \sigma((C\log M-k_0,2M+k_0);\ 2,p,\mathcal{G}_0)$$
$$\geq 1 - P\{\exists \text{ vacant horizontal crossing on } \mathcal{G}_0^* \text{ of } [0,C\log M-k_0-\Lambda] \times [0,2M+k_0+\Lambda]\}$$

for some constant $\Lambda$ (which depends on $\mathcal{G}_0 = \mathbb{Z}^2$ only). Moreover, as at the end of the proof of Lemma 5.4, a horizontal crossing on $\mathcal{G}_0^*$ of $[0,C\log M-k_0-\Lambda] \times [0,2M+k_0+\Lambda]$ has to contain one of the vertices $v = (0,\ell)$, $0 \leq \ell \leq 2M+k_0+\Lambda$. If such a $v$ is part of a vacant horizonta crossing of $[0, C\log M-k_0-\Lambda] \times [0,2M+k_0+\Lambda]$, then its vacant component an $\mathcal{G}_0^*$, $W^*(v)$, must contain at least $C\log M-k_0-\Lambda$ vertices. Thus, the right hand side of (5.98) equals at least

$$1 - \sum_{\ell=0}^{2M+k_0+\Lambda} P\{\#W^*((0,\ell)) \geq C\log M-k_0-\Lambda\}.$$

Now Theorem 5.1 applied to $\mathcal{G}_0^*$ shows that (by virtue of (5.61) and (5.64)).

$$P\{\#W^*(0,\ell) \geq C\log M-k_0-\Lambda\} \leq K_4 M^{-K_5C}$$

uniformly in $\ell$, for some constants $K_4,K_5$ which depend only on the probability measure $P$. Thus for $C > K_5^{-1}$ the right hand side of (5.98) is greater than $\frac{1}{2}$ eventually. From the FKG inequality, Proposition 4.1, and (5.97) we now obtain

(5.99) $$P\{\#\bigcup_{w\varepsilon F_M} W_M(w,0) \geq C_5\,\theta(0)(M/k_0)^2 \text{ and there exists an occupied vertical crossing of } [-M,-M + C\log M] \times [-M,M]\}$$
$$\geq \frac{1}{2} P\{\bigcup_{w\varepsilon F_M} W_M(w,0) \geq C_5\theta(0)(M/k_0)^2\}$$
$$\geq \frac{1}{16} C_5\,(3k_0)^{-2}\ \theta(0).$$

Now assume that there exists an occupied vertical crossing $r$ of $[-M,-M+C\log M] \times [-M,M]$. Then any occupied cluster $W_M(v,0)$ in $S(0,M)$

which is connected inside $S(0,M)$ to $w$ in $F_M = \{-M\} \times [-M,M]$, and which contains a vertex in $[-M + C \log M, M] \times [-M,M]$ must intersect $r$. Hence $r$ will be part of any such $W_M(v,0)$. In particular all $W_M(v,0)$ with the above property are connected via $r$ and form a single cluster. On the other hand, any cluster $W_M(v,0)$ which contains a $w$ in $F_M$ but does not intersect $r$ must be contained in $[-M,-M + C \log M) \times [-M,M]$. Hence, all such clusters contain together at most $(C \log M + 1)(2M + 1)$ vertices. Thus, if the event in braces in the first member of (5.99) occurs, then $S(0,M)$ contains a single $W_M(v,0)$ of at least

$$\#\Big( \bigcup_{w \varepsilon F_M} W_M(w,0) - (C \log M + 1)(2M + 1)$$

$$\geq C_5\, \theta(0)(M/k_0)^2 - (C \log M + 1)(2M + 1)$$

vertices. For sufficiently large $M$ this number exceeds $\frac{1}{2} C_5 k_0^{-2}\, \theta(0) M^2$ so that

(5.100) $$P\{ \exists\ v \varepsilon S(0,M) \text{ with } \#W_M(v,0) \geq \tfrac{1}{2} C_5 k_0^{-1}\, \theta(0) M^2 \}$$
$$\geq \frac{1}{16} C_5 (3k_0)^{-2}\ \theta(0)$$

for large $M$. This gives us a $W_M(v,0)$ (with a certain probability) whose cardinality equals at least the lower bound of (5.95). To make sure that $\#W_M(v,0)$ actually falls in the interval (5.95) we once more appeal to (5.68). For each $w$ in $W_M(v,0)$ with $|w(i)-v(i)| > M_0$ for $i = 1$ or $2$, $B(w,M_0)$ occurs. Indeed any such $w$ is connected to $v \notin S(w,M_0)$. Therefore, if $\#W_M(v,0) > 3^4 \theta(0) M^2$, then $B(w,M_0)$ occurs for more than $3^4\, \theta(0) M^2 - (2M_0+1)^2 \geq 2\theta(0)(2M+1)^2 = 2\theta(0)\ \#S(0,M)$ vertices in $S(0,M)$. Thus, by (5.68), for large enough $M$

$$P\{\#W_M(v,0) > 3^4 \theta(0) M^2 \text{ for some } v \varepsilon S(0,M)\}$$
$$\leq K_1 \exp - K_2 (2M+1)^2 \leq 2^{-6} C_5 (3k_0)^{-2}\ \theta(0)\ .$$

By the same argument one has for large $M$

$$P\{\#(W_M(v,0) \cap \Delta S(0,M)) > 20\theta(0)M \quad \text{for some} \quad v \in S(0,M)\}$$
$$\leq P\{B(w,M_0) \text{ occurs for more than } 20\theta(0)M - (2M_0+1)^2$$
$$\geq 2\theta(0)\ \#\Delta S(0,M) \text{ vertices in } \Delta S(0,M)\}$$
$$\leq K_1 \exp - 8K_2 M \leq 2^{-6}\ C_5(3k_0)^{-2}\ \theta(0)\ .$$

These estimates together with (5.100) prove (5.96). □

From here on the proof closely follows Aizenman et al. (1980).

Lemma 5.9. For any vertices $v_1, v_2$ and integers $n_1, n_2 \geq 1$ one has on $\mathbb{Z}^d$

$$\text{(5.101)} \qquad P\{\#W(v_1) = n_1 + n_2\} \geq \pi^{2dn_2} P\{\#W(v_1) = n_1\}$$

and, for some constant $C_{10} = C_{10}(d)$

$$\text{(5.102)} \qquad P\{W(v_1) = n_1 + n_2 + (d+1)k_0\}$$
$$\geq \frac{1}{n_2(d+1)k_0}\ \pi^{C_{10}k_0}\ P\{W(v_1) = n_1\}\ P\{W(v_2) = n_2\}\ .$$

Proof: Let $G_1$ be a connected set of vertices of $\mathbb{Z}^d$ containing $v_1$ with $\#G_1 = n_1$. Let $w_1 = (w_1(1), w_1(2),\dots,w_1(d))$ be a vertex in $G$, with maximal first coordinate, i.e., $w_1(1) \geq w(1)$ for all $w \in G_1$. ($w_1$ is a "right most" point in $G_1$). Then form a connected set $G$ of vertices by adding to $G_1$ the $n_2$ vertices

$w_1 + j\xi_1 = (w_1(1) + j,\ w_1(2),\dots,w_1(d))$ for $j=1,\dots,n_2$. Then $\#G = n_1 + n_2$. As in (5.24)

$$P\{W(v_1) = G_1\} = \prod_{w\in G_1} P\{w \text{ is occupied}\}$$
$$\cdot \prod_{w\in \partial G_1} P\,\{u \text{ is vacant}\}$$

and similarly for $G$. Since $G$ consists of $G_1$ plus $n_2$ vertices, and $\partial G$ consists of $\partial G_1 \setminus \{w_1 + \xi_1\}$ plus at most $(2d-1)n_2$ points it follows that

$$\text{(5.103)} \qquad P\{W(v_1) = G\} \geq \pi^{2dn_2}\ P\{W(v_1) = G_1\}\ .$$

Finally,

(5.104) $$P\{\#W(v_1) = n_1\} = \sum_{\#G_1 = n_1} P\{W(v_1) = G_1\}$$

where the sum runs over all connected $G_1$ with $\#G_1 = n_1$ and containing $v_1$. Since distinct $G_1$'s lead to distinct $G$'s in the above construction we find

$$P\{\#W(v_1) = n_1 + n_2\} \geq \sum_{\#G_1 = n_1} P\{W(v_1) = G\}$$

$$\geq \pi^{2dn_2} \sum_{\#G_1 = n_1} P\{W(v_1) = G_1\} \quad .$$

This proves (5.101).

To prove (5.102) we also bring in a connected set of vertices $G_2$ which contains $v_2$ and with $\#G_2 = n_2$. We take $w_2 = (w_2(1),\ldots, w_2(d))$ as a "left most" point of $G_2$, i.e., one with $w_2(1) \leq w(1)$ for all $w \in G_2$ . We shall now form a connected set $G$ with $\#G = n_1 + n_2 + (d+1)k_0$ by connecting $G_1$ and a translate $G_2'$ of $G_2$ . Let $m_i$ be the unique integer for which

$$(m_i-1)k_0 \leq w_1(i)-w_2(i) < m_ik_0, \; 1 \leq i \leq d.$$

For $G_2'$ we take $G_2 + \sum_1^d m_ik_0\xi_i + k_0\xi_1$. Let $w_2' = w_2 + \sum_1^d m_ik_0\xi_i + k_0\xi_1$. Then

$$w_1(1) + k_0 < w_2'(1) \leq w_1(1) + 2k_0 \; ,$$

$$w_1(i) < w_2'(i) \leq w_1(i) + k_0, \; 2 \leq i \leq d,$$

and we can therefore connect $w_1$ to $w_2'$ by a path $r$ of at most $k_0(d+1)$ vertices, all of which lie in the strip $\{w_1(1) < x(1) < w_2'(1)\}$. By the periodicity assumption (5.60)

$P\{W(w_2) = G_2\}$ = P{all vertices in $G_2$ are occupied and all vertices in $\partial G_2$ are vacant} = P{all vertices in $G_2'$ are occupied and all vertices in $\partial G_2'$ are vacant}

Very much as in (5.103) one obtains from this

$$(5.105) \qquad P\{W(v_1) = G_1 \cup r \cup G_2'\} \geq \pi^{2d(d+1)k_0} P\{W(v_1) = G_1\} \; P\{W(v_2) = G_2\} .$$

We now sum this over all connected sets $G_1$, $G_2$ with $\#G_i = n_i$ and containing $v_i$, $i = 1,2$. By (5.104) the sum of the right hand side will be

$$(5.106) \qquad \pi^{2d(d+1)k_0} P\{\#W(v_1) = n_1\} \; P\{\#W(v_2) = n_2\} .$$

As $G_1$, $G_2$ run over these sets, $G_1 \cup r \cup G_2'$ will run over certain connected sets of vertices $G$, containing $v_1$ and with $n_1 + n_2 < \#G \leq n_1 + n_2 + (d+1)k_0$. It is nevertheless not true that the sum of the left hand side is at most $P\{n_1 + n_2 < \#W(v_1) \leq n_1 + n_2 + (d+1)k_0$, because any given $G$ may arise from many pairs $G_1, G_2$. It is, however, not hard to derive an upper bound for the number of pairs which can give rise to the same $G$. In fact $G_1$ is uniquely recoverable from $G$. One merely has to find the smallest integer $m$ such that $G$ has exactly $n_1$ vertices in the half space $\{x : x(1) \leq m\}$. $G_1$ is then the piece of $G$ in this half space. This is so because $r$ and $G_2'$ lie in $\{x : x(1) > w_1(1)\}$ in our construction. In the same way one can recover $G_2'$ as the piece of $G$ in $\{x : x(1) \geq m'\}$ where $m'$ is the maximal integer for which the above halfspace contains $n_2$ vertices of $G$. Finally $r = G \setminus G_1 \cup G_2'$. When $G_2'$ is known there are at most $n_2$ possible choices for $G_2$, since $G_2$ is obtained from $G_2'$ by a translation which takes one of the $n_2$ vertices of $G_2'$ to $v_2$. From this it follows that the sum of the left hand side of (5.105) over $G_1$ and $G_2$ is at most

$$n_2 P\{n_1 + n_2 < \#W(v_1) \leq n_1 + n_2 + (d+1)k_0\} .$$

Together with (5.106) this proves that there exists an $m$ in $(n_1 + n_2, n_1 + n_2 + (d+1)k_0]$ with

$$P\{\#W(v_1) = m\} \geq \frac{1}{n_2(d+1)k_0} \pi^{2d(d+1)k_0} P\{\#W(v_1) = n_1\} \; P\{\#W(v_2) = n_2\} .$$

An application of (5.101) with $n_1$ replaced by $m$ and $n_2$ by

$n_1 + n_2 + (d+1)k_0 - m$ now yields (5.102). □

<u>Proof of Theorem 5.2.</u> Given an integer $n_1 \geq (d+1)k_0 + 3^{d+2}\,\theta(0)\tilde{M}^d$ we find the largest integer $M$ with

$$3^{d+2}\,\theta(0)M^d + (d+1)k_0 \leq n_1 ,$$

and then find an $m_1$ in the interval

$$[\tfrac{1}{2} C_5 k_0^{-d}\;\theta(0)M^d,\; 3^{d+2}\;\theta(0)M^d] \tag{5.107}$$

for which (5.91) holds. Such an $m_1$ exists by virtue of Lemma 5.7 and 5.8 since $M \geq \tilde{M}$. Next we find the maximal integer $s_1$ for which $s_1(m_1 + (d+1)k_0) \leq n_1$. Since

$$3^{d+2}\;\theta(0)(M+1)^d + (d+1)k_0 > n_1 ,$$

and $m_1$ lies in the interval (5.107), it follows that for $n_1$ greater than some $n_0 = n_0(\theta(0), d, \tilde{M})$

$$m_1 \geq \frac{1}{4} C_5 k_0^{-d}\, 3^{-d-2}\, n_1 . \tag{5.108}$$

Consequently for $n_1 \geq n_0$ and $C_{11} = 4C_5^{-1}\, 3^{d+2}$

$$1 \leq s_1 \leq C_{11}\, k_0^{-d} \tag{5.109}$$

and

$$n_2 := n_1 - s_1(m_1 + (d+1)k_0) \leq \frac{1}{2} n_1 . \tag{5.110}$$

By repeating the above procedure for $n_2$ instead of $n_1$ and so on we can represent $n_1$ as

$$n_1 = \sum s_i(m_i + (d+1)k_0) + t$$

with integers $m_i$ satisfying (5.91) and (5.108), $s_i$ satisfying (5.109), and $t < n_0$. Repeated application of Lemma 5.9 and (5.91) now shows that for some $v \in [0,k_0)^d$

$$P\{\#W(v) = n_1\} \geq \pi^{2dn_0 + C_{10}k_0 \sum s_i}\; \Pi(m_i(d+1)k_0)^{-s_i}\; P\{\#W(v_i) = m_i\}^{s_i}$$

$$\geq \exp\{2dn_0 \log \pi + (C_{10}k_0 \log \pi - \log k_0(d+1)) \sum s_i$$
$$- \sum s_i \log m_i + C_7(\log \pi)k_0^{d-1}(\theta(0))^{1/d} \sum s_i m_i^{(d-1)/d}\} .$$

It is clear that we can fix $n_0$ so large that the inequalities $m_i \geq C_{11}^{-1} k_0^{-d} n_i \geq C_{11}^{-1} k_0^{-d} n_0$ and $s_i \leq C_{11} k_0^d$ (cf. (5.108) and (5.109)) imply that the exponent in the right hand side is at least

$$2C_7(\log \pi)k_0^{d-1} (\theta(0))^{1/d} \sum s_i m_i^{(d-1)/d} + 2dn_0 \log \pi$$

$$\geq 2C_7 C_{11} k_0^{2d-1} \log \pi \, (\theta(0))^{1/d} \sum m_i^{(d-1)/d} + 2dn_0 \log \pi .$$

It is also easy to show from $m_i \leq n_i$ and $n_{i+1} \leq \frac{1}{2} n_i$ (cf. (5.110)) that

$$\sum_{i \geq 1} m_i^{(d-1)/d} \leq \sum_{i \geq 1} n_i^{(d-1)/d} \leq C_{12} n_1^{(d-1)/d} .$$

Since $\Theta \geq \theta(0)$, it follows that (5.63) holds for $n \geq N_0$ with a suitable choice of $N_0$, $C_3 = 3C_7 C_{11} C_{12}$ and $w$ equal to some $w_n \in [0,k_0)^d$. To obtain (5.63) for all $w$ we use Lemma 5.9 once more. By (5.102) with $v_1 = w$, $v_2 = w_{n-1-(d+1)k_0}$

$$P\{\#W(w) = n\} \geq \frac{1}{n(d+1)k_0} \pi^{C_{10}k_0}$$

$$P\{W(w) = 1\} \quad P\{W(w_{n-1-(d+1)k_0}) = n-1 - (d+1)k_0\} .$$

Since

$$P\{W(w) = 1\} = P\{w \text{ is occupied and all its neighbors are vacant}\} \geq \pi^{2d+1} ,$$

and (5.63) holds for $n$ replaced by $n-1 - (d+1)k_0$ and $w = w_{n-1-(d+1)k_0}$, we obtain (5.63), in general, at the expense of increasing $C_3$ and $N_0$ slightly. □

Proof of Theorem 5.3: By Cor. 2.2, if $0 < \#W(v_0) < \infty$, then there exists a vacant circuit $J$ on $\mathcal{G}^*$ surrounding $W(v_0)$. If $\#W(v_0) \geq n$, then $W(v_0)$ contains some vertex $v_1$ with

$$|v_1(i) - v_0(i)| \geq \frac{1}{2} (\sqrt{n/\mu} - 1) \quad \text{for } i = 1 \text{ or } 2,$$

where $\mu$ is as in (5.7). Therefore, the diameter of $J$ - which has

$v_0$ and $v_1$ in its interior - is at least $\frac{1}{2}(\sqrt{n/\mu}-1)$. Let the diameter of J be $L \geq (\sqrt{n/\mu}-1)$. Since J surrounds $v_0$ it intersects the horizontal half line $[0,\infty) \times \{v_0(2)\}$, and if $\Lambda$ is some constant which exceeds the diameter of each edge of $\mathcal{G}^*$, then J contains a vertex $v^*$ of $\mathcal{G}^*$ in the strip

$$S = [-\Lambda,\infty) \times [v_0(2)-\Lambda,\ v_0(2) + \Lambda].$$

Moreover, $|v^*(1)-v_0(1)| \leq L$, since $v_0$ lies in the interior of J. Also, J must contain at least

$$\frac{L}{\Lambda} \geq \frac{1}{\Lambda} \max\{|v^*(1)-v_0(1)|,\ \frac{1}{2}(\sqrt{n/\mu}-1)\}$$

vertices of $\mathcal{G}^*$ and all of those belong to the vacant cluster of $v^*$ on $\mathcal{G}^*$, $W^*(v^*)$. Thus,

$$(5.111)\qquad P_p\{n \leq \#W(v_0) < \infty\}$$
$$\leq \sum_{v^*\varepsilon S} P_p\{\#W^*(v^*) \geq \frac{1}{\Lambda} \max\{|v^*(1)-v_0(1)|,\ \frac{1}{2}(\sqrt{n/\mu}-1)\}\}\ .$$

By virtue of Lemma 4.1 the right hand side of (5.111) can only be increased if we replace p by $p_0$ with $p(i) \geq p_0(i)$, $1 \leq i \leq d$. Moreover, by Theorem 5.1 (applied to $\mathcal{G}^*$) (5.65) implies that

$$(5.112)\qquad P_{p_0}\{\#W^*(v^*) \geq m\} \leq C_1 e^{-C_2 m}\ ,\ m \geq 0,$$

and by the periodicity this estimate is uniform in $v^*$. (5.66) is immediate from (5.111), (5.112), and (5.7). □

## 5.3. Large crosssing probabilities imply that percolation occurs.

Even though this section does not deal with the distribution of #W we include it here, since the proof of next theorem, due to Russo (1981), is in a sense dual to that of Theorem 5.1. The argument works for any graph $\mathcal{G}$ imbedded in $\mathbb{R}^2$ which satisfies the following condition.

Condition C. If e' and e" are edges of $\mathcal{G}$ with endpoints v',w' and v",w", respectively, and e' intersects e" in a point which is not an endpoint of both e' and e", then there exists an edge of $\mathcal{G}$ from v' or w' to v" or w". ///

Condition C holds for instance if $\mathcal{G}$ is one of a matching pair $(\mathcal{G},\mathcal{G}^*)$ based on some $(\mathcal{M},\mathcal{F})$. In such a graph two edges $e'$, $e''$ can intersect in a point which is not an endpoint of both, only if $e'$ and $e''$ both belong to the closure of the same face $F \in \mathcal{F}$ (cf. Comment 2.2. (vii)). This $F$ is close-packed in $\mathcal{G}$ and the endpoints $v'$, $w'$, $v''$, $w''$ of $e'$ and $e''$ must lie on the perimeter of $F$, and there exist an edge of $\mathcal{G}$ between any pair of these vertices. This argument also shows that even the graphs discussed in the Remark in Sect. 2.3 satisfy Condition C.

The reader should note that in the next theorem (5.113) and (5.114) are conditions on the crossing probabilities in the "long direction" of the blocks, while (5.10) is for crossing probabilities in the "short direction".

Theorem 5.4. (Russo 1981) Let $\mathcal{G}$ be a periodic graph imbedded in $\mathbb{R}^2$ which satisfies (2.2)-(2.5) and Condition C. Let $P_p$ be a $\lambda$-parameter periodic probability measure and let $\Lambda$ satisfy (5.8). If for some integers $N_1, N_2 > 2\Lambda$

(5.113) $\quad \sigma((3N_1,N_2);\ 1,p,\mathcal{G}) > 1-7^{-81}$

as well as

(5.114) $\quad \sigma((N_1,3N_2);\ 2,p,\mathcal{G}) > 1-7^{-81}$

then

(5.115) $\quad \theta(p,v) > 0$ for some $v \in \mathcal{G}$.

Remark.

Russo (1981), Prop. 1 uses Theorem 5.4 to show that for periodic site-percolation problems on graphs $\mathcal{G}$ in $\mathbb{R}^2$ which satisfy conditions somewhat stronger than those of Theorem 3.2 no percolation can occur on the critical surface. In other words $\theta(p_0,v) = 0$ for the $p_0$ defined in Theorem 3.2. In particular $\theta(p_H,v) = 0$ in one-parameter problems of this kind. This is of course also a consequence of Theorem 3.2 (see (3.43)). Actually using Theorem 6.1 and a refinement of Russo's argument one can prove this result under more general conditions. Specifically the following left-continuity property holds: Let $(\mathcal{G},\mathcal{G}^*)$ be a matching pair of periodic graphs imbedded in $\mathbb{R}^2$ and $\mathcal{V}_1,\dots,\mathcal{V}_\lambda$ a periodic partition of the vertices of $\mathcal{G}$ such that one of the coordinate axes is an axis of symmetry for $\mathcal{G},\mathcal{G}^*$ and the partition $\mathcal{V}_1,\dots,\mathcal{V}_\lambda$. Let $P_p$ be as in (3.20)-(3.23). If $p_0 \in \mathcal{P}_\lambda$ is such that $p_0 \gg 0$ and $\theta(p,v) = 0$ for all

$p << p_0$, $p \in \mathcal{P}_\lambda$, <u>then</u> $\theta(p_0,v) = 0$ .

There also is a continuity result if $\theta(p_0,v) > 0$, which can be derived from Theorem 12.1. <u>Under the above conditions</u> $p \to \theta(p,v)$ <u>is continuous at all points</u> $p >> 0$ <u>for which</u> $\theta(p,v) > 0$.

We do not proof either of these results.

Finally, it is worth pointing out that Russo (1978) proved that $\theta(.,v)$ is always right continuous for any graph in any dimension. I.e., if $p(i) \downarrow p_0(i)$, $1 \le i \le d$, then $\theta(p,v) \downarrow \theta(p_0,v)$. This is so because $\theta(.,v)$ is the decreasing limit of the sequence of continuous increasing fuctions $p \to P_p\{v$ is connected by an occupied path to some point outside $S(v,M)\}$. (See the lines before Lemma 5.5 for $S(v,M)$.)

<u>Proof of Theorem 5.4.</u> As in Theorem 5.1 we use an auxiliarly graph and set up a correspondence between vertices of this graph and blocks of $\mathcal{G}$ . This time the auxiliarly graph is the simple quadratic lattice $\mathcal{G}_0$ of Ex. 2.1(i). For each occupancy configurations $\omega$ on $\mathcal{G}$ we construct an occupancy configuration on $\mathcal{G}_0$ as follows. If $(i_1,i_2)$ is a vertex of $\mathcal{G}_0$ with $i_1 + i_2$ even, then we take $(i_1,i_2)$ occupied iff there exists an occupied horizontal crossing on $\mathcal{G}$ of

$$[i_1N_1,(i_1+3)N_1] \times [i_2\, N_2,(i_2+1)N_2] \ . \tag{5.116}$$

If $(j_1,j_2)$ is a vertex of $\mathcal{G}_0$ with $j_1 + j_2$ odd we take $(j_1,j_2)$ occupied iff there exists an occupied vertical crossing on $\mathcal{G}$ of

$$[(j_1+1)N_1,\ (j_1+2)N_1] \times [(j_1-1)N_2,\ (j_2+2)N_2] \ . \tag{5.117}$$

We claim that if $(i_1,i_2)$ with $i_1 + i_2$ even and $(j_1,j_2)$ with $j_1 + j_2$ odd are two adjacent vertices of $\mathcal{G}_0$ which are both occupied, then there exists an occupied horizontal crossing $r = (v_0,e_1,\dots,e_\nu,v_\nu)$ of (5.116) and an occupied vertical crossing $s = (w_0,f_1,\dots,f_\rho,w_\rho)$ of (5.117), and any such pairs of crossings must intersect. We check this for the case $j_1 = i_1+1$, $j_2 = i_2$; the other cases are similar. Since $(i_1,i_2)$ is occupied, there exists an occupied horizontal crossing $r$ of (5.116) on $\mathcal{G}$. By Def. 3.1, if $r = (v_0,e_1,\dots,e_\nu,v_\nu)$, then the curve made up from $e_1,\dots,e_\nu$ contains a continuous path in $[i,N_1,(i_1+3)N_1] \times [i_2\, N_2,(i_2+1)N_2]$ which connects the left and right edges of this rectangle. Similarly, there exists an occupied vertical crossing $s = (w_0,f_1,\dots,f_\rho,w_\rho)$ of (5.117), and $s$ contains a continuous curve in $[(j_1+1)N_1,\ (j_1+2)N_1] \times [(j_2-1)N_2,\ (j_2+2)N_2]$ which connects the top and bottom edges of this rectangle. Since

$j_1 = i_1+1$, $j_2 = i_2$, the latter rectangle equals

$$(5.118) \qquad [(i_1+2)N_1, (i_1+3)N_1] \times [(i_2-1)N_2, (i_2+2)N_2] .$$

It is now evident from the relative location of the rectangles (5.116) and (5.118) that $r$ and $s$ intersect.

This proves the claim. By condition C it follows that either $r$ and $s$ intersect in a vertex of $\mathcal{G}$, common to both, or there exists vertices $v$ of $r$ and $w$ of $s$ which are adjacent to each other on $\mathcal{G}$. In either case all the vertices of $r$ and $s$ (which are all occupied) belong to the same occupied component on $\mathcal{G}$. Thus, if $(i_1,i_2)$ and $(j_1,j_2)$ are occupied neighbors on $\mathcal{G}_0$, then necessarily one of them has an even sum of its coordinates, and one an odd sum, and the corresponding blocks on $\mathcal{G}$ contain crossings which belong to the same occupied component on $\mathcal{G}$. Therefore, if $\mathcal{G}_0$ contains an infinite occupied cluster, then so does $\mathcal{G}$. To complete the proof it therefore suffices to show

$$(5.119) \qquad P_p\{\mathcal{G}_0 \text{ contains an occupied cluster}\} > 0,$$

since this will imply (5.115). (5.119) is proved by the standard Peierls argument. Let $W_0$ be the occupied cluster of $(0,0)$ on $\mathcal{G}_0$. By Cor. 2.2., $0 < \#W_0 < \infty$ happens only if there exists a vacant circuit $J$ surrounding $(0,0)$ on $\mathcal{G}_0^*$. $\mathcal{G}_0^*$ is described in Ex. 2.2(i). Every vertex has eight neighbors on $\mathcal{G}_0^*$. The number of self-avoiding paths starting at the origin and containing $n$ vertices is therefore at most $8.7^{n-2}$. The number of circuits of $n$ vertices containing the origin in its interior is therefore at most $8n.7^{n-2}$ (since any such circuit must contain one of the points $(i,0)$, $1 \le i \le n$, as in the argument preceding (5.111)). On the other hand, the probability that any vertex of $\mathcal{G}_0^*$ is vacant is strictly less than $7^{-81}$, by virtue of (5.113) and (5.114). Not all vertices of $\mathcal{G}_0^*$ are independent, but if $\overline{\ell}_1,\dots,\overline{\ell}_t$ are vertices of $\mathcal{G}_0^*$ (and hence of $\mathcal{G}_0$) such that for each $1 \le r, s \le t$, $r \neq s$, there is an $i = 1,2$, with $|\ell_r(i)-\ell_s(i)| \ge 5$ ($\overline{\ell}_r = (\ell_r(1), \ell_r(2))$ then the occupancies of $\overline{\ell}_1,\dots,\overline{\ell}_t$ are independent, because they depend on disjoint sets of vertices of $\mathcal{G}$. Any circuit on $\mathcal{G}_0^*$ of $n$ vertices contains at least $n/81$ such independent vertices, and hence the probability that a given circuit on $\mathcal{G}_0^*$ of $n$ vertices is vacant is at most

$$(7^{-81} - \eta)^{n/81}$$

for some $\eta > 0$. It follows that for a suitably large $N$

(5.120) $P_p$ {there does not exist a vacant circuit on $\mathcal{G}_0^*$ surrounding $(0,0)$ and containing at least $N$ vertices}

$$\geq 1 - \sum_{n \geq N} 8n\, 7^{n-2} (7^{-81} - \eta)^{n/81} \geq \frac{1}{2}.$$

Now the event that there does not exist a vacant circuit of a certain type on $\mathcal{G}_0^*$ is an increasing event for the percolation on $\mathcal{G}$. Thus, by the FKG inequality

(5.121) $P_p${the origin of $\mathcal{G}_0$ is occupied and there does not exist any vacant circuit on $\mathcal{G}_0^*$ surrounding $(0,0)$

$\geq P_p${the origin of $\mathcal{G}_0$ is occupied and there does not exist any vacant circuit on $\mathcal{G}_0^*$ surrounding $(0,0)$ and containing less than $N$ vertices} × {the left hand side of (5.120)}

$$\geq \prod_{\substack{|i_1| \leq N \\ |i_2| \leq N}} P_p\{\text{the vertex } (i_1,i_2) \text{ of } \mathcal{G}_0^* \text{ is occupied}\} \cdot \frac{1}{2} > 0.$$

As we saw above, the event in braces in the first member of (5.121) implies $\#W_0 = \infty$, so that we proved

$$P_p\{\#W_0 = \infty\} > 0$$

which in turn implies (5.119). □

# 6. THE RUSSO-SEYMOUR-WELSH THEOREM.

The object of this chapter is a result which states that if the crossing probabilities of certain rectangles in both the horizontal and vertical direction are bounded away from zero, then so are the crossing probabilities for larger rectangles. This result will then be used to prove the existence of occupied circuits surrounding the origin. The idea is to connect an occupied horizontal crossing of $[0,n_1] \times [0,n_2]$ and an occupied horizontal crossing of $[m,n_1 + m] \times [0,n_2]$ by means of a suitable occupied vertical crossing, in order to obtain a horizontal crossing of $[0,n_1 + m] \times [0,n_2]$. This would be quite simple (compare the proof of Lemma 6.2) if one had a lower bound for the probability of an occupied vertical crossing of $[m,n_1] \times [0,n_2]$, but in the applications one only has estimates for the existence of occupied vertical crossings of rectangles which are wider and/or lower. One therefore has to use some trickery, based on symmetry to obtain the desired connections. Such tricks were developed independently by Russo (1978) and Seymour and Welsh (1978). (See also Smythe and Wierman (1978), Ch. 3 and Russo (1981).) These papers dealt with the one-parameter problems on the graphs $\mathcal{G}_0$ or $\mathcal{G}_1$ (see Ex. 2.1(i) and (ii)) and therefore had at their disposal symmetry with respect to both coordinate axes, as well as invariance of the problem under interchange of the horizontal and vertical direction. We believe that neither of these properties is necessary, but so far we still need at least one axis of symmetry. We also have to restrict ourselves to a planar modification $\mathcal{G}_{p\ell}$ of a graph $\mathcal{G}$ which is one of a matching pair of graphs in $\mathbb{R}^2$.

Throughout this chapter we deal with the following setup:

(6.1) $(\mathcal{G},\mathcal{G}^*)$ is a matching pair based on $(\mathcal{M},\mathcal{F})$ for some mosaic $\mathcal{M}$ satisfying (2.1)-(2.5) and subset $\mathcal{F}$ of its collection of faces (see Sect. 2.2). $\mathcal{G}_{p\ell}$ is the planar modification of $\mathcal{G}$ (see Sect. 2.3).

(6.2) $\mathcal{G}$ and $\mathcal{G}_{p\ell}$ are periodic and the second coordinate axis $L_0: x(1) = 0$ is an axis of symmetry for $\mathcal{G}$ and for $\mathcal{G}_{p\ell}$ (Note that we can construct $\mathcal{G}_{p\ell}$ symmetrically with respect to $L_0$ as soon as $\mathcal{G}$ is symmetric with respect to this axis, by virtue of Comment 2.4(iii).)

(6.3) P is a product measure on $(\Omega_{\mathcal{V}}, \mathcal{B}_{\mathcal{V}})$, where $\mathcal{V}$ is the vertex set of $\mathcal{G}_{p\ell}$ (compare Sect. 3.1). P is symmetric with respect to $L_0$, i.e. if $v = (v(1), v(2))$ is any vertex of $\mathcal{G}_{p\ell}$, then $P\{v = (v(1), v(2))$ is occupied$\}$ $= P\{(-v(1), v(2))$ is occupied$\}$. (It is not required that (2.15), (2.16) be satisfied).

Finally $\Lambda$ is a constant such that

(6.4) diameter of any edge of $\mathcal{G}$ or of $\mathcal{G}_{p\ell}$ is $\leq \Lambda$.

Theorem 6.1. Assume (6.1) - (6.4). Let $\pi \geq 1$ be an integer and assume that $\bar{n} = (n_1, n_2)$ and $\bar{m} = (m_1, m_2)$ are integral vectors for which

(6.5) $\sigma(\bar{n};1,p,\mathcal{G}_{p\ell}) = P_p\{\exists$ an occupied horizontal crossing on $\mathcal{G}_{p\ell}$ of $[0,n_1] \times [0,n_2]\} \geq \delta_1 > 0$ ,

(6.6) $\sigma(\bar{m};2,p,\mathcal{G}_{p\ell}) = P_p\{\exists$ an occupied vertical crossing on $\mathcal{G}_{p\ell}$ of $[0,m_1] \times [0,m_2]\} \geq \delta_2 > 0$ ,

and

(6.7) $$\frac{1}{\pi} \leq \frac{m_i}{n_i} \leq \pi \qquad i = 1,2$$

Then there exist $n_0 = n_0(\mathcal{G},\pi)$, and for each integer $k \geq 1$ an $f = f(\delta_1,\delta_2,\pi,k) > 0$ depending on the indicated parameters only, such that for

(6.8) $$n_i \geq n_0 = n_0(\mathcal{G},\pi)$$

one has

(6.9) $\sigma(kn_1, 2n_2); 1,p,\mathcal{G}_{p\ell}) = P_p\{\exists$ occupied horizontal crossing on $\mathcal{G}_{p\ell}$ of $[0,kn_1]\times[0,2n_2]\} \geq f(\delta_1,\delta_2,\pi,k) > 0$

and

(6.10) $\sigma((\pi + 3)n_1, kn_2); 2,p,\mathcal{G}_{p\ell}) = P_p\{\exists$ occupied vertical crossing on $\mathcal{G}_{p\ell}$ of $[0,(\pi + 3)n_1] \times [0,kn_2]\} \geq f(\delta_1,\delta_2,\pi,k) > 0$ .

Moreover, for fixed $\pi,k$

(6.11) $$\lim_{\substack{\delta_1 \to 1 \\ \delta_2 \to 2}} f(\delta_1,\delta_2,\pi,k) = 1 .$$

Corollary 6.1. Under the hypotheses of Theorem 6.1 (including (6.8))

(6.12) $P_p\{\exists$ occupied circuit on $\mathcal{G}_{p\ell}$ surrounding 0, and inside the annulus $[-2(\pi + 3)n_1, 2(\pi + 3)n_1] \times [-3n_2,3n_2]$ $(-(\pi + 3)n_1, (\pi + 3)n_1) \times (-n_2, n_2)\} \geq f^4(\delta_1,\delta_2,\pi, 4\pi + 12)$.

The very long proof will be broken down into several lemmas. If one is content with proving the theorem only for the case $m_1 = n_1$, $m_2 = n_2 (\pi = 1)$ and under the additional hypothesis that both the x(1) and x(2)-axis are symmetry-axes, then Lemma 6.1 suffices. Since these extra hypotheses hold for most examples the reader is strongly urged to stop with Lemma 6.1 at first reading, or to read the original proofs of Russo (1978) or Seymour and Welsh (1978). The proof of Theorem 6.1 in its full generality is only included for readers interested in technical details, with the hope that it will lead someone to a proof which does not use symmetry.

The principal ideas appear already in the first lemma. These ideas are due to Russo (1978), (1981) and Seymour and Welsh (1978). A very important role is played by an analogue of the strong Markov property, not with respect to a stopping time, but with respect to a lowest occupied horizontal crossing (see step (b) of Lemma 6.1). Harris (1960) seems to have been the first person to use this property.

In each of the lemmas we construct an occupied crossing of a large rectangle by connecting several occupied horizontal and vertical crossings. The existence of suitable crossings will come from (6.5) - (6.7). The difficulty is to make sure that the vertical crossings really intersect the horizontal ones, so that they can all be connected. To do this we shall repeatedly use the FKG inequality (and symmetry considerations) to restrict the locations of the crossings. In other words, if we know that with high probability there exists an occupied crossing of some rectangle, we shall deduce that there is also a high probability for the existence of an occupied crossing with additional restrictions on its location. Lemma 6.3 and the proofs of Lemmas 6.6 - 6.8 exemplify this kind of argument.

Since we only consider paths and crossings on $\mathcal{G}_{p\ell}$ we shall drop the specification "on $\mathcal{G}_{p\ell}$" for paths for the remainder of this chapter. We remind the reader that $\mathcal{G}_{p\ell}$ is planar, and that a path in our terminology has therefore no self intersections (see beginning of Sect. 2.3). We shall suppress the subscript $p$ in $P_p$. (6.1) - (6.4) will be in force throughout this chapter.

Lemma 6.1. Assume

(6.13) $\quad \sigma((\ell_1,\ell_2); 1,p,\mathcal{G}_{p\ell}) \geq \delta_3 > 0$

and

(6.14) $\quad \sigma((\ell_3,\ell_2); 2,p,\mathcal{G}_{p\ell}) \geq \delta_4 > 0$

for some integers $\ell_1,\ell_2,\ell_3 \geq 1$ with[1)]

(6.15) $\quad \ell_3 \leq \frac{3}{2}\ell_1, \quad \ell_1 \geq 32 + 16\Lambda, \quad \ell_2 > \Lambda.$

Then for each $k$ there exists an $f_1(\delta_3,\delta_4,k) > 0$ such that

(6.16) $\quad \sigma((k\ell_1,\ell_2); 1,p,\mathcal{G}_{p\ell}) \geq f_1(\delta_3,\delta_4,k) > 0$

and

(6.17) $$\lim_{\substack{\delta_3 \to 1 \\ \delta_4 \to 1}} f_1(\delta_3,\delta_4,k) = 1 \quad .$$

---

1) The requirement $\ell_3 \leq \frac{3}{2}\ell_1$ can be replaced by $\ell_3 \leq (2-\delta)\ell_1$ for any $\delta > 0$.

Proof: The proof is somewhat lengthy and will be broken down into three steps.

Step (a). Consider a fixed horizontal crossing $r = (v_0, e_1, \ldots, e_\nu, v_\nu)$ of $[0, \ell_1 - 1] \times [0, \ell_2]$ such that $e_\nu$ intersects the right edge, $\{\ell_1 - 1\} \times [0, \ell_2]$, in its interior only. In view of Def. 3.1 and $\ell_1 > 1 + \Lambda$, this implies that $r$ intersects the vertical line $L: x(1) = \ell_1 - 1$ only in the open segment $\{\ell_1 - 1\} \times (0, \ell_2)$. The rather trivial technical reasons for insisting that the intersection of $r$ with $L$ is in this open segment rather than the closed segment $\{\ell_1 - 1\} \times [0, \ell_2]$ will become clear below. For the moment we merely observe that any horizontal crossing $r_1$ of $[0, \ell_1] \times [0, \ell_2]$ contains a path $r$ with the above properties. Indeed we can simply take for $r$ the initial piece of $r_1$ up till and including the first edge $e$ of $r_1$ which intersects $L$. (Note that $L$ is an axis of symmetry of $\mathcal{G}_{p\ell}$ because $L_0: x(1) = 0$ is an axis of symmetry and $\mathcal{G}_{p\ell}$ is periodic with period $\xi_1 = (1,0)$. As explained in Comment 2.4(ii) this implies that $e$ intersects $L$ in exactly one point; $e$ cannot be in case (a) or (b) of that Comment because it has one endpoint strictly to the left of $L$.) Therefore

$$(6.18) \qquad P\{\exists \text{ occupied crossing } r = (v_0, e_1, \ldots, e_\nu, v_\nu) \text{ of } [0, \ell_1 - 1] \times [0, \ell_2] \text{ which intersects } L \text{ only in } \{\ell_1 - 1\} \times (0, \ell_2)\} \geq \sigma((\ell_1, \ell_2); 1, p, \mathcal{G}_{p\ell}) \geq \delta_3 .$$

We shall write $\tilde{e}(\tilde{v})$ for the reflection of an edge $e$ (a vertex $v$) in $L$. $\tilde{r}$ will denote the reflection of $r$ in $L$. Then for $r$ as above $r \cup \tilde{r}$ is a horizontal crossing of $[0, 2\ell_1 - 2] \times [0, \ell_2]$, provided we interpret this statement with a little care. If $v_\nu$ lies on $\{\ell_1 - 1\} \times (0, \ell_2)$ then $r \cup \tilde{r}$ is simply the path $(v_0, e_1, \ldots, e_\nu, v_\nu = \tilde{v}_\nu, \tilde{e}_\nu, \tilde{v}_{\nu-1}, \ldots, \tilde{v}_0)$. As observed above, by Comment 2.4(ii) the only other possibility is that the intersection of $e_\nu$ and $L$ is the midpoint of $e_\nu$. Then $e_\nu = \tilde{e}_\nu$ and $r \cup \tilde{r}$ should be interpreted as the path $(v_0, e_1, \ldots, e_\nu, v_\nu = \tilde{v}_{\nu-1}, \tilde{e}_{\nu-1}, \tilde{v}_{\nu-2}, \ldots, \tilde{v}_0)$. Note that we insisted on $e_\nu$ intersecting $L$ in the open segment $\{\ell_1 - 1\} \times (0, \ell_2)$ precisely to make $r \cup \tilde{r}$ a horizontal crossing of $[0, 2\ell_1 - 2] \times [0, \ell_2]$.

Now we take for $J_2$ the perimeter of $[0, 2\ell_1 - 2] \times [0, \ell_2]$ viewed as a Jordan curve. We further take $B_1 = \{0\} \times [0, \ell_2]$, $B_2 = \{2\ell_1 - 2\} \times [0, \ell_2]$, $A_2 = [0, 2\ell_1 - 2] \times \{0\}$ and $C_2 = [0, 2\ell_1 - 2] \times \{\ell_2\}$. These are the left, right, bottom and top edge of $[0,2\ell_1 - 2] \times [0,\ell_2]$, respectively. These four edges make up $J_2$ and $r \cup \tilde{r}$ satisfies the analogues of (2.23) - (2.25), i.e., all its edges and vertices except for $v_0, e_1, \tilde{e}_1$ and $\tilde{v}_0$ lie in $\text{int}(J_2)$, while $e_1(\tilde{e}_1)$ has exactly one point in common with $B_1(B_2)$. We can therefore define $J_2^+(r \cup \tilde{r})$ $J_2^-(r \cup \tilde{r}))$ as the component of $\text{int}(J_2) \setminus r \cup \tilde{r}$ which contains $C_2(A_2)$ in its boundary, exactly as in Def. 2.11. We also introduce the events[1)]

(6.19) $D(r) := \{ \exists$ path $s = (w_0, f_1, \ldots, f_\rho, w_\rho)$ such that $w_1, \ldots, w_{\rho-1}$ are occupied, $w_0 = v_i$ for some $v_i \in r$, $f_\rho$ intersects $C_2$ in some point $\zeta$, and

$$(f_1 \setminus \{w_0\}, w_1, f_2, \ldots, f_{\rho-1}, w_{\rho-1}, [w_{\rho-1}, \zeta)) \subset \{J_2^+(r \cup \tilde{r}) \cap [\lfloor \tfrac{\ell_1}{8} \rfloor, 2\ell_1 - 2 - \lfloor \tfrac{\ell_1}{8} \rfloor] \times (0,\ell_2)\}\}$$

and $D(\tilde{r})$, defined as $D(r)$, except that one now requires $w_0 = \tilde{v}_i$ for some $v_i \in r$, or equivalently that $w_0$ is a vertex on $\tilde{r}$. We shall prove in this step that

$$P\{D(r)\} \geq 1 - \sqrt{1-\delta_4} \quad . \tag{6.20}$$

Note that (6.19) estimates the probability of the existence of an "occupied connection from $r$ to the upper edge $C_2$ of $[0,2\ell_1 - 2] \times [0,\ell_2]$ above $r \cup \tilde{r}$" and in the rectangle $[\lfloor \frac{\ell_1}{8} \rfloor, 2\ell_1 - 2 - \lfloor \frac{\ell_1}{8} \rfloor] \times [0,\ell_2]$ (see Fig. 6.1).

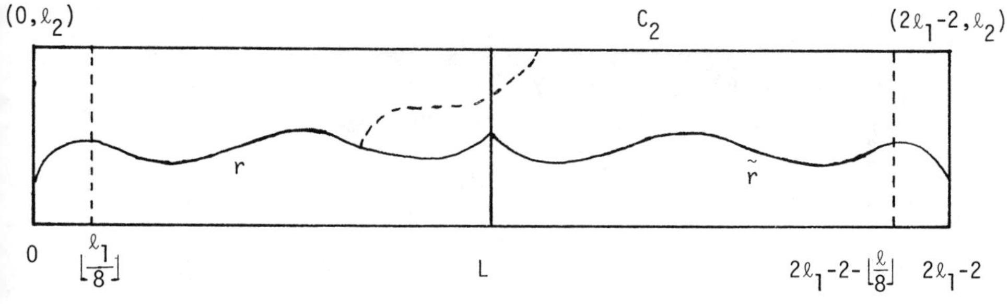


Figure 6.1

1) Recall that $\lfloor a \rfloor$ denotes the largest integer $\leq a$ .

Before starting on the proof of (6.20) proper we first observe that for any two increasing events $E_1, E_2$ one obtains from the FKG inequality

$$P\{E_1 \cup E_2\} = 1 - P\{E_1^c \cap E_2^c\} \le 1 - P\{E_1^c\} P\{E_2^c\}$$

or

$$(6.21) \qquad (1 - P\{E_1\})(1 - P\{E_2\}) \le 1 - P\{E_1 \cup E_2\} .$$

We apply this with $E_1 = D(r)$, $E_2 = D(\tilde{r})$. Since $D(\tilde{r})$ is obtained by "reflecting $D(r)$ in $L$" and $L$ is an axis of symmetry we have $P\{D(\tilde{r})\} = P\{D(r)\}$ and (6.21) becomes

$$P\{D(r)\} \ge 1 - (1 - P\{D(r) \cup D(\tilde{r})\})^{1/2} .$$

For (6.20) it therefore suffices to prove

(6.22) $P\{D(r) \cup D(\tilde{r})\} = P\{\exists$ path $s = (w_0, f_1, \dots, f_\rho, w_\rho)$ such that $w_1, \dots, w_{\rho-1}$ are occupied, $w_0 = v_i$ or $\tilde{v}_i$ for some $i$, $f_\rho$ intersects $C_2$ in some point $\zeta$ and

$$(f_1 \setminus \{w_0\}, w_1, f_2, \dots, f_{\rho-1}, w_{\rho-1}, [w_{\rho-1}, \xi)) \subset \{J_2^+(r \cup \tilde{r}) \cap [\lfloor \tfrac{\ell_1}{8} \rfloor, 2\ell_1 - 2 - \lfloor \tfrac{\ell_1}{8} \rfloor] \times (0, \ell_2)\}\} \ge \delta_4 .$$

To prove (6.22) assume for the moment that there exists an occupied vertical crossing $t = (u_0, g_1, \dots, g_\tau, u_\tau)$ of $[\lfloor \frac{\ell_1}{8} \rfloor, 2\ell_1 - 2 - \lfloor \frac{\ell_1}{8} \rfloor] \times [0, \ell_2]$. Then $t$ contains a continuous curve from the bottom to the top of this rectangle, while $r \cup \tilde{r}$ contains a continuous curve from the left to the right edge of this rectangle. Both these curves are contained in the rectangle and must therefore intersect. Thus $r \cup \tilde{r}$ and $t$ intersect, and since both are paths on the planar graph $\mathcal{G}_{p\ell}$ they intersect in a vertex. Let $u_\alpha$ be the last point of $t$ on $r \cup \tilde{r}$ and let $u_\alpha$ equal $v_i$ or $\tilde{v}_i$, $v_i \in r$. Since $t$ is a vertical crossing of $[\lfloor \frac{\ell_1}{8} \rfloor, 2\ell_1 - 2 - \lfloor \frac{\ell_1}{8} \rfloor] \times [0, \ell_2]$ and $\ell_2 > \Lambda$ $g_\tau$ is the only edge of $t$ which intersects $C_2$. Let $\zeta$ be the first intersection of $g_\tau$ with $C_2$, so that the segment from $u_{\tau-1}$ to $\zeta$ (excluding $\zeta$) is disjoint from $C_2$. Since $C_2$ is part of $Fr(J_2^+(r \cup \tilde{r}))$, and $J_2^+(r \cup \tilde{r})$ as well as $u_{\tau-1}$ lie below $C_2$, it follows that near $\zeta$ the segment of $g_\tau$ from $u_{\tau-1}$ to $\zeta$ lies in $J_2^+(r \cup \tilde{r})$. Moreover, the connected set $g_{\alpha+1} \setminus \{u_\alpha\} \cup g_{\alpha+2} \cup \ldots \cup g_{\tau-1} \cup$ (the segment of $g_\tau$ from $u_{\tau-1}$ to $\zeta$) does not intersect $Fr(J_2^+(r \cup \tilde{r}))$. Consequently $g_{\alpha+1} \setminus \{u_\alpha\}, \ldots, g_{\tau-1}$ and the vertices $u_{\alpha+1}, \ldots, u_{\tau-1}$ on these edges also lie in $J_2^+(r \cup \tilde{r})$. These observations show that the path $(u_\alpha, g_{\alpha+1}, \ldots, g_\tau, u_\tau)$ satisfies the requirements for $s$ in (6.22) (if we take $w_j = u_{\alpha+j}$, $f_j = g_{\alpha+j}$, $\rho = \tau - \alpha$). We have therefore proved that the event in (6.22) occurs whenever there exists an occupied vertical crossing of $[\lfloor \frac{\ell_1}{8} \rfloor, 2\ell_1 - 2 - \lfloor \frac{\ell_1}{8} \rfloor] \times [0, \ell_2]$ and consequently

$$\begin{aligned} P\{D(r) \cup D(\tilde{r})\} &\geq P\{\exists \text{ an occupied vertical crossing of } \\ &\qquad [\lfloor \tfrac{\ell_1}{8} \rfloor, \ 2\ell_1 - 2 - \lfloor \tfrac{\ell_1}{8} \rfloor] \times [0, \ell_2]\} \\ &\geq \sigma((\ell_3, \ell_2); 2, p, \mathcal{G}_{p\ell}) \geq \delta_4 \ . \end{aligned}$$

For the second inequality we used periodicity, $\ell_3 < 2\ell_1 - 2 - 2\lfloor \frac{\ell_1}{8} \rfloor$ (see 6.15)) and the monotonicity property of Comment 3.3(v). This proves (6.22) and (6.20).

<u>Step (b)</u>. We apply Prop. 2.3 with $J$ equal to the perimeter of $[0, \ell_1 - 1] \times [0, \ell_2]$ and $B_1 = \{0\} \times [0, \ell_2]$, $B_2 = \{\ell_1 - 1\} \times [0, \ell_2]$, $A = [0, \ell_1 - 1] \times \{0\}$ and $C = [0, \ell_1 - 1] \times \{\ell_2\}$, and with $S = \mathbb{R}^2 \setminus \{(\ell_1 - 1, 0), (\ell_1 - 1, \ell_2)\}$. Note that $B_2$ here differs from $B_2$ in step (a); in any case $B_1 \cap B_2 = \emptyset$ so that (2.26) holds. Moreover the lines $x(1) = 0$ and $x(1) = \ell_1 - 1$ containing $B_1$ and $B_2$ are axes of symmetry. Prop. 2.3 now tells us that if there exists an occupied horizontal crossing of $[0, \ell_1 - 1] \times [0, \ell_2]$ in $S$, then there exists a lowest such crossing, i.e., an occupied crossing with minimal $J^-(r)$. As in Prop. 2.3 we denote the lowest such crossing by $R$ if it exists. Note that a crossing in $S$ is precisely one which intersects $L$ in the open segment $\{\ell_1 - 1\} \times (0, \ell_2)$. Therefore, by Prop. 2.3 and (6.18), the probability that $R$ exists is at least $\sigma((\ell_1, \ell_2); 1, p, \mathcal{G}_{p\ell}) \geq \delta_3$. For any fixed horizontal crossing $r = (v_0, e_1, \ldots, e_\nu, v_\nu)$ of $[0, \ell_1 - 1] \times [0, \ell_2]$ denote by $Y(r)$ the second coordinate of the last intersection of $r$ with the vertical line $L_1 : x(1) = \lfloor \frac{\ell_1}{8} \rfloor$. Formally, if $e_j$ intersects $L_1$

in $y = (y(1), y(2))$ and the segment of $e_j$ from $y$ to $v_j$ as well as $e_{j+1},\dots,e_\nu$ do not intersect $L_1$ anymore, then $Y(r) = y(2)$. Note that $Y(r)$ is well-defined since $r$ - which goes from $\{x(1) \le 0\}$ to $\{x(1) \ge \ell_1 - 1\}$ - must intersect $L_1$. Finally, we choose $m$ as the conditional $(1-\varepsilon)$ - quantile of $Y(R)$, given that $R$ exists, where

$$\varepsilon = \frac{1}{\delta_3}\{\sqrt{1-\delta_3} - (1-\delta_3)\} .$$

More formally, we choose $m$ such that

$$(6.23) \qquad P\{R \text{ exists and } Y(R) \le m\} \ge (1-\varepsilon)\, P\{R \text{ exists}\}$$
$$= (1-\varepsilon) \times (\text{left hand side of } (6.18))$$
$$\ge (1-\varepsilon) \quad \sigma((\ell_1,\ell_2); 1,p,\mathcal{G}_{p\ell})$$

and

$$(6.24) \qquad P\{R \text{ exists and } Y(R) < m\} \le (1-\varepsilon)P\,\{R \text{ exists}\}$$
$$= (1-\varepsilon) \times (\text{left hand side of } (6.18)).$$

Finally, we take the segments $A_2 = [0, 2\ell_1 - 2] \times \{0\}$ and $C_2 = [0, 2\ell_1 - 2] \times \{\ell_2\}$ as in step (a) and define the horizontal semi-infinite strip $H$ by

$$H = [\lfloor \frac{\ell_1}{8} \rfloor , \infty) \times (0,\ell_2) .$$

In this step we shall prove

(6.25) $P\{ \exists$ an occupied horizontal crossing $r'$ of $[0,\ell_1 - 1] \times [0,\ell_2]$ with $Y(r') \le m$ and $r' \cap L \subset \{\ell_1 - 1\} \times (0,\ell_2)$ and $\exists$ path $s' = (w_0,f_1,\dots,f_\rho, w_\rho)$ such that $w_0,\dots,w_{\rho-1}$ are occupied, $w_0$ is a vertex of $r'$, $f_\rho$ intersects $C_2$ in some point $\zeta$, while $(w_0,f_1,\dots,f_{\rho-1}, w_{\rho-1}, [w_\rho,\zeta)) \subset H\}$

$$\ge (1 - \sqrt{1-\delta_3})(1-\sqrt{1-\delta_4})$$

and

(6.26) $P\{\exists$ an occupied horizontal crossing $r''$ of $[0,\ell_1 - 1] \times [0,\ell_2]$ with $Y(r'') \geq m$ and $r'' \cap L \subset \{\ell_1 - 1\} \times (0,\ell_2)$ and $\exists$ a path $s'' = (u_0,g_1,\ldots,g_\tau, u_\tau)$ such that $u_0,\ldots,u_{\tau-1}$ are occupied, $u_0$ is a vertex of $r''$, $g_\tau$ intersects $A_2$ in some point $\zeta$ while $(u_0,g_1,\ldots,g_{\tau-1},u_{\tau-1}, [u_\tau,\zeta)) \subset H\}$

$$\geq (1 - \sqrt{1-\delta_3})(1 - \sqrt{1-\delta_4}).$$

To prove (6.25) we observe that the event in the left hand side contains the union

(6.27) $\bigcup_{r'} \{R = r'$ and $\exists$ a path $s' = (w_0,f_1,\ldots,f_\rho,w_\rho)$ such that $w_0,\ldots,w_{\rho-1}$ are occupied, $w_0$ is a vertex on $r'$, $f_\rho$ intersects $C_2$ in some point $\zeta$ and $(w_0,f_1,\ldots,f_{\rho-1},w_{\rho-1},[w_\rho,\zeta)) \subset H\}$ ,

where the union in (6.27) is over all horizontal crossings $r'$ of $[0,\ell_1 - 1] \times [0,\ell_2]$ with $Y(r') \leq m$ and which intersect $L$ in $\{\ell_1 - 1\} \times (0,\ell_2)$. The events in (6.27) are clearly disjoint. In addition, if $R = r'$ and $D(r')$ occurs (see (6.19)), then the event in (6.27) corresponding to $r'$ occurs. Indeed, $D(r')$ implies the existence of a path $s = (w_0,f_1,\ldots,f_\rho,w_\rho)$ with $w_1,\ldots,w_{\rho-1}$ occupied, $w_0$ a vertex of $r'$, $f_\rho$ intersecting $C_2$ in a point $\zeta$ and $(f_1 \setminus \{w_0\}, w_1,\ldots,f_{\rho-1},w_{\rho-1},[w_{\rho-1},\zeta)) \subset [\lfloor \frac{\ell_1}{8} \rfloor, \infty) \times (0,\ell_2) = H$. In addition $w_0$ is occupied since it belongs to $r' = R$, and $w_0$ lies on $f_1 \cap r' \subset H$ (since $r'$ lies strictly between the horizontal lines $x(2) = 0$ and $x(2) = \ell_2$ to the right of $L_1$) . Therefore $s$ satisfies all requirements for $s'$. It follows from these observations that the left hand side of (6.25) is no less than

(6.28) $$\sum_{\substack{Y(r') \leq m \\ r' \cap L \subset \{\ell_1 - 1\} \times (0,\ell_2)}} P\{R = r'\} \; P\{D(r') \mid R = r'\} \; .$$

The "strong Markov property" to which we referred earlier is that $\{R = r'\}$ and $D(r')$ are independent. This is true, because by Prop. 2.3 $\{R = r'\}$ depends only on the occupancies of vertices in

$\bar{J}^-(r') \cup \{v: v$ is a vertex of $\mathcal{G}_{p\ell}$ with its reflection $\tilde{v}$ in $L_0: x(1) = 0$ or $L: x(1) = \ell_1 - 1$ belonging to $\bar{J}^-(r')$ and such that $e \cap J \subset \bar{J}^-(r')$ for some edge $e$ of $\mathcal{G}_{p\ell}$ between $v$ and $\tilde{v}\}$. Here $J$ is still the perimeter of $[0,\ell_1 - 1] \times [0,\ell_2]$ and $\bar{J}$ is the closure of $\text{int}(J)$, i.e., $[0,\ell_1 - 1] \times [0,\ell_2]$. One easily sees that all these vertices lie in $\bar{J}_2^-(r' \cup \tilde{r}')$ plus possibly a collection of points in the half plane $x(1) < 0$ (note that the endpoint of $r'$ lies on $\tilde{r}'$ in all cases; the notation here is as in step (a)). On the other hand the definition (6.19) shows that $D(r')$ depends only on vertices in $J_2^+(r' \cup \tilde{r}')$. Thus $\{R = r'\}$ and $D(r')$ depend on disjoint sets of vertices so that they are indeed independent. It now follows from (6.20), (6.23) and (6.13) that (6.28) is at least

$$\sum_{\substack{Y(r') \le m \\ r' \cap L \subset \{\ell_1 - 1\} \times (0,\ell_2)}} P\{R = r'\} \, P\{D(r')\}$$

$$\ge (1 - \sqrt{1-\delta_4}) \, P\{R \text{ exists and } Y(R) \le m\}$$

$$\ge (1 - \sqrt{1-\delta_4}) \, (1-\varepsilon) \, \sigma((\ell_1,\ell_2);1,p,\mathcal{G}_{p\ell})$$

$$\ge (1-\varepsilon)\delta_3 \, (1 - \sqrt{1-\delta_4}) = (1 - \sqrt{1-\delta_3}) \, (1 - \sqrt{1-\delta_4}) \, .$$

This proves (6.25).

The proof of (6.26) is essentially obtained from (6.25) by interchanging the role of "top and bottom" or rather the role of the positive and negative second coordinate axis. The lowest occupied horizontal crossing now has to be replaced by the highest occupied horizontal crossing, i.e., the roles of $A$ and $C$ have to be interchanged. We are not using symmetry with respect to the first coordinate axis, but merely saying that the same proof works when we make the above change, except for one step. The analogue of (6.23) which we need is the following: Let $R^+$ be the highest occupied horizontal crossing of $[0,\ell_1 - 1] \times [0,\ell_2]$ which intersects $L$ in $\{\ell_1 - 1\} \times (0,\ell_2)$. In other words, $R^+$ is the occupied horizontal crossing $r$ of the above type with minimal $J^+(r)$. $R^+$ exists by Prop. 2.3 as soon as there exists an occupied horizontal crossing of $[0,\ell_1 - 1] \times [0,\ell_2]$ in $S = \mathbb{R}^2 \setminus \{(\ell_1 - 1,0), (\ell_1 - 1,\ell_2)\}$ (Just interchange $A$ and $C$). We want

$$(6.29) \qquad P\{R^+ \text{ exists and } Y(R^+) \geq m\} \geq (1-\varepsilon)\delta_3 .$$

Once one has (6.29) to replace (6.23), the proof of (6.26) becomes a copy of that of (6.25).

We now deduce (6.29) from (6.24). First observe that $R^+$ exists iff $R$ exists iff there exists any occupied horizontal crossing of $[0,\ell_1 - 1] \times [0,\ell_2]$ in $S$. Second, if such crossings exist, then

$$(6.30) \qquad Y(R^+) \geq Y(r) \geq Y(R)$$

for any occupied horizontal crossing $r$ of $[0,\ell_1 - 1] \times [0,\ell_2]$ in $S$. We only have to prove the right hand inequality in (6.30); the left hand inequality will then follow by interchanging the role of $A$ and $C$. To obtain this right hand inequality note that the piece of $R$ from its last intersection $\zeta_1 := (\lfloor \frac{\ell_1}{8} \rfloor, Y(R))$ with $L_1$ to its unique intersection, $\zeta_2$ say, with the line $L: x(1) = \ell_1 - 1$ forms a crosscut of the rectangle $F := (\lfloor \frac{\ell_1}{8} \rfloor, \ell_1 - 1) \times (0,\ell_2)$ (see Fig. 6.2).

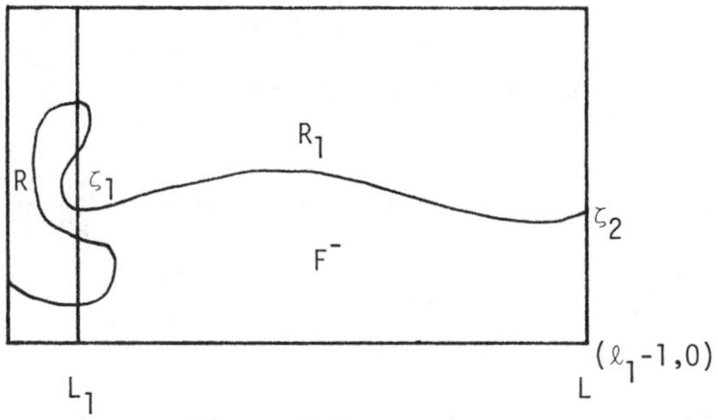


Figure 6.2

Let us write $R_1$ for the piece of $R$ between $\zeta_1$ and $\zeta_2$. Thus $R_1$ divides $F$ into two Jordan domains. The lower one, which we denote by $F^-$ is bounded by $R_1$, the segment of $L$ from $\zeta_2$ to $(\ell_1 - 1,0)$, the horizontal segment at the bottom from $(\ell_1 - 1,0)$ to $(\lfloor \frac{\ell_1}{8} \rfloor, 0)$ and the segment of $L_1$ from $(\lfloor \frac{\ell_1}{8} \rfloor, 0)$ to $\zeta_1$. Any point in $F^-$ which is close enough to $R_1$ can be connected by a continuous curve in $F^- \setminus R$ to the segment of $L$ below $\zeta_2$, i.e., the segment from $\zeta_2$ to $(\ell_1 - 1,0)$. This is obvious if $R$ is a polygonal path. In general one can obtain this from the fact that $\overline{F^-}$ can be mapped homeomorphically onto the closed unit disc (see Newman (1951), Theorem VI. 17.1 or use conformal mapping as in Hille (1962), Theorem 17.5.3). Since the segment of $L$ from $\zeta_2$ to $(\ell_1 - 1, 0)$ belongs to $Fr(J^-(R))$ and not to $Fr(J^+(R))$ it follows that all points of $F^-$ close to $R_1$ belong to $J^-(R)$. Consequently for any occupied horizontal crossing $r$ of $[0,\ell_1 - 1] \times [0,\ell_2]$ in $S$, the piece between the last intersection of $r$ with $L_1$ and the first intersection with $L$ cannot enter $F^-$, because such a crossing $r$ satisfies $r \cap \bar{J} \subset \bar{J}^+(R)$ (see (2.27)). In particular, the last intersection of $r$ with $L_1$, $(\lfloor \frac{\ell_1}{8} \rfloor, Y(r))$, cannot lie strictly below $\zeta_1$ on $L_1$. This just says $Y(r) \geq Y(R)$, and therefore proves (6.30).

Now we apply (6.21) with $E_1(E_2)$ the event that there exists an occupied horizontal crossing $r$ of $[0,\ell_1 - 1] \times [0,\ell_2]$ in $S$ with $Y(r) < m$ $(Y(r) \geq m)$. $E_1 \cup E_2$ is the event that there is some occupied horizontal crossing of $[0,\ell_1 - 1] \times [0,\ell_2]$ in $S$ and this has probability at least $\delta_3$ by (6.18). Also, by (6.30) $P\{E_1\}$ is given by the left hand side of (6.24), and hence is at most $(1 - \varepsilon) P\{E_1 \cup E_2\}$. Thus, by (6.30) and (6.21)

$$P\{R^+ \text{ exists and } Y(R^+) \geq m\} \geq P\{\exists \text{ an occupied horizontal crossing } r \text{ of } [0,\ell_1-1] \times [0,\ell_2] \text{ in } S \text{ with } Y(r) \geq m\}$$

$$= P\{E_2\} \geq 1 - \frac{1-P\{E_1 \cup E_2\}}{1-P\{E_1\}} \geq 1 - \frac{1-P\{E_1 \cup E_2\}}{1-(1-\varepsilon)P\{E_1 \cup E_2\}}$$

$$1 - \frac{1-\delta_3}{1-(1-\varepsilon)\delta_3} = 1 - \sqrt{1-\delta_3} = (1-\varepsilon)\delta_3 .$$

This is precisely (6.29), and as stated above, implies (6.26).

<u>Step (c)</u>. In this step, we complete the proof of the lemma from (6.25) and (6.26). Assume that the events in braces in the left hand sides of (6.25) and (6.26) both occur. Then $r' \cup s'$ contains in $H$ a continuous curve from $(\lfloor \frac{\ell_1}{8} \rfloor, Y(r'))$ = last intersection of $r'$ with $L_1$ to the upper edge of $H$, $[\lfloor \frac{\ell_1}{8} \rfloor, \infty) \times \{\ell_2\}$. Also $r'' \cup s''$ contains in $H$ a continuous curve from $(\lfloor \frac{\ell_1}{8} \rfloor, Y(r''))$ to the lower edge of $H$, $[\lfloor \frac{\ell_1}{8} \rfloor, \infty) \times \{0\}$. Moreover, $Y(r'') \geq m \geq Y(r')$, so that the second curve begins above the first curve on $L_1$ and ends

below the first curve. Thus these curves intersect, necessarily in a vertex and in H. Since all vertices of $s' \cup s''$ in H are occupied it follows that $r'$ $r''$, $s' \cap H$ and $s'' \cap H$ all belong to one occupied component and $(r' \cup s' \cup r'' \cup s'') \cap H$ contains a continuous curve,

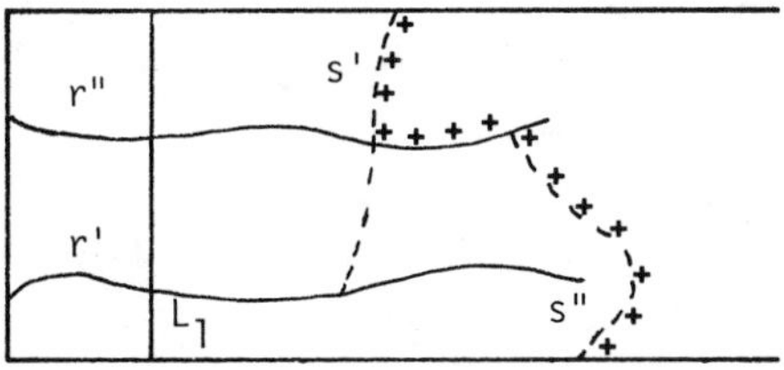


Figure 6.3 $r'$ and $r''$ are solidly drawn, $s'$ and $s''$ are dashed. The curve $\psi$ is indicated by + signs.

$\psi$ say, in H which connects the upper and lower edge of H. If $\psi$ contains any point on or to the right of the vertical line $L_2 : x(1) = \lfloor \frac{\ell_1}{8} \rfloor + M$ for a given integer M (to be specified later) then $r' \cup s' \cup r'' \cup s''$ contains an occupied horizontal crossing of

(6.31) $$[0, \lfloor \frac{\ell_1}{8} \rfloor + M - \Lambda] \times [0, \ell_2]$$

If, on the other hand, $\psi$ lies strictly to the left of $L_2$, then we must bring in a further path. Assume in this case that there also exists an occupied horizontal crossing $r'''$ of

(6.32) $$[\lfloor \frac{\ell_1}{8} \rfloor - 1, \lfloor \frac{\ell_1}{8} \rfloor + M] \times [0, \ell_2]$$

If $\psi$ lies entirely to the left of $L_2$, then $\psi$ lies in the rectangle

$$[\lfloor \frac{\ell_1}{8} \rfloor , \lfloor \frac{\ell_1}{8} \rfloor + M] \times [0, \ell_2]$$

and connects the top and bottom edges of this rectangle. Thus $\psi$ intersects $r'''$ to the right of $L_1$ and $r', r'', r'''$, $s' \cap H$ and $s'' \cap H$ all belong to one occupied component in this situation. Since $r'$ begins on or to the left of $x(1) = 0$ and $r'''$ ends on or to the right of $x(1) = \lfloor \frac{\ell_1}{8} \rfloor + M$, we see that now $r' \cup r'' \cup r''' \cup s' \cup s''$ contains an occupied horizontal crossing of the rectangle (6.31). Consequently

$$\sigma((\lfloor \frac{\ell_1}{8} \rfloor + M - \Lambda, \ell_2); 1,p,\mathcal{G}_{p\ell}) \geq P\{\text{the events in (6.25) and (6.26) both occur and there exists an occupied horizontal crossing } r''' \text{ of the rectangle (6.32)}\} .$$

By the FKG inequality, (6.25), (6.26) and periodicity we finally obtain from this

$$(6.33) \qquad \sigma((\lfloor \frac{\ell_1}{8} \rfloor + M - \Lambda, \ell_2); 1,p,\mathcal{G}_{p\ell}) \geq (1 - \sqrt{1-\delta_3})^2 (1 - \sqrt{1-\delta_4})^2 \sigma((M + 1,\ell_2); 1,p,\mathcal{G}_{p\ell}) .$$

We apply this first with $M = M_0 := \ell_1 - 1$. Then by (6.13)

$$(6.34) \qquad \sigma((\lfloor \frac{\ell_1}{8} \rfloor + \ell_1 - \Lambda - 1, \ell_2);1,p,\mathcal{G}_{p\ell}) \geq \delta_3(1 - \sqrt{1-\delta_3})^2 (1 - \sqrt{1-\delta_4})^2 .$$

We now use (6.33) with $M = M_1 := M_0 + \lfloor \frac{\ell_1}{8} \rfloor - \Lambda - 2$, and use the estimate (6.34) for the last factor in the right hand side of (6.33). We can repeat this procedure and successively obtain lower bounds for $\sigma((M_{j+1} + 1, \ell_2);1,p,\mathcal{G}_{p\ell})$ in terms of $\sigma((M_j + 1, \ell_2);1,p,\mathcal{G}_{p\ell})$, where

$$M_j = \ell_1 - 1 + j(\lfloor \frac{\ell_1}{8} \rfloor - \Lambda - 1) .$$

By induction on $j$ one sees that these lower bounds tend to one when $\delta_3 \uparrow 1$ and $\delta_4 \uparrow 1$. Since $M_{16k} \geq k\ell_1$ this implies (6.16) and (6.17) for a suitable $f_1$ (cf Comment 3.3 (v)). □

Lemma 6.2. Assume (6.13) holds as well as

$$(6.35) \qquad \sigma((\ell_1,\ell_4); 2,p,\mathcal{G}_{p\ell}) \geq \delta_5 > 0$$

for some integers $\ell_1,\ell_2,\ell_4 \geq 1$ with[1])

$$(6.36) \qquad \ell_2 \leq \frac{98}{100} \ell_4 , \ \ell_4 \geq 300 .$$

---

1) The requirement $\ell_2 \leq \frac{98}{100} \ell_4$ can be replaced by $\ell_2 \leq (1-\delta)\ell_4$ for any $\delta > 0$ .

<u>Then for each</u> $k$ <u>there exists an</u> $f_2(\delta_3,\delta_5,k) > 0$ <u>such that</u>

(6.37) $$\sigma((\ell_1,k\ell_4);\ 2,p,\mathcal{G}_{p\ell}) \geq f_2(\delta_3,\delta_5,k) > 0$$

and

(6.38) $$\lim_{\substack{\delta_3 \to 1 \\ \delta_5 \to 1}} f_2(\delta_3,\delta_5,k) = 1 \ .$$

<u>Remark.</u>

The reader should note that the crossing probabilities in (6.13) and (6.35) are for rectangles of the same horizontal size $\ell_1$, while in (6.13) and (6.14) they are for rectangles of the same vertical size. Also, this lemma estimates the probability of "long" vertical crossings, while Lemma 6.1 deals with "long" horizontal crossings. This lemma is much simpler than the last one and does not rely on symmetry. The simplification comes from the assumption that $\ell_4$ is greater than $\ell_2$, by a fixed fraction. In contrast to this, (6.15) allowed $\ell_1 \leq \ell_3$ .

<u>Proof</u>: To prove (6.37), we observe that if there exist occupied vertical crossings of $r'$ and $r''$ of $[0,\ell_1] \times [0, M + 1]$ and $[0,\ell_1] \times [M - \ell_2 - 1, 2M - \ell_2]$ , for some integer $M$, and an occupied horizontal crossing $t$ of $[0,\ell_1] \times [M - \ell_2,M]$, then $t$ must intersect $r'$ as well as $r'$ in the open rectangle $(0,\ell_1) \times (M - \ell_2,M)$ (see Fig. 6.4). It follows that in this situation $r' \cup r'' \cup t$ contains a vertical crossing of $[0,\ell_1] \times [0,2M - \ell_2]$. Thus, again from the FKG inequality, periodicity and (6.13), we obtain

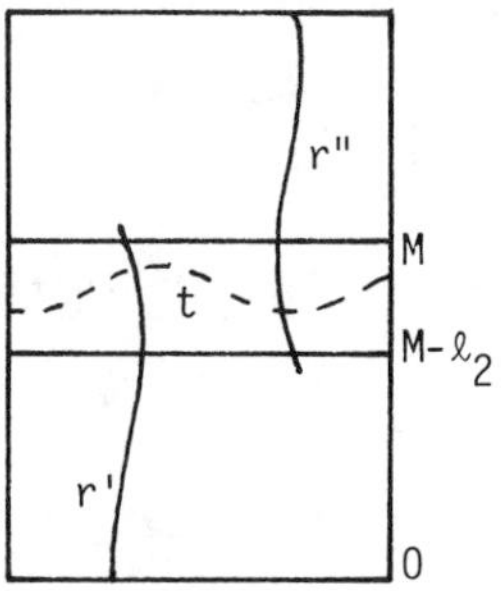


Figure 6.4.

(6.39) $$\sigma((\ell_1, 2M - \ell_2); 2,p,\mathcal{G}_{p\ell})$$

$$\geq \sigma((\ell_1, M + 1); 2,p,\mathcal{G}_{p\ell})$$

$$P\{\exists \text{ occupied vertical crossing of } [0,\ell_1] \times [M-\ell_2-1, 2M-\ell_2]\}$$

$$P\{\exists \text{ occupied horizontal crossing of } [0,\ell_1] \times [M-\ell_2, M]\}$$

$$\geq \{\sigma((\ell_1, M + 1); 2,p,\mathcal{G}_{p\ell})\}^2 \ \delta_3 \quad .$$

We use this in the same way as (6.33). We first take $M = M_0 := \ell_4 - 1$. Then by (6.35) the right hand side of (6.39) is at least $\delta_3 \, \delta_5^2$. This is also a lower bound for

(6.40) $$\sigma((\ell_1, M_j + 1); 2,p,\mathcal{G}_{p\ell})$$

when $j = 1$ and $M_j := \lfloor (1.01)^j \ell_4 \rfloor$ (use (6.36)). Once we have a lower bound for a given $j$ we substitute it into the right hand side of (6.39) to obtain a lower bound for (6.40) with $M_j + 1$ replaced by $2M_j - \ell_2$. Since $2M_j - \ell_2 \geq M_{j+1} + 1$ this is also a lower bound for (6.40) with $M_j$ replaced by $M_{j+1}$. Again we see by induction on $j$ that the lower bound for (6.40) obtained after $j$ iterations of this procedure tends to one when $\delta_3$ and $\delta_5 \to 1$. (6.37) and (6.38) follow from this. □

<u>Lemma 6.3</u>. <u>Assume (6.13) holds. Let</u> $s > 0$ <u>be an integer. Then one has</u>

(6.41) $$\sigma((\ell_1, \tfrac{302}{s} \ell_2 + 2); 1,p,\mathcal{G}_{p\ell}) = P\{\exists \text{ an occupied horizontal crossing of } [0,\ell_1] \times [0, \tfrac{302}{s} \ell_2 + 2]\}$$

$$\geq \delta_6 := 1 - (1-\delta_3)^{(s+2)^{-2}}$$

<u>or for some</u> $300 \leq j \leq s$ <u>the following estimate holds:</u>[1]

---

1) $\lceil a \rceil$ denotes the smallest integer $\geq a$.

(6.42) $P\{\ \exists$ occupied horizontal crossing of $[0,\ell_1] \times [0, \lceil \frac{j+2}{s} \ell_2 \rceil + 2]$ and $\exists$ occupied vertical crossing of $[0,\ell_1] \times [\lceil \frac{\ell_2}{s} \rceil + 1, \lfloor \frac{j+1}{s} \ell_2 \rfloor]\}$

$$\geq \delta_6 = 1 - (1-\delta_3)^{(s+2)^{-2}} .$$

<u>This lemma does not depend on symmetry and the role of the horizontal and vertical direction may be interchanged.</u>

<u>Proof</u>: Let $r = (v_0, e_1, \ldots, e_\nu, v_\nu)$ be an occupied horizontal crossing of $[0,\ell_1] \times [0,\ell_2]$. Let $\zeta_1$ be the last intersection of $e_1$ with the left edge, $\{0\} \times [0,\ell_2]$, of this rectangle, and $\zeta_\nu$ the first intersection of $e_\nu$ with the right edge, $\{\ell_1\} \times [0,\ell_2]$. Then the segment $[\zeta_1, v_1]$ of $e_1$, together with the edges $e_2, \ldots, e_{\nu-1}$ and the segment $[v_{\nu-1}, \zeta_\nu]$ of $e_\nu$ form a continuous curve inside $[0,\ell_1] \times [0,\ell_2]$, connecting the left and right edge. Let $y_\ell(r)$ and $y_h(r)$ be the minimum and maximum value, respectively, of the second coordinates of the points on this curve. Also, let $E(j_1,j_2)$ for $0 \leq j_1, j_2 \leq s$ be the event

$$\{\ \exists \text{ occupied horizontal crossing } r \text{ of } [0,\ell_1] \times [0,\ell_2] \text{ with } \lfloor \frac{j_1}{s} \ell_2 \rfloor < y_\ell(r) \leq \lfloor \frac{(j_1+1)}{s} \ell_2 \rfloor \text{ and } \lceil \frac{j_2}{s} \ell_2 \rceil \leq y_h(r) \leq \lceil \frac{(j_2+1)}{s} \ell_2 \rceil\} .$$

Any horizontal crossing $r$ of $[0,\ell_1] \times [0,\ell_2]$ has $0 \leq y_\ell(r) \leq y_h(r) \leq \ell_2$ , so that if there exists an occupied horizontal crossing of $[0,\ell_1] \times [0,\ell_2]$, then one of the events $E(j_1,j_2)$, $-1 \leq j_1, j_2 \leq s$ must occur. Exactly as in (6.21) we obtain from the FKG inequality and (6.13)

$$1-\delta_3 \geq P\{(\cup E(j_1,j_2))^c\} \geq \Pi\ (1-P\{E(j_1,j_2)\}) \tag{6.43}$$

The union and product in (6.43) run over $-1 \leq j_1, j_2 \leq s$ and hence contain at most $(s+2)^2$ elements. Therefore, for some $-1 \leq j_1, j_2 \leq s$

$$P\{E(j_1,j_2)\} \geq \delta_6 := 1 - (1-\delta_3)^{(s+2)^{-2}} . \tag{6.44}$$

Assume now that (6.44) holds for some $j_1 < j_2 - 300$. If $E(j_1,j_2)$ occurs for these $j_1,j_2$ then there exists an occupied horizontal crossing $r = (v_0,e_1,\dots,e_\nu,v_\nu)$ of $[0,\ell_1] \times [0,\ell_2]$ with

$\lfloor j_1 s^{-1}\ell_2 \rfloor < y_\ell(r) \le \lfloor (j_1+1)s^{-1}\ell_2 \rfloor$ and

$\lceil j_2 s^{-1}\ell_2 \rceil \le y_h(r) < \lceil (j_2+1)s^{-1}\ell_2 \rceil$. By Def. 3.1 of a crossing, $r$ is then also an occupied horizontal crossing of

$[0,\ell_1] \times [\lfloor \frac{j_1}{s}\ell_2 \rfloor, \lceil \frac{j_2+1}{s}\ell_2 \rceil]$. But also

$y_\ell(r) \le \lfloor (j_1+1)s^{-1}\ell_2 \rfloor < \lceil j_2 s^{-1}\ell_2 \rceil \le y_h(r)$ implies that some edge $e_\alpha$ of $r$ intersects the segment $[0,\ell_1] \times \{\lfloor (j_1+1)s^{-1}\ell_2 \rfloor\}$ and some edge $e_\beta$ intersects the segment $[0,\ell_1] \times \{\lceil j_2 s^{-1}\ell_2 \rceil\}$. Choose $\alpha$ and $\beta$ such that $|\beta-\alpha|$ is minimal. For the sake of argument let $\alpha \le \beta$. Then the piece $(v_\alpha,e_{\alpha+1},\dots,e_\beta,v_\beta)$ of $r$ is an occupied vertical crossing of $[0,\ell_1] \times [\lfloor (j_1+1)s^{-1}\ell_2 \rfloor, \lceil j_2 s^{-1}\ell_2 \rceil]$ (see Fig. 6.5). Thus for $j = j_2 - j_1 - 1$ the left hand side of (6.42) is (by virtue of the periodicity and the monotonicity property of Comment 3.3(v)) at least

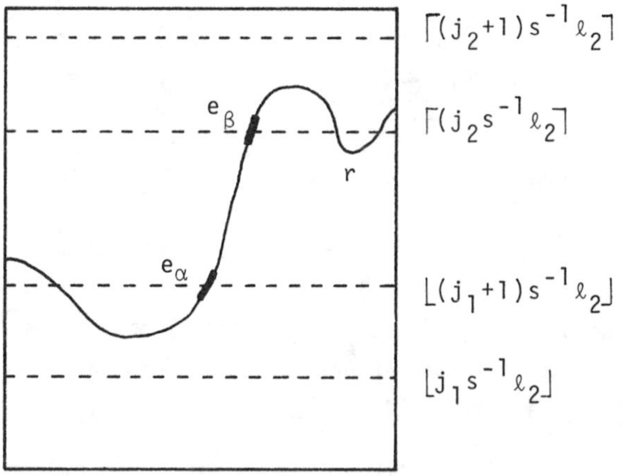


Figure 6.5. The boldly drawn pieces of $r$ represent the edges $e_\alpha$ and $e_\beta$.

$P\{\ \exists$ occupied horizontal crossing of $[0,\ell_1] \times [\lfloor \frac{j_1}{s} \ell_2 \rfloor, \lceil \frac{j_2+1}{s} \ell_2 \rceil]$ and $\exists$ occupied vertical crossing of $[0,\ell_1] \times [\lfloor \frac{j_1+1}{s} \ell_2 \rfloor, \lceil \frac{j_2}{s} \rceil]\} \geq P\{E(j_1,j_2)\} \geq \delta_6$ .

Thus, (6.44) for some $j_1 < j_2-300$ implies (6.42) for a $j \geq 300$. If, on the other hand, (6.44) holds for some $j_1 \geq j_2 - 300$ then the first part of the above argument and periodicity show that (6.41) holds. □

Lemma 6.4. Assume (6.13) and (6.14) hold for some integers $\ell_1,\ell_2,\ell_3 \geq 1$ with

(6.45) $$\ell_3 \leq t\ell_1, \ell_1 \geq 302 + 32\Lambda,\ \ell_2 > \Lambda$$

for some $t$. Then for each $k$ there exists an $f_3(\delta_3,\delta_4,t,k) > 0$ such that

(6.46) $$\sigma((k\ell_1,\ell_2);1,p,\mathcal{G}_{p\ell}) \geq f_3(\delta_3,\delta_4,t,k) > 0$$

and

(6.47) $$\lim_{\substack{\delta_3 \to 1 \\ \delta_4 \to 1}} f_3(\delta_3,\delta_4,t,k) = 1 .$$

For $t = \frac{3}{2}$ this is Lemma 6.1. Here we relax condition (6.15) considerably.

Proof: For $\ell_3 \leq 3\ell_1/2$ Lemma 6.1 already implies (6.46) and (6.47), so that we may assume $\ell_3 \geq 3\ell_1/2$ . We now apply Lemma 6.3 with the horizontal and vertical direction interchanged. Take $s = \lceil 302\ell_3\ell_1^{-1} \rceil \leq 303\ell_3\ell_1^{-1} \leq 303t$ . We then have

$$\sigma((\frac{302}{s}\ell_3 + 2,\ \ell_2);\ 2,p,\mathcal{G}_{p\ell}) = P\{\ \exists \text{ occupied vertical crossing of } [0, \tfrac{302}{s}\ell_3 + 2] \times [0,\ell_2]\} \geq \delta_7 := (1-\delta_4)^{(s+2)^{-2}}$$

or for some $j \geq 300$

(6.48) $P\{\ \exists$ occupied vertical crossing of

$[0, \lceil \frac{j+2}{s} \ell_3 \rceil + 2] \times [0, \ell_2]$ and $\exists$ occupied horizontal crossing of $[\lceil \frac{\ell_3}{s} \rceil + 1, \lfloor \frac{j+1}{s} \ell_3 \rfloor] \times [0, \ell_2]\} \geq \delta_7$ .

In the first case (6.14) and (6.15) hold for $\ell_3$ replaced by

$$\lceil \frac{302}{s} \ell_3 \rceil + 2 \leq \frac{302\ell_3}{302\ell_3\ell_1^{-1}} + 3 \leq \frac{3}{2}\ell_1 ,$$

and $\delta_4$ by $\delta_7$. Thus in this case (6.46) and (6.47) follow from (6.16), (6.17) and the fact that $\delta_7 \to 1$ as $\delta_4 \to 1$ (uniformly under the condition $s \leq 303t$ implied by (6.45)).

In the second case (6.48) implies the following replacements of (6.13) and (6.14):

$$\sigma((\lfloor \frac{j}{s} \ell_3 \rfloor -3, \ell_2); 1, p, \mathcal{G}_{p\ell}) \geq \delta_7$$

(use periodicity again) and

$$\sigma((\lceil \frac{j+2}{s} \ell_3 \rceil + 2, \ell_2); 2, p, \mathcal{G}_{p\ell}) \geq \delta_7 \quad .$$

Thus $\ell_1$ is replaced by

$$\lfloor \frac{j}{s} \ell_3 \rfloor -3 \geq \frac{j\ell_3}{303\ell_3\ell_1^{-1}} - 4 \geq \frac{300}{303}\ell_1 - 4 \geq 32 + 16\Lambda$$

and $\ell_3$ by

$$\lceil \frac{j+2}{s} \ell_3 \rceil + 2 \leq \frac{j+2}{s} \ell_3 + 3 \leq \frac{3}{2}(\frac{j}{s} \ell_3 - 4) \leq \frac{3}{2}(\lfloor \frac{j}{s} \ell_3 \rfloor - 3)$$

(recall $\ell_1 \geq 302 + 32\Lambda, j \geq 300$). With these replacements, and $\delta_7$ instead of $\delta_3, \delta_4$, (6.16) and (6.17) give us (6.46) and (6.47). □

Now assume (6.5) and (6.6) hold. Assume also that $m_i, n_i$ satisfy (6.7) for a given $\pi \geq 1$ and take for the remainder of the proof

(6.49) $$s = 400\pi \quad .$$

We then have (6.13) with $\ell_i = n_i$, $\delta_3 = \delta_1$ and by Lemma 6.3 (6.41) holds or (6.42) holds for some $300 \leq j \leq s$. Also (6.14) holds with

$\ell_2 = m_2$, $\ell_3 = m_1$, $\delta_4 = \delta_2$. In the next lemma we take care of the case where (6.41) holds, and then we deal with the case where (6.42) holds in a sequence of reductions in the succeeding lemmas.

Lemma 6.5. Assume (6.6), (6.7) hold and (6.41) for $\ell_i = n_i$, $\delta_3 = \delta_1$ and $s = 400\pi$. Then the conclusion of Theorem 6.1 holds.

Proof: By (6.7) and (6.49)

$$(6.50)\qquad \ell_2' := \frac{302}{s}\ell_2 + 2 = \frac{302}{400\pi} n_2 + 2 \le \frac{7}{8}\frac{n_2}{\pi} \le \frac{7}{8} m_2$$

as soon as $n_2$ exceeds some $n_0(\pi)$. Then by Comment 3.3(v) and (6.6)

$$\sigma((m_1,\ell_2'); 2,p,\mathcal{G}_{p\ell}) \ge \delta_2 ,$$

while by (6.41)

$$\sigma((\ell_1,\ell_2');1,p,\mathcal{G}_{p\ell}) \ge \delta_6 .$$

Since by (6.7) $m_1 \le \pi n_1 = \pi\ell_1$ it now follows from Lemma 6.4 that for $n_1,n_2$ greater than some $n_o(\pi)$ one has

$$(6.51)\qquad \sigma((kn_1,\ell_2'); 1,p,\mathcal{G}_{p\ell}) \ge f_3(\delta_6,\delta_2,\pi,k) .$$

Since (6.41) holds for $\delta_3 = \delta_1$, $\delta_6$ here has to be read as

$$(6.52)\qquad \delta_6 = 1 - (1-\delta_1)^{-(s+2)^{-2}} .$$

(6.51) together with another application of Comment 3.3(v) gives us (6.9).

For (6.10) we use Lemma 6.2. (6.35) with $\ell_1 = m_1$, $\ell_4 = m_2$, $\delta_5 = \delta_2$ holds by virtue of (6.6). Also, if we apply (6.51) with $k = \pi$, then we find (again using Comment 3.3(v))

$$\sigma((m_1,\ell_2'); 1,p,\mathcal{G}_{p\ell}) \ge \sigma((\pi n_1,\ell_2');1,p,\mathcal{G}_{p\ell}) \ge \delta_8 ,$$

where

$$(6.53)\qquad \delta_8 = f_3(\delta_6,\delta_2,\pi,\pi) .$$

This takes the place of (6.13). Since $\ell_2' \le \frac{98}{100} m_2$ (see (6.50)) (6.37) now gives

$$\sigma((m_1,km_2);\, 2,p,\mathcal{G}_{p\ell}) \;\geq\; f_2(\delta_8,\delta_2,k)$$

and hence (6.10). Finally (6.11) follows from (6.38), (6.47) and the fact that $\delta_6 \uparrow$ , $\delta_8 \uparrow 1$ as $\delta_1 \uparrow 1$, $\delta_2 \uparrow 1$ . □

In view of the last lemma and the comments immediately before it we may assume from now on that (6.42) holds for some $300 \leq j \leq s$ and $\ell_1 = n_1$, $\ell_2$, $= n_2$ and $\delta_3 = \delta_1$ . If the first coordinate axis were also an axis of symmetry. Theorem 6.1 would now follow from (6.42) and Lemma 6.4. Without this extra symmetry assumption we must first show that (6.42) can be strengthened to (6.85) below.

For the remainder we take $\ell_1 = n_1$, $\ell_2 = n_2$, $s = 400\pi$, $\delta_3 = \delta_1$ and $300 \leq j \leq s$ such that (6.42) holds for these choices. We shall also use the following abreviations and notations:

$$\ell_5 = \lceil (j+2)s^{-1}\, \ell_2 \rceil + 2 = \lceil (j+2)s^{-1}\, n_2 \rceil + 2;$$

if $r = (v_0,e_1,\dots,e_\nu,v_\nu)$ is a horizontal crossing of $[0,\ell_1] \times [0,\ell_5]$, then $\zeta_1$ denotes the last intersection of $e_1$ with the segment $\{0\} \times [0,\ell_5]$. For any vertical line $L(a)$: $x(1) = a$ with $0 \leq a \leq \ell_1$, $\zeta(a) = \zeta(a,r)$ is the first intersection of $r$ with $L(a)$ and $Y(a) = Y(a,r)$ is the second coordinate of $\zeta(a)$. Thus $\zeta(a) = (a,Y(a))$, and if $\zeta(a) \in e_\rho$, then the segment $[\zeta_1,v_1]$ of $e_1$, together with the edges $e_2,\dots,e_{\rho-1}$ and the segment $[v_{\rho-1},\zeta(a)]$ of $e_\rho$ form a continuous curve inside $[0,a] \times [0,\ell_5]$ connecting the left and right edge of this rectangle. For $a = \ell_1/8$ we denote by $z_\ell(r)$ and $z_h(r)$ the minimum and maximum value, respectively, of the second coordinates of the points of this curve, i.e., of the piece of $r$ from $\zeta_1$ to $\zeta(\ell_1/8)$.

Lemma 6.6. Let $\delta_6$ be as in (6.52). Assume

(6.54) $P\{\exists$ occupied horizontal crossing $r$ of $[0,\ell_1] \times [0,\ell_5]$ with $z_\ell(r) > (.03)\ell_5$ or $z_h(r) < (.97)\ell_5$ and $\exists$ occupied vertical crossing of $[0,\ell_1] \times [\lceil \frac{\ell_2}{5} \rceil + 1, \lfloor \frac{j+1}{s} \ell_2 \rfloor]\} \geq \delta_9 := 1 - \sqrt{1-\delta_6}$ .

Then the conclusion of Theorem 6.1 holds.

Proof: A horizontal crossing $r$ of $[0,\ell_1] \times [0,\ell_5]$ with $z_\ell(r) > (.03)\ell_5$ contains a horizontal crossing of $[0,\ell_1/8] \times [(.03)\ell_5,\ell_5]$. Similarly a horizontal crossing of $[0,\ell_1] \times [0,\ell_5]$ with $z_h(r) < (.97)\ell_5$ contains a horizontal crossing of $[0,\ell_1/8] \times [0,(.97)\ell_5]$. Therefore (6.54) implies

$$P\{\exists \text{ occupied horizontal crossing of } [0, \frac{\ell_1}{8}] \times [(.03)\ell_5,\ell_5] \text{ or of } [0, \frac{\ell_1}{8}] \times [0,(.97)\ell_5]\} \geq \delta_9 \quad .$$

By the FKG inequality, or rather (6.21), this implies

(6.55) $$P\{\exists \text{ occupied horizontal crossing of } [0, \frac{\ell_1}{8}] \times [(.03)\ell_5,\ell_5]\} \geq 1 - \sqrt{1-\delta_9}$$

or

(6.56) $$P\{\exists \text{ occupied horizontal crossing of } [0, \frac{\ell_1}{8}] \times [0,(.97)\ell_5]\} \geq 1 - \sqrt{1-\delta_9} \quad .$$

For the sake of argument let (6.56) hold. From (6.54), Comment 3.3(v) and periodicity it also follows that

(6.57) $$P\{\exists \text{ occupied vertical crossing of } [0,\ell_1] \times [0, \lfloor \frac{j}{s}\ell_2 \rfloor - 3]\} \geq \delta_9 \quad .$$

Since $j \geq 300$, $\ell_2 = n_2$ we have for $n_2$ greater than some $n_0(\pi)$

$$(.97)\ell_5 + 1 \leq (.97)\frac{j+2}{s}\ell_2 + 4 \leq (.98)(\lfloor \frac{j}{s}\ell_2 \rfloor - 3).$$

We are therefore in the same situation as in the beginning of Lemma 6.5 and (6.9) - (6.11) for suitable $f(\cdot)$ follow from Lemmas 6.4, 6.2 and Comment 3.3(v). □

By virtue of the last lemma we only have to consider the case where (6.54) fails. Denote by $E_1$ the event in the left hand side of (6.54) and set

$$E_2 = E_2(\ell_1,\ell_5) = \{\exists \text{ occupied horizontal crossing } r \text{ of } [0,\ell_1] \times [0,\ell_5] \text{ with } z_\ell(r) \leq (.03)\ell_5 \text{ and } z_h(r) \geq (.97)\ell_5 \text{ and } \exists \text{ occupied vertical crossing of } [0,\ell_1] \times [\lceil \frac{\ell_2}{5} \rceil + 1, \lfloor \frac{j+1}{s}\ell_2 \rfloor]\} \quad .$$

Then $E_1 \cup E_2$ is the event in the left hand side of (6.42). Thus if (6.42) holds with $\delta_3 = \delta_1$, but (6.54) fails, then by virtue of (6.21)

$$(6.58) \qquad P\{E_2\} \geq 1 - \frac{(1-\delta_6)}{(1-\delta_6)^{1/2}} = \delta_9 .$$

It therefore remains to derive Theorem 6.1 if (6.58) prevails (with $\ell_1 = n_1$, $\ell_2 = n_2$, $\delta_3 = \delta_1$). First we observe that we may assume an even stronger condition than (6.58). Specifically set

$$E_3(k) \geq E_3(\ell_1,\ell_5,k) = \{ \exists \text{ occupied horizontal crossing}$$

$$r \text{ of } [0,\ell_1] \times [0,\ell_5] \text{ with } z_\ell(r) \leq (.03)\ell_5 ,$$

$$z_h(r) \geq (.97)\ell_5 \text{ and } Y(\lfloor \frac{\ell_1}{2} \rfloor, r) \in [\frac{k\ell_5}{100}, \frac{(k+1)\ell_5}{100}]\} .$$

Since $Y(\lfloor \frac{\ell_1}{2} \rfloor , r) \in [k\ell_5/100, (k+1)\ell_5/100]$ for some $0 \leq k < 100$ it follows from (6.58) that

$$P\{\bigcup_{0 \leq k < 100} E_3(k)\} = P\{E_2\} \geq \delta_9 .$$

As in (6.43), (6.44) this, together with the FKG inequality shows that for some $0 \leq k_1 < 100$

$$(6.59) \qquad P\{E_3(k_1)\} \geq \delta_{10} := 1 - (1-\delta_9)^{1/100} .$$

The next lemma will show that we can assume that the intersections of an occupied horizontal crossing of $[0,\ell_1] \times [0,\ell_5]$ with any line $L(a)$, $\frac{\ell_1}{2} \leq a \leq \ell_1$, lie with high probability in

$$(6.60) \qquad \{a\} \times [\frac{k_1 - 11}{100} \ell_5, \frac{k_1 + 12}{100} \ell_5] .$$

In order to state the lemmas to follow we need to introduce a further integer $t = t(\mathcal{G}_{p\ell})$. By Lemma A.3 there exists a vertex $v_0$ of $\mathcal{G}_{p\ell}$, an integer $\alpha \geq 1$ and a path $v_0$ on $\mathcal{G}_{p\ell}$ from $v_0$ to $v_0 + (\alpha,0)$ such that for all $n \geq 1$ the path on $\mathcal{G}_{p\ell}$ obtained by successively traversing the paths $r_0 + (k\alpha,0)$, $k = 0,1,\dots,n$ (these are translates of $v_0$) is self-avoiding. We take

$$(6.61) \qquad t = 2\lceil \text{diameter of } r_0) \rceil + 1 .$$

For later use we observe that this definition of $t$ guarantees that if $(b_1, b_2)$ is any point of $r_0$ then

(6.62) $$r_0 + (k\alpha,0) \subset [b_1 - t,\infty) \times \mathbb{R} , \; k \geq 0 \; .$$

Lemma 6.7. Assume that (6.59) holds and that there exists an integer $a \in [\frac{\ell_1}{2} , \ell_1]$ for which

(6.63) $$\begin{aligned} P\{ &\exists \text{ occupied horizontal crossing } r' \text{ of} \\ &[0,\ell_1] \times [0,\ell_5] \text{ with } z_\ell(r') \leq (.03)\ell_5 \\ &z_h(r') \geq (.97)\ell_5 \text{ and which intersects } L(a) \text{ in} \\ &\{a\} \times [0, \frac{k_1 - 11}{100} \ell_5] \cup \{a\} \times [\frac{k_1 + 12}{100} \ell_5,\ell_5]\} \\ &\geq \delta_{11} := 1 - (1-\delta_{10})^{1/12t} \end{aligned}$$

Then the conclusion of Theorem 6.1 holds.

Proof: Assume that

(6.64) $$\begin{aligned} P\{ &\exists \text{ occupied horizontal crossing } r' \text{ of} \\ &[0,\ell_1] \times [0,\ell_5] \text{ with } z_\ell(r') \leq (.03)\ell_5 , \\ &z_h(r') \geq (.97)\ell_5 \text{ and which intersects } L(a) \text{ in} \\ &\{a\} \times [0, \frac{k_1 - 11}{100}\ell_5]\} \geq 1 - (1-\delta_{11})^{1/2} \end{aligned}$$

If (6.64) does not hold, then it will become valid after replacing the interval $\{a\} \times [0, (k_1-11)\ell_5/100]$ by $\{a\} \times [(k_1+12)\ell_5/100,\ell_5]$, by virtue of (6.63) and (6.21). In this case one only has to interchange the role of top and bottom in the following argument.

The idea of the proof is now roughly as follows. If $E_3(k)$ occurs then there is an occupied path $r$ with $z_\ell(r) \leq (.03)\ell_5$, $z_h(r) \geq (.97)\ell_5$ and which contains a connection, $\rho$, between the lower edge of the rectangle .

(6.65) $$T := [0, \lfloor \frac{\ell_1}{2} \rfloor] \times [(.03)\ell_5,\ell_5]$$

and the segment

(6.66) $$I := \{\lfloor \frac{\ell_1}{2} \rfloor\} \times [\frac{k_1}{100} \ell_5, \frac{k_1 + 1}{100} \ell_5]$$

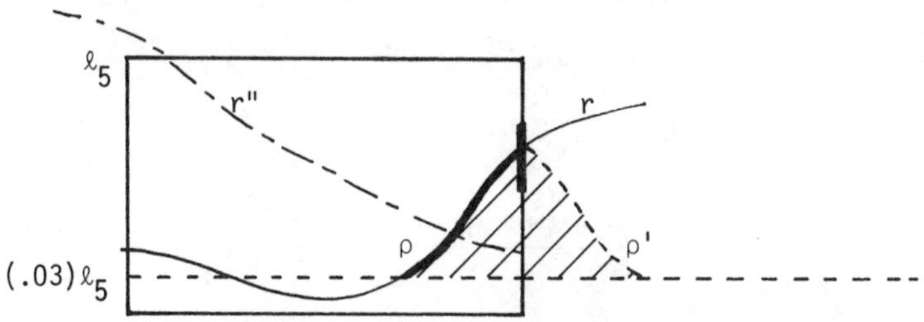


Figure 6.6. The interval I (in the right edge of the rectangle) and the connection $\rho$ are drawn boldly. The reflection $\rho'$ of $\rho$ is dashed (---) —— - —— - denotes r". The hatched region is $\Delta$

in its right edge (see Fig. 6.6). (Note that (6.64) implies $k_1 \geq 11$ so that I lies entirely in the right edge of the rectangle at (6.65). Also, $z_\ell(r) \leq (.03)\ell_5$ guarantees that r intersects the lower edge of this rectangle. Now if the translate by $(\lfloor \ell_1/2 \rfloor - a, \lfloor (.1)\ell_5 \rfloor)$ of the event in (6.64) occurs, then there exists an occupied horizontal crossing r" of

$$(6.67). \quad [\lfloor \frac{\ell_1}{2} \rfloor - a, \lfloor \frac{\ell_1}{2} \rfloor - a + \ell_1] \times [\lfloor (.1)\ell_5 \rfloor , \lfloor (.1)\ell_5 \rfloor + \ell_5]$$

which gets above the upper edge of T (in fact its highest point will be on or above the line $x(2) = (.97)\ell_5 + \lfloor (.1)\ell_5 \rfloor$. Also r" intersects $L(a + \lfloor \frac{\ell_1}{2} \rfloor - a) = L(\lfloor \frac{\ell_1}{2} \rfloor)$ in $\{a\} \times [\lfloor (.1)\ell_5 \rfloor, \frac{k_1 - 11}{100} \ell_5 + \lfloor (.1)\ell_5 \rfloor]$. Thus the intersection of r" with $L(\lfloor \frac{\ell_1}{2} \rfloor)$ lies in the right edge of T below I. Denote by $\Delta$ the "triangle" bounded by $\rho$, its reflection $\rho'$ in $L(\lfloor \frac{\ell_1}{2} \rfloor)$, and the horizontal line $\mathbb{R} \times (.03)\ell_5$. Then from the above observations we see that r" contains a point in $\Delta$ as well as points outside $\Delta$ (to wit points above the upper edge of T). Since r" is a horizontal crossing of the rectangle (6.67) it lies above the line $x(2) = \lfloor (.1)\ell_5 \rfloor - \Lambda > (.03)\ell_5$ and does not intersect the horizontal bottom edge of $\Delta$. In order to enter $\Delta$ r" must therefore intersect $\rho \cup \rho'$. A symmetry argument will show that we may assume r" intersects $\rho$ and hence r. But then $r \cup r''$ will contain an occupied vertical crossing of $[-\ell_1, \ell_1 + \Lambda] \times [(.03)\ell_5, (.97)\ell_5 + \lfloor (.1)\ell_5 \rfloor]$. By periodicity this gives us a lower bound for

(6.68) $P\{\exists$ occupied vertical crossing of

$$[0, 3\ell_1] \times [0, \lfloor (1.04)\ell_5 \rfloor - 2]\} \quad .$$

This will take the place of (6.35) and then the lemma will follow directly from Lemmas 6.4, 6.2.

Now for the details. The symmetry argument is really the main part which needs to be filled in. To do this we shall use Prop. 2.3 and this requires a slight change in the definition of $\rho$ and $\Delta$. At various places we tacitly assume $n_2$, and hence $\ell_5$, large. Let $B_1$ be a continuous path without double points, made up from edges of $\mathcal{G}_{p\ell}$ inside the strip

$$[0, \lfloor \frac{\ell_1}{2} \rfloor] \times ((.03)\ell_5, (.04)\ell_5) \ ,$$

and connecting the left and right edge of this strip. It is easy to see from the periodicity and connectedness of $\mathcal{G}_{p\ell}$ that such a $B_1$ exists as soon as $(.01)\ell_5 \geq 3s^{-1} n_2$ is larger than some constant which depends on $\mathcal{G}_{p\ell}$ only (see Lemma A.3 for a more detailed argument). Let the endpoints of $B_1$ be $(0,c)$ and $(\lfloor \frac{\ell_1}{2} \rfloor, d)$. Next define the straight line segments

$$B_2 = \{\lfloor \frac{\ell_1}{2} \rfloor\} \times [\lfloor (.1)\ell_5 \rfloor, \frac{k_1 + 1}{100} \ell_5] \ ,$$

$$A = \{\lfloor \frac{\ell_1}{2} \rfloor\} \times [d, \lfloor (.1)\ell_5 \rfloor] \quad .$$

Finally, let $C$ be the curve made up of the three segments

$\{0\} \times [c,\ell_5]$, $[0,\lfloor \ell_1/2 \rfloor] \times \{\ell_5\}$ and $\lfloor \ell_1/2 \rfloor \times [(k_1+1)\ell_5/100, \ell_5]$.

Then $B_1$, $A$, $B_2$, $C$ together make up a Jordan curve $J$ which almost equals the perimeter of $T$, except that the lower edge of $T$ has been replaced by $B_1$ (see Fig. 6.7). If $r$ is an occupied horizontal

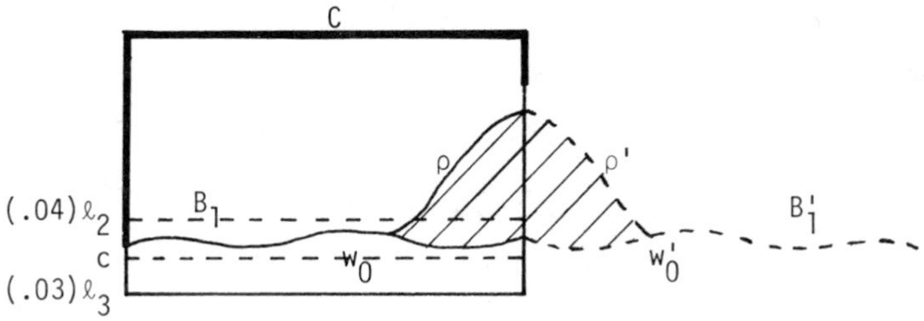


Figure 6.7. $C$ is drawn boldly. The hatched region is $\Delta$.

crossing of $[0,\ell_1] \times [0,\ell_5]$ with $z_\ell(r) \leq (.03)\ell_5$, and $Y(\lfloor \ell_1/2 \rfloor, r) \in [k_1\ell_5/100, (k_1+1)\ell_5/100]$, then since $r$ lies to the left of $L(\lfloor \ell_1/2 \rfloor)$ until it reaches $\zeta(\lfloor \ell_1/2 \rfloor, r)$ and since the piece of $r$ between $L(0)$ and $L(\ell_1/8)$ gets below $\mathbb{R} \times (.03)\ell_5$, $r$ contains an occupied path $\rho = (w_0, f_1, \dots, f_\tau, w_\tau)$ with the following properties:

(6.69) $$w_1, f_2, \dots, f_{\tau-1}, w_{\tau-1} \subset \text{int}(J),$$

(6.70) $$w_0 \in B_1 \text{ and } f_1 \setminus \{w_0\} \subset \text{int}(J),$$

(6.71) $f_\tau$ has exactly one point in common with $J$. This lies in $B_2$ and is either $w_\tau$ or the midpoint of $f_\tau$.

For (6.71) we used Comment 2.4(ii) again. The intersection of $f_\tau$ with $B_2$ is just the point $\zeta(\lfloor \ell_1/2 \rfloor, r) = (\lfloor \ell_1/2 \rfloor, Y(\lfloor \ell_1/2) \rfloor, r))$ in the notation introduced before Lemma 6.6. Also $k_1 \geq 11$. (6.70) holds because $B_1$ is made up from edges of the planar graph $\mathcal{G}_{p\ell}$; the path $r$ on $\mathcal{G}_{p\ell}$ can intersect $B_1$ only in a vertex. $w_0$ is just the first such intersection we reach when going back along $r$ from $\zeta(\lfloor \ell_1/2 \rfloor, r)$ to its initial point. The above shows that

(6.72) $$P\{\exists \text{ occupied path } \rho = (w_0, f_1, \dots, f_\tau, w_\tau) \text{ with the properties (6.69) - (6.71)}\} \geq P\{E_3(k_1)\} \geq \delta_{10}.$$

The properties (6.69) - (6.71) are just the analogues of (2.23) - (2.25) in the present context and we can therefore apply Prop. 2.3 (again with $S = \mathbb{R}^2$). If $J^-(\rho)$ denotes the component of $\text{int}(J) \setminus \rho$ which contains $A$ in its boundary, then we denote by $R$ the path $\rho$ for which $J^-(\rho)$ is minimal among all occupied paths $\rho$ satisfying (6.69) - (6.71). By Prop. 2.3 and (6.72) the probability that $R$ exists is at least $\delta_{10}$. Now for any path $\rho_0$ satisfying (6.69) - (6.71) denote by $\rho_0'$ its reflection in $L(\lfloor \ell_1/2 \rfloor)$. Also write $B_1'$ for the reflection of $B_1$ in $L(\lfloor \ell_1/2 \rfloor)$ and $\Delta = \Delta(\rho_0)$ for the triangular domain bounded by $\rho_0 \cup \rho_0'$ and the piece of $B_1 \cup B_1'$ between $w_0$ and $w_0'$, the reflection of $w_0$ in $L(\lfloor \ell_1/2 \rfloor)$. Now let $\rho_0$ be a given path which satisfies (6.69) - (6.71). Assume the translate of the event in (6.64) by $[\lfloor \ell_1/2 \rfloor - a, \lfloor (.1)\ell_5 \rfloor]$ occurs. Then there exists an occupied horizontal crossing $r''$ of the rectangle in (6.67). Moreover, the piece of $r''$ between $L(\lfloor \ell_1/2 \rfloor - a)$ and $L(\lfloor \ell_1/2 \rfloor - a + \ell_1/8)$ contains a point on or above the line $\mathbb{R} \times \{(.97)\ell_5 + \lfloor (.1)\ell_5 \rfloor\}$ (by virtue of the condition on $z_h(r')$ in (6.64)). Also $r''$ intersects $L(\lfloor \ell_1/2 \rfloor)$ in a point with second coordinate at most

$$\frac{k_1-11}{100}\ell_5 + \lfloor (.1)\ell_5 \rfloor < \frac{k_1}{100}\ell_5 .$$

Lastly, $r''$ lies above the horizontal line $\mathbb{R} \times \{\lfloor (.1)\ell_5 \rfloor - \Lambda\}$ and a fortiori does not intersect $B_1 \cup B_1'$. In particular $r''$ contains a point outside $\Delta$(since $\Delta$ lies below $\mathbb{R} \times \{\ell_5\}$) and a point on $L(\lfloor \ell_1/2 \rfloor)$ inside $\Delta$. Since $r''$ does not intersect $B_1 \cup B_1'$ it must intersect $\rho_0 \cup \rho'_0$, necessarily in a vertex of $\mathcal{G}_{p\ell}$. Therefore $r''$ contains a path $\sigma = (u_0, g_1, \ldots, g_\theta, u_\theta)$ with the properties (6.73) - (6.76) below.

(6.73) $g_1$ intersects the horizontal line $\mathbb{R} \times \{\lfloor (1.07)\ell_5 \rfloor - 1\}$.

(6.74) $(u_0, g_1, \ldots, g_\theta \setminus \{u_\theta\}) = \sigma \setminus \{u_\theta\}$ is contained in the vertical strip $[\lfloor \ell_1/2 \rfloor - a - \Lambda, \lfloor \ell_1/2 \rfloor + a + \Lambda] \times \mathbb{R}$ but outside $\overline{\Delta}(\rho_0)$. (Use the inequality $\lfloor \ell_1/2 \rfloor - a + \ell_1 \le \lfloor \ell_1/2 \rfloor + a$).

(6.75) $u_\theta \in \rho_0 \cup \rho_0'$ .

(6.76) $u_0, \ldots, u_{\theta-1}$ are occupied .

It follows from these observations and (6.64) that

$$P\{\exists \text{ a path } \sigma = (u_0, g_1, \ldots, g_\theta, u_\theta) \text{ satisfying (6.73) - (6.76)}\} \ge 1 - (1-\delta_{11})^{1/2} .$$

Since $L(\lfloor \ell_1/2 \rfloor)$ is an axis of symmetry we obtain exactly as in the derivation of (6.20) from (6.22) that

(6.77) $$P\{\exists \text{ a path } \sigma = (u_0, g_1, \ldots, g_\theta, u_\theta) \text{ satisfying (6.73), (6.74), (6.76) and } u_\theta \in \rho_0\} \ge 1-(1-\delta_{11})^{1/4}.$$

Now, by Prop. 2.3 the event $\{R = \rho_0\}$ depends only on vertices in $\bar{J}^-(\rho_0) \cup$ the reflection of $\bar{J}^-(\rho_0)$ in $L(\lfloor \ell_1/2 \rfloor)$ i.e., on vertices in $\bar{\Delta}(\rho_0)$. The event in (6.79) depends only on a set of vertices which is disjoint from the above one, and is therefore independent of $\{R = \rho_0\}$. As in the proof of (6.25) we now obtain

(6.78) $P\{R$ exists and $\exists$ path $\sigma = (u_0, g_1, \dots, g_\theta, u_\theta)$ which satisfies (6.73) and (6.76), is contained in the vertical strip $[\lfloor \ell_1/2 \rfloor - a - \Lambda, \lfloor \ell_1/2 \rfloor + a + \Lambda]$ and has $u_\theta \in R\}$

$\geq \{1 - (1-\delta_{11})^{1/4}\}\ P\{R$ exists$\}$

$\geq \{1 - (1-\delta_{11})^{1/4}\}\ \delta_{10}$ .

But if $R$ exists, then it is occupied and contains a point on $B_1$. Thus, if the event in the left hand side of (6.78) occurs, then $\sigma \cup R$ contains an occupied vertical crossing of

$$[\lfloor \frac{\ell_1}{2} \rfloor - a - \Lambda - 1, \lfloor \frac{\ell_1}{2} \rfloor + a + \Lambda + 1] \times [(.04)\ell_5, \lfloor (1.07)\ell_5 \rfloor - 1]$$

Since $a \leq \ell_1$ we obtain from periodicity and the monotonicity property in Comment 3.3(v).

$$\sigma((4\ell_1, \lfloor 1.03\ell_5 \rfloor - 3); 2, p, \mathcal{G}_{p\ell})$$
$$\geq \delta_{10} \{1 - (1-\delta_{11})^{1/4}\} \ .$$

This is just (6.35) for the values

$$\ell_4 = \lfloor (1.03)\ell_5 \rfloor - 3, \ \delta_5 = \delta_{10}\{1 - (1-\delta_{11})^{1/4}\} \ ,$$

and $\ell_1$ replaced by $4\ell_1$. But we also have

$$\sigma((\ell_1, \ell_5); 1, p, \mathcal{G}_{p\ell}) \geq \delta_9$$

(by virtue of (6.58)) as replacement for (6.13), and

$$\ell_5 \leq \frac{98}{100} (\lfloor (1.03)\ell_5 \rfloor - 3).$$

We can therefore obtain (6.9) - (6.11) again from Lemmas 6.4 and 6.2 in the same way as in Lemma 6.5. □

One more reduction is necessary. Lemma 6.7 discusses intersections of horizontal crossings with $L(a)$ for a single integer $a$. The next lemma considers the intersections with a vertical strip around such a line.

Lemma 6.8. Assume that (6.59) holds and that for the $t$ of (6.61) there exists an integer $a \in [\frac{5\ell_1}{8}, \frac{7\ell_1}{8}]$ for which

(6.79) $$P\{\exists \text{ occupied horizontal crossing } r' \text{ of } [0,\ell_1] \times [0,\ell_5] \text{ with } z_\ell(r') \le (.03)\ell_5, z_h(r') \ge (.97)\ell_5, \text{ and which contains some vertex } v = (v(1), v(2)) \text{ with } |v(1) - a| \le t \text{ and } v(2) \in [0, \frac{k_1 - 12}{100}\ell_5] \cup [\frac{k_1 + 13}{100}\ell_5, \ell_5]\} \ge \delta_{10}$$

Then the conclusion of Theorem 6.1 holds.

Proof: If the event in (6.79) occurs, then $v(1)$ must lie in one of the intervals $[b,b+1]$, $a - t \le b < a + t$ and $v(2)$ in one of the two intervals $[0, \frac{k_1 - 12}{100}\ell_5]$, $[\frac{k_1 + 13}{100}\ell_5, \ell_5]$. From the by now familiar argument using the FKG inequality it follows that one of these eventualities has a probability at least

$$\delta_{12} := 1 - (1-\delta_{10})^{1/4t} .$$

For the sake of argument let $b$ be an integer with

$$\tfrac{1}{2}\ell_1 \le a - t \le b < a + t < \ell_1$$

and such that

(6.80) $$P\{\exists \text{ occupied horizontal crossing } r' \text{ of } [0,\ell_1] \times [0,\ell_5] \text{ with } z_\ell(r') \le (.03)\ell_5, z_h(r') \ge (.97)\ell_5 \text{ and which contains a vertex } v = (v(1), v(2)) \text{ with } b \le v(1) < b + 1 \text{ and } v(2) \in [0, \frac{k_1 - 12}{100}\ell_5]\} \ge \delta_{12} .$$

If for $a = b$ or $a = b + 1$

(6.81) $$P\{\exists \text{ occupied horizontal crossing } r' \text{ of } [0,\ell_1] \times [0,\ell_5] \text{ with } z_\ell(r') \le (.03)\ell_5,\ z_h(r') \ge (.97)\ell_5 \text{ and which intersects } L(a) \text{ in } \{a\} \times [0, \frac{k_1 - 11}{100}\ \ell_5]\} \ge \delta_{11}$$

then we are done, by virtue of Lemma 6.7. Thus we may assume that (6.81) fails for $a = b$ and $a = b + 1$. The obvious generalization of (6.21) to three events together with (6.80) then gives

(6.82) $$P\{\exists \text{ occupied horizontal crossing } r' \text{ of } [0,\ell_1] \times [0,\ell_5] \text{ which intersects } L(b) \text{ only in } \{b\} \times (\frac{k_1 - 11}{100}\ \ell_5, \ell_5] \text{ and } L(b+1) \text{ only in } \{b+1\} \times (\frac{k_1 - 11}{100}\ \ell_5, \ell_5], \text{ but contains a vertex } v = (v(1), v(2)) \text{ with } b \le v(1) < b + 1,\ 0 \le v(2) \le \frac{k_1 - 12}{100}\ \ell_5\} \ge 1 - \frac{1-\delta_{12}}{(1-\delta_{11})^2} = \delta_{11}\ .$$

When the event in (6.82) occurs, then the piece of $r'$ from the last edge of $r'$ before $v$ which intersects $L(b) \cup L(b+1)$ through the first edge of $r'$ after $v$ which intersects $L(b) \cup L(b+1)$ contains a vertical crossing of $[b,b+1] \times [\frac{k_1 - 12}{100}\ \ell_5, \frac{k_1 - 11}{100}\ \ell_5]$. Thus, (6.82) and periodicity implies

(6.83) $$P\{\exists \text{ occupied vertical crossing of } [0,1] \times [0, \frac{\ell_5}{100} - 2]\} \ge \delta_{11}\ .$$

As before let $\mu$ be the number of vertices of $\mathcal{G}_{p\ell}$ in the unit square $[0,1) \times [0,1)$, and let $\Lambda$ as in (6.4) . Any vertical crossing $r'' = (w_0, f_1, \dots, f_\rho, w_\rho)$ of $[0,1] \times [0, \frac{\ell_5}{100} - 2]$ intersects all the segments $[0,1] \times \{\lfloor \frac{j\ell_5}{300\mu} \rfloor\}$, $1 \le j \le \mu + 1$. Let $w_{i(j)} = (w_{i(j)}(1), w_{i(j)}(2))$ be the last vertex on $r''$ on or below the $j^{th}$ segment of this form. Then

$$0 < w_{i(j)}(1) < 1 \quad , \quad 1 \le j \le \mu + 1,$$

while for $j \neq k$, $1 \le j,k \le \mu + 1$

$$| w_{i(j)}(2) - w_{i(k)}(2)| \ge \frac{\ell_5}{300\mu} - \Lambda - 1 \ge \frac{\ell_5}{400\mu} \quad ,$$

provided $\ell_5$ is large enough, or equivalently, $n_2 \ge n_0(\mathcal{G},\pi)$ for suitable $n_0$. Any such point $w_{i(j)}$ is the translate by a vector $(0,m)$, $m \in \mathbb{Z}$, of some vertex in $[0,1) \times [0,1)$. Thus, by Dirichlet's pigeon hole principle there must be a pair $w_{i(j)}$ and $w_{i(k)}$ with equal first coordinates, i.e., with

$$w_{i(j)} - w_{i(k)} = (0,m) \quad \text{for some integer} \quad m \ge \frac{\ell_5}{400\mu} \quad .$$

Since $1 \le j \le \mu + 1$ and

$$w_{i(j)} \in (0,1) \times [\lfloor \frac{j\ell_5}{300\mu} \rfloor - \Lambda, \lfloor \frac{j\ell_5}{300\mu} \rfloor],$$

there are at most $\lambda := (\Lambda+1)^2 \mu^2(\mu+1)^2$ possibilities for the pair $w_{i(j)}, w_{i(k)}$. Thus, by periodicity and the FKG inequality, (6.83) implies the existence of a vertex $w \in [0,1) \times [0,1)$ and integer $m \ge (400\mu)^{-1}\ell_5$ such that

(6.84) $$P\{ \exists \text{ occupied path in } [0,1] \times \mathbb{R} \text{ from } w \text{ to } w + (0,m)\} \ge \delta_{13} := 1 - (1-\delta_{11})^{1/\lambda} \quad .$$

By periodicity (6.84) remains valid if $w$ is replaced by $w + (0,jm)$. Moreover, if we combine occupied paths from $w + (0,jm)$ to $w + (0,(j+1)m)$ for $j = 0,\dots,\nu - 1$ we obtain an occupied path with possible double points from $w$ to $w + (0,\nu m)$. We can remove the double points by loop-removal (see Sect. 2.1). Since all the paths which we combined lie in the strip $[0,1] \times \mathbb{R}$ we obtain an occupied vertical crossing of $[-1,2] \times [1,\nu m-1]$. Thus, by virtue of the FKG inequality (6.84) implies

$$P\{ \exists \text{ occupied vertical crossing of } [0,3] \times [0,\nu m-2]\} \ge \delta_{13}^{\nu} \quad .$$

This, together with (6.5), implies (6.9) - (6.11)(this time we need only Lemma 6.1). □

Lemma 6.8 was the last reduction. With $t$ fixed as in (6.61) it follows from the preceding lemmas that it suffices to prove Theorem 6.1 under the additional hypotheses that (6.58) holds, but (6.79) fails for every $5\ell_1/8 \le a \le 7\ell_1/8$. Again by (6.21) we may therefore assume that for such $a$ in this interval.

(6.85) $$P\{\exists \text{ occupied horizontal crossing } r \text{ of } [0,\ell_1]\times[0,\ell_5] \text{ with } z_\ell(r) \le (.03)\ell_5,\ z_h(r) \ge (.97)\ell_5, \text{ and which intersects the strip } [a-t,\ a+t]\times\mathbb{R} \text{ only in } [a-t,\ a+t]\times[\frac{k_1-12}{100}\ell_5,\ \frac{k_1+13}{100}\ell_5]\} \ge 1-\frac{1-\delta_9}{1-\delta_{10}} \ge \delta_{10}.$$

<u>Lemma 6.9</u>. <u>If (6.85) holds for every integer</u> $a \in [\frac{5\ell_1}{8}, \frac{7\ell_1}{8}]$, <u>then the conclusion of Theorem 6.1 holds</u>.

<u>Proof</u>: Assume $0 \le k_1 \le 50$. The case $50 < k_1 < 100$ again only involves an interchange of the role of top and bottom. If the event in (6.85) occurs, then the segment of $r$ between the points where $z_\ell(r)$ and $z_h(r)$ are achieved lies (by definition of $z_\ell$ and $z_h$) in the vertical strip $[0,\ell_1/8]\times\mathbb{R}$. Consequently, by periodicity and (6.85).

(6.86) $$P\{\exists \text{ occupied vertical crossing } r' \text{ of } [\lfloor\tfrac{11}{16}\ell_1\rfloor - 1,\ \lceil\tfrac{13}{16}\ell_1\rceil + 1]\times[-(.01)\ell_5,\ (.93)\ell_5 - 1]\} \ge \delta_{10}.$$

We shall again use Prop. 2.3 to find the "right most" of the vertical crossings in (6.86). More precisely, let $v_0 \in [0,1)\times[0,1)$, $\alpha$ and $r_0$ have the properties discussed before the definition (6.61) of $t$; (see also Lemma A.3). For a suitable choice of the integers $\nu_1,\nu_2$ and $m$ the path obtained by traversing successively $r_0 + (\nu_1 + j\alpha, \nu_2)$, $j = 0,1,\dots,m$ will be a self-avoiding path $s$ on $\mathcal{G}_{p\ell}$ in the horizontal strip $\mathbb{R}\times(-(.01)\ell_5, 0)$ (provided $n_2 \ge n_0(\mathcal{G},\pi)$ again) which intersects both the vertical lines

$$L(\lfloor\tfrac{11}{16}\ell_1\rfloor - 1) \quad\text{and}\quad L(\lceil\tfrac{13}{16}\ell_1\rceil + 1).$$

Denote by $B_1$ the segment of the path $s$ from its last intersection with $L(\lfloor 11\ell_1/16 \rfloor - 1)$ to its first intersection with $L(\lceil 13\ell_1/16 \rceil + 1)$. Similarly $s'$ will be a path in the horizontal strip $\mathbb{R} \times (.92)\ell_5 -1, (.93)\ell_5 -1)$ obtained by traversing successively $r_0 + (\nu_3 + j\alpha, \nu_4)$ , $j = 0,1,\dots,m$, and $B_2$ will be the segment of $s'$ from its last intersection with $L(\lfloor \frac{11}{16} \ell_1/16 \rfloor - 1)$ to its first intersection with $L(\lceil 13\ell_1/16 \rceil + 1)$ (see Fig. 6.8).

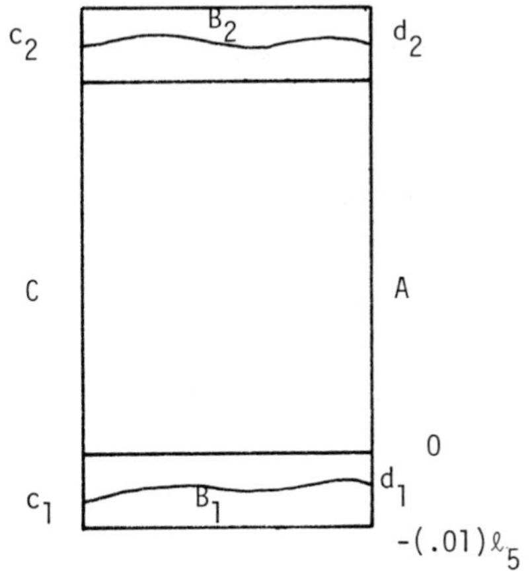


Figure 6.8

By property (6.62), if a vertical line $L(b)$ intersects $B_2$ in a point of $r_0 + (\nu_3 + j_0\alpha, \nu_4)$ then

(6.87) the paths $r_0 + (\nu_3 + j\alpha, \nu_4)$, $j_0 \le j \le m$, are contained in the halfplane $[b-t,\infty) \times \mathbb{R}$.

We denote the endpoints of $B_i$, $i = 1,2$, by

$$(\lfloor \tfrac{11}{16} \ell_1 \rfloor - 1, c_i) \text{ and } (\lceil \tfrac{13}{16} \ell_1 \rceil + 1, d_i).$$

Furthermore $A$ denotes the straightline segment $\{\lceil 13\ell_1/16 \rceil + 1\} \times [d_1, d_2]$ and $C$ the straightline segment $\{\lfloor 11\ell_1/16 \rfloor - 1\} \times [c_1, c_2]$. (see Fig. 6.8). The composition of $B_1, A, B_2$ and $C$ is a Jordan curve which we denote by $J$. If the event in (6.86) occurs, then the path $r'$ begins below $B_1$ and ends above $B_2$. Since $\mathcal{G}_{p\ell}$ is planar $r'$ intersects $B_1$ as well as $B_2$ only in vertices of $\mathcal{G}_{p\ell}$ . In particular $r'$ must contain an occupied path $\rho = (w_0, f_1, \ldots, f_\tau, w_\tau)$ with the following two properties

(6.88) $$\rho \setminus \{w_0, w_\tau\} \subset \text{int}(J)$$

(6.89) $$w_0 \in B_1, \; w_\tau \in B_2 \quad .$$

These are the analogues of (2.23) - (2.25). Again we denote the component of $\text{int}(J) \setminus \rho$ which contains $A$ in its boundary by $J^-(\rho)$ whenever $\rho$ is a path satisfying (6.88) and (6.89). Prop. 2.3 with $S = \mathbb{R}^2$ shows that as soon as such an occupied path $\rho$ exists, there also exists one with minimal $J^-(\rho)$ . As in Prop. 2.3 we denote the occupied path $\rho$ for which $J^-(\rho)$ is minimal by $R$ whenever it exists. By Prop. 2.3 and (6.86).

(6.90) $$P\{ \; R \text{ exists } \} \geq P\{ \exists \text{ occupied path } \rho \text{ which satisfies (6.88) and (6.89)} \} \geq \delta_{10} \quad .$$

Now assume that $R$ exists and equals some fixed path $\rho_0 = (w_0, f_1, \ldots, f_\tau, w_\tau)$ . Set

$$b = w_\tau(1) \;, \; a = \lfloor b \rfloor = \lfloor w_\tau(1) \rfloor \;,$$

and denote the highest intersection of $\rho_0$ with $L(b)$ by $(b, b_2)$. Since the endpoint of $\rho_0$, $w_\tau = (w_\tau(1), w_\tau(2))$ lies on $L(b)$ we have $b_2 \geq w_\tau(2)$. We write $I$ for the segment $\{b\} \times [b_2, \lfloor 5\ell_5/4 \rfloor]$ of $L(b)$, and $\rho_1$ for the segment of $\rho_0$ from its initial point $w_0$ to the intersection $(b, b_2)$ of $\rho_0$ and $L(b)$. Then $\rho_1 \cup I$ contains a crosscut of the rectangle

$$T := (\lfloor \tfrac{11}{16} \ell_1 \rfloor - 1, \lceil \tfrac{13}{16} \ell_1 \rceil + 1) \times (0, \lfloor 5\ell_5/4 \rfloor),$$

because $\rho_0$ begins on $B_1$ which lies below the lower edge of this rectangle (see Fig. 6.9). This crosscut divides $T$ in a left and a right component, $w_\tau$ lies on $B_2$, hence belongs to $(r_0 + (\nu_3 + j_0\alpha, \nu_4)$ for some $j_0$. The piece of $B_2$ which belongs to $Fr(J^-(\rho_0))$ then consists of pieces of $r_0 + (\nu_3 + j\alpha, \nu_4)$ with $j_0 \leq j \leq m$. By (6.87) and the construction of $B_2$ $B_2 \cap Fr(J^-(\rho_0))$ contained in the rectangle

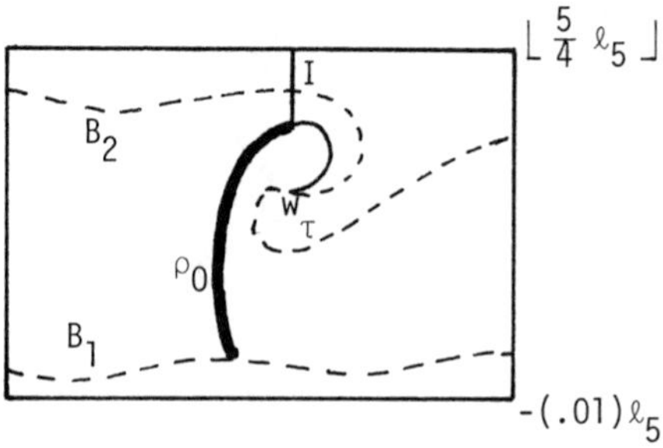


Figure 6.9 $B_1$ and $B_2$ are dashed. $\rho_0$ is drawn solidly; the boldly drawn part of $\rho_0$ is $\rho_1$.

$$[b-t, \lceil \frac{13}{16}\ell_1 \rceil + 1] \times [(.92)\ell_5 - 1, (.93)\ell_5] \quad .$$

We show first that this implies

$$(6.91) \qquad B_2 \cap Fr(J^-(\rho_0)) \cap \text{ left component of } T$$
$$\subset [b - t, b + t - 1] \times [(.92)\ell_5 - 1, (.93)\ell_5]$$

From the preceding it follows that it suffices to show that the left hand side of (6.91) is contained in $(-\infty, b + t - 1] \times \mathbb{R}$. Now assume $x$ is a point of $r_0 + (\nu_3 + j\alpha, \nu_4) \cap Fr(J^-(\rho_0))$ for some $j_0 \le j \le m$. If $r_0 + (\nu_3 + j\alpha, \nu_4)$ lies entirely strictly to the right of $L(b)$, then so do $r_0 + (\nu_3 + j'\alpha, \nu_4)$ for $j' > j$, because $\alpha \ge 1$. In this case there is a path from $x$ to the right edge of $T$ which consists of pieces of $r_0 + (\nu_3 + j'\alpha, \nu_4)$, $j' = j, j+1, \dots, m$. This path neither intersects $I \subset L(b)$, nor does it intersect $\rho_0$, since $\rho_0 \cap B_2 = \{w_\tau\}$. Consequently, $x$ can be connected in $T \setminus \rho_0 \cup I$ to the right edge of $T$, and $x$ cannot lie in the left component of $T$. If on the other hand $r_0 + (\nu_3 + j\alpha, \nu_4)$ is not entirely strictly to the right of $L(b)$, then $r_0 + (\nu_3 + j\alpha, \nu_4) \subset (-\infty, b + t - 1] \times \mathbb{R}$ by the choice of $t$ in (6.61). Thus (6.91) holds.

Assume now that the translate of the event in (6.85) by $(0, \lfloor \frac{\ell_5}{4} \rfloor)$ occurs. Then there exists an occupied horizontal crossing $r$ of

$$[0,\ell_1] \times [\lfloor \frac{\ell_5}{4} \rfloor, \lfloor \frac{\ell_5}{4} \rfloor + \ell_5] = [0,\ell_1] \times [\lfloor \frac{\ell_5}{4} \rfloor, \lfloor \frac{5\ell_5}{4} \rfloor]$$

which intersects the strip $[a - t, a + t] \times \mathbb{R}$ only in

$$[a - t, a + t] \times [\frac{k_1 + 12}{100} \ell_5, \frac{k_1 + 38}{100} \ell_5] .$$

Moreover, $r$ passes through a point $z = (z(1), z(2))$ with

$$0 \le z(1) \le \frac{\ell_1}{8} , \ z(2) \ge (1.22)\ell_5 - 1$$

before it reaches $L(\frac{\ell_1}{8})$. Since this horizontal crossing $r$ begins to the left of $L(\lfloor \frac{11\ell_1}{16} \rfloor - 1)$ and ends to the right of $L(\lceil \frac{13\ell_1}{16} \rceil + 1)$ it must intersect the crosscut of $T$ contained in $\rho_1 \cup I$. We claim that $r$ intersects $\rho_0$, but not $I$, and does not hit $Fr(J^-(\rho_0))$ before it hits $\rho_0$). To prove this claim we first note that $r$ cannot intersect

$$I \cup \{B_2 \cap Fr(J^-(\rho_0)) \cap \text{left component of } T\} ,$$

since this set is contained in

$$[a - t, a + t] \times [(.92)\ell_5 - 1, \lfloor 5\ell_5/4 \rfloor] ,$$

which is disjoint from

$$[a - t, a + t] \times [\frac{k_1 + 12}{100} \ell_5 , \frac{k_1 + 38}{100} \ell_5] .$$

To see this we use (6.91) and the facts $b_2 \ge w(2) \ge (.92)\ell_5 - 1$ (recall that the lower endpoint of $I$, $(b,b_2)$ lies no lower than $w_\tau \in B_2$) and $k_1 \le 50$. In particular $r$ does not intersect $I$ and must intersect $\rho_0$. Moreover, $r$ does not get below the horizontal line $\mathbb{R} \times \{\lfloor \ell_5/4 \rfloor\}$ and therefore cannot hit $B_1$ or the lower edge of $T$. Neither does $r$ get above the top edge of $T$ and therefore cannot enter the right component of $T$ through the upper edge of $T$ without hitting $\rho_0 \cup I$ first. Lastly, since $r$ stays between the upper and lower edge of $T$ and begins to the left of $T$, it cannot reach the right edge of $T$ without hitting $\rho_0 \cup I$. All in all we see that $r$ cannot enter the right component of $T$ without hitting $\rho_0 \cup I$. A fortiori $r$ cannot hit

$$B_2 \cap Fr(J^-(\rho_0)) \cap \text{right component of } T$$

without hitting $\rho_0 \cup I$ first. Combining the above observations we see that $r$ must hit $\rho_0 \cup I$ (and hence $\rho_0$) before hitting the other parts of $Fr(J^-(\rho_0))$ (since these other parts lie in $\mathbb{R} \times (-\infty, 0] \cup B_2 \cup$ right edge of $T$. This substantiates our claim.

An immediate consequence of the claim is that the piece of $r$ from its initial point to its first intersection with $\rho_0$ is a path $s = (u_0, g_1, \dots, g_\sigma, u_\sigma)$ with the following properties:

(6.92) $$s \setminus \{u_\sigma\} = (u_0, g_1, \dots, u_{\sigma-1}, g_\sigma \setminus \{u_\sigma\}) \subset (\bar{J}^-(\rho_0))^c, \quad \text{and} \quad s \cap \rho_0 = \{u_\sigma\}$$

(6.93) $s$ is contained in the horizontal strip
$$[-\Lambda, \ell_1] \times \mathbb{R},$$

(6.94) $s$ contains a point $z = (z(1), z(2))$ with
$$z(2) \geq (1.22)\ell_5 - 1 .$$

and

(6.95) $u_0, \dots, u_{\sigma-1}$ are occupied

Clearly the existence of such a path $s$ depends only on the occupancies of vertices outside $\bar{J}^-(\rho_0)$, and by Prop. 2.3, these are independent of the event $\{R = \rho_0\}$. Just as in the proof (6.25) - in particular the estimates following (6.28) - it follows from this and (6.85) that

(6.96) $$P\{R = \rho_0 \text{ and there exists a path } s \text{ with the properties } (6.92) - (6.95)\} \geq \delta_{10} P\{R = \rho_0\} .$$

Finally observe that if $R = \rho_0$ and there exists a path $s$ with the properties (6.92) - (6.95) then $s$ and $\rho_0$ together contain an occupied path from the initial point of $\rho_0$ on $B_1$, (and hence below $\mathbb{R} \times \{0\}$) via $u_\sigma$ (the intersection of $\rho_0$ and $s$) to $z$ above the horizontal line $\mathbb{R} \times \{(1.22)\ell_5 - 1\}$. This path also lies in the strip $[-\Lambda, \ell_1] \times \mathbb{R}$ and consequently $\rho_0 \cup s$ contains an occupied vertical crossing of $[-\Lambda - 1, \ell_1 + 1] \times [0, (1.22)\ell_5 - 1]$. Thus,

$$P\{\exists \text{ occupied vertical crossing of } [-\Lambda-1, \ell_1+1] \times [0,(1.22)\ell_5 - 1]\} \geq \sum_{\substack{\rho_0 \text{ satisfying} \\ (6.88),\ (6.89).}} P\{R = \rho_0 \text{ and there exists a path } s \text{ with properties (6.92) - (6.95)}\}$$

$$\geq \delta_{10} \sum_{\substack{\rho_0 \text{ satisfying} \\ (6.88),\ (6.89)}} P\{R = \rho_0\} \quad \text{(by (6.96))}$$

$$\geq \delta_{10}^2 \text{ (by (6.90)}.$$

By periodicity this implies for $\ell_1 = n_1 \geq 2\Lambda + 3$,

$$\sigma((2\ell_1, (1.22)\ell_5 - 1); 2, p, \mathcal{G}_{p\ell}) \geq \delta_{10}^2 \ .$$

Since we also have

$$\sigma((\ell_1, \ell_5); 1, p, \mathcal{G}_{p\ell}) \geq \delta_{10}$$

(by virtue of (6.85)), and $(1.22)\ell_5 - 1 \geq \frac{100}{98}\ell_5$ we can now obtain (6.9) - (6.11) from Lemma 6.4 and 6.2 in the same way as in Lemma 6.5 (provided $n_i \geq n_0(\mathcal{G},\pi)$ again). □

As pointed out before Lemma 6.9 takes care of the last case and the proof of Theorem 6.1 is therefore complete. □

Proof of Corollary 6.1. It is easy to see that if $r_1$ and $r_2$ are occupied horizontal crossings of $[-2(\pi+3)n_1, 2(\pi+3)n_1] \times [-3n_2, -n_2]$ and $[-2(\pi+3)n_1, 2(\pi+3)n_1] \times [n_2, 3n_2]$, respectively, and if $r_3$

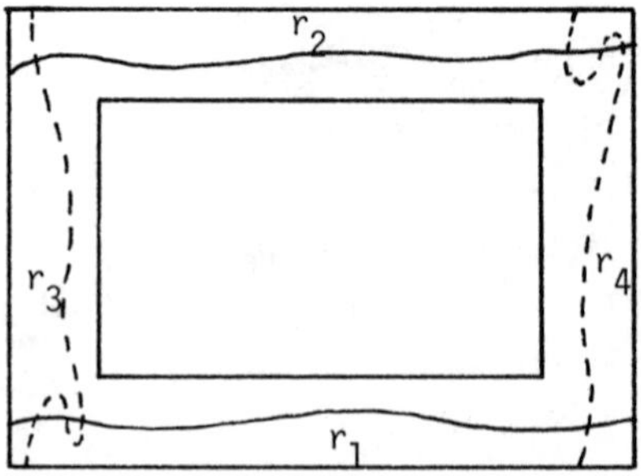


Figure 6.10

and $r_4$ are occupied vertical crossings of $[-2(\pi+3)n_1, -(\pi+3)n_1] \times [-3n_2, 3n_2]$ and $[(\pi+3)n_1, 2(\pi+3)n_1] \times [-3n_2, 3n_2]$, respectively, then $r_1 \cup r_2 \cup r_3 \cup r_4$ contains an occupied circuit surrounding 0 inside the annulus $[-2(\pi+3)n_1, 2(\pi+3)n_1] \times [-3n_2, 3n_2] \setminus (-(\pi+3)n_1, (\pi+3)n_1) \times (-n_2, n_2)$. (See Fig. 6.10).

Therefore the left hand side of (6.12) is at least equal to the probability of such $r_1$-$r_4$ existing. However, by the FKG inequality this is at least

$$\prod_{i=1}^{4} P\{r_i \text{ exists}\} \geq f^4(\delta_1, \delta_2, \pi, 4\pi+12)$$

(by (6.9) and (6.10)).

## 7. PROOFS OF THEOREMS 3.1 AND 3.2.

The first step is to show that for a parameter point $p_0$ which satisfies Condition A or B of Ch. 3 there exist large rectangles for which the crossing probabilities in both the horizontal and vertical direction are bounded away from zero. The RSW theorem will then show that with $P_{p_0}$-probability one there exist arbitrarily large occupied circuits on $\mathcal{G}$ surrounding the origin. From this it follows that there are no infinite vacant clusters on $\mathcal{G}^*$ under $P_{p_0}$[1]. An interchange of the roles of $\mathcal{G}$ and $\mathcal{G}^*$ and of occupied and vacant then shows that there is also no percolation on $\mathcal{G}$ under $P_{p_0}$. This is just the content of (3.43), which is the most important statement in Theorem 3.1(i). Clearly the above implies that for $p'$, $p''$ such that $p'(i) \leq p_0(i) \leq p''(i)$, $i = 1,\dots,\lambda$ also

$$P_{p'}\{\#W(v) = \infty\} = 0 \quad \text{and} \quad P_{p''}\{\#W^*(v) = \infty\} = 0.$$

The above conclusions are basically already in Harris' beautiful paper (Harris (1960)). The first proof that percolation actually occurs for $p'' >> p_0$ is in Kesten (1980a). The proof given below is somewhat simpler because we now use Russo's formula (Prop. 4.2) which only appeared in Russo (1981). Actually we prove the dual statement that for $p' << p_0$ infinite vacant clusters occur on $\mathcal{G}^*$. An easy argument shows that it suffices to show $E_{p'}\{\#W(v)\} < \infty$, and by Theorem 5.1 this will follow once we prove that the crossing-probabilities $\tau(\bar{N};1,p')$ and $\tau(\bar{N};2,p')$ of some large rectangles are small for $p' << p$. This is done by showing that $\frac{d}{dt}\tau(\bar{N};i,p(t))$ is "large" for $0 \leq t \leq 1$, $p(t) = (1-t)p' + tp_0$. By Russo's formula, this amounts to showing that there are many pivotal sites (see Def. 4.2) for the events

(7.1) $\quad A(\bar{N};i) = \{\exists$ occupied crossing in the i-direction of $T(\bar{N};i)\}$.

---

1) In this part we shall use some simplifications suggested by S. Kotani.

This last step is the same as in Kesten (1980a). The pivotal sites for $A(\bar{N};1)$ for instance are found more or less as the sites on the lowest occupied horizontal crossing of $T(\bar{N};1)$ which have a vacant connection on $\mathcal{G}^*$ to the upper edge of $T(\bar{N};1)$ (see Ex. 4.2(iii)). To enable us to talk about a "lowest horizontal crossing" the actual proofs are carried out on $\mathcal{G}_{p\ell}, \mathcal{G}^*_{p\ell}$, rather than on $\mathcal{G}, \mathcal{G}^*$. For the remainder of this chapter $(\mathcal{G},\mathcal{G}^*)$ is a matching pair of periodic graphs imbedded in $\mathbb{R}^2$, based on $(\mathcal{M},\mathcal{F})$ and $\mathcal{G}_{p\ell}, \mathcal{G}^*_{p\ell}$ their planar modifications (see Ch.2.2, 2.3). $\mathcal{V}_1,\dots,\mathcal{V}_\lambda$ is a periodic partition of the vertices of $\mathcal{G}$ (and hence of the vertices of $\mathcal{G}^*$). For $p \in \mathcal{P}_\lambda$, $P_p$ is the corresponding $\lambda$-parameter periodic probability measure (see Ch.3.2). $P_p$ is always extended to a measure on the occupancy configurations of $\mathcal{G}_{p\ell}$ and $\mathcal{G}^*_{p\ell}$ by taking the central vertices of $\mathcal{G}_{p\ell}$ occupied and those of $\mathcal{G}^*_{p\ell}$ vacant, i.e.,

(7.2) $\quad P_p\{\omega(v) = +1\} = 1$ if $v$ is a central vertex of some face $F \in \mathcal{F}$,

(7.3) $\quad P_p\{\omega(v) = -1\} = 1$ if $v$ is a central vertex of some face $F \in \mathcal{F}^*$.

Lastly, we assume that the second coordinate axis is an axis of symmetry for $\mathcal{G}, \mathcal{G}^*$ and the partition $\mathcal{V}_1,\dots,\mathcal{V}_\lambda$. As we saw in Comment 2.4 (iii) we may then also take $\mathcal{G}_{p\ell}$ and $\mathcal{G}^*_{p\ell}$ symmetric with respect to the vertical line $x(1)=0$, and by periodicity also with respect to any line $x(1)=k$, $k \in \mathbb{Z}$. We always assume that $\mathcal{G}_{p\ell}$ and $\mathcal{G}^*_{p\ell}$ have been imbedded in this symmetric way.

<u>Lemma 7.1.</u> <u>Assume that</u> $p_0 \in \mathcal{P}_\lambda$ <u>satisfies Condition A in Ch. 3.3 and that</u>

(7.4) $$\bar{0} \ll p_0 \ll \bar{1} .$$

<u>Then there exists a vector</u> $\bar{\Lambda} = (\Lambda(1),\Lambda(2))$ <u>and a sequence</u> $\{\bar{m}_n = (m_{n1},m_{n2})\}_{n\geq 1}$ <u>of integral vectors such that</u> $m_{ni} \to \infty$ $(n \to \infty,$ $i = 1,2)$ <u>and such that for all large n (with</u> $\delta$ <u>as in Condition A)</u>

(7.5) $$\sigma(\bar{m}_n;1,p_0) \geq \delta \quad \text{and} \quad \sigma(\bar{m}_n+\bar{\Lambda};2,p_0) \geq \delta .$$

<u>Also, for some sequence</u> $\{m^*_n\}_{n\geq 1}$ <u>of integral vectors with</u> $\bar{m}^*_n(i) \to \infty$ $(n \to \infty;\ i = 1,2)$ <u>and a vector</u> $\bar{\Lambda}^*$

(7.6) $\sigma^*(\overline{m}_n^*;1,p_0) \geq \delta$ and $\sigma^*(\overline{m}_n^* + \overline{\Lambda}^*;2,p_0) \geq \delta$

eventually.

Proof: First we show that there exists a constant $C = C(\mathcal{G},p_0)$ such that

(7.7) $\lim_{n\to\infty} \sigma((n,e^{Cn});1,p_0) = 1$ and $\lim_{n\to\infty} \sigma((e^{Cn},n);2,p_0) = 1.$

We prove the first relation in (7.7). Choose $\Lambda_3 = \Lambda_3(\mathcal{G})$ such that each horizontal (vertical) strip of height $\Lambda_3$ (width $\Lambda_3$) possesses a horizontal (vertical) crossing on $\mathcal{M}$ (and hence also on $\mathcal{G}$, as well as on $\mathcal{G}^*$). Such a $\Lambda_3$ exists by Lemma A.3. We also pick a constant $\Lambda = \Lambda(\mathcal{G},\mathcal{G}^*)$ for which

(7.8) diameter (e) $\leq \Lambda$ for each edge e of $\mathcal{G}$ or $\mathcal{G}^*$ or $\mathcal{G}_{p\ell}$ or $\mathcal{G}_{p\ell}^*$.

We set

(7.9) $\mu = \mu(\mathcal{G},\mathcal{G}^*)$ = number of vertices which belong to $\mathcal{G}$ or $\mathcal{G}^*$ in $[0,1)\times[0,1)$.

Now consider the strips

$$S_k := [0,n]\times[2k\Lambda_3,(2k+1)\Lambda_3] .$$

Each $S_k$ contains a horizontal crossing of at most

$$(n+2\Lambda)\Lambda_3\mu \leq 2\Lambda_3\mu n$$

vertices, for n sufficiently large. Therefore

$$\begin{aligned} &P_{p_0}\{\exists \text{ occupied horizontal crossing on } \mathcal{G} \text{ of } S_k\} \\ &\geq [\min_{v\in\mathcal{G}} P_{p_0}\{v \text{ is occupied}\}]^{2\Lambda_3\mu n} \\ &\geq e^{-\gamma n} \end{aligned}$$

for some $\gamma = \gamma(p_0,\mathcal{G}) < \infty$. Finally, since the $S_k$ are disjoint, we have for $C > \gamma$

$$\sigma((n,e^{Cn});1,p_0) = P_{p_0}\{\exists \text{ occupied horizontal crossing on } \mathcal{G}$$
$$\text{of } [0,n]\times[0,e^{Cn}]\} \geq P_{p_0}\{\exists \text{ occupied horizontal crossing on}$$
$$\mathcal{G} \text{ of some } S_k \text{ with } 1 \leq k \leq \frac{1}{2\Lambda_3}e^{Cn}-1\}$$
$$\geq 1-(1-e^{-\gamma n})^{(2\Lambda_3)^{-1}e^{Cn}-1} \to 1 \quad (n\to\infty) .$$

This proves (7.7).

Now let $C$ be such that (7.7) holds. For the sake of argument assume that the implication in (3.36) is valid for $j = 2$. Let $n$ be so large that $\sigma((n,\exp Cn);1,p_0) \geq \frac{1}{2}$. We can then choose $m = m(n)$ as the smallest integer $\leq \exp Cn$ for which

$$\sigma((n,m);1,p_0) \geq \frac{1}{2} . \tag{7.10}$$

In exactly the same way as we proved (7.7) we prove

$$\lim_{n\to\infty} \sigma^*((n,\tfrac{1}{C}\log n);2,p_0) = \lim_{k\to\infty} P\{\exists \text{ vacant vertical crossing of } [0,e^{Ck}]\times[0,k] \text{ on } \mathcal{G}^*\} = 1. \tag{7.11}$$

But if there exists a vacant vertical crossing $r$ of $[0,n_1]\times[0,n_2]$ for some $n_1$, $n_2$, then there cannot be an occupied horizontal crossing $r'$ of $[0,n_1]\times[0,n_2]$. For $r$ and $r'$ would have to intersect, necessarily in a vertex of $\mathcal{M}$ (see Comment 2.2 (vii)) and this vertex in $r \cap r'$ would have to be vacant as well as occupied. This is clearly impossible. Consequently

$$\sigma((n_1,n_2);1,p_0) \leq 1-\sigma^*((n_1,n_2);2,p_0). \tag{7.12}$$

Taking $n_1 = n$, $n_2 = \frac{1}{C}\log n$ we obtian from (7.11) and (7.12) that

$$\sigma((n,\tfrac{1}{C}\log n);1,p_0) \to 0 \quad (n\to\infty).$$

Comparing this with (7.10) and using the monotonicity property of $\sigma$ (Comment 3.3 (v)) we see that

$$m(n) \geq \frac{1}{C}\log n \quad \text{eventually.} \tag{7.13}$$

We now use Prop. 2.2 to prove that the inequality in (7.12) can almost be reversed. More precisely, let

$$\Lambda_4 = \lceil \Lambda_3 + \Lambda \rceil + 1$$

and assume $n_1, n_2 > 2\Lambda_4$. Then for any $p \in \mathcal{P}_\lambda$ one has

$$(7.14) \qquad \sigma((n_1,n_2);1,p) + \sigma^*((n_1 + 2\Lambda_4, n_2 - 2\Lambda_4);2,p) \geq 1$$

as well as

$$(7.15) \qquad \sigma((n_1 + 2\Lambda_4, n_2 - 2\Lambda_4);2,p) + \sigma^*((n_1,n_2);1,p) \geq 1 .$$

We only prove (7.14). For (7.15) we only need to interchange the roles of $\mathcal{G}$ and $\mathcal{G}^*$ and of occupied and vacant. To prove (7.14) we take a self-avoiding vertical crossing $r_1$ on $\mathcal{M}$ of $[-\Lambda_4,-\Lambda-1] \times [0,n_2]$. Such a vertical crossing exists by Lemma A.3 and our choice of $\Lambda_3$. Similarly we take a selfavoiding vertical crossing $r_3$ on $\mathcal{M}$ of $[n_1 + \Lambda + 1, n_1 + \Lambda_4] \times [0,n_2]$ and horizontal crossings $r_2$ and $r_4$ of $[-\Lambda_4, n_1 + \Lambda_4] \times [\Lambda + 1, \Lambda_4]$ and $[-\Lambda_4, n_1 + \Lambda_4] \times [n_2 - \Lambda_4, n_2 - \Lambda - 1]$, respectively (see Fig. 7.1). Once again we remind the reader of the observa-

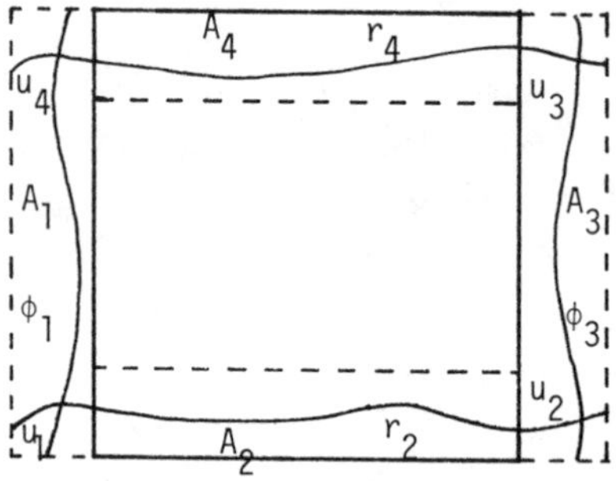


Figure 7.1 The solid rectangle is $[0,n_1] \times [0,n_2]$; the outer dashed rectangle is $[-\Lambda_4, n_1+\Lambda_4] \times [0,n_2]$; the inner dashed rectangle is $[0,n_1] \times [\Lambda_4, n_2-\Lambda_4]$.

tion at the beginning of Sect. 2.3: Since $\mathcal{M}$ is planar, and $r_i$ is self-avoiding, the curve made up from the edges of $r_i$ is a simple curve. $r_1$ contains therefore a simple curve, $\phi_1$ say, inside the rectangle $[-\Lambda_4,-\Lambda-1]\times[0,n_2]$, and connecting the top and bottom edge of this rectangle. Similarly $r_3$ contains a simple curve $\phi_3$ inside $[n_1+\Lambda+1,n_1+\Lambda_4]$, and connecting the top and bottom edge of this rectangle. Now, both $r_2$ and $r_4$ must intersect $\phi_1$ as well as $\phi_3$. Starting from the left endpoint of $r_2$ $(r_4)$ let $u_1$ $(u_3)$ be the last intersection of $r_2$ $(r_4)$ with $\phi_1$ and $u_2$ $(u_4)$ the first intersection of $r_2$ $(r_4)$ with $\phi_3$. Denote the closed segment of $\phi_1$ from $u_4$ to $u_1$ by $A_1$, the closed segment of $r_2$ from $u_1$ to $u_2$ by $A_2$, the closed segment of $\phi_3$ from $u_2$ to $u_3$ by $A_3$, and the closed segment of $r_4$ from $u_3$ to $u_4$ by $A_4$. By construction $A_1$ is strictly to the left of the vertical line $x(1) = -\Lambda$ and $A_3$ to the right of $x(1) = n_1 + \Lambda$. Similarly $A_2$ is below the horizontal line $x(2) = \Lambda_4$ and $A_4$ above $x(2) = \Lambda_4$. In addition, the $A_i$ are simple curves. It is not hard to see from this that the composition of $A_1,A_2,A_3$ and $A_4$ is a Jordan curve, J say. Any path on $\mathcal{G}$ inside $\bar{J} = J \cup \text{int}(J)$ from a vertex on $A_1$ to a vertex on $A_3$ has to contain a horizontal crossing of $[0,n_1]\times[0,n_2]$, since $A_2$ lies strictly above the horizontal line $x(2) = 0$ and $r_4$ strictly below $x(2) = n_2$. If all vertices on $r$ in $\text{int}(J)$ are occupied then $r$ contains an occupied horizontal crossing of $[0,n_1]\times[0,n_2]$. Thus, if there does not exist an occupied horizontal crossing of $[0,n_1]\times[0,n_2]$, then no path $r$ of the above nature can exist. By Prop. 2.2 this implies the existence of a vacant path $r^*$ on $\mathcal{G}^*$ and inside $\bar{J}\setminus A_1 \cup A_3$ with initial point on $\mathring{A}_2$ and final point on $\mathring{A}_4$. Finally, any such path $r^*$ contains a vacant vertical crossing of $[-\Lambda_4,n_1+\Lambda_4]\times[\Lambda_4,n_2-\Lambda_4]$. For the crossing probabilities this implies

$$
\begin{aligned}
1-\sigma((n_1,n_2);1,p) &= P_p\{\text{there does not exist an occupied}\\
&\quad \text{horizontal crossing of } [0,n_1]\times[0,n_2] \text{ on } \mathcal{G}\}\\
&\le P_p\{\exists \text{ vacant vertical crossing of } [-\Lambda_4,n_1+\Lambda_4]\times[\Lambda_4,n_2-\Lambda_4]\\
&\quad \text{on } \mathcal{G}^*\} = \sigma^*((n_1+2\Lambda_4,n_2-2\Lambda_4);2,p)
\end{aligned}
$$

(use periodicity for the last equality). This proves (7.14).

It is easy now to complete the proof. For $n_2 > 2\Lambda_4$ and $m(n)-1 \ge \frac{1}{C}\log n-1 > 2\Lambda_4$ we have (7.10) as well as

$$\sigma((n,m(n)-1);1,p_0) < \frac{1}{2}, \tag{7.16}$$

by virtue of the definition of $m(n)$. Then, by (7.14)

$$\sigma^*((n+2\Lambda_4, m(n)-2\Lambda_4-1);2,p_0) \geq \frac{1}{2} ,$$

and finally, by (3.36) in Condition A

$$\sigma(n+2\Lambda_4-\rho_1^*, m(n)-2\Lambda_4-1-\rho_2^*);2,p_0) \geq \delta .$$

This, together with (7.10) implies (7.5) with $\bar{m}_n = (n,m(n))$ and $\bar{\Lambda} = (2\Lambda_4-\rho_1^*, -2\Lambda_4-1-\rho_2^*)$. When (3.36) holds for $j = 1$, then one merely has to interchange the roles of the first and second coordinate. To prove (7.6) one interchanges the roles of $\mathcal{G}$ and $\mathcal{G}^*$ in the above proof. □

Lemma 7.2. Assume that $p_0$ satisfies (7.4) and Condition A or B in Ch. 3.3. Then there exist sequences of vectors $\{\bar{N}_\ell = (N_{\ell 1}, N_{\ell 2})\}_{\ell \geq 1}$, $\{\bar{M}_\ell = (M_{\ell 1}, M_{\ell 2})\}_{\ell \geq 1}$, and for each integer $k$ a number $\delta_k > 0$ such that

(7.17) $$N_{\ell i} \to \infty \quad , M_{\ell i} \to \infty , \; i = 1,2, \text{ as } \ell \to \infty ,$$

(7.18) $$\sigma((kN_{\ell 1}, N_{\ell 2});1,p_0,\mathcal{G}_{p\ell}) \geq \delta_k > 0,$$

$$\sigma((N_{\ell 1}, kN_{\ell 2});2,p_0,\mathcal{G}_{p\ell}) \geq \delta_k > 0,$$

and

(7.19) $$\sigma^*((kM_{\ell 1}, M_{\ell 2});1,p_0,\mathcal{G}_{p\ell}) \geq \delta_k > 0,$$

$$\sigma^*((M_{\ell 1}, kM_{\ell 2});2,p_0,\mathcal{G}_{p\ell}) \geq \delta_k > 0.$$

Moreover

(7.20) $$P_{p_0}\{ \exists \text{ occupied circuit on } \mathcal{G}_{p\ell} \text{ surrounding } 0$$
$$\text{and inside the annulus } [-2N_{\ell 1}, 2N_{\ell 1}] \times [-2N_{\ell 2}, 2N_{\ell 2}] \setminus$$
$$(-N_{\ell 1}, N_{\ell 1}) \times (-N_{\ell 2}, N_{\ell 2})\} \geq \delta_4^4,$$

and

(7.21) $P_{p_0}\{\exists$ vacant circuit on $\mathcal{G}^*_{p\ell}$ surrounding $0$ and inside the annulus $[-2M_{\ell 1},2M_{\ell 1}]\times[-2M_{\ell 2},2M_{\ell 2}]\setminus(-M_{\ell 1},M_{\ell 1})\times(-M_{\ell 2},M_{\ell 2})\}\geq\delta_4^4.$

Proof: Again we restrict ourselves to proving (7.18) and (7.20). First assume Condition A is satisfied. By the last lemma we then have (7.5). With $\Lambda$ as in (7.8) this implies, by virtue of Lemma 2.1b,

(7.22) $$\sigma((m_{n1}-2\Lambda,m_{n2}+2\Lambda);1,p_0,\mathcal{G}_{p\ell})\geq\delta \quad \text{and}$$
$$\sigma((m_{n1}+\Lambda(1)+2\Lambda,m_{n2}+\Lambda(2)-2\Lambda);2,p_0,\mathcal{G}_{p\ell})\geq\delta$$

(Basically an occupied horizontal crossing on $\mathcal{G}$ is turned into a horizontal crossing on $\mathcal{G}_{p\ell}$ by inserting central vertices of $\mathcal{G}$. These central vertices are occupied with probability one by virtue of (7.2). The resulting horizontal crossing on $\mathcal{G}_{p\ell}$ is therefore again occupied. The same argument applies to vertical crossings.) We can now apply the RSW theorem (Theorem 6.1) with $\pi=2$, $\bar{n}=(m_{n1}-2\Lambda,m_{n2}+2\Lambda)$ and $\bar{m}=(m_{n1}+\Lambda(1)+2\Lambda,m_{n2}+\Lambda(2)-2\Lambda)$. (7.18) is then immediate from (6.9) and (6.10) and the monotonicity properties of $\sigma$ (see Comment 3.3 (v)) with $\bar{N}_\ell=5\bar{m}_\ell$ and $\delta_k=f(\delta,\delta,2,10k)$. (7.20) follows from (7.18), because one can construct a circuit from two horizontal and two vertical crossings of suitable rectangles, as explained in the proof of Cor. 6.1 at the end of Ch. 6. This proves the lemma under Condition A.

Now assume that Condition B holds. Instead of (7.22) we now obtain from (3.38) and Lemma 2.1b

$$\sigma((n_{\ell 1}-2\Lambda,n_{\ell 2}+2\Lambda;1,p_0,\mathcal{G}_{p\ell})\geq\delta \quad \text{and}$$

$$\sigma(a_1n_{\ell 1}+2\Lambda,a_2n_{\ell 2}-2\Lambda);2,p_0,\mathcal{G}_{p\ell})\geq\delta \quad .$$

The Lemma again follows from the RSW theorem (this time with $\pi=2\lceil\max\{a_1,a_2,a_1^{-1},a_2^{-1}\}\rceil$). □

Lemma 7.3. Assume $p\in\mathcal{P}_\lambda$ satisfies

$$\bar{0}\ll p\ll\bar{1}.$$

<u>If for some vertex</u> $v$ <u>of</u> $\mathcal{G}$

(7.23) $$E_p\{\#W(v)\} < \infty ,$$

<u>then for every vertex</u> $w$ <u>of</u> $\mathcal{G}^*$

(7.24) $$P_p\{\#W^*(w) = \infty\} > 0 .$$

<u>Also</u>

(7.25) $$E_p\{\#W^*(w)\} < \infty$$

<u>implies</u>

(7.26) $$P_p\{\#W(v) = \infty\} > 0.$$

<u>Proof</u>: We shall show that (7.23) implies

(7.27) $$P_p\{\text{ an infinite vacant component on } \mathcal{G}^* \text{ inside the first quadrant}\} = 1.$$

This will imply that

$$P_p\{\#W^*(w_1) = \infty\} > 0$$

for some $w_1 \in \mathcal{G}^*$. (7.24) follows then for any $w$ by (4.8) (with $n = \infty$). A similar proof will work for obtaining (7.26) from (7.25).

To prove (7.27) we first use (7.14) with

$$n_1 = 2^k - 2\Lambda_4 \quad , \quad n_2 = 2^{k+1} + 2\Lambda_4 .$$

We obtain

(7.28) $$1-\sigma^*((2^k,2^{k+1});2,p,\mathcal{G}) \le \sigma((2^k-2\Lambda_4,2^{k+1}+2\Lambda_4);1,p,\mathcal{G}).$$

Next we claim that (7.23) implies

(7.29) $$\sum_{k=1}^{\infty} \sigma((2^k+\Lambda_5,2^{k+1}+\Lambda_6);1,p) < \infty$$

for any $\Lambda_5$, $\Lambda_6$. This was essentially already proved in Lemma 5.4. Exactly as at the end of the proof of that lemma (cf. (5.55)) one shows that

$$\sigma((2^k+\Lambda_5,2^{k+1}+\Lambda_6);1,p)$$

$$\leq \mu(2\Lambda+1)(2^{k+1}+\Lambda_6+2\Lambda+1) \sup_{v_0(1)\leq\Lambda} P_p\{W(v_0) \text{ contains a vertex}$$

$$\text{to the right of } x(1) = 2^k+\Lambda_5-\Lambda\}$$

$$\leq \mu(2\Lambda+1)(2^{k+1}+\Lambda_6+2\Lambda+1)$$

$$\cdot \sum_{v_0\varepsilon[0,1)\times[0,1)} P_p\{\#W(v_0) \geq \frac{1}{\Lambda}(2^k+\Lambda_5-2\Lambda)\}$$

(use periodicity for the last inequality). But (7.23) for some $v$ implies

$$E_p\{\#W(v_0)\} < \infty$$

for all $v_0$ (see the Application 4.1 of the FKG inequality) and consequently

$$\sum_{v_0\varepsilon[0,1)\times[0,1)} \sum_k 2^{k+2}P_p\{\#W(v_0) \geq \frac{1}{\Lambda}(2^k+\Lambda_5-2\Lambda)\} < \infty .$$

(7.29) follows.

From the Borel-Cantelli lemma (Renyi (1970) Lemma VII.5.A), (7.28) (7.29) it now follows that

(7.30) $$P_p\{\exists \text{ vacant vertical crossing on } \mathcal{G}^* \text{ of } [0,2^k]\times[0,2^{k+1}] \text{ for all large } k\} = 1.$$

In the same way one sees

(7.31) $$P_p\{\exists \text{ vacant horizontal crossing on } \mathcal{G}^* \text{ of } [0,2^{k+1}]\times[0,2^k] \text{ for all large } k\} = 1.$$

Since a horizontal crossing of $[0,2^{k+1}]\times[0,2^k]$ or of $[0,2^{k+3}]\times[0,2^{k+2}]$ must intersect a vertical crossing of $[0,2^{k+1}]\times[0,2^{k+2}]$, one easily sees that if for all large $k$ there exists a vacant horizontal crossing on $\mathcal{G}^*$ of $[0,2^{2k+1}]\times[0,2^{2k}]$ and a vacant vertical crossing on $\mathcal{G}^*$ of $[0,2^{2k+1}]\times[0,2^{2k+2}]$, then these crossings combine to an infinite vacant cluster on $\mathcal{G}^*$ in the first quadrant. Thus (7.27) follows from (7.30) and (7.31). □

Remark.

(i) The above proof is taken from Smythe and Wierman (1978), Theorem 3.2. Together with parts (ii) and (iii) of Theorem 3.1 it will show that one actually has infinite occupied clusters on $\mathcal{G}$ in the first quadrant under $P_{p''}$ with $p'' >> p_0$, and infinite vacant clusters on $\mathcal{G}^*$ in the first quadrant under $P_{p'}$ with $p' << p_0$.

Proof of Theorem 3.1 (i): With $\overline{M}_\ell$ as in Lemma 7.2 consider the annuli

$$(7.32) \qquad U_\ell := [-2M_{\ell 1}, 2M_{\ell 1}] \times [-2M_{\ell 2}, 2M_{\ell 2}] \setminus (-M_{\ell 1}, M_{\ell 1}) \times (-M_{\ell 2}, M_{\ell 2}).$$

Without loss of generality we may assume these annuli disjoint. In this case the occurrences of occupied circuits in different $U_\ell$ are independent of each other. Therefore, by (7.21) and the Borel-Cantelli Lemma (Renyi (1970), Lemma VII.5.B), with $P_{p_0}$-probability one infinitely many $U_\ell$ contain a vacant circuit on $\mathcal{G}^*_{p\ell}$ surrounding the origin. If $M_{\ell 1} > \Lambda$, $M_{\ell 2} > \Lambda$, and $U_\ell$ contains a vacant circuit on $\mathcal{G}^*_{p\ell}$ surrounding $0$, then by Lemma 2.1a

$$(7.33) \qquad [-2M_{\ell 1}-\Lambda, 2M_{\ell 1}+\Lambda] \times [-2M_{\ell 2}-\Lambda, 2M_{\ell 2}+\Lambda] \setminus$$

$$(-M_{\ell 1}+\Lambda, M_{\ell 1}-\Lambda) \times (-M_{\ell 2}+\Lambda, M_{\ell 2}-\Lambda)$$

contains a vacant circuit on $\mathcal{G}^*$ surrounding $0$. In fact this latter circuit must surround all of $(-M_{\ell 1}+\Lambda, M_{\ell 1}-\Lambda) \times (-M_{\ell 2}+\Lambda, M_{\ell 2}-\Lambda)$. Hence for all $N$

$$(7.34) \qquad P_{p_0}\{ \exists \text{ a vacant circuit on } \mathcal{G}^* \text{ surrounding } [-N,+N] \times [-N,+N]\} = 1.$$

In the same way we obtain arbitrarily large occupied circuits on $\mathcal{G}$, and (3.45) follows. (3.43) is immediate from this, because if $v \in [-N,N] \times [-N,N]$ and $[-N,N] \times [-N,N]$ is surrounded by a vacant circuit $J$ on $\mathcal{G}^*$, then $W(v)$ is contained in $\text{int}(J)$, and hence $\#W(v) < \infty$. In fact any path on $\mathcal{G}$ from $v$ to the complement of $\text{int}(J)$ would have to be intersect $J$, necessarily in a vertex of $\mathcal{G}$ and $\mathcal{G}^*$ (see Comment 2.2 (vii)) and this vertex would have to be vacant. Thus no vertex in $\text{ext}(J)$ or on $J$ can belong to $W(v)$. Similarly

$\#W^*(v)$ is shown to be finite with probability one.

Finally, (3.44) is a consequence of (3.43) and Lemma 7.3. □

Lemma 7.4. *Assume* $p_0$ *satisfies (7.4) and Condition A or B. Let* $\delta_k$, $\{\bar{N}_\ell\}$ *and* $\{\bar{M}_\ell\}$ *be as in Lemma 7.2 so that (7.17)-(7.21) hold. Then for*

$$p' << p_0 << p''$$

(7.35)
$$\lim_{\ell\to\infty} \tau(2\bar{M}_\ell;i,p',\mathcal{G}) = 0,\ i = 1,2,$$

*and*

(7.36)
$$\lim_{\ell\to\infty} \tau^*(2\bar{N}_\ell;i,p'',\mathcal{G}) = 0,\ i = 1,2,$$

*(see (5.5) and (5.6) for* $\tau$ *and* $\tau^*$).

Proof: We shall only prove (with $\Lambda$ as in (7.8))

(7.37)
$$P_{p'}\{\exists \text{ occupied horizontal crossing on } \mathcal{G}_{p\ell} \text{ of } [\Lambda,2M_{\ell 1}-\Lambda]\times[-\Lambda,6M_{\ell 2}+\Lambda]\} \to 0 \quad (\ell\to\infty).$$

By Lemma 2.1b $\tau(2\bar{M}_\ell;1,p',\mathcal{G}) = P_{p'}\{\exists$ occupied horizontal crossing on $\mathcal{G}$ of $[0,2M_{\ell 1}]\times[0,6M_{\ell 2}]\}$ is bounded by the left hand side of (7.37). Therefore (7.37) will imply (7.35) for $i = 1$. The proofs of (7.35) for $i = 2$ and of (7.36) are similar.

To prove (7.37) take $\Lambda_3$ and $\Lambda_4$ as in the proof of Lemma 7.1. Suppress the subscript $\ell$ for the time being. Very much as in the proof of Lemma 7.1 take self-avoiding vertical crossings $r_1$ and $r_3$ on $\mathcal{M}$ of the strips $[\Lambda,\Lambda_4-1]\times[-\Lambda_4,6M_2+\Lambda_4]$ and $[2M_1-\Lambda_4+1,2M_1-\Lambda]\times[-\Lambda_4,6M_2+\Lambda_4]$, respectively. Also we take horizontal crossings $r_2$ and $r_4$ on $\mathcal{M}$ of $[0,2M_1]\times[-\Lambda_4,-\Lambda-1]$ and $[0,2M_1]\times[6M_2+\Lambda+1,6M_2+\Lambda_4]$, respectively (see Fig. 7.2). Again $\phi_1$ ($\phi_3$) is a simple curve in $[\Lambda,\Lambda_4-1]\times[-\Lambda_4,6M_2+\Lambda_4]$ ($[2M_1-\Lambda_4+1,2M_1-\Lambda]\times[-\Lambda_4,6M_2+\Lambda_4]$) connecting the top and bottom edge of this rectangle. Starting from the left endpoint of $r_2$ ($r_4$) let $u_1$ ($u_4$) be the last intersection of $r_2$ ($r_4$) with $\phi_1$; and $u_2$ ($u_3$) the first intersection of $r_2$ ($r_4$) with $\phi_3$. We denote the closed segment of $\phi_1$ from $u_4$ to $u_1$ by $B_1$, the closed segment of $\phi_3$ from $u_3$ to $u_2$ by $B_2$, the closed segment of $r_2$ from $u_1$ to $u_2$ by $A$ and the closed segment of $r_4$ from $u_4$ to $u_3$

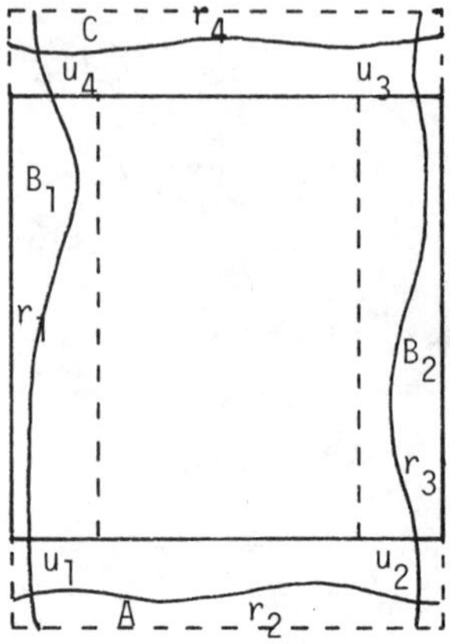


Figure 7.2 The solid rectangle is $[0,2M_1] \times [0,6M_2]$; the outer dashed rectangle is $[0,2M_1] \times [-\Lambda_4, 6M_2+\Lambda_4]$; the inner dashed rectangle is $[\Lambda_4-1, 2M_1-\Lambda_4+1] \times [0,6M_2]$ .

by C. As in Lemma 7.1, as soon as $M_1 > 2\Lambda_4$ the composition of $B_1$, A, $B_2$ and C is a Jordan curve, which we again denote by J. Also

$$(7.38) \qquad [\Lambda_4, 2M_1-\Lambda_4] \times [-\Lambda, 6M_2+\Lambda] \subset \text{int}(J).$$

Any horizontal crossing $\tilde{r}$ on $\mathcal{G}_{p\ell}$ of $[\Lambda, 2M_1-\Lambda] \times [-\Lambda, 6M_2+\Lambda]$ contains some point $v = (v(1), v(2))$ in the interior of the rectangle in the left hand side of (7.38), and hence in int(J). Let $\psi$ be the segment of $\tilde{r}$ from its last intersection with the vertical line $x(1) = \Lambda$ to the first intersection with the line $x(1) = 2M_1-\Lambda$ . Then $\psi$ starts on $x(1) = \Lambda$ to the "left of $B_1$" and when it reaches v it lies to the "right of $B_1$". Since $\psi$ minus its endpoints lies between the horizontal lines $x(2) = -\Lambda$ and $x(2) = 6M_2+\Lambda$, $\psi$ must intersect $B_1$ between its initial point and v. (Note that $B_1$ runs from $u_1$ below $x(2) = -\Lambda$ to $u_4$ above $x(2) = 6M_2+\Lambda$.) Similarly the piece of $\psi$ between v and its final point must intersect $B_2$. The piece of $\tilde{r}$ between the last intersection before v with $B_1$ and the first intersection after v with $B_2$ is therefore a path $r = (v_0, e_1, \ldots, e_\nu, v_\nu)$ on $\mathcal{G}_{p\ell}$

with the following properties:

(7.39) $$(v_1,e_2,\dots,e_{\nu-1},v_{\nu-1}) \subset \mathrm{int}(J),$$

(7.40) $e_1$ intersects $J$ only in the point $v_0 \in B_1$,

(7.41) $e_\nu$ intersects $J$ only in the point $v_\nu \in B_2$.

Thus if we introduce the event

$$E = \{\exists \text{ occupied path } r = (v_0,e_1,\dots,e_\nu,v_\nu) \text{ on } \mathcal{G}_{p\ell} \text{ with the properties (7.39)-(7.41)}\},$$

then the left hand side of (7.37) is bounded by $P_{p'}\{E\}$.

We now introduce

$$N_0 = N_0(E,\omega) = \#\text{ of pivotal sites for } (E,\omega) \text{ which are vertices of } \mathcal{M}$$

and

$$p(t) = tp_0+(1-t)p',\ 0 \le t \le 1.$$

Since $E$ is an increasing event we can apply Russo's formula (4.22) to obtain

(7.42) $$\frac{d}{dt} P_{p(t)}\{E\} \ge \inf_{v\in\mathcal{M}}\{P_{p_0}\{v \text{ is occupied}\} - P_{p'}\{v \text{ is occupied}\}\} \cdot E_{p(t)}\{N_0\}.$$

Since $p' << p_0$ and $P_{p_0}$ and $P_{p'}$ are periodic, the constant

(7.43) $$\alpha := \inf_{v\in\mathcal{M}}\{P_{p_0}\{v \text{ is occupied}\} - P_{p'}\{v \text{ is occupied}\}\}$$

is strictly positive. We now write (7.42) as

$$(P_{p(t)}\{E\})^{-1} \frac{d}{dt} P_{p(t)}\{E\} \ge \alpha\, E_{p(t)}\{N_0|E\},$$

and integrate over $t$ from $0$ to $1$. We obtain the inequality

(7.44) $$P_{p'}\{E\} \le P_{p_0}\{E\}\exp-\alpha \int_0^1 E_{p(t)}\{N_0|E\}dt \le \exp-\alpha \int_0^1 E_{p(t)}\{N_0|E\}dt.$$

It therefore suffices to prove

(7.45) $\quad E_{p(t)}\{N_0|E\} \to \infty$ uniformly in $t$ as $\overline{M} \to \infty$

through the sequence $\overline{M}_\ell$ ,

for this will imply that the left hand sides of (7.44) and (7.37) tend to 0 as $\ell \to \infty$.

We follow the lines of Kesten (1980a) to prove (7.45). (7.39)-(7.41) are just (2.23)-(2.25) in the present set up. $E$ is the event that there exists at least one occupied path $r$ with these properties. Proposition 2.3 (with $S = \mathbb{R}^2$) states that if $E$ occurs, then there exists a unique minimal occupied path $r$ satisfying (7.39)-(7.41), i.e., a path $r$ for which the component of $\text{int}(J)\setminus r$ with $A$ in its boundary is as small as possible (see Def. 2.11 and 2.12). As in Prop. 2.3 we denote the minimal occupied path satisfying (7.39)-(7.41) by $R$. In Kesten (1980a) the suggestive term "lowest (occupied) left-right crossing" was used for $R$ because there we could take for $J$ the perimeter of a rectangle. The above comments imply

(7.46) $$E = \cup\{R = r\} ,$$

where the union is over all paths $r = (v_0, e_1, \dots, e_\nu, v_\nu)$ on $\mathcal{G}_{p\ell}$ which satisfy (7.39)-(7.41). Next we use Ex. 4.2 (iii) to find pivotal sites for $E$. We restrict ourselves to pivotal sites which are vertices of $\mathcal{M}$, because these are the only ones counted in $N_0$. A vertex $v$ of $\mathcal{M}$ on $R \cap \text{int}(J)$ which has a "vacant connection on $\mathcal{G}_{p\ell}$ to $\mathring{C}$ above $r$" is pivotal for $E$. To be more specific, for any path $r$ on $\mathcal{G}_{p\ell}$ which satisfies (7.39)-(7.41) and vertex $v$ of $\mathcal{M}$ on $r \cap \text{int}(J)$ we shall say that $v$ has a <u>vacant connection to $\mathring{C}$ above $r$</u> if there exists a vacant path $s^\star = (v_0^\star, e_1^\star, \dots, e_\rho^\star, v_\rho^\star)$ on $\mathcal{G}_{p\ell}^\star$ which satisfies (7.47)-(7.49) below.

(7.47) there exists an edge $e^\star$ of $\mathcal{G}_{p\ell}^\star$ between $v$ and $v_0^\star$ such that $\mathring{e}^\star \subset J^+(r)$

(7.48) $$v_\rho^\star \in \mathring{C}$$

(7.49) $$(v_0^\star, e_1^\star, \dots, v_{\rho-1}^\star, e_\rho^\star \setminus \{v_\rho^\star\}) = s^\star \setminus \{v_\rho^\star\} \subset J^+(r)$$

(see Def. 2.11 for $J^+(r)$). Note that $\rho = 0$ is permitted in (7.47)-(7.49). In this case $s^\star$ reduces to the single point $\{v_0^\star\}$ and (7.49) becomes vacuous. (7.47)-(7.49) are merely the conditions (4.13)-(4.15) with $R$ replaced by $r$, except that in (7.47) we require $e^*$ to belong to $\mathcal{G}^*_{p\ell}$ rather than to $\mathcal{M}_{p\ell}$, as in (4.13). The latter change does not constitute a real change from (4.13) since we assumed here that $v$ is a vertex of $\mathcal{M}$, i.e., of $\mathcal{G}^*$ and $\mathcal{G}^*_{p\ell}$. If such a $v$ is connected by an edge $e^*$ to the vertex $v^*_0$ of $\mathcal{G}^*_{p\ell}$ then $e^*$ automatically belongs to $\mathcal{G}^*_{p\ell}$. (The vacant connections defined here correspond to the weak cut sets with respect to $r$ of Kesten (1980a).) Ex. 4.2 (iii) now shows that any vertex $v$ of $\mathcal{M}$ on $R \cap \text{int}(J)$ with a vacant connection to $\mathring{C}$ above $R$ is pivotal for $E$. Thus

$$N_0 \geq \#\text{ of vertices } v \text{ of } \mathcal{M} \text{ on } R \cap \text{int}(J) \text{ which have a vacant connection to } \mathring{C} \text{ above } R.$$

For the remainder of the proof we use the abbreviation

(7.50) $$N(r) = N(r,\omega) = \#\text{ of vertices of } \mathcal{M} \text{ on } r \cap \text{int}(J) \text{ which have a vacant connection to } \mathring{C} \text{ above } r.$$

Then $N_0(E,\omega) \geq N(R,\omega)$, and by virtue of (7.46)

(7.51) $$E_{p(t)}\{N_0|E\} \geq \sum_r P_{p(t)}\{R = r|E\}E_{p(t)}\{N(r)|R = r\} .$$

By Prop. 2.3 the event $\{R = r\}$ depends only on the occupancies of vertices in $\bar{J}^-(r)$ (note that $B_i$ is made up from edges of $\mathcal{M}$ and a fortiori of $\mathcal{M}_{p\ell}$ here). Moreover, for any $v$ on $r$ the existence of a vacant connection from $v$ to $\mathring{C}$ above $r$ depends only on the occupancies of the vertices in $J^+(r) \cup \mathring{C}$, (see (7.48), (7.49)) which is disjoint from $\bar{J}^-(r)$. This allows us to drop the condition $R = r$ in the last expectation in the right hand side of (7.51). More precisely

(7.52) $$E_{p(t)}\{N(r)|R = r\} = \sum_{\substack{v \in r \cap \text{int}(J) \\ v \text{ a vertex of } \mathcal{M}}} P_{p(t)}\{v \text{ has a vacant connection to } \mathring{C} \text{ above } r|R = r\}$$

$$= \sum_{\substack{v \in r \cap \text{int}(J) \\ v \text{ a vertex of } \mathcal{M}}} P_{p(t)}\{v \text{ has a vacant connection to } \mathring{C} \text{ above } r\} .$$

Clearly

$$\{\ \exists \text{ vacant connection from } v \text{ to } \mathring{C} \text{ above } r\}$$

is a decreasing event. Lemma 4.1 shows that the $P_{p(t)}$-measure of any decreasing event is decreasing in $t$. It follows that the last member of (7.52) is also decreasing in $t$. Thus for $0 \le t \le 1$

(7.53) $$E_{p(t)}\{N(r) | R = r\} \ge E_{p_0}\{N(r)\}.$$

Substituting this estimate into (7.51) and using

$$\sum_r P_{p(t)}\{R = r | E\} = 1 \qquad \text{(see (7.46))}$$

we obtain

(7.54) $$E_{p(t)}\{N_0 | E\} \ge \min_r E_{p_0}\{N(r)\},$$

where the minimum is over all paths $r$ on $\mathcal{G}_{p\ell}$ satisfying (7.39)-(7.41). Fix such an $r$. Let its initial point on $B_1$ be $v_0$ and its final point on $B_2$ be $v_\nu$ and consider the following curves on $\mathcal{M}$ (and hence on $\mathcal{M}_{p\ell}$): $\tilde{B}_1 := C$, $\tilde{A} :=$ closed segment of $B_1$ between $u_4$ and $v_0$, $\tilde{B}_2 := r$, $\tilde{C} :=$ closed segment of $B_2$ between $v_\nu$ and $u_3$ (see Fig. 7.3). Together these curves form a Jordan curve, which we

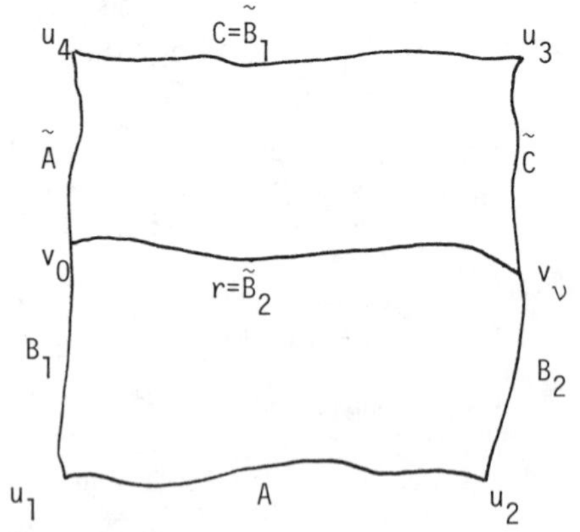


Figure 7.3

denote by $\tilde{J}$, and which is precisely $Fr(J^+(r))$. Now let $v \in r \cap int(J) \in \overset{\ell}{B}_2$ be a vertex of $\mathcal{M}$ and consider vacant paths $\tilde{s}^* = (v, e^*, v_0^*, e_1^*, \ldots, e_\rho^*, v_\rho^*)$ on $\mathcal{G}_{p\ell}^*$ which satisfy

(7.55) $\qquad \tilde{s}^*$ minus its endpoints $\subset int(\tilde{J})$

and

(7.56) $\quad$ one endpoint of $\tilde{s}^*$ lies on $\mathring{\tilde{B}}_1$ and one endpoint of $\tilde{s}^*$ lies on $\mathring{\tilde{B}}_2$ .

(Paths of this type correspond to the strong cut sets of Kesten (1980a).) Clearly if there exists such a vacant path, then its endpoint on $r = \tilde{B}_2$ has a vacant connection to $\mathring{C}$ above $r$. We again want to apply Prop. 2.3, this time with $\mathcal{G}_{p\ell}$ replaced by $\mathcal{G}_{p\ell}^*$ and $J, A, B_1, C, B_2$ replaced by $\tilde{J}, \tilde{A}, \tilde{B}_1, \tilde{C}$ and $\tilde{B}_2$, respectively. Analogously to Def. 2.11 we set for any path $\tilde{s}^*$ satisfying (7.55) and (7.56)

$$\tilde{J}^-(\tilde{s}^*)(\tilde{J}^+(\tilde{s}^*)) = \text{component of } int(\tilde{J}) \setminus \tilde{s}^* \text{ with } \tilde{A}(\tilde{C}) \text{ in its boundary.}$$

Prop. 2.3 will give us an $\tilde{s}^*$ with minimal $\tilde{J}^-(\tilde{s}^*)$. For later estimates (see (7.64), (7.65) and their use at the end of the proof) it is important that this minimal path is not too far to the right. We shall therefore consider only vacant connections in the vertical strip

$$\chi := [\Lambda_4+1, M_1+\Lambda_4+1] \times \mathbb{R} \ .$$

We remind the reader that for any subset $S$ of $\mathbb{R}^2$ $\tilde{s}^* \subset S$ means that all edges (and hence all vertices) of $\tilde{s}^*$ lie in $S$. We need to consider the event

$$F(r) := \{ \exists \text{ vacant path } \tilde{s}^* \text{ on } \mathcal{G}_{p\ell}^* \text{ which satisfies (7.55), (7.56) and } \tilde{s}^* \subset \chi \} \ .$$

From Propositon 2.3, applied to $\mathcal{G}_{p\ell}^*$ rather than $\mathcal{G}_{p\ell}$ and with $S$ taken as the strip $\chi$ above we conclude that when $F(r)$ occurs there is a unique $\tilde{s}^*$ with minimal $\tilde{J}^-(\tilde{s}^*)$ among the vacant paths on $\tilde{\mathcal{G}}_{p\ell}^*$ which satisfy (7.55), (7.56) and are contained in $\chi$. We denote this path by $S^*$. (Intuitively, $S^*$ is the "left-most vacant vertical crosscut" of $int(\tilde{J})$ in $\chi$.) As we saw above $S^*$ provides us with a vacant connection from its endpoint on $\mathring{\tilde{B}}_2 = r \backslash \{w_1, w_2\}$ to $\mathring{C}$ above $r$. Before we estimate the number of sites which have such a connection we estimate the probability of having at least one such site by estimating the probability that $S^*$ exists, which equals $P_{p_0}\{F(r)\}$. Let $(u_0^*, f_1^*, \dots, f_\tau^*, u_t^*)$ be a vacant path on $\mathcal{G}_{p\ell}^*$ with

(7.57) $$u_0^* \in A,$$

(7.58) $$u_\tau^* \in \tilde{B}_1 = C,$$

(7.59) $$(f_1^* \backslash \{u_0^*\}, u_1^*, \dots, u_{\tau-1}^*, f_\tau^* \backslash \{u^*\}) \subset \text{int}(J) \cap \chi .$$

Since $\chi$ is closed any such path lies entirely in $\chi$; and since $B_1$ and $B_2$ separate $A$ and $C$ on $J$ the path must intersect $r$. The last intersection of this path on $\mathcal{G}_{p\ell}^*$ with $r$ - which is a path on $\mathcal{G}_{p\ell}$ - is necessarily a vertex of $\mathcal{G}_{p\ell}^*$ and of $\mathcal{G}_{p\ell}$ (see Comment 2.3(v)). Thus this last intersection of $(u_0^*, f_1^*, \dots, f_\tau^*, u_\tau^*)$ with $r$ is one of the $u_i^*$, say $u_\sigma^*$, and also equals one of the $v_j$, but not $v_0$ or $v_\nu$ since the latter two lie on $B_1 \cup B_2$, hence outside $\chi$. One now easily sees that if one takes $\tilde{s}^* = (u_\sigma^*, f_{\sigma+1}^*, \dots, f_\tau^*, u_\tau^*)$ then the requirements (7.55) and (7.56) are fulfilled. Of course this $\tilde{s}^*$ is also contained in $\chi$ to that

(7.60) $$P_{p_0}\{F(r)\} \geq P_{p_0}\{\exists \text{ vacant path } (u_0^*, f_1^*, \dots, f_\tau^*, u_\tau^*) \text{ on } \mathcal{G}_{p\ell}^* \text{ with the properties (7.57)-(7.59)}\}.$$

In turn it is easy to see that any vacant vertical crossing on $\mathcal{G}_{p\ell}^*$ of $[\Lambda_4+1, M_1+\Lambda_4+1] \times [-\Lambda_4, 6M_2+\Lambda_4]$ contains a path with the properties (7.57)-(7.59). Indeed any such vertical crossing contains a continuous curve $\psi$ which connects the horizontal lines $x(2) = -\Lambda_4$ (which lies below $r_2$) and $x(2) = 6M_2+\Lambda_4$ (which lies above $r_4$) (see Fig. 7.2). $\psi$ therefore intersects $r_2$ in a point of $A$ and $r_4$ in a point of $\tilde{B}_1$; $\psi$ also lies in $\chi$. Combining this observation with (7.60) we obtain

(7.61) $$P_{p_0}\{F(r)\} \geq P_{p_0}\{\exists \text{ vacant vertical crossing on } \mathcal{G}_{p\ell}^* \text{ of } [\Lambda_4+1, M_1+\Lambda_4+1] \times [-\Lambda_4, 6M_2+\Lambda_4]\}$$
$$\geq \sigma^*((M_1, 7M_2); 2, p_0, \mathcal{G}_{p\ell}) \geq \delta_7 ,$$

as soon as $M_1, M_2 > 2\Lambda_4+1$, by virtue of (7.19). By Prop. 2.3 also

$$P_{p_0}\{S^\star \text{ exists}\} = P_{p_0}\{F(r)\} \geq \delta_7 \quad . \tag{7.62}$$

The next step in estimating $E_{p_0}\{N(r)\}$ is to write

$$E_{p_0}\{N(r)\} \geq \sum_{\tilde{s}^\star} P\{S^\star = \tilde{s}^\star\} E_{p_0}\{N(r) | S^\star = \tilde{s}^\star\} \tag{7.63}$$

$$\geq \delta_7 \min_{\tilde{s}^\star} E_{p_0}\{N(r) | S^\star = \tilde{s}^\star\} ,$$

where $\tilde{s}^\star$ ranges over all paths on $\mathcal{G}^\star_{p\ell}$ which lie in $\chi$ and satisfy (7.55) and (7.56). For the remainder of the proof we fix a path $\tilde{s}^\star = (v, e^\star, \dots, e^\star_\rho, v^\star_\rho)$ on $\mathcal{G}^\star_{p\ell}$ which lies in $\chi$ and satisfies (7.55) and (7.56). The initial point $v = (v(1), v(2))$ lies on $r$ and is a vertex of $\mathcal{M}$ while $v^\star_\rho$ lies on $C \cap \chi \subset \mathring{C}$ . Let the annulus $U_k$ be defined as in (7.32) and let $V_k$ be $U_k$ translated by $(\lfloor v(1) \rfloor, \lfloor v(2) \rfloor)$, i.e.,

$$V_k = [\lfloor v(1) \rfloor - 2M_{k1}, \lfloor v(1) \rfloor + 2M_{k1}] \times [\lfloor v(2) \rfloor - 2M_{k2}, \lfloor v(2) \rfloor + 2M_{k2}] \setminus$$

$$(\lfloor v(1) \rfloor - M_{k1}, \lfloor v(1) \rfloor + M_{k1}) \times (\lfloor v(2) \rfloor - M_{k2}, \lfloor v(2) \rfloor + M_{k2}).$$

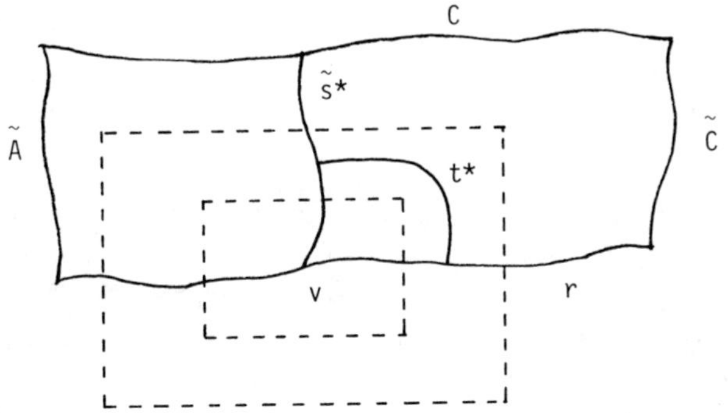


Figure 7.4 $V_k$ is the region between the dashed rectangles.

We restrict ourselves to $k$ with

(7.64) $\quad M_{k1} > 1,\ M_{k2} > 1 \ \text{and}\ 2M_{k1} < M_{\ell 1}-2\Lambda_4-1 \ .$

(Note the $M_{\ell 1}$ in the last expression in (7.64); we reintroduced to subscript $\ell$ to distinguish $\overline{M}_k$ and $\overline{M}_\ell$.) Under (7.64) $v$ lies inside the center rectangle

$$(\lfloor v(1)\rfloor - M_{k1}, \lfloor v(1)\rfloor + M_{k1}) \times (\lfloor v(2)\rfloor - M_{k2}, \lfloor v(2)\rfloor + M_{k2})$$

of $V_k$. Moreover, since $\tilde{s}^* \subset \chi$ , $v(1) \le M_{\ell 1}+\Lambda_4+1$ and consequently

(7.65) $\quad v(1)+2M_{k1} < 2M_{\ell 1}-\Lambda_4 \ .$

Assume now that there exists a path $t^* = (w,g^*,w_0^*,g_1^*,\dots,g_\sigma^*,w_\sigma^*)$ on $\mathcal{G}_{p\ell}^*$ with the following properties:

(7.66) $\quad w \in V_k$, $w$ is a vertex on $r \cap \text{int}(J)$

(7.67) $\quad w_\sigma^* \in C \setminus \{v_\rho^*\}$ or $w_\sigma^*$ lies on $\tilde{s}^*$ ,

(7.68) $\quad (g^* \setminus \{w\}, w_0^*,\dots,w_{\sigma-1}^*, g_\sigma^* \setminus \{w_\sigma^*\})$

$$= t^* \setminus \{w, w_\sigma^*\} \subset \tilde{J}^+(\tilde{s}^*) \cap V_k$$

and

(7.69) $\quad w_0^*,\dots,w_{\sigma-1}^*$ are vacant, and if $w \ \ \in C\setminus\{v_\rho^*\}$ then also $w_\sigma^*$ is vacant.

Again we allow $\sigma = 0$, $t^* = (w,g^*,w_0^*)$, in which case (7.68) reduces to $\mathring{g}^* \subset \tilde{J}^+(\tilde{s}^*) \cap V_k$. We claim that if such a $t^*$ exists and $S^* = \tilde{s}^*$, then $w$, the initial point of $t^*$, has a vacant connection to $\mathring{C}$ above $r$. This is obvious if $w_\sigma^* \in C \setminus \{v_\rho^*\}$ (see (7.47)-(7.49)) and recall that $\tilde{J}^+(\tilde{s}^*) \subset \text{int}(\tilde{J}) = J^+(r)$; also $w_\sigma^* \in$ closure of $(\tilde{J}^+(\tilde{s}^*) \cap V_k) \cap (C \setminus v_\rho^*)$ implies $w_\sigma^* \in \mathring{C}$ (use (7.65).) But also in the other case – when $w_\sigma^*$ lies on $\tilde{s}^*$ – it is easy to substantiate this claim. Indeed, if $w_\sigma^* = v_i^*$ for some $0 \le i \le \rho$ then $t_1^* := (w_0^*,g_1^*,\dots,g_\sigma^*,w_\sigma^* = v_i^*, e_{i+1}^*,\dots,e_\rho^*,v_\rho^*)$ is a path on $\mathcal{G}_{p\ell}^*$ consisting of $t^* \setminus g_1^*$ followed by a piece of $\tilde{s}^*$. It is self-avoiding since $t \setminus \{w_\sigma^*\}$ does not intersect $\tilde{s}^*$ (see (7.68)). There is an edge $g^*$ of $\mathcal{G}_{p\ell}^*$ from $w$ to $w_0^*$ with $\mathring{g} \in J^+(r)$, while $t_1^*$ ends at $v_\rho^* \in \mathring{C}$. Also $t_1^* \setminus \{v_\rho^*\} \subset J^+(r)$ by

(7.68) and (7.55). Finally $t_1^*$ is vacant by (7.69) and the fact that $\tilde{s}^* = S^*$ is vacant whenever $S^*$ exists. Thus indeed $w$ has a vacant connection to $\mathcal{C}$ above $r$. The last conceivable case with $w_\sigma^* = v$ cannot occur, since $v \notin V_k$ while $w_\sigma^*$ is the endpoint of $g^*$ or $g_\sigma^*$, hence $w_\sigma^* \in \overline{V}_k = V_k$, by (7.68). This proves our claim.

As before we may assume the $U_k$ of (7.32) disjoint. Then the $V_k$ are also disjoint and then distinct $V_k$ for which there exist a $t^*$ as above provide us with distinct vertices of $\mathcal{M}$ on $r$ which have a vacant connection above $r$ to $\mathcal{C}$. In view of the definition (7.50) we therefore have

$$(7.70) \qquad E_{p_0}\{N(r)\,|\,S^* = \tilde{s}^*\} \geq \sum_{\substack{k \text{ satisfying} \\ (7.64)}} P_{p_0}\{\ \exists \text{ path } t^* \text{ which satisfies (7.66)-(7.69)} \,|\, S^* = \tilde{s}^*\}\ .$$

We now complete our proof by showing

$$(7.71) \qquad P_{p_0}\{\ \exists \text{ path } t^* \text{ which satisfies (7.66)-(7.69)} \,|\, S^* = \tilde{s}^*\} \geq \delta_4^4\ ,$$

whenever (7.64) holds and $\tilde{s}^* \subset \chi$ satisfies (7.55) and (7.56). This will indeed imply (7.45) by means of (7.54), (7.63), (7.70) and the fact that the number of $k$ which satisfy (7.64) tends to $\infty$ as $\ell \to \infty$. Now for the proof of (7.71). To begin with observe that we may drop the condition $S^* = \tilde{s}^*$, because the existence of a path $t^*$ which satisfies (7.66)-(7.69) depends only on the occupancies of vertices in $\tilde{J}^+(\tilde{s}^*) \cap V_k$ or vertices on $C \setminus \{v_\rho^*\}$ which are an endpoint of some edge of $\mathcal{G}_{p\ell}^*$ with interior in $\tilde{J}^+(\tilde{s}^*)$. None of these vertices lie in $\tilde{\overline{J}}^-(\tilde{s}^*)$. The only vertices for which this is possibly in doubt are those on $C \setminus \{v_\rho^*\}$. However, these vertices would have to be in $\tilde{\overline{J}}^+(\tilde{s}^*)$, since they are an endpoint of an edge with interior in $\tilde{J}^+(s^*)$. But the only vertex on $C$ in $\tilde{\overline{J}}^+(s^*) \cap \tilde{\overline{J}}^-(s^*)$ is $v_\rho^*$, the final point of $\tilde{s}^*$. On the other hand, by Prop. 2.3 the event $\{S^* = \tilde{s}^*\}$ depends only on the occupancies of vertices in $\tilde{\overline{J}}^-(\tilde{s}^*)$. Therefore the conditional probability in (7.71) is the same as the unconditional probability. Next let $c^*$ be a vacant circuit on $\mathcal{G}_{p\ell}^*$ surrounding the point $(\lfloor v(1) \rfloor, \lfloor v(2) \rfloor)$ and with all its edges and vertices in $V_k$. We want to show that if such a $c^*$ exists, then it contains a $t^*$ with the properties (7.66)-(7.69). This is intuitively clear from Fig. 7.4 if one takes into account that by (7.65) the right edge of $V_k$ is on the vertical line $x(1) = \lfloor v(1) \rfloor + 2M_{k1} < 2M_{\ell 1} - \Lambda_4$, while $\tilde{C}$ is part of $r_3$ and hence to the right of the vertical line $x(1) = 2M_{\ell 1} - \Lambda_4$. A formal proof was given in Kesten (1980a) Lemma 3 for the case where the upper edge of $V_k$ also lies below $C = \tilde{B}_1$ (as depicted in Fig. 7.4). Here we shall appeal to Lemma A.2. Let $J_1$ be $Fr(\tilde{J}^+(\tilde{s}^*))$, viewed as a Jordan curve. $J_1$ is made up of the following four arcs: $A_{11} = \{v\}$ (i.e., consisting of the single point $v$ only), $A_{12} = \tilde{s}^*$ followed by the piece of $C$ from $v_\rho^*$ to $u_3$ ($v_\rho^*$ is the intersection of $\tilde{s}^*$ and $C$, $u_3$ is the intersection of $C$ and $\tilde{C}$; see Fig. 7.3 and 7.5), $A_{13} = \tilde{C}$ and $A_{14}$ = piece of $r$ between $v_\nu$ and $v$ ($v_\nu$ is the intersection of $r$ and $\tilde{C}$, $v$ is the intersection of $r$ and $\tilde{s}^*$ (see Fig. 7.3-7.5). For $J_2$ we take $c^*$, viewed as a Jordan curve. Then

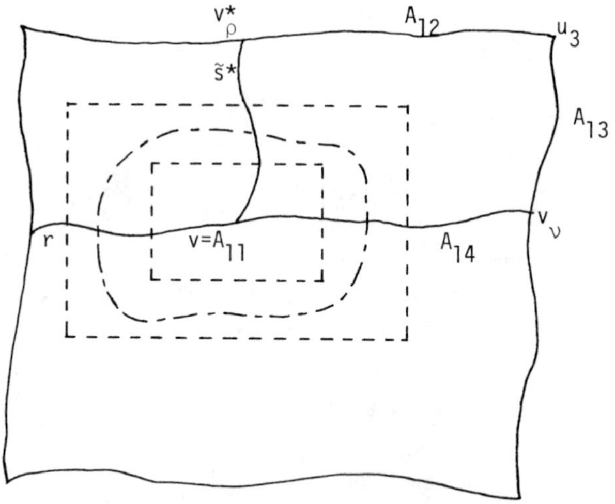


Figure 7.5 $U_k$ is the region between the dashed rectangles. — - — - denotes the circuit $c^*$.

under (7.64) $c^*$ also surrounds $v$, i.e., $A_{11} = \{v\} \subset \text{int}(J_2)$, and $A_{13} = \tilde{C} \subset \text{ext}(J_2)$, since by the above $\tilde{C}$ lies outside the exterior boundary of $V_k$ whenever (7.64) and hence (7.65) holds. Therefore, by Lemma A.2 $c^*$ contains an arc, $t^*$ say, with one endpoint each on

$\mathring{A}_{12} \subset \tilde{s}^\star \cup \mathring{C}$ and $\mathring{A}_{14} \subset r$, and such that $\tilde{t}^\star$ minus its endpoints is contained in $\text{int}(J_1) = \tilde{J}^+(\tilde{s}^\star)$. If $t^\star = (w, g^\star, w_0^\star, \dots, g_\sigma^\star, w_\sigma^\star)$ with $w$ the endpoint on $r$ and $w_\sigma^\star$ the endpoint on $\mathring{A}_{12}$, then $t^\star$ satisfies (7.66)-(7.69) (recall that $c^\star \subset V_k$ and that $c^\star$ is vacant; also $w \in \mathring{A}_{14} \subset \text{int}(J)$). Thus the existence of $c^\star$ implies the existence of $t^\star$ as desired. Consequently,

(7.72)
$$P_{p_0}\{\exists \text{ path } t^\star \text{ which satisfies (7.66)-(7.69)} \mid S^\star = \tilde{s}^\star\}$$
$$= P_{p_0}\{\exists \text{ path } t^\star \text{ which satisfies (7.66)-(7.69)}\}$$
$$\geq P_{p_0}\{\exists \text{ vacant circuit on } \mathcal{G}_{p\ell}^\star \text{ surrounding } (\lfloor v(1) \rfloor, \lfloor v(2) \rfloor) \text{ and inside } V_k\}.$$

Since $V_k$ is just the translate by $(\lfloor v(1) \rfloor, \lfloor v(2) \rfloor)$ of $U_k$, the last member of (7.72) equals the left hand side of (7.21) (with $\ell$ replaced by $k$), by virtue of periodicity. Thus (7.71) follows from (7.72) and (7.21). The proof is complete. □

Remark.

(ii) In Ch. 10 it will be necessary to have an estimate for the conditional distribution of $N(r)$, given $\{R = r\}$ under $P_{p(t)}$, instead of just for the conditional expectation of $N(r)$. This estimate was already given in Kesten (1980a), Steps (i) and (ii) in the proof of Prop. 1. We shall want to restrict ourselves in Ch. 10 to counting only vertices with vacant connections in

$$\Gamma = \Gamma_\ell := [\tfrac{1}{2} M_{\ell 1}, \tfrac{3}{2} M_{\ell 1}] \times \mathbb{R} .$$

More precisely let $N_\Gamma(r)$ be the number of vertices $v$ of $\mathcal{G}_{p\ell}$ on $r$ for which there exists a vacant path $s^\star = (v_0^\star, e_1^\star, \dots, e_\rho^\star, v_\rho^\star)$ on $\mathcal{G}_{p\ell}^\star$ which satisfies the following properties

(7.73) there exists an edge $e^\star$ of $\mathcal{M}_{p\ell}$ between $v$ and $v_0^\star$ such that $\mathring{e}^\star \subset J^+(r) \cap \Gamma$,

(7.74)
$$v_\rho^\star \in \mathring{C}$$

(7.75)
$$(v_0^\star, e_1^\star, \dots, e_{\rho-1}^\star \setminus \{v_\rho^\star\}) = s^\star \setminus \{v_\rho^\star\} \subset J^+(r) \cap \Gamma .$$

(Note that we dropped the restriction $v \in \mathcal{M}$, and therefore only require $e^*$ is an edge of $\mathcal{M}_{p\ell}$ in (7.73)). Let $r$ be as in (7.39)-(7.41) and

$$\Gamma' = [\frac{3}{4} M_{\ell 1}, \frac{5}{4} M_{\ell 1}] \times \mathbb{R} \quad .$$

The desired estimate is that for $\ell$ greater than some $\ell_0(m)$

(7.76) $$P_{p(t)}\{N_\Gamma(r) \geq m | R = r\}$$
$$\geq \frac{1}{2} P_{p_0}\{ \exists \text{ at least one } v \text{ on } r \text{ and a vacant path } s^* \text{ which satisfy (7.73)-(7.75) with } \Gamma \text{ replaced by } \Gamma'\} ,$$

uniformly in $r$, $0 \leq t \leq 1$. We briefly indicate the trivial changes necessary in the proof of Lemma 7.4 to obtain (7.76). Instead of (7.52) and (7.53) we have

$$P_{p(t)}\{N_\Gamma(r) \geq m | R = r\} = P_{p(t)}\{N_\Gamma(r) \geq m\} \geq P_{p_0}\{N_\Gamma(r) \geq m\} .$$

Also, for fixed $r$ we again consider vacant paths $\tilde{s}^*$ satisfying (7.55) and (7.56) with the right hand side of (7.55) replaced by $\text{int}(\tilde{J}) \cap \Gamma'$. Again $S^*$ will be the left-most of all these paths. Then there exists at least one $v$ on $r$ and a vacant path $s^*$ which satisfies (7.73)-(7.75) with $\Gamma$ replaced by $\Gamma'$ whenever $S^*$ exists. Instead of (7.63) we get

$$P_{p_0}\{N_\Gamma(r) \geq m\}$$
$$\geq P_{p_0}\{S^* \text{ exists}\} \cdot \min_{\tilde{s}^*} P_{p_0}\{N_\Gamma(r) \geq m | S^* = s^*\}$$

Now if $\tilde{s}^* \subset \Gamma'$ then its endpoint $v$ on $r$ lies in $\Gamma'$. Thus, if we strengthen (7.64) to

(7.77) $$M_{k1} > 1, M_{k2} > 1 \text{ and } 2M_{k1} < \frac{1}{4} M_{\ell 1} - 1 ,$$

then the whole annulus $V_k$ lies inside $\Gamma$. Instead of (7.70) we therefore obtain

(7.78) $\quad P_{p_0}\{N_\Gamma(r) \geq m | S^* = s^*\} \geq P_{p_0}\{$# of $k$ satisfying (7.77) for which there exists a path $t^*$ which satisfies (7.66)-(7.69) at least $m | S^* = \tilde{s}^*\}$

As in the proof of (7.72) we may drop the condition $S^* = s^*$ and replace "path $t$ which satisfies (7.66)-(7.69)" by "vacant circuit in $V_k$" in (7.78). In other words the right hand side of (7.78) is at least

(7.79) $\quad P_{p_0}\{$# of $k$ satisfying (7.77) for which $V_k$ contains a vacant circuit on $\mathcal{G}^*_{p\ell}$ surrounding $\lfloor v \rfloor$ is at least $m\}$ .

However, the $P_{p_0}$-probability that any fixed $V_k$ contains a vacant circuit on $\mathcal{G}^*_{p\ell}$ surrounding $\lfloor v \rfloor$ is at least $\delta_4^4$ (cf. (7.21) and Lemma 4.1) and the different $V_k$ are disjoint. Vacant circuits in different $V_k$ occur therefore independent of each other. Moreover, as $\ell \to \infty$ the number of $k$ which satisfies (7.77) also tends to $\infty$. If we call this number $\nu$, then the number of $k$ satisfying (7.77) for which $V_k$ contains a vacant circuit on $\mathcal{G}^*_{p\ell}$ surrounding $\lfloor v \rfloor$ has just a binomial distribution corresponding to $\nu$ trials with success probability $\geq \delta_4^4$ . Clearly the probability that such a variable is $\geq m$ tends to 1 as $\nu \to \infty$. Thus (7.79) is at least 1/2 for all large $\ell$. This implies (7.76). ///

Proof of Theorem 3.1 (ii) and (iii). It suffices to prove part (ii), since part (iii) then follows by interchanging the roles of $\mathcal{G}$, $p$ and "occupied" with those of $\mathcal{G}^*$, $\bar{1}-p$ and "vacant", respectively.

(3.46) follows from (7.35), Theorem 5.1 and Lemma 7.3. To see this note that (7.35) implies (5.10) with $\bar{N} = 2\bar{M}_\ell$, $\ell$ large and $p = p'$ . Thus by (5.11)

(7.80) $$P_{p'}\{\#W(v) = \infty\} = 0,$$

which is the first relation in (3.46). It is also immediate from (5.11) that (3.48) holds. To obtain the second relation in (3.46) pick a $p \in \mathcal{P}_\lambda$ such that $p' << p << p_0$. Then automatically $\bar{0} << p << \bar{1}$ and by the above (applied to $p$ instead of $p'$) also

$$E_p\{\#W(v)\} < \infty .$$

Lemma 7.3 now shows

$$P_p\{\#W^*(v) = \infty\} > 0.$$

But $\{\#W^*(v) = \infty\}$ is a decreasing event so that Lemma 4.1 implies

$$P_{p'}\{\#W^*(v) = \infty\} \geq P_p\{\#W^*(v) = \infty\} > 0 .$$

The second relation in (3.46) follows. Finally, we have from Lemma 4.1 and (7.34)

(7.81) $P_{p'}\{\ \exists$ a vacant circuit on $\mathcal{G}^*$ surrounding

$[N,N]\times[-N,N]\} \geq P_{p_0}\{\ \exists$ vacant circuit on $\mathcal{G}^*$ surrounding

$[-N,N]\times[-N,N] = 1$ for all $N$.

If $v_1$ and $v_2$ are two vertices of $\mathcal{G}^*$ in $[-N,N]\times[-N,N]$ and $\#W^*(v_1) = \#W^*(v_2) = \infty$, then there exist vacant paths, $\pi_1^*$ and $\pi_2^*$ say, on $\mathcal{G}^*$ from $v_1$ to $\infty$ and from $v_2$ to $\infty$, respectively. Both these paths have to intersect any vacant circuit $c^*$ on $\mathcal{G}^*$ which surrounds $[-N,N]\times[-N,N]$ (and hence $v_1$ and $v_2$). The intersection of $\pi_i^*$ and $c^*$ does not have to be a vertex of $\mathcal{G}^*$, but nevertheless $\pi_i^*$ and $c^*$ must contain a pair of neighboring vertices on $\mathcal{G}^*$, as explained in Comment 2.2 (vii). Consequently $c^*$ has to belong to $W^*(v_i)$ for $i = 1,2$. Thus, if a vacant circuit $c^*$ as above exists, then $W^*(v_1)$ and $W^*(v_2)$ have $c^*$ in common and $W^*(v_1) = W^*(v_2)$. Thus (7.81) shows $W^*(v_1) = W^*(v_2)$ whenever $\#W^*(v_1) = \#W^*(v_2) = \infty$ so that there is at most one infinite vacant cluster on $\mathcal{G}^*$. The fact that there actually exists an infinite vacant cluster follows from Birkhoff's ergodic theorem (Walters (1982) Theorem 1.14) since for fixed $v \in \mathcal{G}^*$

$$\frac{1}{n}\sum_{k=0}^{n} I[\#W^*(v+k\xi_1) = \infty] \to P_{p'}\{\#W^*(v) = \infty\} > 0 \quad \text{a.e. } [P_{p'}]$$

(compare Harris (1960), Lemma 5.1 and Lemma 3.1). (3.47) is immediate from these considerations. □

<u>Proof of Theorem 3.2</u>. Let $p_1 \in \mathcal{P}_\lambda$ be such that the set in the right hand side of (3.56) is nonempty, so that $t_0$ in (3.56) is well defined. Assume further that $\overline{0} << p_0 = t_0 p_1 << \overline{1}$. We shall now give an indirect proof of

(7.82) $$\liminf_{n\to\infty} \sigma^*((d_2n,d_3n);1,p_0) > 0$$

and

(7.83) $$\liminf_{n\to\infty} \sigma^*((c_2n,c_3n);2,p_0) > 0 \quad .$$

Assume for the sake of argument that (7.82) fails. Then there exists a sequence $n_\ell \to \infty$ such that

$$\lim_{\ell\to\infty} \sigma^*((d_2n_\ell,d_3n_\ell);1,p_0) = 0$$

and by (3.55) also

$$\lim_{\ell\to\infty} \sigma^*((n_\ell,d_1n_\ell);2,p_0) = 0.$$

If this is the case, then we see from (7.14) and (7.15) that

(7.84) $$\lim_{\ell\to\infty} \sigma((n_\ell-2\Lambda_4,d_1n_\ell+2\Lambda_4);1,p_0) = 1$$

as well as

$$\lim_{\ell\to\infty} \sigma((d_2n_\ell+2\Lambda_4,d_3n_\ell-2\Lambda_4);2,p_0) = 1.$$

By virtue of Lemma 2.1b the probabilities of occupied horizontal and vertical crossings on $\mathcal{G}_{p\ell}$ of suitable rectangles also tend to 1. More precisely, the existence of an occupied horizontal crossing on $\mathcal{G}$ of $[0,n-2\Lambda_4]\times[0,d_1n+2\Lambda_4]$ implies the existence of an occupied horizontal crossing on $\mathcal{G}_{p\ell}$ of $[\Lambda,n-2\Lambda_4-\Lambda]\times[-\Lambda,d_1n+2\Lambda_4+\Lambda]$. Therefore (7.84) implies

$$\lim_{\ell\to\infty} \sigma((n_\ell-2\Lambda_4-2\Lambda-1,d_1n_\ell+2\Lambda_4+2\Lambda+1);1,p_0,\mathcal{G}_{p\ell}) = 1.$$

Similarly

$$\lim_{\ell\to\infty} \sigma((d_2n_\ell+2\Lambda_4+2\Lambda+1,d_3n_\ell-2\Lambda_4-2\Lambda-1);2,p_0,\mathcal{G}_{p\ell}) = 1.$$

By virtue of the RSW theorem (Theorem 6.1) (and Comment 3.3 (v)) there must exist a $\pi$ (depending on $d_1,d_2,d_3$ only) such that for all $k$

$$\lim_{\ell\to\infty} \sigma((kn_\ell,(\pi+3)n_\ell);1,p_0,\mathcal{G}_{p\ell}) = \lim_{\ell\to\infty} \sigma((\pi+3)n_\ell,kn_\ell);2,p_0,\mathcal{G}_{p\ell}) = 1.$$

By Lemma 2.1a we can now go back to $\mathcal{G}$ to obtain

(7.85) $\lim_{\ell\to\infty} \sigma((kn_\ell,(\pi+4)n_\ell);1,p_0,\mathcal{G}) = \lim_{\ell\to\infty} \sigma(((\pi+4)n_\ell,kn_\ell);2,p_0,\mathcal{G}) = 1.$

Finally, by (7.12) we have for any integers $m_1$, $m_2$

(7.86) $$\sigma((m_1,m_2);1,p_0)+\sigma^*((m_1,m_2);2,p_0) \le 1$$

and by interchanging the horizontal and vertical direction also

(7.87) $$\sigma((m_1,m_2);2,p_0)+\sigma^*((m_1,m_2);1,p_0) \le 1.$$

(7.85)-(7.87) show that

$$\lim_{\ell\to\infty} \sigma^*((kn_\ell,(\pi+4)n_\ell);2,p_0) = \lim_{\ell\to\infty} \sigma^*(((\pi+4)n_\ell,kn_\ell);1,p_0) = 0.$$

If we take $N_\ell = (\pi+4)n_\ell$ and $k = 3\pi+12$ this implies

(7.88) $$\tau^*((N_\ell,N_\ell);i,p_0,\mathcal{G}) = \tau((N_\ell,N_\ell);i,\overline{1}-p_0,\mathcal{G}^*) \to 0$$

as $\ell \to \infty$ for $i = 1,2$. Indeed $(3\pi+12)n_\ell = 3N_\ell$ so that

$$\tau^*((N_\ell,N_\ell);1,p_0,\mathcal{G}) = P_{p_0}\{\exists \text{ vacant horizontal crossing on } \mathcal{G}^* \text{ of } [0,N_\ell]\times[0,3N_\ell]\} = \sigma^*((\pi+4)n_\ell,(3\pi+12)n_\ell);1,p_0),$$

and similarly for the vertical direction. In particular (7.88) allows us to pick on $N$ with

$$\tau((N,N);i,\overline{1}-p_0,\mathcal{G}^*) \le \frac{1}{2}\kappa(2),\ i = 1,2,$$

where $\kappa(2)$ is defined by (5.9). By continuity we can then also find a $0 < t_1 < t_0$ such that $\overline{0} \ll t_1p_1 \ll \overline{1}$ and

(7.89) $$\tau^*((N,N);i,t_1p_1,\mathcal{G}) = \tau^*((N,N);i,\overline{1}-t_1p_1,\mathcal{G}^*) \le \kappa(2).$$

This, however, contradicts the definition of $t_0$ via Theorem 5.1. Indeed (7.89) and Theorem 5.1 applied to $\mathcal{G}^*$ show

(7.90) $$P_{t_1p_1}\{\#W^*(v) \ge n\} \le C_1e^{-C_2n},\ n \ge 0$$

for any vertex $v$ of $\mathcal{G}^*$, which implies

$$\lim_{n\to\infty} \sigma^*((n+2\Lambda_4, a_1n-2\Lambda_4); t_1p_1, 2) = 0,$$

by the same argument as at the end of the proof of Lemma 5.4 (especially (5.55)). Together with (7.14) this finally gives

$$\lim_{n\to\infty} \sigma((n, a_1n); t_1p_1, 1) = 1,$$

contradicting (3.56) since $t_1 < t_0$. It follows that (7.82) must hold and (7.83) is proved in the same way. (3.39) for some choice of $\delta$, $\overline{m}_\ell$ is now immediate from (7.82) and (7.83). (Note however, that the $b_1, b_2$ for which (3.39) holds are not the $b_1, b_2$ of (3.53).)

Interchanging the role of $\mathcal{G}$ and $\mathcal{G}^*$ one proves in the same way that

$$\liminf_{n\to\infty} \sigma((b_2n, b_3n); 1, p_0) = 0$$

implies for some $t_2 > t_0$ with $\overline{0} << t_2p_1 << \overline{1}$

$$\lim_{n\to\infty} \sigma((n, a_1n); 1, t_2p_1) = \lim_{n\to\infty} \sigma((n, b_1n); 2, t_2p_1) = 0.$$

Again this contradicts (3.56), since $t_2 > t_0$. Hence

$$\liminf_{n\to\infty} \sigma((b_2n, b_3n); 1, p_0) > 0$$

and similarly

$$\liminf_{n\to\infty} \sigma((a_2n, a_3n); 2, p_0) > 0.$$

Thus also (3.38) holds, i.e., Condition B is fulfilled for $p_0$. $\square$

## 8. POWER ESTIMATES.

In this chapter we study the behavior of the percolation probability and the expected size of an occupied cluster in a one-paremeter problem. As defined in Ch. 3 this means that we consider probability measures for which

$$P_p\{v \text{ is occupied}\} = p$$

is the same for all vertices $v$ of the studied graph $\mathcal{G}$, and the occupancies of all vertices are independent. We want to know the asymptotic behavior of

$$\theta(p) = \theta(p,z_0) = P_p\{\#W(z_0) = \infty\}$$

and of [1])

$$E_p\{\#W(z_0);\ \#W(z_0) < \infty\}$$

as $p$ approaches the critical probability $p_H$ (see Sect. 3.4). By analogy with results in statistical mechanics, and on the basis of numerical evidence (see Stauffer (1979) and Essam (1980)) it is generally believed that

$$(8.1) \qquad \theta(p) \sim C_0(p-p_H)^{\beta} \quad , \quad p \downarrow p_H ,$$

$$(8.2) \qquad E_p\{\#W(z_0);\ \#W(z_0) < \infty\} \sim C_+(p-p_H)^{-\gamma+} \ , \ p \downarrow p_H$$

and

$$(8.3) \qquad E_p\{\#W(z_0)\} \sim C_-(p_H-p)^{-\gamma-} \ , \ p \uparrow p_H$$

for suitable constants $C_0$ $C_\pm$ and $0 < \beta, \gamma_\pm < \infty$. Similar power laws are conjectured for other quantities. It is also conjectured that the so-called critical exponents $\beta, \gamma_\pm$ do not depend (or

---

1) $E\{X;A\}$ stands for $E\{X\,I_A\}$, i.e., the integral of $X$ over the set $A$.

depend very little) on the detailed structure of $\mathcal{G}$, but depend (almost) entirely on the dimension of $\mathcal{G}$ only. In other words, these exponents should be (almost) the same for all periodic graphs $\mathcal{G}$ imbedded in $\mathbb{R}^d$ with one particular $d$. As far as the author knows powerlaws like (8.1)-(8.3) have been established mathematically for very few models, and not at all for any of the percolation models discussed in this monograph. It is not even clear how strictly (8.1) should be interpreted. Does it mean

$$\lim_{p \downarrow p_H} \frac{\theta(p)}{(p-p_H)^\beta} = c_0 \neq 0 ,$$

or

$$\frac{\theta(p)}{(p-p_H)^\beta} \quad \text{is a slowly varying function of } p-p_H \text{ as } p \downarrow p_H,$$

or perhaps only

$$\lim_{p \downarrow p_H} \frac{\log \theta(p)}{\log (p-p_H)} = \beta \quad ?$$

A similar comment applies to (8.2), (8.3) and other conjectured power laws. The best we can prove so far is that the left hand sides of (8.1)-(8.3) are bounded above and below by suitable powers of $|p-p_H|$ for percolation problems on certain two dimensional graphs $\mathcal{G}$. We believe that the method of proof will work for many graphs in the plane in which the horizontal and vertical direction play symmetric roles, but to simplify matters somewhat we restrict ourselves here to site - and bond - percolation on the simple quadratic lattice. The graph for site percolation on $\mathbb{Z}^2$ is $\mathcal{G}_0$ of Ex. 2.1 (i). In keeping with the tenor of these notes we treat bond percolation on $\mathbb{Z}^2$ in its equivalent version as site percolation on the graph $\mathcal{G}_1$ of Ex. 2.1 (ii) (see Sect. 2.5, especially Ex. 2.5 (ii)). We also deal with the matching graph $\mathcal{G}_0^*$ of $\mathcal{G}_0$ described in Ex. 2.2 (i) and the matching graph $\mathcal{G}_1^*$ of $\mathcal{G}_1$. $\mathcal{G}_1^*$ is isomorphic to $\mathcal{G}_1$ (see Ex. 2.2 (ii)). When $\mathcal{G} = \mathcal{G}_i^*$, $i = 0$ or $1$, then $\mathcal{G}^*$ will be the graph $\mathcal{G}_i$ itself, in accordance with Comment 2.2 (v).

The principal result of this chapter is the following theorem.

<u>Theorem 8.1</u>. <u>For one-parameter site-percolation on</u> $\mathcal{G} = \mathcal{G}_0$, $\mathcal{G}_1$, $\mathcal{G}_0^*$ <u>or</u> $\mathcal{G}_1^*$ <u>there exist constants</u> $0 < C_i, \beta_i, \gamma_i < \infty$ <u>such that for</u> $p_H = p_H(\mathcal{G})$ <u>one has</u>

(8.4) $C_3(p-p_H)^{\beta_1} \le \theta(p) \le C_4(p-p_H)^{\beta_2}$ , $p \ge p_H$ ,

(8.5) $C_5(p_H-p)^{-\gamma_1} \le E_p\{\#W\} \le C_6(p_H-p)^{-\gamma_2}$ , $p \le p_H$ ,

and

(8.6) $C_7(p-p_H)^{-\gamma_3} \le E_p\{\#W;\ \#W < \infty\} \le C_8(p-p_H)^{-\gamma_4}$ , $p > p_H$ .

In the course of proving this theorem we derive the following estimates, some of which will be used in the next chapter.

Theorem 8.2. For one-parameter site-percolation on $\mathcal{G} = \mathcal{G}_0, \mathcal{G}_1, \mathcal{G}_0^*$, or $\mathcal{G}_1^*$ there exist constants $0 < C_i, \gamma_i < \infty$ such that uniformly for $0 \le p \le 1$

(8.7) $P_p\{n \le \#W < \infty\} \le C_9 n^{-\gamma_5}$

and

(8.8) $E_p\{(\#W)^{\frac{1}{2}\gamma_5}\ ;\ \#W < \infty\} \le C_{10}$ .

Also, at $p = p_H = p_H(\mathcal{G})$

(8.9) $C_{11}n^{\gamma_6 - 1} \le P_{p_H}\{\#W \ge n\} = P_{p_H}\{n \le \#W < \infty\} \le C_9 n^{-\gamma_5}$ .

Remark .

For $\mathcal{G} = \mathcal{G}_1$ or $\mathcal{G}_1^*$ $p_H(\mathcal{G}) = \frac{1}{2}$ by Application 3.4 (ii). Also, by Application 3.4 (iv) (see also Russo (1981))

$$p_H(\mathcal{G}_1) = 1 - p_H(\mathcal{G}_1^*) .$$

In the graphs considered here all vertices play the same role so that $\theta(p,z_0)$ and the distribution of $\#W(z_0)$ are the same for all vertices $z_0$ . Therefore no reference to $z_0$ is necessary in the theorem. Finally, for $p \le p_H$ $\#W < \infty$ with $P_p$-probability one (see Theorem 3.1 (ii)). Therefore, for $p \le p_H$ (8.8) simply becomes

$$E_p\{(\#W)^{\frac{1}{2}\gamma_5}\} \le C_{10} .$$ ///

In each of (8.4)-(8.6) one of the inequalities is much easier to prove than the other one. In (8.4) the first inequality is the difficult one. To motivate our principal lemma we shall work backwards from this inequality. Assume then that we want to prove

$$\theta(p) \ge C_3(p-p_H)^{\beta_1} , \quad p \ge p_H .$$

First we fix a vertex $z_0$ . If $\mathcal{G} = \mathcal{G}_0$ or $\mathcal{G}_0^*$ we take $z_0 = (0,0)$ , the origin, and if $\mathcal{G} = \mathcal{G}_1$ or $\mathcal{G}_1^*$ we take $z_0 = (\frac{1}{2},0)$ . We introduce the following notation. For any vertex $v = (v(1),v(2))$ of $\mathcal{G}$

$$(8.10) \qquad S(v,M) = [v(1)-M,\ v(1)+M] \times [v(2)-M,\ v(2)+M]$$

(a square around $v$). The topological boundary of $S(v,M)$ is denoted by

$$(8.11) \qquad \Delta S(v,M) = \{x = (x(1),x(2)) : |x(1)-v(1)| = M\ ,\ |x(2)-v(2)| \le M \text{ or } |x(1)-v(1)| \le M\ ,\ |x(2)-v(2)| = M\}\ .$$

If some point $y \in \Delta S(z_0,M)$ belongs to an edge in $W = W(z_0)$ , then $W$ can be finite only if there exists a vacant circuit on $\mathcal{G}^*$ surrounding $z_0$ and $y$ , by virtue of Cor. 2.2. Such a circuit $c^*$ must contain at least $M$ vertices. (e.g. if $y$ is on the top edge of $\Delta S$ , then $c^*$ must contain a vertex below the horizontal line $x(2) = 0$ and a vertex above the horizontal line $x(2) = M$.) Consequently, for any $M$

$$\theta(p) \ge P_p\{\ \exists \text{ occupied path on } \mathcal{G} \text{ from } z_0 \text{ to some } y \text{ on } \Delta S(v_0,M) \text{ but there does not exist a vacant circuit on } \mathcal{G}^* \text{ surrounding } z_0 \text{ and containing at least } M \text{ vertices}\}\ .$$

By the FKG inequality this implies

$$(8.12) \qquad \theta(p) \ge P_p\{\ \exists \text{ occupied path on } \mathcal{G} \text{ from } z_0 \text{ to some } y \text{ on } \Delta S(z_0,M)\}\ .\ P_p\{\text{there does not exist a vacant circuit on } \mathcal{G}^* \text{ surrounding } 0 \text{ and containing at least } M \text{ vertices}\}.$$

It is not hard to prove (see Smythe and Wierman (1978), formula (3.34); a better estimate is in Lemma 8.4 below) that the first factor in the right hand side of (8.12) is at least $C_{12}/M$ for any $p \ge p_H$ . To estimate the second factor, observe that any circuit on $\mathcal{G}^*$ surrounding $z_0$ and containing $\ell \ge M$ vertices must intersect the first coordinate axis in one of the vertices $(j,0)$ $((j + \frac{1}{2}, 0))$ , $1 \le j \le \ell$ , if $\mathcal{G} = \mathcal{G}_0$ or $\mathcal{G}_0^*(\mathcal{G}_1$ or $\mathcal{G}_1^*)$ . If $\mathcal{G} = \mathcal{G}_0$ or $\mathcal{G}_0^*$ and there exists a vacant circuit on $\mathcal{G}^*$ through $(j,0)$ which contains $\ell$ vertices, then $W^*(j,0)$ , the vacant component of $(j,0)$ on $\mathcal{G}^*$ contains at least $\ell$ vertices. Consequently

(8.13) $$\theta(p) \geq P_p\{\exists \text{ occupied path on } \mathcal{G} \text{ from } z_0 \text{ to some } y \text{ on } \Delta S(z_0,M)\}\{1 - \sum_{\ell=M}^{\infty} \sum_{j=1}^{\ell} P_p\{\#W^*(j,0) \geq \ell\}\}$$

$$= P_p\{\exists \text{ occupied path on } \mathcal{G} \text{ from } z_0 \text{ to some } y \text{ on } \Delta S(z_0,M)\}\{1 - \sum_{\ell=M}^{\infty} \ell P_p\{\#W^*(z_0) \geq \ell\}\}$$

(8.13) remains valid when $\mathcal{G} = \mathcal{G}_1$ or $\mathcal{G}_1^*$. The difficult part is now to find a good upper bound for

$$P_p\{\#W^*(z_0) \geq \ell\}$$

when $p > p_H$, but $p$ close to $p_H$. For this we use Theorem 5.1, applied to $\mathcal{G}^*$. By Theorem 3.1 (iii), for $p > p_H$

$$E_p\{\#W^*(z_0)\} < \infty$$

and thus, by Theorem 5.1 (with the role of occupied and vacant interchanged)

(8.14) $$P_p\{\#W^*(z_0) \geq \ell\} \leq C_1 e^{-C_2 \ell}$$

and the problem is reduced to getting a grip on $C_1, C_2$. Lemma 5.3 shows that we can take

(8.15) $$C_1 = \left(\frac{7}{5}\right)^2 (50e) \quad , \quad e^{-C_2} = 2^{-A} \quad ,$$

where

(8.16) $$A = \frac{1}{49} \frac{1}{N^2}$$

as soon as $N$ is so large that

(8.17) $$\tau^*((N,N);\, i,\, p,\, \mathcal{G}) \leq \kappa = \frac{1}{4} (50e)^{-121} \quad , \; i = 1,2 \quad .$$

Actually (5.42) still contains the quantity

(8.18) $$\tau^*((N,N);\, 1,\, p,\, \mathcal{G}) + \tau^*((N,N);\, 2,\, p,\, \mathcal{G})$$

but one easily sees from (5.46) that our upper bound (8.14) is increasing in the quantity (8.18), and we may therefore substitute $2\kappa$ for the quantity (8.18), as long as (8.17) holds. On the graphs which we consider here the horizontal and vertical directions are equivalent so that it suffices to choose $N$ such that (8.17) holds for $i = 1$. For any such $N$ (8.14)-(8.16) yield

(8.19) $$P_p\{\#W^*(z_0) \geq \ell\} \leq C_1 \exp - \left(\frac{\log 2}{49} \frac{1}{N^2} \ell\right) .$$

To find an $N$ for which (8.17) holds we reexamine the proof of Theorem 3.1. Specifically we shall go back to Russo's formula in the form (7.44). We write $E^* = E^*(N)$ for the event

(8.20) $$E^* = \{ \exists \text{ vacant horizontal crossing on } \mathcal{G}^*_{p\ell} \text{ of } [0,N] \times [0,3N]\}$$

and $N_0^*$ for the number of pivotal sites on $\mathcal{M}$ for $E^*$. (Here and in the sequel, we view $(\mathcal{G},\mathcal{G}^*)$ as a matching pair, based on $(\mathcal{M},\mathcal{F})$ as described in Sect. 2.2. The planar modifications $\mathcal{G}_{p\ell}$ and $\mathcal{G}^*_{p\ell}$ were defined in Sect. 2.3.)

Note that we are dealing with crossings on $\mathcal{G}^*_{p\ell}$ rather than $\mathcal{G}^*$ in (8.20). The planar modifications of the graphs are useful whenever we want to use the RSW theorem (Theorem 6.1) as we shall have to do repeatedly here. For the present graphs we always choose the central vertices in $\mathcal{G}^*_{0,p\ell}$ and $\mathcal{G}^*_{1,p\ell}$ at points of the form $(k_1 + \frac{1}{2}, k_2 + \frac{1}{2})$ , $k_i \in \mathbb{Z}$ , and in $\mathcal{G}_{1,p\ell}$ at points $(k_1,k_2)$ , $k_i \in \mathbb{Z}$. The edges incident to the central vertices are straight line segments as illustrated in Fig. 8.1. Of course $\mathcal{G}_{0,p\ell} = \mathcal{G}_0$, and $\mathcal{G}^*_{1,p\ell}$ is obtained by translating $\mathcal{G}_{1,p\ell}$ by $(\frac{1}{2},\frac{1}{2})$ . One of the simplifications

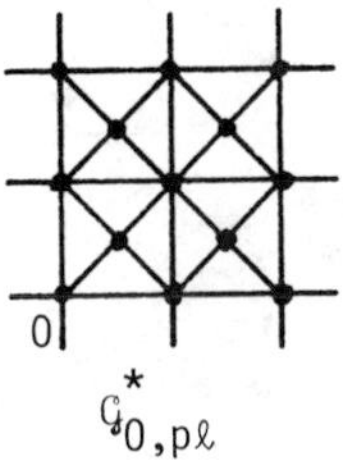


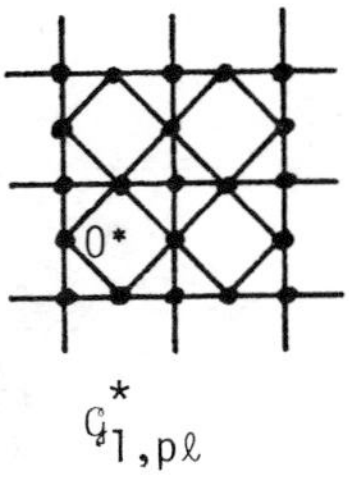


Figure 8.1 Illustration of $\mathcal{G}^*_{0,p\ell}$ and $\mathcal{G}^*_{1,p\ell}$ . Each black circle represents a vertex. In $\mathcal{G}^*_{1,p\ell}$ the origin is marked by *; it is not a vertex of $\mathcal{G}^*_{1,p\ell}$ .

obtained by this construction is that for each of the graphs $\mathcal{G}_0$ and $\mathcal{G}_1$ an edge of $\mathcal{G}_{p\ell}$ or of $\mathcal{G}^*_{p\ell}$ intersects each vertical line $x(1) = n$ or horizontal line $x(2) = n$, $n \in \mathbb{Z}$, in a vertex of $\mathcal{G}_{p\ell}$ or $\mathcal{G}^*_{p\ell}$, respectively. It is not hard to check the proof of Lemma 2.1b and to verify that for the special graphs $\mathcal{G}_0, \mathcal{G}_1, \mathcal{G}^*_0$ and $\mathcal{G}^*_1$ the existence of a vacant horizontal crossing on $\mathcal{G}^*$ of $[0,N] \times [0,3N]$ implies the existence of a vacant horizontal crossing on $\mathcal{G}^*_{p\ell}$ of $[0,N] \times [0,3N]$ [1]. (One just inserts central sites of $\mathcal{G}^*_{p\ell}$ wherever necessary; these are vacant by our convention (7.3)). Therefore

$$\begin{aligned}(8.21)\qquad \tau^*((N,N);\ 1,p,\mathcal{G}) &= \tau((N,N);\ 1,q,\mathcal{G}^*)\\ &\leq \tau((N,N);\ 1,q,\mathcal{G}^*_{p\ell}) = P_p\{E^*(N)\} \quad (q = 1-p)\ .\end{aligned}$$

We now apply Russo's formula (4.22) as we did in (7.42)-(7.44). $\mathcal{G}^*_{p\ell}$, $E^*$ are substituted for $\mathcal{G}$ and $E$, respectively. We also have to replace $p$ by $q = P_p\{v$ is vacant$\}$. The quantity $\alpha$ in (7.43) is to be replaced by

$$\inf_{v \in \mathcal{M}} (P_{p_H}\{v \text{ is vacant}\} - P_p\{v \text{ is vacant}\}) = p - p_H ,$$

and if we take $p(t) = tp_H + (1-t)p$ then we find exactly as in (7.44)

$$\begin{aligned}(8.22)\qquad \tau^*((N,N);\ 1,p,\mathcal{G}) &\leq P_p\{E^*(N)\}\\ &\leq \exp - (p-p_H) \int_0^1 E_{p(t)}\{N^*_0 | E^*\}dt\ ,\ p > p_H\ .\end{aligned}$$

In the present setup a vacant horizontal crossing on $\mathcal{G}^*_{p\ell}$ of $[0,N] \times [0,3N]$ is a vacant path $r^* = (v^*_0, e^*_1, \ldots, e^*_\nu, v^*_\nu)$ on $\mathcal{G}^*_{p\ell}$ with the properties (8.23)-(8.25) :

$$(8.23)\qquad (v^*_1, e^*_2, \ldots, e^*_{\nu-1}, v^*_{\nu-1}) \subset \text{int}\ (J)\ ,$$

where $J$ is the perimeter of $[0,N] \times [0,3N]$ viewed as a Jordan curve.

(8.24) $e^*_1$ intersects $J$ only in the point $v^*_0$ which belongs to $\{0\} \times [0,3N]$ .

---

[1] This fact is not at all crucial; it merely allows us to do away with $\Lambda$ on most places in the proof. Also we do not have to construct $J$ laboriously as in Lemmas 7.1 and 7.4.

(8.25) $e^*_\nu$ intersects $J$ only in the point $v^*_\nu$ which belongs to $\{N\} \times [0,3N]$.

Note that $v^*_1 \subset \text{int}(J)$ and (8.24) together imply $e^*_1 \setminus \{v^*_0\} \subset \text{int}(J)$. Similarly (8.23) and (8.25) imply $e^*_\nu \setminus \{v^*_\nu\} \subset \text{int}(J)$ . By Prop. 2.3, whenever $E^*$ occurs, then there exists a unique vacant horizontal crossing $r^*$ of $[0,N] \times [0,3N]$ for which the component of $\text{int}(J) \setminus r^*$ below $r^*$ (i.e., with the lower edge of $J = [0,N] \times \{0\}$ in its boundary) is minimal. We shall denote this lowest vacant horizontal crossing by $R^*$ . As in (7.46)

$$E^* = \cup\{R^* = r^*\} ,$$

where the union is over all paths $r^* = (v^*_0, e^*_1,\dots,e^*_\nu, v^*_\nu)$ on $\mathcal{G}^*_{p\ell}$ which satisfy (8.23)-(8.25) . Also, when $\{R^* = r^*\}$ occurs, and $v^*$ is a vertex of $\mathcal{M}$ on $r^* \cap \text{int}(J)$ , then $v^*$ is pivotal for $E^*$ whenever it has an occupied connection to $\mathring{C}:= (0,N) \times \{3N\}$ above $r^*$ . Analogously to Lemma 7.4 we mean by this that there exists a path $s = (v_0,e_1,\dots,e_\rho,v_\rho)$ on $\mathcal{G}_{p\ell}$ such that

(8.26) there exists an edge $e$ of $\mathcal{G}_{p\ell}$ between $v^*$ and $v_0$ such that $\mathring{e} \subset J^+(r^*)$

(8.27) $$v_\rho \in \mathring{C} ,$$

(8.28) $$(v_0,e_1,\dots,e_\rho \setminus \{v_\rho\}) \subset J^+(r^*) ,$$

and

(8.29) all vertices of $s$ are occupied,

where $J^+(r^*)$ is the component of $\text{int}(J) \setminus r^*$ with $C = [0,N] \times \{3N\}$ in its boundary (compare (7.47)-(7.49)).

Still following the proof of Lemma 7.4 we now set

(8.30) $N^*(r^*) = N^*(r^*,N) = \#$ of vertices $v^*$ of $\mathcal{M}$ on $r^* \cap \text{int}(J)$ which have an occupied connection to $\mathring{C}$ above $r^*$.

Exactly as in (7.54) we then have

$$E_{p(t)}\{N^*_0|E^*\} \geq \min_{r^*} E_{p_H}\{N^*(r^*)\} ,$$

where the minimum is over all paths $r^*$ on $\mathcal{G}^*_{p\ell}$ satisfying (8.23)-(8.25). Together with (8.22) this yields

(8.31) $\tau^*((N,N);1,p,\mathcal{G}) \leq \exp - (p-p_H) \min_{r^*} E_{p_H}(N^*(r^*,N))$ ,

and we finally must estimate how fast

(8.32) $$\min_{r^*} E_{p_H}(N^*(r^*,N))$$

grows with $N$.

The argument so far has been largely a repetition of the proof of Lemma 7.4 with $\mathcal{G}^*_{p\ell}$ and "vacant" taking the place of $\mathcal{G}_{p\ell}$ and "occupied". One could continue to imitate the proof of Lemma 7.4. For this we would first show that there exists $\delta_k > 0$ such that

(8.33) $\sigma((k\ell,\ell);\ 1,p_H(\mathcal{G}),\ \mathcal{G}_{p\ell}) \geq \delta_k > 0 \quad , \quad \ell \geq 1$ ,

and

(8.34) $P_{p_H(\mathcal{G})}\{\ \exists$ occupied circuit on $\mathcal{G}_{p\ell}$ surrounding $0$ and inside the annulus $[-2\ell,2\ell] \times [-2\ell,2\ell] \setminus (-\ell,\ell) \times (-\ell,\ell) \geq \delta_4^4$ , $N \geq 1$ .

((8.33) and (8.34) will be needed in any case and will be demonstrated below; see Lemma 8.1). (8.33) and (8.34) are just (7.18) and (7.20) for the present graphs; they show that we may take $\bar{N}_\ell = (\ell,\ell)$ in (7.18) and (7.20) . However, for Lemma 7.4 we wanted disjoint annuli so that we rather take $\bar{N}_\ell = (2^{2\ell},2^{2\ell})$ . The analogues of (7.62), (7.70) and (7.72) then yield

(8.35) $\min_{r^*} E_{p_H}\{N^*(r^*,N)\} \geq \delta'(\#$ of $k$ with $N_k < \frac{1}{2}N) \geq \delta'' \log N$

for some $\delta', \delta'' > 0$ . When this estimate is substituted in (8.31) one obtains

$$\tau^*((N,N);\ 1,p,\mathcal{G}) \leq N^{-\delta''(p-p_H)} ,$$

so that (8.17) holds when $N \geq \exp C(p-p_H)^{-1}$ for some constant $C$. Next, by (8.19) this would give

$$\sum_{\ell=M}^{\infty} \ell\ P_p\{\#W^*(v_0) \geq \ell\} \leq \frac{1}{2}$$

whenever

$$M \geq \exp\{(2+\varepsilon)\ C\ (p-p_H)^{-1}\}$$

for fixed $\varepsilon > 0$ and $p$ close to $p_H$. Finally, (8.13) with an estimate of order $M^{-1}$ for the first factor in the right hand side would show

$$\theta(p) \geq \exp - \{(2+\varepsilon)C((p-p_H)^{-1}\} \quad , \quad p \downarrow p_H$$

Obviously this is much weaker than the left hand inequality in (8.4). The reason for this is the poor lower bound (8.35) for (8.32). Retracing the above steps we see that we will obtain the first inequality of (8.4) when we improve (8.35) to

$$\min_{r^*} E_{p_H} \{N^*(r^*,N)\} \geq CN^{(2+\varepsilon)/\beta_1} .$$

The principal step of our proof is therefore to obtain this improvement on Lemma 7.4. It is established in Lemma 8.3.

Lemma 8.1. For $\mathcal{G} = \mathcal{G}_0, \mathcal{G}_1, \mathcal{G}_0^*$, or $\mathcal{G}_1^*$ and integral $k$ there exists a $\delta_k > 0$ such that

(8.36) $$\sigma((k\ell,6\ell); 1, p_H(\mathcal{G}),\mathcal{G}_{p\ell}) = \sigma((6\ell,k\ell); 2, p_H(\mathcal{G}),\mathcal{G}_{p\ell}) \geq \delta_k$$

and

(8.37) $$P_{p_H(\mathcal{G})}\{\exists \text{ occupied circuit on } \mathcal{G}_{p\ell} \text{ surrounding the origin in } [-12\ell, 12\ell] \times [-12\ell,12\ell] \setminus (-6\ell,6\ell) \times (-6\ell,6\ell)\} \geq \delta_4^4 , \ell \geq 1 .$$

Remarks.

(i) This lemma proves (8.33) and (8.34) with $\ell$ replaced by $6\ell$. Using monotonicity properties such as in Comment 3.3 (v) we could obtain (8.33) and (8.34) for all $\ell$, but this will not be needed.

(ii) For $\mathcal{G} = \mathcal{G}_0$ or $\mathcal{G}_0^*$ this lemma was proved by Russo (1981) by means of Theorem 5.4. For $\mathcal{G} = \mathcal{G}_1$ or $\mathcal{G}_1^*$ the lemma was proved by Seymour and Welsh (1978), but formulated for bond percolation. Their argument for $\mathcal{G}_1$ runs roughly as follows in our notation: By a simple variant of Prop. 2.2

(8.38) $$\sigma((\ell,\ell); 1,p,\mathcal{G}_{1,p\ell}) + P_p\{\exists \text{ vacant vertical crossing on } \mathcal{G}_{1,p\ell}^* \text{ of } [\tfrac{1}{2}, \ell-\tfrac{1}{2}] \times [\tfrac{1}{2},\ell-\tfrac{1}{2}]\} \geq 1$$

(compare (7.14). Now use the fact that $\mathcal{G}^*_{1,p\ell}$ is just $\mathcal{G}_{1,p\ell}$ shifted by $(\frac{1}{2}, \frac{1}{2})$ and the fact that the horizontal and vertical direction play identical roles on $\mathcal{G}_{1,p\ell}$ to obtain

$$P_p\{\exists \text{ vacant vertical crossing of } [\tfrac{1}{2}, \ell-\tfrac{1}{2}] \times [\tfrac{1}{2}, \ell-\tfrac{1}{2}] \text{ on } \mathcal{G}^*_{1,p\ell}\} = P_{1-p}\{\exists \text{ occupied vertical crossing of } [0,\ell-1] \times [0,\ell-1] \text{ on } \mathcal{G}_{1,p\ell}\} = \sigma((\ell-1,\ell-1);1,1-p,\mathcal{G}_{1,p\ell}) .$$

Together with (8.38) this gives for $p = \frac{1}{2}$

$$\sigma((\ell,\ell);\ 1,\ \tfrac{1}{2},\ \mathcal{G}_{1,p\ell}) + \sigma((\ell-1,\ell-1);\ 1,\ \tfrac{1}{2},\ \mathcal{G}_{1,p\ell}) \geq 1$$

so that for each N

$$\sigma((m,m);\ 1,\ \tfrac{1}{2},\ \mathcal{G}_1) \geq \tfrac{1}{2} \quad \text{for } m = \ell-1 \text{ or } m = \ell .$$

This is essentially (8.36) for $k = 6$ , since $p_H(\mathcal{G}_1) = \frac{1}{2}$ (see Application 3.4 (ii)). From this one can easily obtain Lemma 8.1 by means of the RSW theorem.

Our proof below is essentially as in Russo (1981), and works simultaneously for all the $\mathcal{G}$ under consideration. The only difference is that we use Theorem 5.1 instead of Theorem 5.4.

Proof of Lemma 8.1. Theorem 5.1 implies

$$\tau((\ell,\ell);\ i,p_H(\mathcal{G}),\ \mathcal{G}) \geq \kappa = \kappa(2) \text{ for } i=1 \text{ and } i=2, \tag{8.39}$$

for otherwise by (5.11)

$$E_{p_H}(\#W) < \infty .$$

But this is impossible since $p_H \geq p_T$ and by (5.17)

$$E_{p_T}(\#W) = \infty ,$$

while $E_p\{\#W\}$ increases with $p$ (Lemma 4.1). Thus (8.39) holds. However, for the graphs $\mathcal{G}$ considered in this lemma the horizontal and vertical direction play identical roles so that

$$\sigma((\ell_1,\ell_2);1,\ p,\ \mathcal{G}) = \sigma((\ell_2,\ell_1);\ 2,\ p,\ \mathcal{G}) . \tag{8.40}$$

In particular

$$\sigma((\ell,3\ell);\ 1,\ p_H,\mathcal{G}) = \sigma((3\ell,\ell);\ 2,\ p_H,\ \mathcal{G}) =$$
$$\tau((\ell,\ell);\ 1,\ p_H,\mathcal{G}) = \tau((\ell,\ell);\ 2,\ p_H,\ \mathcal{G}) \geq \kappa$$

We also saw above (see the argument before (8.21)) that the existence of an occupied horizontal (vertical) crossing of a rectangle $[0,\ell_1]\times[0,\ell_2]$ on $\mathcal{G}$ implies the existence of such a crossing on $\mathcal{G}_{p\ell}$ ($\ell_1$, $\ell_2$ integral). Thus

$$\sigma((\ell,3\ell);1,p_H(\mathcal{G}),\mathcal{G}_{p\ell}) \geq \sigma((\ell,3\ell);1,p_H(\mathcal{G}),\mathcal{G}) \geq \kappa ,$$

$$\sigma((3\ell,\ell);2,p_H(\mathcal{G}),\mathcal{G}_{p\ell}) \geq \sigma((3\ell,\ell);2,p_H(\mathcal{G}),\mathcal{G}) \geq \kappa .$$

(8.36) and (8.37) now follow from Theorem 6.1 and (the proof of) Corollary 6.1. □

We need some preparation for Lemma 8.2. Let $a$ and $\Theta$ each be a vertex of $\mathcal{G}_{p\ell}$ or of $\mathcal{G}^*_{p\ell}$, and $\ell$, $N$ integers $\geq 0$ such that

(8.41) $$S(a,3.2^{\ell}) \subset S(\Theta,N)$$

(see (8.10) for $S$ and (8.11) for $\Delta S$). Let $r = (v_0,e_1,\dots,e_\nu,v_\nu)$ and $s = (w_0,f_1,\dots,f_\sigma,w_\sigma)$ be two paths on $\mathcal{G}_{p\ell}$ with the following properties:

(8.42) $$v_0 = a, \quad v_\nu \in \Delta S(\Theta,N),$$

(8.43) $$(v_0,e_1,\dots,v_{\nu-1},e_\nu \setminus \{v_\nu\}) = e\setminus\{v_\nu\} \subset \mathring{S}(\Theta,N),$$

(8.44) $$w_0 = a, \quad w_\sigma \in \Delta S(\Theta,N),$$

(8.45) $$(w_0,f_1,\dots,w_{\sigma-1},f_\sigma \setminus \{w_\sigma\}) = s\setminus\{w_\sigma\} \subset \mathring{S}(\Theta,N),$$

(8.46) $$r \cap s = \{a\} .$$

If (8.42)-(8.46) hold then $r$ and $s$ are two paths in $S(\Theta,N)$ from $a$ to $\Delta S(\Theta,N)$ which intersect only in $a$. (This can only happen if $a$ is a vertex of $\mathcal{G}_{p\ell}$.) The reverse of $r$ followed by $s$ is a simple curve which divides $\mathring{S}(\Theta,N)$ into two components, each of which is bounded by this simple curve and one of the arcs of $\Delta S(\Theta,N)$ between $w_\sigma$ and $v_\nu$ (see Fig. 8.2). Denote these components in arbitrary order $S' = S'(\Theta,r,s)$ and $S'' = S''(\Theta,r,s)$.

<u>Def. 8.1</u>. For any subset $R$ of $S(\Theta,N)$ and vertex $v_i$ on $r$ we say that $v_i$ is <u>connected to $s$ in $R$</u> if $v_i = a$ or if there exists a path $t = (u_0,g_1,\dots,g_\tau,u_\tau)$ on $\mathcal{G}_{p\ell}$ which satisfies

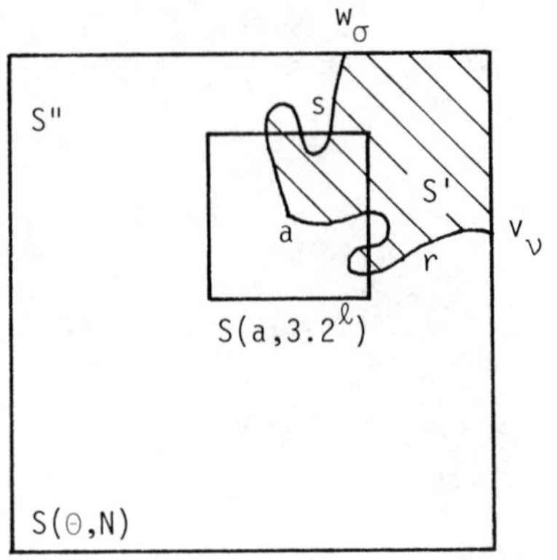


Figure 8.2 The outer square is $S(\Theta,N)$; the inner square is $S(a,3.2^\ell)$. $S'$ is the hatched region.

(8.47) $$(g_1 \setminus \{u_0\}, u_1, \ldots, u_{\tau-1}, g_\tau \setminus \{u_\tau\}) = t \setminus \{u_0, u_\tau\} \subset R,$$

(8.48) $$u_0 = v_i \text{ and } u_\tau = w_j \text{ on } s \text{ for some } 1 \le j \le \sigma,$$

and

(8.49) $$u_1, \ldots, u_{\tau-1} \text{ are occupied.}$$ ///

Next we set

(8.50) $$Y(v_i,a,\ell,r,s) = \begin{cases} 1 & \text{if } v_i \text{ is connected to } s \text{ in } S'(\Theta,r,s) \cap S(a,3.2^\ell), \\ 0 & \text{otherwise,} \end{cases}$$

and

(8.51) $$Z(\ell) = \min E_{p_H}(\mathcal{G})\{\sum_{\substack{v_i \varepsilon r \cap S(a,3.2^\ell) \\ v_i \text{ a vertex of } \mathcal{M}}} Y(v_i,a,\ell,r,s) \mid \omega(v) = \varepsilon(v),\ v \varepsilon \overline{S}''(\Theta,r,s)\},$$

where the min in (8.51) is over all $a$, $\Theta$, $N$, $r$, $s$ which satisfy (8.41)-(8.46) and over all choices of +1 or -1 for $\varepsilon(v)$ with $v$

a vertex of $\mathcal{G}_{p\ell}$ in $\bar{S}''$. Note that the sum (8.51) is simply the number of vertices of $\mathcal{M}$ or $r$ inside $S(a,3.2^{\ell})$ which are connected to $s$ in $S' \cap S(a,3.2^{\ell})$. This sum depends only on occupancies of vertices in $S'$, and hence is independent of $\{\omega(v): v \in \bar{S}''\}$. Thus, the conditioning in the expectation in the right hand side of (8.51) does not influence the expectation. It is nevertheless useful for the proof of the next lemma to introduce this conditioning.

We shall also need an analogue of $Z$ when $r$ is replaced by a path on $\mathcal{G}^*_{p\ell}$ (instead of on $\mathcal{G}_{p\ell}$). In other words $r = (v^*_0, e^*_1, \dots, e^*_\nu, v^*_\nu)$ will now be a path on $\mathcal{G}^*_{p\ell}$ which satisfies

(8.52) $$v^*_0 = a,\ v^*_\nu \in \Delta S(\Theta,N)$$

and

(8.53) $$(v^*_0, e^*_1, \dots, v^*_{\nu-1}, e^*_1 \setminus \{v^*_\nu\}) = r^* \setminus \{v^*_\nu\} \subset \mathring{S}(\Theta,N).$$

$s = (w_0, f_1, \dots, f_\sigma, w_\sigma)$ will again be a path on $\mathcal{G}_{p\ell}$ which satisfies (8.44) and (8.45). Analogously to (8.46) we require

(8.54) $$r^* \cap s = \{a\} ,$$

which can happen only if $a$ is a vertex of $\mathcal{G}$ and $\mathcal{G}^*$, i.e., a vertex of $\mathcal{M}$. Def. 8.1 can be copied without change for vertices $v^*_i$ on $r^*$ instead of vertices $v_i$ on $r$. Finally $Y^*(v^*_i, a, \ell, r^*, s)$ is defined as in (8.50) by replacing $v_i$ and $r$ by $v^*_i$ and $r^*$. Similarly $Z^*(\ell)$ is defined by replacing $Y(v_i, a, \ell, r, s)$ by $Y^*(v^*_i, a, \ell, r^*, s)$ and $\bar{S}''(\Theta, r, s)$ by $\bar{S}''(\Theta, r^*, s)$ in (8.51).

<u>Lemma 8.2</u>. <u>There exist constants</u> $0 < C_{12}, \alpha_1 < \infty$ , <u>such that for</u> $\mathcal{G} = \mathcal{G}_0, \mathcal{G}_1, \mathcal{G}^*_0$ <u>or</u> $\mathcal{G}^*_1$

(8.55) $$Z(\ell) \geq C_{12} 2^{\alpha_1 \ell} , \quad \ell \geq 0,$$

<u>and</u>

(8.56) $$Z^*(\ell) \geq C_{12} 2^{\alpha_1 \ell} , \quad \ell \geq 0 .$$

<u>Proof:</u> We restrict ourselves to (8.55) since the proof of (8.56) is practically the same. Throughout we fix $\mathcal{G}$ as one of the four graphs $\mathcal{G}_0$, $\mathcal{G}_1$, $\mathcal{G}^*_0$ or $\mathcal{G}^*_1$ . If $\mathcal{G} = \mathcal{G}^*_i$, then $\mathcal{G}^* = \mathcal{G}_i$, $i = 0,1$.

The idea of the proof is very similar to the last part of the proof of Lemma 7.4 (but $s^*$ is now replaced by $s$). Let $r$ and $s$ be as in (8.42)-(8.46). Again we start with considering disjoint annuli centered at $\lfloor a \rfloor := (\lfloor a(1) \rfloor, \lfloor a(2) \rfloor)$ $(a = (a(1),a(2)) = v_0 = w_0)$. In view of (8.37) suitable annuli to take now are

$$V_k := S(\lfloor a \rfloor, 6.2^{2k}) \setminus \mathring{S}(\lfloor a \rfloor, 6.2^{2k-1}).$$

As in the argument for (7.72) we estimate the probability of some $v_i$ being connected in $V_k$ to $s$ by the probability of there existing an occupied circuit surrounding $\lfloor a \rfloor$ in $V_k$. Assume now that there is a vertex $v_{i_k}$ of $r$ in $V_k$ which is connected by a path $t = (u_0, g_1, \dots, g_\tau, u_\tau)$ in $V_k \cap S'(\Theta, r, s)$ to $s$. In Lemma 7.4 we only used the estimate that $V_k$ contains at least the one vertex $v_{i_k}$ of $r$ connected to $s$, in this situation. Here we shall be less casual with our estimation. Let $u_\tau$, the final point of $t$, equal $w_j$ on $s$. Consider the path $s_k$ consisting of $t$ followed by $(w_j, f_{j+1}, \dots, f_\sigma, w_\sigma)$ (a tail piece of $s$). Just as $s$ itself, $s_k$ is

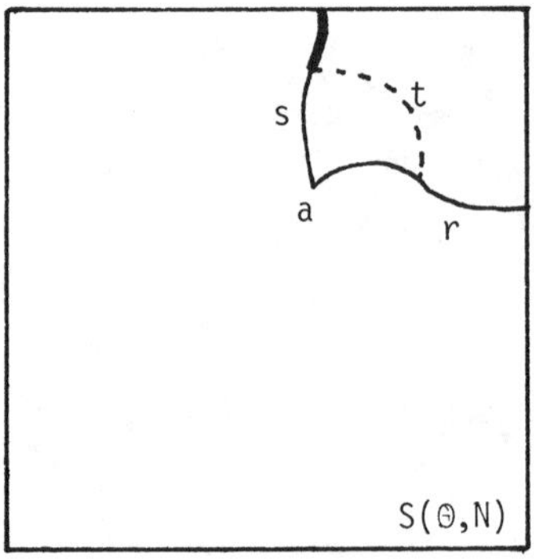


Figure 8.3 $r$ and $s$ are drawn as solid curves. $t$ is dashed. $s_k$ is the composition of $t$ and the boldly drawn part of $s$.

a path on $S(\Theta,N)$ from a point of $r$ to $\Delta S(\Theta,N)$, and $s_k$ intersects $r$ only in the initial point $v_{i_k}$ of $s_k$. Therefore $s_k$ can take over the role of $s$. If some $v_i$ is connected to $s_k$ in $S'(\Theta,r,s)$

then $v_i$ is connected to $s$ itself in $S'$. We can therefore obtain new points connected to $s$, by looking for points which are connected to $s_k$. This is done by considering the annuli

$$S(\lfloor v_{i_k} \rfloor, 6.2^{2m}) \setminus \mathring{S}(\lfloor v_{i_k} \rfloor, 6.2^{2m-1})$$

centered at $\lfloor v_{i_k} \rfloor := (\lfloor v_{i_k}(1) \rfloor, \lfloor v_{i_k}(2) \rfloor)$. This procedure can be repeated and we obtain something resembling a branching process in which the first generation consists of the $v_{i_k}$. Each vertex $v$ which in some generation has been found to be connected to $s$ by a path $\tilde{s}$ "produces" a next generation of vertices connected to $s$, namely the ones connected to $\tilde{s}$ inside suitable annuli centered at $\lfloor v \rfloor$. Closer scrutiny would show that we are dealing with a supercritical branching process with mean number of offspring per individual equal to $m > 1$, say. Estimating $Z(\ell)$ would then amount to estimating the total number of individuals in the branching process after $\varepsilon\ell$ generations, for some $\varepsilon > 0$. This number would have an expectation

$$m^{\varepsilon\ell} = 2^{\ell(\varepsilon \log m/\log 2)}.$$

This is precisely the kind of estimate claimed in (8.55). Rather than follow the above outline in detail we shall prove the recursion relation

$$Z(\ell) \geq (1 + \delta_{30}^4) Z(\ell - 3), \quad \ell \geq 4, \tag{8.57}$$

with $\delta_{30}$ as in (8.36). This corresponds roughly to decomposing the branching process into the separate branching processes generated by the individuals of the first generation of the original branching process. The $(\varepsilon\ell)$-th generation of the former branching process is the sum of the $(\varepsilon\ell-1)$-th generation for the latter branching process.

Now for the detailed proof of (8.57). Fix $a$, $\Theta$, $N$, $\ell$, $r$ and $s$ such that (8.41)-(8.46) hold. Obviously (8.41)-(8.46) continue to hold when $\ell$ is replaced by $\ell-3$ in (8.41), and also

$$Y(v_i, a, \ell, r, s) \geq Y(v_i, a, \ell-3, r, s) \quad \text{for} \quad v_i \in S(a, 3.2^{\ell-3}).$$

Consequently

(8.58) $$E_{p_H}\{\sum_{\substack{v_i \varepsilon r \cap S(a,3.2^{\ell-3}) \\ v_i \varepsilon \mathcal{M}}} Y(v_i,a,\ell,r,s)|\omega(v) = \varepsilon(v), v \varepsilon \bar{S}"\}$$

$$\geq E_{p_H}\{\sum_{\substack{v_i \varepsilon r \cap S(a,3.2^{\ell-3}) \\ v_i \varepsilon \mathcal{M}}} Y(v_i,a,\ell-3,r,s)|\omega(v) = \varepsilon(v), v \varepsilon \bar{S}"\}$$

$$\geq Z(\ell-3).$$

Next define the closed annulus

(8.59) $$V := S(\lfloor a \rfloor, 3(2^{\ell-1} + 2^{\ell-3})) \setminus \mathring{S}(\lfloor a \rfloor, 3(2^{\ell-1} - 2^{\ell-3}))$$

$$\subset \mathring{S}(a,3.2^{\ell}) \subset \mathring{S}(\Theta,N),$$

where as above $a = (a(1),a(2))$, $\lfloor a \rfloor = (\lfloor a(1) \rfloor, \lfloor a(2) \rfloor)$. We shall apply Prop. 2.3 with $S$ taken equal to $V$. For $J$ we take the perimeter of $S'(\Theta,r,s)$ and for the arcs $B_1$, $A$, $B_2$, $C$ making up $J$ we take

(8.60) $B_1$ = reverse of $r$, $A = \{a\}$ (a single point), $B_2 = s$ and

$C$ = arc of $\Delta S(\Theta,N)$ from $w_\sigma$ to $v_\nu$ in the boundary of $S'(\Theta,r,s)$.

We shall be concerned with the collection of paths $t = (u_0,g_1,\dots,g_\tau,u_\tau)$ on $\mathcal{G}_{p\ell}$ which satisfy

(8.61) $$t \subset V,$$

(8.62) $$(g_1 \setminus \{u_0\}, u_1, \dots, u_{\tau-1}, g_\tau \setminus \{u_\tau\}) = t \setminus \{u_0,u_\tau\} \subset S'(\Theta,r,s),$$

(8.63) $u_0$ is some vertex $v_i$ on $r$ with $0 < i < \nu$,

and

(8.64) $u_\tau$ is some vertex $w_j$ on $s$ with $0 < j < \sigma$.

Let $G(r,s)$ be the event

$$G(r,s) = \{\exists \text{ occupied path } t \text{ on } \mathcal{G}_{p\ell} \text{ which satisfies (8.61)-(8.64)}\}.$$

The properties (8.62)-(8.64) are the properties (2.23)-(2.25) in the present set up. Therefore Prop. 2.3 can be applied, and on the event $G(r,s)$ there exists a unique occupied path $t$ satisfying (8.61) -(8.64) for which

$$J^-(t) = \text{component of } \operatorname{int}(J)\setminus t \text{ with } \{a\} \text{ in its boundary}$$
$$= \text{component of } S'(\Theta,r,s)\setminus t \text{ with } \{a\} \text{ in its boundary}$$

is minimal. We shall denote this path with minimal $J^-(t)$ by $T$ whenever it exists. Then Prop. 2.3 implies

$$G(r,s) = \cup \{T = t\}, \tag{8.65}$$

where the union is over all $t$ satisfying (8.61)-(8.64) (compare (7.46)). Also, as in (7.72), any occupied circuit $c$ on $\mathcal{G}_{p\ell}$ and in $V$, surrounding $\lfloor a \rfloor$, contains an occupied path $t$ satisfying (8.61) -(8.64). (This time apply Lemma A.2 with $J_1 = J$, $J_2 = c$ and note that, by virtue of (8.59) and $\ell \geq 4$

$$c \subset V \subset \mathring{S}(\Theta,N), \quad a = v_0 = w_0 \notin V;$$

consequently any vertex $v_i$ of $r$ on $c$ must have $0 < i < \nu$ and any vertex $w_j$ of $s$ one must have $0 < j < \sigma$ and hence the requirements $0 < i < \nu$ in (8.63) and $0 < j < \sigma$ in (8.64) are automatically fulfilled.) It follows that

$$P_p\{G(r,s)\} \geq P_p\{\exists \text{ occupied circuit on } \mathcal{G}_{p\ell} \text{ in } V \text{ and surrounding } \lfloor a \rfloor\} . \tag{8.66}$$

As in the proof of Cor. 6.1 from Theorem 6.1 one can find an occupied circuit in $V$ surrounding $\lfloor a \rfloor$ as soon as there exist occupied vertical crossings on $\mathcal{G}_{p\ell}$ of the two rectangles (one corresponding to the plus signs and one to the minus signs)

$$[\lfloor a(1) \rfloor \pm 3.2^{\ell-1} - 3.2^{\ell-3}, \lfloor a(1) \rfloor, \pm 3.2^{\ell-1} + 3.2^{\ell-3}] \times$$
$$[\lfloor a(2) \rfloor - 3(2^{\ell-1} + 2^{\ell-3}), \lfloor a(2) \rfloor + 3(2^{\ell-1} + 2^{\ell-3})] ,$$

as well as occupied horizontal crossings on $\mathcal{G}_{p\ell}$ of the two rectangles

$$[\lfloor a(1) \rfloor - 3(2^{\ell-1} + 2^{\ell-3}), \lfloor a(1) \rfloor + 3(2^{\ell-1} + 2^{\ell-3})] \times$$
$$[\lfloor a(2) \rfloor \pm 3.2^{\ell-1} - 3.2^{\ell-3}, \lfloor a(2) \rfloor \pm 3.2^{\ell-1} + 3.2^{\ell-3}].$$

By the FKG inequality and (8.36) the right hand side of (8.66) is therefore at least $\delta_{30}^4$, when $p = p_H(\mathcal{G})$. In other words

(8.67) $$P_{p_H(\mathcal{G})}\{G(r,s)\} \geq \delta_{30}^4 .$$

Now let $t = (u_0, g_1, \ldots, g_\tau, u_\tau)$ be a fixed path satisfying (8.61)-(8.64) (no reference to the occupancies of the $u_i$ is made at the moment). Then $t$ is a crosscut of $J$ and divides $\text{int}(J) = S'(\Theta,r,s)$ into two components. The one which contains $\{a\}$ in its boundary we denoted above as $J^-(t)$, while the one with $C$ in its boundary is denoted as usual by $J^+(t)$ (see Fig. 8.4). It is important to give

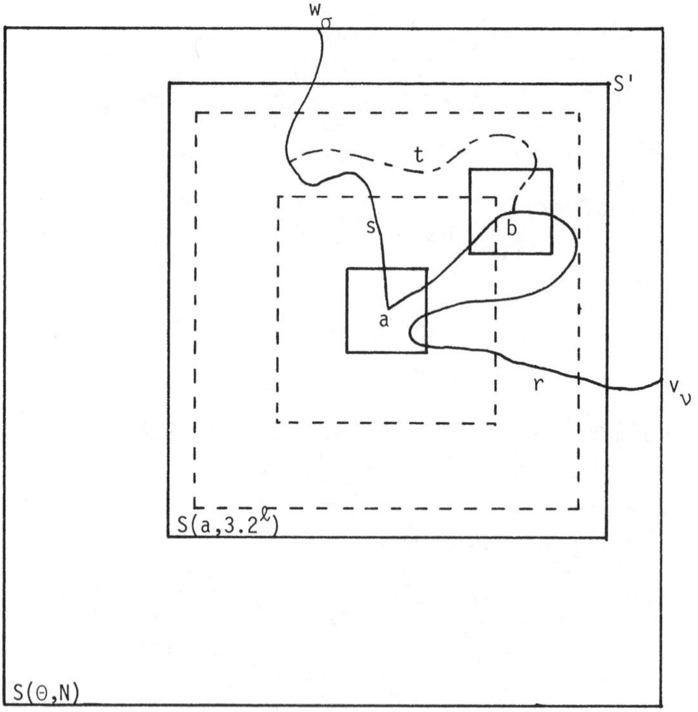


Figure 8.4 V is the annulus between the dashed lines. The small squares centered at a and b are $S(a,3.2^{\ell-3})$ and $S(b,3.2^{\ell-3})$. r and s are drawn solidily; t is indicated by — - — - — .

another equivalent description of $J^+(t)$. Let $u_0 = v_{i_0}$ and denote by $r_0$ the subpath $(v_{i_0}, e_{i_0+1}, \ldots, e_\nu, v_\nu)$ of $r$. Let $u_\tau = w_{j_0}$ and denote by $s_0$ the following path, consisting of $t$ and the piece of $s$ from $w_{j_0}$ on:

$$s_0 = (u_0, g_1, \ldots, g_\tau, u_\tau = w_{j_0}, f_{j_0+1}, w_{j_0+1}, \ldots, f_\sigma, w_\sigma).$$

Finally, we write $b$ for $u_0 = v_{i_0}$. Then the paths $r_0$ and $s_0$ on $\mathcal{G}_{p\ell}$ satisfy the following analogues of (8.42)-(8.46)

$$v_{i_0} = b,\ v_\nu \in \Delta S(\Theta, N),$$

$$(v_{i_0}, e_{i_0+1}, \ldots, e_\nu \setminus \{v_\nu\}) = r_0 \setminus \{v_\nu\} \subset \mathring{S}(\Theta, N),$$

$$u_0 = b,\ \ w_\sigma \in \Delta S(\Theta, N),$$

$$(u_0, g_1, \ldots, g_\tau, u_\tau = w_{j_0}, f_{j_0+1}, \ldots, w_{\sigma-1}, f_\sigma \setminus \{w_\sigma\})$$

$$= s_0 \setminus \{w_\sigma\} \subset \mathring{S}(\Theta, N) \quad (\text{use } \ t \subset V \subset \mathring{S}(\Theta, N)),$$

$$r_0 \cap s_0 = \{b\}\ .$$

In addition, since $b = u_{i_0} \in V$ (8.41) implies

$$S(b, 3.2^{\ell-3}) \subset S(a, 3.2^\ell) \subset S(\Theta, N). \tag{8.68}$$

Therefore $r_0$, $s_0$ and $b$ can take over the roles of $r$, $s$ and $a$, respectively. In particular the simple curve consisting of the reverse of $r_0$ followed by $s_0$ divides $\mathring{S}(\Theta, N)$ into two components $S'(\Theta, v_0, s_0)$ and $S''(\Theta, r_0, s_0)$, where we now choose $S'(\Theta, r_0, s_0)$ to be that component with the arc $C$ between $w_\sigma$ and $v_\nu$ in its boundary. (This arc is also in the boundary of $S'(\Theta, r, s)$; see (8.60).) Also

$$E_{p_H}\{\sum_{\substack{v_i \in r_0 \cap S(b, 3.2^{\ell-3}) \\ v_i \in \mathcal{M}}} Y(v_i, b, \ell-3, r_0, s_0) \mid \omega(v) = \varepsilon(v),\ v \in \overline{S}''(\Theta, r_0, s_0)\} \geq Z(\ell-3). \tag{8.69}$$

We claim that $S'(\Theta,r_0,s_0)$ is the same as $J^+(t)$. This follows immediately from the fact that these two Jordan domains have the same boundary. Indeed, the boundary of $J^+(t)$ consists of $t$, the piece of $s$ between its intersection with $t$, i.e., $w_{j_0}$, and its endpoint $w_\sigma$ (these two pieces make up $s_0$), the arc $C$ and the piece of $r$ from $u_\nu$ to the intersection $u_{i_0}$ of $r$ and $t$. These same curves make up the boundary of $S'(\Theta,r_0,s_0)$. It immediately follows from this claim that

(8.70) $$S'(\Theta,r_0,s_0) = J^+(t) \subset \mathrm{int}(J) = S'(\Theta,r,s)$$

and

(8.71) $$\bar{S}''(\Theta,r,s) \cup \bar{J}^-(t) \subset \bar{S}''(\Theta,r_0,s_0) .$$

Let us now assume that in addition to (8.61)-(8.64) $t$ satisfies

(8.72) $$u_1,\dots,u_{\tau-1} \text{ are occupied .}$$

Then $t$ satisfies (8.47)-(8.49) with $i = i_0$ and

$$R = V \cap S'(\Theta,r,s) \subset \mathring{S}(a,3.2^\ell) \cap S'(\Theta,r,s)$$

(see (8.62) and (8.59)). Thus $v_{i_0}$ is connected to $s$ in $S'(\Theta,r,s) \cap S(a,3.2^\ell)$ and $Y(v_{i_0},a,\ell,r,s) = 1$. However, more is true. We claim that if $t$ satisfies (8.61)-(8.64) and (8.72) and $v_i \in r$ is connected to $s_0$ in $S'(\Theta,r_0,s_0) \cap S(b,3.2^{\ell-3})$, then $v_i$ is also connected to $s$ in $S'(\Theta,r,s) \cap S(a,3.2^\ell)$. In formulas

(8.73) $$Y(v_i,b,\ell-3,r_0,s_0) = 1 \text{ implies } Y(v_i,a,\ell,r,s) = 1.$$

To prove (8.73) assume that $v_i \in r$, and that $t_0 = (x_0,h_1,x_2,\dots,h_\rho,x_\rho)$ is a path on $\mathcal{G}_{p\ell}$ satisfying

(8.74) $$t_0 \setminus \{x_0,x_\rho\} \subset S'(\Theta,r_0,s_0) \cap S(b,3.2^{\ell-3}),$$

(8.75) $$x_0 = v_i \text{ and } x_\rho = \text{some vertex of } s_0 \text{ other than } u_0,$$

(8.76) $$x_1,\dots,x_{\rho-1} \text{ are occupied.}$$

Observe first that (8.68) and (8.70) imply

(8.77) $S'(\Theta,r_0,s_0) \cap S(b,3.2^{\ell-3}) \subset S'(\Theta,r,s) \cap S(a,3.2^{\ell})$.

Thus, $t_0 \setminus \{x_0,x_\rho\}$ is also contained in the right hand side of (8.77), and if its final point $x_\rho$ equals a vertex $w_j$ of $s$ with $1 \leq j \leq \sigma$ (i.e., other than $w_0$) then $v_i$ is connected in $S'(\Theta,r,s) \cap S(a,2^{\ell})$ to $s$, i.e., $Y(v_i,a,\ell,r,s) = 1$. The next case to check is when $x_\rho$ is a vertex of $s_0$ other than $w_1,\dots,w_\sigma$ or $u_0$. Then $x_\rho$ must be one of the vertices $u_1,\dots,u_\tau$. Moreover, $u_\tau = w_{j_0}$ for some $0 < j_0 < \sigma$ (see (8.64)). Let $x_\rho = u_{k_0}$, $1 \leq k_0 \leq \tau$ and define $t_1 := (x_0,h_1,\dots,h_\rho,x_\rho = u_{k_0},g_{k_0+1},\dots,g_\tau,u_\tau)$. $t_1$ consists of $t_0$ followed by a tail piece of $t$. All vertices of $t_1$ other than its initial and final point are occupied, on account of (8.72) and (8.76). Moreover

$$t_1 \setminus \{x_0,u_\tau\} \subset S'(\Theta,r,s) \cap S(a,3.2^{\ell})$$

by virtue of (8.74), (8.77), (8.62), (8.61) and (8.59). Thus, again $Y(v_i,a,\ell,r,s) = 1$. The last case to check for (8.73) is when $v_i = b = v_{i_0} = u_0$. But in this case we already saw, just before (8.73) that $Y(v_{i_0},a,\ell,r,s) = 1$, so that (8.73) has been verified.

The proof of (8.57) is now merely a matter of assembling some of the above results. If there exists a path $t = (u_0,g_1,\dots,g_\tau,u_\tau)$ on $\mathcal{G}_{p\ell}$ which satisfies (8.61)-(8.64) and (8.72) then $b = u_0 \in V$. Then, by definition of $V$,

$$|a(i)-b(i)| \geq 3(2^{\ell-1}-2^{\ell-3})-1$$

and $S(a,3.2^{\ell-3})$ and $S(b,3.2^{\ell-3})$ are disjoint. Thus, by (8.73)

(8.78) $$\sum_{\substack{v_i \in r \cap S(a,3.2^{\ell}) \\ v_i \in \mathcal{M}}} Y(v_i,a,\ell,r,s)$$

$$\geq \sum_{\substack{v_i \in r \cap S(a,3.2^{\ell-3}) \\ v_i \in \mathcal{M}}} Y(v_i,a,\ell,r,s) + \sum_{\substack{v_i \in r \cap S(b,3.2^{\ell-3}) \\ v_i \in \mathcal{M}}} Y(v_i,a,\ell,r,s)$$

$$\geq \sum_{\substack{v_i \in r \cap S(a,3.2^{\ell-3}) \\ v_i \in \mathcal{M}}} Y(v_i,a,\ell,r,s) + \sum_{\substack{v_i \in r \cap S(b,3.2^{\ell-3}) \\ v_i \in \mathcal{M}}} Y(v_i,b,\ell-3,r_0,s_0).$$

Now , as we saw before, the left hand side of (8.78) is independent of the $\omega(v)$ with $v \in \bar{S}''(\Theta,r,s)$. Therefore, by virtue of (8.58)

$$(8.79)\quad E_{P_H(\mathcal{G})}\{\sum_{\substack{v_i \in r \cap S(a,3.2^{\ell}) \\ v_i \in \mathcal{M}}} Y(v_i,a,\ell,r,s) \mid \omega(v) = \varepsilon(v), v \in \bar{S}''(\Theta,r,s)\}$$

$$= E_{P_H(\mathcal{G})}\{\sum_{\substack{v_i \in r \cap S(a,3.2^{\ell}) \\ v_i \in \mathcal{M}}} Y(v_i,a,\ell,r,s)\}$$

$$\geq Z(\ell-3) + \sum_t P_{P_H(\mathcal{G})}\{T = t\} \quad .$$

$$E_{P_H(\mathcal{G})}\{\sum_{\substack{v_i \in r \cap S(u_0,3.2^{\ell-3}) \\ v_i \in \mathcal{M}}} Y(v_i,u_0,\ell-3,r_0,s_0) \mid T = t\} \ ,$$

where the sum is over those path $t$ which satisfy (8.61)-(8.64), $u_0$ is the initial point of $t$ and $r_0$, $s_0$ are defined in terms of $r$, $s$ and $t$ as above. However, by Prop. 2.3 the event $\{T = t\}$ depends only on the occupancies of the vertices in $\bar{J}^-(t) \subset \bar{S}''(\Theta,r_0,s_0)$ (see (8.71)). Therefore

$$E_{P_H(\mathcal{G})}\{\sum_{\substack{v_i \in r \cap S(u_0,3.2^{\ell-3}) \\ v_i \in \mathcal{M}}} Y(v_i,u_0,\ell-3,r_0,s_0) \mid T = t\}$$

$$\geq \min_{\varepsilon(\cdot)} E_{P_H(\mathcal{G})}\{\sum_{\substack{v_i \in r \cap S(u_0,3.2^{\ell-3}) \\ v_i \in \mathcal{M}}} Y(v_i,u_0,\ell-3,r_0,s_0) \mid \omega(v) = \varepsilon(v),\ v \in \bar{S}''(\Theta,r_0,s_0)\}$$

$$\geq Z(\ell-3).$$

Substitution of this estimate into (8.79) and using (8.65) and (8.67) yields

$$E_{P_H(\mathcal{G})}\{\sum_{\substack{v_i \in r \cap S(a,3.2^{\ell}) \\ v_i \in \mathcal{M}}} Y(v_i,a,\ell,r,s) \mid \omega(v) = \varepsilon(v), v \in \bar{S}''(\Theta,r,s)\}$$

$$\geq Z(\ell-3)(1+P_{P_H(\mathcal{G})}\{G(r,s)\}) \geq (1+\delta_{30}^4)Z(\ell-3).$$

(8.57) now follows by minimizing over $a,\Theta,N,r,s$ and $\varepsilon(\cdot)$.

To obtain (8.55) from (8.57) we merely have to show that $Z(\ell) > 0$ for each $\ell \geq 0$. This is easy to see, though, since by Def. 8.1 always $Y(a,a,\ell,r,s) = 1$. If $a$ is a central vertex of $\mathcal{G}$ - and hence lies inside a face $F$ of $\mathcal{M}$, but is not a vertex of $\mathcal{M}$ (see Sect. 2.3) - then $a$ is not to be counted as one of the $v_i$ in the sum in (8.51). However, in this case $r$ and $s$ both have vertices on the perimeter of $F$, and these vertices belong to $\mathcal{G}$ (and hence $\mathcal{M}$). In particular there will be a vertex $v$ of $\mathcal{M}$ on $r$ and a vertex $w$ of $\mathcal{M}$ on $s$ on the perimeter of $F$, such that an open arc of the perimeter of $F$ from $v$ to $w$ lies inside $S'(\Theta,r,s) \cap S(a,3.2^{\ell})$. (See Fig. 8.5 for an illustration which applies when $\mathcal{G} = \mathcal{G}_0^*, \mathcal{G}_1$ or $\mathcal{G}_1^*$; $a$ cannot be a central vertex when $\mathcal{G} = \mathcal{G}_0$.)

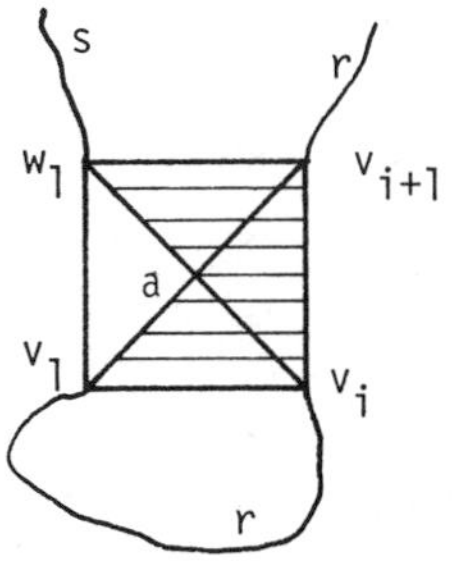


Figure 8.5 The center is the vertex $a$; it is a central vertex in the square, which is a face $F$ of $\mathcal{M}$. The hatched region belongs to $S'(\Theta,N)$. The edges from $a$ to $v_1$ and from $v_i$ to $v_{i+1}$ belong to $r$. The edge from $a$ to $w_1$ is the first edge of $s$. In this illustration the open edge between $v_{i+1}$ and $w_1$ belongs to $S'(\Theta,r,s) \cap S(a,3.2^{\ell})$ and $Y(v_{i+1},a,\ell,r,s) = 1$.

This open arc contains at most two vertices of $\mathcal{G}$ and hence the vertices on this open arc are all occupied with a probability at least $(p_H(\mathcal{G}))^2$. If this happens, then $Y(v,a,\ell,r,s) = 1$. Consequently

$$Z(\ell) \geq (p_H(\mathcal{G}))^2 > 0.$$

This completes the proof. □

We remind the reader that $N^*(r^*) = N^*(r^*,N)$ was defined in (8.30).

Lemma 8.3. There exist a constant $0 < C_{13} < \infty$ such that for $\mathcal{G}$ equal to $\mathcal{G}_0$, $\mathcal{G}_1$, $\mathcal{G}_0^*$ or $\mathcal{G}_1^*$ and any path $r^* = (v_0^*,e_1^*,\dots,e_\nu^*,v_\nu^*)$ on $\mathcal{G}_{p\ell}^*$ which satisfies (8.23)-(8.25) one has

$$E_{p_H(\mathcal{G})}N^*(r^*,N) \geq C_{13}N^{\alpha_1}, \tag{8.80}$$

$$\tau^*(N,N);i,p,\mathcal{G}) \leq \exp-C_{13}(p-p_H(\mathcal{G}))N^{\alpha_1},\ p > p_H,\ i = 1,2 \tag{8.81}$$

and

$$\tau((N,N);i,p,\mathcal{G}) \leq \exp-C_{13}(p_H(\mathcal{G})-p)N^{\alpha_1},\ p < p_H,\ i = 1,2. \tag{8.82}$$

Proof: Again fix $\mathcal{G}$. Let $J$ be the perimeter of $[0,N]\times[0,3N]$ viewed as a Jordan curve, and set

$$A = [0,N]\times\{0\} = \text{bottom edge of } J,$$

$$C = [0,N]\times\{3N\} = \text{top edge of } J.$$

Also fix a path $r^* = (v_0^*,e_1^*,\dots,e_\nu^*,v_\nu^*)$ on $\mathcal{G}_{p\ell}^*$ which satisfies (8.23)-(8.25). It will turn out to be convenient to estimate the left hand side of (8.80) somewhat indirectly, by means of the expected number of occupied connections above $r^*$ to the interior of

$$C_1 := [0,N]\times\{4N\}$$

(rather than to $C$ itself). To be more specific, let $J_1$ be the perimeter of $[0,N]\times[0,4N]$. Then $A$ is also the bottom edge of $J_1$ and $C_1$ is the top edge of $J_1$. The path $r^*$ is also a horizontal crossing of $J_1$, and we define $J_1^-(r^*)$ and $J_1^+(r^*)$ as the components of $\text{int}(J_1)\setminus r^*$ with $A$ and $C_1$ in their boundary, respectively. We say that a vertex $v^*$ on $r^*\cap\text{int}(J) = r^*\cap\text{int}(J_1)$ has an occupied connection to $\mathring{C}_1$ above $r^*$ if there exists a path $s = (v_0,e_1,\dots,e_\rho,v_\rho)$ on $\mathcal{G}_{p\ell}$ which satisfies (8.26)-(8.29) with $J$ and $C$ replaced by $J_1$ and $C_1$. Analogously to (8.30) we write $N_1^*(r^*,N)$ for the number of vertices $v^*$ of $\mathcal{M}$ on $r^*\cap\text{int}(J_1)$ which have an occupied connection above $v^*$ to $\mathring{C}_1$. If $v^*$ has an occupied connection $s = (v_0,e_1,\dots,e_\rho,v_\rho)$ above $r^*$ to $\mathring{C}_1$, then $s$ must intersect $\mathring{C}$, necessarily in one of the $v_i$ (see Fig. 8.6). If $i_0$ is the smallest index $i$ with $v_{i_0}\in C$, then $(v_0,e_1,\dots,e_{i_0},v_{i_0})$

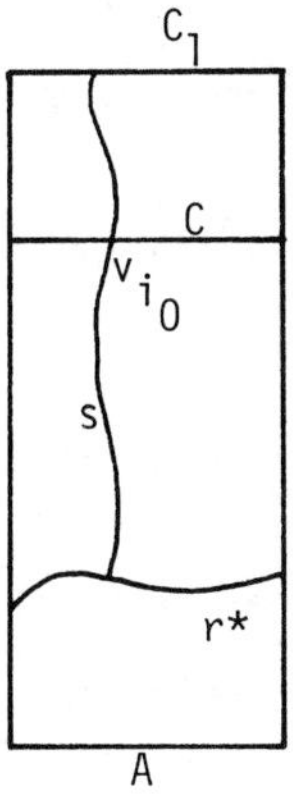


Figure 8.6

(an initial piece of $s$) is an occupied connection above $r^*$ from $v^*$ to $\overset{\circ}{C}$. Thus any vertex counted in $N_1^*(r^*,N)$ must also be counted in $N^*(r^*,N)$ so that

(8.83) $$N^*(r^*,N) \geq N_1^*(r^*,N).$$

The first step in estimating the expectation of $N_1$ is again an imitation of Lemma 7.4. Let $\ell$ be the unique integer for which

(8.84) $$3.2^{\ell} < \frac{N}{2} \leq 3.2^{\ell+1}$$

and let

$$\chi = [1, 3.2^{\ell}+1] \times \mathbb{R}\ .$$

We denote by $F^*(r^*)$ the event that there exists an occupied path $\tilde{s} = (w_0, f_1, \ldots, f_\sigma, w_\sigma)$ on $\mathcal{G}_{p\ell}$ with the following properties:

(8.85) $w_0$ is a vertex of $\mathcal{M}$ on $r^* \cap \mathrm{int}(J) \cap \chi$

(8.86) $$w_\sigma \in C_1 \cap \chi \subset \overset{\circ}{C}_1$$

(8.87) $$(f_1 \setminus \{w_0\}, w_1, f_2, \ldots, w_{\sigma-1}, f_\sigma \setminus \{w_\sigma\})$$
$$= \tilde{s} \setminus \{w_0, w_\sigma\} \subset J_1^+(r^*) \cap \chi\ .$$

Of course $w_0$ has an occupied connecton to $\mathring{C}_1$ above $r^*$, whenever such an $\tilde{s}$ exists. Furthermore, if we denote the perimeter of the Jordan domain $J_1^+(r^*)$ by $J_2$, then such an $\tilde{s}$ is a crosscut of $J_1^+(r^*) = \text{int}(J_2)$ and divides this domain into two components, $J_2^L(\tilde{s})$ and $J_2^R(\tilde{s})$ say. $J_2^L(\tilde{s})$ $(J_2^R(\tilde{s}))$ is the component with a piece of the left edge of $J_1$, $\{0\} \times [0,4N]$, (the right edge of $J_1$, $\{N\} \times [0,4N]$ ) in its boundary. By Prop. 2.3, if $F^*(r^*)$ occurs, then there is a unique occupied connection $\tilde{s}$ with the properties (8.85)-(8.87) with minimal $J_2^L(\tilde{s})$. We shall call this the "left-most occupied connection" and denote it by $\tilde{S}$ whenever it exists. As in (7.60) any occupied vertical crossing $t$ on $\mathcal{G}_{p\ell}$ of $[1,3.2^{\ell}+1] \times [0,4N]$ contains an occupied connection from some point of $r^*$ to $\mathring{C}_1$ inside $X$. Thus

$$\text{(8.88)} \quad P_{p_H}\{\tilde{S} \text{ exists}\} = P_{p_H}\{F^*(r^*) \text{ occurs}\}$$

$$\geq P_{p_H}\{\exists \text{ occupied vertical crossing on } \mathcal{G}_{p\ell} \text{ of } [1,3.2^{\ell}+1] \times [0,4N]\}$$

$$\geq \sigma((3.2^{\ell},3.2^{\ell+4});2,p_H,\mathcal{G}_{p\ell}) \geq \delta_{96} \cdot$$

For the one but last inequality we used (8.84) and Comment 3.3 (v), while the last inequality comes from (8.36).

Now let $\tilde{s}$ be a fixed path satisfying (8.85)-(8.87). This brings us to the setup for Lemma 8.2. Take $a = w_0$, $\Theta = (-3N,0)$ and $r_1^*$ = the piece of $r^*$ from $w_0$ to the right edge $\{N\} \times [0,4N]$ of $J_1$ (i.e., if $w_0 = v_i^*$, then $r_1 = (w_0 = v_i^*, e_{i+1}^*, \dots, e_\nu^*, v_\nu^*))$. Then (8.42)-(8.46) with $r$ replaced by $r_1$, $s$ replaced by $\tilde{s}$ and $N$ replaced by $4N$ are clearly satisfied, since

$$S(\Theta,4N) = [-7N,N] \times [-4N,4N] \supset [0,N] \times [0,4N]$$

and the top right corners of the two rectangles coincide. (8.41) is replaced by

$$S(a,3.2^{\ell}) \subset S(\Theta,4N),$$

which holds by virtue of (8.84) and the fact that $a = w_0$ lies in

$$r^* \cap X \subset [0,3.2^{\ell}+1] \times [0,3N].$$

We now take for $S'(\Theta,r_1,\tilde{s})$ the component of $S(\Theta,4N) \setminus r_1 \cup \tilde{s})$ $= [-7N,N] \times [-4N,4N] \setminus r_1 \cup \tilde{s}$ which is in the "upper right corner" of

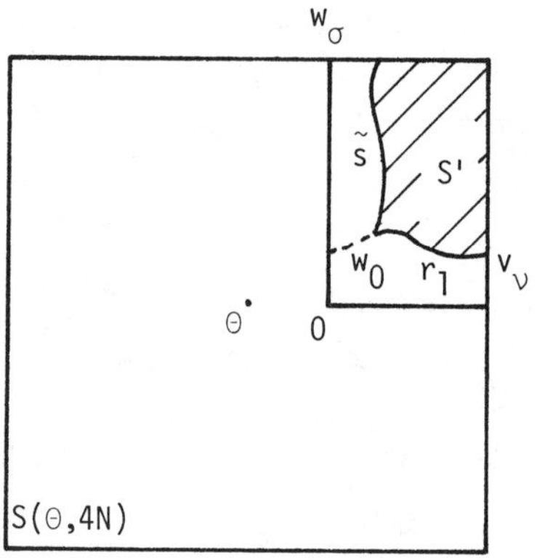


Figure 8.7. $r$ consists of the dashed curve followed by $r_1$. $S'(\Theta,r_1,\tilde{s}) = J_2^R(\tilde{s})$ is the hatched region.

$S(\Theta,4N)$, i.e., the component which is bounded by $r_1 \cup \tilde{s}$ and the arc of $\Delta S(\Theta,4N)$ from $w_\sigma$ to $v_\nu$ which goes through the upper right corner $(N,4N)$ of $S(\Theta,4N)$ (see Fig. 8.7). The latter arc is also an arc of $J_2$ and one easily sees that $S'(\Theta,r_1,\tilde{s})$ is precisely $J_2^R(\tilde{s})$. $S''(\Theta,r_1,\tilde{s})$ will be the other component of $S(\Theta,4N)\setminus r_1 \cup \tilde{s}$. Then (8.56) implies

$$(8.89)\quad E_{p_H}\{\#\text{ of vertices of } \mathcal{M} \text{ on } r_1 \cap S(a,3.2^\ell) \text{ connected to } \tilde{s} \text{ in } S'(\Theta,r_1,\tilde{s}) \cap S(a,3.2^\ell) \,|\, \omega(v) = \varepsilon(v),\ v \in \bar{S}''(\Theta,r_1,\tilde{s})\} \geq C_{12} 2^{\alpha_1 \ell}$$

for any choice of $\varepsilon(v) = \pm 1$, $v \in \bar{S}''$ .

We can derive the required estimate (8.80) easily from (8.89) by an argument already used in Lemma 7.4. Firstly

$$(8.90)\quad E_{p_H}\{N^*(r^*,N)\} \geq E_{p_H}\{N_1^*(r^*,N)\}$$
$$= \sum_{\tilde{s}} P_{p_H}\{\tilde{S} = \tilde{s}\} E_{p_H}\{N_1^*(r^*,N) \,|\, \tilde{S} = \tilde{s}\}$$
$$\geq P_{p_H}\{\tilde{S} \text{ exists}\} \min_{\tilde{s}} E_{p_H}\{N_1^*(r^*,N) \,|\, \tilde{S} = \tilde{s}\}$$
$$\geq \delta_{96} \min_{\tilde{s}} E_{p_H}\{N_1^*(r^*,N) \,|\, \tilde{S} = \tilde{s}\} \qquad \text{(by (8.88))}.$$

The sum and minimum in (8.90) are over all $\tilde{s}$ satisfying (8.85)-(8.87). Secondly, any vertex $v$ on $r_1 \cap S(a,3.2^\ell)$ which is connected to $\tilde{s}$ in $S'(\Theta,r_1,\tilde{s}) \cap \overset{\circ}{S}(a,3.2^\ell)$ (in the sense of Def. 8.1) has an occupied connection above $r^*$ to $C_1$. The argument for this is practically identical to the argument following (7.66)-(7.69) in Lemma 7.4. Consequently

$$N_1^*(r^*,N) \geq \# \text{ of vertices of } \mathcal{M} \text{ on } r_1 \cap S(a,3.2^\ell) \text{ which is connected to } \tilde{s} \text{ in } S'(\Theta,r_1,\tilde{s}) \cap S(a,3.2^\ell).$$

Lastly, by Prop. 2.3 the event $\tilde{S} = \tilde{s}$ depends only on the occupancies of the vertices in

$$\overline{J}_2^L(\tilde{s}) \subset \overline{J}_2 \setminus J_2^R(\tilde{s}) \subset S(\Theta,4N) \setminus S'(\Theta,r_1,\tilde{s}) = \overline{S}''(\Theta,r_1,\tilde{s}).$$

Consequently

$$E_{p_H}\{N_1^*(r^*,N) \mid \tilde{S} = s\} \geq \min_{\varepsilon} E_{p_H}\{\# \text{ of vertices of } \mathcal{M} \text{ on } r_1 \cap S(a,3.2^\ell) \text{ connected to } \tilde{s}' \text{ in } S'(\Theta,r_1,\tilde{s}) \cap S(a,3.2^\ell) \mid \omega(v) = \varepsilon(v),\ v \in \overline{S}''(\Theta,r_1,\tilde{s})\} .$$

This, together with (8.90), (8.89) and (8.84), gives

$$E_{p_H}\{N^*(r^*,N)\} \geq \delta_{96} C_{12} \left(\frac{N}{12}\right)^{\alpha_1} ,$$

whence (8.80).

(8.81) is immediate from (8.80) and (8.31) (and the symmetry between horizontal and vertical for the graphs under consideration). Finally (8.82) is nothing but (8.81) with $\mathcal{G}^*$ and "vacant" replaced by $\mathcal{G}$ and "occupied". (Recall that

$$P_p\{v \text{ vacant}\} = 1-p = 1-P_p\{v \text{ occupied}\}$$

and

$$(8.91) \qquad p_H(\mathcal{G}) = 1-p_H(\mathcal{G}^*)$$

for the graphs of this chapter, by virtue of Applications ii) and iv) in Sect. 3.4.) $\square$

Another application of Lemma 8.2 will be needed for Theorems 8.1 and 8.2. It provides us with a lower bound for $P_{p_H}(B(N))$, where

(8.92) $$B(N) := \{\ \exists \text{ occupied path on } \mathcal{G} \text{ in } S(z_0,N) \text{ which connects } z_0 \text{ with a point on } \Delta S(z_0,N)\}\ .$$

Here $z_0$ is as before, i.e., $z_0$ = the origin if $\mathcal{G}$ is $\mathcal{G}_0$ or $\mathcal{G}_0^*$, and $z_0 = (\frac{1}{2},0)$ if $\mathcal{G}$ is $\mathcal{G}_1$ or $\mathcal{G}_1^*$.

Lemma 8.4. There exists a constant $0 < C_{14} < \infty$ such that

(8.93) $$P_{p_H}\{B(N)\} \geq C_{14}N^{\alpha_1 - 1}\ .$$

Remark.

It is easy to use the argument at the end of the proof below and (8.36) to obtain

$$P_{p_H}\{B(N)\} \geq C_{14}N^{-1}\ .$$

Such an estimate already appears in Smythe and Wierman (1978), formula (3.34). However, to obtain the lower bounds in (8.5) and (8.6) it is crucial to have an estimate like (8.93) which decreases only as a power of $N$ which is strictly larger than the minus first power. Lemma 8.5 below will give an upper bound for $P_{p_H}\{B(N)\}$ which decreases like a negative power of N. It is not known whether there exists an $\alpha$ for which $N^{\alpha}P_{p_H}\{B(N)\}$ has a nonzero (but finite) limit as $N \to \infty$. If such an $\alpha$ exists it must lie strictly between zero and one by (8.93) and (8.101). This is closely related to questions about the behavior of $P_{p_H}\{\#W \geq N\}$ for large N, or the cluster exponent $\tau$ of Stauffer (1979).

Proof of Lemma 8.4. For simplicity take $\mathcal{G}$ equal to $\mathcal{G}_0$, $\mathcal{G}_0^*$ or $\mathcal{G}_1$ so that $\mathcal{G}_{p\ell}$ has edges along the lines $x(i) = k$, $i = 1,2$, $k \in \mathbb{Z}$. Since the left hand side of (8.93) has the same value on $\mathcal{G}_1$ as on $\mathcal{G}_1^*$ these choices for $\mathcal{G}$ suffice.

Fix $\ell$ as the unique integer with

(8.94) $$2^{\ell+2} \leq N < 2^{\ell+3}\ .$$

Consider the collection of occupied vertical crossings on $\mathcal{G}_{p\ell}$ of $[-2^{\ell},2^{\ell}] \times [0,N]$, i.e., the collection of occupied paths

$s = (w_0, f_1, \dots, f_\sigma, w_\sigma)$ on $\mathcal{G}_{p\ell}$ which satisfy

$$(8.95)\qquad (f_1 \setminus \{w_0\}, w_1, \dots, w_{\sigma-1}, f_\sigma \setminus \{w_\sigma\}) = s \setminus \{w_0, w_\sigma\} \subset (-2^\ell, 2^\ell) \times (0, N),$$

$$(8.96)\qquad w_0 \in [-2^\ell, 2^\ell] \times \{0\} \quad \text{and}$$

$$w_\sigma \in [-2^\ell, 2^\ell] \times \{N\} \quad .$$

Denote by $F$ the event that there exists at least one such occupied crossing. Then, by (8.36) and Comment 3.3 (v)

$$(8.97)\qquad P_{p_H}\{F\} = \sigma((2^{\ell+1}, N); 2, p_H, \mathcal{G}_{p\ell}) \geq \delta_{32} \quad .$$

Let $J$ be the perimeter of $[-2^\ell, 2^\ell] \times [0, N]$ and $A = \{-2^\ell\} \times [0, N]$ its left edge, $C = \{2^\ell\} \times [0, N]$ its right edge. For any crossing $s$ satisfying (8.95) and (8.96) $J^\pm(s)$ are defined as before (see Def. 2.11). Prop. 2.3 tells us that whenever $F$ occurs there is a unique left-most occupied crossing $s$ of $J$, i.e., an occupied path $s$ with minimal $J^-(s)$ among all occupied paths satisfying (8.95) and (8.96). We denote this left-most crossing by $S$ whenever it exists.

Now let $s = (w_0, f_1, \dots, f_\sigma, w_\sigma)$ be a fixed path on $\mathcal{G}_{p\ell}$ satisfying (8.95) and (8.96). We shall apply Lemma 8.2 with the following choices: $\Theta$ = the origin, $a = w_0$, $r$ = the path along the first coordinate axis, $x(2) = 0$, from $w_0$ to the point $(N, 0)$ on the right edge of $S(\Theta, N)$. $N$ and $\ell$ satisfy (8.94), so that (8.41) holds since $a = w_0 = (w_0(1), 0)$ with $-2^\ell \leq w_0(1) \leq 2^\ell$ (by (8.96)). We view $r$ as a path on $\mathcal{G}_{p\ell}$. (8.42)-(8.46) are trivially fulfilled for $r$ and $s$. For $S'(\Theta, r, s)$ we take the "upper right corner" of $S(\Theta, N) \setminus r \cup s$, i.e., the component of $S(\Theta, N) \setminus r \cup s$ which contains the corner vertex $(N, N)$ in its boundary (see Fig. 8.8). $S''(\Theta, N)$ is the other component of $S(\Theta, N) \setminus r \cup s$. It is clear that $Fr(J^-(s))$ intersects $Fr(S'(\Theta, N))$ only in the path $s$, which is common to both these boundaries. Moreover, the point $(N, N)$ of $Fr(S')$ lies in $ext(J^-(s))$. Consequently $Fr(S') \subset$ closure of $ext(J^-(s))$. Therefore $J^-(s)$ either lies entirely in $S'$ or entirely in $S''$. Since $A \subset Fr(J^-(s))$ can be connected by a horizontal line segment to the left edge $\{-N\} \times [-N, +N]$ of $S(\Theta, N)$ without entering $S'$ it follows that

$$(8.98)\qquad J^-(S) \subset S''(\Theta, r, s).$$

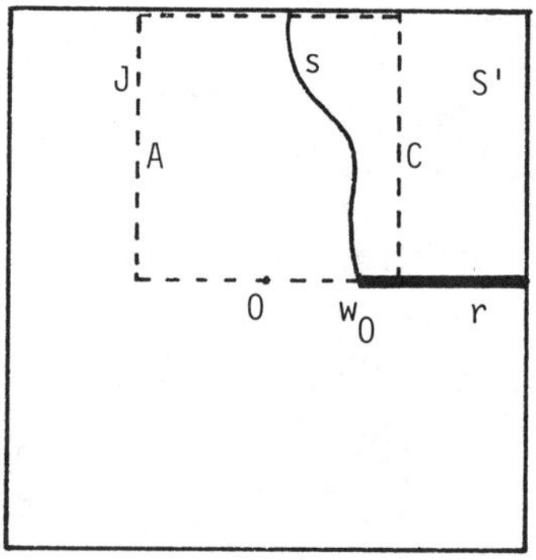


Figure 8.8 r is the boldly drawn path. J is the dashed rectangle. The large square is $S(\Theta,N)$.

We shall write $B$ for the upper edge, $[-N,N]\times\{N\}$, of $S(\Theta,N)$. We shall say that a vertex $v$ of $\mathcal{M}$ in $S(\Theta,N)$ has an occupied connection to $B$ if there exists an occupied path $t=(u_0,g_1,\dots,g_\rho,u_\rho)$ on $\mathcal{G}_{p\ell}$ which satisfies

$$(g_1\setminus\{u_0\},u_1,\dots,u_{\rho-1},g_\rho\setminus\{u_\rho\}) = t\setminus\{u_0,u_\rho\}\subset \mathring{S}(\Theta,N),$$

$$u_0 = v \quad\text{and}\quad u_\rho \in B.$$

Assume now that $\{S = s\}$ occurs so that $s$ is occupied. Exactly as in the argument following (7.66)-(7.69) one now sees that any vertex $v$ of $\mathcal{M}$ on $r$ which is connected to $s$ in $S'(\Theta,r,s)\cap S(a,3.2^\ell)$ (in the sense of Def. 8.1) automatically has an occupied connection to $B$. Therefore

(8.99) $$E_{P_H}\{\#\text{ of vertices of } \mathcal{M} \text{ on } r \text{ which have an occupied connection to } B \mid S = s\}$$

$$\geq E_{P_H}\{\sum_{\substack{v_i\in r\cap S(a,3.2^\ell)\\ v_i\in\mathcal{M}}} Y(v_i,a,\ell,r,s)\mid S = s\}\ .$$

Proposition 2.3 shows that the event $\{S = s\}$ depends only on the occupancies of vertices in $\bar{J}^-(s)\subset\bar{S}''(\Theta,r,s)$ (see (8.98)). Consequently the right hand side of (8.99) is at least

$$\min_{\varepsilon} E_{p_H}\{\sum_{\substack{v_i \varepsilon r \cap S(a,3.2^\ell) \\ v_i \varepsilon \mathcal{M}}} Y(v_i,a,\ell,r,s) | \omega(v) = \varepsilon(v), v \;\varepsilon\; \overline{S}''(\Theta,r,s)\}$$

$$\geq Z(\ell) \geq C_{12} 2^{\alpha_1 \ell} \geq C_{12} 2^{-3\alpha_1} N^{\alpha_1}$$

(see (8.55) and (8.94)). Finally, since $r \subset [-N,+N] \times \{0\}$,

(8.100) $E_{p_H}\{$# of vertices of $\mathcal{M}$ on $[-N,N] \times \{0\}$ which have an occupied connection to $B\}$

$$\geq \sum_s P_{p_H}\{S = s\} E_{p_H}\{\text{\# of vertices of } \mathcal{M} \text{ on } r \text{ which are connected to } s \text{ in } S'(\Theta,r,s) \cap S(w_0,3.2^\ell) | S = s\}$$

$$\geq C_{12} 2^{-3\alpha_1} N^{\alpha_1} \sum_s P_{p_H}\{S = s\}$$

$$\geq C_{12} 2^{-3\alpha_1} N^{\alpha_1} P_{p_H}\{F\} \geq \delta_{32} C_{12} 2^{-3\alpha_1} N^{\alpha_1} .$$

In (8.100) the sum is over all $s$ which satisfy (8.95) and (8.96), and the last inequality relies on (8.97). (8.93) follows from (8.100) since any vertex $v$ of $\mathcal{M}$ on $[-N,N] \times \{0\}$ which has an occupied connection to $B$ also is connected by an occupied path on $\mathcal{G}_{p\ell}$ to a vertex on $\Delta S(v,N)$, because $B$ lies in the complement of $\mathring{S}(v,N)$. From Lemma 2.1a we see that any such $v$ is then also connected by an occupied path on $\mathcal{G}$ to a point on $\Delta S(v,N-1)$. The probability of this event is $P_{p_H}\{B(N-1)\}$, the same for all $v$ of $\mathcal{M}$ on $[-N,N] \times \{0\}$. There are at most $(2N+1)$ such vertices $v$ on $[-N,N] \times \{0\}$, so that the left hand side of (8.100) is at most equal to $(2N+1)P_{p_H}\{B(N-1)\}$. (8.93) follows. □

We turn to the upper bound for $P_{p_H}\{B(N)\}$. The method for this estimation is due to Russo (1978) and Seymour and Welsh (1978).

<u>Lemma 8.5</u>. <u>There exist constants</u> $0 < C_{15}, \alpha_2 < \infty$ <u>such that</u>

(8.101) $$P_{p_H}\{B(N)\} \leq C_{15} N^{-\alpha_2} .$$

<u>Proof</u>: Consider the disjoint annuli

(8.102) $$V_\ell := S(0,3.2^{2\ell})\setminus \mathring{S}(0,3.2^{2\ell-1}) \quad \text{for}$$
$$\ell = 1,2,\dots,\ell_0 := \left\lfloor \frac{\log \frac{1}{3}(N-2)}{2 \log 2} \right\rfloor .$$

These are all contained in $S(z_0,N-1)$. If any one of them contains a vacant circuit $c^*$ on $\mathcal{G}^*_{p\ell}$ surrounding the origin, then there cannot exist an occupied path on $\mathcal{G}$ from $z_0$ to a point on $\Delta S(z_0,N)$. Indeed such an occupied path would start at $z_0$ in the interior of $c^*$ and end in the exterior of $c^*$, and hence would have to intersect $c^*$. But if a path on $\mathcal{G}$ intersects a path on $\mathcal{G}^*_{p\ell}$, then the two paths must have a vertex of $\mathcal{G}$ in common (cf. Comment 2.3 (v)). In our case there would have to be a vertex on $c^*$ (hence vacant) which would also be a vertex on an occupied path from $z_0$ to $\Delta S(z_0,N)$, which is impossible.

It follows from the above that

(8.103) $$P_p\{B(N)\} \le P_p\{\text{there is no vacant circuit on } \mathcal{G}^*_{p\ell} \text{ surrounding the origin in any } V_\ell,\ 1 \le \ell \le \ell_0\}$$
$$= \prod_{\ell=1}^{\ell_0} P_p\{\text{there is no vacant circuit on } \mathcal{G}^*_{p\ell} \text{ surrounding the origin in } V_\ell\} .$$

But (8.37) applied to $\mathcal{G}^*$ (and with $\ell$ replaced by $2^{2\ell-2}$) states

$$P_{p_H(\mathcal{G}^*)}\{\exists \text{ occupied circuit on } \mathcal{G}^*_{p\ell} \text{ surrounding the origin in } V_\ell\} \ge \delta_4^4 , \quad \ell \ge 1.$$

It we interchange "occupied" and "vacant" and take (8.91) into account, this means

(8.104) $$P_{p_H(\mathcal{G})}\{\text{there is no vacant circuit on } \mathcal{G}^*_{p\ell} \text{ surrounding the origin in } V_\ell\} \le 1-\delta_4^4 , \quad \ell \ge 1.$$

Substituting this estimate into the right hand side of (8.103) yields

$$P_{p_H(\mathcal{G})}\{B(N)\} \le (1-\delta_4^4)^{\ell_0} ,$$

from which (8.101) is immediate. □

<u>Proof of (8.4)</u>. The left hand inequality will be seen to follow quickly from (8.13), (8.93), (8.19) and (8.81). Indeed, by virtue of (8.81), (8.17) holds for

$$N = C_{16}(p-p_H(\mathcal{G}))^{-1/\alpha_1} .$$

(We continue to denote by $C_k$ various finite but strictly positive constants which depends on $\mathcal{G}$ only.) (8.19) now shows that

$$(8.105) \qquad P_p\{\#W^*(z_0) \geq \ell\} \leq C_1 \exp - C_{17}(p-p_H(\mathcal{G}))^{2/\alpha_1}\ell \quad ,p > p_H(\mathcal{G}).$$

Since

$$(8.106) \qquad \sum_{\ell=M}^{\infty} \ell e^{-x\ell} = -\frac{d}{dx}\Big(\sum_{\ell=M}^{\infty} e^{-x\ell}\Big) = \frac{e^{-xM}}{1-e^{-x}}\Big(M+\frac{1}{1-e^{-x}}\Big)$$

one easily sees from this that

$$\sum_{\ell=M}^{\infty} \ell P_p\{\#W^*(z_0) \geq \ell\} \leq \frac{1}{2}$$

as soon as

$$(8.107) \qquad M \geq C_{18}(p-p_H(\mathcal{G}))^{-3/\alpha_1} .$$

Thus, by (8.13), and the definition (8.92) of $B(M)$

$$\theta(p) \geq \frac{1}{2} P_p\{B(M)\}, \quad p > p_H$$

for any $M$ which satisfies (8.107). Finally, since $B(M)$ is an increasing event we obtain from Lemma 4.1 and (8.93)

$$\theta(p) \geq \frac{1}{2} P_p\{B(M)\} \geq \frac{1}{2} P_{p_H(\mathcal{G})}\{B(M)\}$$

$$\geq \frac{1}{2} C_{14}\{C_{18}(p-p_H(\mathcal{G}))^{-3/\alpha_1}\}^{\alpha_1-1}, \; p > p_H(\mathcal{G}) .$$

This gives the left hand inequality in (8.4).

The right hand inequality in (8.4) is much easier to prove. Indeed, if $\#W(z_0) = \infty$ then $z_0$ is connected by occupied paths to $\Delta S(z_0,N)$ for all $N$. Consequently, for each $N$

$$\theta(p) \leq P_p\{B(N)\} .$$

However, $B(N)$ is an increasing event which depends only on the occupancies of vertices in $S(z_0,N)$, and for our graphs there are at most $2(2N+1)^2$ vertices of $\mathcal{G}$ in $S(z_0,N)$. Thus for $p_1 \le p_2$ (4.2) applied to $f = I_{B(N)}$ gives

$$(8.108)\qquad P_{p_2}\{B(N)\} \le \left(\frac{p_2}{p_1}\right)^{2(2N+1)^2} P_{p_1}\{B(N)\} .$$

If we use (8.108) with $p_1 = p_H < p_2 = p$ then we obtain from (8.101)

$$\theta(p) \le \left(\frac{p}{p_H}\right)^{2(2N+1)^2} P_{p_H}\{B(N)\} \le \left(\frac{p}{p_H}\right)^{2(2N+1)^2} C_{15}N^{-\alpha_2},\ p \ge p_H .$$

This holds for all $N$, and the right hand inequality of (8.4) now follows by choosing

$$N = \left\lfloor \left(\log \frac{p}{p_H}\right)^{-1/2} \right\rfloor \sim (p_H)^{1/2}(p-p_H)^{-1/2},\ p > p_H . \qquad \square$$

<u>Proof of the left hand inequalities in (8.5) and (8.6)</u>. Whenever $B(N)$ occurs, then $W(z_0)$ contains an occupied path from $z_0$ to $\Delta S(z_0,N)$, and any such path contains at least $N$ vertices of $\mathcal{G}$. Therefore

$$E_p\{\#W;\#W < \infty\} \ge NP_p\{B(N) \text{ occurs and } \exists \text{ vacant circuit on } \mathcal{G}^*_{p\ell} \text{ surrounding } 0 \text{ in } V_{\ell_0+3}\} .$$

Here $V_\ell$ and $\ell_0$ are as in (8.102) and we again use the fact that any vacant circuit on $\mathcal{G}^*_{p\ell}$ which surrounds $z_0$ must contain all of $W(z_0)$ in its interior (cf. proof of Lemma 8.5). But $B(M)$ depends only on the vertices in $S(z_0,N) \subset S(0,N+1)$ in the graphs $\mathcal{G}$ under consideration. Moreover $S(0,N+1)$ is disjoint from $V_{\ell_0+3}$ for $N > 5$. It follows that for $N > 5$

$$E_p\{\#W;\#W < \infty\} \ge NP_p\{B(N)\} \cdot P_p\{\exists \text{ vacant circuit on } \mathcal{G}^*_{p\ell} \text{ surrounding } 0 \text{ in } V_{\ell_0+3}\}.$$

Now we first take $p \ge p_H$. Then we obtain from the fact that $B(N)$ is an increasing event and (4.1), (8.93)

$$(8.109)\qquad E_p\{\#W;\#W < \infty\} \ge N\, C_{14}N^{\alpha_1-1} \cdot P_p\{\exists \text{ vacant circuit on } \mathcal{G}^*_{p\ell} \text{ surrounding } 0 \text{ in } V_{\ell_0+3}\} .$$

Next we use Lemma 4.1 with $f$ the indicator function of the event that there exists a vacant circuit on $\mathcal{G}^*_{p\ell}$ surrounding $0$ in $V_{\ell_0+3}$. This event depends only on the occupancies of the vertices of $\mathcal{G}^*_{p\ell}$ in $V_{\ell_0+3}$. Actually, it depends only on the vertices of $\mathcal{M}$ (or $\mathcal{G}^*$) in $V_{\ell_0+3}$, since the other vertices of $\mathcal{G}^*_{p\ell}$ are all vacant by our convention (7.3). There are at most $C_{19}N^2$ vertices of $\mathcal{G}^*$ in $V_{\ell_0+3}$. Therefore by the version of (4.2) for decreasing $f$, and (8.104)

$$\begin{aligned} &P_p\{\exists \text{ vacant circuit on } \mathcal{G}^*_{p\ell} \text{ surrounding } 0 \text{ in } V_{\ell_0+3}\} \\ &\geq \left(\frac{1-p}{1-p_H}\right)^{C_{19}N^2} P_{p_H}\{\exists \text{ vacant circuit on } \mathcal{G}^*_{p\ell} \text{ surrounding } 0 \\ &\qquad\qquad \text{in } V_{\ell_0+3}\} \\ &\geq \left(\frac{1-p}{1-p_H}\right)^{C_{19}N^2} \delta_4^4, \quad p \geq p_H . \end{aligned}$$

From this and (8.109) we obtain

$$E_p\{\#W;\#W < \infty\} \geq NC_{14}N^{\alpha_1-1}\left(\frac{1-p}{1-p_H}\right)^{C_{19}N^2} \delta_4^4, \ p \geq p_H .$$

The left hand inequality in (8.6) follows by taking

$$N = \left\lfloor \left(\log \frac{1-p_H}{1-p}\right)^{-1/2} \right\rfloor \sim (1-p_H)^{1/2}(p-p_H)^{-1/2}, \ p > p_H .$$

To obtain the left hand inequality of (8.5) we take $p \leq p_H$. Then

$$P_p\{\#W(z_0) < \infty\} = 1-\theta(p) = 1.$$

(This is true even at $p = p_H$ by Sect. 3.3 or by (8.4).) We therefore have the simple bound

$$\begin{aligned} E_p\{\#W\} &\geq NP_p\{B(N)\} \\ &\geq N\left(\frac{p}{p_H}\right)^{2(2N+1)^2} P_{p_H}\{B(N)\} \qquad \text{(see (8.108))} \\ &\geq N\left(\frac{p}{p_H}\right)^{2(2N+1)^2} C_{14}N^{\alpha_1-1} . \end{aligned}$$

This time we take

$$N = \lfloor (\log \frac{p_H}{p})^{-1/2} \rfloor \sim p_H^{1/2}(p_H-p)^{-1/2}, \; p < p_H . \qquad \square$$

Proof of right hand inequalities in (8.5) and (8.6). The right hand inequality in (8.5) comes from (8.105) with $\mathcal{G}$ and $\mathcal{G}^*$ interchanged and "occupied" and "vacant" interchanged. With these changes (8.105) turns into

$$(8.110) \qquad P_p\{\#W(z_0) \geq \ell\} \leq C_1 \exp - C_{17}(p_H(\mathcal{G})-p)^{2/\alpha_1} \ell \;, \; p < p_H(\mathcal{G})$$

(recall (8.91)). The right hand inequality in (8.5) is now obtained by summing over $\ell$.

For the right hand inequality in (8.6) we need one more observation. Since $S(z_0,N)$ contains no more than $2(2N+1)^2$ vertices of $\mathcal{G}$, $\#W(z_0) > 2(2N+1)^2$ implies that $W(z_0)$ must contain vertices outside $S(z_0,N)$. This can only happen if $z_0$ is connected by an occupied path to the exterior of $S(z_0,N)$, and hence $B(N)$ occurs. If in addition $\#W(z_0) < \infty$, then - as we saw in the derivation of (8.12) - there must exist a vacant circuit on $\mathcal{G}^*$ surrounding $z_0$ and containing at least $N$ vertices of $\mathcal{G}^*$. Therefore

$$(8.111) \qquad P_p\{2(2N+1)^2 < \#W(z_0) < \infty\} \leq P_p\{B(N) \text{ and there exists a vacant circuit on } \mathcal{G}^* \text{ surrounding } z_0 \text{ and containing at least } N \text{ vertices}\} .$$

By the estimate used for the second factor in the right hand side of (8.12) we obtain by means of (8.105), (8.106)

$$\begin{aligned}(8.112) \qquad & P_p\{2(2N+1)^2 < \#W(z_0) < \infty\} \\ & \leq \sum_{\ell=N}^{\infty} \ell P_p\{\#W^*(z_0) \geq \ell\} \\ & \leq \sum_{\ell=N}^{\infty} C_1 \ell \exp - C_{17}(p-p_H(\mathcal{G}))^{2/\alpha_1} \ell \;, \; p > p_H(\mathcal{G}) \\ & \leq C_{20}(p-p_H(\mathcal{G}))^{-2/\alpha_1}\{N+(p-p_H(\mathcal{G}))^{-2/\alpha_1}\} \\ & \qquad \cdot \exp - C_{17}(p-p_H(\mathcal{G}))^{2/\alpha_1} N .\end{aligned}$$

Since

$$E_p\{\#W(z_0);\#W(z_0) < \infty\} \le 2+16 \sum_{N=0}^{\infty} (N+1)P_p\{2(2N+1)^2 < \#W(z_0) < \infty\}$$

the right hand inequality in (8.6) follows easily. □

The above proofs of (8.4)-(8.6) constitute the proof of Theorem 8.1.

Proof of Theorem 8.2. We begin with the proof of (8.7). For $p \le p_H$ we have the simple estimate

$$P_p\{n \le \#W(z_0) < \infty\} \le P_p\{B(\tfrac{1}{2}(\tfrac{n-1}{2})^{\frac{1}{2}} - \tfrac{1}{2})\} \text{ (by (8.111))}$$

$$\le P_{p_H}\{B(\tfrac{1}{2}(\tfrac{n-1}{2})^{1/2} - \tfrac{1}{2})\} \text{ (since } B \text{ is an increasing event)}$$

$$\le C_{19}n^{-\alpha_2} \quad \text{(by (8.101))} \quad .$$

For $p > p_H$ we estimate (8.7) more or less in the same way, as long as $p$ is close to $p_H$, and by means of (8.112) for $p-p_H$ large. To be specific, take

$$m = \frac{1}{3}\min(n^{1/2}, n^{\alpha_1/16}).$$

Then, for large $n$ $2(2m+1)^2 < n$ so that by (8.111), (8.108) and (8.101)

(8.113) $$P_p\{n \le \#W(z_0) < \infty\} \le P_p\{2(2m+1)^2 < \#W(z_0) < \infty\}$$

$$\le P_p\{B(m)\} \le (\frac{p}{p_H})^{2(2m+1)^2} P_{p_H}\{B(m)\}$$

$$\le C_{15}(\frac{p}{p_H})^{2(2m+1)^2} m^{-\alpha_2} \quad , \quad p > p_H \ .$$

For

$$0 < p-p_H \le n^{-\alpha_1/8}$$

the factor

$$(\frac{p}{p_H})^{2(2m+1)^2} \le \exp\{2(2m+1)^2\log(1+p_H^{-1}n^{-\alpha_1/8})\}$$

is bounded, so that (8.7) holds with $\gamma_5 = \min(\alpha_2/2, \alpha_1\alpha_2/16)$ for such $p$. On the remaining interval

$$p-p_H \ge n^{-\alpha_1/8} \quad ,$$

we use (8.112) with

$$N = \frac{1}{3} n^{1/2} \geq \frac{1}{3}(p-p_H)^{-4/\alpha_1} \quad .$$

This gives

$$P_p\{n \leq \#W(z_0) < \infty\} \leq P_p\{2(2N+1)^2 \leq \#W(z_0) < \infty\}$$

$$\leq C_{21}N^{3/2}\exp - C_{17}N^{1/2} = O(n^{-\gamma_5}),$$

for any choice of $\gamma_5 > 0$.

The above proves (8.7) in all cases. (8.8) and the last inequality in (8.9) are immediate from (8.7). Finally, the left hand inequality in (8.9) follows from the observation - made already in the proof of the left hand inequalities in (8.5) and (8.6) - that $\#W(z_0) \geq n$ on the event $B(n)$. Thus, by Lemma 8.4

$$P_{p_H}\{\#W(z_0) \geq n\} \geq P_{p_H}\{B(n)\} \geq C_{14}n^{\alpha_1 - 1} \quad .$$

□

## 9. THE NATURE OF THE SINGULARITY AT $p_H$.

The arguments of Sykes and Essam (1964) which led them (not quite rigorously) to values for $p_H(\mathcal{G})$ for certain graphs were based on "the average number of clusters per site". In a one parameter problem with

$$(9.1) \qquad P_p\{v \text{ is occupied}\} = p$$

for all vertices $v$ this average is, of course, a function, $\Delta(p,\mathcal{G})$ say, of $p$. Sykes and Essam's motivation for introducing this function lay in analogies with statistical mechanics, and on the basis of such analogies they assumed that $\Delta(p)$ has exactly one singularity as a function of $p$, and that this singularity is located at $p = p_H$. This assumption was actually their only non rigorous step. They then proved that for a matching pair of graphs $(\mathcal{G},\mathcal{G}^*)$ one has the remarkable relationship

$$(9.2) \qquad \Delta(p,\mathcal{G}) - \Delta(1-p,\mathcal{G}^*) = \text{a polynomial in } p.$$

It was for this relation that Sykes and Essam introduced matching pairs of graphs. They then proceeded to locate $p_H$, which was presumably the singularity of $\Delta$, by means of (9.2) for certain matching pairs in which $\mathcal{G}$ and $\mathcal{G}^*$ have a close relation. E.g. for bond percolation on $\mathbb{Z}^2$, $\mathcal{G}_1^*$ is isomorphic to $\mathcal{G}_1$ and hence $\Delta(\cdot,\mathcal{G}_1) = \Delta(\cdot,\mathcal{G}_1^*)$.

In this chapter we shall first give the precise definition and show the existence of $\Delta(p)$, following Grimmett (1976) and Wierman (1978). We then derive the Sykes-Essam relation (9.2) and show that for the matching pairs $(\mathcal{G},\mathcal{G}^*)$ to which Theorem 3.1 applies $\Delta(p,\mathcal{G})$ is analytic in $p$ for $p \neq p_H(\mathcal{G})$. This justifies part of the Sykes-Essam assumption: For various matching pairs $\Delta(\cdot,\mathcal{G})$ has at most one singularity, and if there is one it must be at $p_H(\mathcal{G})$. Unfortunately we have been unable to show that $\Delta(\cdot,\mathcal{G})$ has any singularity at $p_H$ as a function of $p$ only. (There is an obvious singularity if one brings in additional variables; compare the study of the function $f(h)$ in Kunz and Souillard (1978) or Remark 9.3 (iv) below.) We shall prove that for site- or bond-percolation on $\mathbb{Z}^2$ $\Delta(p)$ is twice continuously differentiable at all $p \in [0,1]$, including at $p_H$. The belief is (see Stauffer (1979), formula (6a) and Essam (1980), Formula (2.22)) that $\Delta(p)$ also satisfies a power law, i.e.,

$$\Delta(p,\mathcal{G}) \sim C_0 |p-p_H|^{2-\alpha_\pm}, \quad p \to p_H,$$

for some $0 < \alpha_\pm < 1$ ($\alpha_+$ corresponding to $p \downarrow p_H$ and $\alpha_-$ to $p \uparrow p_H$). In particular $(\frac{d}{dp})^3 \Delta(p)$ should blow up as $p \to p_H$. So far we have been unable to show that any derivative of $\Delta$ fails to exist at $p_H$.

## 9.1 The existence of $\Delta(p)$.

Intuitively, the average number of clusters per site should be the limit (in some sense) of

$$(9.3) \qquad (\# \text{ of sites in } B_n)^{-1} (\# \text{ of occupied clusters in } B_n)$$

as $B_n$ runs through a sequence of blocks which increase to the whole space. Sykes and Essam (1964) did not show that such a limit exists. This was first done by Grimmett (1976), and an expression for the limit was given by Wierman (1978). Their results follow quickly from the ergodic theorem and are reproduced in Theorem 9.1. Of course we must first define the expression in (9.3) properly.

Def. 9.1. For a block $B = \prod_1^d [a_i,b_i]$ and a vertex $v$ of $\mathcal{G}$ in $B$, the occupied cluster of $v$ (on $\mathcal{G}$) in $B$ is the union of all edges and vertices of $\mathcal{G}$ which belong to an occupied path on $\mathcal{G}$ contained in $B$ and with initial point $v$. ///

This is the obvious analogue of Def. 2.7. Note that two vertices $v_1$ and $v_2$ may belong to different occupied clusters in $B$, even though they belong to the same occupied cluster on the graph as a whole. This will happen if and only if there exists one or more occupied paths from $v_1$ to $v_2$, but all such paths go outside of $B$. When counting the number of occupied clusters in $B$ the clusters of $v_1$ and $v_2$ will be counted as two separate clusters in this situation.

We also need the following notation. For any block $B = \Pi[a_i,b_i]$ and $v$ a vertex of $\mathcal{G}$ in $B$ we set

$$(9.4)\qquad \Gamma(v,B) = \begin{cases} 0 \text{ if } v \text{ is vacant,} \\ (\#\text{ of vertices of } \mathcal{G} \text{ in the occupied} \\ \text{cluster of } v \text{ in } B)^{-1} \text{ if } v \text{ is occupied.} \end{cases}$$

Also

$$(9.5)\qquad \Gamma(v) = \begin{cases} 0 \text{ if } v \text{ is vacant,} \\ (\#W(v))^{-1} \text{ if } v \text{ is occupied.} \end{cases}$$

(If $\#W(v) = \infty$, then $\Gamma(v) = 0$.)

Theorem 9.1. Let $\mathcal{G}$ be a periodic graph imbedded in $\mathbb{R}^d$ with $\mu$ = number of vertices of $\mathcal{G}$ in $[0,1)^d$. Let $P_p$ be the one-parameter probability distribution on the occupancy configurations of $\mathcal{G}$ determined by (9.1) and let $B(n_1,\dots,n_d) = [0,n_1]\times\dots\times[0,n_d]$. Then

$$(9.6)\qquad \frac{\#\text{ of occupied clusters in } B(n_1,\dots,n_d)}{\#\text{ of vertices of } \mathcal{G} \text{ in } B(n_1,\dots,n_d)}$$

$$\to \frac{1}{\mu} \sum_{v\in[0,1)^d} E_p\{\frac{1}{\#W(v)}\,;\,\#W(v) \geq 1\}$$

$$= \frac{1}{\mu} \sum_{v\in[0,1)^d} \sum_{n=1}^{\infty} \frac{1}{n} P_p\{\#W(v) = n\} \quad ,$$

as $n_1 \to \infty,\dots,n_d \to \infty$ independently. The convergence in (9.6) holds a.e. $[P_p]$ and in every $L_r(P_p)$, $r > 0$.

Special case: When all vertices of $\mathcal{G}$ play the same role such as on the graphs $\mathcal{G}_0$, $\mathcal{G}_1$, $\mathcal{G}_0^*$ and $\mathcal{G}_1^*$ considered in the last chapter, then the right hand side of (9.6) reduces to

$$\sum_{n=1}^{\infty} \frac{1}{n} P_p\{\#W(v) = n\} .$$

## Remarks.

(i) Theorem 9.1 remains valid if $B(n_1,\dots,n_d)$ is replaced by the box $[-n_1,n_1]\times\dots\times[-n_d,n_d]$ which is symmetric with respect to the origin. This follows easily by writing $[-n_1,n_1]\times\dots\times[-n_d,n_d]$ as the union of $2^d$ boxes, to each of which one can apply Theorem 9.1 after an interchange of the positive and negative direction along a number of coordinate axes.

(ii) One can easily generalize Theorem 9.1 to $\lambda$-parameter periodic probability measures $P_p$, but we shall have no use for this generalization.

Proof of Theorem 9.1. By the periodicity of $\mathcal{G}$

$$\lim \frac{1}{n_1 \cdots n_d} (\# \text{ of vertices of } \mathcal{G} \text{ in } B(n_1,\ldots,n_d)) = \mu .$$

It is also clear that

(9.7) $$\# \text{ of occupied clusters in } B(n_1,\ldots,n_d) = \sum_{v \in B(n_1,\ldots,n_d)} \Gamma(v, B(n_1,\ldots,n_d)),$$

since for any occupied cluster $W$ in $B$, containing exactly the $n$ vertices $v_1,\ldots,v_n \in B$, the right hand side of (9.7) contains

$$\Gamma(v_1,B) + \Gamma(v_1,B) + \ldots + \Gamma(v_n,B) = n \times \frac{1}{n} = 1.$$

It is clear from the definitions (9.4) and (9.5) that

(9.8) $$\Gamma(v,B) \geq \Gamma(v), \quad v \in B.$$

Moreover, the ergodic theorem (Dunford and Schwartz (1958), Theorem VIII.6.9 or Tempel'man (1972), Theorem 6.1 and Cor. 6.2; see also Harris (1960), Lemma 3.1) applied to the bounded function $\Gamma$ shows that

$$\frac{1}{n_1 n_2 \cdots n_d} \sum_{0 \leq k_i < n_i} \Gamma(v + \sum_1^d k_i \xi_i) \to E_p\{\Gamma(v)\} \quad \text{a.e. } [P_p]$$

as $n_1,\ldots,n_d \to \infty$ for every $v \in [0,1)^d$. Since

$$E_p\{\Gamma(v)\} = \sum_{n=1}^{\infty} \frac{1}{n} P_p\{\#W(v) = n\}$$

it follows that

(9.9) $$(\# \text{ of vertices in } B(n_1,\ldots,n_d))^{-1} \sum_{v \in B(n_1,\ldots,n_d)} \Gamma(v) \to \frac{1}{\mu} \sum_{v \in [0,1)^d} \sum_{n=1}^{\infty} \frac{1}{n} P_p\{\#W(v) = n\} \quad \text{a.e. } [P_p].$$

This together with (9.7) and (9.8) also shows that

$$(9.10)\quad \liminf_{n_i\to\infty} \frac{\#\text{ of occupied clusters in } B(n_1,\dots,n_d)}{\#\text{ of vertices of } \mathcal{G} \text{ in } B(n_1,\dots,n_d)}$$

$$\geq \frac{1}{\mu} \sum_{v\in[0,1)^d} \sum_{n=1}^{\infty} \frac{1}{n} P_p\{\#W(v) = n\} \text{ , a.e. } [P_p].$$

To obtain a bound in the other direction we note that $\Gamma(v,B) = \Gamma(v)$ whenever $W(v)$ is contained entirely in $B$. Consequently

$$(9.11)\quad \#\text{ of occupied clusters in } B(n_1,\dots,n_d)$$

$$= \sum_{v\in B(n_1,\dots,n_d)} \Gamma(v,B(n_1,\dots,n_d))$$

$$\leq \sum_{v\in B(n_1,\dots,n_d)} \Gamma(v) + \#\text{ of occupied clusters in } B(n_1,\dots,n_d)$$

which are part of an occupied cluster on $\mathcal{G}$ which contains vertices outside $B(n_1,\dots,n_d)$.

The last term in the right hand side of (9.11) is bounded by $z\times$ the number of vertices of $\mathcal{G}$ in $\partial(B(n_1,\dots,n_d))$, i.e., $z\times$ the number of vertices outside $B(n_1,\dots,n_d)$ but adjacent to a vertex in $B(n_1,\dots,n_d)$. This is so because each occupied component which contains vertices inside and outside $B$ must contain a vertex in $\partial B$ (cf. (2.3) for $z$). If $\Lambda \geq$ diameter of any edge of $\mathcal{G}$, then any $v \in \partial B$ satisfies

$$-\Lambda \leq v(j) \leq n_j+\Lambda \quad \text{for} \quad 1 \leq j \leq d \quad \text{and}$$

$$-\Lambda \leq v(i) < 0 \quad \text{or} \quad n_i < v(i) \leq n_i+\Lambda \quad \text{for some} \quad 1 \leq i \leq d.$$

Thus the last term in (9.11) is bounded by

$$\#\partial(B(n_1,\dots,n_d)) \leq 2\mu(\Lambda+1)\left(\frac{1}{n_1}+\frac{1}{n_2}+\dots+\frac{1}{n_d}\right) \prod_1^d (n_j+2\Lambda+1).$$

This together with (9.11) and (9.9) shows

$$\limsup_{n_i\to\infty} \frac{\#\text{ of occupied clusters in } B(n_1,\dots,n_d)}{\#\text{ of vertices of } \mathcal{G} \text{ in } B(n_1,\dots,n_d)}$$

$$\leq \frac{1}{\mu} \sum_{v\in[0,1)^d} \sum_{n=1}^{\infty} \frac{1}{n} P_p\{\#W(v) = n\}, \text{ a.e. } [P_p].$$

Thus the convergence in (9.6) holds a.e. $[P_p]$. The convergence in

$L_r(P_p)$ follows from this since the left hand side of (9.6) lies between zero and one. □

9.2 The Sykes-Essam relation for matching graphs.

In view of Theorem 9.1 we define for any periodic graph $\mathcal{G}$ and one-parameter probability measure $P_p$ the "average number of occupied clusters per site" as

$$(9.12)\qquad \Delta(p) = \Delta(p,\mathcal{G}) = \frac{1}{\mu} \sum_{v\in[0,1)^d} \sum_{n=1}^{\infty} \frac{1}{n} P_p\{\#W(v) = n\}$$

$$= \frac{1}{\mu} \sum_{v\in[0,1)^d} E_p\{\frac{1}{\#W(v)} ; \#W(v) \geq 1\} .$$

We now prove (9.2).

<u>Theorem 9.2.</u> <u>Let</u> $(\mathcal{G},\mathcal{G}^*)$ <u>be a matching pair of periodic groups in</u> $\mathbb{R}^2$. <u>Then there exists a polynomial</u> $\Phi(p) = \Phi(p,\mathcal{G})$ <u>for which</u>

$$(9.13)\qquad \Delta(p,\mathcal{G}) - \Delta(1-p,\mathcal{G}^*) = \Phi(p,\mathcal{G}),\ 0 \leq p \leq 1.$$

Remarks.

(iii) The pair $(\mathcal{G}^*,\mathcal{G})$ is also a matching pair (Comment 2.2 (v)). It is obvious from (9.13) that the corresponding $\Phi(p,\mathcal{G}^*)$ is given by

$$(9.14)\qquad \Phi(p,\mathcal{G}^*) = -\Phi(1-p,\mathcal{G}).$$

(iv) The proof below will give an explicit expression for $\Phi$:

$$(9.15)\qquad \Phi(p,\mathcal{G}) = C_1' + (1-C_2')p + (C_3-C_2'')p^2$$

$$-\frac{1}{\mu} \sum_{n=1}^{\infty} (1-p)^n \gamma_n(\mathcal{M},\mathcal{F}) + \frac{1}{\mu} \sum_{n=1}^{\infty} p^n \gamma_n^*(\mathcal{M},\mathcal{F}),$$

where $C_i$ and $C_i'$ are given in (9.21)-(9.25) and

$\gamma_n(\mathcal{M},\mathcal{F})(\gamma^*(\mathcal{M},\mathcal{F}))$ = # of central vertices in $[0,1)\times[0,1)$ of a face $F$ of $\mathcal{M}$ in $\mathcal{F}$ (not in $\mathcal{F}$) with exactly $n$ vertices of $\mathcal{M}$ on the perimeter of $F$.

For example, when $\mathcal{G} = \mathcal{G}_0$, the simple quadratic lattice (see Ex. 2.1(i) and Ex. 2.2 (i)) one has $\mu = 1$, $\gamma_n = 0$ for all $n$, $\gamma_m^* = 0$ for $m \neq 4$

while $\gamma_4^* = 1$, and

$$\Phi(p,\mathcal{G}_0) = p - 2p^2 + p^4 ,$$
$$\Phi(p,\mathcal{G}_0^*) = 1 + (1-4)p + (4-2)p^2 - (1-p)^4 = p - 4p^2 + 4p^3 - p^4 . \qquad ///$$

Proof: Sykes and Essam's proof works with $\mathcal{G}$ directly. We find it easier to work with $\mathcal{G}_{p\ell}$ and so we shall first prove

(9.16) $\quad \Delta(p,\mathcal{G}_{p\ell}) - \Delta(1-p,\mathcal{G}_{p\ell}^*)$ is a polynomial in $p$, $\Phi(p,\mathcal{G}_{p\ell})$ say.

Following Sykes and Essam (1964) we first define the occupied and vacant graphs. For some mosaic $\mathcal{M}^\circ$ and subset $\mathcal{F}^\circ$ of its faces, let $(\mathcal{G}^\circ,\mathcal{G}^{\circ *})$ be the matching pair based on $(\mathcal{M}^\circ,\mathcal{F}^\circ)$, and let $\mathcal{G}_{p\ell}^\circ$, $\mathcal{G}_{p\ell}^{\circ *}$ and $\mathcal{M}_{p\ell}^\circ$ be the corresponding planar modifications as in Sect. 2.3. Any occupancy configuration $\omega$ of $\mathcal{M}^\circ$ is also an occupancy configuration of $\mathcal{G}^\circ$ and $\mathcal{G}^{\circ *}$, and can be extended to an occupancy configuration of $\mathcal{M}_{p\ell}^\circ$, $\mathcal{G}_{p\ell}^\circ$ and $\mathcal{G}_{p\ell}^{\circ *}$ by taking all central vertices of a face of $\mathcal{M}^\circ$ in $\mathcal{F}^\circ$ (not in $\mathcal{F}^\circ$) as occupied (vacant) as we did in (2.15), (2.16). For a fixed configuration $\omega$ we define $\mathcal{G}^\circ$ ($\omega$, occupied) as the graph whose vertex set consists of the occupied vertices of $\mathcal{G}^\circ$ and whose edge set consists of all edges of $\mathcal{G}^\circ$ connecting two occupied vertices of $\mathcal{G}^\circ$. $\mathcal{G}_{p\ell}^\circ$ ($\omega$, occupied) is defined in the same way by replacing $\mathcal{G}^\circ$ by $\mathcal{G}_{p\ell}^\circ$. Similarly $\mathcal{G}^{\circ *}$ ($\omega$, vacant) and $\mathcal{G}_{p\ell}^{\circ *}$ ($\omega$, vacant) are defined by replacing $\mathcal{G}^\circ$ by $\mathcal{G}^{\circ *}$ and $\mathcal{G}_{p\ell}^{\circ *}$, respectively, and "occupied" by "vacant". Note that the components of $\mathcal{G}^\circ$ ($\omega$, occupied) are precisely the occupied clusters of $\mathcal{G}^\circ$, and similarly the components of $\mathcal{G}^{\circ *}$ ($\omega$, vacant) are the vacant clusters of $\mathcal{G}^{\circ *}$.

Now, let our periodic pair $(\mathcal{G},\mathcal{G}^*)$ be based on $(\mathcal{M},\mathcal{F})$, a periodic mosaic and periodic subset of its faces. We shall apply Euler's relation to the planar graph $\mathcal{G}_{p\ell}$ ($\omega$, occupied), or rather to a "truncated modification" of this graph, which we construct as follows. Let $J^n$ be a circuit made up of edges of $\mathcal{M}_{p\ell}$, surrounding $(\Lambda_3,n-\Lambda_3) \times (\Lambda_3,n-\Lambda_3)$, and contained in the annulus

(9.17) $$[0,n] \times [0,n] \setminus (\Lambda_3,n-\Lambda_3) \times (\Lambda_3,n-\Lambda_3).$$

Here $\Lambda_3$ is a suitably large constant depending on $\mathcal{M}_{p\ell}$ only; we constructed this kind of circuit already in the proof of Lemma 7.1. Let $\mathcal{M}_{p\ell}^n$ be the graph obtained by removing from $\mathcal{M}_{p\ell}$ all edges and vertices which are not contained in $\bar{J}^n = J^n \cup \text{int}(J^n)$. Thus $\mathcal{M}_{p\ell}^n$ has exactly one unbounded face, namely $\text{ext}(J^n)$, and the other faces of $\mathcal{M}^n_{p\ell}$ are exactly the faces of $\mathcal{M}_{p\ell}$ in $\text{int}(J^n)$. The unbounded face of $\mathcal{M}^n_{p\ell}$ contains no vertices and does not intersect any edges of $\mathcal{M}^n_{p\ell}$. An occupancy configuration $\omega$ of $\mathcal{M}_{p\ell}$ can be restricted to an occupancy configuration on $\mathcal{M}^n_{p\ell}$ and the corresponding graph $\mathcal{G}^n_{p\ell}$ ($\omega$, occupied) is then defined as above. It is a planar graph since it is a subgraph of the planar graph $\mathcal{G}_{p\ell}$. We therefore have Euler's relation

$$V^n_{p\ell} - E^n_{p\ell} + F^n_{p\ell} = C^n_{p\ell} + 1 \ , \tag{9.18}$$

where $V^n_{p\ell}$, $E^n_{p\ell}$, $F^n_{p\ell}$ and $C^n_{p\ell}$ are the number of vertices, edges, faces and components of $\mathcal{G}^n_{p\ell}$ ($\omega$, occupied), respectively. (Cf. Bollobás (1979), Theorem I.11 if $C^n_{p\ell} = 1$; the general case follows easily by induction on $C^n_{p\ell}$.) We need to look closer at $F^n_{p\ell}$. Note first that each vacant vertex of $\mathcal{M}_{p\ell}$ must be a vertex of $\mathcal{G}^*_{p\ell}$, since the only vertices of $\mathcal{M}_{p\ell}$ which do not belong to $\mathcal{G}^*_{p\ell}$ are central vertices of some face in $\mathcal{F}$, and these have all been taken as occupied. Therefore, if a face $F$ of $\mathcal{G}^n_{p\ell}$ ($\omega$, occupied) contains a vacant vertex of $\mathcal{M}^n_{p\ell}$, then it belongs to $\mathcal{G}^{n*}_{p\ell}$ ($\omega$, vacant), and in this case $F$ contains at least one component of $\mathcal{G}^*_{p\ell}$ ($\omega$,vacant). Some examples will convince the reader that in this case $F$ contains exactly one component of $\mathcal{G}^{n*}_{p\ell}$ ($\omega$, vacant). A formal statement and proof of this fact is given in Prop. A.1 in the Appendix. Thus, if $C^{n*}_{p\ell}$ denotes the number of components of $\mathcal{G}^{n*}_{p\ell}$ ($\omega$, vacant)

$$F^n_{p\ell} = C^{n*}_{p\ell} + \#\text{ of faces of } \mathcal{G}^n_{p\ell}\ (\omega,\text{ occupied}) \text{ which contain no vacant vertex of } \mathcal{M}^n_{p\ell}. \tag{9.19}$$

Let us call the faces of $\mathcal{G}^n_{p\ell}$ ($\omega$, occupied) which contain no vacant vertex of $\mathcal{M}^n_{p\ell}$ empty faces. Recall now that $\mathcal{M}_{p\ell}$ is completely triangulated (Comment 2.3 (vi)). In other words each face of $\mathcal{M}_{p\ell}$ is a "triangle", bounded by three edges of $\mathcal{M}_{p\ell}$, and containing exactly three vertices of $\mathcal{M}_{p\ell}$ on its perimeter. We claim that the bounded empty faces of $\mathcal{G}^n_{p\ell}$ ($\omega$, occupied) are precisely those triangular faces of $\mathcal{M}_{p\ell}$ in $\text{int}(J_n)$ with all three of its boundary vertices belonging to $\mathcal{G}_{p\ell}$ and occupied. Such faces are therefore also faces of $\mathcal{G}_{p\ell}$. To see this consider a face $G$ of $\mathcal{G}^n_{p\ell}$ ($\omega$, occupied) and let $e$ be an edge of $\mathcal{M}_{p\ell}$ in $\text{Fr}(G)$. $e$ necessarily is an edge of $\mathcal{G}_{p\ell}$ in $\bar{J}_n$, and its endpoints, $v_1$ and $v_2$, say, are necessarily occupied. $\mathring{e}$ belongs to the boundary of exactly two triangular faces, $F_1$ and $F_2$ say, of $\mathcal{M}_{p\ell}$. Each $F_i$ belongs to a unique face, $G_i$ say, of $\mathcal{G}^n_{p\ell}$ ($\omega$, occupied). $\mathring{e}$ belongs only to the boundary of $G_1$ and $G_2$, but not to the boundary of any other face of $\mathcal{G}^n_{p\ell}$ ($\omega$, occupied), so that $G$ is one of $G_1$ or $G_2$ ($G_1 = G_2$ is possible, though). Let $w_i$ the third vertex of $\mathcal{M}_{p\ell}$ on the perimeter of $F_i$ (in addition to $v_1$ and $v_2$). If $F_i$ lies in $\text{ext}(J_n)$ then $F_i$ is contained in the unbounded face of $\mathcal{G}^n_{p\ell}$, and hence also in the unbounded face of $\mathcal{G}^n_{p\ell}$ ($\omega$, occupied). In this case $G_i$ equals the unbounded face of $\mathcal{G}^n_{p\ell}$ ($\omega$, occupied). If $F_i \subset \text{int}(J_n)$ and $w_i$ is occupied, then in particular $w_i$ cannot be a central vertex of $\mathcal{G}^*_{p\ell}$, since these are taken vacant. Therefore all vertices on the perimeter of $F_i$ belong to $\mathcal{G}^n_{p\ell}$ and are occupied, and consequently belong to $\mathcal{G}^n_{p\ell}$ ($\omega$, occupied). In this case $F_i$ is itself a face of $\mathcal{G}^n_{p\ell}$ ($\omega$, occupied) and $G_i = F_i$. Finally if $F_i \subset \text{int}(J_n)$ but $w_i$ is vacant, then $G_i$ contains the vacant vertex $w_i$. (Since no edges of $\mathcal{G}^n_{p\ell}$ ($\omega$, occupied) are incident to $w_i$, so that a full neighborhood of $w_i$ belongs to one face of $\mathcal{G}^n_{p\ell}$ ($\omega$, occupied); this face must therefore contain $F_i$ and cannot be any other face than $G_i$.) The only bounded empty faces of $\mathcal{G}^n_{p\ell}$ ($\omega$, occupied) which we encountered in the above list was the triangle $F_i$, in the case where $w_i$ was occupied and $F_i \subset \text{int}(J_n)$. This proves our claim. As a consequence (9.19) can be written as

$$(9.20) \qquad F^n_{p\ell} = C^{n*}_{p\ell} + T^n_{p\ell} + \varepsilon_n ,$$

where

$T^n_{p\ell}$ = # of triangular faces of $\mathcal{M}_{p\ell}$ in $\bar{J}_n$ with all three vertices on their perimeter occupied

and

$$\varepsilon_n = \begin{cases} 1 & \text{if the unbounded face of } \mathcal{G}^n_{p\ell} \ (\omega, \text{occupied}) \text{ is an empty face,} \\ 0 & \text{otherwise.} \end{cases}$$

We substitute (9.20) into (9.18), divide by $\mu n^2$ and take limits as $n \to \infty$. This gives

$$\lim_{n\to\infty} \frac{1}{\mu n^2}[V^n_{p\ell} - E^n_{p\ell} + T^n_{p\ell} + C^{n*}_{p\ell} - C^n_{p\ell}] = 0 \quad \text{a.e. } [P_p].$$

It therefore suffices for (9.16) to show that a.e. $[P_p]$

$$\lim_{n\to\infty} \frac{1}{\mu n^2} V^n_{p\ell} = C_1' + C_1''p ,$$

$$\lim_{n\to\infty} \frac{1}{\mu n^2} E^n_{p\ell} = C_2'p + C_2''p^2 ,$$

$$\lim_{n\to\infty} \frac{1}{\mu n^2} T^n_{p\ell} = C_3p^2 ,$$

$$\lim_{n\to\infty} \frac{1}{\mu n^2} C^n_{p\ell} = \Delta(p,\mathcal{G}) \quad \text{and} \quad \lim_{n\to\infty} \frac{1}{\mu n^2} C^{*n}_{p\ell} = \Delta(1-p,\mathcal{G}^*)$$

for suitable $C_1', C_1'', \dots, C_j$. In fact these relations are easily proved from the ergodic theorem, with the constants $C_i$ and $C_i'$ determined as follows: Order the vertices of $\mathcal{G}_{p\ell}$ lexicographically, i.e., $v = (v(1),v(2))$ precedes $w = (w(1),w(2))$ iff $v(1) < w(1)$ or $v(1) = w(1)$ and $v(2) < w(2)$. Then

(9.21) $C_1' = \frac{1}{\mu}\{\#$ of central vertices of $\mathcal{G}_{p\ell}$ in $[0,1)\times[0,1)\}$,

(9.22) $C_1'' = \frac{1}{\mu}\{\#$ of vertices of $\mathcal{G}$ in $[0,1)\times[0,1)\} = 1$ ,

(9.23) $C_2' = \frac{1}{\mu}\{\#$ of edges of $\mathcal{G}_{p\ell}$ between two vertices, $v_1$ and $v_2$ say, such that $v_1$ precedes $v_2$, $v_1 \in [0,1)\times[0,1)$ and such that $v_1$ or $v_2$ is a central vertex of $\mathcal{G}_{p\ell}\}$

(9.24) $C_2'' = \frac{1}{\mu}\{\#$ of edges of $\mathcal{G}_{p\ell}$ between two vertices, $v_1$ and $v_2$ say, such that $v_1$ precedes $v_2$, $v_1 \in [0,1)\times[0,1)$ and such that $v_1$ and $v_2$ are both non-central vertices of $\mathcal{G}_{p\ell}\}$

(9.25) $C_3 = \frac{1}{\mu}\{\#$ of triangular faces of $\mathcal{G}_{p\ell}$ with vertices $v$, $v_1$ and $v_2$, say, on its perimeter, with $v$ preceding $v_1$ and $v_2$ and $v \in [0,1)\times[0,1))$.

We only prove

(9.26) $$\lim_{n\to\infty} \frac{1}{\mu n^2} T^n_{p\ell} = C_3p^2 .$$

The other relations are proved in a similar way. Now, $J_n$ is contained in the annulus (9.17). Therefore

(9.27) $T^n_{p\ell} \le$ number of triangular faces of $\mathcal{M}_{p\ell}$ contained in $[0,n]\times[0,n]$ with all three vertices on their perimeter occupied,

while the inequality has to be reversed if $[0,n]\times[0,n]$ is replaced by $(\Lambda_3,n-\Lambda_3)\times(\Lambda_3-n-\Lambda_3)$. Now let

$N(v) = \#$ of triangular faces of $\mathcal{M}_{p\ell}$ with vertices $v$, $w_1$ and $w_2$, say, on their perimeter such that $v$ precedes $w_1$ and $w_2$ and such that $v$, $w_1$ and $w_2$ are occupied .

Then the right hand side of (9.27) clearly equals

$$\sum_{v\in[0,1)\times[0,1)} \sum_{\substack{0\le k_1<n \\ 0\le k_2<n}} N(v+k_1\xi_1+k_2\xi_2) + O(n) \tag{9.28}$$

where $\xi_1 = (1,0)$, $\xi_2 = (0,1)$, and the $O(n)$ term is at most equal to the number of triangular faces of $\mathcal{M}_{p\ell}$ whose closure intersects $\mathrm{Fr}([0,n]\times[0,n])$. Thus, by (9.27) and the ergodic theorem (Dunford and Schwartz (1958) Theorem VIII.6.9 or Tempel'man (1972), Theorem 6.1 and Cor. 6.2)

$$\limsup \frac{1}{\mu n^2} T^n_{p\ell} \le \frac{1}{\mu} \sum_{v\in[0,1)\times[0,1)} E_p N(v) \quad \text{a.e. } [P_p]. \tag{9.29}$$

To calculate $\sum E_p N(v)$ we have to recall that $\mathcal{M}_{p\ell}$ is constructed by inserting a central vertex in each face $F$ of $\mathcal{M}$, and by connecting this central vertex $v$ say by an edge to each vertex of $\mathcal{M}$ on the perimeter of $F$. This means that the triangular faces of $\mathcal{M}_{p\ell}$ all have one central vertex $w$ and two non-central vertices $v_1$ and $v_2$ say on their perimeter. If $w$ is a central vertex of $\mathcal{G}^*_{p\ell}$ , i.e., lies in a face $F \notin \mathcal{F}$ , then it is vacant and the triangle with vertices $w$, $v_1$ and $v_2$ cannot contribute to any $N(v)$. If $w$ is a vertex of $\mathcal{G}_{p\ell}$, i.e., lies in a face $F \in \mathcal{F}$, then it is occupied with probability one, the triangle with vertices $w$, $v_1$ and $v_2$ is a face of $\mathcal{G}_{p\ell}$, and all three vertices $w$, $v_1$ and $v_2$ are occupied with probability $p^2$.

Consequently

$$\sum_{v\varepsilon[0,1)\times[0,1)} E_pN(v) = p^2C_3 .$$

Together with (9.29) this shows that

$$\limsup \frac{1}{\mu n^2} T^n_{p\ell} \le C_3p^2 \quad \text{a.e. } [P_p].$$

It follows similarly from the lower bound given after (9.27) that

$$\liminf \frac{1}{\mu n^2} T^n_{p\ell} \ge C_3p^2 \quad \text{a.e. } [P_p].$$

This proves (9.26) and (9.16).

To obtain (9.13) from (9.16) we merely have to show that

(9.30) $$\Delta(p,\mathcal{G}_{p\ell}) - \Delta(p,\mathcal{G}) = \frac{1}{\mu}\sum_{v\varepsilon[0,1)\times[0,1)} \sum_{n=1}^{\infty} (1-p)^n I[v \text{ is a}$$

central vertex of a face of $\mathcal{M}$ in $\mathcal{F}$ with $n$ vertices on its perimeter].

Indeed the right hand side of (9.30) is only a finite sum by (2.3), (2.4), hence a polynomial in $p$. Also, interchanging the roles of $\mathcal{G}$ and $\mathcal{G}^*$,

$$\Delta(1-p,\mathcal{G}^*_{p\ell}) - \Delta(1-p,\mathcal{G}^*) \text{ is a polynomial in } p.$$

To prove (9.30) we use Cor. 2.1. This corollary shows that each occupied cluster on $\mathcal{G}$ belongs to a unique occupied cluster on $\mathcal{G}_{p\ell}$. Moreover, if $W(v_1)$ and $W(v_2)$ are two distinct occupied clusters on $\mathcal{G}$, then the occupied clusters $W_{p\ell}(v_1)$ and $W_{p\ell}(v_2)$ on $\mathcal{G}_{p\ell}$ to which they belong are also disjoint, since by (2.20) any vertex $w$ of $W_{p\ell}(v_1) \cap W_{p\ell}(v_2)$ would have to be a central vertex of $\mathcal{G}$, adjacent to some $w_i \varepsilon W(v_i)$ for $i = 1,2$. But then $w_1$ and $w_2$ would lie on the perimeter of a close-packed face of $\mathcal{G}$ (cf. Comment 2.3 (iv)) and would be adjacent on $\mathcal{G}$ and hence belong to the same cluster. On the other hand it is possible to have an occupied cluster on $\mathcal{G}_{p\ell}$ which does not contain an occupied cluster on $\mathcal{G}$. Again by (2.20), this can occur only if the cluster on $\mathcal{G}_{p\ell}$ contains no vertex $v$ of $\mathcal{G}$ - otherwise it equals $W_{p\ell}(v)$ which contains $W(v)$. Since two central vertices are never adjacent on $\mathcal{G}_{p\ell}$ (Comment 2.3 (iv)) this means that the only occupied clusters on $\mathcal{G}_{p\ell}$ which do not contain a cluster on $\mathcal{G}$ are isolated central vertices, i.e., central vertices of a face $F \varepsilon \mathcal{F}$ with all vertices on the perimeter of $F$ vacant (the central vertex is automatically occupied by (2.15)). From the above observations it follows that

$$\begin{aligned}|&(\#\text{ of occupied clusters on } \mathcal{G}_{p\ell} \text{ on } B(n,n))\\ &-(\#\text{ of occupied clusters on } \mathcal{G} \text{ in } B(n,n))\\ &-(\#\text{ of central vertices of } \mathcal{G}_{p\ell} \text{ in } B(n,n) \text{ which belong to}\\ &\ \text{a face with only vacant vertices on its perimeter})|\\ &\le z\cdot(\#\text{ of vertices of } \mathcal{G}_{p\ell} \text{ in } \partial(B(n,n))\end{aligned}$$

(compare with the estimate for the last term in (9.11)). (9.30) now follows from Theorem 9.1 and another application of the ergodic theorem. □

## 9.3 Smoothness of $\Delta(p)$.

Theorem 9.3. Let $(\mathcal{G},\mathcal{G}^*)$ be a matching pair of periodic graphs in $\mathbb{R}^2$. Then $\Delta(p,\mathcal{G})$ is an analytic function of $p$ outside the interval $[p_T(\mathcal{G}),1-p_T(\mathcal{G}^*)]$ (see (3.63) for $p_T$). If the conditions of Theorem 3.1 are fulfilled for $\lambda = 1$ (i.e., in the one-parameter problem) and some $0 < p_0 < 1$, then $\Delta(p,\mathcal{G})$ is analytic for $p \neq p_H(\mathcal{G}) = p_0$.

Remarks.

(i) In particular if $\mathcal{G} = \mathcal{G}_0$ or $\mathcal{G} = \mathcal{G}_1$, then $\Delta(p,\mathcal{G})$ is analytic, except possibly at $p_H(\mathcal{G})$.

(ii) The proof will also show that $E_p\{\pi(\#W(z_0))\}$ is an analytic function of $p$ on $0 \le p < p_T(\mathcal{G})$, for any polynomial $\pi$. Theorem 5.3 shows that the function $p \to E_p\{\pi(\#W(z_0));\#W(z_0) < \infty\}$ is infinitely often differentiable on $p_H(\mathcal{G}) < p \le 1$ (cf. Russo (1978)). ///

Proof: This theorem is immediate from Theorems 5.1, 9.1 and 9.2. Indeed for $p \le p_1 < p_T(\mathcal{G})$ we have by (5.11) and Lemma 4.1

(9.31) $$P_p\{\#W(z_0) \ge n\} \le P_{p_1}\{\#W(z_0) \ge n\} \le C_1e^{-C_2n}$$

for each vertex $z_0$ and some constants $C_1$, $C_2$ depending on $p_1$ and $\mathcal{G}$ only. Now take $a(n,\ell) = a(n,\ell,z_0)$ as in (5.18), (5.19). By (5.24) (with $q = 1-p$)

(9.32) $$P_p\{\#W(z_0) = n\} = \sum_\ell a(n,\ell)p^nq^\ell = \sum_\ell a(n,\ell)p^n(1-p)^\ell ,$$

and by (5.25) the sum over $\ell$ may be restricted to $\ell = 1,\ldots,zn$. Thus (9.12) can be written as

$$\Delta(p) = \frac{1}{\mu} \sum_{v\varepsilon[0,1)\times[0,1)} \sum_{n=1}^{\infty} \sum_{\ell=1}^{zn} \frac{1}{n} a(n,\ell,v)p^n(1-p)^\ell .$$

It therefore suffices to prove for fixed $z_0$ that

$$\sum_{n=1}^{\infty} \sum_{\ell=1}^{zn} \frac{1}{n} a(n,\ell)p^n(1-p)^\ell$$

is analytic in $p$ on $[0,p_1]$, whenever $p_1 < p_T(\mathcal{G})$. But for any such $p \neq 0$ and a complex number $\zeta$ with

$$(9.33) \qquad |\zeta-p| \leq \delta$$

we have for $\ell \leq zn$

$$|a(n,\ell)\zeta^n(1-\zeta)^\ell| \leq (\frac{p+\delta}{p})^n(\frac{1-p+\delta}{1-p})^\ell \; a(n,\ell)p^n(1-p)^\ell$$

$$\leq (\frac{p+\delta}{p})^n(\frac{1-p+\delta}{1-p})^\ell \; P_p\{\#W(z_0) \geq n\}$$

$$\leq C_1\{e^{-C_2}(\frac{p+\delta}{p})(\frac{1-p+\delta}{1-p})^z\}^n .$$

Thus for $0 < p \leq p_1$, we can choose $\delta$ such that

$$\sum_{n=1}^{\infty} \sum_{\ell=1}^{zn} \frac{1}{n} a(n,\ell)\zeta^n(1-\zeta)^\ell$$

converges uniformly in the disc defined by (9.33). For $p$ close to zero we have the estimate

$$|a(n,\ell)\zeta^n(1-\zeta)^\ell| \leq a(n,\ell)|\zeta|^n \leq \{z^{-z}(z+1)^{z+1}|\zeta|\}^n ,$$

by virtue of (5.22), so that analyticity holds on $|\zeta| < z^z(z+1)^{-z-1}$. A slightly improved version of this last argument already appears in Kunz and Souillard (1978). This proves the analyticity of $\Delta(p,\mathcal{G})$ on $[0,p_T(\mathcal{G}))$ and consequently also of $\Delta(p,\mathcal{G}^*)$ on $[0,p_T(\mathcal{G}^*))$. But then $\Delta(p,\mathcal{G})$ is also analytic on $(1-p_T(\mathcal{G}^*),1]$, by virtue of (9.13). This proves the first statement in the theorem.

If for some $p_0 \varepsilon (0,1)$ Condition A or B of Sect. 3.2 holds, and $\mathcal{G}$ has an axis of symmetry as required in Theorem 3.1, then Theorem 3.1 shows that

$$p_T(\mathcal{G}) = p_H(\mathcal{G}) = p_0 = 1-p_T(\mathcal{G}^*) = 1-p_H(\mathcal{G}^*).$$

In such a case we obtain that $\Delta(p,\mathcal{G})$ is analytic for all $p \neq p_H(\mathcal{G})$ as claimed. □

Theorem 9.4. Let $\mathcal{G} = \mathcal{G}_0, \mathcal{G}_1, \mathcal{G}_0^*$ or $\mathcal{G}_1^*$ (see Ex. 2.1 (i), 2.1 (ii), 2.2 (i), 2.2 (ii) for these graphs). Then $\Delta(p,\mathcal{G})$ is twice continuously differentiable in $p$ on all of $[0,1]$.

Proof: In view of Theorem 9.3 and its proof it suffices to show that

$$\sum_{n=N}^{\infty} \sum_{\ell=1}^{zn} \frac{1}{n} a(n,\ell) \left| \left(\frac{d}{dp}\right)^r p^n(1-p)^\ell \right| \to 0 \quad (N \to \infty)$$

uniformly for $p$ in some neighborhood of $p_H(\mathcal{G})$, and $r = 1,2$. Now, with $q = 1-p$,

$$\frac{d}{dp} p^n(1-p)^\ell = \left(\frac{n}{p} - \frac{\ell}{q}\right) p^n q^\ell ,$$

$$\frac{d^2}{dp^2} p^n(1-p)^\ell = \left(\frac{n}{p} - \frac{\ell}{q}\right)^2 p^n q^\ell - \left(\frac{n}{p^2} + \frac{\ell}{q^2}\right) p^n q^\ell .$$

We shall only prove that

$$\sum_{n=N}^{\infty} \sum_{\ell=1}^{zn} \frac{1}{n} a(n,\ell) \left(\frac{n}{p} - \frac{\ell}{q}\right)^2 p^n q^\ell \to 0 \quad (N \to \infty) \tag{9.34}$$

uniformly in a neighborhood of $p_H$. The other terms can all be handled in the same way. To estimate (9.34) we split the sum over $\ell$ into two pieces: the $\ell$ with

$$\left|\frac{n}{p} - \frac{\ell}{q}\right| \leq n^{\frac{1}{2} + \frac{1}{8}\gamma_5} , \tag{9.35}$$

and the $\ell$ with

$$\left|\frac{n}{p} - \frac{\ell}{q}\right| > n^{\frac{1}{2} + \frac{1}{8}\gamma_5} , \tag{9.36}$$

where $\gamma_5$ is as in Theorem 8.2. The sum over the $\ell$ satisfying (9.35) contributes at most

$$\sum_{n=N}^{\infty} \sum_{\ell=1}^{zn} n^{\frac{1}{4}\gamma_5} a(n,\ell) p^n q^\ell = \sum_{n=N}^{\infty} n^{\frac{1}{4}\gamma_5} P_p\{\#W = n\} \quad \text{(see (9.32))} \tag{9.37}$$

$$\leq N^{-\frac{1}{4}\gamma_5} E_p\{(\#W)^{\frac{1}{2}\gamma_5}; \#W < \infty\} \leq C_{10} N^{-\frac{1}{4}\gamma_5} ,$$

by Theorem 8.2. For the sum over the $\ell$ satisfying (9.36) we use Lemma 5.1. We take

$$x = n^{\frac{1}{8}\gamma_5 - \frac{1}{2}}$$

in (5.23). We then find that the sum over the $\ell$ satisfying (9.36) contributes at most

$$\sum_{n=N}^{\infty} \frac{1}{n}\left(\frac{n}{p}+\frac{zn}{q}\right)^2 zn \exp - \frac{1}{3} n^{\frac{1}{4}\gamma_5} p^2 q ,$$

which obviously tends to zero as $N \to \infty$, uniformly for $p$ in some neighborhood of $p_H(\mathcal{G}) \in (0,1)$. □

Remarks.

(iii) Since we only know that $\gamma_5 > 0$ we cannot push the argument above further to obtain a third derivative of $\Delta(\cdot)$. As observed in the introduction to this Chapter it is assumed that $(\frac{d}{dp})^3 \Delta(p)$ blows up at $p_H$. It should be noted that one needs none of the difficult estimates of Ch. 8 for the present proof if $p \leq p_H(\mathcal{G})$. Indeed, for such $p$ one obtains

$$P_p\{\#W \geq n\} \leq P_{p_H}\{\#W \geq n\} \leq C_{22} n^{-\alpha_2}$$

from the very simple Lemma 8.5 (cf. (8.113)). This is enough to make the above estimates go through for $p \leq p_H(\mathcal{G})$ and to conclude that $\Delta(\cdot)$ has two continuous derivatives on $[0,p_H(\mathcal{G}))$ and these have finite limits as $p \uparrow p_H(\mathcal{G})$. Applying this to $\mathcal{G}^*$ and using Theorem 9.2 we see that there also exist two continuous derivatives on $(p_H(\mathcal{G}),1]$ and that these have finite limits as $p \downarrow p_H(\mathcal{G})$. Thus the hard part of the above theorem is that $\Delta'$ and $\Delta''$ do not have a jump at $p_H$. In fact Grimmett (1981) already gave a simple proof of this for the first derivative. For $\mathcal{G} = \mathcal{G}_1$ we can use the fact that $\mathcal{G}_1^*$ is isomorphic to $\mathcal{G}_1$ whence $\Delta(\cdot,\mathcal{G}_1^*) = \Delta(\cdot,\mathcal{G}_1)$ and

$$\Delta(p,\mathcal{G}_1) = \Delta(1-p,\mathcal{G}_1) + \Phi(p,\mathcal{G}_1) .$$

The polynomial $\Phi$ must be an odd function of $p - \frac{1}{2}$ therefore, and $\Phi''(\frac{1}{2},\mathcal{G}) = 0$ is then automatic. This shows that for $\mathcal{G} = \mathcal{G}_1$ even the second derivative of $\Delta$ must be continuous at $p_H(\mathcal{G}_1) = \frac{1}{2}$. It does not seem possible to handle $\Delta''(p,\mathcal{G}_0)$ in the same simple way.

(iv) Kunz and Souillard (1978) discuss the series

$$\sum_{n=1}^{\infty} e^{-nh}\pi(n)P_p\{\#W = n\} = E_p\{\pi(\#W)e^{-h\#W}\}$$

for a polynomial $\pi$ or $\pi(n) = \frac{1}{n}$. The series converges for all $p \in [0,1]$, $h \geq 0$. It is not analytic in $h$ at $h = 0$, $p > p_H(\mathcal{G})$, whenever $\pi$ is always nonnegative. In fact, if we write $\zeta$ for $e^{-h}$, then

$$\sum e^{-nh}n^{\delta}\, P_p\{\#W = n\} = \sum \zeta^n n^{\delta} P_p\{\#W = n\}$$

is a power series with positive coefficients in $\zeta$, whose radius of convergence equals 1 whenever $p > p_H(\mathcal{G})$ (by Theorem 5.2). The same is true for $p = p_H(\mathcal{G})$ if $\mathcal{G} = \mathcal{G}_0$ or $\mathcal{G}_1$ by (8.9). Such a power series has a singularity at $\zeta = 1$ by Pringsheim's theorem (Hille (1959), Theorem 5.7.1).

We also point out that if we view

$$\Delta(p) = \sum_{n=1}^{\infty} \sum_{\ell} \frac{1}{n} a(n,\ell)p^n q^{\ell}$$

as a function of two independent variables $p$ and $q$, then

$$(9.38) \qquad \frac{\partial^2}{\partial p^2} \sum_{n=1}^{\infty} \sum_{\ell} \frac{1}{n} a(n,\ell)p^n q^{\ell}$$

$$= \frac{1}{p^2} \sum_{n=1}^{\infty} \sum_{\ell} (n-1)a(n,\ell)p^n q^{\ell} = \frac{1}{p^2} E_p\{(\#W-1);\#W < \infty\}$$

on the set $\{q = 1-p\}$. By (5.17) the right hand side of (9.38) blows up as $p \to p_T(\mathcal{G})$. Despite these facts we could not show that $\Delta(p)$ has a singularity at $p = p_H$ when viewed as a function of the single variable $p$.

## 10. INEQUALITIES FOR CRITICAL PROBABILITIES.

We first give a theorem of Hammersley's (1961) stating that for any connected graph $\mathcal{G}$ the critical probability in a one-parameter problem for site-percolation on $\mathcal{G}( = p_H(\mathcal{G})$ in our notation) is at least as large as the critical probability for bond-percolation on $\mathcal{G}( = p_H(\tilde{\mathcal{G}})$, where $\tilde{\mathcal{G}}$ is the covering graph of $\mathcal{G}$; see Sect. 2.5). Actually, the result is obtained by comparing the probabilities that a fixed vertex $z_0$ is connected to some set of vertices $V$ via a path with all vertices occupied, and via a path with all edges open, respectively. The proof given below is from Oxley and Welsh (1979). Hammersley (1980) has generalized this further to mixed bond and site problems (see Remark 10.1(i) below).

Special cases of the above mentioned inequality

$$(10.1) \qquad p_H(\mathcal{G}) \geq p_H(\tilde{\mathcal{G}})$$

are

$$(10.2) \qquad p_H(\mathcal{G}_0) = \text{critical probability for site-percolation on } \mathbb{Z}^2 \geq p_H(\mathcal{G}_1) = \frac{1}{2} .$$

(see Ex. 2.1(i), 2.1(ii) and Application 3.4(ii)) and

$$(10.3) \qquad p_H(\mathcal{T}) = \frac{1}{2} \geq \text{critical probability for bond percolation on the triangular lattice} = 2\sin\frac{\pi}{18} .$$

(see Ex. 2.1(iii) and Applications 3.4(i) and (iii)). In (10.3) we clearly have a strict inequality, and various data (Essam (1972)) indicate that $p_H(\mathcal{G}_0) \approx .59$ so that one long expected (10.2) to be a strict inequality as well. Higuchi (1982) recently gave the first proof of this strict inequality. Intuitively, the most important basis for a comparison of $p_H(\mathcal{G}_0)$ and $p_H(\mathcal{G}_1)$ is the fact that $\mathcal{G}_0$ can be realized as a subgraph of $\mathcal{G}_1$; one obtains (an isomorphic copy of) $\mathcal{G}_0$ by deleting certain edges from $\mathcal{G}_1$, see Fig. 2.1 and 2.2. and Fisher (1961). The principal result of this chapter implies that for many pairs of periodic graphs $\mathcal{H}$, $\mathcal{G}$ with $\mathcal{H}$ a subgraph of $\mathcal{G}$ one has

$$(10.4) \qquad p_H(\mathcal{H}) \quad > \quad p_H(\mathcal{G}).$$

Of course one always has $p_H(\mathcal{H}) \geq p_H(\mathcal{G})$ whenever $\mathcal{H}$ is a subgraph of $\mathcal{G}$. The strength of Theorems 10.2 and 10.3 is that they give a strict inequality in many examples such as (10.2) and (10.3) (see Ex. 10.2(i), (ii)). Theorem 10.2 is actually much more general, and also gives strict inclusions for the percolative regions in some multiparameter percolation problems (see Ex. 10.2(i) below). The price for the generality is a very involved combinatorial argument in Sect. 10.3. The reader is advised to look first at the simple special case treated in Higuchi (1982).

## 10.1 Comparison of bond and site problems.

Let $\mathcal{G}$ be any graph with vertex (edge) set $\mathcal{V}(\mathcal{E})$, and let $P_p$ be the one-parameter probability measure on the occupancy configurations of its sites, given by

$$P_p = \Pi \ \mu_v$$

with (3.61), as in Sect. 3.4. For a vertex $z_0$ of $\mathcal{G}$ and a set of vertices $V$ of $\mathcal{G}$ set

$$\sigma_p(z_0,V) = \sigma_p(z_0,V,\mathcal{G}) = P_p\{\ \exists \text{ path } (v_0,e_1,\dots,e_\nu,v_\nu) \text{ with } v_0 = z_0,\ v_\nu \in V \text{ and all its vertices occupied} \mid z_0 \text{ is occupied}\} \ .$$

Analogously, we define $\tilde{P}_p$ as a measure on the configurations of passable and blocked edges of $\mathcal{G}$. As in Sect. 3.1 we take

$$\tilde{P}_p = \Pi \ \mu_e$$

and

$$\mu_e\{\omega(e) = 1\} = 1 - \mu_e\{\omega(e) = -1\} = p \ .$$

Also, with $z_0$ and $V$ as above we set

$$\beta_p(z_0,V) = \beta_p(z_0,V,\mathcal{G}) = \tilde{P}_p\{\ \exists \text{ path } (v_0,e_1,\dots,e_\nu,v_\nu)$$
$$\text{with } z_0 = v_0,\ v_\nu \in V \text{ and all its edges passable}\}$$

Lastly we remind the reader that $\theta(p,z_0)$ was defined in (3.25), and define here its analogue

$$\tilde{\theta}(p,z_0) := \tilde{P}_p\{\ \exists \text{ infinitely many vertices connected to } z_0$$
$$\text{by a path with all its edges passable}\}\ .$$

<u>Theorem 10.1. Let $\mathcal{G}$ be any connected graph, $z_0$ a fixed vertex of $\mathcal{G}$, and $V$ a collection of vertices of $\mathcal{G}$. Then</u>

(10.5) $$\sigma_p(z_0,V) \le \beta_p(z_0,V)\ ,\quad 0 \le p \le 1\ .$$

<u>Moreover,</u>

(10.6) $$\theta(p,z_0) \le p\tilde{\theta}(p,z_0)\ ,$$

<u>and consequently</u>

(10.7) $$p_H(\mathcal{G}) \ge p_H(\tilde{\mathcal{G}})\ ,$$

<u>where $\tilde{\mathcal{G}}$ is the covering graph of $\mathcal{G}$</u> .

<u>Proof</u>: We only have to prove (10.5). One then obtains (10.6) by taking for $V$ the set

$$V_n := \{v:\ v \text{ a vertex of } \mathcal{G} \text{ such that all paths from}$$
$$z_0 \text{ to } v \text{ contain at least } n \text{ vertices}\}\ .$$

and letting $n \to \infty$. Indeed one has the simple relations

$$\theta(p,z_0) = \lim_{n\to\infty} P_p\{z_0 \text{ is connected by an occupied path}$$
$$\text{to } V_n\} = \lim_{n\to\infty} p\,\sigma_p(z_0,V_n),$$

$$\tilde{\theta}(p,z_0) = \lim_{n\to\infty} \beta_p(z_0,V_n)\ .$$

(10.7) in turn follows from (10.6), the definition (3.62) of $p_H(\mathcal{G})$ and the corresponding formula

$$p_H(\tilde{\mathcal{G}}) = \sup\{p \in [0,1] : \tilde{\theta}(p,z_0) = 0\} \quad .$$

(Here we use the fact that bond percolation on $\mathcal{G}$ is equivalent to site percolation on $\tilde{\mathcal{G}}$, as proved in Prop. 3.1.)

For proving (10.5) we shall drop the restriction that $\mathcal{G}$ is connected. It suffices then to consider only finite graphs $\mathcal{G}$, by virtue of the following simple limit relation. Let $\mathcal{G}_n$ be the graph obtained from $\mathcal{G}$ by deleting all vertices in $V_n$ and all edges incident to some vertex in $V_n$. Then clearly

$$\sigma_p(z_0,V,\mathcal{G}) = \lim_{n\to\infty} \sigma_p(z_0,V \cap \mathcal{G}_n,\mathcal{G}_n) \ .$$

We now prove (10.5) for a finite graph $\mathcal{G}$ by induction on the number of edges in $\mathcal{G}$. First assume $\mathcal{G}$ has one edge $e$ only. If $z_0 \in V$ then $\sigma_p(z_0,V,\mathcal{G}) \geq P_p\{z_0$ is occupied $| z_0$ is occupied$\} = 1$. Thus $\sigma_p(z_0,V) = 1$ and similarly $\beta(z_0,V) = 1$. If $z_0 \notin V$ and $e$ is not incident to $z_0$, then both sides of (10.5) are zero. If $e$ connects $z_0$ with a vertex $z_1$, then both sides of (10.5) are still zero if $z_1 \notin V$. If, however, $z_1 \in V$, then (10.5) follows from

$$\sigma_p(z_0,V) = P_p\{z_0 \text{ and } z_1 \text{ are occupied} \mid z_0 \text{ is occupied}\}$$

$$= p = \tilde{P}_p\ \{e \text{ is passable}\} = \beta_p(z_0,V)$$

(since $z_0$ can be connected only to $z_1$). Now assume that (10.5) has been proven for all graphs with $m$ or fewer edges, and let $\mathcal{G}$ have (m+1) edges. As before the case with $z_0 \in V$ is trivial. Assume $z_0 \notin V$. If there is no edge incident to $z_0$, then again $\sigma_p(z_0,V) = \beta_p(z_0,V) = 0$ . Otherwise let $e$ be an edge with endpoints $z_0$ and some other vertex, $z_1$ say. Introduce the following two graphs:

$\mathcal{G}^d$ = graph obtained by deleting $\mathring{e} = e\setminus\{z_0,z_1\}$ from $\mathcal{G}$,

$\mathcal{G}^c$ = graph obtained by contracting $e$,i.e, deleting $\mathring{e} = e\setminus\{z_0,z_1\}$, but identitying $z_1$ with $z_0$ .

$\mathcal{G}^c$ has as vertex set the vertex set of $\mathcal{G}$ minus $z_1$, and has as many edges from $z_0$ to $v$ as there are edges in $\mathcal{G}$ from $z_0$ or $z_1$ to $v$. Both $\mathcal{G}^d$ and $\mathcal{G}^c$ have at most $m$ edges. Next, denote by $B(z_0,V,\mathcal{G})$ $(S(z_0,V,\mathcal{G}))$ the event that there exists a path $(v_0,e_1,\ldots,e_\nu,v_\nu)$ with $v_0 = z_0$, $v_\nu \in V$ and all its bonds or edges passable (all its sites or vertices occupied). One easily sees that if $e$ is blocked, then $B(z_0,V,\mathcal{G})$ occurs if and only if $B(z_0,V,\mathcal{G}^d)$ occurs, since any passable path from $z_0$ to $V$ does not contain $e$. Therefore

$$\tilde{P}_p\{B(z_0,V,\mathcal{G}) \text{ and } e \text{ blocked}\} = (1-p)\tilde{P}_p\{B(z_0,V,\mathcal{G}^d)\} = (1-p)\beta_p(z_0,V,\mathcal{G}^d)$$

Similarly, if $z_1$ is vacant and $S(z_0,V,\mathcal{G})$ occurs, then there is an occupied path on $\mathcal{G}$ from $z_0$ to $V$, which does not go through $e$, because any path which does not go through $z$, cannot contain $e$ either. In other words $z_1$ must be vacant and on the graph $\mathcal{G}^d$ minus the vertex $z_1$(and the edges incident to $z_1$ on $\mathcal{G}$ there must exist an occupied path from $z_0$ to $V$. Since this occupied path is automatically a path on $\mathcal{G}^d$ we have

$$P_p\{S(z_0,V,\mathcal{G}) \text{ and } z_1 \text{ is vacant} \mid z_0 \text{ is occupied}\} ,$$

$$\leq (1-p)\sigma_p(z_0,V,\mathcal{G}^d) .$$

Next consider the case in which $e$ is passable. Then, if $B(z_0,V,\mathcal{G}^c)$ occurs, also $B(z_0,V,\mathcal{G})$ occurs. Indeed, if $(z_0,e_1,v,\ldots,e_\nu,v_\nu)$ is a passable path on $\mathcal{G}^c$ from $z_0$ to $v_\nu \in V$, then either $(z_0,e_1,v_1,\ldots,e_\nu,v_\nu)$ or $(z_0,e,z_1,e_1,v_1,\ldots,e_\nu,v_\nu)$ is a passable path on $\mathcal{G}$ from $z_0$ to $v_\nu$. (We abuse notation somewhat here by using the same symbol for an edge or vertex on $\mathcal{G}$ and the corresponding edge or vertex, respectively on $\mathcal{G}^c$. Also if $z_1 \in V$ on $\mathcal{G}$, then on $\mathcal{G}^c$ the vertex $z_0$, resulting from identifying $z_0$ and $z_1$ on $\mathcal{G}$, belongs to $V$). Conversely it is just as easy to go from a passable path on $\mathcal{G}$ to a passable path with possible double points on $\mathcal{G}^c$ by removal of the edge $e$ and identifying $z_0$ and $z_1$. Therefore

$$P_p\{B(z_0,V,\mathcal{G}) \text{ and } e \text{ passable}\} = p\,\beta_p(z_0,V,\mathcal{G}^c) .$$

Finally, if $z_1$ is occupied, then $S(z_0,V,\mathcal{G})$ implies that there exists an occupied path on $\mathcal{G}^c$ from $z_0$ to $V$. By considering separately the cases $z_1 \in V$ and $z_1 \notin V$ one obtains

$$P_p\{S(z_0,V,\mathcal{G}) \text{ and } z_1 \text{ occupied} | z_0 \text{ is occupied}\} = p\,\sigma_p(z_0,V,\mathcal{G}^c) .$$

Finally, by the induction hypothesis

$$\beta_p(z_0,V,\mathcal{G}^c) \geq \sigma_p(z_0,V,\mathcal{G}^c) \quad \text{and}$$

$$\beta_p(z_0,V,\mathcal{G}^d) \geq \sigma_p(z_0,V,\mathcal{G}^d) .$$

Putting all these inequalities together we obtain

$$\beta_p(z_0,V,\mathcal{G}) = \tilde{P}_p\{B(z_0,V,\mathcal{G}) \text{ and } e \text{ is blocked}\}$$

$$+ \tilde{P}_p\{B(z_0,V,\mathcal{G}) \text{ and } e \text{ is passable}\}$$

$$= (1-p)\,\beta_p(z_0,V,\mathcal{G}^d) + p\,\beta_p(z_0,V,\mathcal{G}^c)$$

$$\geq (1-p)\,\sigma_p(z_0,V,\mathcal{G}^d) + p\,\sigma_p(z_0,V,\mathcal{G}^c)$$

$$\geq P_p\{S(z_0,V,\mathcal{G}) \text{ and } z_1 \text{ vacant} \mid z_0 \text{ is occupied}\}$$

$$+ P_p\{S(z_0,V,\mathcal{G}) \text{ and } z_1 \text{ occupied} \mid z_0 \text{ is occupied}$$

$$= \sigma_p(z_0,V,\mathcal{G}).$$

□

Remark .

(i) We can also ask for the probability

$\gamma(p,p',z_0,V) := P\{\ \exists$ path $(v_0,e_1,\ldots,e_\nu,v_\nu)$ with

$v_0 = z_0$, $v_\nu \in V$ and all its edges passable and all its vertices occupied$\}$ ,

when each vertex is occupied with probability $p$ and each edge is passable with probability $p'$ (all edges and all vertices independent) . Hammersley (1980) gives the following generalization of a result of McDiarmid (1980).

(10.8) $\gamma(\delta p,p',z_0,V) \leq \gamma(p,\delta p',z_0,V)$, $0 \leq \delta,p,p' \leq 1$ .

Here is Hammerersley's quick proof of (10.8). Let $\mathcal{H}$ be the random graph obtained by deleting each site other than $z_0$ of $\mathcal{G}$ with probability $1-p$ and each edge of $\mathcal{G}$ with probability $1-p'$. $\mathcal{H}$ may have some edges for which only one or no endpoint is a vertex of

$\mathcal{H}$ . Despite this slight generalization (10.5) remains valid for $\mathcal{H}$ since one can simple ignore all edges which do not have a vertex of $\mathcal{H}$ for both of their endpoints. Now take the expectation over $\mathcal{H}$ of the inequality

$$\sigma_\delta(z_0,V;\mathcal{H}) \leq \beta_\delta(z_0,V;\mathcal{H}) \quad .$$

This gives (10.8). E.g. in the left hand side one can pass through an edge only if it remained in $\mathcal{H}$; this event has probability $p'$. One can go through a vertex only if it stayed in $\mathcal{H}$ and is now occupied in $\mathcal{H}$; this event has probability $\delta p$. Thus

$$E\ \sigma_\delta(z_0,V,\mathcal{H}) = \gamma(\delta p,p',z_0,V)\ .$$

Similarly

$$E\ \beta_\delta(z_0,V;\mathcal{H}) = \gamma(p,\delta p',z_0,V).$$

(10.5) can be recovered from (10.8) by taking $p = p' = 1$, since

$$\sigma_\delta(z_0,V) = \gamma(\delta,1,z_0,V) \quad \text{and} \quad \beta_\delta(z_0,V) = \gamma(1,\delta,z_0,V)\ .$$

## 10.2 Strict inequalities for a graph and a subgraph .

The set-up in this section will be the following.

(10.9) $(\mathcal{G},\mathcal{G}^*)$ is a matching pair of periodic graphs in $\mathbb{R}^2$, based on $(\mathcal{M},\mathcal{F})$,

(10.10) $\mathcal{V}_1,\dots,\mathcal{V}_\lambda$ is a periodic partition of the vertices of $\mathcal{M}$,

and $P_p$ is the $\lambda$-parameter probability measure defined as in (3.22), (3.23). We further assume that

(10.11) one of the coordinate axes, call it $L$, is an axis of symmetry for $\mathcal{G},\mathcal{G}^*$ and the partition $\mathcal{V}_1,\dots,\mathcal{V}_\lambda$.

We shall later be interested in subgraphs $\mathcal{H}$ of $\mathcal{G}$ and the inequality (10.4). For the time being, though, we concentrate on comparing the percolation probabilities on $\mathcal{G}$ (or rather $\mathcal{G}_{p\ell}$) under two different probability measures. We shall show after Theorem 10.2 how the case of a subgraph $\mathcal{H}$ of $\mathcal{G}$ fits into our framework. For a little while our attention will be on $\mathcal{G}_{p\ell}$. $\mathcal{W}$ will be a periodic subclass of the vertices of $\mathcal{G}_{p\ell}$. Unfortunately we have to impose an ugly and complicated looking technical condition. It is a purely combinatorial condition, whose purpose is to guarantee that sufficiently many sites in $\mathcal{W}$ can be pivotal for the occurrence of occupied horizontal and vertical crossings on $\mathcal{G}_{p\ell}$ of large rectangles. Despite its forbidding appearance the condition is rather mild, as the examples after Theorem 10.2 will show. We shall also show by example that some condition of this form is needed to obtain the inequality (10.4). Before formulating the condition we remind the reader of some of the constants $\Lambda, \Lambda_i$ introduced earlier. These depend on $\mathcal{M}, \mathcal{G}, \mathcal{G}^*$, $\mathcal{G}_{p\ell}$ and $\mathcal{G}^*_{p\ell}$ only.

(10.12) $\qquad \Lambda \geq$ diameter of any edge of $\mathcal{G}, \mathcal{G}^*, \mathcal{G}_{p\ell}$ or $\mathcal{G}^*_{p\ell}$.

$\Lambda_3$ and $\Lambda_5 \geq 1$ are such that each horizontal (vertical) strip of height $\Lambda_3$(width $\Lambda_3$) posseses a horizontal (vertical) crossing on $\mathcal{M}$ (and hence also on $\mathcal{G}$ as well as on $\mathcal{G}^*$) with the property that for any two points $y_1, y_2$ on the crossing the diameter of the segment of the crossing between $y_1$ and $y_2$ is at most

$$\Lambda_5(|y_1 - y_2| + 1) .$$

Such $\Lambda_3$, $\Lambda_5$ exist by Lemma A.3 (Note that this lemma allows us to construct crossings which consist of translates of a fixed path independent of the length of the strip.) As before $\Lambda_4 = \lceil \Lambda_3 + \Lambda \rceil + 1$. We also choose $\Lambda_6$ such that any two vertices of $\mathcal{G}_{p\ell}(\mathcal{G}^*_{p\ell})$ within distance $\Lambda_3 + 10\Lambda$ of each other can be connected by a path on $\mathcal{G}_{p\ell}(\mathcal{G}^*_{p\ell})$ of diameter $\leq \Lambda_6$. Further we use the following abbreviations

$$\Lambda_7 = \Lambda_3 + 4\Lambda \quad ,$$

$$\Lambda_8 = (3\Lambda_5 + 1)(2\Lambda_6 + 4\Lambda_3 + 10\Lambda + 1) .$$

Lastly we make the following definitions.

<u>Def. 10.1</u>. A path $(v_0, e_1, \ldots, e_\nu, v_\nu)$ on $\mathcal{G}_{p\ell}$ is called <u>minimal</u>

if for any $i < j$ for which $v_i$ and $v_j$ are adjacent on $\mathcal{G}_{p\ell}$ one has $j = i + 1$.

Def. 10.2. A shortcut of one edge of the path $(v_0,e_1,\dots,e_\nu,v_\nu)$ on $\mathcal{G}_{p\ell}$ is an edge $e$ of $\mathcal{G}_{p\ell}$ between two vertices $v_i$ and $v_j$ on the path with $j \geq i + 2$.

Comment.

(i) A path is minimal exactly when it has no shortcuts of one edge. ///

Now let $\mathfrak{w}$ be a periodic subclass of the vertices of $\mathcal{G}_{p\ell}$.

Condition D. For some vertex $x = (x(1), x(2)) \in \mathfrak{w}$ there exists a constant $\Delta \geq 2\Lambda_8$, a minimal path $U = (u_0,e_1,\dots,e_\rho,u_\rho)$ on $\mathcal{G}_{p\ell}$ and a path $V^* = (v_0,e_1,\dots,e^*_\sigma,v^*_\sigma)$ on $\mathcal{G}^*_{p\ell}$ such that the following conditions are satisfied:

a) $x = u_{i_0}$ for some $i_0$, i.e., U goes through x.

b) If i and $j \geq i + 2$ are such that $u_i$ and $u_j$ lie on the perimeter of a single face $F \in \mathfrak{F}$, whose central vertex does not belong to $\mathfrak{w}$, then either $i + 2 \leq j \leq i_0$ or $i_0 \leq i \leq j - 2$,

c) U is a horizontal crossing of

$$B = B(x) := [x(1) - \Delta,\ x(1) + \Delta] \times [x(2) - \Delta,\ x(2) + \Delta].$$

U lies below the horizontal line $\mathbb{R} \times \{x(2) + \Delta - \Lambda_8\}$. Moreover, $(u_{i_0} = x, e_{i_0+1},\dots,e_\rho,u_\rho)$ lies to the right of the vertical line $\{x(1) - \Delta + \Lambda_8\} \times \mathbb{R}$, while $(u_0,e_1,\dots,e_{i_0},u_{i_0} = x)$ lies to left of the vertical line $\{x(1) + \Delta - \Lambda_8\} \times \mathbb{R}$,

d) $V^*$ connects x to the top edge of B inside the strip $[x(1) - \Delta + \Lambda_8,\ x(1) + \Delta - \Lambda_8] \times \mathbb{R}$, i.e., $(v^*_0,e^*_1,\dots,e^*_\sigma,v^*_\sigma)$ are contained in this strip, $(v^*_0,e^*_1,\dots,e^*_{\sigma-1},v^*_{\sigma-1}) \subset \mathring{B}(x)$, but $e^*_\sigma$ intersects $[x(1) - \Delta + \Lambda_8, x(1) + \Delta - \Lambda_8] \times \{x(2) + \Delta\}$. Moreover, $v^*_0$ and x are adjacent on $\mathcal{M}_{p\ell}$.

e) U and $V^*$ have no vertex in common.

Comments.

(ii) Basically a),c),d) and e) state that there exists a horizontal crossing U of B(x) on $\mathcal{G}$ through x, and a connection $V^*$ from x to the top edge of B above U. There are some restrictions on the location of U and V*, and U has to be minimal. However, condition b) may put a crucial restriction of another kind on U. Basically it requires that the pieces of U before and after x should not come too close to each other in a certain sense. On the other hand, condition b) is vacuous if $\mathcal{F} = \emptyset$ or if all central vertices of $\mathcal{G}_{p\ell}$ belong to $\mathfrak{w}$. This happens in several of the examples below. The reader is urged to look at these examples to get a feeling for Condition D. Example v) also illustrates that some restriction is necessary to obtain (10.4).

(iii) In condition c) and d) there is an asymmetry between the roles of the horizontal and vertical direction, and between the roles of the positive and negative vertical direction. This was merely done not to complicate the conditions still further. One can always interchange the positive and negative direction of an axis, or the first and second coordinate axis by rotating the graph over 180° or 90°. ///

We now turn to a discussion of the probability measures to be considered. We assume that $p_0 \in \mathcal{P}_\lambda$ is such that

$$\bar{0} \ll p_0 \ll \bar{1} \tag{10.13}$$

and that $P_{p_0}$ is given by (3.22), (3.23) with $p = p_0$. Further

(10.14) Condition A or B of Sect. 3.3 is satisfied for $p_0$.

As usual we extend $P_{p_0}$ to a probability measure on the occupancy configurations of $\mathcal{M}_{p\ell}$ by means of (7.2) and (7.3). The extended measure $P_{p_0}$ is still a product measure of the form (3.22), (3.23) with $\mathfrak{v}$ = vertex set of $\mathcal{M}_{p\ell}$. We shall also consider another probability measure, $P_{p'}$, on the occupancy configurations of $\mathcal{M}_{p\ell}$. $P_{p'}$ too will be a product measure:

$$P_{p'} = \prod_{\substack{v \text{ a vertex} \\ \text{of } \mathcal{M}_{p\ell}}} \nu_v \tag{10.15}$$

with $\nu_v$ a probability measure on $\{-1, +1\}$. We assume that

$$\nu_v = \mu_v \quad \text{for } v \notin \mathfrak{w} \tag{10.16}$$

but

(10.17) $\nu_v\{\omega(v) = 1\} < \mu_v\{\omega(v) = 1\}$ , $v \in \mathfrak{w}$ ,

where $\mathfrak{w}$ is a periodic subset of vertices of $\mathcal{G}_{p\ell}$ . $P_{p'}$ is also assumed periodic, i.e.,

(10.18) $\nu_v = \nu_w$ if $w = v + k_1\xi_1 + k_2\xi_2$ for some

$$k_1, k_2 \in \mathbb{Z} .$$

Thus, $P_{p'}$ {v is occupied} takes still only a finite number of values, on periodic subclasses of the vertices. We think of these values as the components of a vector p', thereby justifying the notation $P_{p'}$ . Note, however, that p' can have more (or fewer) components than p; $P_{p'}$ does not have to be a $\lambda$-parameter probability measure. Also, for a central vertex v of $\mathcal{G}_{p\ell}$ which belongs to $\mathfrak{w}$ (10.17) and (7.2) imply

(10.19) $\nu_v\{\omega(v) = 1\} < 1 = \mu_v\{\omega(v) = 1\}$ .

We are therefore no longer restricting ourselves to measures in which all central vertices of $\mathcal{G}_{p\ell}$ are occupied with probability one. However, by (10.16) and (7.3) we still have

(10.20) $\nu_v\{\omega(v) = -1\} = \mu_v\{\omega(v) = -1\} = 1$ for every central vertex of $\mathcal{G}^*_{p\ell}$ .

It is also worth pointing out that (10.15) - (10.17) imply

$$P_{p'}\{v \text{ is occupied}\} \leq P_{p_0}\{v \text{ is occupied}\}$$

for all vertices v of $\mathcal{M}_{p\ell}$ .

Theorem 10.2. Assume $\mathcal{G}, \mathcal{G}^*, \mathfrak{v}_1, \dots, \mathfrak{v}_\lambda$ satisfy (10.9) - (10.11) and that $\mathfrak{w}$ is a periodic subset of the vertices of $\mathcal{G}_{p\ell}$ such that Condition D holds. Further let $p_0$ be such that (10.13) and (10.14) hold, and assume that $P_{p_0}$ is extended such that (7.2) and (7.3) hold for $p = p_0$. Let $P_{p'}$ be defined by (10.15) and satisfy (10.16) and (10.17). Then, for any vertex $z_0$ of $\mathcal{G}_{p\ell}$

(10.21) $E_{p'}\{\#W_{p\ell}(z_0)\} < \infty$ and $P_{p'}\{\#W_{p\ell}(z_0) = \infty\} = 0$,

where $W_{p\ell}(z_0)$ is the occupied cluster on $\mathcal{G}_{p\ell}$ of $z_0$.

We now explain how this result can be applied to deal with subgraphs $\mathcal{H}$ of $\mathcal{G}$. We will consider subgraphs $\mathcal{H}$ of $\mathcal{G}$ formed by one or both of the following two procedures in succession:

(10.22) Remove all vertices of $\mathcal{G}$ in some periodic subclass $\mathcal{V}_0$ of the vertices of $\mathcal{G}$. Also remove all edges incident to any vertex of $\mathcal{V}_0$.

(10.23) Remove the close-packing in all faces of $\mathcal{F}_0$, where $\mathcal{F}_0$ is a periodic subset of $\mathcal{F}$.

Note that we do not make any symmetry requirements for $\mathcal{H}$ with respect to any line. The periodicity requirement in (10.22) for $\mathcal{V}_0$ means of course that (3.18) holds for $\mathcal{V}_0$, while for $\mathcal{F}_0$ in (10.23) it means that if $F \in \mathcal{F}_0$ then also $F + k_1\xi_1 + k_2\xi_2 \in \mathcal{F}_0$ for any integers $k_1, k_2$. To remove the close packing of $F$ means to remove all edges which run through the interior of $F$ and connect two vertices on the perimeter of $F$. Recall that these edges where inserted to manufacture $\mathcal{G}$ from $\mathcal{M}$ (see Sect. 2.2).

Now let $p_0$ satisfy (10.13) and (10.14) ((10.14) is a condition on $p_0$ and $\mathcal{G}$). $P_{p_0}$ also induces a probability measure on the occupancy configurations of $\mathcal{H}$(we merely have to restrict $P_{p_0}$ to the vertices of $\mathcal{H}$, i.e., to $\bigcup_i^{\lambda} \mathcal{V}_i \setminus \mathcal{V}_0$ ). To define $P_{p'}$ in the present situation we take

(10.24) $\mathcal{W} = \mathcal{V}_0 \cup \{$the central vertices of faces $F \in \mathcal{F}_0\}$ ($\mathcal{W}$ is a subset of the vertex set of $\mathcal{G}_{p\ell}$. $\mathcal{V}_0 = \emptyset$ if only (10.23) is applied to form $\mathcal{H}$; also $\mathcal{F}_0 = \emptyset$ if only (10.22) is applied to form $\mathcal{H}$).

Next, we take for $v$ a vertex of $\mathcal{M}_{p\ell}$

(10.25) $P_{p'}\{v$ is occupied$\} = P_{p_0}\{v$ is occupied$\}$ if $v \notin \mathcal{W}$,

and

(10.26) $P_{p'}$ {v is occupied} = 0 if $v \in \mathcal{W}$ .

Later on we shall show the easy fact that percolation on $\mathcal{H}$ under $P_{p_0}$ is equivalent to percolation on $\mathcal{G}_{p\ell}$ under $P_{p'}$, and that (10.15) - (10.18) hold for the above $\mathcal{W}$ and $P_{p'}$. This then leads to the following result for subgraphs $\mathcal{H}$.

Theorem 10.3. Assume $\mathcal{G}, \mathcal{G}^*, \mathcal{V}_1, \dots, \mathcal{V}_\lambda$ satisfy (10.9) - (10.11) and $p_0$ satisfies (10.13) and (10.14). Let $\mathcal{H}$ be a subgraph of $\mathcal{G}$ formed by one or both of the procedures (10.22), (10.23) and assume Condition D holds with $\mathcal{W}$ as in (10.24). Then, for any $p_1$ in some open neighborhood (in $\mathcal{P}_\lambda$) of $p_0$ and any vertex $z_0$ of $\mathcal{H}$:

$$E_{p_1} \{\#(\text{occupied cluster of } z_0 \text{ on } \mathcal{H})\} < \infty ,$$

$$P_{p_1} \{\#(\text{occupied cluster of } z_0 \text{ on } \mathcal{H}) = \infty\} = 0 .$$

Special case. In a one-parameter problem (i.e., $\lambda = 1$) with $\mathcal{G}$ and $\mathcal{H}$ as in Theorem 10.3 one obtains

$$p_H(\mathcal{H}) > p_H(\mathcal{G}) .$$

## Examples.

Before turning to the proofs we illustrate the use of Theorems 10.2 and 10.3 and the verifiability of condition D with a few examples.

(i) Let $\mathcal{G} = \mathcal{G}_1$, the graph corresponding to bond percolation on $\mathbb{Z}^2$, imbedded as in Fig. 2.3 (see Ex. 2.1(ii); the vertices are located at $(i + \frac{1}{2}, i_2)$ and $(i_1, i_2, + \frac{1}{2})$, $i_1, i_2 \in \mathbb{Z}$). $\mathcal{G}_{1,p\ell}$ has in addition vertices at $(i_1, i_2)$, $i_1, i_2 \in \mathbb{Z}$. (see Ex. 2.3(ii) where the same graph is discussed, but rotated over 45°). $\mathcal{G}^*_{1,p\ell}$ is shown in Fig. 10.1 below. It has vertices at $(i_1, i_2 + \frac{1}{2})$, $(i_1 + \frac{1}{2}, i_2)$, $(i_1 + \frac{1}{2}, i_2 + \frac{1}{2})$, $i_1, i_2 \in \mathbb{Z}$. For $\mathcal{W}$ we take the vertices of $\mathcal{G}_{1,p\ell}$ on $\mathbb{Z}^2$, i.e.,

$$\mathcal{W} = \{(i_1, i_2) : i_1, i_2 \in \mathbb{Z}\} .$$

We easily see that condition D holds in this example with x = the origin. For U we take a path from $(-\Delta, 0)$ to $(\Delta, 0)$ along the first

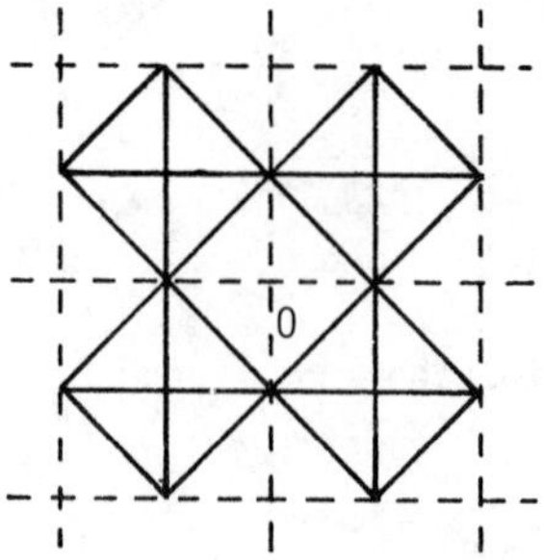


Figure 10.1 $\mathcal{G}^*_{1,p\ell}$ . The solid segments are the edges of $\mathcal{G}^*_{1,p\ell}$ . The dashed lines are the lines $x(1) = k_1$ or $x(2) = k_2$ , $k_i \in \mathbb{Z}$ .

coordinate axis. For $V^*$ we take the path from $v^*_0 = (0, \frac{1}{2})$ along the 45° line to $(\frac{1}{2}, 1)$ and then upwards along the vertical line $x(1) = \frac{1}{2}$ to the point $(\frac{1}{2}, \Delta)$ (see Fig. 10.2). b) is automatically fulfilled since $\mathcal{W}$ contains all central vertices of $\mathcal{G}_{p\ell}$ .

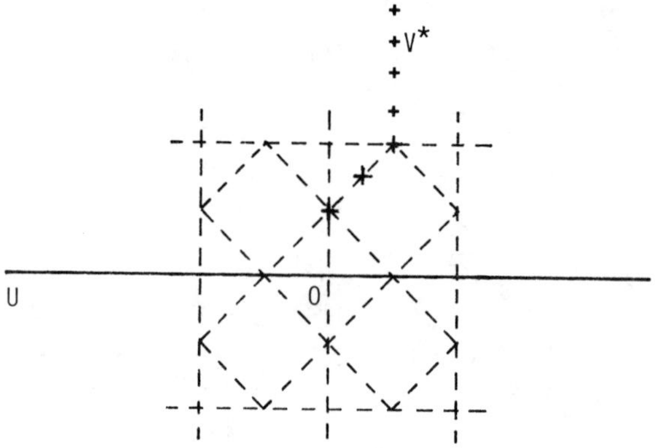


Figure 10.2 The dashed lines represent edges of $\mathcal{G}_{1,p\ell}$ . The path $U$ is drawn solidly. The path $V^*$ is indicated by +++ ; it runs on $\mathcal{G}^*_{1,p\ell}$ .

Now as in Application 3.4(ii), let

$$\mathcal{U}_1 = \{i_1 + \frac{1}{2}, i_2) : i_1, i_2 \in \mathbb{Z}\} ,$$
$$\mathcal{U}_2 = \{(i_1, i_2 + \frac{1}{2}) : i_1, i_2 \in \mathbb{Z}\} .$$

We consider the corresponding two-parameter problem, as defined in (3.20) - (3.23). Take $p_0 = (p_0(1), p_0(2))$ such that

$$p_0(1) + p_0(2) = 1,\ 0 < p_0(i) < 1,\ i = 1,2 .$$

By Application 3.4(ii) condition A holds for such a $p_0$. By Theorem 10.2 we therefore have

(10.27) $$E_{p'}\{\#W_{p\ell}(z_0)\} < \infty$$

for any $P_{p'}$ of the form (10.15) with

(10.28) $$P_{p'}\{v \text{ is occupied}\} = p_0(i),\ v \in \mathcal{V}_i,\ i = 1,2, .$$

(10.29) $$P_{p'}\{(i_1,i_2) \text{ is occupied}\} < 1,\ i_1,i_2 \in \mathbb{Z} .$$

Actually the set of $p >> 0$ in parameter space where (10.27) holds is open, by Cor. 5.1. Thus (10.27) continues to hold when $p_0$ in (10.28) and is replaced by $p_1$ sufficiently close to $p_0$, even when $p_1(1) + p_1(2) > 1$. The best illustration for this is provided by Theorem 10.3. We now define $\mathcal{H}$ as the subgraph of $\mathcal{G}$, obtained by removing the close packing of all the faces which contain a point $(i_1, i_2)$, $i_1,i_2 \in \mathbb{Z}$). (Thus, if we call this last collection of faces $\mathcal{F}_0$, then we only apply (10.23) with this $\mathcal{F}_0$). The resulting $\mathcal{H}$ is clearly isomorphic to $\mathcal{G}_0$, the simple quadratic lattice, and $\mathcal{V}_1$ and $\mathcal{V}_2$ are such that the resulting two-parameter problem on $\mathcal{H}$ is precisely the two-parameter problem for site-percolation on $\mathbb{Z}^2$ considered in Application 3.4(iv). We conclude from Theorem 10.3 that no percolation occurs under $P_{p_1}$ for $p_1 = (p_1(1), p_1(2)$, in some neighborhood of $p_0$. In particular, <u>the non-percolative region for two-parameter site-percolation on $\mathbb{Z}^2$ contains the (anti-) diagonal</u>

$$\{p: 0 \leq p(i) \leq 1,\ p(1) + p(2) = 1\}$$

<u>strictly in its interior</u>. Strictly speaking we only obtain this conclusion from Theorem 10.3 for $0 << p << 1$. However, we already know from Application 3.4(iv) that no percolation occurs for $0 \leq p(1) \leq p_H(\mathcal{G}_0^*)$, $p(2) = 1$, and hence by monotonicity (Lemma 4.1) no percolation occurs for $0 \leq p(1) \leq p_H(\mathcal{G}_0^*)$, $p(2) \geq 1 - p_H(\mathcal{G}_0^*)$ (see Fig. 3.8). Similarly no percolation occurs for $1-p_H(\mathcal{G}_1^*) \leq p(1) \leq 1$, $0 \leq p(2) \leq p_H(\mathcal{G}_0^*)$.

When restricted to $p(1) = p(2)$ the above shows that there is no percolation in a neighborhood of $p(1) = p(2) = \frac{1}{2}$. This shows that (10.2) is really a strict inequality .

(ii) This time let $\mathcal{G}$ be the triangular lattice. In order to obtain the familiar picture we imbed this lattice in such a way that its faces are equilateral triangles (i.e., we use the imbedding of Fig. 2.4 rather than the one for $\mathcal{J}$ described in Ex. 2.1(iii).) $\mathcal{G}_{p\ell} = \mathcal{G}$ in this case. Let the vertices be located at

$$(k_1 + \frac{k_2}{2}, \frac{k_2}{2}\sqrt{3}), \; k_1, k_2 \in \mathbb{Z},$$

and take

$$\mathfrak{w} = \{2k_1 + k_2, k_2\sqrt{3}\}, \; k_1, k_2 \in \mathbb{Z}.$$

In a way $\mathfrak{w}$ consists of every other point; see Fig. 10.3.

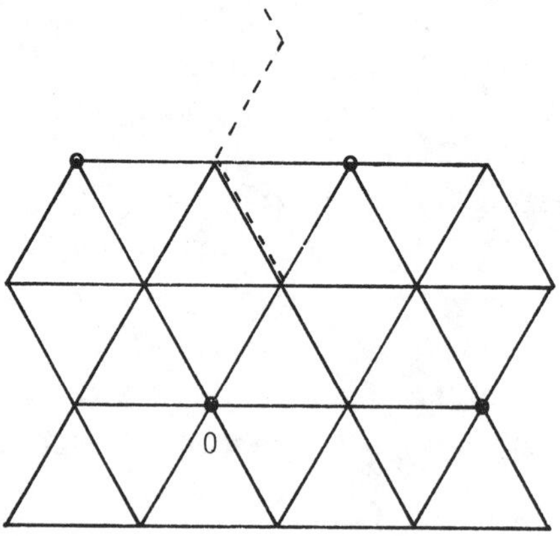


Figure 10.3 The triangular lattice with the points of $\mathfrak{w}$ indicated by circles. $V^*$ is the dashed path.

Again condition D is easily seen to hold with $x$ = the origin. For $U$ we take again a path from $(-\Delta,0)$ to $(\Delta,0)$ along the first coordinate axis. For $V^*$ we take a path with "zig-zags" upward from the point $(\frac{1}{2}, \frac{1}{2}\sqrt{3})$ alternatingly through points $(\frac{1}{2}, (j - \frac{1}{2})\sqrt{3})$ and $(0, j\sqrt{3})$, $j = 1,2,\dots,\Delta$.

We may therefore apply Theorem 10.3 to the one-parameter problem on $\mathcal{G}$. We know from application 3.4(i) that $p_0 = \frac{1}{2}$ = critical probability for site-percolation on $\mathcal{G}$ satisfies condition A. Let $\mathcal{H}$ be the graph obtained by removing the vertices in $\mathfrak{w}$ from $\mathcal{G}$.(Thus we apply only (10.22) with $\mathfrak{v}_0 = \mathfrak{w}$.) We conclude that $p_H(\mathcal{H}) > \frac{1}{2}$.

However, one easily sees that removing the sites in $\mathcal{W}$ from $\mathcal{G}$ yields the Kagome lattice of Ex. 2.5(i) for $\mathcal{H}$. This is the covering graph of the hexagonal lattice, so that $p_H(\mathcal{H})$ = critical probability for bond percolation on the hexagonal lattice $= 1 - 2\sin\frac{\pi}{18}$ (see Prop. 3.1 and Application 3.4(iii).). Thus, we obtained the obvious inequality $1-2\sin\frac{\pi}{18} = p_H(\mathcal{H}) > \frac{1}{2}$.

Since by Application 3.4(iii) the critical probability for bond-percolation on the triangular lattice equals one minus the critical probability for bond percolation on the hexagonal lattice, we also have

$$p_H(\text{bond percolation on triangular lattice}) < \frac{1}{2} .$$

This is precisely (10.3) with a strict inequality.

(iii) In this example we compare $\mathbb{Z}^3$ with $\mathbb{Z}^2$. We concentrate on site-percolation, but practically the same argument works for bond-percolation on $\mathbb{Z}^3$, or even the restriction of $\mathbb{Z}^3$ to $\mathbb{Z}^2 \times \{0,1\}$ (i.e., two layers of $\mathbb{Z}^2$). The latter graph contains the following graph $\mathcal{G}$, which is obtained by decorating one out of nine faces of $\mathcal{G}_0$ (see Ex. 2.1(i) for $\mathcal{G}_0$). Each face $(i_1, i_1+1) \times (i_2, i_2+1)$ with both $i_1 \equiv 1 \pmod 3$ and $i_2 \equiv 1 \pmod 3$ is decorated as shown in Fig. 10.4.

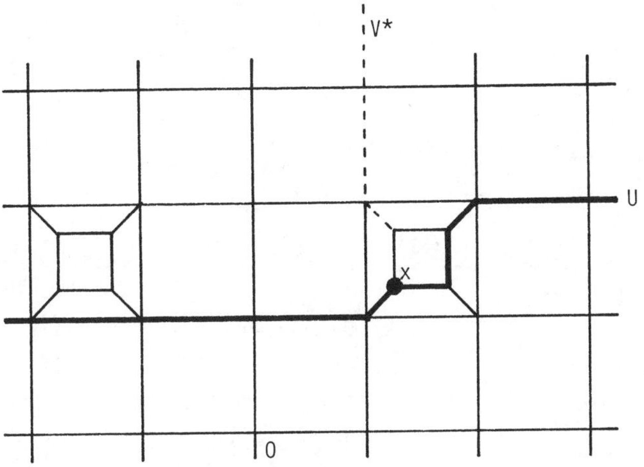


Figure 10.4 The graph $\mathcal{G}$, obtained from $\mathcal{G}_0$ by the indicated decorations. The blackened circle is the vertex $x$. The boldly drawn path is $U$. The path $V^*$ is dashed.

$\mathcal{G}$ is a mosaic so that we can view $\mathcal{G}$ as one of a matching pair based on $(\mathcal{G},\emptyset)$. In this case $\mathcal{G} = \mathcal{G}_{p\ell}$. Both coordinate axes are axes of symmetry for $\mathcal{G}$. For the subgraph $\mathcal{H}$ we take $\mathcal{G}_0$ = the simple square lattice. This corresponds to applying (10.22) only, with $\mathcal{V}_0$ = the collection of vertices used in decorating $\mathcal{G}_0$ when forming $\mathcal{G}$. Condition D b) is vacuous since $\mathcal{F} = \emptyset$, and Fig. 10.4 illustrates that the other parts of Condition D can also easily be satisfied for any choice of $x \in \mathcal{V}_0$. Since $\mathcal{G}$ is invariant under a rotation over 90° around the origin, it is immediate that (3.52) - (3.55) hold for the one-parameter problem on $\mathcal{G}$; compare Applications 3.4(iv) and (v). As in those Applications it follows from Theorem 3.2 that Condition B of Sect. 3.3 holds for $p_0 = p_H(\mathcal{G})$. We therefore conclude from the one-parameter case of Theorem 10.3 that

(10.30) $$p_H(\text{site-percolation on } \mathbb{Z}^3)$$
$$\leq p_H(\text{site-percolation on two layers of } \mathbb{Z}^2) \leq p_H(\mathcal{G})$$
$$< p_H(\text{site-percolation on } \mathbb{Z}^2) = p_H(\mathcal{G}_0).$$

To obtain a similar conclusion for bond-percolation on $\mathbb{Z}^3$ we compare the covering graph $\tilde{\mathcal{G}}$ of $\mathcal{G}$ with the covering graph of $\mathbb{Z}^2$, (see Ex. 2.5(ii)). We draw some faces of $\tilde{\mathcal{G}}$ in Fig. 10.5. The central square in this figure corresponds to one of the decorated faces in $\mathcal{G}$. $\mathcal{H}$ is now formed from $\tilde{\mathcal{G}}$ by removing all vertices of $\mathcal{H}$ which correspond to edges of the decorations. These vertices are marked by solid circles in Figure 10.5. We leave it to the reader to verify that $\mathcal{H}$ is nothing but $\mathcal{G}_1$. We therefore conclude in the same way as in (10.30) that

$$p_H(\text{bond-percolation on } \mathbb{Z}^3) < \frac{1}{2} = p_H(\mathcal{G}_1)$$

(see Application 3.4(ii) for the last equality).

(iv) The graph $\mathcal{G}$ in this example will be $\mathcal{D}^*$, the matching graph of the diced lattice $\mathcal{D}$. $\mathcal{D}$ was introduced in Ex. 2.1(v); $\mathcal{D}^*$ is illustrated in Fig. 10.6. One can think of $\mathcal{D}^*$ as a "decoration" of the hexagonal lattice. Note that $\mathcal{D}^*$ is not identical with the matching graph of the hexagonal graph, because $\mathcal{D}^*$ has a vertex in the center of each hexagon (the solid circles in Fig. 10.6). $\mathcal{D}^*_{p\ell}$ is also drawn in Fig. 10.6. It has a central vertex in each face of $\mathcal{D}$ (see Fig. 2.7; these central vertices are indicated by the open

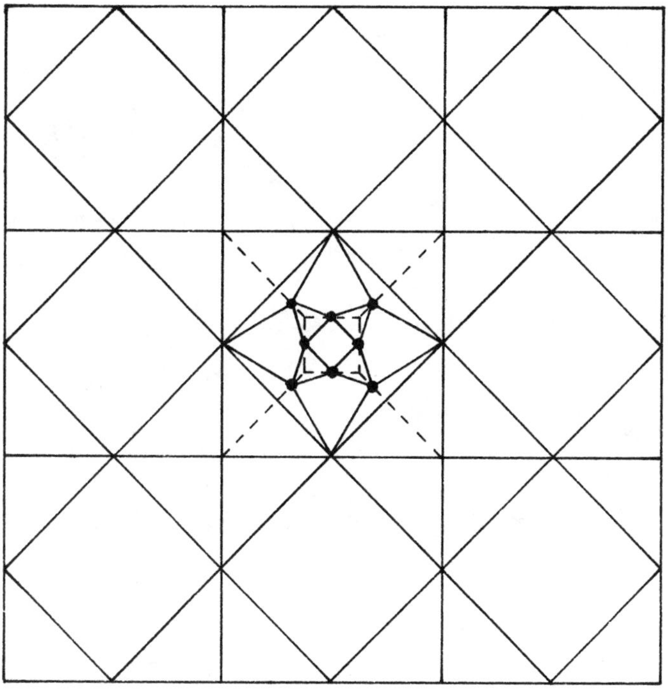

Figure 10.5 The covering graph $\tilde{\mathcal{G}}$ of $\mathcal{G}$ . The dashed edges form the decoration of one face of $\mathcal{G}_0$ .

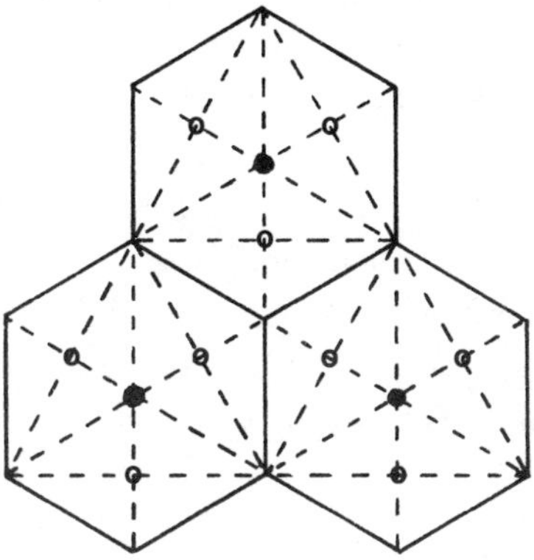

Figure 10.6 $\mathcal{D}^*$ drawn as a "decoration" of a hexagonal lattice. The "decoration" is indicated by dashed lines. There is a vertex of $\mathcal{D}^*$ at each center of the hexagons (drawn as a solid circle). There is no vertex of $\mathcal{D}^*$ at the open circles; however, there is a vertex of $\mathcal{D}^*_{p\ell}$ at each open circle.

circles in Fig. 10.6). For $\mathfrak{W}$ we take the collection of these central vertices. Condition D again holds. We content ourselves with a picture of a possible choice for U and V* in Fig. 10.7 for x an arbitrary vertex in $\mathfrak{W}$ . Note that Condition D b) is again vacuous since $\mathfrak{W}$ contains all central vertices of $\mathcal{G}_{p\ell} = \mathcal{D}^*_{p\ell}$ . Also $(\mathcal{D}^*)^* = \mathcal{D}$ and $\mathcal{D}_{p\ell} = \mathcal{D}$ .

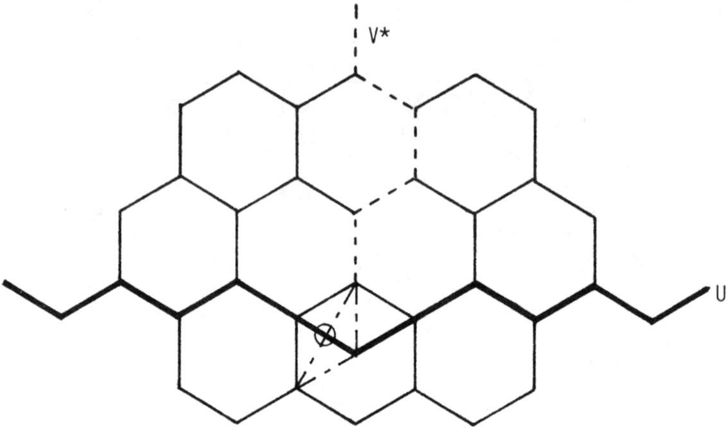


Figure 10.7 The open circle is the vertex x . The boldly drawn path is U . The dashed path is V* . The edges indicated by — - — belong to $\mathcal{D}_{p\ell}$ .

Once more we apply Theorem 10.3. This time we take for $\mathcal{H}$ the graph obtained by removing the close packing in all faces of $\mathcal{D}^*$, i.e., we apply only (10.23) with $\mathcal{F}_0$ all faces of $\mathcal{D}$. The resulting $\mathcal{H}$ is just $\mathcal{D}$ itself. $p_0 = p_H(\mathcal{D}^*)$ satisfies condition B when $\mathcal{G}$ is taken $\mathcal{D}^*$ ( by Application 3.3(v) and Theorem 3.2 ). (Actually we checked (3.52) - (3.55) for $\mathcal{G} = \mathcal{D}$. However, (3.52) - (3.55) remain unchanged when $\mathcal{G}$ is replaced by $\mathcal{G}^*$ and p by 1-p. Thus (3.52)-(3.55) hold when $\mathcal{G} = \mathcal{D}^*$.) Theorem 3.2 then shows that Condition B holds for $p_0 = p_H(\mathcal{D}^*)$. The conclusion of the one-parameter case of Theorem 10.3 is now

$$p_H(\mathcal{D}) > p_H(\mathcal{D}^*) \quad .$$

But by Theorems 3.2 and 3.1 $P_H(\mathcal{D}) = 1-p_H(\mathcal{D}^*)$ so that we find

$$p_H(\mathcal{D}) > \frac{1}{2} > p_H(\mathcal{D}^*).$$

From Fig. 10.7 one also sees that Condition D is fulfilled if we take $\mathcal{G} = \mathcal{D}$, and $\mathfrak{w}$ the collection of the centers of the hexagons. If $\mathcal{D}$ is imbedded as described in Ex. 2.1(v) these are the points

$$((k_1 + \frac{\ell}{2})\sqrt{3}\ ,\ 3(k_2 + \frac{1}{2}\ell)),\ k_i \in \mathbb{Z}\ ,\ \ell = 0 \text{ or } 1\ ;$$

in Fig. 10.6 this means that we remove the solid circles. If we apply (10.22) with $\mathfrak{v}_0 = \mathfrak{w}$ the resulting graph is the hexagonal lattice and we obtain

$$p_H(\text{hexagonal lattice}) > p_H(\text{diced lattice}) > \frac{1}{2}\ .$$

(these are critical probabilities for site-percolation).

<u>Remark</u> .

i) The procedure illustrated in this example will work in many examples of matching pairs $(\mathcal{G},\mathcal{G}^*)$ based on $(\mathcal{M},\emptyset)$ to yield

$$p_H(\mathcal{G}) = p_H(\mathcal{M}) > \frac{1}{2} > p_H(\mathcal{G}^*)\ .$$

Indeed apply Theorem 10.3 with $\mathcal{G}$ replaced by $\mathcal{G}^*$, and $\mathcal{F}_0$ the collection of all faces of $\mathcal{M}$ . When removing the close-packing from $\mathcal{G}^*$ in all faces of $\mathcal{M}$ as in (10.23), the resulting subgraph $\mathcal{H}$ is just $\mathcal{M}$, or $\mathcal{G}$. Lastly one uses $p_H(\mathcal{G}) + p_H(\mathcal{G}^*) = 1$, assuming Theorem 3.1 or 3.2 applies. One could have obtained $p_H(\mathcal{G}_0) > \frac{1}{2}$ in Ex. 10.2(i) above in this way. ///

v) This "negative" example shows that some kind of condition like Condition D has to be imposed. We take for $\mathcal{H}$ a mosaic, and for $\mathcal{G}$ a graph obtained by decorating a periodic subclass of faces of $\mathcal{H}$ . Choose the decoration in a face $F$ such that it is attached to only one vertex $v$ , or two adjacent vertices $v'$ , $v''$, of $\mathcal{H}$ on the

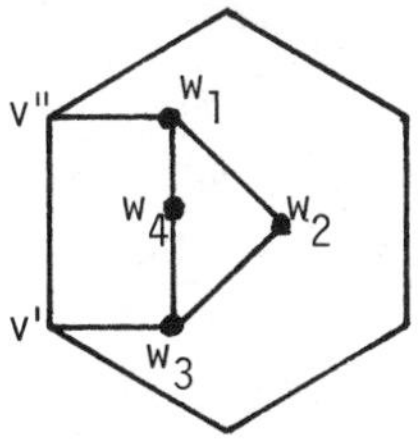


Figure 10.8. $F$ is the interior of the hexagon, which is a face of $\mathcal{H}$. The vertices $w_1$-$w_4$ and the edges in $F$ have been used to "decorate" $F$.

perimeter of F, e.g. as in Fig. 10.8. Even though $\mathcal{H}$ is a subgraph of $\mathcal{G}$ one always has $p_H(\mathcal{H}) = p_H(\mathcal{G})$. Indeed in site-percolation, in the situation of Fig. 10.8, the decoration could be of help in forming an infinite occupied cluster only if $v'$ and $v''$ are both occupied. But in this case $v'$ and $v''$ belong to that same cluster even if no decoration is present. Condition D fails because there exists no minimal path through any of the added vertices in F which starts and ends ouside F.

Remark .

ii) The theorems of this section give no strict inequality if $\mathcal{H}$ is obtained from $\mathcal{G}$ by removing edges of $\mathcal{M}$ or partial close-packings only. If we remove one of the edges introduced when close-packing a face of $\mathcal{M}$, then we usually cannot find a subgraph $\mathcal{H}_{p\ell}$ which serves as the planar modification of $\mathcal{H}$, and we therefore have trouble in defining a "lowest" horizontal occupied crossing. On the other hand, if an edge e of $\mathcal{M}$ (and it translates by integral vectors) is removed to form $\mathcal{H}$, then one can artifically turn this into a situation where one removes a vertex. One introduces a new kind of vertex for $\mathcal{M}$, situated somewhere on $\overset{\circ}{e}$, and connected only to the endpoints of e. The new vertex should be occupied with probability one on $\mathcal{G}$, and it is this vertex which is removed to form $\mathcal{H}$. However, this introduces a new vertex on the perimeter of some faces of $\mathcal{M}$, and therefore $\mathcal{G}$ may no longer be obtained from the modified $\mathcal{M}$ by close-packing faces. Nevertheless we believe a more complicated proof may work when only edges of $\mathcal{M}$ are removed from $\mathcal{G}$ to form $\mathcal{H}$. ///

Proof of Theorem 10.2. The proof consists of two parts. First a combinatorial, or topological, part which derives another ugly condition - Condition E stated in Step (ii) - from Condition D. We begin with a probabilistic part, and defer the derivation of Condition E from Condition D to a separate section (to make it easier to skip the unpleasant and not very interesting part of the argument).

The probabilistic part begins like the proof of Lemma 7.4. By virtue of Theorem 5.1 it suffices for (10.21) to prove

$$\lim_{\ell\to\infty} \tau(2\overline{M}_\ell;\ i,p',\mathcal{G}_{p\ell}) = 0\ ,\ i = 1,2,$$

for some sequence $\overline{M}_\ell = (M_{\ell 1}, M_{\ell 2})$ with

$$M_{\ell i} \to \infty\ (\ell \to \infty)\ ,\ i = 1,2,$$

In this whole proof we restrict ourselves to horizontal crossings, i.e., we prove only

$$(10.31) \qquad \lim_{\ell \to \infty} \tau(2\overline{M}_\ell; 1, p', \mathcal{G}_{p\ell}) = 0$$

for suitable $\overline{M}_\ell$. The same proof can be used to show

$$\lim_{\ell \to \infty} \tau(2M_\ell; 2, p', \mathcal{G}_{p\ell}) = 0 ;$$

the asymmetry between the horizontal and vertical direction in Condition D discussed in Comment 10. 2(iii) will play no role in the proof of (10.31).

Let $\tilde{E}$ be the event that there exists an occupied horizontal crossing on $\mathcal{G}_{p\ell}$ of a certain large rectangle. We want to show that $P_{p'}\{\tilde{E}\}$ is small. As in Lemma 7.4 this is essentially done by showing $\frac{d}{dt} P_{p(t)}\{\tilde{E}\}$ is large with $p(t) = tp_0 + (1-t)p'$. Russo's formula (4.22) reduces this to proving that the number of pivotal sites in $\mathfrak{w}$ for $\tilde{E}$ is large. This is really the content of (10.62), which is our principal new estimate here. From Lemma 7.4 and Remark 7(ii) we know that with high probability there are many pivotal sites for $\tilde{E}$ on the lowest occupied horizontal crossing of the large rectangle. (10.62) claims that many of these have to belong to $\mathfrak{w}$. The proof of this is based on the idea that if few of the pivotal sites belong to $\mathfrak{w}$, then one can make local modifications in the occupancy configuration so as to obtain many pivotal sites in $\mathfrak{w}$. To obtain (10.62) one has to make the modifications in such a way that one can more or less go back, i.e., reconstruct the original occupancy configuration from the modified one. For this one first has to locate the sites whose occupancy has been modified. To achieve this we must have good control over the changes in the lowest occupied crossing under our modifications of the occupancy configuration. The various parts of Condition E give the necessary control.

Before we can even formulate Condition E we need a preparatory step.

Step (i). Since $p_0$ satisfies (10.13) and (10.14) the conclusion of Lemma 7.2 holds. For the remainder of this chapter we choose $\overline{M}_\ell$ and $\delta_k > 0$ such that (7.17), (7.19) and (7.21) hold. For

large $\ell$ we construct a Jordan curve $J_\ell$ on $\mathcal{M}$ close to the perimeter of $[0,2M_{\ell 1}] \times [0,12M_{\ell 2}]$ by the method of Lemma 7.4. Specifically, we find simple curves $\phi_1$ and $\phi_3$ on $\mathcal{M}$ which connect the top and bottom edges of the strips
$[0,\Lambda_3] \times [-\Lambda_4, 12M_{\ell 2} + \Lambda_4]$ and $[2M_{\ell 1} - \Lambda_3, 2M_{\ell 1}] \times [-\Lambda_4, 12M_{\ell 2} + \Lambda_4]$, respectively. Such curves can be found as parts of

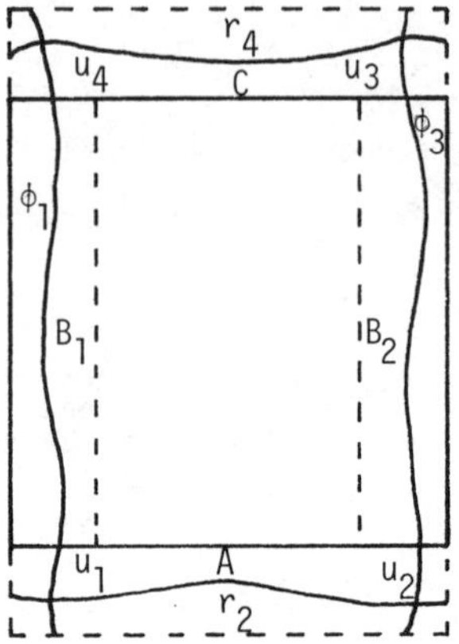


Figure 10.9 The solid rectangle is $[0,2M_{\ell 1}] \times [0,12M_{\ell 2}]$; the outer dashed rectangle is $[0,2M_{\ell 1}] \times [-\Lambda_4, 12M_{\ell 2}+\Lambda_4]$; the inner dashed rectangle is $[\Lambda_3, 2M_{\ell 1}-\Lambda_3] \times [0,12M_{\ell 2}]$.

vertical crossings of these strips. Also we take self-avoiding horizontal crossings $r_2$ and $r_4$ on $\mathcal{M}$ of the strips
$[0, 2M_{\ell 1}] \times [-\Lambda_4, -1]$ and $[0,2M_{\ell 1}] \times [12M_{\ell 2} + 1, 12M_{\ell 2} + \Lambda_4]$, respectively. Starting from the left endpoint of $r_2(r_4)$ let $u_1(u_4)$ be the last intersection of $r_2(r_4)$ with $\phi_1$; and $u_2(u_3)$ the first intersection of $r_2(r_4)$ with $\phi_3$(see Fig. 10.9). As in Lemma 7.4 we denote the closed segment of $\phi_1$ from $u_4$ to $u_1$ by $B_1$, the closed segment of $\phi_3$ from $u_2$ to $u_3$ by $B_2$, the closed segment of $r_2$ from $u_1$ to $u_2$ by $A$ and the closed segment of $r_4$ from $u_3$ to $u_4$ by $C$(again see Fig. 10.9). $J_\ell$ is the Jordan curve consisting of $B_1, A, B_2$ and $C$. We shall be considering paths $r = (v_0, e_1, \dots, e_\nu, v_\nu)$ on $\mathcal{G}_{p\ell}$ with the properties (7.39)- (7.41) (with $J_\ell$ for $J$ in these ). For brevity we shall refer to such paths simply as <u>crosscuts of $\text{int}(J_\ell)$</u> in this chapter. For any such

path we define, as in Def. 2.11 $J_\ell^-(r)(J_\ell^+(r))$ as the component of $\text{int}(J_\ell)\setminus r$ with $A(C)$ in its boundary.

With any crosscut $r$ which in addition satisfies

$$r \subset [0,2M_{\ell 1}] \times [-\infty,6M_{\ell 2}], \tag{10.32}$$

(roughly speaking this means that $r$ lies in the lower half of $\bar{J}$) we shall associate a crosscut $r^\#$ which also satisfies (7.34) -(7.41) and which lies "above" r. This associated $r^\#$ is found by means of a specially chosen circuit $K$ on $\mathcal{G}_{p\ell}$ and surrounding the origin. To choose $K$ recall that $\Delta$ is chosen in Condition D and set

$$\begin{aligned} \Lambda_9 &= 20(\Lambda_5 + \Lambda_6 + \Lambda_7 + \Lambda_8 + \Lambda + \Delta + 1), \\ \Theta &= (6\Lambda_5 + 1)\,(3\Lambda_9 + \Lambda_6 + 4\Lambda_3 + 7\Lambda + 1). \end{aligned} \tag{10.33}$$

Next take for $K$ a circuit on $\mathcal{G}_{p\ell}$ surrounding the origin in the annulus

$$[-2\Theta - \Lambda_3, 2\Theta + \Lambda_3] \times [-2\Theta - \Lambda_3, 2\Theta + \Lambda_3]\setminus (-2\Theta,2\Theta) \times (-2\Theta,2\Theta). \tag{10.34}$$

Such a circuit can be constructed in the manner of $J_\ell$ above from two vertical crossings $s_1$ and $s_2$ on $\mathcal{G}_{p\ell}$ of $[-2\Theta - \Lambda_3, -2\Theta] \times [-2\Theta - \Lambda_3,2\Theta + \Lambda_3]$ and $[2\Theta,2\Theta + \Lambda_3] \times [-2\Theta - \Lambda_3, 2\Theta + \Lambda_3]$, together with two horizontal crossings $s_2$ and $s_4$ on $\mathcal{G}_{p\ell}$ of $[-2\Theta - \Lambda_3, 2\Theta + \Lambda_3] \times [-2\Theta - \Lambda_3, -2\Theta]$ and $[-2\Theta - \Lambda_3, 2\Theta + \Lambda_3] \times [2\Theta, 2\Theta + \Lambda_3]$, respectively. By our choice of the constant $\Lambda_5$ (just after (10.12)) we can take the $s_i$ such that for any two points $y_1,y_2$ on one $s_i$, there is a segment of $s_i$ connecting $y_1$ and $y_2$ with diameter $\leq \Lambda_5(|y_1-y_2| + 1)$. We claim that any pair of points $y_1,y_2$ on $K$ is then connected by an arc of $K$ of diameter at most

$$3\Lambda_5(|y_1-y_2| + 2\Lambda_3 + 1)\ . \tag{10.35}$$

This is obvious of $y_1,y_2$ lie on one $s_i$. When $y_1$ lies on $s_1$, $y_2$ on $s_2$ and $u$ is the intersection of $s_1$ and $s_2$ on $K$, then $u$ lies in $[-2\Theta - \Lambda_3, -2\Theta] \times [-2\Theta - \Lambda_3, -2\Theta]$, $y_1$ to the left of $\mathbb{R} \times \{-2\Theta\}$ and $y_2$ below $\{-2\Theta\} \times \mathbb{R}$. From this it is not hard to see that

$$|y_i-u| \le |y_1-y_2| + 2\Lambda_3 \quad , \; i = 1,2,$$

One therefore obtains the estimate (10.35) for the arc which goes from $y_1$ to $u$ along $s_1$ and then from $u$ to $y_2$ along $s_2$. When $y_1$ lies on $s_1$ and $y_2$ on $s_3$, then $y_1$ lies to the left of the vertical line $x(1) = -2\Theta$ and $y_2$ to the right of $x(2) = 2\Theta$. In this case

$$3(|y_1-y_2| + 2\Lambda_3) \ge 12\Theta + 6\Lambda_3 \ge \text{diameter of the annulus (10.34)}$$

Since $K$ is contained in the annulus, (10.35) is obvious in this case too ($\Lambda_5$ has to be $\ge 1$ by its definition). Thus we showed (10.35) in all typical cases.

We also want to arrange matters such that

(10.36) $$K \text{ is minimal,}$$

in the sense that if $v_1$ and $v_2$ are two vertices of $\mathcal{G}_{p\ell}$ on $K$ which are adjacent on $\mathcal{G}_{p\ell}$, then $K$ contains an edge of $\mathcal{G}_{p\ell}$ from $v_1$ to $v_2$. (This is the obvious extension of Def. 10.1 to a circuit). If $K$ is not minimal, then we can make it minimal by inserting a number of suitable shortcuts of one edge. E.g., if $v_1$ and $v_2$ are adjacent and $e$ is an edge of $\mathcal{G}_{p\ell}$ between them, but $K$ itself does not contain such an edge, then we can replace $K$ by one of the arcs of $K$ between $v_1$ and $v_2$ and the edge $e$. Since diameter $(e) \le \Lambda$, the new circuit will still surround the square

(10.37) $$(-2\Theta + \Lambda, 2\Theta - \Lambda) \times (-2\Theta + \Lambda, 2\Theta + \Lambda),$$

and lie inside the square

(10.38) $$[-2\Theta - \Lambda_3 - \Lambda, 2\Theta + \Lambda_3 + \Lambda] \times [-2\Theta - \Lambda_3 - \Lambda, 2\Theta + \Lambda_3 + \Lambda].$$

(Of course this holds only if we combine $e$ with one of the two arcs of $K$ between $v_1$ and $v_2$; it fails for the other arc). Also the estimate (10.35) changes only a little. Any two points $y_1, y_2$ on the new circuit are now connected by an arc of the new circuit with diameter at most

(10.39) $$3\Lambda_5(|y_1-y_2| + 2\Lambda_3 + 3\Lambda + 1).$$

These observations remain valid even if we replace several arcs of $K$ by shortcuts. Indeed, denote for the time being the circuit obtained after the insertion of shortcuts by $K'$. Then any $y \in K'$ lies within $\Lambda$ of some vertex $z \in K \cap K'$. In particular, if $y_1, y_2 \in K'$, then there exist $z_1, z_2 \in K \cap K'$, $|z_1-z_2| \le |y_1-y_2| + 2\Lambda$. Also some arc of $K$ between $z_1$ and $z_2$ has diameter $\le 3\Lambda_5(|z_1-z_2| + 2\Lambda_3 + 1)$. One can now find an arc of $K'$ from $y_1$ to $y_2$ which is within distance $\Lambda$ from the arc of $K$ from $z_1$ to $z_2$. (10.39) is immediate from this, as well as the fact that $K'$ lies outside (10.37) and inside (10.38). We drop the prime in $K'$ and for the remainder we assume that $K$ is a fixed circuit inside (10.38), which surrounds (10.37), satisfies (10.36) and the estimate (10.39).

For any vertex $v = (v(1), v(2))$ of $\mathcal{G}_{p\ell}$ we set

$$K(v) = K + \lfloor v(1) \rfloor \xi_1 + \lfloor v(2) \rfloor \xi_2 .$$

$K(v)$ is the translate of $K$ by $(\lfloor v(1)\rfloor, \lfloor v(2) \rfloor)$ and therefore $v \in \text{int}(K(v))$. For any crosscut $r = (v_0, e_1, \dots, e_\nu, v_\nu)$ on $\mathcal{G}_{p\ell}$ of $J_\ell$ which satisfies (10.32) (in addition to (7.39) - (7.41)) we set

(10.40) $$\mathcal{E}(r) = \bar{J}_\ell^-(r) \cup \bigcup_w \bar{K}(w),$$

where the union runs over the vertices $w = (w(1), w(2))$ of $\mathcal{G}_{p\ell}$ on $r$ which satisfy

(10.41) $$\tfrac{1}{2}M_{\ell 1} - \Theta - 2\Lambda \le w(1) \le \tfrac{3}{2}M_{\ell 1} + \Theta + 2\Lambda ,$$

and $\bar{K} = \text{int}(K) \cup K$. Also $\mathfrak{F}(r)$ denotes the component of $\text{int}(J_\ell) \setminus \mathcal{E}(r)$ with $C$ in its boundary. Note that $\mathcal{E}(r)$ is a somewhat fattened up (near $r$) version of $\bar{J}_\ell^-(r)$. $\mathcal{E}(r)$ still lies below the horizontal line $x(2) = 6M_{\ell 2} + 2\Theta + \Lambda_3 + \Lambda$ (by (10.32) and (10.38)) so that for all large $\ell$ $\mathfrak{F}(r)$ is well defined and even contains a whole strip of $\text{int}(J)$ near its upper edge $C$($C$ lies above $x(2) = 12M_{\ell 2}$). We claim that for sufficiently large $\ell$ there exists a crosscut $r^\#$ on $\mathcal{G}_{p\ell}$ which satisfies (7.39) - (7.41) and

(10.42) $$\mathfrak{F}(r) = J_\ell^+(r^\#),$$

(10.43) $$\overline{J}_\ell^-(r) \subset \overline{J}_\ell^-(r^\#),\ J_\ell^+(r^\#) \subset J_\ell^+(r),$$

and

(10.44) $$r^\# \subset r \cup \bigcup_w K(w)\ ,$$

where the union in (10.44) runs over the same $w$ as in (10.40). Of course $r^\#$ will simply be the "lower part" of the boundary of $\mathfrak{F}(r)$. A formal proof of the existence of $r^\#$ proceeds by induction. Assume the vertices which enter in the union in (10.40) are $w_1,\dots,w_m$. Let

$$\mathcal{E}_k = \overline{J}_\ell^-(r) \cup \bigcup_{i=1}^{k} \overline{K}(w_i),$$

and $\mathfrak{F}_k$ the component of $\text{int}(J_\ell) \setminus \mathcal{E}_k$ with $C$ in its boundary. Assume we already proved that $\mathfrak{F}_k = J_\ell^+(r_k)$ for some $r_k$ on $\mathcal{G}_{p\ell}$ satisfying (7.39) - (7.41) and

(10.45) $$\overline{J}_\ell^-(r) \subset \overline{J}_\ell^-(r_k),\ r_k \subset r \cup \bigcup_1^k K(w_i)\ .$$

This statement is true for $k = 0$ if we take $\mathcal{E}_0 = \overline{J}_\ell^-(r)$, $\mathfrak{F}_0 = J_\ell^+(r)$, $r_0 = r$. We now show that the statement is then also true for $k$ replaced by $k+1$. We shall find $r_{k+1}$ by a method similar to the construction of $r$ from $r_1$ and $r_2$ in the beginning of the proof of Prop. 2.3 (see the Appendix). $\mathcal{E}_{k+1} = \mathcal{E}_k \cup \overline{K}(w_{k+1})$. For large enough $\ell$ $K(w_{k+1})$ does not intersect the left and right pieces $B_1$ and $B_2$ of $J$ by virtue of (10.41). If $\alpha$ is an arc of $K(w_{k+1})$ which lies in $J^+(r_k)$ except for its endpoints, $v_1$ and $v_2$, which lie on $r_k$ (see Fig. 10.10) then replace the piece of $r_k$ between $v_1$ and $v_2$ by $\alpha$. This gives a new crosscut, $\tilde{r}_k$ say, of $\text{int}(J_\ell)$ such that

$$\tilde{r}_k \subset \overline{J}_\ell^+(r_k) \text{ and } r_k \subset \overline{J}_\ell^-(\tilde{r}_k)\ .$$

The proof of this statement is the same as for (A.38) - (A.40). If $K(w_{k+1})$ still contains a point above $\tilde{r}_k$, and hence an arc above $\tilde{r}_k$,

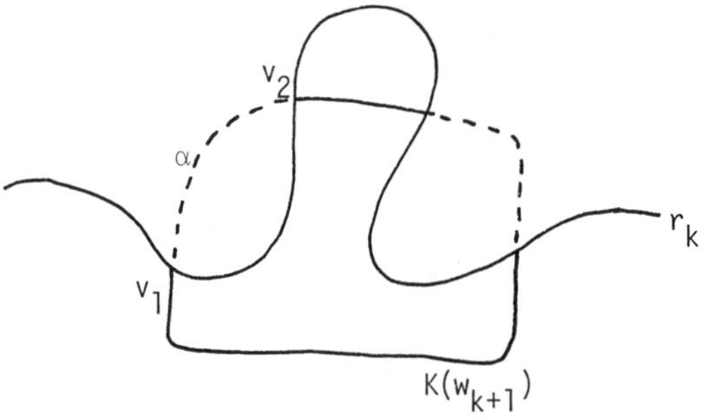


Figure 10.10 The two dashed pieces of the circuit $K(w_{k+1})$ lie in $J_\ell^+(r_k)$.

i.e., in $J^+(\tilde{r}_k)$, we repeat the procedure until we arrive at a crosscut $r_{k+1}$, made up from pieces of $r_k$ and $K(w_{k+1})$ such that $K(w_{k+1})$ contains no more points of $J_\ell^+(r_{k+1})$. It is clear from the construction and the induction hypothesis (10.45) that

$$r_{k+1} \subset r_k \cup K(w_{k+1}) \subset r \cup \bigcup_1^{k+1} K(w_i), \tag{10.46}$$

Also, as in (A.38)

$$r_{k+1} \subset \bar{J}^+(r_k)$$

and this implies, just as (A.38) implies (A.39),

$$\bar{J}_\ell^-(r) \subset \bar{J}_\ell^-(r_k) \subset \bar{J}_\ell^-(r_{k+1}) \tag{10.47}$$

(of course (10.45) is used for the first inclusion). Finally, we must show that $\mathfrak{J}_{k+1} = J_\ell^+(r_{k+1})$. But, by (10.46) $r_{k+1} \subset \mathcal{E}_{k+1}$. Therefore, the connected subset $\mathfrak{J}_{k+1}$ of $\text{int}(J_\ell) \setminus \mathcal{E}_{k+1} \subset \text{int}(J_\ell) \setminus r_{k+1}$ with $C$ in its boundary is contained in $J_\ell^+(r_{k+1})$. To prove the inclusion in the other direction, let $y \in J_\ell^+(r_{k+1})$. Then $y$ can be connected by a continuous curve, $\phi$ say, to $C$, such that $\phi$ minus its endpoint on $C$ lies in $J_\ell^+(r_{k+1}) \subset J_\ell^+(r_k)$ (by (10.47); compare (A.40)). Thus $y \in J_\ell^+(r_k)$ and $y \notin \bar{J}^-(r_k)$. But neither can $y$ lie in $\bar{K}(w_{k+1})$. Indeed, the endpoint of $\phi$ on $C$ lies in $\text{ext}(K(w_{k+1}))$ (recall that $\mathcal{E}(r)$ lies below $x(2) = 6M_{\ell 2} + 2\Theta + \Lambda_3 + \Lambda$). If $y \in \bar{K}(w_{k+1})$, then $\phi$ would intersect $K(w_{k+1})$, and since $\phi$ minus its endpoint on $C$ lies in $J^+_\ell(r_{k+1})$, this would imply that $K(w_{k+1})$ still contains a point of $J^+_\ell(r_{k+1})$, contrary to our construction of $r_{k+1}$. Thus

$$y \notin \bar{J}^-_\ell(r_k) \cup \bar{K}(w_{k+1}) .$$

Since $y$ was arbitrary in $J^+(r_{k+1})$ ,and $\mathcal{E}_{k+1} \subset \bar{J}^-_\ell(r_k) \cup \bar{K}(w_{k+1})$ by the induction hypothesis, and $\bar{K}(w_i) \cap \mathfrak{F}_k = \emptyset$ for $i \le k$ we now have

$$J^+_\ell(r_{k+1}) \subset \text{int}(J_\ell) \setminus \mathcal{E}_{k+1} .$$

Further, since $J^+_\ell(r_{k+1})$ is connected and contains $C$ in its boundary we also have

$$J^+_\ell(r_{k+1}) \subset \mathfrak{F}_{k+1} ,$$

and therefore

$$J^+_\ell(r_{k+1}) = \mathfrak{F}_{k+1} . \tag{10.48}$$

as desired.

Now that we have shown how to obtain $r_{k+1}$ from $r_k$ we can take $r^\# = r_m$, the crosscut obtained after the last $K(w)$ has been added. (10.42) - (10.44) are then just (10.48) with $k+1 = m$ and (10.45) with $k = m$ (plus the simple observation

$$J^+_\ell(r^\#) = \text{int}(J_\ell) \setminus \bar{J}^-_\ell(r^\#) \subset \text{int}(J_\ell) \setminus \bar{J}^-_\ell(r) \subset J^+_\ell(r)$$

for the second part of (10.43)).

<u>Step (ii)</u>. In this step we formulate Condition E, by means of the path $r^\#$. Throughout we shall assume $M_{\ell 1}$, $M_{\ell 2}$ large enough so that the construction of Step (i) can be carried out. The specific properties of $r^\#$ will only be used later; for the time being we only use the fact that to each $r$ with properties (7.39) - (7.41) and (10.32) we have assigned an $r^\#$ in a specific way. Now assume that $\omega$ is an occupancy configuration on $\mathcal{M}_{p\ell}$ with all central vertices of faces $F \in \mathfrak{F}$ ($F \notin \mathfrak{F}$) occupied (vacant), and such that there exists an occupied crosscut of $\text{int}(J_\ell)$ which also satisfies (10.32). Analogously to Lemma 7.4 we shall say that a vertex $a$ on $r$ has a vacant connection to $\mathring{C}$ above $r$ inside a set $\Gamma$ if there

exists a vacant path $s^* = (w_0^*, f_1^*, \dots, f_\tau^*, w_\tau^*)$ on $\mathcal{G}_{p\ell}^*$ which satisfies the following conditions (10.49) - (10.51) :

(10.49) there exists an edge $f^*$ of $\mathcal{M}_{p\ell}$ between a and $w_0^*$ such that $\mathring{f}^* \subset J_\ell^+(r) \cap \Gamma$ ,

(10.50) $$w_\tau^* \in \mathring{C} \quad ,$$

(10.51) $$(w_0^*, f_1^*, \dots, w_{\tau-1}^*, f_\tau^* \setminus \{w_\tau^*\}) = s^* \setminus \{w_\tau^*\}) \subset J_\ell^+(r) \cap \Gamma \,.$$

When $\Gamma = \mathbb{R}^2$ (so that the restrictions due to $\Gamma$ are vacuous) we simply talk about a vacant connection from a to $\mathring{C}$ above r.

Once there exists some occupied r which satisfies (7.39)-(7.41) and (10.32) we know from Prop. 2.3 that there then also exists a unique such r with minimal $J_\ell^-(r)$. We denote this path by $R = (v_0, e_1, \dots, e_\nu, v_\nu)$. Associated with R is a path $R^\#$ as in Step (i). Now assume $a^\#$ is a vertex of $R^\#$ which has a vacant connection to $\mathring{C}$ above $R^\#$ inside

$$\Gamma_\ell : = [\tfrac{1}{2}M_{\ell 1}, \tfrac{3}{2}M_{\ell 1}] \times \mathbb{R} \,.$$

Finally assume that $x \in \mathfrak{w}$ is such that Condition D holds for this x, and set

$$\mathfrak{w}_0 = \{x + k_1\xi_1 + k_2\xi_2 : k_i \in \mathbb{Z}, i = 1,2,\} \,.$$

Since $\mathfrak{w}$ was assumed periodic, $\mathfrak{w}_0 \subset \mathfrak{w}$ . Moreover, by the periodicity assumptions in (10.9) Condition D remains valid when x is replaced by any element of $\mathfrak{w}_0$ .

We now formulate Condition E. It requires that for suitable constants $\kappa_i$ we can find a configuration $\tilde{\omega}$ which satisfies (10.53) - (10.57). The specific values of the $\kappa_i$ are unimportant. We only need $0 < \kappa_i < \infty$ and that the $\kappa_i$ depend only on $\mathcal{G}_{p\ell}, \mathcal{G}_{p\ell}^*$ and $\Delta$ but not on $\ell, \omega, R, a^\#$, $p_0$ or p'.

<u>Condition E</u>. Let $\ell \geq \kappa_0$ and let $\omega$ be an occupancy configuration on $\mathcal{M}_{p\ell}$ which has an occupied crosscut of $\text{int}(J_\ell)$ and is such that

(10.52) all central vertices of $\mathcal{G}_{p\ell}$ outside $\mathfrak{w}$ are occupied, while all central vertices of $\mathcal{G}_{p\ell}^*$ are vacant.

Let R be the occupied crosscut of $\text{int}(J_\ell)$ with $J_\ell^-(R)$ minimal and let $R^{\#}$ be associated to $R$ as in Step (i). Then for every vertex $a^{\#}$ on $R^{\#}$ which has a vacant connection to $\mathring{C}$ above $R^{\#}$ inside $\Gamma_\ell$ there exists an occupancy configuration $\tilde{\omega} = \tilde{\omega}(\omega, a^{\#})$ on $\mathcal{M}_{p\ell}$ with the following properties (10.53) - (10.57).

(10.53) $\tilde{\omega}(v) = \omega(v)$ for all vertices $v$ of $\mathcal{M}_{p\ell}$ with $|v(i) - a^{\#}(i)| > \kappa_1$ for $i \geq 1$ or 2.

(Recall that $\tilde{\omega}(v)$ is the value of $\tilde{\omega}$ at the vertex $v$ of $\mathcal{M}_{p\ell}$, and similarly for $\omega(v)$; the more explicit notation $\tilde{\omega}(\omega, a^{\#})(v)$ for $\tilde{\omega}(v)$ should not be necessary.)

(10.54) If $v$ is a central vertex of $\mathcal{G}_{p\ell}$ which does not belong to $\mathfrak{w}$, and hence $\omega(v) = 1$, then $\tilde{\omega}(v) = 1$.

(10.55) If $v$ is a central vertex of $\mathcal{G}^*_{p\ell}$, and hence $\omega(v) = -1$, then $\tilde{\omega}(v) = -1$.

(10.56) In the configuration $\tilde{\omega}$ there exists an occupied crosscut $\tilde{R}$ of $\mathrm{int}(J_\ell)$ satisfying (7.39) - (7.41) and with $J_\ell^-(\tilde{R})$ minimal among all such crosscuts. Moreover on $\tilde{R}$ there exists a vertex $\tilde{x}$ from $\mathfrak{w}_0$ with a vacant (in the configuration $\tilde{\omega}$) connection $Y^*$ to $\mathring{C}$ above $\tilde{R}$, and such that $|\tilde{x}-a^{\#}| \leq \kappa_2$.

(10.57) Any vertex $y$ from $\mathfrak{w}_0$ which lies on the $\tilde{R}$ of (10.56) and which has a vacant connection to $\mathring{C}$ above $\tilde{R}$ in the configuration $\tilde{\omega}$ satisfies (a) or (b) below.

a) $y$ lies on $R$ and has a vacant connection to $\mathring{C}$ above $R$ in the configuration $\omega$.

b) $|y-a^{\#}| \leq \kappa_3$. ///

We merely add one explanatory comment. The requirements (10.54) and (10.55) just guarantee that $\tilde{\omega}$ also satisfies (10.52). By (7.2), (7.3), and (10.16) the condition (10.52) has to be satisfied with $P_{p_0}$-probability one as well as with $P_{p'}$-probability one. If we did not have (10.52) for $\tilde{\omega}$, then the simple estimate (10.64) would fail. Unfortunately, (10.54) necessitates much extra work; "strong minimality" and "shortcuts of two edges" are used in Steps (iv) - (ix) only for (10.54). The purpose of the other requirements in Condition E should become evident in the next step.

Step (iii). In this step we derive (10.21) from Condition E. As we observed above it suffices to prove

$$\lim_{\ell \to \infty} \tau(2\overline{M}_\ell; i, p', \mathcal{G}_{p\ell}) = 0 \ , \ i = 1,2,$$

and we shall only deal with (10.31). The proof of (10.31) mimicks the proof of (7.35), at least initially. We restrict ourselves to $i = 1$. Analogously to Lemma 7.4 we shall drop the subscript $\ell$ for the time being, and set

$$E = \{ \exists \text{ occupied path } r = (v_0, e_1, \dots, e_\nu, v_\nu) \text{ on } \mathcal{G}_{p\ell} \text{ with the properties (7.39) - (7.41) and (10.32)} \} .$$

Note that we have added the requirement (10.32); this was absent in the definition of $E$ in Lemma 7.4. Moreover, $J$ as defined in Step (i) differs somewhat from the $J$ in Lemma 7.4. Nevertheless the argument used in Lemma 7.4 still shows that

$$\tau(2\overline{M}_\ell; 1, p', \mathcal{G}_{p\ell}) \leq P_{p'}\{E\} ,$$

so that it suffices to prove

$$\lim_{\ell \to \infty} P_{p'}\{E\} = 0 \ . \tag{10.58}$$

In addition to $E$ we also introduce the event in which the restriction (10.32) is dropped. We denote this by $E_1$:

$$E_1 = \{ \exists \text{ occupied path } r = (v_0, e_1, \dots, e_\nu, v_\nu) \text{ on } \mathcal{G}_{p\ell} \text{ with the properties (7.39) - (7.41)} \} .$$

Analogously to Lemma 7.4 we write for any $r$ which satisfies (7.39)-(7.41)

$N(r) = N(r,\omega) = \#$ of vertices of $\mathcal{G}_{p\ell}$ in $\mathfrak{w}_0$ and on $r \cap \text{int}(J)$ which have a vacant connection to $\mathring{C}$ above $r$ .

Again note the slight differences with (7.50); the fact that we only count vertices in $\mathfrak{w}_0$ is crucial. If $E$ occurs then all the vertices of $R$ counted in $N(R,\omega)$ are pivotal for $(E_1,\omega)$, by Ex. 4.2(iii). Set

$$p(t) = t\, p_0 + (1-t)p'$$

and for $x$ as in the last step

$$\alpha = P_{p_0}\{x \text{ is occupied}\} - P_{p'}\{x \text{ is occupied}\} .$$

Then, since $\mathfrak{w}_0$ consists of the translates of $x$ by integral vectors we have

$$\alpha = \min_{v \in \mathfrak{w}_0} \{P_{p_0}\{v \text{ is occupied}\} - P_{p'}\{v \text{ is occupied}\}\}$$

and by assumption (10.17) $\alpha > 0$. By Russo's formula (Prop. 4.2) we have as in (7.42), and (7.51).

$$(10.59) \quad \frac{d}{dt} P_{p(t)}\{E_1\} \geq \alpha\, E_{p(t)}\{\# \text{ of pivotal sites in } \mathfrak{w}_0 \text{ for } E_1\} \geq \alpha\, E_{p(t)}\{N(R);\ E \text{ occurs}\} .$$

We must now find a lower bound for the right hand side of (10.59) Assume that $E$ occurs, and that $R = r$ for a path $r$ satisfying (7.39) - (7.41) and (10.32). If $r^{\#}$ be the path associated to $r$ as in Step (i), set

$M(r^{\#})$ = number of vertices $a^{\#}$ on $r^{\#}$ which have a vacant connection to $\mathring{C}$ above $r^{\#}$ inside $\Gamma$.

Our first estimate is that for each $m$ we can choose $\ell_0 = \ell_0(m)$ such that for all $\ell \geq \ell_0$ and all $0 \leq t \leq 1$.

$$(10.60) \qquad P_{p(t)}\{E \text{ occurs and } M(R^{\#}) \geq m\} \geq P_{p'}\{E\}\, \frac{1}{2}\, \delta_{27} ,$$

where $\delta_{27}$ is as in (7.19). To see this we observe that as in (7.46), (7.51).

$$P_{p(t)}\{E \text{ occurs and } M(R^{\#}) \geq m\} .$$

$$\geq \sum_r P_{p(t)}\{R = r, R^{\#} = r^{\#}\}\, P_{p(t)}\{M(r^{\#}) \geq m \mid R = r,\ R^{\#} = r^{\#}\}$$

where the sum is over all paths $r$ which satisfy (7.39) - (7.41) and (10.32) and $r^{\#}$ is the path associated to $r$ by Step (i). By definition of $M(R^{\#})$ and vacant connections. (see (10.49)- (10.51)) $M(r^{\#})$ depends only on the occupancies of vertices outside $\bar{J}^{-}(r^{\#})$. On the other hand the event $\{R = r, R^{\#} = r^{\#}\} = \{R = r\}$, since $r^{\#}$ and $R^{\#}$ are the paths which are associated uniquely to $r$ and $R$, respectively. Further, by Prop. 2.3 $\{R = r\}$ depends only on occupancies of the vertices in $\bar{J}^{-}(r) \subset \bar{J}^{-}(r^{\#})$ (by (10.43)). Therefore, for fixed $r^{\#}$ satisfying (7.39)-(7.41).

$$P_{p(t)}\{M(r^{\#}) \geq m \mid R = r,\ R^{\#} = r^{\#}\} = P_{p(t)}\{M(r^{\#}) \geq m\} .$$

Now as in Remark 7(ii) to Lemma 7.4 (especially (7.76)) we have for all sufficiently large $\ell$

(10.61) $P_{p(t)}\{M(r^{\#}) \geq m\} \geq \frac{1}{2} P_{p_0}\{\ \exists$ at least one vertex $a^{\#}$ on $r^{\#}$ with a vacant connection to $\mathring{C}$ above $r^{\#}$ inside $\Gamma'\}$,

where

$$\Gamma' = \Gamma'_{\ell} = [\tfrac{3}{4} M_{\ell 1}, \tfrac{5}{4} M_{\ell 1}] \times \mathbb{R}$$

Moreover, exactly as in (7.61), the probability in the right hand side of (10.61) is at least

$$P_{p_0}\{\ \exists \text{ vacant vertical crossing on } \mathcal{G}^{*}_{p\ell} \text{ of } [\tfrac{3}{4} M_{\ell 1}, \tfrac{5}{4} M_{\ell 1}] \times [-\Lambda_4, 12M_{\ell 2} + \Lambda_4]$$

$$\geq \sigma^{*}((\tfrac{1}{2}M_{\ell 1} - 1), 13M_{\ell 2}); 2, p_0, \mathcal{G}_{p\ell}) \geq \delta_{27} .$$

(10.60) follows by combining these observations with the facts

$$E = \bigcup_{r} \{R = r,\ R^{\#} = r^{\#}\} ,$$

where the union runs over all $r$ which satisfy (7.39)-(7.41) and (10.32), and

$$P_{p(t)}\{E\} \geq P_{p'}\{E\} \quad , 0 \leq t \leq 1 ,$$

which follows from Lemma 4.1 and the fact that $E$ is an increasing event.

The second important estimate for our proof concerns the event

$$G(m,\eta) := \{E \text{ occurs}, \ M(R^{\#}) \geq m, \text{ but } N(R) \leq \eta m\} .$$

We shall show that for some $\tau_1, \tau_2$ independent of $\eta$, $m$ and $\ell$(but dependent on $p_0$ and $p'$).

$$(10.62) \qquad P_{p(t)} \{G(m,\eta)\} \leq \tau_1(\eta + \frac{\tau_2}{m}) , \quad \frac{1}{4} \leq t \leq \frac{3}{4} ,$$

for all sufficiently large $\ell$. Before proving (10.62) we show that it quickly implies (10.58). Indeed, on the event

$$\{E \text{ occurs}, \ M(R^{\#}) \geq m, \text{ but } G(m,\eta) \text{ fails}\}$$

one has $N(R) > \eta m$, so that by (10.60) and (10.62)

$$\begin{aligned} & E_{p(t)}\{N(R); E \text{ occurs}\} \\ & \geq \eta m(P_{p(t)}\{E \text{ occurs}, M(R^{\#}) \geq m\} - P_{p(t)}\{G(m,\eta)\}) \\ & \geq \eta m(\tfrac{1}{2}\delta_{27} P_{p'}\{E\} - \tau_1\eta - \frac{\tau_1\tau_2}{m}), \qquad \frac{1}{4} \leq t \leq \frac{3}{4} . \end{aligned}$$

Thus, by (10.59), for large $\ell$

$$\begin{aligned} 1 & \geq \int_{1/4}^{3/4} \frac{d}{dt} P_{p(t)} \{E_1\} \, dt \\ & \geq \alpha\eta m \int_{1/4}^{3/4} (\tfrac{1}{2} \delta_{27} P_{p'}\{E\} - \tau_1\eta - \frac{\tau_1\tau_2}{m}) \, dt \\ & = \frac{1}{2} \alpha\eta m \, (\tfrac{1}{2} \delta_{27} P_{p'}\{E\} - \tau_1\eta - \frac{\tau_1\tau_2}{m}) . \end{aligned}$$

Consequently, for all $\eta, m$

$$\limsup_{\ell \to \infty} \{\tfrac{1}{2} \delta_{27} P_{p'}\{E\} - \tau_1\eta - \frac{\tau_1\tau_2}{m})\} \leq \frac{2}{\alpha\eta m} ,$$

or equivalently

$$\limsup_{\ell \to \infty} P_{p'}\{E\} \leq \frac{2}{\delta_{27}} (\frac{2}{\alpha\eta m} + \tau_1\eta + \frac{\tau_1\tau_2}{m})$$

By first choosing $\eta$ small, then $m$ large we obtain the desired (10.58). As we saw above this implies (10.31) and (10.21).

Theorem 10.2 has been reduced to (10.62) which we now prove by means of Condition E. Let

$$H(\lambda,\eta) = \{E \text{ occurs}, M(R\#) = \lambda, \text{ but } N(R) \leq \eta m\} .$$

Then

$$(10.63) \qquad G(m,\lambda) = \bigcup_{\lambda \geq m} H(\lambda,\eta) .$$

Let $\omega$ be a configuration in $H(\lambda,\eta)$ which satisfies (10.52). Then by definition of $M(.)$, in the configuration $\omega$ there are $\lambda$ vertices on $R^{\#}$ which have a vacant connection to $\mathring{C}$ above $R^{\#}$ inside $\Gamma$. Denote these by $a_1^{\#},\dots,a_\lambda^{\#}$ in an arbitrary order. To each one of these there is assigned by Condition E a configuration $\tilde{\omega}(\omega,a_j^{\#})$ with the properties (10.53)-(10.57). Let S be any square. Denote by $\omega_S$ the set of all configurations which agree with $\omega$ at all sites in S. We show first that there exists a constant $\tau_3 > 0$ (which depends on p' and $p_0$, but not on $\ell$, S,$\omega$, R or $a^{\#}$) such that

$$(10.64) \qquad P_{p(t)}\{\tilde{\omega}_S(\omega, a_j^{\#})\} \geq \tau_3 P_{p(t)}\{\omega_S\}, \quad \frac{1}{4} \leq t \leq \frac{3}{4} .$$

This is easy to see, since $\tilde{\omega}(\omega, a_j^{\#})$ is obtained from $\omega$ by changing at most $\kappa_4$ sites for some $\kappa_4$ depending on the graph only, by (10.53). Moreover, if v is a site with $\omega(v) = +1$, $\tilde{\omega}(v) = -1$, then either v is not a central site of $\mathcal{G}_{p\ell}$, or it is a central site of $\mathcal{G}_{p\ell}$ which belongs to $\mathfrak{w}$ (by (10.54)). In the former case, for $t \geq 1/4$

$$P_{p(t)}\{v \text{ is vacant}\} \geq t\, P_{p_0}\{v \text{ is vacant}\}$$
$$\geq \frac{1}{4} P_{p_0}\{v \text{ is vacant}\} > 0,$$

since $p_0 \ll \bar{1}$ (see (10.13)). In the latter case, for $t \leq 3/4$

$$P_{p(t)}\{v \text{ is vacant}\} \geq (1-t)\, P_{p'}\{v \text{ is vacant}\}$$
$$\geq \frac{1}{4} \nu_v\{\omega(v) = -1\} > 0$$

by (10.17). On the other hand, if $\omega(v) = -1$ and $\tilde{\omega}(v) = +1$, then by (10.55) v is not a central vertex of $\mathcal{G}^*_{p\ell}$. Therefore, for

$t \geq 1/4$

$$P_{p(t)}\{v \text{ is occupied}\} \geq \frac{1}{4} P_{p_0}\{v \text{ is occupied}\} > 0,$$

this time by $p_0 >> \bar{0}$ (see (10.13)). Therefore, in all cases, if $v$ has a different state in $\tilde{\omega}$ then in $\omega$, then

$$P_{p(t)}\{v \text{ is in the state prescribed by } \tilde{\omega}\}$$
$$\geq \delta P_{p(t)}\{v \text{ is in the state prescribed by } \omega\}$$

for some $\delta = \delta(p_0,p') > 0$. Consequently (10.64) holds with $\tau_3 = \delta^{\kappa_4}$.

Next we note that for fixed $\ell$ we can choose $S$ so large that all events which we consider only depend on the configuration in $S$. Indeed we are only interested in $\omega(v)$ for $v$ in $\bar{J} = J \cup \text{int}(J)$, and $\tilde{\omega}(v) = \omega(v)$ except possibly for $v$ with $|v(i) - a^{\#}(i)| \leq \kappa_1$ for some $a^{\#} \in J$ (see (10.53)). The last property also allows us to choose $\tilde{\omega}_S(\tilde{\omega},a^{\#})$ as a function of $\omega_S$ and $a^{\#}$ only (when $S$ is large enough). Accordingly we denote it by $\tilde{\omega}_S(\omega_S,a^{\#})$ below. We also repeat the observation that by (7.2), (7.3) and (10.16) the condition (10.52) holds with $P_{p_0}$-probability one as well as with $P_{p'}$-probability one. Consequently it also holds with $P_{p(t)}$-probability one for all $0 \leq t \leq 1$. We therefore conclude from (10.64) that

$$(10.65) \qquad P_{p(t)}\{H(\lambda,n)\} = \sum_{\omega_S} P_{p(t)}\{\omega_S\}$$
$$\leq \frac{1}{\tau_3\lambda} \sum_{\omega_S} \sum_{j=1}^{\lambda} P_{p(t)}\{\tilde{\omega}_S(\omega_S,a_j^{\#})\} ,$$

where $\sum_{\omega_S}$ is the sum over all configurations $\omega_S$ in $S$ for which $H(\lambda,n)$ occurs, and (10.52) holds inside $S$. We now rearrange the double sum in the last member of (10.65); on the outside we sum over the possible "values" of $\tilde{\omega}_S(\omega_S,a_j^{\#})$, and inside we sum over the $\omega_S$ and $j$ for which $\tilde{\omega}_S(\omega_S,a_j^{\#})$ equals a specified configuration. This yields

$$P_{p(t)}\{H(\lambda,\eta)\} \le \frac{1}{\tau_3\lambda} \sum_{\bar{\omega}_S} P_{p(t)}\{\bar{\omega}_S\} \,.\, (\text{number of pairs } \omega_S \text{ and } a^{\#} \text{ on } R^{\#}(\omega_S) \text{ with } \tilde{\omega}_S(\omega_S,a^{\#}) = \bar{\omega}_S \text{ and } \omega_S \text{ such that } H(\lambda,\eta) \text{ occurs}).$$

The sum over $\bar{\omega}_S$ runs over all possible configurations in S, and we have written $R^{\#}(\omega_S)$ for $R^{\#}(\omega)$, again because $R^{\#}$ depends on $\omega_S$ only for large S. If we sum the last inequality over $\lambda \ge m$, then we obtain, by virtue of (10.63),

$$P_{p(t)}\{G(m,\eta)\} \le \frac{1}{\tau_3 m} \sum_{\bar{\omega}_S} P_{p(t)}\{\bar{\omega}_S\}.\, (\text{number of pairs } \omega_S \text{ and } a^{\#} \text{ on } R^{\#}(\omega_S) \text{ with } \bar{\omega}_S(\omega_S,a^{\#}) = \bar{\omega}_S \text{ and } \omega_S \text{ such that } G(m,\eta) \text{ occurs}).$$

Finally we shall prove that for any given $\bar{\omega}_S$ there are at most $\kappa_5(\eta m + \kappa_6)$ pairs $\omega_S$ and $a^{\#}$ on $R^{\#}(\omega_S)$ with $\tilde{\omega}_S(\omega_S,a^{\#}) = \bar{\omega}_S$ and such that $G(m,\eta)$ occurs in $\omega_S$. This will imply

$$P_{p(t)}\{G(m,\eta)\} \le \frac{1}{\tau_3 m} \kappa_5(\eta m + \kappa_6),$$

which is the desired (10.62) ($\kappa_5$ and $\kappa_6$ depend only on $\kappa_1$-$\kappa_3$ and $\mathcal{G}_{p\ell}$).

Now fix a configuration $\bar{\omega}_S$ in S and let $\omega_S$ be a configuration such that $G(m,\eta)$ occurs and let $a^{\#}$ lie on $R^{\#}(\omega_S)$ such that $\tilde{\omega}_S(\omega_S,a^{\#}) = \bar{\omega}_S$. Then $a^{\#}$ has to be a vertex with a vacant connection to $\mathring{C}$ above $R^{\#}(\omega_S)$ (these were the only $a^{\#}$ for which we ever considered $\tilde{\omega}(\omega, a^{\#})$). By (10.56) $\tilde{\omega}_S(\omega_S,a^{\#}) = \bar{\omega}_S$ must then be such that it has a lowest crosscut $\tilde{R}$ of J and a vertex $\tilde{x}$ from $\mathcal{W}_0$ with a vacant connection to $\mathring{C}$ above $\tilde{R}$ in configuration $\bar{\omega}_S$ and such that $|\tilde{x}(i) - a^{\#}(i)| \le \kappa_2$. Now we are only given $\bar{\omega}_S$, and know neither $R,R^{\#}$ nor $a^{\#}$. However $\tilde{R}$ is the lowest crosscut in configuration $\bar{\omega}_S$, and hence there is at most one possibility for $\tilde{R}$ for a given $\bar{\omega}_S$. Next we must check how many possibilities there are for $\tilde{x}$. By (10.57), if $\bar{\omega}_S$ arose as $\tilde{\omega}_S(\omega_S,a^{\#})$, then the number of vertices from $\mathcal{W}_0$ on $\tilde{R}$ with a vacant connection above $\tilde{R}$ to $\mathring{C}$ in $\bar{\omega}_S$ is limited. It either is of the type described in (10.57)(a) or (10.57)(b). There are at most $\eta m$ vertices of type

(10.57)(a) in int(J) if $\omega_S$ is such that $G(m,\eta)$ occurs (because by definition $N(R,\omega_S) \le \eta m$ in this case). Also, there are at most $\kappa_6$ vertices of type (10.57)(b) or on $\tilde{R} \cap J$. Thus, any $\overline{\omega}_S$ which can arise from an $\omega_S$ for which $G(m,\eta)$ occurs has at most $\eta m + \kappa_6$ vertices in $\mathcal{W}_0$ with a vacant connection above $\tilde{R}(\overline{\omega}_S)$ to $\mathcal{E}$ in configuration $\overline{\omega}_S$. Thus, there are at most $\eta m + \kappa_6$ choices for $\tilde{x}$ for any $\overline{\omega}_S$ which can arise at all. But once we picked $\tilde{x}$, we have at most $\kappa_7$ choices for $a^\#$ by (10.56). Finally, if we know $\overline{\omega}_S = \tilde{\omega}_S(\omega_S,a^\#)$ and $a^\#$, then there are at most $\kappa_8$ possibilities for $\omega_S$, because (by (10.53)) $\omega_S$ differs from $\tilde{\omega}_S(\omega_S,a^\#) = \overline{\omega}_S$ only in a fixed neighborhood of $a^\#$. In total, starting with $\overline{\omega}_S$ we can make at most $(\eta m + \kappa_6)\kappa_7\kappa_8$ choices for $\tilde{x}$, $a^\#$ and $\omega_S$. This bound completes the proof of (10.62) and Theorem 10.2 (modulo the derivation of Condition E from Condition D in the next section). □

Proof of Theorem 10.3. The principal idea was already explained before the statement of the theorem. Let $\mathcal{K}$ be the graph obtained from $\mathcal{M}$ by close-packing only the faces F in $\mathcal{F}_1 := \mathcal{F} \setminus \mathcal{F}_0$, where $\mathcal{F}_0$ is as in (10.23). ($\mathcal{F}_0 = \emptyset$ if $\mathcal{H}$ is obtained by applying only (10.22)). Clearly $\mathcal{K}$ is one of a matching pair of graphs, based on $(\mathcal{M},\mathcal{F}_1)$, and $\mathcal{K}$ is a subgraph of $\mathcal{G}$, while $\mathcal{H}$ is the subgraph of $\mathcal{K}$ obtained by removing all vertices in $\mathcal{V}_0$($\mathcal{V}_0$ as in (10.22); again $\mathcal{V}_0 = \emptyset$ if only (10.23) is applied to construct $\mathcal{H}$). An occupied cluster on $\mathcal{H}$ is an occupied cluster on $\mathcal{K}$ which does not contain any vertices of $\mathcal{V}_0$, and hence remains unchanged if all vertices in $\mathcal{V}_0$ are made vacant with probability one. Moreover Cor. 2.1 applied to $\mathcal{K}$ shows that for any vertex $z_0$ of $\mathcal{K}$

$$\begin{aligned}&\#(\text{occupied cluster of } z_0 \text{ on } \mathcal{K})\\ &\le (\#\text{occupied cluster of } z_0 \text{ on } \mathcal{K}_{p\ell}).\end{aligned}$$

Therefore

$$\begin{aligned}(10.66)\qquad &E_{p_0}(\#(\text{occupied cluster of } z_0 \text{ on } \mathcal{H}))\\ &\le E(\#(\text{occupied cluster of } z_0 \text{ on } \mathcal{K}_{p\ell}))\ ,\end{aligned}$$

where in the right hand side we make vertices in $\mathcal{V}_0$ vacant with probability one, and for other vertices of $\mathcal{K}_{p\ell}$ we use the measure

$P_{p_0}$ . However, $\mathcal{K}_{p\ell}$ is just $\mathcal{G}_{p\ell}$ with the central vertices of faces in $\mathcal{F}_0$ (and the edges incident to these vertices removed). The right hand side of (10.66) therefore equals

(10.67) $\quad E_{p'}(\#(\text{occupied cluster of } z_0 \text{ on } \mathcal{G}_{p\ell})$ ,

where

$P_{p'}\{v$ is occupied$\} = 0$ if $v \in \mathcal{V}_0$ or if $v$ is a central vertex of a face $F \in \mathcal{F}_0$ ,

while

$P_{p'}\{v$ is occupied$\} = P_{p_0}\{v$ is occupied$\}$ for all other vertices $v$ of $\mathcal{G}_{p\ell}$ .

With $\mathfrak{w}$ as in (10.24), these are just the relations (10.25) and (10.26), which in turn say that $P_{p'}$ is of the form (10.15) and satisfies (10.16) and (10.17). Indeed, for $v \in \mathfrak{w}$ we now have

$$\begin{aligned} \nu_v\{\omega(v) = 1\} &= P_{p'}\{\omega(v) = 1\} = 0 < \mu_v\{\omega(v) = 1\} \\ &= P_{p_0}\{\omega(v) = 1\} , \end{aligned}$$

because of $p_0 >> \bar{0}$ and (7.2). Thus Theorem 10.2 applies and (10.67) is finite. But then also the left hand side of (10.66) is finite. Theorem 10.3 now follows from Cor. 5.1 applied to the graph $\mathcal{H}$ . □

## 10.3 Derivation of Condition E from Condition D.

In this section we fill the gap left in the proof of Theorem 10.2. The proof is broken down into six steps, numbered (iv)-(ix) (because we already had Steps (i)-(iii) of the proof of Theorem 10.2). Condition E says that one can make a local modification in the occupancy configuration around a site $a^{\#}$ on $R^{\#}$ with a vacant connection in $\mathring{C}$. The modified configuration is to have a site from $\mathfrak{w}_0$ (defined in step (ii)) with a vacant connection above the lowest horizontal crossing in the new configuration. Basically this is obtained by translating the point $x$ together with the paths $U$ and $V^*$ of condition D and "splicing in" the translate of $U$ into the lowest crossing $R$ and connecting the translate of $V^*$ to the vacant connection from $a^{\#}$ to $\mathring{C}$. A good part of the construction takes place in $\text{int}(K(a))$ (see Step (i) for an $a$ with $a^{\#}$ on $K(a)$. We begin with a method for making well controlled connections between (endpoints of) paths.

Step (iv). By a corridor $\mathcal{K}$ of width $\Lambda_7$ we mean the union of a finite sequence of rectangles $D_0,\dots,D_\lambda$ or $D_1,\dots,D_\lambda$ of the form

$$D_{2i} = [a_{2i},a_{2i}+\Lambda_7]\times[b_{2i},b_{2i}+k_{2i}], \tag{10.68}$$

$$D_{2i+1} = [a_{2i+1},a_{2i+1}+k_{2i+1}]\times[b_{2i},b_{2i}+\Lambda_7] \tag{10.69}$$

with $k_{2i},k_{2i+1} \geq 2\Lambda_7$ and arbitrary $a_j$, $b_j$, and satisfying the connectivity condition that $D_j$ and $D_{j+1}$ have a corner in common and intersect in a square of size $\Lambda_7 \times \Lambda_7$. However, $D_{j-1}$ and $D_{j+1}$ must have disjoint interiors; see Fig. 10.11. The first edge of the corridor

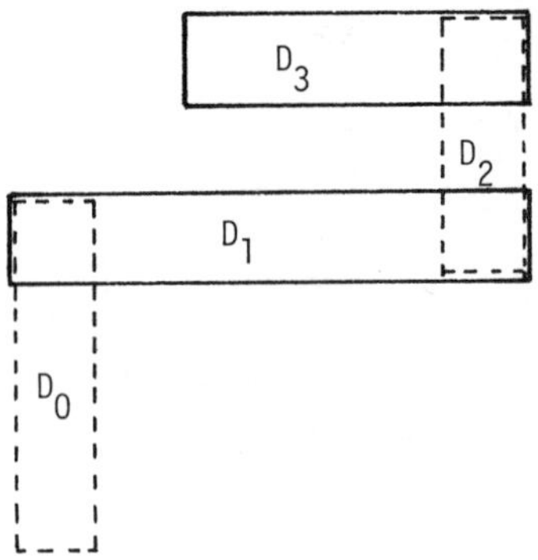


Figure 10.11 A typical corridor. The solid rectangles have odd indices, the dashed rectangles have even indices.

$\mathcal{K} = \bigcup_{i=0}^{\lambda} D_i$ will be the short edge of $D_0$ which does not belong to $D_1$, i.e., $[a_0,a_0+\Lambda_7]\times\{b_0\}$ or $[a_0,a_0+\Lambda_7]\times\{b_0+k_0\}$, whichever one is disjoint from $D_1$. The last edge of $\mathcal{K}$ is that short edge of $D_\lambda$ which does not belong to $D_{\lambda-1}$. A similar definition holds if $\mathcal{K} = \bigcup_{i=1}^{\lambda} D_i$ (which starts with a rectangle of odd index). For the duration of this proof only we shall call a path $r = (v_0, e_1, \dots, e_\nu, e_\nu)$ on $\mathcal{G}_{p\ell}$ strongly minimal if it is minimal (see Def. 10.1), and if in addition for any $i < j$ such that $v_i$ and $v_j$ are vertices of $\mathcal{M}$ which are not adjacent on $\mathcal{M}$, but lie on the perimeter of one face $F \in \mathcal{F}$ whose central vertex $u$ does not belong to $\mathfrak{w}$, one has $j = i+2$ and $v_{i+1}$ is a central vertex of $\mathcal{G}_{p\ell}$ which does not belong to $\mathfrak{w}$. In a strongly minimal path two vertices on the perimeter of a single face $F \in \mathcal{F}$ whose central vertex does not belong to $\mathfrak{w}$ are always connected in one of two ways: either by a single edge of the path which belongs to the perimeter of $F$, or by two successive edges of the path which go through a central vertex of $\mathcal{G}_{p\ell}$ not in $\mathfrak{w}$. Note that two vertices $v_i$ and $v_j$ may be simultaneously on the perimeter of several faces and that there may be several central vertices which are adjacent to both $v_i$ and $v_j$; for this reason we did not require $v_{i+1} = u$ in the above definition. In analogy with Def. 10.2 we shall call a shortcut of two edges of the path $(v_0, e_1, \dots, e_\nu, v_\nu)$ a string $e, u, f$ of an edge, vertex and edge of $\mathcal{G}_{p\ell}$ such that for some $i < j$, $v_i$ and $v_j$ are not adjacent on $\mathcal{G}_{p\ell}$, $v_i$ and $u$ ($u$ and $v_j$) are the endpoints of $e(f)$ and $u$ is a central vertex of $\mathcal{G}_{p\ell}$ which does not belong to $\mathfrak{w}$, and is different from all the $v_i$, $0 \le i \le \nu$. (Since a central vertex has only non-central neighbors (Comment 2.3(iv)) $v_i$ and $v_j$ have to lie on the perimeter of some face $F \in \mathcal{F}$ of $\mathcal{M}$ if there is a shortcut of two edges between them.)

A minimal path for which there do not exist shortcuts of two edges is strongly minimal. However, the converse is not quite true. A strongly minimal path $(v_0, e_1, \dots, e_\nu, v_\nu)$ can have a shortcut of two edges $e, u, f$ between two vertices $v_i$ and $v_j$, but this can happen only if $j = i+2$, $v_i$ and $v_j$ lie on the perimeter of a face $F_1 \in \mathcal{F}$ of $\mathcal{M}$ and $v_{i+1}$ is the central vertex of $F_1$, but does not belong to $\mathfrak{w}$. In this case $u$ has to be the central vertex of another face $F_2 \in \mathcal{F}$ of $\mathcal{M}$, $u$ must be outside $\mathfrak{w}$ and $v_i$, $v_{i+2}$ must lie on the perimeter of $F_2$, as well as on the perimeter of $F_1$.

In this step we prove that for every corridor $\mathcal{K}$ of width $\Lambda_7$ there exists a strongly minimal path $r = (v_0, e_1, \dots, e_\nu, v_\nu)$ on $\mathcal{G}_{p\ell}$ such that

(10.70) $\quad r \subset \mathcal{K}$ and $v_0(v_\nu)$ are within distance $3\Lambda$ from the first (last) edge of $\mathcal{K}$.

This statement remains true if $\mathcal{G}_{p\ell}$ is replaced by $\mathcal{G}^*_{p\ell}$. Note that no statements about the occupancy of $r$ are made. The proof is carried out only for $\mathcal{G}_{p\ell}$ and only by means of a single case illustration. Assume $\mathcal{K} = \bigcup_{i=0}^{2\nu} D_i$ and that a corner on the top edge of $D_0$, $[a_0,a_0+\Lambda_7]\times\{b_0+k_0\}$, is also a corner of $D_1$. Then the first edge of $\mathcal{K}$ is the bottom edge of $D_0$, $[a_0,a_0+\Lambda_7]\times\{b_0\}$. Assume also that $D_{2\nu-1}$ and $D_{2\nu}$ have a corner in common which lies on the bottom edge of $D_{2\nu}$. Then the last edge of $\mathcal{K}$ is the top edge of $D_{2\nu}$, $[a_{2\nu},a_{2\nu}+\Lambda_7]\times\{b_{2\nu}+k_{2\nu}\}$. To find a strongly minimal $r$ satisfying (10.70) let $s_{2i}$ be a vertical crossing on $\mathcal{G}_{p\ell}$ of

$$\tilde{D}_{2i} := [a_{2i}+2\Lambda,a_{2i}+\Lambda_7-2\Lambda]\times[b_{2i}+2\Lambda,b_{2i}+k_{2i}-2\Lambda]$$

and $s_{2i+1}$ a horizontal crossing on $\mathcal{G}_{p\ell}$ of

$$\tilde{D}_{2i+1} := [a_{2i+1}+2\Lambda,a_{2i+1}+k_{2i+1}-2\Lambda]\times[b_{2i+1}+2\Lambda,b_{2i+1}+\Lambda_7-2\Lambda].$$

All these crossings exist by our choice of $\Lambda_3$ and $\Lambda_7 = \Lambda_3+4\Lambda$. Now, since $D_j$ and $D_{j+1}$ intersect in a $\Lambda_7\times\Lambda_7$ square, $\tilde{D}_j$ and $\tilde{D}_{j+1}$ intersect in a $(\Lambda_7-4\Lambda)\times(\Lambda_7-4\Lambda) = \Lambda_3\times\Lambda_3$ square. The latter square is crossed horizontally by $s_j$ and vertically by $s_{j+1}$, if $j$ is odd. Thus $s_j$ and $s_{j+1}$ intersect, necessarily in a vertex of $\mathcal{G}_{p\ell}$. A similar argument works for even $j$. We can therefore put together pieces of $s_0,\dots,s_{2\nu}$ to obtain a path $\tilde{s} = (\tilde{u}_0,\tilde{f}_1,\dots,\tilde{f}_\sigma,\tilde{u}_\sigma)$ with possible double points, which satisfies

$$(10.71)\qquad (\tilde{u}_1,\tilde{f}_2,\dots,\tilde{f}_{\sigma-1},\tilde{u}_{\sigma-1}) \subset \tilde{\mathcal{K}} := \bigcup_{i=0}^{2\nu} \tilde{D}_i$$

and

$$(10.72)\qquad \tilde{f}_1 \text{ intersects } [a_0+2\Lambda,a_0+\Lambda_7-2\Lambda]\times\{b_0+2\Lambda\}, \quad \text{while } \tilde{f}_\sigma \text{ intersects } [a_{2\nu}+2\Lambda,a_{2\nu}+\Lambda_7-2\Lambda]\times\{b_{2\nu}+k_{2\nu}-2\Lambda\}$$

(see Fig. 10.12 for $\nu = 1$). By loop removal, as described in Sect. 2.1 we can make $\tilde{s}$ into a self-avoiding path, without changing its initial or endpoint. Since loop removal only takes away pieces of a path, we obtain after loop removal a self-avoiding path, which we shall denote by $s = (u_0,f_1,\dots,f_\tau,u_\tau)$, which satisfies the analogue of (10.71), i.e.,

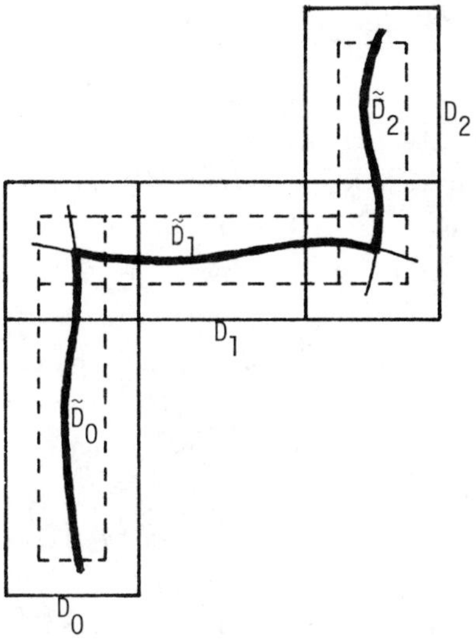


Figure 10.12 An illustration of $\mathcal{K}$, $\tilde{\mathcal{K}}$ and $\tilde{s}$ for $\nu = 1$. The solid rectangles are the $D_i$, the dashed ones the $\tilde{D}_i$. The boldly drawn path is $\tilde{s}$.

(10.73) $$(u_1, f_1, \dots, u_{\tau-1}, u_{\tau-1}) \subset \tilde{\mathcal{K}} .$$

However (10.72) need not be valid any longer. Nevertheless $u_0 = \tilde{u}_0$, $u_\tau = \tilde{u}_\sigma$ so that, by (10.72) and (10.12)

(10.74) $u_0$ is within distance $\Lambda$ of $[a_0+2\Lambda, a_0+\Lambda_7-2\Lambda] \times \{b_0+2\Lambda\}$, and $u_\sigma$ is within distance $\Lambda$ of $[a_\nu+2\Lambda, a_\nu+\Lambda_7-2\Lambda] \times \{b_{2\nu}+k_{2\nu}-2\Lambda\}$.

We shall now replace $s$ by a minimal path, by introducing shortcuts of one edge, whenever necessary. Specifically, assume $s$ is not minimal. Let $u_i$ be the first vertex which is adjacent on $\mathcal{G}_{p\ell}$ to a $u_j$ with $j \geq i+2$. Take the highest $j$ with this property and replace the piece $f_{i+1}, u_{i+1}, \dots, f_{j-1}$ of $s$ by a single edge of $\mathcal{G}_{p\ell}$ from $u_i$ to $u_j$. By repeated application of this procedure we obtain a minimal path from $u_0$ to $u_\tau$, which we still denote by $s = (u_0, f_1, \dots, f_\tau, u_\tau)$. Since its vertices form a subset of the vertices of the original $s$ we have (see (10.73))

(10.75) $$\{u_1,\dots,u_{\tau-1}\} \subset \tilde{\mathcal{K}} .$$

Of course (10.74) remains valid.

If $s$ is not strongly minimal we also introduce shortcuts of two edges. This time we take the smallest $i$ for which there exists a $j \geq i+2$ such that $u_i$ and $u_j$ lie on the perimeter of a face $F \in \mathcal{F}$, whose central vertex does not belong to $\mathfrak{w}$, but not such that $j = i+2$ and $u_{i+1}$ a central vertex of $\mathcal{G}_{p\ell}$ outside $\mathfrak{w}$. Again we take the maximal $j$ with this property, and replace the piece $f_{i+1}, u_{i+1}, \dots, f_{j-1}$ of $s$ by a piece of two edges and a vertex in between, e, u, f say, with $u$ the central vertex of $F$ and $e(f)$ the edge from $u_i$ to $u$ (from $u$ to $u_j$). The insertion of this piece of two edges neither introduces double points, nor destroys the minimality of $s$. Indeed if $u$ were equal to $u_k$ for some $k < i$, then by the minimality of $s$ this would require $i = k+1$ and $j = k+1$ (since $u_k$ would then be adjacent to $u_i$ and $u_j$). This is clearly impossible, as is $u = u_i$. A similar argument excludes $u = u_k$ with $k \geq j$. Thus the new path has no double points. Also, if $u$ is adjacent to some $u_k$ with $k < i$ then $u_k$ has to lie on the perimeter of $F$ (the central vertex of $F$ is adjacent only to vertices on the perimeter of $F$). Then $u_k$ and $u_j$ with $j > k+2$ lie on the perimeter of $F$ whose central vertex $u$ is outside $\mathfrak{w}$. This contradicts the choice of $u_i$ as the first vertex with such a property. Thus $u$ is not adjacent to $u_k$ with $k < i$ and a similar argument works for $k > i$. Consequently the new path is minimal, as claimed. After a finite number of insertions of shortcuts of two edges we arrive at a strongly minimal path $r = (v_0, e_1, \dots, e_\nu, v_\nu)$ with $v_0 = u_0$, $v_\nu = u_\tau$. We claim that this path $r$ satisfies (10.70). $r$ satisfies the last part of (10.70) by virtue of (10.74). But also $r \subset \mathcal{K}$ follows. Indeed any edge or shortcut of two edges has diameter at most $2\Lambda$, by virtue of (10.12). Therefore $r$ contains only points within distance $2\Lambda$ from some vertex $u_1, \dots, u_{\tau-1}$, i.e.,

$$r \subset (2\Lambda)\text{-neighborhood of } \tilde{\mathcal{K}} \subset \mathcal{K} \quad (\text{see (10.75)}).$$

Thus $r$ has the properties claimed in (10.70). It is clear that the whole argument goes through unchanged on $\mathcal{G}^*_{p\ell}$.

We shall use the above procedure for making a path strongly minimal a few more times. We draw the readers attention to two aspects of the procedure. Firstly, we do not insert a shortcut of two edges between any pair of vertices $u_i$ and $u_{i+2}$ if $u_{i+1}$ is already a central vertex of some face $F \in \mathfrak{F}$ of $\mathcal{M}$, with $u_{i+1} \notin \mathfrak{U}$ . Secondly, the procedure is carried out in a specific order, first loop removal, then insertion of shortcuts of one edge and finally insertion of shortcuts of two edges. In all three of these subprocedures we work from the initial vertex of the path to the final one.

Step (v). In this step we make a remark about combining strongly minimal paths. Let $r = (v_0, e_1, \ldots, e_\nu, v_\nu)$ and $s = (u_0, f_1, \ldots, f_\sigma, u_\sigma)$ be strongly minimal paths on $\mathcal{G}_{p\ell}$ such that

$$|v_\nu - u_0| \leq \Lambda_7 + 6\Lambda .$$

By definition of $\Lambda_6$ (see the lines following (10.12)) there then exists a path $t$ on $\mathcal{G}_{p\ell}$ from $v_\nu$ to $u_0$ with diameter $(t) \leq \Lambda_6$ . Now consider the path (with possible double points) consisting of $r$, $t$ and $s$ (in this order) and make it into a strongly minimal path from $v_0$ to $u_\sigma$. The procedure for making the path strongly minimal consists of loop removal and insertion of shortcuts of one or two edges as described for $\tilde{s}$ and $s$ in the last step. Denote the resulting strongly minimal path from $v_0$ to $u_\sigma$ by $\langle r,t,s \rangle$ . Then the following holds.

(10.76) $\langle r,t,s \rangle$ contains all vertices $u_i$ of $s$ for which

$$(\text{distance from } u_j \text{ to } r) > \Lambda_6 + 2\Lambda \quad \text{for all } j > i,\ j \leq \sigma .$$

To prove (10.76) observe that $u_i$ can be removed from $s$ during loop removal only if $u_i$ belongs to a loop which starts on $r \cup t$ and ends with a $u_j$, $j > i$, because $s$ itself is self-avoiding. But this means that $u_j$ equals some vertex on $r \cup t$. In this case the distance from $u_j$ to $r$ is $\leq \Lambda_6$, since any point of $t$ is within distance $\Lambda_6$ from the initial point of $t$, which equals the endpoint $v_\nu$ of $r$. Next assume $u_i$ is removed when a shortcut of one or two edges is inserted. One endpoint of the shortcut has to be a vertex of the combination of $r$, $t$ and $s$ following $u_i$. This has to be a $u_j$ with $j > i$. If the shortcut has any point in common with $r \cup t$ then the above argument again gives us (10.76), in view of the fact that the diameter of the shortcut is at most $2\Lambda$. Finally any shortcut disjoint from $r \cup t$ would be a shortcut for $s$ itself, and no such shortcuts are inserted because $s$ was already strongly minimal. Thus (10.76) always holds.

Assume now that $s$ lies within distance $2\Lambda$ from some rectangle $B$, and that $r$ lies outside $B$ (in addition to the assumptions on $r$ and $s$ already made in the beginning of this step). Then $\langle r,t,s\rangle$ also has the following property:

(10.77) $\langle r,t,s\rangle$ contains only points of $r \cup s$ plus points within distance $\Lambda_6+4\Lambda$ from each of $r$, $s$ and $\mathrm{Fr}(B)$.

The proof of (10.77) is essentially contained in the proof of (10.76). Certainly $t$ lies within distance $\Lambda_6$ from each of its endpoints, $v_\nu$ (which lies on $r$) and $u_0$ (which lies on $s$). Moreover $u_0$ lies inside $B$ or within $2\Lambda$ from $\mathrm{Fr}(B)$. In the former case $t$ runs from the outside of $B$ to a point inside $B$ and hence intersects $\mathrm{Fr}(B)$. In both cases $t$ lies within $\Lambda_6+2\Lambda$ from $\mathrm{Fr}(B)$. The only points on $\langle r,t,s\rangle$ which do not belong to $r \cup t \cup s$ are points of certain shortcuts. If the shortcut contains a point of $t$ or runs from a point of $r$ to a point of $s$, then the above argument again shows that all points of the shortcut are within distance $\Lambda_6+4\Lambda$ from $r$, $s$ and from $\mathrm{Fr}(B)$. Finally, as we saw in the proof of (10.76) no shortcuts from a point of $s$ to a point of $s$ are inserted, and for the same reason no shortcuts from a point of $r$ to a point of $r$ are inserted. This takes care of all possible cases and proves (10.77).

Step (vi). This very long step gives a number of preparatory steps for the description of the local modifications of occupancy configurations which figure in Condition E. The basic objective is to construct a path $\tilde{R}$ which is a crosscut of $\mathrm{int}(J_\ell)$ and which differs only slightly from the "lowest occupied crosscut" $R$ of $\mathrm{int}(J_\ell)$ and, most importantly, contains a translate $\tilde{x}$ of the vertex $x$ in Condition D, such that $\tilde{x}$ has (almost) a vacant connection to $\mathring{C}$ above $\tilde{R}$. We choose for $\tilde{x}$ a translate of $x$, such that $\tilde{x}$ is not too far away from $R$ and is near a point $a^\#$ which has a vacant connection $s^*$ to $\mathring{C}$ above $R$ (actually above $R^\#$). To obtain $\tilde{R}$ we replace a piece of $R$ by a curve on $\mathcal{G}_{p\ell}$ which contains $\tilde{x}$. To construct the vacant connection from $\tilde{x}$ to $\mathring{C}$ we construct a connection on $\mathcal{G}^*_{p\ell}$ from $\tilde{x}$ to the initial point of $s^*$, near $a^\#$, and then continue along $s^*$ to $\mathring{C}$. Unfortunately, the details are complicated and the reader is advised to refer frequently to Figure 10.13-10.17 to try and see what is going on.

Now for the details. Let $\omega$ be an occupancy configuration in which the event $E$ occurs (see Step (iii) for $E$). Let $R = (v_0, e_1, \dots, e_\nu, v_\nu)$ be the occupied crosscut of $\text{int}(J_\ell)$ with minimal $J_\ell^-(R)$ among all occupied crosscuts which satisfy (7.39)-(7.41) and (10.32). Associated with it is a crosscut $R^\#$ satisfying (7.39)-(7.41) and (10.42)-(10.44) (with $r$, $r^\#$ replaced by $R$, $R^\#$) as in Step (i). Assume further that $a^\# \in R^\#$ has a vacant connection $s^* = (w_0^*, f_1^*, \dots, f_\tau^*, w_\tau^*)$ to $\mathring{C}$ above $R^\#$ in $\Gamma_\ell$.

We shall now use the specific properties of $R^\#$ to prove that the following relations hold ($K$ is the special circuit of Step (i) and $K(a) = K + \lfloor a(1) \rfloor \xi_1 + \lfloor a(2) \rfloor \xi_2$ as before):

(10.78) $$(\text{distance from } a^\# \text{ to } R) \geq \Theta \quad ,$$

(10.79) $$a^\# \in K(a) \text{ for some vertex } a \text{ on } R \text{ with}$$
$$\frac{1}{2} M_{\ell 1} - \Theta - 2\Lambda \leq a(1) \leq \frac{3}{2} M_{\ell 1} + \Theta + 2\Lambda \text{ , and}$$

(10.80) $$s^* \subset \text{ext } K(a).$$

Assume that (10.78) fails. Then we can find some point $b$ on $R$ with $|a^\# - b| < \Theta$ and hence for some vertex $w$ of $\mathcal{G}_{p\ell}$ on $R$ ($w$ can be taken as an endpoint of the edge containing $b$)

$$|w_0^* - w| \leq |w_0^* - a^\#| + |a^\# - b| + |b - w|$$
$$< \Theta + 2\Lambda \quad .$$

Since $K$ surrounds the square (10.37) this means that $w_0^* \in \text{int}(K(w))$. Further, from $w_0^* \in \Gamma_\ell$ we obtain

$$\frac{1}{2} M_{\ell 1} - \Theta - 2\Lambda \leq w(1) \leq \frac{3}{2} M_{\ell 1} + \Theta + 2\Lambda \quad .$$

In other words $\overline{K}(w) \subset \mathcal{E}(R)$ (see (10.40) and (10.41)). This, however, is impossible since $\mathcal{E}(R)$ is disjoint from $\mathfrak{F}(R)$ (by definition of $\mathfrak{F}(R)$), while by (10.42) $\mathfrak{F}(R) = J_\ell^+(R^\#)$. Thus $w_0^*$, which is a point of $J_\ell^+(R^\#)$ (see (10.51)) cannot lie in $\mathcal{E}(R)$. This contradiction implies that (10.78) holds.

(10.79) is now easy. By virtue of (10.44) $a^\# \in R^\#$ lies on $R$ or on some $K(a)$ for which (10.79) holds. $a^\# \in R$ is excluded by (10.78). Also (10.80) follows, since $s^* \setminus \{w_\tau^*\} \subset J_\ell^+(R^\#)$ (see (10.51)), and as we saw above $J_\ell^+(R^\#) = \mathcal{F}(R)$ is disjoint from all $\overline{K}(a)$ which can arise in (10.79). Moreover $w_\tau^* \in \overset{\circ}{C}$ (by (10.50)) lies above the line $x(2) = 12M_{\ell 2}$ (see Step (i)) and outside $\overline{K}(a)$ since $R$ satisfies (10.32).

For the remainder fix a vertex $a$ of $\mathcal{G}_{p\ell}$ on $R$ such that (10.78)-(10.80) hold. For the sake of argument assume that $a^\#$ lies on the "left half of the lower edge of $K(a)$", i.e.,

$$a^\#(1) \leq a(1), \quad a^\#(2) \leq a(2) - 2\Theta + \Lambda \quad ; \tag{10.81}$$

see Fig. 10.13. Similar arguments will apply in the other cases. Let $x \in \mathbb{W}$ have the properties listed in Condition D and choose $k_1, k_2 \in \mathbb{Z}$

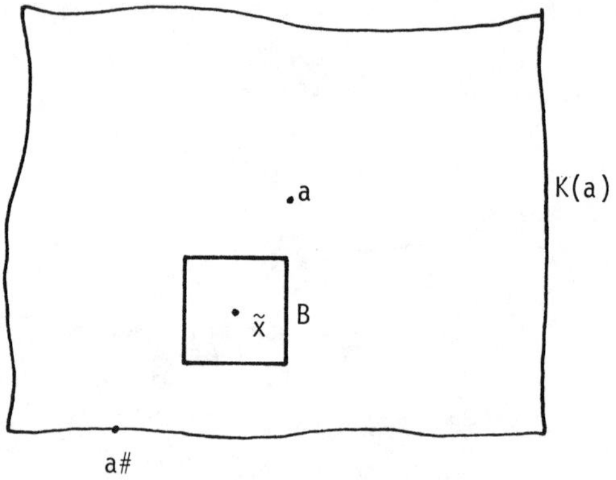


Figure 10.13

such that $\tilde{x} := x + (k_1, k_2)$ lies in the closed unit square centered at

$$a^\# + (5\Lambda_7 + 2\Lambda_8 + 3\Lambda + \Delta + 1, \Lambda_6 + \Lambda_5 + \Lambda_3 + 10\Lambda + \Delta + 1). \tag{10.82}$$

Then, by the periodicity $\tilde{x}$ also has the properties listed in Condition D. We can therefore find $B = B(\tilde{x})$ and paths $U$ on $\mathcal{G}_{p\ell}$, $V^*$ on $\mathcal{G}_{p\ell}^*$ such that a)-e) of Condition D (with $\tilde{x}$ for $x$) hold. We note that by (10.37) and (10.38) $K(a)$ lies in the annulus

$$\mathbb{G} := [\lfloor a(1) \rfloor -2\Theta-\Lambda_3-\Lambda, \lfloor a(1) \rfloor +2\Theta+\Lambda_3+\Lambda]$$
$$\times [\lfloor a(2) \rfloor -2\Theta-\Lambda_3-\Lambda, \lfloor a(2) \rfloor +2\Theta+\Lambda_3+\Lambda]$$
$$\setminus (\lfloor a(1) \rfloor -2\Theta+\Lambda, \lfloor a(1) \rfloor +2\Theta-\Lambda)$$
$$\times (\lfloor a(2) \rfloor -2\Theta+\Lambda, \lfloor a(2) \rfloor +2\Theta-\Lambda).$$

By (10.81), (10.82) and (10.33) $B = B(\tilde{x})$ lies in the interior of the inner boundary of $\mathbb{G}$. In fact

(10.83) $$\text{distance } (B,\mathbb{G}) > \Lambda_6+6\Lambda \quad .$$

We now want to "splice $U$ into $R$" and connect $V^*$ to $s^*$. We first connect those endpoints of $U$ and $V^*$ near the perimeter of $B$ to $K(a) \subset \mathbb{G}$, by paths which run to the outside of $\mathbb{G}$. These paths should not interfere with each other, nor should they be too far away from $B$ (for purposes of the construction to follow). We put these paths inside three corridors $\mathcal{K}_\ell$, $\mathcal{K}_r$ and $\mathcal{K}^*$ of width $\Lambda_7$. A typical illustration of these corridors is shown in Fig. 10.14. Formally, we require that they have the properties (10.84)-(10.92) below.

(10.84) The corridors are disjoint from $\overset{\circ}{B}$ (= interior of $B(\tilde{x})$).

(10.85) The first edge of $\mathcal{K}_\ell (\mathcal{K}_r)$ is on the left (right) edge of $B$, i.e., on $\{\tilde{x}(1)-\Delta\} \times [\tilde{x}(2)-\Delta,\tilde{x}(2)+\Delta]$ $(\{\tilde{x}(1)+\Delta\} \times [\tilde{x}(1)-\Delta,x(2)+\Delta])$. Moreover the first edge of $\mathcal{K}_\ell$ $(\mathcal{K}_r)$ intersects the edge $e_1$ $(e_\rho)$ of $U$ (cf. Condition Dc). Finally the distance between $\mathcal{K}_\ell$ $(\mathcal{K}_r)$ and $\{u_{i_0},\dots,u_\rho\}$ $(\{u_0,\dots,u_{i_0}\})$ is at least $\Lambda_6+9\Lambda$, while the distance between $\mathcal{K}_\ell \cup \mathcal{K}_r$ and $V^*$ is at least $\Lambda_6+5\Lambda$ .

(10.86) The first edge of $\mathcal{K}^*$ is on the top edge of $B$, in the segment $[\tilde{x}(1)-\Delta+\Lambda_8,\tilde{x}(1)+\Delta-\Lambda_8] \times \{\tilde{x}(2)+\Delta\}$ and intersects the edge $e^*_\sigma$ of $V^*$. The distance between $\mathcal{K}^*$ and $U$ is at least $\Lambda_8$.

(10.87) Let $D_\ell$ be the last rectangle in the corridor $\mathcal{K}_\ell$. It is of the even-indexed type (10.68) and intersects $\mathbb{G}$ only in the latter's bottom strip

$[\lfloor a(1)\rfloor-2\Theta-\Lambda_3-\Lambda, \lfloor a(1)\rfloor+2\Theta+\Lambda_3+\Lambda] \times [\lfloor a(2)\rfloor-2\Theta-\Lambda_3-\Lambda,$ $\lfloor a(2)\rfloor-2\Theta+\Lambda])$. The intersection of $D_\ell$ and this bottom strip is a rectangle of size $\Lambda_7 \times (\Lambda_3+2\Lambda)$. The last edge of $\mathcal{K}_\ell$ lies in the exterior of $\mathbb{G}$, at a distance $\geq 3\Lambda$ from $\mathbb{G}$. $D_\ell$ lies to the right of the vertical line $\{\lfloor a(1)\rfloor-2\Theta+3\Lambda\} \times \mathbb{R}$, i.e., more than $2\Lambda$ units to the right of the left strip of $\mathbb{G}$. Lastly, all points of $\mathcal{K}_\ell$ within distance $2\Lambda$ from $\mathbb{G}$ lie in $D_\ell$.

(10.88) Either (10.87) also holds with $\mathcal{K}_\ell$ replaced by $\mathcal{K}_r$ and $D_\ell$ by the last rectangle $D_r$ of $\mathcal{K}_r$, or $D_r$ is of the odd-indexed type (10.69) and intersects $\mathbb{G}$ only in the latter's left strip, $[\lfloor a(1)\rfloor-2\Theta-\Lambda_3-\Lambda, \lfloor a(1)\rfloor-2\Theta+\Lambda]$ $\times [\lfloor a(2)\rfloor-2\Theta-\Lambda_3-\Lambda, \lfloor a(2)\rfloor+2\Theta+\Lambda_3+\Lambda]$. In this case the intersection of $D_r$ and the left strip is a rectangle of size $(\Lambda_3+2\Lambda)\times\Lambda_7$, the last edge of $\mathcal{K}_r$ lies in the exterior of $\mathbb{G}$ at a distance $\geq 3\Lambda$ from $\mathbb{G}$. Also all points of $\mathcal{K}_r$ within distance $2\Lambda$ of $\mathbb{G}$ lie in $D_r$, and $D_r$ lies above the horizontal line $\mathbb{R}\times\{\lfloor a(2)\rfloor-2\Theta$ $+3\Lambda\}$ (i.e., more than $2\Lambda$ units above the bottom strip of $\mathbb{G}$).

(10.89) $a^\# \in \mathcal{K}^* \cap K(a) \subset \mathcal{K}^* \cap \mathbb{G}$; $\mathcal{K}^* \cap \mathbb{G}$ lies below the horizontal line $\mathbb{R}\times\{\lfloor a(2)\rfloor-\Theta\}$.

(10.90) The distance between any pair of the corridors $\mathcal{K}_\ell$, $\mathcal{K}_r$ and $\mathcal{K}^*$ is at least $\Lambda_8$ ($\Lambda_8$ is defined before Condition D).

(10.91) All three corridors $\mathcal{K}_\ell$, $\mathcal{K}_r$ and $\mathcal{K}^*$ lie within distance $\Lambda_9$ of $a^\#$ ($\Lambda_9$ is defined in (10.33)).

(10.92) $\mathcal{K}^* \cap K(a)$ lies "between $\mathcal{K}_\ell \cap \mathbb{G}$ and $\mathcal{K}_r \cap \mathbb{G}$". More precisely, if $b$ is any point of $\mathcal{K}^* \cap K(a)$, then any continuous curve from $\mathcal{K}_\ell$ to $\mathcal{K}_r$ inside $\mathbb{G}$ of diameter $\leq \Theta$ intersects the line segment $b+t(1,1)$, $-2\Lambda_3-4\Lambda \leq t$ $\leq 2\Lambda_3+4\Lambda$.

These horrendous conditions are actually not difficult to satisfy as illustrated in Fig. 10.14 for the case where $a^\#$ is sufficiently far away from the left edge of $\mathbb{G}$ so that (10.87) can be satisfied for $\mathcal{K}_\ell$ as well as $\mathcal{K}_r$. We content ourselves with this figure and a few minor comments indicating why (10.84)-(10.92) can be satisfied. For

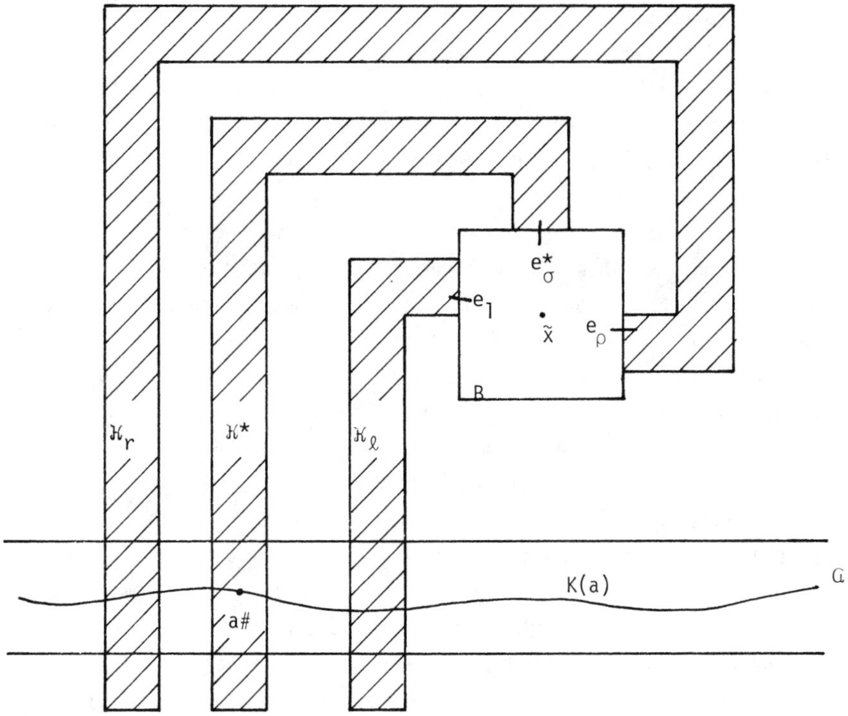


Figure 10.14 The hatched regions are the corridors $\mathcal{K}_r$, $\mathcal{K}_\ell$ and $\mathcal{K}^*$.

(10.85) and (10.86) we remind the reader that $e_1$, $e_\rho$ and $e^*_\sigma$ intersect the left, right and top edge of B, respectively, by Condition D. Moreover, $U = (u_0, e_1, \dots, e_\rho, u_\rho)$ lies below the horizontal line $\mathbb{R} \times \{\tilde{x}(2) + \Delta - \Lambda_8\}$, while $V^*$ lies in the vertical strip $[\tilde{x}(1) - \Delta + \Lambda_8, \tilde{x}(1) + \Delta - \Lambda_8] \times \mathbb{R}$. Lastly $(u_{i_0}, e_{i_0+1}, \dots, u_\rho)$ lies to the right of $\{x(1) - \Delta + \Lambda_8\} \times \mathbb{R}$ and $(u_0, e_1, \dots, u_{i_0})$ lies to the left of $\{x(1) + \Delta - \Lambda_8\} \times \mathbb{R}$. (10.91) can be satisfied by (10.33) and because

$$(10.93) \qquad |a^\#(i) - \tilde{x}(i)| \le 5(\Lambda_5 + \Lambda_6 + \Lambda_7 + \Lambda_8 + \Lambda + \Delta + 1)$$

(see (10.82)). Lastly, with regard to (10.92) we remark that the segment $b + t(1,1)$, $|t| \le 2\Lambda_3 + 4\Lambda$, is on a 45° line through $b$ and cuts $\mathbb{G}$ "close to" the lower strip of $\mathbb{G}$. Also $\mathcal{K}_\ell \cap \mathbb{G}$ and $\mathcal{K}_r \cap \mathbb{G}$ lie close to the lower edge of $\mathcal{G}$. A path from $\mathcal{K}_\ell \cap \mathcal{G}$ to $\mathcal{K}_r \cap \mathcal{G}$ of diameter $\leq \Theta$, has to remain below the horizontal line $x(2) = \lfloor a(2) \rfloor - \Theta + \Lambda$ (by (10.87)). Therefore such a path cannot intersect the segment $\{\lfloor a(1) \rfloor\} \times [\lfloor a(2) \rfloor + 2\Theta - \Lambda, \lfloor a(2) \rfloor + 2\Theta + \Lambda_3 + \Lambda\}$ which cuts the top strip of $\mathcal{G}$. This segment together with the segment $b+t(1,1), |t| \leq 2\Lambda_3+4\Lambda$ divide $\mathcal{G}$ into two components, whenever $b \in \mathcal{K}^* \cap \mathcal{G}$ (by (10.89)). (10.92) basically says that $\mathcal{K}_\ell \cap \mathcal{G}$ and $\mathcal{K}_r \cap \mathcal{G}$ do not lie in the same component of $\mathcal{G}$ when $\mathcal{G}$ is cut by these two segments. This is obviously the case when $\mathcal{K}_\ell$, $\mathcal{K}_r$ and $\mathcal{K}^*$ are located as in Fig. 10.14.

It should be obvious that the precise values of the various constants $\Lambda_i$ and $\Theta$ are without significance.

Once the corridors $\mathcal{K}_\ell$, $\mathcal{K}_r$ and $\mathcal{K}^*$ have been chosen we choose strongly minimal paths $r_i$ on $\mathcal{G}_{p\ell}$ inside $\mathcal{K}_i$, $i = \ell$ or $r$, which start within distance $3\Lambda$ from its first edge and end within distance $3\Lambda$ from its last edge, by the method of Step (iv) (see (10.70)). Since the last edge of $\mathcal{K}_i$ is at least $3\Lambda$ units outside $\mathcal{G}$ (by (10.87), (10.88)), the endpoint of $r_i$ lies in the exterior or on the exterior boundary of $\mathcal{G}$. The first point of $r_i$ lies within $3\Lambda$ from $B$ and therefore inside the inner boundary of $\mathcal{G}$ and at distance $> 3\Lambda$ from this inner boundary (by (10.83)). Hence $r_i$ intersects $K(a)$. A fortiori, there exists a first vertex of $r_i$, $b_i$ say, which can be connected to a vertex of $K(a)$, $c_{\alpha(i)}$ say, by a path of two edges on $\mathcal{G}_{p\ell}$. We connect $b_i$ to $c_{\alpha(i)}$ by such a path of two edges. If possible we take for the intermediate vertex between $b_i$ and $c_{\alpha(i)}$ a central vertex of $\mathcal{G}_{p\ell}$ which does not belong to $\mathfrak{w}$. Also we connect the initial point of $r_\ell$ $(r_r)$ to $u_1$ $(u_{\rho-1})$ by a path $t_\ell$ $(t_r)$ on $\mathcal{G}_{p\ell}$ of diameter $\leq \Lambda_6$. This can be done by one choice of $\Lambda_6$ since the initial point of $r_\ell$ is within $3\Lambda$ from the first edge of $\mathcal{K}_\ell$, which intersects $e_1$ by (10.85). Thus the distance between the initial point of $r_\ell$ and $u_1$ is at most $4\Lambda+\Lambda_7$. A similar statement holds for $r_r$ and $u_{\rho-1}$. Next we make the piece of $U$ from $u_1$ to $u_{\rho-1}$ into a strongly minimal path, $\tilde{U}$ say, which still runs from $u_1$ to $u_{\rho-1}$, by insertion of shortcuts of two edges if necessary (see the method used for the path $s$ in Step (iv); recall that $U$ is minimal by Condition D). Now consider the following path on $\mathcal{G}_{p\ell}$ (with possible double points) from $c_{\alpha(\ell)}$ to $c_{\alpha(r)}$: From $c_{\alpha(\ell)}$ go via two edges to the vertex $b_\ell$ of $r_\ell$, traverse $r_\ell$ backwards, then go along $t_\ell$ to $u_1$, along $\tilde{U}$ from $u_1$ to $u_{\rho-1}$, along $t_r$ to the initial point of $r_r$, then along $r_r$ to the vertex $b_r$ of $r_r$, and finally via two edges to $c_{\alpha(r)}$ (see

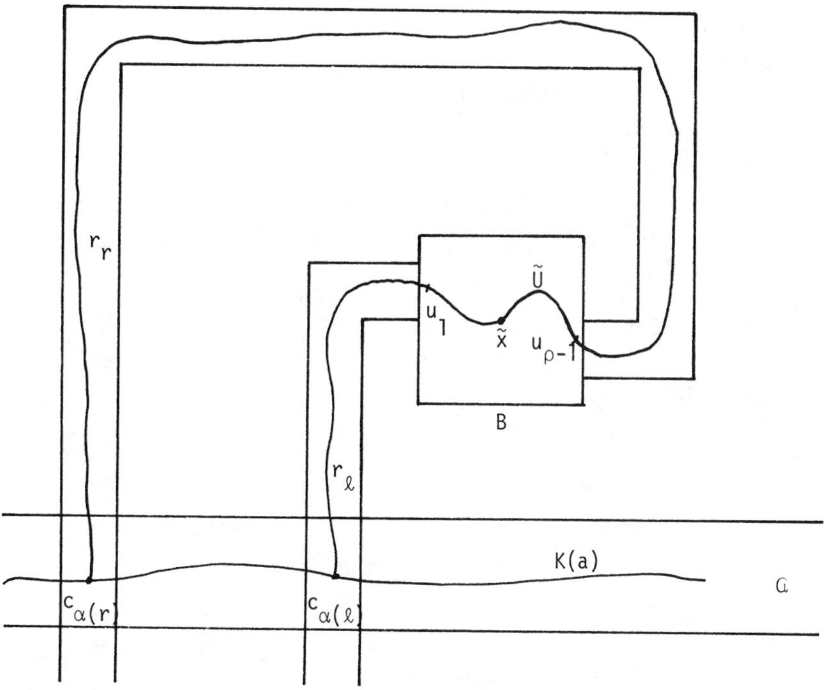


Figure 10.15

Fig. 10.15). This whole path is made into a strongly minimal path $\tilde{X}$ in the following way. First make $r_i$ till $b_i$ plus the two-edge connection from $b_i$ to $c_{\alpha(i)}$ into a strongly minimal path, $\tilde{r}_i$ say, by the method applied to the path s in Step (iv). Since $r_i$ itself was already strongly minimal, and since $b_i$ is the first point on $r_i$ which can be connected by two edges to K(a), one easily sees that no loops have to be removed, nor shortcuts of one edge have to be inserted during the formation of $\tilde{r}_i$. Moreover, at most one shortcut of two edges has to be inserted to obtain a strongly minimal $\tilde{r}_i$. Indeed, if the connection from $b_i$ to $c_{\alpha(i)}$ goes through the vertex $y_i$ of $\mathcal{G}_{p\ell}$, then the only shortcut which may have to be inserted is from some vertex on the piece of $r_i$ between its initial point and $b_i$ to $y_i$. Note that such a shortcut lies within $3\Lambda$ from K(a) and hence further than $2\Lambda$ away from $U$ (by virtue of (10.83)). Now that $\tilde{r}_i$ and $\tilde{U}$ have been formed we first combine $\tilde{r}_\ell$, $t_\ell$ and $\tilde{U}$ into the strongly minimal path $<\tilde{r}_\ell,t_\ell,\tilde{U}>$ as in Step (v) (see (10.76)). Finally we obtain the strongly minimal path $\tilde{X}$ as the combination $<<\tilde{r}_\ell,t_\ell,\tilde{U}>,t_t,\tilde{r}_r>$ of this last path with $t_r$ and $\tilde{r}_r$.

It will be very important that one has

(10.94) $\qquad \tilde{x}$ is a vertex on $\tilde{X}$,

as we now prove. Firstly $\tilde{x}$ cannot be removed when $U$ is turned into the strongly minimal path $\tilde{U}$. This is so because $U$ is already minimal by hypothesis (see Condition D), and $\tilde{x} = u_{i_0}$ could be removed only by insertion of a shortcut of two edges, and only if such a shortcut runs from $u_i$ to $u_j$ with $i < i_0 < j$. By Condition D b) no such shortcuts exist. Secondly, when we form $<\tilde{r}_\ell,t_\ell,\tilde{U}>$ from $\tilde{r}_\ell$, $t_\ell$ and $\tilde{U}$, by the method of Step (v), then $\tilde{x} = u_{i_0}$ is not removed, on account of (10.76) and (10.85). Indeed, all points $u_{i_0+1},\dots,u_\rho$ have a distance of at least $\Lambda_6+9\Lambda$ to $r_\ell \subset \mathcal{K}_\ell$. Thus, also any shortcuts introduced in the formation of $\tilde{U}$ and ending at one of $u_{i_0+1},\dots,u_\rho$ have distance at least $\Lambda_6+5\Lambda$ to $\tilde{r}_i$ (which lies within $2\Lambda$ from $r_i$). Thirdly, when $\tilde{r}_r$, $t_r$ and $<\tilde{r}_\ell,t_\ell,\tilde{U}>$ are combined to $<<\tilde{r}_\ell,t_\ell,\tilde{U}>,t_r,\tilde{r}_r> = \tilde{X}$, then $\tilde{x}$ is still maintained. This is so because no intersections or shortcuts between $\tilde{r}_\ell \cup t_\ell$ and $\tilde{r}_r \cup t_r$ exist, the distance between these two sets being at least

$$\Lambda_8-2\Lambda_6-4\Lambda > 6\Lambda ,$$

by virtue of (10.90). Also the distance between $u_1,\dots,u_{i_0-1}$, or any shortcuts ending at one of these points, and $\tilde{r}_r$ is at least $\Lambda_6+5\Lambda$, by (10.85) again. As in the proof of (10.76) one obtains from this that $\tilde{x}$ will not be removed when forming $\tilde{X}$. This proves (10.94).

We set

(10.95) $\qquad \tilde{X}_i(\tilde{x})$ = closed segment of $\tilde{X}$ between $c_{\alpha(i)}$ on $K(a)$ and $\tilde{x}$, $i = \ell$ or $r$.

The proof of (10.94) just completed also shows that

(10.96) $\qquad$ There exist no shortcuts of two edges for $\tilde{X}$ with one endpoint each on of $\tilde{X}_\ell(\tilde{x})\setminus\{\tilde{x}\}$ and $\tilde{X}_r(\tilde{x})\setminus\{\tilde{x}\}$ .

We also leave it to the reader to use (10.83), (10.77) and the description of $\tilde{X}$ - especially the statements about $\tilde{r}_i$ before the proof of (10.94) - to verify that

(10.97) any vertex on $\tilde{X}$ which can be connected to $K(a)$ by one or two edges of $\mathcal{G}_{p\ell}$ lies within distance $2\Lambda$ of $\{c_{\alpha(\ell)}, c_{\alpha(r)}\}$.

For later purposes it is also useful to know that

(10.98) $$\tilde{X} \setminus \{c_{\alpha(\ell)}, c_{\alpha(r)}\} \subset \operatorname{int}(K(a)).$$

To prove this we go back to the construction of $\tilde{r}_i$. This is made from the piece of $r_i$ from its initial point to $b_i$, a two-edge connection from $b_i$ via the vertex $y_i$ to $c_{\alpha(i)}$, and possibly a shortcut from $y_i$ via a central vertex, $y_i'$ say, to a vertex, $y_i''$ say, on the piece of $r_i$ between its initial point and $b_i$. Since $r_i$ from its initial point to $b_i$ lies in $\operatorname{int}(K(a))$, we see that also $\tilde{r}_i \setminus c_{\alpha(i)} \subset \operatorname{int}(K(a))$, unless $y_i$ or $y_i'$ belongs to $K(a)$. However $y_i$ cannot lie on $K(a)$ by the minimality properties of $b_i$, for if $y_i \in K(a)$, then $b_i$ would be connectable to $K(a)$ by a single edge. Similarly $y_i \notin K(a)$, because $y_i''$ cannot be connected to $K(a)$ by a single edge. Thus

$$\tilde{r}_\ell \cup \tilde{r}_r \setminus \{c_{\alpha(\ell)}, c_{\alpha(r)}\} \subset \operatorname{int}(K(a))$$

and also

$$t_\ell \cup \tilde{U} \cup t_r \text{ lie in } \operatorname{int}(K(a)), \text{ even at a distance } > 4\Lambda \text{ from } K(a)\ .$$

(Again recall (10.83) and the fact that $t_\ell$ $(t_r)$ has one endpoint at $u_1$ $(u_{\rho-1})$.) Finally any shortcuts inserted while making $\tilde{X}$ from $\tilde{r}_\ell$, $t_\ell$, $\tilde{U}$, $t_r$, $\tilde{r}_r$ lie in $\operatorname{int}(K(a))$ by (10.83) and (10.77) with its proof (recall that there are no shortcuts between $\tilde{r}_0 \cup t_0$ and $\tilde{r}_\nu \cup t_\nu$).

It is our objective to make (most of) $\tilde{X}$, including $\tilde{x}$, part of the "lowest" occupied horizontal crosscut of $J_\ell$ in the modified occupancy configuration. Before we can do this we also have to describe part of the path which will form the vacant connection from $\tilde{x}$ to $\mathring{C}$ in the modified configuration. Specifically we construct a path on $\mathcal{G}_{p\ell}^*$ from $v_0^*$ (= the initial point of $V^*$) to $w_0^*$ (= the initial point of $s^*$). We first take a path $r^*$ on $\mathcal{G}_{p\ell}^*$ in $\mathcal{H}^*$ which begins within distance $3\Lambda$ from the first edge of $\mathcal{H}^*$ and ends within $\Lambda_7+3\Lambda$ from

$a^{\#}$. This can be done by virtue of (10.89) and the fact that $\mathcal{K}^*$ has width $\Lambda_7$. We connect $v^*_\sigma$ to the first point of $r^*$ by a path on $\mathcal{G}^*_{p\ell}$ of diameter $\leq \Lambda_6$. We also connect the final point of $r^*$ to $w^*_0$ by a path on $\mathcal{G}^*_{p\ell}$ of diameter $\Lambda_6$. This can be done since $|a^{\#}-w^*_0| \leq \Lambda$ (cf. (10.49)) so that the distance from the last point of $r^*$ to $w^*_0$ is at most $\Lambda_7+4\Lambda$. Now take the path (with possible double points) from $v^*_0$ to $w^*_0$ which proceeds via $V^*$, the connection between $v^*_\sigma$ and the first point of $r^*$, $r^*$ and finally the connection from the last point of $r^*$ to $w^*_0$. Make it self-avoiding by loop-removal (it is not important that it become (strongly) minimal). The resulting path on $\mathcal{G}^*_{p\ell}$, will still run from $v^*_0$ to $w^*_0$. Call it $X^*$. We shall need the fact that

(10.99) $\qquad X^*$ is disjoint from $\tilde{X}$.

This follows from the following remarks, Firstly $\tilde{U}$ and $V^*$ have no point in common by virtue of Condition De) and the fact that the only vertices which can lie on $\tilde{U}\backslash U$ are central vertices of $\mathcal{G}_{p\ell}$, and hence are not on the path $V^*$ on $\mathcal{G}^*_{p\ell}$. Secondly, all points of $\tilde{X}(X^*)$ further away than $\Lambda_6+4\Lambda$ from $\mathcal{K}_\ell \cup \mathcal{K}_r$ $(\mathcal{K}^*)$ must belong to $\tilde{U}(V^*)$. Finally points within $\Lambda_6+4\Lambda$ from $\mathcal{K}_\ell \cup \mathcal{K}_r$ $(\mathcal{K}^*)$ cannot belong to $X^*(\tilde{X})$ by (10.90), (10.85) and (10.86).

We now start on making (most of) $\tilde{X}$ part of the lowest crossing. In order to achieve this we want to connect $\tilde{X}$ with $R$. Note first that

(10.100) $\qquad \tilde{X}$ is disjoint from $R$,

because by construction $\tilde{X}$ lies within $\Lambda_6+4\Lambda$ from $B \cup \mathcal{K}_\ell \cup \mathcal{K}_r$, hence within

$$\Lambda_6+4\Lambda+2\Lambda_9$$

from $a^{\#}$ (see (10.91) and (10.33)), which is less than the distance from $R$ to $a^{\#}$ (by (10.78)). Despite (10.100) $R$ is not too far away from $\tilde{X}$. Indeed $R$ contains the vertex $a$ in the interior of $K(a)$, while for large enough $\ell$, the initial (final) point of $R$ on $B_1(B_2)$ has first coordinate $\leq \Lambda_3$ $(\geq 2M_{\ell 1}-\Lambda_3)$, and therefore lies in $\text{ext}(K(a))$ for all sufficiently large $\ell$. (See Step (i) for $B_i$ and recall that $a$ satisfies (10.79).) Thus $R$ intersects $K(a)$ at least twice. We next derive some information about the location of these intersections. Let $K_{\#}$ be the arc of $K(a)$ from $c_{\alpha(\ell)}$ to $c_{\alpha(r)}$ through $a^{\#}$. We claim that

(10.101) $\text{diameter}(K_{\#}) \leq 6\Lambda_5(2\Lambda_9+2\Lambda_3+5\Lambda+1) < \Theta$ ,

and

(10.102) $$\mathcal{H}^* \cap K(a) \subset K_{\#} .$$

To prove (10.101) and (10.102) let $b$ be any point of $\mathcal{H}^* \cap K(a)$. Then, by (10.91)

$$|b-c_{\alpha(i)}| \leq |b-b_i| + |b_i-c_{\alpha(i)}| \leq 2\Lambda_9+2\Lambda, \ i = \ell,r,$$

since $b_i \in \mathcal{H}_i$ and $b_i$ is connected to $c_{\alpha(i)}$ by two edges. Thus, by the construction of $K$ - in particular by (10.39) - $b$ and $c_{\alpha(\ell)}$ are connected by an arc, $\phi$ say, of $K(a)$ of diameter at most

(10.103) $$3\Lambda_5(2\Lambda_9+2\Lambda_3+5\Lambda+1).$$

First we must show that this arc does not contain $c_{\alpha(r)}$. Assume to the contrary that moving along $\phi$ from $c_{\alpha(\ell)}$ to $b$ one passes $c_{\alpha(r)}$ before reaching $b$. Then the subarc $\phi'$ of $\phi$ from $c_{\alpha(\ell)}$ to $c_{\alpha(r)}$ does not contain $b$. However, $b_i \in \mathcal{H}_i$ and $|b_i-c_{\alpha(i)}| \leq 2\Lambda$ . Thus by (10.87), (10.88) $b_i$ lies in the last rectangle $D_i$ of $\mathcal{H}_i$ . Since the location of $D_\ell$ is at least $2\Lambda$ units to the right of the left strip of $\mathcal{G}$ (see (10.87)) and within $\Lambda_9$ of $a^{\#}$ (see (10.91)) - which lies to the left of $a$ (see (10.81)) - it follows that $c_{\alpha(\ell)}$ (which lies within $2\Lambda$ from $D_\ell \subset \mathcal{H}_\ell$) lies in the lower strip of $\mathcal{G}$. Hence, $c_{\alpha(\ell)}$ can be connected to some point of $D_\ell$ by a horizontal line segment in the lower strip of $\mathcal{G}$ and of length $\leq 2\Lambda$. Similarly, $c_{\alpha(r)}$ can be connected to a point of $D_r \subset \mathcal{H}_r$ by a straight line segment in $\mathcal{G}$ (horizontal or vertical) of length $\leq 2\Lambda$ . $\phi'$ together with the two straight line segments from $c_{\alpha(i)}$ to $\mathcal{H}_i$ form a continuous curve in $\mathcal{G}$ from $\mathcal{H}_\ell$ to $\mathcal{H}_r$ of diameter $\leq 4\Lambda$ plus the expression in (10.103). Since this diameter is at most $\Theta$, (10.92) implies that the curve must intersect the segment $b+t(1,1)$, $|t| \leq 2\Lambda_3+4\Lambda$. The two straight line segments which were added to $\phi'$ lie within $2\Lambda$ of $\mathcal{H}_\ell \cup \mathcal{H}_r$, and by virtue of (10.90) do not intersect the segment $b+t(1,1)$, $|t| \leq 2\Lambda_3+4\Lambda$, which lies within $2\Lambda_3+4\Lambda$ from $\mathcal{H}^*$. Thus $\phi'$ already intersects the segment in some point $b'$, whose distance from $b$ is at most $2\Lambda_3+4\Lambda$. Again by the construction of $K$ and the estimate (10.39), $b'$ is connected to $b$ by an arc, $\psi$ say, of $K(a)$ of diameter at most

(10.104) $$3\Lambda_5(4\Lambda_3+7\Lambda+1).$$

Now by our assumption the curve $\phi$ starting at $c_{\alpha(\ell)}$ first passes through $b'$, then through $c_{\alpha(r)}$ and then ends at $b$. $\psi$ cannot be the piece of $\phi$ from $b'$ through $c_{\alpha(r)}$ to $b$, in fact $\psi$ cannot contain $c_{\alpha(r)}$, for then by (10.90) its diameter would be at least

$$|c_{\alpha(r)}-b| \geq \text{distance } (\mathcal{K}_r,\mathcal{K}^*)-2\Lambda \geq \Lambda_8-2\Lambda \ ,$$

which exceeds (10.104). Thus, the piece of $\phi$ from $b'$ to $b$ and $\psi$ have to be two arcs of $K(a)$ from $b'$ to $b$, exactly one of which contains the point $c_{\alpha(r)}$ of $K(a)$. This can only be if together these two arcs make up all of the Jordan curve $K(a)$, and if at least one of these arcs has a diameter $\geq \frac{1}{2}$ diameter $(K(a)) \geq 2\Theta-\Lambda$ (see (10.37)). Since this is not the case we have derived a contradiction from the assumption that $\phi$ contains the point $c_{\alpha(r)}$. Thus the path $\phi$ from $c_{\alpha(\ell)}$ to $b$ does not contain $c_{\alpha(r)}$. In the same way we find an arc $\theta$ of $K(a)$ from $b$ to $c_{\alpha(r)}$ of diameter at most equal to the expression in (10.103) and not containing $c_{\alpha(\ell)}$. $\phi$ followed by $\theta$ gives us an arc of $K(a)$ from $c_{\alpha(\ell)}$ to $c_{\alpha(r)}$ through $b$ and of diameter at most equal to the right hand side of (10.101). This arc must be the same for all choices of $b$ in $\mathcal{K}^* \cap K(a)$. Otherwise, as above, $K(a)$ would be the union of two different arcs from $c_{\alpha(\ell)}$ to $c_{\alpha(r)}$, each with diameter at most equal to the right hand side of (10.101). This, however, contradicts the fact that diameter $(K(a))$ $\geq 4\Theta-2\Lambda$ . But for $b = a^{\#}$ the arc from $c_{\alpha(\ell)}$ to $c_{\alpha(r)}$ through $a^{\#}$ is just $K_{\#}$ so that (10.101) and (10.102) follow.

We shall use two consequences of (10.101) and (10.102). These are

$$\text{(10.105)} \qquad R \cap K_{\#} = \emptyset$$

and

$$\text{(10.106)} \qquad X^* \cap K(a) \subset K_{\#} \text{ and hence } X^* \cap K(a) \cap R = \emptyset \ .$$

(10.105) is immediate from (10.101) since $a^{\#} \in K_{\#}$ has distance at least $\Theta$ to $R$ (see (10.78)). The second statement in (10.106) will follow from the first part and (10.105). As for the first part of (10.106), by (10.83) and the construction of $X^*$, any point $c$ of $X^* \cap K(a)$ lies on $r^* \cap K(a) \subset \mathcal{K}^* \cap K(a)$ or lies on the connection of diameter $\leq \Lambda_6$ from the endpoint of $r^*$ to $w_0^*$. Since $|w_0^*-a^{\#}| \leq \Lambda$ , any point $c$ of $X^* \cap K(a)$ lies within distance $\Lambda_6+\Lambda$ from some point $b$ in $\mathcal{K}^* \cap K(a)$. Again by the estimate (10.39) $b$ is then connected to $c$ by an arc $\zeta$ of $K(a)$ of diameter at most

$$3\Lambda_5(\Lambda_6+2\Lambda_3+4\Lambda+1) < \Lambda_8-2\Lambda .$$

On the other hand $b$ is connected to $c_{\alpha(\ell)}$ and $c_{\alpha(r)}$ by two arcs of $K(a)$ of diameter at least

$$\lim_{i=\ell,r} |c_{\alpha(i)}-b| \geq \min_{i=\ell,r} \text{distance}(\mathcal{K}_i,\mathcal{K}^*)-2\Lambda \geq \Lambda_8-2\Lambda$$

(see (10.90)), and as we saw in the proof of (10.101) and (10.102) these arcs have only the point $b$ in common and together make up $K_\#$. $\zeta$ must start out following one of these arcs, and the endpoint of $\zeta$ must come before the endpoint of this arc since

$$\min_{i=\ell,r} |c_{\alpha(i)}-b| > \text{diameter}(\zeta).$$

Consequently $\zeta$ is contained in one of the above arcs from $b$ to $c_{\alpha(i)}$, $i = \ell$ or $r$, and a fortiori $\zeta$ is contained in $K_\#$. This proves (10.106).

We now know that $R$ intersects $K(a)\setminus K_\#$ at least twice (see the lines immediately preceding (10.101), and (10.105)). Therefore if one moves along the arc of $K(a)$ from $c_{\alpha(\ell)}$ to $c_{\alpha(r)}$ which is not $K_\#$, then one passes through at least two points of $R$. Let $R = (v_0,e_1,\dots,e_\nu,v_\nu)$ and let $v_{\beta(\ell)}$ $(v_{\beta(r)})$ be the first (last) point of $R$ one meets in going along $K(a)\setminus K_\#$ from $c_{\alpha(\ell)}$ to $c_{\alpha(r)}$. Denote by $K_i$, $i = \ell$ or $r$, the (closed) arc of $K(a)$ between $c_{\alpha(i)}$ and $v_{\beta(i)}$ which does not contain $K_\#$ (see Fig. 10.16). From the above description we see that $v_{\beta(\ell)} \neq v_{\beta(r)}$, and

(10.107) $$K_i \cap K_\# = \{c_{\alpha(i)}\} \quad K_\ell \cap K_r = \emptyset ,$$

$$K_i \cap R = \{v_{\beta(i)}\} \quad K_\# \cap R = \emptyset .$$

We can now define a new crosscut $\overline{R}$ of $\text{int}(J_\ell)$ which contains $\tilde{X}$ "spliced into $R$" (see Step (i) for $J_\ell$). The path $\overline{R}$ on $\mathcal{G}_{p\ell}$ consists of several pieces. We start with the piece of $R$ from $v_0$ to $v_{\beta(\ell)}$ or $v_{\beta(r)}$, whichever comes first. Let $\gamma$ and $\delta$ be such that

$$\beta(\gamma) = \min(\beta(\ell),\beta(r)), \quad \beta(\delta) = \max(\beta(\ell),\beta(r)) .$$

Thus $\{\gamma,\delta\} = \{\ell,r\}$ and the first piece of $\overline{R}$ is the piece of $R$ from $v_0$ to $v_{\beta(\gamma)}$. $v_{\beta(\gamma)}$ is an endpoint of $K_\gamma$. We now continue $\overline{R}$ along $K_\gamma$ to its other endpoint $c_{\alpha(\gamma)}$. Next we move along $\tilde{X}$ to

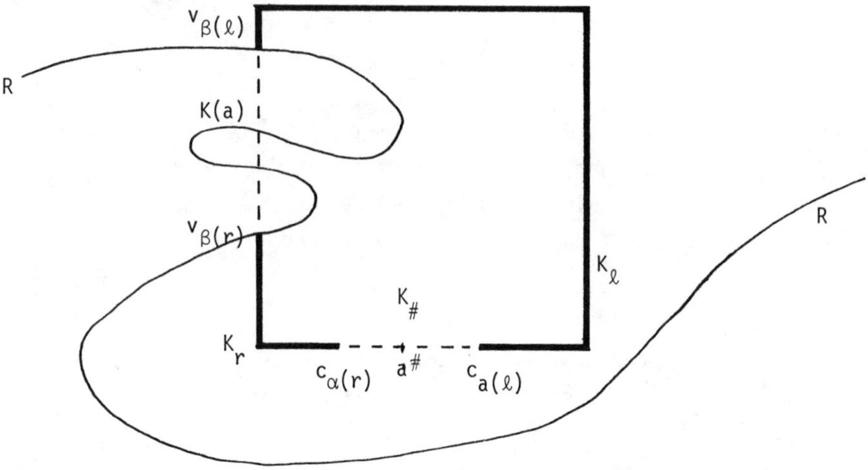


Figure 10.16 Schematic diagram. The dashed and boldly drawn curves together make up the circuit K(a) . The boldly drawn pieces of K(a) are the arcs $K_\ell$ and $K_r$ , while $K_\#$ is the arc between $K_\ell$ and $K_r$ which contains $a^\#$ .

$c_{\alpha(\delta)}$ (recall that $\tilde{X}$ is a path with endpoints $c_{\alpha(\ell)}$ and $c_{\alpha(r)}$). From $c_{\alpha(\delta)}$ we move along $K_\delta$ to $v_{\beta(\delta)}$. The last piece of $\bar{R}$ is the piece of R from $v_{\beta(\delta)}$ to $v_\nu$. The curve traversed in this way from $v_0$ to $v_\nu$ is $\bar{R}$. It is made up of paths on $\mathcal{G}_{p\ell}$, and as we shall now show,

$$\bar{R} \text{ has no double points.}$$

Indeed, since R itself has no double points, and the same holds for the arcs $K_\ell$ and $K_r$ of K(a) and for the path $\tilde{X}$, the only way $\bar{R}$ can have a double point is when $\tilde{X}$ intersects $R \cup K_\ell \cup K_r$ in a point distinct from its endpoints $c_{\alpha(\ell)}$ and $c_{\alpha(r)}$, or if $K_i$ intersects R in a point other than $v_{\alpha(i)}$, $i = \ell$ or r. All these possibilities are ruled out though by (10.100), (10.98) and (10.107). Thus $\bar{R}$ is indeed a self-avoiding path on $\mathcal{G}_{p\ell}$ from $v_0$ to $v_\nu$ . We stress that $\bar{R}$ contains the vertex $\tilde{x}$ of $\tilde{X}$ (see (10.94)).

We want to show that $\bar{R}$ is a crosscut of $J_\ell$, i.e.,

(10.108) $$\bar{R}\setminus\{v_0,v_\nu\} \subset \text{int}(J_\ell),\ v_0 \in B_1, v_\nu \in B_2 .$$

In addition we want to know that $\bar{R}$ lies above $R$, i.e.,

(10.109) $$\bar{R} \subset \bar{J}^+_\ell(R) \text{ and } J^+_\ell(\bar{R}) \subset J^+_\ell(R).$$

We begin with the first inclusion in (10.109). It is clear that the two pieces of $R$ from $v_0$ to $v_{\beta(\gamma)}$ and from $v_{\beta(\delta)}$ to $v_\nu$ belong to $\bar{J}^+_\ell(R)$. Thus, for the first inclusion in (10.109) we only have to show that the connected curve consisting of $K_\ell$, $\tilde{X}$ and $K_r$ lies in $\bar{J}^+_\ell(R)$. As we just saw, (10.100), (10.98) and (10.107) imply that this curve only has its endpoints, $v_{\beta(\ell)}$ and $v_{\beta(r)}$, on $R$. It therefore suffices to show that $K_\ell \cup \tilde{X} \cup K_r \ \{v_{\beta(\ell)}, v_{\beta(r)}\}$ does not intersect $\text{Fr}(J^+(R))$, but contains some point of $J^+_\ell(R)$. As a first step we show

$$a^\# \in J^+_\ell(R).$$

To see this note that $a^\# \in R^\# \setminus R \subset \bar{J}^+_\ell(R)\setminus R$, by virtue of (10.43), (10.78). But neither does $a^\#$ belong to the pieces $B_1, B_2$ or $C$ of $J_\ell$ because $B_1(B_2)$ lies to the left (right) of the vertical line $\{\Lambda_3\} \times \mathbb{R}$ $(\{2M_{\ell 1}-\Lambda_3\} \times \mathbb{R})$ and $C$ lies above the horizontal line $\mathbb{R} \times \{12M_{2\ell}\}$ (see Step (i)), while $a^\# \in K(a)$ with

$$\frac{1}{2} M_{\ell 1}-\Theta-2\Lambda \le a(1) \le \frac{3}{2} M_{\ell 1}+\Theta+2\Lambda$$

(see (10.79)), and $a \in R$, whence

$$a(2) \le 6M_{\ell 2}$$

(see (10.32) and beginning of this Step). Thus, for sufficiently large $\ell$

(10.110) $$\text{distance } (a^\#, B_1 \cup B_2 \cup C) \ge \min\ (\tfrac{1}{2}M_{\ell 1}-\Theta-2\Lambda-\Lambda_3), 6M_{\ell 2}\} - \text{diameter } \bar{K}(a) > 2 \text{ diameter } \bar{K}(a) + \Lambda.$$

We have now shown that $a^\#$ does not belong to $\text{Fr}(J^+_\ell(R)) \subset R \cup B_1 \cup B_2 \cup C$, so that indeed $a^\# \subset J^+_\ell(R)$.

Next, (10.110) shows that $\bar{K}(a) = K(a) \cup \text{int}(K(a))$ does not intersect $B_1 \cup B_2 \cup C$. This and (10.105) imply that $K_\#$ does not intersect $Fr(J_\ell^+(R))$, and since $a^\# \varepsilon K_\#$ we see that

$$c_{\alpha(i)} \varepsilon K_\# \subset J_\ell^+(R), \; i = \ell, r.$$

By virtue of (10.107) we then obtain also

$$K_i \setminus \{v_{\beta(i)}\} \subset J_\ell^+(R), \; i = \ell, r.$$

Finally, we already saw in (10.98) and (10.100) that

$$\tilde{X} \subset \overline{K(a)} \setminus R,$$

which is disjoint from $Fr(J_\ell^+(R))$. Thus also

$$\tilde{X} \subset J_\ell^+(R).$$

This proves the first inclusion of (10.109). In the course of its proof we also saw that $K_\ell \cup \tilde{X} \cup K_r \subset \overline{K}(a)$ does not intersect $B_1 \cup B_2 \cup C$. But neither can $K_\ell \cup \tilde{X} \cup K_r$ intersect the arc $A$ of $J_\ell$ since $A \subset \overline{J_\ell^-}(R) \cap J_\ell$, while

$$K_\ell \cup \tilde{X} \cup K_r \setminus \{v_{\beta(\ell)}, v_{\beta(r)}\} \subset J_\ell^+(R).$$

Also

$$v_{\beta(i)} \varepsilon R \setminus (B_1 \cup B_2) \subset \text{int}(J_\ell) \quad .$$

Thus $K_\ell \cup \tilde{X} \cup K_r \subset \text{int}(J_\ell)$. Since $R$ is a crosscut of $J_\ell$, (7.39) - (7.41) show that $R \setminus \{v_0, v_\nu\} \subset \text{int}(J_\ell)$, $v_0 \varepsilon B_1$, $v_\nu \varepsilon B_2$. (10.108) is now obvious. Finally, the second inclusion in (10.109) follows from the first one, in the same way as (A.40) follows from (A.38) in the Appendix.

As a final step before defining the modified configuration $\tilde{\omega}$ we construct a connection on $\mathcal{G}^*_{p\ell}$ to $\mathring{C}$ above $\overline{R}$. This connection, call it $Y^*$, will consist of $X^*$ - which runs from $v_0^*$ to $w_0^*$ - followed by $s^*$ - which runs from $w_0^*$ to $w_\tau^* \varepsilon \mathring{C}$ (see beginning of this step). Actually $X^*$ followed by $s^*$ could still have double points; $Y^*$ is the path obtained by loop-removal from the composition of $X^*$ and $s^*$. To show that $Y^*$ is a connection from $\tilde{x}$ to $\mathring{C}$ above $\overline{R}$ note first that $Y^*$ ends at $w_\tau^* \varepsilon \mathring{C}$ and that $s^* \setminus \{w_\tau^*\} \subset J_\ell^+(R^\#)$, because by assumption $s^*$ is a vacant connection of $a^\#$ to $\mathring{C}$ above $R^\#$. Thus, by (10.43) $s^* \setminus \{w_\tau^*\} \subset J_\ell^+(R)$ and a fortiori $s^* \setminus \{w_\tau^*\}$ does not intersect $R$. But neither does $s^*$ intersect $K_\ell \cup \tilde{X} \cup K_r \subset \overline{K(a)}$ by virtue of (10.80). Thus, $s^*$ does not intersect the crosscut $\overline{R}$ of $J_\ell$ and ends on $\mathring{C}$. Since some neighborhood of $\mathring{C}$ intersected with $\text{int}(J_\ell)$ belongs to $J^+(\overline{R})$ and $s^* \setminus \{w_\tau^*\} \subset \text{int}(J_\ell)$ we conclude

(10.111) $$s^*\setminus\{w^*_\tau\}\subset J^+_\ell(\overline{R}) .$$

Neither can $X^*$ intersect $\overline{R}$. To see this, observe that we already know that $X^*$ is disjoint from $\tilde{X}$ (see (10.99)) and that $X^*\cap K(a)\subset K_\#$ (see (10.106)). Also $X^*$ does not contain the points $c_{\alpha(\ell)}$ and $c_{\alpha(r)}$ of $K(a)$ since by construction any point of $X^*$ lies on $V^*$ or is within distance $\Lambda_6$ from $\mathcal{H}^*$, while $c_{\alpha(i)}$ has a distance at least $\Lambda_8-2\Lambda$ from $\mathcal{H}^*$ by (10.90), and $V^*\subset \text{int}(K(a))$ by (10.83). This means that

$$X^*\cap(K_\ell\cup K_r)=X^*\cap K(a)\cap(K_\ell\cup K_r)\setminus\{c_{\alpha(\ell)},c_{\alpha(r)}\}$$

$$\subset K_\#\cap(K_\ell\cup K_r)\setminus\{c_{\alpha(\ell)},c_{\alpha(r)}\}=\emptyset\quad\text{(see (10.107))}.$$

Lastly, to show that $X^*$ is disjoint from $R$ we can copy the proof of (10.100) verbatim. $X^*$ too lies within distance $\Lambda_6+4\Lambda+2\Lambda_9$ from $a^\#$. On the one hand, this together with (10.110) shows that $X^*$ does not intersect $B_1\cup B_2\cup C$ for large $\ell$. On the other hand, together with (10.78) this gives

(10.112) $$\text{distance}(X^*,R)\geq\Theta-(\Lambda_6+4\Lambda+2\Lambda_9)>2\Lambda .$$

Thus $X^*$ is disjoint from $\overline{R}\cup B_1\cup B_2\cup C$ and a fortiori from $\text{Fr}(J^+_\ell(\overline{R}))$. Since we already saw that the endpoint $w^*_0\in s^*$ of $X^*$ belongs to $J^+_\ell(\overline{R})$, it follows that all of $X^*$ lies in $J^+_\ell(\overline{R})$. Combined with (10.111) this gives the desired conclusion

(10.113) $$Y^*\setminus\{w^*_\tau\}\subset J^+_\ell(\overline{R}).$$

We note also that the initial point of $Y^*$ = initial point of $X^*=v^*_0$ which is adjacent on $\mathcal{M}_{p\ell}$ to $\tilde{x}$ by Condition Dd) (with $x$ replaced by $\tilde{x}$). Thus $Y^*$ is indeed a connection on $\mathcal{G}^*_{p\ell}$ from $\tilde{x}$ to $\mathring{C}$ above $\overline{R}$. Note that we do not claim $Y^*$ to be vacant, though.

Figure 10.17 illustrates the end result of our construction of $\overline{R}$ and $Y^*$. In Fig. 10.17 we have more or less drawn the various pieces in the same relative location as in Fig. 10.13-10.16.

<u>Step (vii)</u>. We are finally ready to describe the modification $\tilde{\omega}$ of the occupancy configuration $\omega$. We remind the reader that $\omega$ satisfies (10.52). We form $\tilde{\omega}$ by means of the following steps:

(a) Make all sites on $\overline{R}$ which are vacant in $\omega$ occupied in $\tilde{\omega}$.

(b) Make vacant all sites of $\mathcal{G}_{p\ell}$ which lie in $\overline{J^-_\ell(\overline{R})\setminus\overline{R}}$ and which

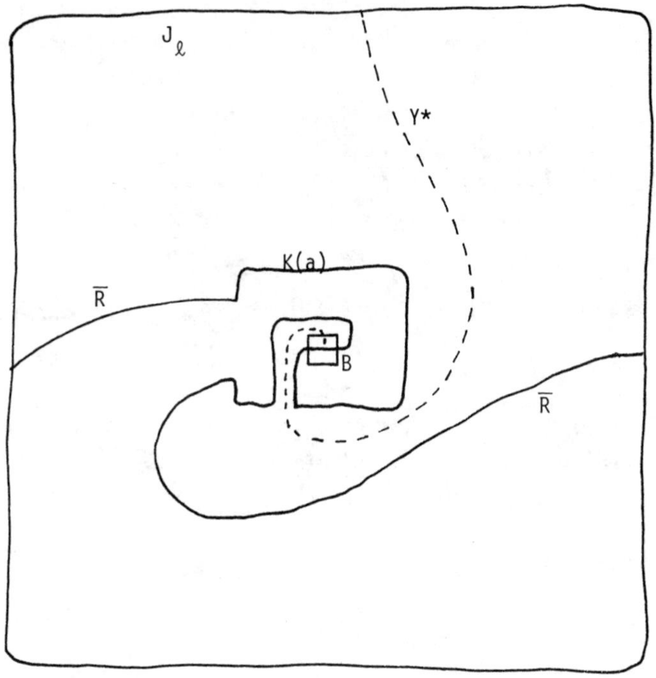


Figure 10.17 The outer circuit is $J_\ell$ . The solidly drawn crosscut is $\overline{R}$ . The dashed path is $Y^*$ . The small square near the center is $B = B(\tilde{x})$, which has $\tilde{x}$ as its center .

can be connected to a vertex on $K_\ell \cup \tilde{X} \cup K_r$ via one or two edges of $\mathcal{G}_{p\ell}$. Excluded from this change are central vertices of $\mathcal{G}_{p\ell}$ which do not belong to $\mathfrak{w}$.

(c) Make all vertices on $Y^*$ vacant.

(d) Make occupied all non-central vertices of $\mathcal{G}^*_{p\ell}$ which lie in $J^+_\ell(\overline{R}) \setminus Y^*$ and which are connected to a point of $X^*$ via one or two edges of $\mathcal{G}^*_{p\ell}$ .

No other changes than the ones listed in (a)-(d) are made in the configuration $\omega$ to obtain $\tilde{\omega}$.

Before we can start on the verification of Condition E we must show that the steps (a)-(d) are compatible, i.e., that they do not require a certain vertex to be made occupied as well as vacant. This is easy, however. Indeed (a) only involves vertices on $\overline{R}$, (b) only vertices in $\overline{J^-_\ell(\overline{R})} \setminus \overline{R}$ and (c) and (d) only vertices in $J^+_\ell(\overline{R}) \cup \mathring{C}$ (by virtue of (10.113)). Thus, Steps (a), (b) and the pair (c) and (d) deal with disjoint sets of vertices. It is also clear that Steps (c) and (d) deal with disjoint sets of vertices. Therefore no conflict exists between any of the required modifications.

We denote by $\tilde{\omega}$ the occupancy configuration which results from $\omega$ by Steps (a)-(d). We check in this step that (10.53)-(10.55) hold for $\tilde{\omega}$. (10.54) is immediate from steps (a)-(d) and the fact that $Y^*$ is a path on $\mathcal{G}^*_{p\ell}$, hence does not contain any central vertices of $\mathcal{G}_{p\ell}$. Thus, in none of the steps is an occupied central vertex of $\mathcal{G}_{p\ell}$ outside $\mathfrak{w}$ made vacant. Also (10.55) is immediate if we take into account that $\overline{R}$ is a path on $\mathcal{G}_{p\ell}$ and hence does not contain central vertices of $\mathcal{G}^*_{p\ell}$. Lastly, (10.53) follows from the fact that $R$ is already occupied and $s^*$ already vacant in the configuration $\omega$ (see beginning of Step (vi), where $R$ and $s^*$ are introduced). Therefore (a) requires only changes of vertices on $K_\ell \cup \tilde{X} \cup K_r \subset \overline{K}(a)$. Also (c) requires only changes of vertices on $X^*$, which by construction lies within distance $\Lambda_6$ from $\overline{K(a)} \cup \mathcal{K}^*$; in turn $\mathcal{K}^*$ lies within distance $\Lambda_9$ from $\overline{K(a)}$ by (10.91) and (10.79). The changes in (b) and (d) lie within $2\Lambda$ from the set $K_\ell \cup \tilde{X} \cup K_r$ or $X^*$. Consequently $\tilde{\omega}(v) \neq \omega(v)$ is only possible for a $v$ within $\Lambda_6+\Lambda_9+2\Lambda$ from $\overline{K(a)}$, which contains $a^{\#}$, and which has diameter $\leq 8\Theta+4\Lambda_3+4\Lambda$ (see (10.38)). This proves (10.53).

<u>Step (viii)</u>. In this step we verify (10.56). The essential part is to show that in the configuration $\tilde{\omega}$ there exists a lowest occupied crosscut $\tilde{R}$ of $\text{int}(J_\ell)$ on $\mathcal{G}_{p\ell}$, which almost equals the path $\overline{R}$, and in particular contains $\tilde{x}$. The existence of a lowest occupied crosscut $\tilde{R}$ of $\text{int}(J_\ell)$ - i.e., an occupied path $\tilde{R}$ on $\mathcal{G}_{p\ell}$ which satisfies (7.39)-(7.41) and such that $J^-_\ell(\tilde{R})$ is minimal among all such paths - follows from Prop. 2.3, because $\overline{R}$ is an occupied crosscut on $\mathcal{G}_{p\ell}$ of $J_\ell$ in $\tilde{\omega}$ (by (10.108) and Step (viia)). Let $\tilde{R} = (y_0,h_1,\dots,h_\lambda,y_\lambda)$. We remind the reader that $R = (v_0,e_1,\dots,e_\nu,v_\nu)$ and that the pieces $(v_0,e_1,\dots,e_{\beta(\gamma)},v_{\beta(\gamma)})$ and $(v_{\beta(\delta)},e_{\beta(\delta)+1},\dots,e_\nu,v_\nu)$ of $R$ are also the first and last piece of $\overline{R}$; between these pieces $\overline{R}$ consists of the composition of $K_\ell$, $\tilde{X}$, and $K_r$ (or this path in reverse). We shall now prove the following statements:

(10.114) $\quad (y_0,h_1,\dots,h_{\beta(\gamma)},y_{\beta(\gamma)}) = (v_0,e_1,\dots,e_{\beta(\gamma)},v_{\beta(\gamma)}),$

(10.115) $\quad (y_{\lambda-\nu+\beta(\delta)},h_{\lambda-\nu+\beta(\delta)+1},\dots,h_\lambda,y_\lambda)$

$$= (v_{\beta(\delta)},e_{\beta(\delta)+1},\dots,e_\nu,v_\nu),$$

(10.116) Any $y_i$ with $\beta(\gamma) < i < \lambda-\nu+\beta(\delta)$ lies within distance $\Lambda$ of a vertex on $K_\ell \cup \tilde{X} \cup K_r$,

(10.117) $\tilde{x}$ is one of the $y_i$ .

Of course (10.114)-(10.116) say that $\tilde{R}$ shares its beginning and last piece with $R$ and $\overline{R}$ and in between deviates only little from $\overline{R}$.

To prove (10.114)-(10.117) we first must assemble some facts about the non-existence of certain shortcuts for $\tilde{R}$. It is convenient to use the following notation. $R(\gamma) = (v_0, e_1, \dots, e_{\beta(\gamma)}, v_{\beta(\gamma)})$, the beginning piece of $R$ and $\overline{R}$; $R(\delta) = (v_{\beta(\delta)}, e_{\beta(\delta)+1}, \dots, e_\nu, v_\nu)$, the last piece of $R$ and $\overline{R}$. Let $z$ be an arbitrary point of $R(\gamma) \setminus v_{\beta(\gamma)}$. Since $R$ and $\overline{R}$ are crosscuts of $\text{int}(J_\ell)$ which have the piece $R(\gamma)$ in common, there exist arbitrarily small neighborhoods $N$ of $z$ such that

$$N \cap \text{int}(J_\ell) \setminus R = N \cap \text{int}(J_\ell) \setminus R(\gamma) = N \cap \text{int}(J_\ell) \setminus \overline{R}$$

and such that $N \cap \text{int}(J_\ell) \setminus R$ consists of two components, $N^+$ and $N^-$ say, with

(10.118) $$N^+ \subset J_\ell^+(R), \quad N^- \subset J_\ell^-(R).$$

We claim that for any such $N$ also

(10.119) $$N^+ \subset J_\ell^+(\overline{R}), \quad N^- \subset J_\ell^-(\overline{R}).$$

This is easy to see from (10.109). Indeed (10.109) implies

$$J_\ell^-(R) = \text{int}(J_\ell) \setminus \overline{J_\ell^+(R)} \subset \text{int}(J_\ell) \setminus \overline{J_\ell^+(\overline{R})} = J_\ell^-(\overline{R})$$

and hence

$$N^- \subset J_\ell^-(\overline{R}).$$

But $N \cap \text{int}(J_\ell) \setminus \overline{R}$ consists of the two connected sets $N^-$ and $N^+$, and $N \cap \text{int}(J_\ell) \setminus \overline{R}$ must intersect $J_\ell^+(\overline{R})$ as well as $J_\ell^-(\overline{R})$ (since $N$ is a neighborhood of a point $z$ on the crosscut $\overline{R}$ of $\text{int}(J_\ell)$; see Newman (1951), Theorem V.11.7). Thus both inclusions in (10.119) must hold.

We use (10.119) to prove that if $\omega$ satisfies (10.52) then

(10.120) there does not exist a shortcut of one or two edges of $\overline{R}$ inside $\overline{J_\ell^-(\overline{R})}$, which has one endpoint among $v_0, v_1, \dots, v_{\beta(\gamma)-1}, v_{\beta(\delta)+1}, \dots, v_\nu$ .

(See Def. 10.2 and Step (iv), for the definition of shortcuts.) Suppose first that the edge $e$ of $\mathcal{G}_{p\ell}$ is a shortcut of $\overline{R}$ of one edge which runs from some $v_i$, $0 \le i \le \beta(\gamma)-1$ to a vertex $u$ of $\overline{R}$, and is such that $e \subset \overline{J_\ell^-}(\overline{R})$. Then by Def. 10.2 $e$ is not an edge of $\overline{R}$ itself, since $u$ is a vertex of $\overline{R}$ which is not the immediate predecessor or successor of $v_i$ on $\overline{R}$. But then $\mathring{e}$ is disjoint from $\overline{R}$. $\mathring{e}$ also cannot belong to $J_\ell$ because then both $v_i$ and $u$ must belong to $J_\ell \cap \overline{R} = \{v_0, v_\nu\}$ and the vertices $v_0$ and $v_\nu$ on $B_1$ and $B_2$ respectively (see (7.40), (7.41)) are too far apart to be connected by the single edge $e$. Thus, by the planarity of $\mathcal{G}_{p\ell}$, $\mathring{e}$ is also disjoint from $J_\ell$. Since $e \subset \overline{J_\ell^-}(\overline{R})$ this implies $\mathring{e} \subset J_\ell^-(\overline{R})$. Therefore, if $N$ is a neighborhood of $v_i$ for which (10.118) and (10.119) hold, then $\mathring{e} \cap N \subset N^- \subset J_\ell^-(R)$. Consequently $\mathring{e} \subset J_\ell^-(R)$ entirely. On the other hand $u$ is a vertex on $\overline{R} \subset \overline{J_\ell^+}(R)$ (by (10.109)) so that $u \in \overline{J_\ell^-}(R) \cap \overline{J_\ell^+}(R) = R$. This means that $e$ connects $v_i$ with $u$, two vertices of $R$, while $\mathring{e}$ lies strictly below $R$, i.e., in $J_\ell^-(R)$. Replacing the arc of $R$ between $v_i$ and $u$ by $e$ then gives an occupied crosscut of $J_\ell$ which lies in $\overline{J_\ell^-}(R)$ and which is not equal to $R$. This contradicts the choice of $R$ as the occupied (in the configuration $\omega$) crosscut of $\text{int}(J_\ell)$ with minimal $J_\ell^-(R)$; see Prop. 2.3. Thus, no shortcut of one edge for $\overline{R}$ exists which lies inside $\overline{J_\ell^-}(\overline{R})$ and has one endpoint among $v_0, \dots, v_{\beta(\gamma)-1}$.

Next suppose that $e, u, f$ is a shortcut of two edges for $\overline{R}$ inside $\overline{J_\ell^-}(\overline{R})$ which starts at some $v_i$, $0 \le i \le v_{\beta(\gamma)-1}$. In this case $u$ must be a central vertex of $\mathcal{G}_{p\ell}$ which neither belongs to $\mathfrak{w}$ nor is one of the vertices $v_j$, $0 \le j \le \beta(\gamma)$ of $\overline{R}$. This again excludes the possibility that $e$ belongs to $R$ or to $J_\ell$ (since $J_\ell$ lies on $\mathcal{M}$ and contains therefore no central vertices; see Step (i)). As above this implies $\mathring{e} \subset J_\ell^-(R)$. On the other hand the endpoint other than $u$ of $f$ lies on $\overline{R} \subset \overline{J_\ell^+}(R)$ (see (10.109)). Consequently $\mathring{e}, u, f$ intersects $R$, necessarily in a vertex, $w$ say, of $\mathcal{G}_{p\ell}$. Thus $e$ followed by $f$ contains a path, $t$ say, from $v_i$ to $w$, $t$ lies in $J_\ell^-(R)$, except for its endpoints $v_i$ and $w$ on $R$. $t$ can contain at most one vertex not on $R$, to wit the vertex $u$. But as a central vertex of $\mathcal{G}_{p\ell}$ not in $\mathfrak{w}$, $u$ is occupied in the configuration $\omega$ (by (10.52)). Thus we would have the occupied path $t$ below $R$ connecting the two vertices $v_i$ and $w$ on $R$. As above this contradicts the minimality of $R$. This proves the cases of (10.120) where the shortcut has one endpoint among $v_i$, $0 \le i \le \beta(\gamma)-1$. The same argument can be used for the $v_i$ with

$\beta(\delta)+1 \leq i \leq \nu$ .

We conclude from (10.120) that any shortcuts for $\overline{R}$ in $\overline{J}_\ell^-(\overline{R})$ have to have their endpoints on $K_\ell \cup \tilde{X} \cup K_r$ (this includes $v_{\beta(\gamma)}$ and $v_{\beta(\delta)}$). $K_\ell$ and $K_r$ are pieces of $K(a)$, hence minimal paths (see (10.36)). $\tilde{X}$ was even taken strongly minimal in Step (vi). There can still be shortcuts for $\overline{R}$ between these three pieces. Some of these will be harmless but we have to rule out shortcuts between points on "opposite sides of $\tilde{x}$". Shortcuts from $\tilde{X}_\ell(\tilde{x})\setminus\{\tilde{x}\}$ to $\tilde{X}_r(\tilde{x})\setminus\{\tilde{x}\}$ are already ruled out by (10.96) (see (10.95) for the definition of $\tilde{X}_\ell$ and $\tilde{X}_r$). We now prove

(10.121) there do not exist shortcuts of one or two edges of $\overline{R}$ inside $\overline{J}_\ell$ with one endpoint on $\tilde{X}_\ell(\tilde{x})$ and the other on $K_r$ or with one endpoint on $\tilde{X}_r(\tilde{x})$ and the other on $K_\ell$.

Again we give an indirect proof of (10.121). Assume that $e$ or $(e,u,f)$ is a shortcut of $\overline{R}$ connecting a vertex $z_1$ on $K_\ell$ with a vertex $z_2$ on $\tilde{X}_r(\tilde{x})$. Then by (10.97)

$$|z_2-c_{\alpha(\ell)}| \leq 2\Lambda \quad \text{or} \quad |z_2-c_{\alpha(r)}| \leq 2\Lambda \ .$$

Since by construction $c_{\alpha(\ell)}$ lies on $K(a)$ and within $2\Lambda$ from $b_\ell \in \mathcal{K}_\ell$ it has distance $> 2\Lambda$ from $\tilde{X}_r(\tilde{x})$, by (10.90) and (10.83). ($\tilde{X}_r$ contains only points within $2\Lambda$ from $U$ or within $\Lambda_6+4\Lambda$ from $r_r \subset \mathcal{K}_r$, as in (10.77).) Thus

$$|z_2-c_{\alpha(r)}| \leq 2\Lambda \quad \text{and} \quad |z_1-c_{\alpha(r)}| \leq |z_1-z_2| + |z_2-c_{\alpha(r)}| \leq 4\Lambda \ .$$

By the estimate (10.39), there must then exist an arc $K_1$ of $K(a)$ from $z_1$ to $c_{\alpha(r)}$ with

$$\text{(10.122)} \qquad \operatorname{diameter}(K_1) \leq 3\Lambda_5(7\Lambda+2\Lambda_3+1).$$

Now, since $z_1 \in K_\ell$ one arc between $z_1$ and $c_{\alpha(r)}$ contains $c_{\alpha(\ell)}$ and the arc $K_\#$ from $c_{\alpha(\ell)}$ to $c_{\alpha(r)}$ (see Fig. 10.18). Since the diameter of $K_\#$ is at least (see (10.90))

$$|c_{\alpha(\ell)}-c_{\alpha(r)}| \geq |b_\ell-b_r|-4\Lambda \geq \operatorname{distance}(\mathcal{K}_\ell,\mathcal{K}_r)-4\Lambda \geq \Lambda_8-4\Lambda,$$

which exceeds the right hand side of (10.122). Thus $K_1$ must be the other arc of $K(a)$ from $z_1$ to $c_{a(r)}$. However, this second arc of $K(a)$ from $z_1$ to $c_{\alpha(r)}$ has to contain $K_r$ from $v_{\beta(r)}$ to $c_{\alpha(r)}$

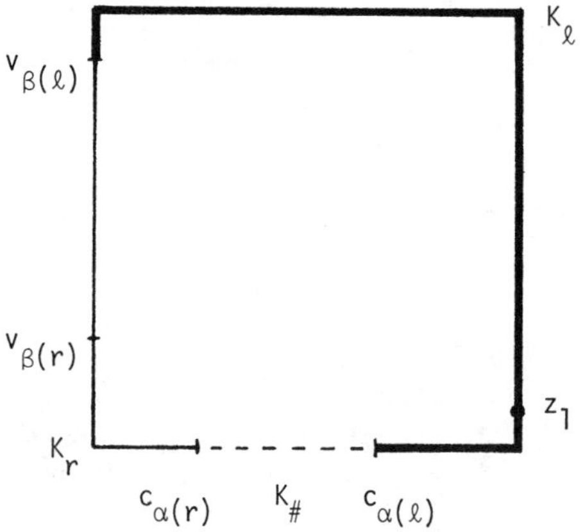


Figure 10.18 Schematic diagram of $K(a)$ indicating the relative location of various points. $K_\ell$ is boldly drawn; $K_\#$ is dashed.

and this has diameter at least

$$(10.123)\qquad |v_{\beta(r)}-c_{\alpha(r)}| \geq |v_{\beta(r)}-a^\#| - |c_{\alpha(r)}-a^\#| \geq \Theta-\Lambda_9-2\Lambda$$

since $|v_{\beta(r)}-a^\#| \geq \Theta$ (by (10.78)) and

$$|c_{\alpha(r)}-a^\#| \leq |c_{\alpha(r)}-b_r| + |b_r-a^\#| \leq 2\Lambda+\Lambda_9 ,$$

(by (10.91)). But the right hand side of (10.123) also exceeds the right hand side of (10.122), so that neither arc of $K(a)$ from $z_1$ to $c_{\alpha(r)}$ is possible for $K_1$. This contradiction proves that there is no shortcut of $\bar{R}$ from a vertex on $K_\ell$ to a vertex on $\tilde{X}_r(x)$. The same argument shows that there is no shortcut from $K_r$ to $\tilde{X}_\ell(x)$ and therefore proves (10.121).

Our final claim about shortcuts is that if $\omega$ satisfies (10.52), then

(10.124) there do not exist shortcuts of one or two edges for $\bar{R}$ in $\bar{J}_\ell^-(\bar{R})$ with one endpoint on each of $K_\ell$ and $K_r$ .

We prove (10.124) for shortcuts of two edges, the case of a shortcut of one edge being similar, but easier. Assume $(e,u,f)$ is a shortcut of two edges for $\overline{R}$ in $J_\ell^-(\overline{R})$, which starts at $z_1$ on $K_\ell$ and ends at $z_2$ on $K_r$. Let $K_2$ be the arc of $K(a)$ which connects $z_1$ to $z_2$ and is contained in $K_\ell \cup K_\# \cup K_r$ (see Fig. 10.19). As above

$$\text{(10.125)} \qquad \text{diameter}(K_2) \geq \text{diameter}(K_\#) \geq \Lambda_8 - 4\Lambda > 3\Lambda_5(5\Lambda+2\Lambda_3+1).$$

On the other hand the estimate (10.39), together with the fact $|z_1 - z_2| \leq 2\Lambda$, implies that there exists an arc $K_3$ of $K(a)$ from $z_1$ to $z_2$ with

$$\text{diameter}(K_3) \leq 3\Lambda_5(5\Lambda+2\Lambda_3+1).$$

Thus $K_3$ is not $K_2$, but $K_3$ must be the arc through $v_{\beta(\ell)}$ and $v_{\beta(r)}$ (see Fig. 10.19). Now consider the closed curve $G$ consisting

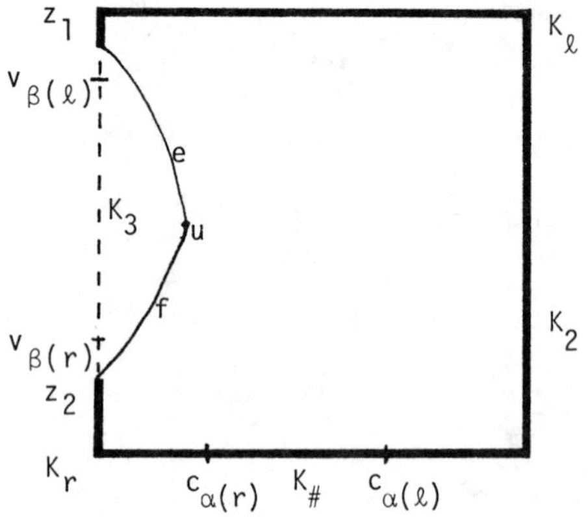


Figure 10.19 Schematic diagram of $K(a)$ indicating the relative location of various parts. $K_2$ is boldly drawn, $K_3$ is dashed.

of $K_2$ from $z_1$ to $z_2$ followed by $f$ and $e$. $G$ is a path with possible double points on $\mathcal{G}_{p\ell}$. We first show that

(10.126) $\qquad G$ is a simple Jordan curve.

Since $K(a)$ is a simple Jordan curve, the only way $G$ could have a double point is when $u \in K_2 \subset K_\ell \cup K_\# \cup K_r$. But $u \notin K_\ell \cup K_r \subset \overline{R}$ because if $(e,u,f)$ is a shortcut of two edges for $\overline{R}$, then $u$ is not a vertex of $\overline{R}$ (see Step (iv)). But also $u \varepsilon K_{\#}$ is impossible for then $e$ and $f$ are edges with both endpoints on $K(a)$, and therefore[1] $e$ followed by $f$ would be an arc of $K(a)$ from $z_1$ to $z_2$ containing a point of $K_{\#}$. This could only happen if $e$ followed by $f$ constitutes the arc $K_2$ - which would go through the point $u$ of $K_{\#}$ - and consequently diameter $(K_2) \leq 2\Lambda$ . Since this is excluded by (10.125), it follows that (10.126) holds.

Next we observe that $a \varepsilon \text{int}(G)$. This must be so because by definition of $K(a)$ $a \varepsilon \text{int}(K(a))$ at a distance at least $2\Theta-\Lambda-1$ from any point of $K(a)$ (see (10.37)). On the other hand $G$ is formed from $K(a)$ by replacing the arc $K_3$ between $z_1$ and $z_2$ by $e \cup f$. Since

$$\text{diameter}(K_3)+\text{diameter}(e)+\text{diameter}(f)$$

$$\leq 3\Lambda_5(5\Lambda+2\Lambda_3+1)+2\Lambda < \Theta < 2\Theta-\Lambda-1 \quad ,$$

this replacement cannot take $a$ from $\text{int}(K(a))$ to $\text{ext}(G)$.

We now have the point $a$ of $R$ (see (10.79)) in $\text{int}(G)$, while $v_0 \varepsilon B_1$ is outside $G$, because $B_1$ is to the left of the vertical line $x(1) = \Lambda_3$ (see Step (i)) and

$$a(1) \geq \frac{1}{2} M_{\ell 1}-\Theta-2\Lambda > \text{diameter}(G)+\Lambda_3$$

for large $\ell$ (see (10.79)). Similarly, $v_\nu$ is outside $G$. Therefore $R$ must intersect $G$ in at least two distinct vertices of $\mathcal{G}_{p\ell}$, such that $R$ intersects $\text{int}(G)$ in arbitrarily small neighborhoods of each of these vertices. By (10.105) $R$ does not intersect $K_{\#}$, while by choice of $K_\ell$ and $K_r$ $R$ intersects $K_\ell \cup K_r$ only in $v_{\beta(\ell)}$ and $v_{\beta(r)}$ (see (10.107)). If $v_{\beta(\ell)}$ $(v_{\beta(r)})$ belongs to $G$ at all, then it must equal $z_1$ $(z_2)$, and in particular, belong to $e$ $(f)$ (see Fig. 10.19 and recall that $u \notin K_2$). It follows from this and from $G \subset K_\ell \cup K_{\#} \cup K_r \cup e \cup f$ that $R \cap G$ is contained in $e \cup f$. Starting at $v_0$ $R$ must therefore enter $\text{int}(G)$ through a vertex on $e \cup f$ and exit again through another vertex of $e \cup f$ to reach $v_\nu$. Since $e \cup f$ contains only the three vertices $z_1$, $u$ and $z_2$, $R$ must intersect $\text{int}(G)$ as well as $\text{ext}(G)$ in arbitrarily small neighborhoods of one of the $z_i$.

---

1) A little care is needed here because we allowed multiple edges between a pair of vertices. However, in the present case $u$ is a central vertex of $\mathcal{G}_{p\ell}$, and the construction of $\mathcal{G}_{p\ell}$ in Sect. 2.3 is such that there exists exactly one edge in $\mathcal{G}_{p\ell}$ between a central vertex and any of its neighbors.

For the sake of argument let this happen at $z_1$. Then $z_1$ belongs to $K_\ell \cap R = \{v_{\beta(\ell)}\}$ , i.e., $z_1 = v_{\beta(\ell)}$ and one of the edges $e_{\beta(\ell)}$ or $e_{\beta(\ell)+1}$ of $R$ has its interior in int(G) and the other in ext(G). This means that $R$ intersects $G$ transversally at $z_1 = v_{\beta(\ell)}$. But the arc $K_\ell$ from $v_{\beta(\ell)}$ to $c_{\alpha(\ell)}$ belongs to G, since $z_1 = v_{\beta(\ell)}$ and $z_2 \in K_r$ (see Fig. 10.19). As we saw in the proof of (10.109) this arc belongs to $J_\ell^+(R)$, or more precisely

$$K_\ell \setminus \{v_{\beta(\ell)}\} \subset J_\ell^+(R).$$

This, together with the transversality of $R$ and $G$ at $v_{\beta(\ell)}$ forces

$$\mathring{e} \subset J_\ell^-(R).$$

We are now in the same situation as in the proof (10.120). $\mathring{e}$ would have to be part of a path below $R$ of one or two edges, and occupied in the configuration $\omega$. No such path exists by the minimality of $J_\ell^-(R)$ and Prop. 2.3. (10.124) follows from this contradiction.

With (10.96), (10.120), (10.121) and (10.124) in hand, it is now relatively simple to prove (10.114)-(10.117). Assume first (10.114) fails and let $\xi$ be the smallest index with $h_\xi \neq e_\xi$. Then $1 \le \xi \le \beta(\gamma)$. Since $\tilde{R}$ satisfies (7.39)-(7.41) $\mathring{h}_\xi \subset \text{int}(J_\ell)$. Now consider first the case $\xi \ge 2$. Then by the minimality of $\xi$, $y_{\xi-1} = v_{\xi-1} \in R$ as well as $y_{\xi-1} = v_{\xi-1} \in \bar{R}$. Since $h_\xi \neq e_\xi$ and $\mathcal{G}_{p\ell}$ is planar, it follows that $\mathring{h}$ does not intersect $\bar{R}$, and for all sufficiently small neighborhoods $N$ of $v_{\xi-1}$

$$\mathring{h}_\xi \cap N \subset (\tilde{R} \cap N) \setminus (J_\ell \cup \bar{R}). \tag{10.127}$$

On the other hand $\tilde{R}$ is the occupied crosscut of $\text{int}(J_\ell)$ in the configuration $\tilde{\omega}$ with $J_\ell^-(\tilde{R})$ minimal. In particular

$$\tilde{R} \subset \overline{J_\ell^-(\bar{R})} \ , \tag{10.128}$$

since also $\bar{R}$ is an occupied crosscut of $\text{int}(J_\ell)$ in $\tilde{\omega}$, (by Step (viia); see also (2.27)). Thus, by (10.127) and (10.128),

$$\mathring{h}_\xi \cap N \subset N \cap (\overline{J_\ell^-(\bar{R})} \setminus \text{Fr}(J_\ell^-(\bar{R})) = N \cap J_\ell^-(\bar{R}).$$

In view of (10.118) and (10.119) this means also

$$\mathring{h}_\xi \cap N \subset N \cap J_\ell^-(R)$$

for suitable $N$. Since $h_\xi \neq e_\xi$ implies also that $\mathring{h}_\xi$ does not intersect $R$ - again because $\mathcal{G}_{p\ell}$ is planar - it follows that

(10.129) $$\overset{\circ}{h}_\xi \subset J_\ell^-(R).$$

Exactly the same argument works if $\xi = 1$ and $y_0$ lies on $\overline{R}$, for then $y_0 \in \overline{R} \cap B_1 = \{v_0\}$, i.e., $y_0 = v_0$. On the other hand, if $y_0$ does not lie on $\overline{R}$, then automatically $\xi = 1$ and $h_1$ cannot reach $\overline{R}$ or $R$ before $y_1$, i.e., $\overset{\circ}{h}_1 = \overset{\circ}{h}_\xi$ is again disjoint from $Fr(J_\ell^-(\overline{R}))$ and from $Fr(J_\ell^-(R))$ (use the analogue of (7.40) for $\tilde{R}$). Since also

$$h_1 \subset \tilde{R} \subset \overline{J}^-(\overline{R}),$$

the initial point $y_0$ of $h$ belongs to the part of $B_1$ in $Fr(J_\ell^-(\overline{R}))\setminus \overline{R}$, which is the segment between $u_1$ and $v_0$ (apply (7.40) to $\overline{R}$ and see Fig. 10.9). But this segment of $B_1$ from $u_1$ to $v_0$ also equals $Fr(J_\ell^-(R))\setminus R$ so that $\overset{\circ}{h}_1$ belongs to $J_\ell^-(R)$ near $y_0$. (10.129) therefore holds in the case $\xi = 1$ as well.

To derive a contradication from (10.129) we consider the set

$$\Xi := \{\text{vertices of } \mathcal{G}_{p\ell} \text{ which are vacant in } \omega \text{ but occupied in } \tilde{\omega}\}.$$

If $\tilde{R}$ has no vertex in $\Xi$, then $\tilde{R}$ is also an occupied crosscut of $\text{int}(J_\ell)$ in the configuration $\omega$. In this case (2.27) shows that $\tilde{R} \subset \overset{\circ}{\overline{J}}{}_\ell^+(R)$, and therefore $\tilde{R}$ cannot contain any part of any edge - such as $h_\xi$ - strictly below $R$. Thus, if (10.114) fails, and hence (10.129) holds, then $\tilde{R}$ must contain a vertex in $\Xi$. Let $\pi$ be the smallest index with $y_\pi \in \Xi$. Now observe that by Steps (viia)-(viid) and (10.109)

$$\Xi \subset \overline{J}_\ell^+(\overline{R}) \subset \overline{J}_\ell^+(R).$$

Also, all vertices on $R$ are occupied in $\omega$, hence are outside $\Xi$, so that

(10.130) $$\Xi \subset \overline{J}_\ell^+(R)\setminus R, \text{ whence } \quad \Xi \cap \overline{J}_\ell^-(R) = \emptyset .$$

By definition of $\xi$ and (10.129), $y_0,\dots,y_{\xi-1} \in \overline{J}_\ell^-(R)$ (even when $\xi = 1$) and hence by (10.130) $\pi \geq \xi$. We claim that

(10.131) $$y_i \notin R \quad \text{for} \quad \xi \leq i \leq \pi .$$

Indeed, if (10.131) would fail and $j$ would be the smallest index $\geq \xi$ with $y_j \in R$, then $j \leq \pi$ and the path $(y_{\xi-1},h_\xi,\dots,h_j,y_j)$ minus its endpoints $y_{\xi-1},y_j$ would lie in $J_\ell^-(R)$ (by (10.129)) and have all its vertices $y_\xi,\ldots,y_{j-1}$ occupied in $\omega$ since $j \le \pi$. This would again contradict the minimality of $J_\ell^-(R)$ in the configuration $\omega$. Thus (10.131) holds. On the other hand, by (10.129), the path $(y_{\xi-1},h_\xi,\ldots,h_\pi,y_\pi)$ starts with $\overset{\circ}{h}_\xi$ in $J_\ell^-(R)$, and by (10.130) cannot reach $\Xi$ without intersecting $R$. This contradiction proves the impossibility of (10.129). Thus (10.114) must hold.

(10.115) must hold for the same reasons as (10.114). We merely have to interchange the roles of $B_1$ and $v_0$ with the roles of $B_2$ and $v_\nu$.

Next we prove (10.116) and (10.117). Let $\bar{R} = (\bar{y}_0,\bar{h}_1,\ldots,\bar{h}_\kappa,\bar{y}_\kappa))$. We already know from (10.114) and the definition of $\bar{R}$ that

$$y_i = \bar{y}_i = v_i,\ 0 \le i \le \beta(\gamma), \text{ and } h_j = \bar{h}_j = e_j,\ 1 \le j \le \beta(\gamma).$$

Now assume for a certain $i$

(10.132) $y_i = \bar{y}_j$ for some $j$ with $y_i = \bar{y}_j \in K_\ell \cup \tilde{X} \cup K_r$ .

By (10.114) this holds for $i = j = \beta(\gamma)$. If $h_{i+1}$ is an edge of $\bar{R}$, then we can simply move along $h_{i+1}$ to $y_{i+1}$ and then (10.132) also holds with $y_i$ replaced by $y_{i+1}$ (unless $y_{i+1} \notin K_\ell \cup \tilde{X} \cup K_r$). The case of interest is the one where $h_{i+1}$ is not an edge of $\bar{R}$. First consider the case where $y_{i+1}$ again belongs to $\bar{R}$. Then the edge $h_{i+1}$ forms a shortcut of one edge for $\bar{R}$. It lies necessarily below $\bar{R}$, i.e., in $\overline{J_\ell^-}(\bar{R})$ because of (10.128). By (10.120), (10.121), (10.124) the endpoints of $h_{i+1}$, $y_i = \bar{y}_j$ and $y_{i+1} = \bar{y}_k$ say, must in this case both belong to $K_\ell \cup \tilde{X}_\ell(\tilde{x})$, both to $K_r \cup \tilde{X}_r(\tilde{x})$, or both to $\tilde{X}$. The last case cannot occur because $\tilde{X}$ is a minimal path, by construction. In the other two cases $\tilde{x}$ does not occur between $\bar{y}_j$ and $\bar{y}_k$ on $\bar{R}$ since $\tilde{X}_i(\tilde{x})$ is the piece of $\tilde{X}$ between $\tilde{X} \cap K_i$ and $\tilde{x}$, $i = \ell$ or $r$, by the definition (10.95). Note that $\tilde{x} = \bar{y}_j$ or $\tilde{x} = \bar{y}_k$ is not excluded, though. In any case, if we replace the segment of $\bar{R}$ between $\bar{y}_j$ and $\bar{y}_k$ by $h_{i+1}$ then $\tilde{x}$ still lies on the modified path. Moreover, $y_{i+1} = \bar{y}_k$ will again be a vertex of $\tilde{R}$ on $\bar{R}$, and as long as $y_{i+1} \in K_\ell \cup \tilde{X} \cup K_r$ we are back to (10.132) with $y_i$, $\bar{y}_j$ replaced by $y_{i+1}$, $\bar{y}_k$.

The other possibility allowed by (10.132) is that $y_{i+1}$ does not belong to $\bar{R}$. Since $y_{i+1} \in \tilde{R} \subset \overline{J_\ell^-}(\bar{R})$ (by (10.128)) this implies $y_{i+1} \in \overline{J_\ell^-}(\bar{R}) \setminus \bar{R}$. Also, since $y_{i+1} \in \tilde{R}$ it must be occupied in the configuration $\tilde{\omega}$, and by Step (viib) this means that $y_{i+1}$ has to be a central vertex of $\mathcal{G}_{p\ell}$ which does not belong to $\mathfrak{w}$. The neighbor $y_{i+2}$ of $y_{i+1}$ is then not a central vertex of $\mathcal{G}_{p\ell}$ (Comment 2.3(iv)). Again by Step (viib) it follows that $y_{i+2}$ cannot lie in $\bar{J}_\ell^-(\bar{R})\setminus\bar{R}$. Since $y_{i+2}$ is an endpoint of $h_{i+1}$ - which starts at $y_{i+1} \in \bar{J}^-(\bar{R})\setminus\bar{R}$ - we have $y_{i+2} \in \bar{J}_\ell^-(\bar{R})$, and hence $y_{i+2} \in \bar{R}$, say $y_{i+2} = \bar{y}_k$. Thus, in this case either $\bar{y}_j$ and $\bar{y}_k$ are successive points of $\bar{R}$ or $(h_{i+1},y_{i+1},h_{i+2})$ is a shortcut of two edges for $\bar{R}$ in $\bar{J}_\ell^-(R)$. Again, if we replace the segment of $\bar{R}$ between $\bar{y}_j$ and $\bar{y}_k$ by $(h_{k+1},y_{i+1},h_{i+2})$, then we do not remove $\tilde{x}$. This is obvious if $\bar{y}_k$ and $\bar{y}_j$ are successive points on $\bar{R}$, while the argument is essentially as above in case $(h_{i+1},y_{i+1},h_{i+2})$ is a shortcut for $\bar{R}$. The only new case to consider this time is the one where the shortcut runs between two points of $\tilde{X}$. But then (10.96) guarantees that $\tilde{x}$ is not removed during the replacement. Once again, with $\bar{y}_k$ we are back at (10.132) with $y_i$, $\bar{y}_j$ replaced by $y_{i+2}$, $\bar{y}_k$ . Starting with $y_{\beta(\gamma)}$ , which satisfies (10.132) we use the above argument until we arrive at $y_{\lambda-\nu+\beta(\delta)} = \bar{y}_{\kappa+\nu+\beta(\delta)}$ after which

$$(y_{\lambda-\nu+\beta(\delta)},h_{\lambda-\nu+\beta(\delta)+1},\dots,h_\lambda,y_\lambda)$$

$$= (\bar{y}_{\kappa-\nu+\beta(\delta)},\bar{h}_{\kappa-\nu+\beta(\delta)+1},\dots,\bar{h}_\kappa,\bar{y}_\kappa)$$

$$= (v_{\beta(\delta)},e_{\beta(\delta)+1},\dots,e_\nu,v_\nu)$$

by (10.115) and the definition of $\bar{R}$. It follows from this that $\tilde{R}$ is formed from R by replacing a number of pieces of $\bar{R}$ between two vertices of $\bar{R}$ on $K_\ell \cup \tilde{X} \cup K_r$ by pieces of $\tilde{R}$ of one or two edges. None of these replacements results in the removal of $\tilde{x}$. This proves (10.116) and (10.117).

Finally we complete the proof of (10.56). The existence of the crosscut $\tilde{R}$ of $\text{int}(J_\ell)$ with minimal $J_\ell^-(\tilde{R})$, and containing $\tilde{x}$ from $\mathfrak{w}_0$ we already proved (see especially (10.117)). We know from (10.93) and (10.33) that

$$|\tilde{x}-a^{\#}| \le \Theta \quad .$$

Also, we showed at the end of Step (vi) that $Y^*$ is a connection on $\mathcal{G}_{p\ell}^*$ from $\tilde{x}$ to $\mathring{C}$ above $\bar{R}$. But $\tilde{R} \subset \bar{J}_\ell^-(\bar{R})$ (see (10.128)) and this implies

$$J_\ell^+(\bar{R}) \subset J_\ell^+(\tilde{R}) \tag{10.133}$$

as shown by the derivation of (A.41) from (A.38). Thus $Y^*$ is also a connection from $\tilde{x}$ to $\overset{\circ}{C}$ above $\tilde{R}$. Moreover it is vacant in the configuration $\tilde{\omega}$ by Step (viic). Thus, everything claimed in (10.56) has been verified.

Step (ix). In this step we complete the deduction of Condition E by verifying (10.57). Let $y \in \mathfrak{w}_0$ be a vertex of $\tilde{R}$ and let $Z^* = (z_0^*, k_1^*, \dots, k_\theta^*, z_\theta^*)$ be a vacant connection on $\mathcal{G}_{p\ell}^*$ (in the configuration $\tilde{\omega}$) from $y$ to $\overset{\circ}{C}$ above $\tilde{R}$ (cf. the definition (10.49)-(10.51) with $\Gamma = \mathbb{R}^2$). If $y$ is not one of the $v_i$ with $0 \le i < \le \beta(\gamma)-1$ or $\beta(\delta)+1 \le i \le \nu$, then by (10.114)-(10.116) $y$ lies within distance $\Lambda$ from $K_\ell \cup \tilde{X} \cup K_r \subset \overline{K}(a)$. Since $a^\# \in K(a)$, (b) of (10.57) holds for such $y$ with $\kappa_3$ = diamter(K)+$\Lambda$ . Thus we may restrict ourselves to $y = v_i \in \overline{R}$ with $0 \le i < \beta(\gamma)$; the case where $y = v_i$ with $\beta(\delta) < i \le \nu$ is similar.

We begin by showing that

(10.134) $\quad Z^*$ is a vacant connection (in $\tilde{\omega}$) from $y$ to $\overset{\circ}{C}$ above $\overline{R}$.

The point of (10.134) is that $Z^*$ is even above $\overline{R}$, not only above $\tilde{R}$. To see (10.134) we observe that (by requirement (10.49)) there exists an edge $k^*$ of $\mathcal{M}_{p\ell}$ between $y$ and $z_0^*$ such that $\overset{\circ}{k}{}^* \subset J_\ell^+(\tilde{R})$. Thus for any small neighborhood $N$ of $y$

$$\overset{\circ}{k}{}^* \cap N \subset N \cap J_\ell^+(\tilde{R}).$$

However, now that we have (10.114) we can use the argument which derives (10.119) from (10.118) - with (10.133) or (10.128) replacing (10.109) - to obtain also

$$N \cap J_\ell^+(\tilde{R}) = N \cap J_\ell^+(\overline{R})$$

for suitable small neighborhoods $N$ of $y$. For such $N$ one has

$$\overset{\circ}{k}{}^* \cap N \subset N \cap J_\ell^+(\overline{R}).$$

Thus, near $y$ $\overset{\circ}{k}{}^*$ lies in $J_\ell^+(\overline{R})$, and then all of $\overset{\circ}{k}{}^*$ lies in $J_\ell^+(\overline{R})$. This is the analogue of (10.49) for $Z^*$ and $\overline{R}$ instead of $s^*$ and $r$. The analogue of (10.50) is $z_\theta^* \in \overset{\circ}{C}$, which is true because $Z^*$ is a connection to $\overset{\circ}{C}$. To prove (10.134) it therefore suffices to show

(10.135) $$Z^* \setminus \{z_\theta^*\} \subset J_\ell^+(\overline{R}).$$

Since $\overset{\circ}{k} \subset J_\ell^+(\overline{R})$ and $z_0^*$ is an endpoint of $k$, hence in $\overline{J}_\ell^+(\overline{R})$, and since $Z^* \setminus \{z_\theta^*\} \subset \text{int}(J_\ell)$ (by (10.51) with $r$ replaced by $\tilde{R}$), (10.135) can fail only if some point of $Z^*$ lies on $\overline{R}$. The first intersection of $Z^*$ and $\overline{R}$ has to be one of the vertices $z_i^*$ in this case, say $z_\xi^*$. $z_\xi^*$ also has to be a vertex of $\overline{R}$. This is not possible for then $z_\xi^*$ has to vacant in the configuration $\tilde{\omega}$, being on $Z^*$, as well as occupied, being a vertex of $\overline{R}$, which is occupied in $\tilde{\omega}$, by Step (viia). Thus (10.135) and (10.134) hold.

We now introduce

$$\Xi^* := \{\text{vertices of } \mathcal{G}_{p\ell}^* \text{ which are occupied in } \omega \text{ but vacant in } \tilde{\omega}\} .$$

If $Z^*$ has no vertex in $\Xi^*$, then $Z^*$ is also vacant in the configuration $\omega$. Moreover $J_\ell^+(\overline{R}) \subset J_\ell^+(R)$, as we saw in (10.109), so that in this case, by virtue of (10.134) $Z^*$ is a vacant connection from $y$ to $\overset{\circ}{C}$ above $R$ in the configuration $\omega$. Thus in this case (a) of (10.57) holds. There remains the case where $Z^*$ has a vertex in $\Xi^*$. We shall now show that (a) of (10.57) must hold in this case as well. To prove this, let $z_\eta^*$ be the first vertex of $Z^*$ in $\Xi^*$. By Step (vii)(a)-(d),

$$\Xi^* \cap (\overline{J}_\ell^+(\overline{R}) \setminus \overline{R}) \subset Y^* .$$

Actually, we saw in the proof of (10.53) at the end of Step (vii) that Step (viic) requires only changes in the occupancies of vertices on $X^*$. Therefore

$$\Xi^* \cap (\overline{J}_\ell^+(\overline{R}) \setminus \overline{R}) \subset X^*. \tag{10.136}$$

In particular $z_\eta^*$ is a vertex on $X^* \cap Y^*$ and we can define $\pi$ as the smallest index $i \leq \eta$ with $z_i^* \in X^* \cap Y^*$. Since $z_0^*$ and $z_1^*$ are within distance $2\Lambda$ of $y \in R$, and since (10.112) shows that distance $(X^*,R) > 2\Lambda$, $z_0^*$ and $z_1^*$ cannot lie on $X^*$. Therefore

$$2 \leq \pi \leq \eta \quad .$$

Now $z_{\pi-1}^*$ and $z_{\pi-2}^*$ both lie in $J_\ell^+(\overline{R})$ (by (10.135)) and they can be connected by one or two edges of $\mathcal{G}_{p\ell}^*$ to $z_\pi^* \in X^*$. Being vertices of $Z^*$, $z_{\pi-1}^*$ and $z_{\pi-2}^*$ have to be vacant in the configuration $\tilde{\omega}$. In view of Step (viid) this means that both $z_{\pi-1}^*$ and $z_{\pi-2}^*$ have to be central vertices of $\mathcal{G}_{p\ell}^*$ or belong to $Y^*$. If $z_{\pi-1}^* \in Y^*$, then

$$z_{\pi-1}^* \in Y^* \setminus X^* \subset s^*$$

(see the construction of $Y^*$ towards the end of Step (vi)). If $z^*_{\pi-1}$ is the vertex $w^*_\phi$ of $s^*$, then

$$(10.137)\qquad (z^*_0, k^*_1, \dots, k^*_{\pi-1}, z^*_{\pi-1} = w^*_\phi, f^*_{\phi+1}, \dots, f^*_\tau, w^*_\tau)$$

is a path with possible double points on $\mathcal{G}^*_{p\ell}$, consisting of the beginning piece of $Z^*$, until an intersection of $Z^*$ and $s^*$, and a final piece of $s^*$ from this intersection of $s^*$ with $Z^*$ to $w^*_\tau \in \mathring{C}$. This path is vacant in the configuration $\omega$, since $z^*_0, \dots, z^*_{\pi-1}$ do not lie in $\Xi^*$ and are vacant in $\tilde{\omega}$, while $s^*$ is a vacant connection in $\omega$ from $a^\#$ to $\mathring{C}$ above $R^\#$ (see beginning of Step (vi)). Also, as we saw above

$$\mathring{k}^* \subset J^+_\ell(\bar{R}) \subset J^+_\ell(R) \quad (\text{cf. } (10.109)),$$

$$(z^*_0, k^*_1, \dots, k^*_{\pi-1}, z^*_{\pi-1}) \subset Z^* \setminus \{z^*_\theta\} \subset J^+_\ell(\bar{R}) \subset J^+_\ell(R)$$
$$(\text{cf. } (10.135), (10.109)),$$

and finally, because $s^*$ is a connection to $\mathring{C}$ above $R^\#$

$$(w^*_\phi, f^*_{\phi+1}, \dots, f^*_\tau \setminus \{w^*_\tau\}) \subset s^* \setminus \{w^*_\tau\} \subset J^+_\ell(R^\#) \subset J^+_\ell(R) \quad (\text{cf.} (10.43)).$$

It follows from this that the path in (10.137) after loop-removal, to make it self-avoiding, forms a vacant connection in $\omega$ from $y$ to $\mathring{C}$ above $R$. Thus, if $z^*_{\pi-1} \in Y^*$, then (a) of (10.57) holds. The same argument works if $z^*_{\pi-2} \in Y^*$. This leaves only the case where neither $z^*_{\pi-1} \in Y^*$ nor $z^*_{\pi-2} \in Y^*$. This case, however, cannot arise, for as we saw above this would require both $z^*_{\pi-1}$ and $z^*_{\pi-2}$ to be central vertices of $\mathcal{G}^*_{p\ell}$. Since $z^*_{\pi-1}$ and $z^*_{\pi-2}$ are neighbors on $\mathcal{G}^*_{p\ell}$ this is impossible (Comment 2.3 (iv)). We have thus proved (10.57) in all cases and completed the proof of Condition E.

# 11. RESISTANCE OF RANDOM ELECTRICAL NETWORKS.

## 11.1 Bounds for resistances of networks.

Many people have studied the electrical resistance of a network made up of random resistors. It was realized quite early that critical phenomena occur, and that there is a close relation with percolation theory, in special cases where the individual resistors can have infinite resistance (or zero resistance). We refer the reader to Kirkpatrick (1978) and Stauffer (1979) for a survey of much of this work. In these introductory paragraphs we shall assume that the reader knows what the resistance of a network is, but we shall come back to a description of resistance in Sect. 11.3.

A typical problem in which the relation with percolation is apparent is the following. Consider the graph $\mathbb{Z}^d$, with vertices the integral vectors in $\mathbb{R}^d$, and edges between two vertices $v_1$ and $v_2$ iff $|v_1-v_2| = 1$. Assume each edge of $\mathbb{Z}^d$ is a resistance of 1 ohm with probability $p$, and is removed with probability $q = 1-p$. As usual all edges are assumed independent of each other. Let $\mathcal{H}_n$ be the restriction of the resulting random network to the cube of size $n$, $B_n = [0,n]^d$. What is the behavior for large $n$ of the resistance in $\mathcal{H}_n$ between the left and right face of $B_n$? More precisely let

$$(11.1) \qquad A^0 = A_n^0 = \{v = (v(1),\dots,v(d)): v(1) = 0, 0 \le v(i) \le n, \; 2 \le i \le d\}$$

be the left face of $B_n$ and

$$(11.2) \qquad A^1 = A_n^1 = \{v = (v(1),\dots,v(d)): v(1) = n, 0 \le v(i) \le n, \; 2 \le i \le d\}$$

the right face. Form a new network from $\mathcal{H}_n$ by identifying as one vertex $a_0$ all vertices of $\mathbb{Z}^d$ in $A^0$, and by identifying all vertices of $\mathbb{Z}^d$ in $A^1$ as another vertex $a_1$. This means that we view all edges of $\mathcal{H}_n$ which run between the hyperplanes $x(1) = 0$ and $x(1) = 1$ as having the common endpoint $a_0$ in $x(1) = 0$. In "reality" one would have to connect all vertices in $A^0$ by wires made from some super material which has zero electrical resistance. The same has to be done for the vertices in $A^1$. $R_n$ is the resistance in $\mathcal{H}_n$ between $a_0$ and $a_1$ after this identification of vertices.

For small $p$ there will with high probability be no path at all in $\mathcal{H}_n$ connecting $A_n^0$ with $A_n^1$. Of course $R_n = \infty$ if no such path exists. Therefore

$$P_p\{R_n = \infty\} \to 1 \quad \text{as} \quad n \to \infty \qquad \text{for small } p.$$

On the other extreme, if $p = 1$, $\mathcal{H}_n$ becomes the restriction of $\mathbb{Z}^d$ to $B_n$. One easily verifies that in this situation $V(x) := x(1)/n$ is the potential at $x$ when $A_n^0$ $(A_n^1)$ is given the potential $0(1)$ by means of an external voltage source. Indeed Kirchhoff's and Ohm's laws give that $V(\cdot)$ is the unique function which satisfied

$$\sum_{\substack{y \in B_n : y \\ \text{adjacent to } x}} (V(y)-V(x)) = 0, \; x \in B_n \setminus A_n^0 \cup A_n^1$$

(i.e., $V(\cdot)$ is harmonic on $B_n \setminus A_n^0 \cup A_n^1$) and which has boundary value $0(1)$ on $A_n^0$ $(A_n^1)$ (see Feynman et al (1963), Sect. I.25.4,5 and II.22.3, Nerode and Shank (1961) or Slepian (1968), Ch. 7.3; also Sect. 11.3 below). Thus, by Ohm's law the current leaving $A^0$ equals $(n+1)^{d-1} \frac{1}{n}$. (There are $(n+1)^{d-1}$ edges of resistance 1 ohm between $A_n^0$ and the hyperplane $x(1) = 1$ in $B_n$; the potential difference across each edge is $1/n$.) Thus, if $p = 1$, $R_n = n(n+1)^{1-d}$. It is therefore reasonable to conjecture that $n^{d-2}R_n$ converges in some sense to a finite and non-zero (random) limit as $n \to \infty$, at least when $p$ is large enough. We do not know how to prove such a result, but the results in this chapter establish that $n^{2-d}$ gives the correct order of magnitude of $R_n$ when $p > \frac{1}{2}$. For $d = 2$ we obtain much more precise information on $R_n$ for all $p$.

Of course removing an edge $e$ is equivalent to giving $e$ an infinite resistance. A dual problem arises when each edge of $\mathbb{Z}^d$ is a resistor of 1 ohm (has zero resistance) with probability $p(q = 1-p)$. The resistance $R_n$ between $A_n^0$ and $A_n^1$ of the restriction to $B_n$ of $\mathbb{Z}^d$ will now be zero as soon as there exists a single path in $B_n$ containing only edges of zero resistance and connecting $A_n^0$ with $A_n^1$. The probability of $\{R_n = 0\}$ will therefore tend to one as $n \to \infty$ for large enough p, but for small $p$ $n^{d-2}R_n$ should be bounded away from zero.

In the theorems below we shall combine both situations. In fact we shall allow for an arbitrary distribution of the resistances of the individual edges. We restrict ourselves to the graph $\mathbb{Z}^d$, and for most of the results even to $\mathbb{Z}^2$. It is clear, however, that a good part of the method of proof used for $\mathbb{Z}^2$ will work when $\mathbb{Z}^2$ is replaced by another graph $\mathcal{G}$ imbedded in $\mathbb{R}^2$ which is one of a matching pair $(\mathcal{G},\mathcal{G}^*)$ for which $p_T(\mathcal{G}) = p_S(\mathcal{G}) = 1-p_T(\mathcal{G}^*)$.

Before formulating our results we point out that continuum analogues of the resistance problem have been studied as well. For instance Papanicolaou and Varadhan (1979) and Golden and Papanicolaou (1982) (see especially Appendix) assume that the conductivity of a certain material is a random process, indexed by position in $\mathbb{R}^d$ (rather than time). This process is assumed stationary. Under suitable assumptions the asymptotic behavior of the conductivity of $B_n$ between $A_n^0$ and $A_n^1$ for the random medium is the same as that of a certain deterministic "effective" medium. Golden and Papanicolaou (1982) give bounds for the conductivity of the effective medium. A related sequence of bounds for the conductivity in a composite medium can be found in Milton (1981). However, these bounds seem to apply only for a material of two components, both of which have a finite non-zero conductivity.

We turn to the precise formulation of our theorems. It turns out that in the first mentioned problem a good way to estimate $R_n$ is to find a lower bound for the number of disjoint paths in $\mathcal{H}_n$ from $A_n^0$ to $A_n^1$. In other words, we try to find many disjoint conducting paths (i.e., paths each of whose edges has finite resistance) in $B_n$ from the left to the right face. This part of the analysis is pure percolation theory. For a closer match with the previous chapters we treat this part as a site percolation problem. Let $\mathcal{G}$ be a periodic graph imbedded in $\mathbb{R}^d$. By definition of $p_S = p_S(\mathcal{G})$ (see (3.65)) the probability under $P_p$ that there exists any occupied path on $\mathcal{G}$ in $B_n$ from $A_n^0$ to $A_n^1$ tends to zero (as $n \to \infty$) whenever $p < p_S$. For many of the graphs in $\mathbb{R}^2$ which we considered the same probability tends to one when $p > p_S$. We now define a new critical probability as the dividing point where lots of disjoint occupied paths in $B_n$ from $A_n^0$ to $A_n^1$ begin to appear. Specifically, we want of the order of $n$ such paths. With $P_p$ the one-parameter probability measure defined by (3.22) and (3.61) and i-crossings as in Def. 3.1 we define

(11.3) $$\hat{p}_R = \hat{p}_R(\mathcal{G}) = \inf\{p: \exists\ C(p) > 0 \text{ such that } P_p\{\exists\ C(p)n \text{ disjoint occupied 1-crossings of } [0,n]^d \text{ for all large } n\} = 1\}.$$

Clearly $\hat{p}_R \geq p_S$. It is also not hard to show that in general (cf. (1.16))

$$p_R \leq \hat{p}_R .$$

This is an easy consequence of the fact that the harmonic mean is less than or equal to the arithmetic mean. The proof of this relation between $p_R$ and $\hat{p}_R$ is implicit in the proof of Theorem 11.2 (see the lines preceding (11.81). We shall not make this proof any more explicit. Instead we concentrate on the much harder and more crucial relation

$$\hat{p}_R = p_S \quad ,$$

which holds for many graphs in $\mathbb{R}^2$. Since we are also interested in an estimate for $C(p)$ in (11.3) in terms of powers of $(p-p_H(\mathcal{G}))$ we want to appeal to the results of Ch. 8. We therefore restrict ourselves to proving $\hat{p}_R = p_S$ only for the graphs $\mathcal{G}_0$, $\mathcal{G}_1$, $\mathcal{G}_0^*$ and $\mathcal{G}_1^*$ introduced in Ex. 2.1(i), 2.1(ii), 2.2(i) and 2.2(ii). (See, however, Remark (i) below.)

Theorem 11.1. Let $\mathcal{G}$ be one of the graphs $\mathcal{G}_0$, $\mathcal{G}_1$, $\mathcal{G}_0^*$ or $\mathcal{G}_1^*$ and let $P_p$ be the one-parameter probability measure on the occupancy configurations of $\mathcal{G}$ of the form (3.22) and specified by (3.61). Then for some universal constants $0 < C_i, \delta_i < \infty$ one has

(11.4) $$P_p\{\exists \text{ at least } C_1(p-p_H(\mathcal{G}))^{\delta_1} n \text{ disjoint occupied horizontal crossings on } \mathcal{G} \text{ of } [0,m]\times[0,n]\} \geq 1-C_2(m+1)\exp\{-C_3(p-p_H(\mathcal{G}))^{\delta_2} n\} ,$$

whenever $p \geq p_H(\mathcal{G})$.

Remarks.

(i) The proof given below can be used to show that for any $\mathcal{G}$ which is one of a matching pair of periodic graphs in $\mathbb{R}^2$ there exist constants $0 < C_i = C_i(p,\mathcal{G}) < \infty$ for which

(11.5) $$P_p\{\exists \text{ at least } C_1 n \text{ occupied horizontal crossings on } \mathcal{G} \text{ of } [0,m]\times[0,n], \text{ no pair of which has a vertex in common}\} \geq 1-C_2 m \exp -C_3 n,$$

whenever $p > 1-p_T(\mathcal{G}^*)$.

(ii) The proof below for Theorem 11.1 is largely taken from Grimmett and Kesten (1982). The estimate in the latter paper does, however, differ slightly from (11.4). It replaces $C_1(p-p_H(\mathcal{G}))^{\delta_1}n$ inside the braces in (11.4) by $(\mu-\varepsilon)n$, where $\mu$ is the time constant of a certain first-passage percolation problem (see Smythe and Wierman (1978) for such problems) and then shows that on $\mathbb{Z}^2$ the number of edge disjoint occupied crossings of $[0,m]\times[0,n]$ is actually of the order $\mu n$ for $n^{-1}\log m$ small. The fact that one can give a lower bound of the form $C_1(p-p_H(\mathcal{G}))^{\delta_1}$ for the time constant $\mu$ of the first passage percolation under consideration was pointed out to the author by J. T. Cox (private communication ). It is this observation which leads to the $C_1(p-p_H(\mathcal{G}))^{\delta_1}n$ in the left hand side of (11.4). Grimmett and Kesten (1982) do not pursue the dependence on $p$ of the various constants, but instead are interested in the exponential bound (11.5) with $C_1$ as large as possible (all the way up to $\mu$). ///

We return to the resistance problem on $\mathbb{Z}^d$. We shall assume that each edge has a resistance $R(e)$ with all $R(e)$, $e$ an edge of $\mathbb{Z}^d$, independent random variables, all with the same distribution given as follows:

(11.6) $$P\{R(e) = 0\} = p(0),$$

(11.7) $$P\{R(e) = \infty\} = p(\infty),$$

and for any Borel set $B \subset (0,\infty)$

(11.8) $$P\{R(e) \in B\} = \int_B dF(x)$$

for some measure $F$ on $(0,\infty)$ with total mass $1-p(0)-p(\infty)$.

In the next two theorems $\theta_d(p)$ will denote the percolation probability for bond-percolation on $\mathbb{Z}^d$ under the measure $P_p$ according to which all edges are independently open or passable (blocked) with probability $p(q = 1-p)$. Thus, for any edge $e$ of $\mathbb{Z}^d$

$$\theta_d(p) = P_p\{e \text{ belongs to an infinite open cluster}\}.$$

Also $p_{S,d}$ will be the critical probability of (3.65) for bond-percolation on $\mathbb{Z}^d$. In Theorem 11.2 we take $d = 2$ so that in (11.11) $\theta_2(p)$ also equals the percolation probability for site-percolation on $\mathcal{G}_1$, i.e., $\theta_2(p) = P_p\{v$ belongs to an infinite occupied cluster on $\mathcal{G}_1\}$ for $v$ any vertex of $\mathcal{G}_1$ and $P_p$ given by (3.22) and (3.61) with $\mathcal{V}$ the vertex set of $\mathcal{G}_1$ (compare Ch. 3.1; $\mathcal{G}_1$ is introduced in Ex. 2.1(ii)).

Theorem 11.2. Assume the edges of $\mathbb{Z}^2$ have independent resistances with distribution given by (11.6)-(11.8). Let $R_n$ be the resistance between $A_n^0$ and $A_n^1$ of the network in $B_n$. Then

(11.9) $$P\{R_n = 0 \text{ eventually}\} = 1 \quad \text{if} \quad p(0) > \frac{1}{2},$$

(11.10) $$P\{R_n = \infty \text{ eventually}\} = 1 \quad \text{if} \quad p(\infty) > \frac{1}{2}.$$

Moreover there exist constants $0 < C_i, \delta_i < \infty$ such that if $p(0) < \frac{1}{2}$ and $p(\infty) < \frac{1}{2}$, then

(11.11) $$P\Big\{C_4 \frac{(\frac{1}{2} - p(0))^{2\delta_1}}{\theta_2(1-p(\infty))} \Big\{\int_{(0,\infty)} \frac{1}{x}\, dF(x)\Big\}^{-1} \le \liminf_{n\to\infty} R_n$$

$$\le \limsup_{n\to\infty} R_n \le C_5 \frac{\theta_2(1-p(0))}{(\frac{1}{2} - p(\infty))^{2\delta_1}} \int_{(0,\infty)} x\, dF(x)\Big\} = 1,$$

($\delta_1$ is the same as in (11.4)).

Corollary 11.1. Let the set up be the same as in Theorem 11.2. Then there exist constants $0 < C_i, \delta_i < \infty$ such that for $p(0) = 0$, $p(\infty) < \frac{1}{2}$ one has

(11.12) $$P\Big\{C_6 (\tfrac{1}{2} - p(\infty))^{-\delta_3} \Big\{\int_{(0,\infty)} \frac{1}{x}\, dF(x)\Big\}^{-1} \le \liminf R_n$$

$$\le \limsup R_n \le C_5 (\tfrac{1}{2} - p(\infty))^{-2\delta_1} \int_{(0,\infty)} x\, dF(x)\Big\} = 1.$$

If, on the other hand, $p(0) < \frac{1}{2}$, $p(\infty) = 0$, then

(11.13) $$P\Big\{C_4 (\tfrac{1}{2} - p(0))^{2\delta_1} \Big\{\int_{(0,\infty)} \frac{1}{x}\, dF(x)\Big\}^{-1} \le \liminf R_n$$

$$\le \limsup R_n \le C_7 (\tfrac{1}{2} - p(0))^{\delta_3} \int_{(0,\infty)} x\, dF(x)\Big\} = 1.$$

Remarks.

(iii) If $\int_{(0,\infty)} \frac{1}{x}\, dF(x) = \infty$ then $\{\int_{(0,\infty)} \frac{1}{x}\, dF(x)\}^{-1}$ is to be interpreted as zero, and the lower bounds for $R_n$ in (11.11)-(11.13) become vacuous. Similarly the upper bounds become vacuous if $\int_{(0,\infty)} x\, dF(x) = \infty$. Nevertheless it is possible to use Theorem 11.2 to obtain non-trivial bounds for $R_n$ in such cases by truncation. For example, assume that $\int x\, dF(x) = \infty$ and $p(0) < \frac{1}{2}$, $p(\infty) < \frac{1}{2}$. Define $m$ as the unique finite number for which

$$F((m,\infty)) \leq \frac{1}{2}(\frac{1}{2} - p(\infty)) \leq F([m,\infty)).$$

Now take for each edge $e$

$$R'(e) = R(e) \quad \text{if} \quad R(e) < m,$$

$$R'(e) = \infty \quad \text{if} \quad R(e) > m \quad (\text{including } R(e) = \infty) .$$

If $R(e) = m$, then randomize again for $R'(e)$ and take

$$R'(e) = m \quad \text{with probability} \quad F([m,\infty)) - \frac{1}{2}(\frac{1}{2} - p(\infty))$$

and

$$R'(e) = \infty \quad \text{with probability} \quad \frac{1}{2}(\frac{1}{2} - p(\infty)) - F((m,\infty)).$$

Again the randomizations for $R'(e)$ when $R(e) = m$ are done independently for all edges. Then $R'(e) \geq R(e)$ for all $e$, and if $R_n'$ denotes the resistance between $A_n^0$ and $A_n^1$ in $B_n$ when we use the $R'(e)$ instead of the $R(e)$ then (see Lemma 11.4 below)

$$R_n' \geq R_n .$$

Since

$$P\{R'(e) = \infty\} = p(\infty) + \frac{1}{2}(\frac{1}{2} - p(\infty)),$$

we obtain from (11.11) applied to $R_n'$

(11.14)
$$P\{\limsup R_n \leq \limsup R_n' \leq C_5 2^{2\delta_1} \frac{\theta_2(1-p(0))}{(\frac{1}{2} - p(\infty))^{2\delta_1}} \int_{(0,m]} x\, dF(x)\} = 1$$

whenever $m > 0$. In a similar way one can truncate $R(e)$ near zero to obtain a nonzero lower bound for $\liminf R_n$ when $p(0) < \frac{1}{2}$ and $\int \frac{1}{x}\, dF(x) = \infty$.

(iv) Theorem 11.2 as stated gives no information when $p(0) = \frac{1}{2}$ or $p(\infty) = \frac{1}{2}$. Actually, from (11.11) and simple monotonicity arguments one obtains

(11.15) $P\{\lim R_n = \infty\} = 1$ if $p(0) < \frac{1}{2} = p(\infty)$

and

(11.16) $P\{\lim R_n = 0\} = 1$ if $p(0) = \frac{1}{2} > p(\infty)$.

For example, to obtain (11.15) one merely has to randomize $R(e)$ when $R(e) = \infty$ and to take

$$R''(e) = \begin{cases} 1 & \text{with probability } \varepsilon \\ \infty & \text{with probability } 1-\varepsilon , \end{cases}$$

but to take $R''(e) = R(e)$ when $R(e) < \infty$ (11.15) is then obtained by applying (11.11) to the $R''(e)$ instead of $R(e)$ and taking the limit as $\varepsilon \downarrow 0$.

Finally, when $p(0) = p(\infty) = \frac{1}{2}$, $F$ = zero measure, then

(11.17) $$\lim_{n\to\infty} P\{R_n = 0\} = \lim_{n\to\infty} P\{R_n = \infty\} = \frac{1}{2} .$$

We shall not prove (11.17), but merely note that if each $R(e) = 0$ or $\infty$ then also $R_n = 0$ or $\infty$, and $R_n = 0$ if and only if there is a path in $B_n$ from $A_n^0$ to $A_n^1$ all of whose edges have zero resistance. The probability of this event is precisely the sponge-crossing probability $S_{1/2}(n+1,n+1)$ of Seymour and Welsh (1978) and Seymour and Welsh (1978, pp.233, 234) already show $S_{1/2}(n+1,n+1) \geq S_{1/2}(n,n+1) = \frac{1}{2}$.

(v) When $p(0) = p(\infty) = 0$ percolation theory does not really enter. One can then trivially estimate $R_n$ from above by the resistance of the network consisting of the $(n+1)$ parallel (disjoint) paths $\{k\} \times [0,n]$, $k = 0,\dots,n+1$. A very much simplified version of the proofs of Theorems 11.2 and 11.3 then yields

(11.18) $$\{\int_{(0,\infty)} \frac{1}{x}\, dF(x)\}^{-1} \leq \liminf R_n \leq \limsup R_n \leq \int_{(0,\infty)} x\, dF(x).$$

This bound has apparently been known for a long time (see Milton (1981) and its references).

(vi) It seems very likely that $\lim n^{d-2} R_n$ exists in some sense. Golden and Papanicolaou (1982), Appendix, show that $R_n$ converges in $L^2(P)$ when $d = 2$, $p(0) = p(\infty) = 0$ and $F$ concentrated on an interval $[a,b]$, $0 < a < b < \infty$. Their proof actually deals with the continuum analogue but appears to apply as well in our set up. Straley (1977) uses duality arguments to discuss the case $d = 2$, $p(0) = p(\infty) = 0$, $P\{R(e) = a\} = P\{R(e) = b\} = \frac{1}{2}$ for some $0 < a < b < \infty$. These arguments show that in whatever sense $R_n$ has a limit, the value of the limit should be $(a\, b)^{1/2}$. In particular by the above result of Golden and Papanicolaou $E\{R_n - (ab)^{1/2}\}^2 \to 0$ as $n \to \infty$. ///

For $d > 2$ our results are quite incomplete.

Theorem 11.3. Assume the edges of $\mathbb{Z}^d$ have independent resistances with distribution given by (11.6)-(11.8). Let $R_n$ be the resistance between $A_n^0$ and $A_n^1$ of the network in $B_n$. Then

$$P\{R_n = 0 \text{ eventually}\} = 1 \quad \text{if} \quad p(0) \geq \frac{1}{2} \tag{11.19}$$

and

$$P\{R_n = \infty \text{ eventually}\} = 1 \quad \text{if} \quad 1-p(\infty) < p_{S,d}\,. \tag{11.20}$$

Moreover, there exist constants $0 < C_i, \delta_i < \infty$ such that

$$P\{\liminf n^{d-2} R_n \geq \frac{1-p(\infty)}{\theta_d(1-p(\infty))} \{\int_{(0,\infty)} \frac{1}{x}\, dF(x)\}^{-1}\} = 1 \tag{11.21}$$

$$\text{if} \quad p(0) = 0,$$

and

$$P\{\limsup n^{d-2} R_n \leq \frac{C_9}{(\frac{1}{2} - p(\infty))^{2\delta_1}} \int_{(0,\infty)} x\, dF(x)\} = 1 \tag{11.22}$$

$$\text{if} \quad p(0) < \frac{1}{2} \text{ and } p(\infty) < \frac{1}{2}\,.$$

($\delta_1$ is the same as in (11.4).)

## 11.2 Proof of Theorem 11.1.

We shall only prove a weakened version of (11.4). This will suffice for Theorems 11.2 and 11.3. Instead of obtaining $C_1(p-p_H(\mathcal{G}))^{\delta_1} n$ disjoint occupied crossings of $[0,m] \times [0,n]$ as desired in (11.4) we only obtain this many crossings no pair of which has a vertex in common. Thus the occupied crossings are only vertex-disjoint. For a planar graph such as $\mathcal{G}_0$ this means that the crossings are actually disjoint, but not for a non-planar graph such as $\mathcal{G}_1$. To obtain disjoint crossings one should carry out the argument below (with a number of complicating modifications) on $\mathcal{G}_{p\ell}$.

Now for the proof of the weakened version of (11.4). We restrict ourselves to the case $\mathcal{G} = \mathcal{G}_1$, the other cases being quite similar. We take for $A_1$ the zig zag curve strictly to the left of $\{0\} \times [0,n]$, starting at $(-1,\frac{1}{2})$, going to $(-\frac{3}{2},1)$, then to $(-1,\frac{3}{2})$ and extended periodically, with final point $(-1,n-\frac{1}{2})$. Similarly $A_3$ is a zig-zag curve strictly to the right of $\{m\} \times [0,n]$, from $(m+1,\frac{1}{2})$ to $(m+1,n-\frac{1}{2})$ (see Fig. 11.1). Also $A_2$ is a zig-zag curve from $(-1,\frac{1}{2})$ to $(m+1,\frac{1}{2})$ lying strictly above $[0,m] \times \{0\}$ and obtained by periodic repetition of the segments from $(-1,\frac{1}{2})$ to $(-\frac{1}{2},1)$ to $(0,\frac{1}{2})$ etc. $A_4$ is a similar path strictly below $[0,m] \times \{n\}$ from $(-1,n-\frac{1}{2})$ to $(m+1,n-\frac{1}{2})$. The composition of $A_1$-$A_4$ is a Jordan curve on $\mathcal{M}$, where $\mathcal{M}$ is the mosaic on which $\mathcal{G}_1$ is based ($\mathcal{M}$ is $\mathbb{Z}^2$ rotated over 45° and

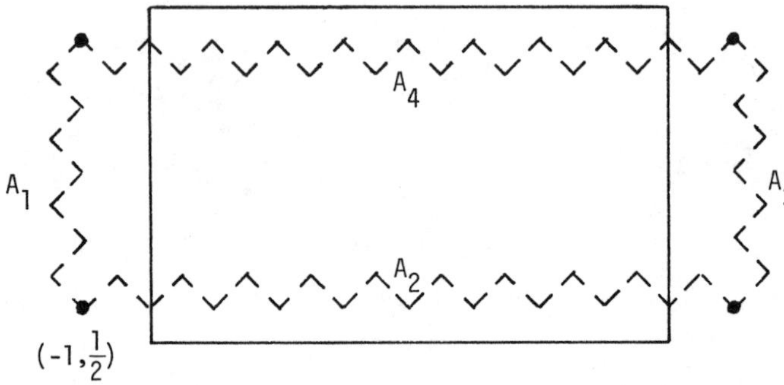


Figure 11.1 The solid rectangle is $[0,m] \times [0,n]$
The dashed curve is $J$.

translated by $(\frac{1}{2},0)$. $\mathcal{G}_1$ is imbedded as in Ex. 2.1(ii); see Fig.2.3). Any path on $\mathcal{G}_1$ in $\bar{J} = J \cup \text{int}(J)$ from a vertex on $A_1$ to a vertex on $A_3$, and with all its sites in $\bar{J} \setminus A_1 \cup A_3$ occupied, contains an occupied crossing on $\mathcal{G}_1$ of $[0,m] \times [0,n]$. Moreover, if two such paths in $\bar{J}$ have no vertex in common in $\bar{J} \setminus A_1 \cup A_3$, then they have no vertex in common in $[0,m] \times [0,n]$. It therefore suffices to find a lower bound on the maximal number of paths on $\mathcal{G}_1$ in $\bar{J}$ from $A_1$ to $A_3$ with only occupied vertices in $\bar{J} \setminus A_1 \cup A_3$, and such that any pair of these paths has no common vertices in $\bar{J} \setminus A_1 \cup A_3$.

To find the desired lower bound fix an occupancy configuration $\omega$ and form the graph $\mathcal{G}_J(\omega)$, which is basically the restriction of the occupied part of $\mathcal{G}$ to $\bar{J}$, with the vertices on $A_1$ identified as one vertex $\hat{1}$, and similarly for the vertices on $A_3$. More precisely, the vertex set of $\mathcal{G}_J(\omega)$ consists of the collection of vertices $v$ of $\mathcal{G}$ in $\bar{J}\setminus A_1 \cup A_3$ which are occupied in $\omega$ plus two vertices which we denote by $\hat{1}$ and $\hat{3}$. There is an edge between two vertices $v'$ and $v''$ of $\mathcal{G}_J(\omega)$ (other than $\hat{1}$ and $\hat{3}$) iff there is an edge between them in $\mathcal{G}$. There is no edge between $\hat{1}$ and $\hat{3}$, and there is an edge between $v$ and $\hat{1}(\hat{3})$ if there is an edge in $\mathcal{G}$ between $v$ and some vertex on $A_1(A_3)$. We shall now apply Menger's Theorem - which is a version of the max flow-min cut theorem, see Bollobás (1979), Theorem III.5(i) - to $\mathcal{G}_J(\omega)$. In the terminology of Bollobás, the number of independent paths from $\hat{1}$ to $\hat{3}$ in $\mathcal{G}_J(\omega)$ equals the maximal number of paths on $\mathcal{G}_J(\omega)$ from $A_1$ to $A_3$ which are pairwise vertex-disjoint on $\bar{J}\setminus A_1 \cup A_3$. In turn, this is precisely the maximal number of paths on $\mathcal{G}_1$ in $\bar{J}$ from $A_1$ to $A_3$ all of whose vertices in $\bar{J}\setminus A_1 \cup A_3$ are occupied and which are pairwise vertex-disjoint on $\bar{J}\setminus A_1 \cup A_3$. By Menger's Theorem this number equals the minimum of the cardinalities of sets of vertices of $\mathcal{G}_J(\omega)$ which separate $\hat{1}$ from $\hat{3}$. (A set $V$ of vertices in $\mathcal{G}_J(\omega)\setminus\{\hat{1},\hat{3}\}$ separates $\hat{1}$ from $\hat{3}$ if after removal of $V$ there no longer exists a path from $\hat{1}$ to $\hat{3}$ on $\mathcal{G}_J(\omega)$). Let us denote by $L$ this minimum cardinality of separating sets. Now consider the collection of all paths $r^* = (v_0^*, e_1^*, \ldots, e_\nu^*, v_\nu^*)$ on $\mathcal{G}^*$ which satisfy

$$r^* \subset \bar{J}\setminus A_1 \cup A_3 \tag{11.23}$$

and

$$v_0^* \text{ lies on } \mathring{A}_2,\ v_\nu^* \text{ lies on } \mathring{A}_4 . \tag{11.24}$$

Denote by $M$ the minimal number of occupied vertices on any such path. We shall use Prop. 2.2 to show that

$$L = M.$$

First pick a path $r^*$ which satisfies (11.23) and (11.24) and which contains only $M$ occupied vertices. If we modify $\omega$ by making these $M$ vertices vacant, then $r^*$ becomes vacant and then by Prop. 2.2 there is no longer a path on $\mathcal{G}$ in $\bar{J}$ from $A_1$ to $A_3$ with all its vertices in $\bar{J}\setminus A_1 \cup A_3$ occupied. Equivalently, removal of the $M$ occupied vertices on $r^*$ separates $A_1$ from $A_3$, so that the occupied vertices on $r^*$ form a set which separates $\hat{1}$ from $\hat{3}$ in $\mathcal{G}_J(\omega)$, whence $L \le M$. Conversely, let $V$ be a set of $L$ vertices which separates $\hat{1}$ from $\hat{3}$ on $\mathcal{G}_J(\omega)$. View $V$ also as a set of vertices of $\mathcal{G}_1$ and let $\tilde{\omega}$ be the occupancy configuration obtained by making the vertices in $V$ vacant. Making the vertices of $V$ vacant amounts to removing them from $\mathcal{G}_J(\omega)$, i.e., $\mathcal{G}_J(\tilde{\omega})$ does not contain any vertex from $V$. Since $V$ was a separating set $\hat{1}$ and $\hat{3}$ are not connected by a path on $\mathcal{G}_J(\tilde{\omega})$. Therefore, in the configuration $\tilde{\omega}$, $A_1$ and $A_3$ are not connected by a path on $\mathcal{G}_1$ in $\bar{J}$ with all its vertices on $\bar{J} \setminus A_1 \cup A_3$ occupied. By Prop. 2.2 this means that there exists a path $r^*$ on $\mathcal{G}^*$ which satisfies (11.23) and (11.24) and which is vacant in the configuration $\tilde{\omega}$. Since $\tilde{\omega}$ differs from $\omega$ only on the vertices of $V$, it follows that $r^*$ has at most $\#V = L$ occupied vertices in the configuration $\omega$. Thus, $M \le L$ and $M = L$ as claimed.

So far we have shown that

(11.25) number of vertex-disjoint occupied horizontal crossings on $\mathcal{G}$ of $[0,m] \times [0,n]$ in the configuration

$\ge$ maximal number of paths on $\mathcal{G}_J(\omega)$ from $\hat{1}$ to $\hat{3}$, such that no pair has a vertex in common in $\bar{J} \setminus A_1 \cup A_3$

$= L = M.$

Thus, the left hand side of (11.25) can be less than $C_1(p - p_H(\mathcal{G}_1))^{\delta_1}$ $= C_1(p - \frac{1}{2})^{\delta_1} n$ only if also $M < C_1(p - \frac{1}{2})^{\delta_1} n$. Now note that $A_4$ lies on or above the horizontal line $\mathbb{R} \times \{n-1\}$. Therefore, $M_{\circ} < C_1(p - \frac{1}{2})^{\delta_1} n$ can happen only if one of the $(2m+3)$ vertices $v^*$ of $\mathring{A}_2$ is connected to the horizontal line $\mathbb{R} \times \{n-1\}$ by a path on $\mathcal{G}_1^*$ containing fewer than $C_1(p - \frac{1}{2})^{\delta_1} n$ occupied vertices. Consequently

(11.26) $P_p\{$maximal number of vertex-disjoint occupied horizontal crossings on $\mathcal{G}_1$ of $[0,m] \times [0,n]$ is less than $C_1(p - \frac{1}{2})^{\delta_1} n\}$

$\le (2m+3) \max_{v^*(2) \le 1} P_p\{\exists$ path on $\mathcal{G}_1^*$ from $v^*$ to the half plane $\mathbb{R} \times [n-1, \infty)$ which contains fewer than $C_1(p - \frac{1}{2})^{\delta_1} n$ occupied vertices$\}$.

To estimate the right hand side of (11.26) we use a slightly strengthened verions of (5.48) or Lemma 1 of Kesten (1980b). For a closer agreement with the notation of Lemma 5.4 we interchange the role of $\mathcal{G}$ and $\mathcal{G}^*$ as well as the role of "occupied" and "vacant" and the role of the first and second coordinate. Theorem 11.1 is then immediate from (11.26) and the Proposition below. (Recall that $p_H(\mathcal{G}^*) = 1-p_H(\mathcal{G})$ for $\mathcal{G} = \mathcal{G}_0$ or $\mathcal{G}_1$ by Applications 3.4(iv) and (ii).) □

Proposition 11.1. Let $\mathcal{G}$ be one of the graphs $\mathcal{G}_0$, $\mathcal{G}_1$, $\mathcal{G}_0^*$ or $\mathcal{G}_1^*$ and let $P_p$ be the one-parameter probability measure on the occupancy configurations of $\mathcal{G}$ of the form (3.22) and specified by (3.61). Then for some universal constants $0 < C_i, \delta_i < \infty$ one has for any vertex $v$ of $\mathcal{G}$ with $v(1) \leq 0$ and $p \leq p_H = p_H(\mathcal{G})$

$$P_p\{\exists \text{ path from } v \text{ to } [n,\infty)\times\mathbb{R} \text{ on } \mathcal{G} \text{ which contains fewer than } C_6(p_H-p)^{\delta_1}n \text{ vacant vertices}\} \leq 10 \exp -C_7(p_H-p)^{\delta_2}n. \tag{11.27}$$

Proof: As in Lemma 5.4 we set for any vertex $u$ of $\mathcal{G}$ and integer $M$

$$S_0 = S_0(v,M) = \{w \text{ a vertex of } \mathcal{G}: |w(j)-v(j)| \leq M,\ j = 1,2\},$$

$$S_1 = S_0 \cup \partial S_0 = \{w \text{ a vertex of } \mathcal{G}: w \in S_0 \text{ or } w \text{ adjacent to a vertex in } S_0\}.$$

Instead of $A(u,m)$ in (5.47) we now define for positive integers $n$ and $k$ the event

$$A(v,n,k) = \{\exists \text{ a path on } \mathcal{G} \text{ from a neighbor of } v \text{ to a } w \text{ with } w(1) \geq n \text{ which contains at most } k \text{ vacant vertices}\}.$$

We repeat the definition of $g$ from Lemma 5.4.

$$g(v,w,M) = P_p\{\exists \text{ occupied path } (w_0,e_1,\dots,e_\rho,w_\rho) \text{ on } \mathcal{G} \text{ with } w_0\mathcal{G}v,\ w_\rho \notin S_0(v,M) \text{ one of the } w_i \text{ equal to } w\}.$$

The principal estimate is the following strengthened version of (5.48).[1] For $v(1) < n-M$ and $k \geq 0$,

---

[1] One could also use the argument of Lemma 1 in Kesten (1980b), which avoids the use of the random set R. However, the present argument is a closer parallel to Ch. 5 and needs essentially no new steps.

(11.28) $$P_p\{A(v,n,k)\} \leq \sum_{w\varepsilon S_1(v,M)} g(v,w,M)P_p\{A(w,n,k)\}$$

$$+ \sum_{w\varepsilon S_1(v,M)} P_p\{A(w,n,k-1)\} .$$

To prove (11.28) let $E$ be the event

$$E = \bigcup_{w\varepsilon S_1(v,M)} A(w,n,k-1).$$

Clearly the second term in the right hand side of (11.28) is an upper bound for $P_p\{E\}$ so that we only have to estimate $P_p\{A(v,n,k)\setminus E\}$. Assume then that $A(v,n,k)\setminus E$ occurs and that $r = (v_0,e_1,\dots,e_\nu,v_\nu)$ is a path on $\mathcal{G}$ with $v_0$ adjacent to $v$, $v_\nu(1) \geq n$ and such that $r$ contains at most $k$ vacant vertices. Since $v_\nu(1) \geq n > v(1)+M$, $v_\nu$ must lie outside $S_0(v,M)$ and there exists a smallest index $a$ with $v_a \notin S_0(v,M)$. Since $v_{a-1} \varepsilon S_0(v,M)$ we still have $v_a \varepsilon \partial S_0 \subset S_1$. Since $E$ does not occur $(v_{a+1},e_{a+2},\dots,e_\nu,v_\nu)$ must contain more than $(k-1)$ vacant vertices (otherwise $A(v_a,n,k-1)$ would occur). But then $(v_0,e_1,\dots,e_{a-1},v_a)$ cannot contain any vacant vertex, because $r$ contains at most $k$ vacant vertices. Consequently with $R$ defined as in Lemma 5.4 $v_a \varepsilon R$. As in Lemma 5.4 let $b \geq a$ be the last index with $v_b \varepsilon R$. Then the path $(v_{b+1},e_{b+2},\dots,e_\nu,v_\nu)$ has all its vertices outside $R$, its initial point, $v_{b+1}$, is adjacent to $v_b \varepsilon R$ and its final point $v_\nu$ satisfies $v_\nu(1) \geq n$. Moreover this path is a subpath of $r$ and therefore contains at most $k$ vacant sites so that $A(v_b,n,k)$ occurs. Thus, as in (5.49)

$P_p\{A(v,n,k)\setminus E\} \leq \sum_{w\varepsilon S_1} P_p\{w \varepsilon R$ and $\exists$ a path $(w_0,f_1,\dots,f_\rho,w_\rho)$ on $\mathcal{G}$ with $w_0 \mathcal{G} w$, $w_\rho(1) \geq n$, $w_i \notin R$ for $0 \leq i \leq \rho$ and at most $k$ of the $w_i$, $0 \leq i \leq \rho$, are vacant$\}$.

One can now copy the argument following (5.48) practically word for word to obtain

(11.29) $$P_p\{A(v,n,k)\setminus E\} \leq \sum_{w\varepsilon S_1} g(v,w,M)P_p\{A(w,n,k)\};$$

one only has to replace "occupied path" in the definition (5.50) of $J$ by "path with at most $k$ vacant vertices". The right hand side of (11.29) is just the first sum in the right hand side of (11.28) so that (11.28) follows.

In order to exploit (11.28) we must now choose $M$ such that (5.51) holds. This time we must also keep track of the dependence of $M$ on $p$. But, for every $v, w, M$

$$g(v,w,M) \le P_p\{\text{some neighbor of } v \text{ is connected by an occupied path on } \mathcal{G} \text{ to } \partial S_0(v,M)\} \le P_p\{\exists \text{ on occupied horizontal crossing of } [v(1)-M,v(1)-1]\times[v(2)-M,v(2)+M] \text{ or of } [v(1)+1,v(1)+M]\times[v(2)-M,v(2)+M]\} + P_p\{\exists \text{ an occupied vertical crossing of } [v(1)-M,v(1)+M]\times[v(2)-M,v(2)-1] \text{ or of } [v(1)-M,v(1)+M]\times[v(2)+1,v(2)+M]\},$$

since any path from a neighbor of $v$ to $\partial S_0(v,M)$ must cross either the left or right "half", or the bottom or top "half" of $S_0(v,M)$. With the notation of (5.5) we therefore conclude from Comment 3.3(v) and Lemma 8.3 that

$$\begin{aligned} g(v,w,M) &\le 2\tau((M-1,M-1);1,p)+2\tau((M-1,M-1);2,p) \\ &\le 4 \exp -C_{13}(p_H-p)(M-1)^{\alpha_1} . \end{aligned} \tag{11.30}$$

Since $S_1(v,M)$ contains at most $2(2M+3)^2$ vertices of $\mathcal{G}_1$ we have

$$\sum_{w\varepsilon S_1(v,M)} g(v,w,M) \le 8(2M+3)^2 \exp -C_{13}(p_H-p)(M-1)^{\alpha_1} \le \frac{3}{4} \tag{11.31}$$

for

$$M = C_8(p_H-p)^{-2/\alpha_1} \tag{11.32}$$

for some suitable $C_8$, which depends on $C_{13}$ only ($C_{13}$ is as in Lemma 8.3).

From here on the proof is identical with that of Prop. 1 of Kesten (1980b). We choose $M$ such that (11.32) and hence (11.31) hold. We rewrite (11.28) as

$$P_p\{A(v,n,k)\} \le \sum_{w_1,y_1} h(v,w_1,y_1)P_p\{A(v+w_1,n,k-y_1)\}, \tag{11.33}$$

where $w_1$ runs over those points in the square $[-M-1,M+1]\times[-M-1,M+1]$ for which $v+w_1 \varepsilon S_1(v,M)$ and $y_1$ takes the values $0$ or $1$. Finally

$$h(v,w_1,y_1) = \begin{cases} 1 & \text{if } y_1 = 1 , \\ g(v,v+w_1,M) & \text{if } y_1 = 0 . \end{cases}$$

Next we observe that

$$P_p\{A(w,n,-1)\} = 0 \quad \text{if} \quad w(1) \le n$$

since no non-empty path from $w$ to $[n,\infty) \times \mathbb{R}$ can have a negative number of vertical sites. Consequently, by iterating (11.33) we obtain for any $\ell \ge 1$

$$(11.34) \qquad P_p\{A(v,n,k)\} \le \sum_{\substack{w_1,y_1 \\ w_1(1) \ge n-M, y_1 \le k}} h(v,w_1,y_1)$$

$$+ \sum_{\substack{w_1,y_1 \\ w_1(1) < n-M, y_1 \le k}} h(v,w_1,y_1) \sum_{w_2,y_2} h(v+w_1,w_2,y_2)$$

$$\cdot\, P_p\{A(v+w_1+w_2,n,k-y_1-y_2)\}$$

$$\le \dots \le \sum_{j=1}^{\ell} \sum{}^{(j)} \prod_{i=1}^{j} h(v+w_1+\dots+w_{i-1},w_i,y_i)$$

$$+ \sum_{\substack{w_1(1)+\dots+w_t(1) < n-M \\ \text{for } t \le \ell, \text{ and } y_1+\dots+y_\ell \le k}} \prod_{i=1}^{\ell} h(v+w_1+\dots+w_{i-1},w_i,y_i) ,$$

where $\sum^{(j)}$ is the sum over $w_1,\dots,w_j,y_1,\dots,y_j$ with $w_1(1)+\dots+w_t(1) < n-M$ for $t < j$ but $w_1(1)+\dots+w_j(1) \ge n-M$ and $y_1+\dots+y_j \le k$. Of course all sums in (11.34) are also restricted to $w_i \in [-M-1,M+1] \times [-M-1,M+1]$, $v+w_1+\dots+w_i \in S_1(v+w_1+\dots+w_{i-1},M)$ and $y_i \in \{0,1\}$. Next we take

$$\lambda = \log 16 + 2\log(2M+3)$$

so that, by (11.31)

$$\phi(\lambda) := \max_u \sum_{\substack{u+w \in S_1(u,M) \\ y \in \{0,1\}}} h(u,w,y)e^{-\lambda y}$$

$$\le \max_u \sum_{u+w \in S_1(u,M)} g(u,u+w,M) + e^{-\lambda} 2(2M+3)^2$$

$$\le \frac{3}{4} + 2(2M+3)^2 e^{-\lambda} = \frac{7}{8} .$$

For this choice of $\lambda$

$$\sum{}^{(j)} \prod_{i=1}^{j} h(v+w_1+\ldots+w_{i-1},w_i,y_i)$$

$$\leq e^{\lambda k} \sum_{\substack{y_i\varepsilon\{0,1\} \\ v+w_1+\ldots+w_i\varepsilon S_1(v+w_1+\ldots+w_{i-1},M)}} \prod_{i=1}^{j} \{e^{-\lambda y_i} h(v+w_1+\ldots+w_{i-1},w_i,y_i)\}$$

$$\leq e^{\lambda k}(\phi(\lambda))^j \leq e^{\lambda k}(\tfrac{7}{8})^j ,$$

because $y_1+\ldots+y_j \leq k$ in $\sum{}^{(j)}$. Similarly the last term in (11.34) is at most

$$e^{\lambda k}(\tfrac{7}{8})^{\ell} .$$

Finally, observe that $w_i(1) \leq M+1$, so that for $v(1) \leq 0$, $v(1)+w_1(1) +\ldots+w_j(1) \geq n-M$ can occur only for $j \geq (n-M)(M+1)^{-1}$. Consequently, by virtue of (11.34)

$$P_p\{A(v,n,k)\} \leq \lim_{\ell\to\infty} e^{\lambda k} \sum_{\frac{n-M}{M+1}\leq j\leq \ell} (\tfrac{7}{8})^j \leq 10e^{\lambda k}(\tfrac{7}{8})^{n/(M+1)},$$

whenever $v(1) \leq 0$.

If we take

$$k = \frac{1}{2\lambda}(\frac{n}{M+1})\log\frac{8}{7} \sim \{\frac{\alpha_1}{8C_8}\log(\tfrac{8}{7})(p_H-p)^{2/\alpha_1}(-\log(p_H-p))^{-1}\}n,\ p\uparrow p_H ,$$

then we find for $v(1) \leq 0$ and suitable $C_9$

$$P_p\{A(v,n,C_9(p_H-p)^{3/\alpha_1}n)\} \leq 10(\tfrac{7}{8})^{\frac{n}{2(M+1)}} \leq 10(\tfrac{7}{8})^{\frac{1}{4C_8}(p_H-p)^{2/\alpha_1}n} .$$

This is just (11.27) with $\delta_1 = \frac{3}{\alpha_1}$, $\delta_2 = \frac{2}{\alpha_1}$ and suitable $C_6$, $C_7$. □

## 11.3. Properties of resistances.

Before we start the proof of Theorem 11.2 we describe how the resistance of a network is related to the resistances of the individual edges. As we have done all along we assume that there are no loops (i.e., edges whose endpoints coincide) in the graph. If $v$ is a vertex and $e$ an edge incident to $v$ then we write $w(e,v)$ for the endpoint other than $v$ of $e$. $R(e)$ is the resistance of the edge $e$. To find the resistance between the sets of vertices $A^0$ and $A^1$ of a finite graph $\mathcal{G}$ one wants to find a potential function $V(\cdot)$ on the vertices of $\mathcal{G}$, which equals 0 on $A^0$ and one on $A^1$, and corresponding currents through the edges. The size of the resistance between $A^0$ and $A^1$ is then equal to the reciprocal of the total current flowing out of $A^0$. If $v$ and $w$ are the endpoint of an edge $e$ let $I(v,e)$ denote the current flowing from $v$ to $w$ along $e$. Ohm's and Kirchhoff's laws (see Feynman et al (1963), Sect. I.25.4,5 and II.22.3, Slepian (1968)) say that the potential and currents have to satisfy

$$I(v,e) = -I(w(e,v),e), \tag{11.35}$$

$$V(w(e,v))-V(v) = R(e)\cdot I(v,e), \tag{11.36}$$

$$\sum_{\substack{e \text{ incident} \\ \text{to } v}} I(v,e) = 0 \quad \text{if} \quad v \notin A^0 \cup A^1 . \tag{11.37}$$

Finally, there is the boundary condition which we imposed

$$V(v) = 0 \quad \text{if} \quad v \in A^0 \quad \text{and} \quad V(v) = 1 \quad \text{if} \quad v \in A^1. \tag{11.38}$$

To discuss the uniqueness and existence of $V$ and $I$ assume first that $R(e) > 0$ for all $e$. $R(e) = \infty$ is allowed, in which case we have to interpret (11.36) as

$$I(v,e) = 0. \tag{11.39}$$

In this case (11.36) makes no statement about the potential difference between the endpoints of $e$. However, if $R(e) \neq 0$ we can rewrite (11.36) as

$$I(v,e) = \frac{V(w(e,v))-V(v)}{R(e)} \tag{11.40}$$

and substitution of (11.40) into (11.37) shows that (11.37) is equivalent to

$$V(v) = \frac{\sum_e \frac{V(w(e,v))}{R(e)}}{\sum_e \frac{1}{R(e)}}, \quad v \notin A^0 \cup A^1 , \tag{11.41}$$

where the sums in numerator and denominator of (11.41) run over edges $e$ incident to $v$. Therefore, $w(e,v)$ runs over all neighbors of $v$ and (11.41) says that $V(v)$ is a weighted average over the values of $V(\cdot)$ at the neighbors of $v$. $V(w)/R(e)$ and $1/R(e)$ are interpreted as zero if $R(e) = \infty$. Thus, $V(v)$ is really an average of $V(\cdot)$ over those neighbors of $v$ which are connected to $v$ by an edge of finite resistance. (If no such edges exist, then $V(v)$ is not determined by (11.35)-(11.37), but this will turn out to be unimportant.) It is well known from the theory of harmonic functions that the mean value property (11.41) implies a maximum principle; many of the proofs of this fact in the continuous case can be transcribed easily for our situation (see for instance Helms (1969), Theorem 1.12 and also Doyle and Snell (1982), Sect. 2.2). We shall use the following formulation of the maximum principle. Let $\mathbb{C}$ be a collection of vertices disjoint from $A^0 \cup A^1$ and let $\partial_f \mathbb{C}$ denote the set of vertices of $w \notin \mathbb{C}$ which are connected to a vertex in $\mathbb{C}$ by an edge of finite resistance. Then

$$(11.42) \qquad \min_{w \in \partial_f \mathbb{C}} V(w) \leq V(v) \leq \max_{w \in \partial_f \mathbb{C}} V(w)$$

for every vertex $v$ in $\mathbb{C}$ which is connected to $\partial_f \mathbb{C}$ by a conducting path. Here, and in the remainder of this chapter, a <u>conducting path</u> is a path all of whose edges have finite resistance. If we take for $\mathbb{C}$ the set

$$\mathbb{C}_0 = \text{set of all vertices outside } A^0 \cup A^1 ,$$

then (11.42) implies that there is at most one possible value for $V(v)$ at any $v$ connected to $A^0 \cup A^1$ by a conducting path (apply (11.42) to the difference $V'-V''$ of a pair of solutions to (11.35)-(11.39); $V'-V''$ has to vanish on $\partial_f \mathbb{C}_0 \subset A^0 \cup A^1$). The fact that there exists a solution of (11.38) and (11.41) is well known (see Slepian (1968), Ch.7) and is also very easy to prove probabilistically, since $V(v)$ can be interpreted as the probability of hitting $A^1$ before $A^0$ when starting at $v$, for a certain Markov chain (see Doyle and Snell (1982), Sect. 2.7). Once we have $V(\cdot)$, (11.39) and (11.40) give us $I(\cdot)$. The resistance $R$ between $A^0$ and $A^1$ is then defined as the reciprocal of the total current flowing out of $A^0$, i.e.,

$$(11.43) \qquad R = \{\sum_e I(v,e)\}^{-1} = \{\sum_e \frac{V(w(e,v))}{R(e)}\}^{-1} ,$$

The sums in (11.43) run over all edges $e$ with one endpoint $v \in A^0$ and the other endpoint $w(e,v) \notin A^0$. Note that the right hand side of (11.43) is uniquely determined, despite the fact that $V(w)$ is not unique for a vertex $w$ which is not connected to $A^0 \cup A^1$ by a conducting path. Indeed if $w(e,v)$ is such a vertex, then necessarily $R(e) = \infty$ and the corresponding contribution to (11.43) is zero, no matter how $V(w)$ is chosen.

There are some complications when we allow $R(e) = 0$ for some edges. For such edges $e$ (11.40) is no longer meaningful, and (11.36) merely says

(11.44) $$V(w(e,v))-V(v) = 0.$$

In this case one can proceed as follows. Sum (11.37) over $v \in \mathcal{C}$ for any set $\mathcal{C}$ disjoint from $A^0 \cup A^1$. If one takes into account that for $v,w \in \mathcal{C}$ connected by an edge $e$ the sum will contain $I(v,e)+I(w,e) = 0$, one obtains

(11.45) $$\sum_e I(v,e) = 0, \quad \mathcal{C} \cap (A^0 \cup A^1) = \emptyset,$$

where the sum in (11.45) runs over all $e$ with one endpoint $v \in \mathcal{C}$ and the other endpoint $w(e,v) \notin \mathcal{C}$. In words (11.45) says that the net current flowing out of any set $\mathcal{C}$ disjoint from $A^0 \cup A^1$ must equal zero. Now define two vertices $v_1$ and $v_2$ of $\mathcal{G}$ as equivalent iff $v_1 = v_2$ or $v_1$ and $v_2$ are connected by a path all of whose edges have zero resistance (i.e., iff there is a short circuit between $v_1$ and $v_2$). Let $C_1, C_2, \dots$ be the equivalence classes of vertices with respect to this equivalence relation. By (11.36), or (11.44), all vertices $v$ in a single class $C$ must have the same potential $V(v)$. We shall write $V(C)$ for this value. Now form a new graph $\mathcal{K}$ by identifying the vertices in an equivalence class. Thus $\mathcal{K}$ has vertex set $\{C_1, C_2, \dots\}$ and the edges of $\mathcal{K}$ between $C_i$ and $C_j$ are in one to one correspondence with the edges of $\mathcal{G}$ connecting a vertex of $C_i$ with a vertex of $C_j$. From the above observations we obtain the following analogue for (11.36)-(11.38).

(11.46) $V(C_j)-V(C_i) = R(e)\cdot I(v,e)$, when $v \in C_i$ is connected to $w \in C_j$ by $e$, $i \neq j$.

(11.47) $\sum_e I(v,e) = 0$, wherever $C_i \cap (A^0 \cup A^1) = \emptyset$ and the sum is over all edges $e$ with one endpoint $v$ in $C_i$ and the other endpoint $w(e,v) \notin C_i$.

(11.48) $$V(C_i) = 0 \quad \text{when} \quad C_i \cap A^0 \neq \emptyset$$

(11.49) $$V(C_i) = 1 \quad \text{when} \quad C_i \cap A^1 \neq \emptyset .$$

(11.35) remains unchanged, and (11.46) again is interpreted as (11.39) when $R(e) = \infty$. Of course (11.48) and (11.49) can be simultaneously valid only if there exists no $C_i$ which intersects both $A^0$ and $A^1$. However, this case can arise only if $A^0$ and $A^1$ are connected by a path all of whose edges have zero resistance. (We shall call such a path a short circuit between $A^0$ and $A^1$.) In this case the resistance between $A^0$ and $A^1$ is taken to be zero. If there is no $C_i$ which intersects $A^0$ and $A^1$, then solving (11.46)-(11.49) just amounts to solving on $\mathcal{H}$ the problem which we solved above for $\mathcal{G}$. We merely have to replace $A^0$ $(A^1)$ by the collection of $C_i$ which intersect $A^0$ $(A^1)$. Note that by definition of the $C_i$ any edge from $C_i$ to $C_j$, $i \neq j$, has a strictly positive resistance. Thus, as before $V(C_i)$ is uniquely determined for any $C_i$ which contains a vertex which is connected to $A^0 \cup A^1$ by a conducting path. For any choice of $V(C_i)$ we then find $I(v,e)$ for $v \in C_i$, $e$ incident to $v$, but with $w(e,v) \in C_j$ with $j \neq i$. The resistance between $A^0$ and $A^1$ in $\mathcal{G}$ can now be defined as the reciprocal of the current flowing out of the union of all $C_i$ which intersect $A^0$. In analogy to (11.43) this becomes

$$(11.50) \qquad \{\sum I(v,e)\}^{-1} = \{\sum \frac{V(C_j)}{R(e)}\}^{-1} ,$$

where the sum is over all edges $e$, having one end point in some $C_i$ which intersects $A^0$ while its other endpoint lies in some $C_j$ with $C_j \cap A^0 = \emptyset$; in the left hand side $v$ is the endpoint of $e$ in $C_i$, and $C_j$ in the right hand side is the class which contains $w(e,v)$. Just as in (11.43) the sums in (11.50) are uniquely determined.

Even though (11.50) does define the resistance between $A^0$ and $A^1$, when $R(e)$ can vanish for some edges $e$, it would be more intuitive if one could use the middle expression in (11.43) to define the resistance, also in the present case. This is indeed possible, but some more observations are required to see this. The currents between a pair of vertices in the same $C_i$ have not yet been determined, and in fact are not uniquely determined by the equations (11.35)-(11.38). If there are several paths of zero resistance between two vertices there is no reason why the current should be divided into any particular way between these paths. However, there do exist solutions to (11.35)-(11.38). We merely have to take

(11.51) $$V(v) = V(C_i) \quad \text{when} \quad v \in C_i ,$$

where $V(C_i)$ satisfies (11.46)-(11.49). Then (11.38) is automatically true. Next define

(11.52) $$I(v,e) = \frac{V(w(e,v))-V(v)}{R(e)} = \frac{V(C_j)-V(C_i)}{R(e)} \quad \text{when } e \text{ is an}$$

edge with endpoints $v \in C_i$ and $w(e,v) \in C_j$ with $i \neq j$.

(11.52) makes sense since $R(e) \neq 0$ for an edge $e$ with endpoints in different $C_i$ and $C_j$. (11.51) and (11.52) guarantee that (11.36) holds, no matter how we choose $I(v,e)$ for an edge $e$ with both endpoints in the same $C_i$ and (11.35) is already satisfied for $v$ and $w(e,v)$ in different $C_i$ and $C_j$. We now merely have to choose $I(v,e)$ for edges $e$ with both endpoints in one $C_i$, in such a way that (11.35) and (11.37) hold. (11.37) can be written as

(11.53) $$\sum_{\substack{e \text{ such that} \\ w(e,v) \in C_i}} I(v,e) = - \sum_{\substack{e \text{ such that} \\ w(e,v) \notin C_i}} I(v,e),$$

$$\text{for} \quad v \in C_i \setminus A^0 \cup A^1 ,$$

for all $C_i$ which contain at least two vertices. The right hand side of (11.53) has already been determined in (11.52). To satisfy (11.35) we choose for each edge $e$ with endpoints $v$, $w$ in $C_i$ one of the endpoints as the first one, $v$ say. Then we take $I(v,e)$ as an independent variable and set $I(w,e) = -I(v,e)$. Then for each $C_i$ which does not intersect $A^0 \cup A^1$ the expressions obtained in the left hand side of (11.53) as $v$ ranges over $C_i$, contain each independent variable exactly twice, once with coefficient $+1$ and once with coefficient $-1$. Thus, the sum of the left hand side of (11.53) over $v$ in $C_i$ vanishes. The same is true for the sum of the right hand sides, by virtue of (11.47) if $C_i \cap (A^0 \cup A^1) = \emptyset$. By induction on the number of variables one easily sees that (11.53) has at least one solution which satisfies (11.35), and (11.37). If $C_i$ intersects $A^0 \cup A^1$, then rewrite (11.37) or (11.53) as

(11.54) $$\sum_{\substack{e \text{ such that} \\ w(e,v) \in C_i \setminus A^0 \cup A^1}} I(v,e) = - \sum_{\substack{e \text{ such that} \\ w(e,v) \notin C_i}} I(v,e)$$

$$- \sum_{\substack{e \text{ such that} \\ w(e,v)\in C_i\cap(A^0\cup A^1)}} I(v,e), \quad v \in C_i\setminus(A^0 \cup A^1).$$

The above argument used for (11.53) now shows that (11.54) has a solution satisfying (11.35) if and only if the sum of the right hand sides of (11.54) over $v \in C_i\setminus(A^0 \cup A^1)$ vanishes, i.e., iff we choose $I(v,e)$ for $v \in C_i\setminus A^0 \cup A^1$, and $w(e,v) \in C_i \cap (A^0 \cup A^1)$ such that

$$(11.55) \qquad - \sum_{v\in C_i\setminus(A^0\cup A^1)} \; \sum_{\substack{e \text{ such that} \\ w(e,v)\in C_i\cap(A^0\cup A^1)}} I(v,e)$$

$$= \sum_{w\in C_i\cap(A^0\cup A^1)} \; \sum_{\substack{e \text{ such that} \\ v(e,w)\in C_i\setminus(A^0\cup A^1)}} I(w,e)$$

$$= \sum_{v\in C_i\setminus(A^0\cup A^1)} \; \sum_{\substack{e \text{ such that} \\ w(e,v)\notin C_i}} I(v,e).$$

Thus we can always solve (11.35)-(11.38), and any solution has to be chosen such that (11.55) holds.

Now that we have shown that there is a solution to (11.35)-(11.38) we can show that the left hand side of (11.50) equals the middle expression in (11.43) by the following general argument. Let $\mathcal{D}$ be any set of vertices which contains $A^0$ and is disjoint from $A^1$. We claim that for any such $\mathcal{D}$

$$(11.56) \qquad R = \{\textstyle\sum_{\mathcal{D}} I(v,e)\}^{-1} = \{\textstyle\sum_{A^0} I(v,e)\}^{-1} ,$$

where $\sum_{\mathcal{D}}$ runs over all edges $e$ with one endpoint $v \in \mathcal{D}$ and the other endpoint $w(e,v)$ outside $\mathcal{D}$. In accordance with this notation, the last member of (11.56) is just the middle member of (11.43) $\sum_{\mathcal{D}} I(v,e)$ represents the current flowing out of $\mathcal{D}$. To prove (11.56) we apply (11.45) with $\mathcal{C} = \mathcal{D}\setminus A^0$. By our choice of $\mathcal{D}$, $\mathcal{C}$ is disjoint from $A^0 \cup A^1$. (11.45) can now be rewritten as

$$(11.57) \qquad \textstyle\sum_1 I(v,e) = - \sum_1 I(w(e,v),e) = \sum_2 I(v,e)$$

where $\sum_1$ runs over all edges $e$ with one endpoint $v$ in $A^0$ and the other endpoint $w(e,v)$ in $\mathcal{D}\setminus A^0$, while $\sum_2$ runs over all edges $e$ with one endpoint $v$ in $\mathcal{D}\setminus A^0$ and the other endpoint $w(e,v)$ outside $\mathcal{D}$. Now add to both sides of (11.57) the sum $\sum_3 I(v,e)$ over all edges $e$ with one endpoint $v$ in $A_0$ and the other endpoint $w(e,v)$ outside $\mathcal{D}$. Then

$$\sum_1 I(v,e) + \sum_3 I(v,e)$$

is just the sum in the middle member of (11.43). On the other hand

$$\sum_2 I(v,e) + \sum_3 I(v,e)$$

is just $\sum_{\mathcal{D}} I(v,e)$, so that (11.56) follows.

We return to (11.50). Take $\mathcal{D} = \cup C_i$ where the union is over all $C_i$ which intersect $A^0$. We ruled out the case in which some $C_i$ intersects $A^0$ and $A^1$; we took the resistance between $A^0$ and $A^1$ zero in this case. With this case ruled out we see that $\mathcal{D} = \cup C_i$ is indeed disjoint from $A^1$ so that (11.56) applies. But for this $\mathcal{D}$, $\sum_{\mathcal{D}}$ is just the sum in the left hand side of (11.50). Thus the middle member of (11.43) can be used to define $R$, even if $R(e)$ can vanish for some $e$ (as long as there is no short circuit between $A^0$ and $A^1$).

It is worth pointing out that for a finite graph $\mathcal{G}$ the above definition of $R$ implies

(11.58) $\quad R = 0$ if and only if there is a short circuit between $A^0$ and $A^1$

and

(11.59) $\quad R = \infty$ if and only if there is no conducting path from $A^0$ to $A^1$.

(11.58) is immediate from (11.56), since we have taken all currents finite, as long as there is no path from $A^0$ to $A^1$ with all its edges of zero resistance. For (11.59), assume first that $r = (v_0, e_1, \dots, e_\nu, v_\nu)$ is a conducting path from $A^0$ to $A^1$, i.e., with $v_0 \in A^0$, $v_\nu \in A^0$. By going over to a subpath we may assume $v_i \notin A^0 \cup A^1$ for $1 \le i \le \nu-1$. Of course $r$ is also self-avoiding. Then $\sum\{V(v_{i+1})-V(v_i)\} = V(v_\nu)-V(v_0) = 1$ by (11.38)). Thus for some $j$ $V(v_{j+1})-V(v_j) > 0$, and since $R(e_{j+1}) < \infty$ also $I(v_j,e_{j+1}) > 0$. If we take $\mathcal{D} = A_0 \cup \{v_0,\dots,v_j\}$ then the middle sum in (11.56) contains the term $I(v_j,e_{j+1}) > 0$, so that $R < \infty$. Conversely, if $R < \infty$, take $\mathcal{D} = A^0 \cup \{v: v$ is connected to $A^0$ by a conducting path$\}$.

Then $\mathcal{D}$ must contain a vertex on $A^1$. Indeed all edges $e$ with one endpoint $v$ in $\mathcal{D}$ and the other endpoint $w(e,v)$ outside $\mathcal{D}$ must have infinite resistance (otherwise we should add $w(e,v)$ to $\mathcal{D}$). But then $\sum_{\mathcal{D}} I(v,e) = 0$, which contradicts $R < \infty$, unless $\mathcal{D} \cap A^1 \neq \emptyset$. But $\mathcal{D}$ intersects $A^1$ if and only if there is a conducting path from $A^0$ to $A^1$. This proves (11.59).

With these preparations it is not hard to prove the following four lemmas. The first two and the fourth lemma are intuitively obvious from their electrical interpretation and reading of their proofs should be postponed. In all four lemmas we take the assignment of resistances to the edges as fixed, i.e., non-random.

Lemma 11.1. *Let $\mathcal{G}$ be a finite planar graph and $R$ the resistance between two disjoint subsets $A^0$ and $A^1$ of $\mathcal{G}$. Assume that $e_0$ is an edge of $\mathcal{G}$ such that $\mathring{e}_0$ is surrounded by a circuit $r = (v_0, e_1, \dots, e_\nu, v_\nu)$ (with $v_i \neq v_j$, $i \neq j$, except for $v_0 = v_\nu$) with*

$$R(e_i) = 0, \ 1 \leq i \leq \nu ,$$

*and such that $A^0 \cup A^1$ contains no vertex in the interior of $r$. Then $R$ is unchanged if $R(e_0)$ is replaced by zero.*

Proof: As before we may exclude the case in which $A^0$ and $A^1$ are connected by a path of zero resistance. In that case $R = 0$ and this is even more true when $R(e)$ is set equal to zero. Thus in this case there is nothing to prove. In the other case let $V(r)$ be the potential at $v$ when all vertices of $A^0$ $(A^1)$ are given the potential zero (one). $R$ can then be calculated as the resistance between $A^0$ and $A^1$ on the graph $\mathcal{H}$ obtained by identifying vertices in a single equivalence class $C_i$ all of whose vertices are connected by paths of zero resistance; see the argument preceding (11.50). By assumption all vertices on $r$ will belong to one such equivalence class, say $C_{i_0}$. Moreover, the vertices inside the circuit $r$ either belong to $C_{i_0}$ or to some $C_j$ which can be connected to $A^0 \cup A^1$ only via $C_{i_0}$ (by the planarity of $\mathcal{G}$). Let $C_{j_1}, \dots, C_{j_\lambda}$ be the classes other than $C_{i_0}$ which contain vertices inside $r$. Then all vertices of $\mathcal{G}$ in $\bigcup_{\alpha=1}^{\lambda} C_{j_\alpha}$ lie in $\text{int}(r)$. The boundary on $\mathcal{H}$ of the set of vertices $\{C_{j_1}, \dots, C_{j_\lambda}\}$ of $\mathcal{H}$ is the one point $C_{i_0}$ (see Def. 2.8). By the maximum principle (11.42) applied to $\mathcal{K}$ it follows that

$$V(C_{j_\alpha}) = V(C_{i_0}) \tag{11.60}$$

for all $C_{j_\alpha}$ which are connected to $C_{i_0}$ by a conducting path, $1 \leq \alpha \leq \lambda$. We shall now show that this implies that $R$ is unchanged if all vertices in the interior of $r$ are removed from $\mathcal{G}$. Then $C_{i_1},\dots,C_{i_\lambda}$ are removed from $\mathcal{K}$, and $C_{i_0}$ becomes the class of vertices on $r$ or outside $r$, but connected to $r$ by a path of zero resistance. To see that this removal does not effect $R$ note that (11.46)-(11.49) remain satisfied with the values of $V(C_i)$ and $I(v,e)$ unchanged as long as $i$ and $j$ are restricted to the complement of $\{j_1,\dots,j_\lambda\}$, and of course $e$ such that its endpoints $v$ and $w$ do not belong to the interior of $r$. This is so because an edge from some $v \in C_i$ with $i \notin \{j_1,\dots,j_\lambda\}$ and $v \notin \text{int}(r)$ to some $w \in \text{int}(r)$ can exist only if $v$ is a vertex on $r$ and hence $v \in C_{i_0}$. In this case $I(v,e)$ is zero anyway, either because $R(e) = \infty$, or by virtue of (11.60). Thus the term corresponding to $e$ be dropped from (11.47) without changing the left hand side of (11.47). But, then the right hand side of (11.50) does not change either when the vertices inside $r$ are removed, again because $C_{j_1},\dots,C_{j_\lambda}$ do not contribute to the sum in the right hand side of (11.50). Indeed if $C_{j_\alpha}$ contains a vertex $w$ connected to some $v \in A_0$ by an edge $e$ and $C_{j_\alpha} \cap A^0 = \emptyset$, then $v$ must belong to $C_{i_0}$, and $V(C_{i_0}) = 0$ by (11.48). The term $V(C_{j_\alpha})/R(e)$ again vanishes, either because $R(e) = \infty$ or because of (11.60). Thus $R$ is indeed unchanged if all vertices in the interior of $r$ are removed, and this has been proven without any reference to the value of $R(e_0)$. Since $e_0$ is no longer part of the network after removal of the vertices in $\text{int}(r)$, the value of $R$ is independent of $R(e_0)$. $\square$

Lemma 11.2. *Let $\mathcal{G}$, $A^0$, $A^1$ and $R$ be as in Lemma 11.1, and let*

$$\mathcal{C}_1 = A^0 \cup A^1 \cup \{v \in \mathcal{G}: v \text{ is connected to } A^0 \text{ by a conducting path}\}.$$

*Then $R$ is unchanged if we replace $R(e)$ by infinity for each edge $e$ which does not have both endpoints in $\mathcal{C}_1$.*

Proof: Since the current is zero in any edge with infinite resistance, the right hand sides of (11.43) and (11.50) involve only the values of $V(w)$ with $w \in \mathcal{C}_1$ - terms which do not involve such $w$ give zero contributions. It therefore suffices to show that $V(\cdot)$ is uniquely determined on $\mathcal{C}_1$, and that its values on $\mathcal{C}_1$ are unchanged if we take $R(e) = \infty$ for each edge $e$ which does not have both endpoints in $\mathcal{C}_1$. Let us first assume $R(f) > 0$ for all edges $f$. Then the restriction of $V(\cdot)$ to $\mathcal{C}_1$ satisfies (11.41) and (11.38) on $\mathcal{C}_1$. Moreover, for $v \in \mathcal{C}_1$, an edge $e$ incident to $v$ only gives a non-zero contribution to the sums in the right hand side of (11.41) if its second endpoint $w(e,v)$ also lies in $\mathcal{C}_1$. Consequently we can view the restriction of $V(\cdot)$ to $\mathcal{C}_1$ as the solution for the potential on the graph $\mathcal{G}_{|\mathcal{C}_1}$ say, whose vertex set is $\mathcal{C}_1$ and whose edge set is the set of edges of $\mathcal{G}$ between two points of $\mathcal{C}_1$. Under (11.38) this problem on $\mathcal{G}_{|\mathcal{C}_1}$ has a unique solution for the same reasons as in the original problem on $\mathcal{G}$. (Note that the maximum principle (11.42) only involves edges of $\mathcal{G}_{|\mathcal{C}_1}$ when $\mathcal{C} \subset \mathcal{C}_1$.) Thus $V_{|\mathcal{C}_1}$ does not change if we change the resistance of edges which do not have both endpoints in $\mathcal{C}_1$, provided we do not change $\mathcal{C}_1$. In particular $\mathcal{C}_1$ does not change if we set $R(e) = \infty$ for some of these edges. This proves the lemma if all edges have a strictly positive resistance.

To prove the lemma when some $R(e)$ may vanish we merely have to apply the preceding argument to the graph $\mathcal{K}$ whose vertices are the equivalence classes $C_j$ introduced after (11.45). (Note that if $C_j$ has any point in $\mathcal{C}_1$, then $C_j \subset \mathcal{C}_1$.) $\square$

For the next lemma we remind the reader that as a planar graph, $\mathbb{Z}^2$ has a dual graph, $(\mathbb{Z}^2)_d$ (see Sect. 2.6, especially Ex. 2.6(i)). $(\mathbb{Z}^2)_d$ can be thought of as the graph with vertices at $(i+\frac{1}{2}, j+\frac{1}{2})$, $i,j \in \mathbb{Z}$, and $(i_1+\frac{1}{2}, j_1+\frac{1}{2})$, $(i_2+\frac{1}{2}, j_2+\frac{1}{2})$ connected by an edge if and only if $|i_1-i_2| + |j_1-j_2| = 1$. Each edge $e^*$ of $(\mathbb{Z}^2)_d$ intersects exactly one edge $e$ of $\mathbb{Z}^2$ and vice versa. If $e$ and $e^*$ are associated in this manner we shall assign to $e^*$ the resistance $S(e^*) = 1/R(e)$. In this way, each assignment of resistances on $\mathbb{Z}^2$ induces a unique assignment of resistances on $(\mathbb{Z}^2)_d$. Finally, let $R([a_1,a_2] \times [b_1,b_2])$ $(S([a_1,a_2] \times [b_1,b_2]))$ be the resistance between the left and right edge (top and bottom edge) of $[a_1,a_2] \times [b_1,b_2]$ of the network consisting of the edges of $\mathbb{Z}^2$ $((\mathbb{Z}^2)_d)$ in $[a_1,a_2] \times [b_1,b_2]$.

Lemma 11.3 which is taken from Straley (1977) gives a duality relation between resistances on $\mathbb{Z}^2$ and $(\mathbb{Z}^2)_d$.

Lemma 11.3. If $S(e^*) = 1/R(e)$ for all pairs of edges $e$ of $\mathbb{Z}^2$ and $e^*$ of $(\mathbb{Z}^2)_d$ which intersect, then for integral $a_1 < a_2$, $b_1 < b_2$,

$$R([a_1,a_2]\times[b_1,b_2]) = \{S([a_1+\tfrac{1}{2},a_2-\tfrac{1}{2}]\times[b_1-\tfrac{1}{2},b_2+\tfrac{1}{2}])\}^{-1} . \tag{11.61}$$

Proof: For the time being assume

$$0 < R([a_1,a_2]\times[b_1,b_2]) < \infty . \tag{11.62}$$

Let $V(v)$ denote the potential at $v$ and $I(v,e)$ the current from $v$ to $w(e,v)$ along $e$ in the network consisting of the restriction of $\mathbb{Z}^2$ to $[a_1,a_2]\times[b_1,b_2]$ when all vertices on $A^0 := \{a_1\}\times[b_1,b_2]$ are given potential zero, and all vertices on $A^1 := \{a_2\}\times[b_1,b_2]$ are given potential one. As explained, $V(\cdot)$ and $I(\cdot,\cdot)$ have to satisfy (11.35)-(11.38) on $[a_1,a_2]\times[b_1,b_2]$. Even though this may not uniquely determine $V$ and $I$, $R([a_1,a_2]\times[b_1,b_2])$ is uniquely given by (11.43), with $\mathcal{G}$ = restriction of $\mathbb{Z}^2$ to $[a_1,a_2]\times[b_1,b_2]$. We first extend $V(\cdot)$ also to the points $[a_1+1,a_2-1]\times\{b_1-1\}$ and $[a_1+1,a_2-1]\times\{b_2+1\}$, just below and just above $[a_1,a_2]\times[b_1,b_2]$. We do this by setting

$$V((i,b_1-1)) = V((i,b_1)),\ V((i,b_2+1)) = V((i,b_2)), \tag{11.63}$$

$$a_1+1 \le i \le a_2+1 .$$

To maintain (11.35)-(11.37) we also set

$$I(v,e) = I(w,e) = 0 \text{ when } v = (i,b_1-1),\ w = (i,b_1) \tag{11.64}$$

or $v = (i,b_2+1)$, $w = (i,b_2)$, and $e$ the edge between $v$ and $w$.

Now let $e$ and $e^*$ be a pair of edges of $\mathbb{Z}^2$ and $(\mathbb{Z}^2)_d$, respectively, which intersect in their common midpoint $m$. Let the endpoints of $e$ be $v$ and $w$. When $e$ is rotated counterclockwise over an angle $\frac{\pi}{2}$, then $e$ goes over into $e^*$. Let $v$ $(w)$ go over into $v^*$ $(w^*)$ under this rotation (see Fig. 11.2 for some illustrations). We then set for $e^* \subset [a_1+\frac{1}{2},a_2-\frac{1}{2}]\times[b_1-\frac{1}{2},b_2+\frac{1}{2}]$

$$J(v^*,e^*) = -J(w^*,e^*) = V(w)-V(v) \tag{11.65}$$

$$W(w^*)-W(v^*) = I(v,e), \tag{11.66}$$

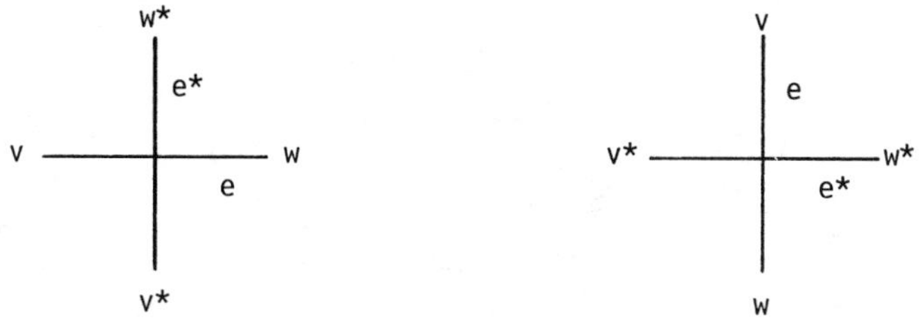


Figure 11.2

(11.67) $W(v^*) = 0$ for $v^* = (i+\frac{1}{2}, b_1 - \frac{1}{2})$, $a_1 \le i \le a_2 - 1$.

We claim that (11.65)-(11.67) define a potential $W$ and current $J$ on the network $(\mathbb{Z}^2)_d$ restricted to $[a_1+\frac{1}{2}, a_2-\frac{1}{2}] \times [b_1-\frac{1}{2}, b_2+\frac{1}{2}]$. Moreover

(11.68) $W(\cdot) = 0$ on $[a_1+\frac{1}{2}, a_2-\frac{1}{2}] \times \{b_1-\frac{1}{2}\}$

and $W(\cdot) = \frac{1}{R}$ on $[a_1+\frac{1}{2}, a_2-\frac{1}{2}] \times \{b_2+\frac{1}{2}\}$,

where $R = R([a_1,a_2] \times [b_1,b_2])$. To substantiate this claim we must first show that (11.66) and (11.67) are consistent and define the function $W(\cdot)$ unambiguously. First, we obtain from (11.64) that if $e^*$ is the edge from $v^* = (i_1 - \frac{1}{2}, b_1 - \frac{1}{2})$ to $w^* = (i_1 + \frac{1}{2}, b_1 - \frac{1}{2})$ which intersects the edge $e$ from $v = (i_1, b_1 - 1)$ to $w = (i_1, b_1)$ then $I(v,e) = 0$. Hence (11.66) tells us to take $W(w^*) = W(v^*)$ in this case. This is in agreement with the constancy of $W(\cdot)$ on $[a_1+\frac{1}{2}, a_2-\frac{1}{2}] \times \{b_1-\frac{1}{2}\}$ as required by (11.67). Next we must verify that if $r^* = (v_0^*, e_1^*, \dots, e_\nu^*, v_\nu^*)$ (with $v_\nu^* = v_0^*$) is a simple closed path on $(\mathbb{Z}^2)_d$ restricted to $[a_1+\frac{1}{2}, a_2-\frac{1}{2}] \times [b_1-\frac{1}{2}, b_2+\frac{1}{2}]$, then

$$\sum_{i=0}^{\nu-1} \{W(v_{i+1}^*) - W(v_i^*)\}$$

as defined by (11.66) indeed has the value zero. In other words, if $v_i^*$ ($v_{i+1}^*$) is the image of $v_i$ ($w_i$) after rotating the edge $e_{i+1}$ from $v_i$ to $w_i$ counterclockwise over $\frac{\pi}{2}$ around the common midpoint of $e_{i+1}^*$ and $e_{i+1}$, then we must show

(11.69) $$\sum_{i=0}^{\nu-1} I(v_i, e_{i+1}) = 0.$$

Once we prove this we can define $W(v^*)$ as

$$(11.70)\qquad W(v^*) = \sum_{i=0}^{\lambda-1} \{W(v^*_{i+1})-W(v^*_i)\} = \sum_{i=0}^{\lambda-1} I(v_i,w_i)$$

for any path $(v^*_0,e^*_1,\dots,e^*_\lambda,v^*_\lambda)$ in $[a_1+\frac{1}{2},a_2-\frac{1}{2}]\times[b_1-\frac{1}{2},b_2+\frac{1}{2}]$ with $v^*_0$ on $[a_1+\frac{1}{2},a_2-\frac{1}{2}]\times\{b_1-\frac{1}{2}\}$ and $v^*_\lambda = v^*$; all the sums in (11.70) will have the same value. To prove (11.69) whenever $r = (v^*_0,e^*_1,\dots,e^*_\nu,v^*_\nu)$ is a simple closed curve is easy. Since the interior of $r^*$ is the union of a finite number of unit squares of the form $(c-\frac{1}{2},c+\frac{1}{2})\times(d-\frac{1}{2},d+\frac{1}{2})$ it follows from standard topological arguments (see Newman (1951), Ch.V.1-V.5, especially Theorem V.21) that it suffices to verify (11.69) if $r^*$ describes the perimeter of such a unit square. Thus, it suffices to take $\nu = 4$, $v^*_0 = v^*_4 = (c-\frac{1}{2},d-\frac{1}{2})$, $v^*_1 = (c+\frac{1}{2},d-\frac{1}{2})$, $v^*_2 = (c+\frac{1}{2},d+\frac{1}{2})$, $v^*_3 = (c-\frac{1}{2},d+\frac{1}{2})$ (see Fig. 11.3) and $e^*_{i+1}$ = the edge from $v^*_i$ to $v^*_{i+1}$. However, in this case $e^*_{i+1}$ is obtained by rotating the edge $e_{i+1}$ from $v$ to $w_i$ counterclockwise over $\frac{\pi}{2}$, where

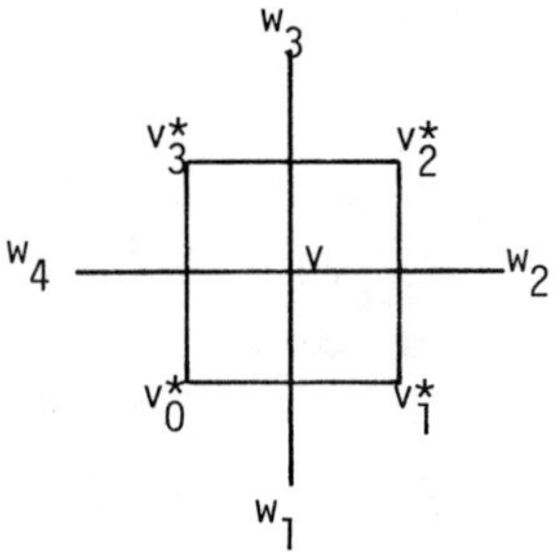


Figure 11.3

$v = (c,d)$, and $w_1,\dots,w_4$ runs over the four neighbors of $v$. Thus (11.69) reduces to

$$\sum_{\substack{e \text{ incident}\\ \text{to } v \text{ on } \mathbb{Z}^2}} I(v,e) = 0 ,$$

which is just Kirchhoff's law (11.37). Thus (11.69) holds, and $W(\cdot)$ is well defined. It satisfies the first relation in (11.68) by virtue of (11.67). The second rotation in (11.68) is verified as follows.

For $v^* = (i_1 + \frac{1}{2}, b_2 + \frac{1}{2})$ and $e_j$ the edge from $(i_1, b_1+j)$ to $(i_1+1, b_1+j)$ we obtain from (11.70)

$$(11.71) \qquad W(v^*) = \sum_{j=0}^{b_2-b_1} I((i_1, b_1+j), e_j) ,$$

which is the total current flowing from left to right through the segment $C = \{i_1\} \times [b_1, b_2]$ in $\mathbb{Z}^2 \cap [a_1, a_2] \times [b_1, b_2]$. This is precisely $1/R$ when $i_1 = a_1$, by definition of $R$ (see (11.43)). However, (11.45) shows that if $e_j'$ denotes the edge from $(i_1, b_1+j)$ to $(i_1-1, b_1+j)$, then

$$\sum_{j=0}^{b_2-b_1} I((i_1, b_1+j), e_j) + \sum_{j=0}^{b_2-b_1} I((i_1, b+j), e_j') = 0, \; a_1 < i_1 < a_2.$$

Since by (11.35) $I((i_1, b_1+j), e_j') = -I((i_1-1, b+j), e_j')$ this says that (11.71) has the same value for all $a_1 \le i_1 < a_2$. (Intuitively, this merely says that the total current flowing into $C$ from the left equals the total current flowing out to the right from $C$.) This proves (11.68).

It is also obvious that

$$W(w^*(e^*, v)) - W(v^*) = I(v, e) = \frac{V(w(e, v)) - V(v)}{R(e)} = S(e^*) J(v^*, e^*),$$

when $e^*$ intersects $e$ by (11.66), (11.36) and (11.65), provided $R(e) \neq 0$. Thus in this case $W$ and $J$ satisfy the analogue of (11.36). If $R(e) = 0$ then $S(e^*) = \infty$ and in this case the analogue of (11.36) requires $J(v^*, e^*) = 0$ (see (11.39)). This is also satisfied, since $R(e) = 0$ implies $V(w(e, v)) - V(v) = 0$ by (11.36) and then $J(v^*, e^*) = 0$ by (11.65). Thus $W$ and $J$ satisfy Ohm's law. Finally, we must verify Kirchhoff's law for $J$, i.e.,

$$(11.72) \qquad \sum_{\substack{e^* \text{ incident} \\ \text{to } v^* \text{ on } (\mathbb{Z}^2)_d}} J(v^*, e^*) = 0, \text{ for}$$
$$v^* \in [a_1 + \tfrac{1}{2}, a_2 - \tfrac{1}{2}] \times (b_1 + \tfrac{1}{2}, b_2 - \tfrac{1}{2}) .$$

If $v^* = (c + \frac{1}{2}, d + \frac{1}{2})$ with $a_1 < c < a_2$, then by (11.65), (11.72) simply reduces to the relation

$$\sum_{i=0}^{3} \{V(v_{i+1}) - V(v_i)\} = 0,$$

where $v_0 = v_4 = (c+1, d)$, $v_1 = (c, d)$, $v_2 = (c, d+1)$, $v_3 = (c+1, d+1)$.

This relation trivially holds since $v_0 = v_4$. If $c = a_1$, then there is no edge in our network between $(c+\frac{1}{2}, d+\frac{1}{2})$ and $(c-\frac{1}{2}, d+\frac{1}{2})$. Thus the term $\{V(v_2)-V(v_1)\} = V((c,d+1))-V((c,d)) = V((a_2,d+1))-V((a_1,d))$ has to be dropped from the last sum. However, this term is zero anyway, by virtue of (11.38). Thus (11.72) remains valid even when $c = a_1$, and a similar argument applies when $c = a_2$. Thus $J$ and $W$ satisfy the analogues of (11.35)-(11.38) as desired. ((11.35) is trivial from (11.65).) Thus $RJ(\cdot)$ can be taken as the current in $(\mathbb{Z}^2)_d \cap [a_1+\frac{1}{2}, a_2-\frac{1}{2}] \times [b_1-\frac{1}{2}, b_2+\frac{1}{2}]$ when the potential on $[a_1+\frac{1}{2}, a_2-\frac{1}{2}] \times \{b_1-\frac{1}{2}\}$ is set equal to zero and on $[a_1+\frac{1}{2}, a_2-\frac{1}{2}] \times \{b_2+\frac{1}{2}\}$ equal to one, and when $e^*$ has resistance $S(e^*) = 1/R(e)$. Consequently, by the definition (11.43) and (11.65)

$$S([a_1+\tfrac{1}{2}, a_2-\tfrac{1}{2}] \times [b_1-\tfrac{1}{2}, b_2+\tfrac{1}{2}])$$

$$= \{\sum_{a_1 \le i < a_2} RJ((i+\tfrac{1}{2}, b_1-\tfrac{1}{2}), (i+\tfrac{1}{2}, b_1+\tfrac{1}{2}))\}^{-1}$$

$$= \frac{1}{R}\{\sum_{a_1 \le i < a_2} (V((i+1,b_1)-V(i,b_1))\}^{-1}$$

$$= \frac{1}{R}\{V(a_2,b_1)-V(a_1,b_1)\}^{-1} .$$

Since $V$ was taken zero (one) on $\{a_1\} \times [b_1,b_2] (a_2 \times [b_1,b_2])$ this proves (11.61) whenever (11.62) holds.

By (11.58) the case $R([a_1,a_2] \times [b_1,b_2]) = 0$ occurs if and only if there exists a path $r = (v_0, e_1, \dots, e_\nu, v_\nu)$ on $\mathbb{Z}^2 \cap [a_1,a_2] \times [b_1,b_2]$ from $A^0$ to $A^1$ such that $R(e_i) = 0$ for all $1 \le i \le \nu$. Let $\mathcal{D}$ be the part of $[a_1+\frac{1}{2}, a_2-\frac{1}{2}] \times [b_1-\frac{1}{2}, b_2+\frac{1}{2}]$ below $r$. Each edge of $(\mathbb{Z}^2)_d \cap [a_1+\frac{1}{2}, a_2-\frac{1}{2}] \times [b_1-\frac{1}{2}, b_2+\frac{1}{2}]$ leaving $\mathcal{D}$ has to be an edge $e^*$ which intersects some $e_i$, $1 \le i \le \nu$, and therefore has $S(e^*) = \infty$. Thus, no current can leave $\mathcal{D}$ in the network $(\mathbb{Z}^2)_d \cap [a_1+\frac{1}{2}, a_2-\frac{1}{2}] \times [b_1-\frac{1}{2}, b_2+\frac{1}{2}]$. Thus by (11.56) applied to this network $S([a_1+\frac{1}{2}, a_1-\frac{1}{2}] \times [b_1-\frac{1}{2}, b_2+\frac{1}{2}]) = \infty$. Thus (11.61) also holds if $R = 0$.

Finally, if $R([a_1,a_2] \times [b_1,b_2]) = \infty$, then by (11.59) there is no conducting path from $A^0$ to $A^1$ in $[a_1,a_2] \times [b_1,b_2]$. By Prop. 2.2, or somewhat more directly by Whitney's theorem (see Smythe and Wierman (1978), proof of Theorem 2.2) it follows that there is then a path $r^*$ on $(\mathbb{Z}^2)_d \cap [a_1+\frac{1}{2},a_2-\frac{1}{2}]\times[b_1-\frac{1}{2},b_2+\frac{1}{2}]$ all of whose edges have zero resistance and which connects the bottom edge $[a_1+\frac{1}{2},a_2-\frac{1}{2}]$ $\times \{b_1-\frac{1}{2}\}$ with the top edge $[a_1+\frac{1}{2},a_2-\frac{1}{2}]\times\{b_2+\frac{1}{2}\}$. (Prop. 2.2 is somewhat clumsier than Whitney's theorem here, because it requires transference of the problem to the covering graph.) The existence of $r^*$ shows that $S([a_1+\frac{1}{2},a_2-\frac{1}{2}]\times[b_1-\frac{1}{2},b_2+\frac{1}{2}]) = 0$. This confirms (11.61) in the last case. □

The reader probably does not need to be reminded that when two vertices $v'$ and $v''$ are connected only by a path $(v' = v_0,e_1,\ldots,e_\nu,v_\nu = v'')$ then the resistance between $v'$ and $v''$ is $\sum_1^\nu R(e_i)$. (The resistances $R(e_1),\ldots,R(e_\nu)$ are in series in this case; see Feynman et al (1963), Sect. I.25.5 and II.22.3.) Also, if $v'$ and $v''$ are connected exactly by $k$ paths $r_1,\ldots,r_k$ which are pairwise disjoint (except for the common endpoints $v'$ and $v''$) then these paths form parallel resistances. If the edges in $r_j$ are $\{e_{ji}\}$, then the resistance of $r_j$ is $\sum_i R(e_{ji})$ and the resistance between $v'$ and $v''$ is

$$\left(\sum_j \left\{\sum_i R(e_{ji})\right\}^{-1}\right)^{-1}$$

(see Feynman et al (1963), Sect. I.25.5 and II.22.3).

Finally we make repeated use of the following monotonicity property.

Lemma 11.4. If $R_1(e)$ and $R_2(e)$ are two assignments of resistances to the edges of $\mathcal{G}$ and $R_1$, $R_2$ the corresponding values of the resistance between $A^0$ and $A^1$, then

(11.73) $$R_1(e) \le R_2(e) \text{ for all } e \text{ implies } R_1 \le R_2.$$

Proof: Despite its intuitive content, we have no intuitive proof of (11.73). A quick proof for (11.73) when

(11.74) $$0 < R_1(e) \le R_2(e) \quad \text{for all } e$$

can be found in Griffeath and Liggett (1983), Theorem 2.1. It is based on the fact that under (11.74) the expression

$$(R_i)^{-1} = \sum_e \frac{V_i(w(e,v))}{R(e)}$$

given in (11.43) for the reciprocal of $R_i$ can also be written as

$$\frac{1}{2} \min_h \sum_{e \in \mathcal{G}} \frac{\{h(v)-h(w)\}^2}{R_i(e)}, \quad i = 1,2. \tag{11.75}$$

Here $V_i(\cdot)$ is the potential function corresponding to the resistances $R_i(e)$, $v$ and $w$ denote the endpoints of $e$, while the min in (11.75) is over all functions $h$ from the vertex set of $\mathcal{G}$ into $[0,1]$ which satisfy

$$h(v) = 0 \text{ if } v \in A^0, \; h(v) = 1 \text{ if } w \in A^1.$$

(11.75) is usually called Dirichlet's principle. Its proof works as long as all edges have a strictly positive resistance; edges with infinite resistance do not cause difficulties. Clearly, (11.73) follows immediately from (11.75) whenever (11.74) holds[1]. When $R_1(e)$ and/or $R_2(e)$ can be zero we have to use a limiting procedure. Let

$$R^\varepsilon(e) = R(e)+\varepsilon, \; R_i^\varepsilon(e) = R_i(e)+\varepsilon$$

and denote by $R^\varepsilon$, $R_i^\varepsilon$ the corresponding resistance between $A^0$ and $A^1$. Then by (11.73) $R_1^\varepsilon \le R_2^\varepsilon$ for all $\varepsilon > 0$. It therefore suffices to show that

$$R^\varepsilon \downarrow R^0 = R \text{ as } \varepsilon \downarrow 0. \tag{11.76}$$

(11.76) is very easy if there exists a short circuit between $A^0$ and $A^1$. For in this case we defined $R$ as zero, while

$R^\varepsilon \le \varepsilon$ (number of edges in any path from $A^0$ to $A^1$ all of whose edges have zero resistance)

(apply (11.73) with $R_1(e) = R^\varepsilon(e)$ and $R_2(e) = R^\varepsilon(e)$ for $e$ belonging to some short circuit between $A^0$ and $A^1$ and $R_2(e) = \infty$ otherwise).

For the remainder of this lemma assume that there is no short circuit between $A^0$ and $A^1$. Observe that by the maximum principle (11.42) $0 \le V^\varepsilon(v) \le 1$ for all $v$ in the set $\mathcal{C}_1$ of Lemma 11.2. (Of course $V^\varepsilon$ and $I^\varepsilon$ denote the potential and current when $R^\varepsilon(e)$ is

---

[1] An alternative approach to (11.73) is via Thomson's principle, which is a dual to Dirichlet's principle (see Doyle and Snell (1982), Sect. 2.9). This works well as long as all edges have finite resistance. In this approach one has to prove an analogue of (11.76) as resistances increase to $\infty$.

the resistance of $e$, and the boundary condition (11.38) is imposed.) Note that $\mathbb{C}_1$ is the same for all $\varepsilon$ and that we showed in the proof of Lemma 11.2 that $R^\varepsilon$ is determined by $V_{|\mathbb{C}_1}$. Now let $\varepsilon_n$ be any sequence decreasing to 0. Since $V^\varepsilon_{|\mathbb{C}_1}$ is uniformly bounded we can pick a subsequence (which for convenience we still denote by $\{\varepsilon_n\}$) such that $V^\varepsilon_{|\mathbb{C}_1}$ converges to some function $\tilde{V}$ on $\mathbb{C}_1$ as $\varepsilon$ runs through the subsequence $\{\varepsilon_n\}$. If $e$ is any edge with $R^0(e) = R(e) > 0$ and its endpoints $v$ and $w$ in $\mathbb{C}_1$, then

$$I^{\varepsilon_n}(v,e) = \frac{V^{\varepsilon_n}(w)-V^{\varepsilon_n}(v)}{R^{\varepsilon_n}(e)}$$

(see (11.40)) also converges to some $\tilde{I}(v,e)$ and

$$\tilde{V}(w)-\tilde{V}(v) = R(e)\tilde{I}(v,e).$$

The main difficulty is to show that

$$\tilde{V}(w(e,v)) = \tilde{V}(v) \quad \text{if} \quad R(e) = 0 \text{ and } v \in \mathbb{C}_1 . \tag{11.77}$$

This does not follow from the above arguments but comes from the following separate argument. Let $C_i$ be an equivalence class of vertices, i.e., a maximal class of vertices which are connected by paths of zero resistance (see the text following (11.45)). Either $C_i \subset \mathbb{C}_1$ or $C_i$ is disjoint from $\mathbb{C}_1$, by definition of $C_i$ and $\mathbb{C}_1$. We are interested in the case with $C_i \subset \mathbb{C}_1$ and $\#C_i > 1$. Let $v \in C_i \setminus (A^0 \cup A^1)$ and write (11.41) for $V^\varepsilon$ as follows

$$V^\varepsilon(v) = \frac{\frac{1}{\varepsilon}\sum_0 V^\varepsilon(w(e,v)) + \sum_1 \frac{V^\varepsilon(w(\varepsilon,v))}{R(e)+\varepsilon}}{\sum_0 \frac{1}{\varepsilon} + \sum_1 \frac{1}{R(e)+\varepsilon}} ,$$

where $\sum_0$ is the sum over edges $e$ incident to $v$ with $R(e) = 0$ (and hence $R^\varepsilon(e) = \varepsilon$) and $\sum_1$ is the sum over edges $e$ incident to $v$ with $R(e) > 0$. By letting $\varepsilon$ run through the sequence $\{\varepsilon_n\}$ we obtain - whenever $\#C_i > 1$ and hence $\sum_0$ nonempty -

$$\tilde{V}(v) = \frac{\sum_0 V(w(e,v))}{\sum_0 1}, \quad v \in C_i \setminus (A^0 \cup A^1). \tag{11.78}$$

Thus on $C_i \setminus (A^0 \cup A^1)$ $\tilde{V}(v)$ is the average over its neighbors connected to $v$ by an edge of zero resistance. Of course, all these neighbors have to belong to $C_i$ as well, by definition of $C_i$. Now assume that $C_i$ is disjoint from $A^1$ and that $\tilde{V}$ achieves its maximum over $C_i$ at $v_0 \in C_i$. If $v_0 \in A^0$, then $\tilde{V}(v_0) = 0$ (by (11.38)) and hence $\tilde{V}(i) \equiv 0$ on $C_i$. If $v_0 \notin A^0$, then by (11.78) $\tilde{V}(w) = \tilde{V}(v_0)$ at each point $w$ which is connected to $v_0$ by a path of zero resistance. Thus also in this case $\tilde{V}(\cdot)$ has the constant value $\tilde{V}(v_0)$ on $C_i$. The same argument with $\min\limits_{v \in C_i} \tilde{V}(v)$ replacing $\max\limits_{v \in C_i} \tilde{V}(v)$ works when $C_i$ is disjoint from $A^0$. In the last possible case when $C_i$ intersects $A^0$ and $A^1$ we already proved (11.76), so that this case does not have to be considered. We have therefore proved (11.77) and (11.76) follows quickly now. Indeed, (11.77) shows that $\tilde{V}$ is constant on any $C_i$. If we denote this constant value by $\tilde{V}(C_i)$, then one immediately sees that $\tilde{V}$ and $\tilde{I}$ must satisfy (11.46)-(11.49), at least when we restrict ourselves to $\mathcal{G}_{|\mathcal{C}_1}$ as in Lemma 11.2. These equations have the unique solution $V_{|\mathcal{C}_1}$. Thus $\tilde{V}_{|\mathcal{C}_1} = V_{|\mathcal{C}_1}$ and (see (11.50))

$$R = \{\sum \frac{\tilde{V}(C_j)}{R(e)}\}^{-1} \tag{11.79}$$

where the sum is over all edges $e$ of $\mathcal{G}_{|\mathcal{C}_1}$ having one endpoint in some $C_i$ which intersects $A^0$ while the other endpoint lies in a $C_j$ which is disjoint from $A^0$. The fact that we may restrict the sum to edges of $\mathcal{G}_{|\mathcal{C}_1}$ is in the proof of Lemma 11.2. But also, by (11.56) with $\mathcal{D} = A^0 \cup \{C_i : C_i$ intersects $A^0\}$, we have

$$R^{\varepsilon} = \{\sum \frac{V^{\varepsilon}(w(e,v))-V^{\varepsilon}(v)}{R^{\varepsilon}(e)}\}^{-1}, \tag{11.80}$$

where the sum runs over all edges $e$ of $\mathcal{G}_{|\mathcal{C}_1}$ with one endpoint $v$ in some $C_i$ which intersects $A^0$, and the other endpoint $w(e,v)$ in a $C_j$ which does not intersect $A^0$. Again the restriction to edges of $\mathcal{G}_{|\mathcal{C}_1}$ rather than $\mathcal{G}$ makes no difference. Now let $\varepsilon \to 0$ through the sequence $\varepsilon_n$. $V^{\varepsilon_n}(v)$ converges to $\tilde{V}(C_i) = V(C_i) = 0$ if $v$ belongs to a $C_i$ which intersects $A^0$, and $V^{\varepsilon_n}(w) \to \tilde{V}(C_j) = V(C_j)$ if $w \in C_j$. Moreover $R(e) > 0$ for each $e$ appearing in the right hand side of (11.80). Thus, the right hand side of (11.80) converges to the right hand side of (11.79). This proves (11.76) and the lemma. □

## 11.4 Proofs of Theorems 11.2 and 11.3.

We remind the reader that $B_n = [0,n]\times[0,n]$, $A_n^0 = \{0\}\times[0,n]$, $A_n^1 = \{n\}\times[0,n]$ and $R_n$ is the resistance of $\mathbb{Z}^2 \cap B_n$ between $A_n^0$ and $A_n^1$.

Proof of Theorem 11.2. To prove (11.9) recall that, by (11.58), $R_n = 0$ as soon as there exists any path on $\mathbb{Z}^2 \cap B_n$ from $A_n^0$ to $A_n^1$ all of whose edges have zero resistance. The probability of this event is at least equal to

$$P_{p(0)}\{\exists \text{ occupied horizontal crossing on } \mathcal{G}_1 \text{ of } [0,n]\times[0,n]\}$$

$$= \sigma((n,n);\ 1,p(0),\mathcal{G}_1),$$

as one can see from the relation between bond-percolation on $\mathbb{Z}^2$ and site-percolation on its covering graph $\mathcal{G}_1$ (see Comment 2.5(iii) and Prop. 3.1). By (7.14) and the definition (3.33) this shows

$$P\{R_n = 0\} \geq 1-\sigma^*((n+2\Lambda_4,n-2\Lambda_4);2,p(0);\mathcal{G}_1)$$

$$= 1-\sigma((n+2\Lambda_4,n-2\Lambda_4);2,1-p(0),\mathcal{G}_1^*)$$

for some constant $\Lambda_4 = \Lambda_4(\mathcal{G}_1)$. Finally $p(0) > \frac{1}{2} = p_H(\mathcal{G}_1)$ is equivalent to $1-p(0) < \frac{1}{2} = p_H(\mathcal{G}_1^*) = p_T(\mathcal{G}_1^*)$ (see Application 3.4 (ii)). Thus by Theorem 5.1 (see also the end of proof of Lemma 5.4)

$$\sigma(n+2\Lambda_4,n-2\Lambda_4,2,1-p(0),\mathcal{G}_1^*) \leq C_1(2n+4\Lambda_4)e^{-C_2 n}$$

for $p(0) > \frac{1}{2}$. (11.9) follows from these estimates and the Borel-Cantelli lemma (see Renyi (1970) Lemma VII.5A).

The proof of (11.10) is very similar. By (11.59) $R_n = \infty$ whenever there does not exist a conducting path on $\mathbb{Z}^2 \cap B_n$ from $A_n^0$ to $A_n^1$. Again by the relation between bond-percolation on $\mathbb{Z}^2$ and site-percolation on $\mathcal{G}_1$, as in Comment 2.5(iii) we get from this

$$P\{R_n = \infty\} \geq 1-\sigma((n-2,n+2));\ 1,1-p(\infty),\mathcal{G}_1).$$

For $1-p(\infty) < \frac{1}{2} = p_H(\mathcal{G}_1) = p_T(\mathcal{G}_1)$ we again get from Theorem 5.1

$$P\{R_n = \infty\} \geq 1-C_1 e^{-C_2 n} .$$

An application of the Borel-Cantelli lemma now proves (11.10).

For the upper bound in (11.11) we shall use Theorem 11.1 and Lemmas 11.1 and 11.4. Note that the proof below works just as well if $B_n$ is replaced by $[0,n]\times[0,n-m]$ and $A_n^0$ by $\{0\}\times[0,n-m]$, $A_n^1$ by $\{n\}\times[0,n-m]$ for any fixed integer $m$. This will be relevant for the proof of the lower bound in (11.11) later on. Now let $M$ be some large integer and assume we can find $k$ paths $r^1,\dots,r^k$ in $[0,n]\times[M,n-M]$ $\subset B_n$ from $A_n^0$ to $A_n^1$ such that $R(e)<\infty$ for each edge $e$ appearing in any of these paths, and such that $r^i$ and $r^j$ have no edge in common. By Lemma 11.1 we do not change $R_n$ if we replace $R(e)$ by

$$\tilde{R}(e) := \begin{cases} 0 & \text{if } \overset{\circ}{e} \text{ is surrounded by a circuit } r \text{ or } \\ & \mathbb{Z}^2 \text{ which lies in } B_n \text{ and all of whose} \\ & \text{edges have zero resistance,} \\ R(e) & \text{otherwise .} \end{cases}$$

After this replacement, $\tilde{R}^j$ := resistance of the path $r^j$ equals

$$\sum_i \tilde{R}(e_i^j),$$

where $e_1^j, e_2^j,\dots$ are the successive edges in $r^j$ (see the lines preceding Lemma 11.4). But the paths $r^1,\dots,r^k$ are almost parallel resistances between $A_n^0$ and $A_n^1$. They can fail to be parallel because the paths can intersect in vertices. If two edges $e_i^j$ and $e_k^\ell$ have an endpoint $v$ in common we can think of this as a link of zero resistance between an endpoint of $e_i^j$ and $e_k^\ell$. Removing the link is equivalent to giving it infinite resistance. By Lemma 11.4 this removal can only increase the resistance of the network. Thus $R_n$ has at most the value of the resistance of the network consisting of $k$ parallel resistances $r^1,\dots,r^k$, i.e.,

$$R_n \le \{\frac{1}{\tilde{R}^1}+\dots+\frac{1}{\tilde{R}^k}\}^{-1} .$$

Since the harmonic mean of positive quantities is no more than their arithmetic mean (by Jensen's inequality; cf. Rudin (1966), Theorem 3.3), and since all $e_i^j$ are distinct and contained in $[0,n]\times[M,n-M]$ and have finite resistance (by our choice of $r^1,\dots,r^k$), we obtain

$$(11.81)\qquad R_n \le \frac{1}{k^2}\sum_{j=1}^{k}\tilde{R}^j = \frac{1}{k^2}\sum_{j=1}^{k}\sum_i \tilde{R}(e_i^j)$$

$$\leq \frac{1}{k^2} \sum_{e \subset [0,n] \times [M,n-M]} \tilde{R}(e) I[R(e) < \infty] .$$

Finally, denote by $m(e) = (m_1(e), m_2(e))$ the midpoint of the edge $e$, and by $I(e) = I_M(e)$ the indicator function of the event

$\{\mathring{e}$ does not lie inside any circuit on $\mathbb{Z}^2$ made up of edges with zero resistance and contained in the square $[m_1(e)-M+1, m_1(e)+M-1] \times [m_2(e)-M+1, m_2(e)+M-1]\}$ .

Then

$$\tilde{R}(e) I[R(e) < \infty] \leq R(e) I[R(e) < \infty] I_M(e) \quad \text{for } e \subset [M,n-M] \times [M,n-M], \tag{11.82}$$

$$\tilde{R}(e) I[R(e) < \infty] \leq R(e) I[R(e) < \infty] \quad \text{for all } e \subset B_n . \tag{11.83}$$

By the ergodic theorem (Tempel'man (1972), Theorem 6.1, Cor. 6.2 or Dunford and Schwartz (1958), Theorem VIII. 6.9; also use Harris (1960), Lemma 3.1 and the fact that $R(e) \geq 0$)

$$\lim_{n\to\infty} \frac{1}{2n^2} \sum_{e \subset [M,n-M]^2} R(e) I[R(e) < \infty] I_M(e) = E\{R(e_0) I[R(e_0) < \infty] I_M(e_0)\} \tag{11.84}$$

with probability one ($e_0$ is an arbitrary fixed edge). Furthermore, if

$$\int_{(0,\infty)} x \, dF(x) = E\{R(e_0) I[R(e_0) < \infty]\} < \infty \tag{11.85}$$

then by Birkhoff's ergodic theorem (Walters (1982), Theorem 1.14)

$$\lim_{n\to\infty} \frac{1}{n} \sum_{e \subset [0,M] \times [0,n]} R(e) I[R(e) < \infty] = 2(M+1) E\{R(e_0) I[R(e_0) < \infty]\} < \infty$$

and consequently

$$\lim_{n\to\infty} \frac{1}{2n^2} \sum_{e \subset [0,M] \times [0,n]} R(e) I[R(e) < \infty] = 0 \tag{11.86}$$

with probability one. Also, under (11.85) the ergodic theorem implies

$$(11.87)\qquad \frac{1}{2n^2}\sum_{e\subset[n-M,n]\times[0,n]}\{R(e)I[R(e)<\infty]\}$$

$$= \frac{1}{2n^2}\sum_{e\subset B_n}\{R(e)I[R(e)<\infty]\}$$

$$- \frac{1}{2n^2}\sum_{\mathring{e}\subset[0,n-M)\times[0,n]}\{R(e)I[R(e)<\infty]\}$$

$$\to \int_{(0,\infty)} x\,dF(x) - \int_{(0,\infty)} x\,dF(x) = 0 \qquad (n\to\infty)$$

with probability one. Of course, we may assume that (11.85) holds, since the upper bound in (11.11) is vacuous otherwise. It follows from (11.82)-(11.87) that

$$\limsup_{n\to\infty}\frac{1}{2n^2}\sum_{e\subset[0,n]\times[M,n-M]}\tilde{R}(e)I[R(e)<\infty]$$

$$\le E\{R(e_0)I[R(e_0<\infty)]I_M(e_0)\}\ .$$

Together with (11.81) this implies for each fixed $M$

$$(11.88)\qquad \limsup R_n \le 2\limsup\left(\frac{n}{k(n,M)}\right)^2 E\{R(e_0)I[R(e_0)<\infty]I_M(e_0)\},$$

where

$k(n,M)$ = maximal number of edge-disjoint conducting paths in $[0,n]\times[M,n-M]$ from $A_n^0$ to $A_n^1$.

(We call $r^1,\dots,r^k$ edge-disjoint if $r^i$ and $r^j$ have no common edges for $i\neq j$.) A simple translation of (11.4) from site-percolation on $\mathcal{G}_1$ to bond percolation on $\mathbb{Z}^2$ as in Comment 2.5(iii) gives for large $n$

$$P\{k(n,M)\ge\frac{1}{2}C_1(\tfrac{1}{2}-p(\infty))^{\delta_1}n\}\ge 1-2C_2 n\exp-C_3(\tfrac{1}{2}-p(\infty))^{\delta_2}n\ .$$

(Recall that $p_H(\mathcal{G}_1)=\frac{1}{2}$ by Application 3.4(ii) and that $P\{R(e)<\infty\}$ $=1-p(\infty)$.) Thus, by the Borel-Cantelli lemma

$$\limsup\left(\frac{n}{k(n,M)}\right)\le\frac{2}{C_1}\left(\tfrac{1}{2}-p(\infty)\right)^{-\delta_1}$$

with probability one, for each $M$. In view of (11.88) this gives

$$\limsup R_n \le \frac{8}{C_1^2}\left(\tfrac{1}{2}-p(\infty)\right)^{-2\delta_1}\lim_{M\to\infty}E\{R(e_0)I[R(e_0)<\infty]I_M(e_0)\}$$

with probability one. We complete the proof of the upper bound in (11.11) by showing that

(11.89) $$\lim_{M\to\infty} E\{R(e_0)I[R(e_0) < \infty]I_M(e_0)\} = \frac{1}{1-p(0)}\,\theta_2(1-p(0))\int_{(0,\infty)} x\,dF(x).$$

To prove (11.89) we observe that

(11.90) $I_M(e_0) \downarrow I[e_0$ is not surrounded by a circuit on $\mathbb{Z}^2$ made up of edges with zero resistance], $M \uparrow \infty$.

Now consider the following bond-percolation problem on $(\mathbb{Z}^2)_d$. Call and edge $f^*$ of $(\mathbb{Z}^2)_d$ open if the edge $f$ of $\mathbb{Z}^2$ which intersects $f^*$ has non-zero resistance, and blocked otherwise. Then, if the open cluster of $e_0^*$ on $(\mathbb{Z}^2)_d$ is non-empty and finite, it must be contained inside a circuit on $\mathbb{Z}^2$ made up of zero resistances. This follows from Whitney's Theorem (Whitney 1933), Theorem 4) as explained in Harris (1960), Lemma 7.1 and Appendix 2. Compare also Example 1 in Hammersley (1959). We proved an analogue for site-percolation in Cor. 2.2. and the above result can be obtained from Cor. 2.2. by the usual translation from bond-percolation on $(\mathbb{Z}^2)_d$ (which is isomorphic to $\mathbb{Z}^2$) to site-percolation on the covering graph $\mathcal{G}_1$ of $\mathbb{Z}^2$ (see Comment 2.5 (iii) and Prop. 3.1). The open cluster of $e_0^*$ is non-empty iff $e_0^*$ is open, or equivalently iff $R(e_0) > 0$. Moreover, the probability that any edge is open is $1-p(0)$. It follows from these observations, that the expectation of the limit of $I_M(e_0)$ in (11.90) is just

$$P\{\text{open cluster of } e_0^* \text{ on } (\mathbb{Z}^2)_d \text{ is infinite} \mid e_0^* \text{ is open}\} = \frac{\theta_2(1-p(0))}{1-p(0)}.$$

(11.89) is immediate from this since $R(e_0)$ is independent of $I_M(e_0)$. This completes the proof of the upper bound in (11.11).

The lower bound in (11.11) can be proved by a direct argument which does not rely on $\mathbb{Z}^2$ being self-dual (see Remark 11.4(i) below for an indication of such a proof). Here we shall merely appeal to the fact that by Lemma 11.3

$$\frac{1}{R_n} = S([\tfrac{1}{2}, n-\tfrac{1}{2}] \times [-\tfrac{1}{2}, n+\tfrac{1}{2}]).$$

However, $(\mathbb{Z}^2)_d$ is isomorphic to $\mathbb{Z}^2$ so that $S([\tfrac{1}{2}, n-\tfrac{1}{2}] \times [-\tfrac{1}{2}, n+\tfrac{1}{2}])$

has the same distribution as $R([0,n+1]\times[0,n-1])$ when the distribution of an individual edge is given by

$$(11.91)\qquad \begin{aligned} P\{R(e) = 0\} &= p(\infty), \\ P\{R(e) = \infty\} &= p(0), \\ P\{R(e) \in B\} &= \int_{\frac{1}{x}\in B} dF(x),\ B \subset (0,\infty). \end{aligned}$$

(Compare (11.6)-(11.8) and recall that $S(e^*) = 1/R(e)$ in Lemma 11.3.) The lower bound in (11.11) now follows by applying the upper bound in (11.11) to $R([0,n+1]\times[0,n-1])$ when the distribution of $R(e)$ is as given by (11.91) instead of (11.6)-(11.8). (Note that the upper bound applies just as well to $R([0,n+1]\times[0,n-1])$ as to $R_n = R([0,n]\times[0,n])$ as pointed out in the beginning of the proof of (11.11).) □

Corollary 11.1 is immediate from (11.11) and (8.4).

Proof of Theorem 11.3. We do not give a detailed proof of (11.22). Its proof is a simplified version of the proof of the upper bound in (11.11). This time we do not use Lemma 11.1 and do not replace $R(e)$ by $\tilde{R}(e)$. We simply find enough edge disjoint conducting paths from $A_n^0$ to $A_n^1$ by applying Theorem 11.1 to the restrictions of $B_n$ to planes specified by fixing $x(3),\dots,x(d)$, i.e., to graphs which are the restrictions of $\mathbb{Z}^d$ to $[0,n]\times[0,n]\times\{i(3)\}\times\dots\times\{i(d)\}$, with $0 \le i(3) \le n,\dots,$ $0 \le i(d) \le n$.

(11.19) is quite trivial. As in (11.9) $R_n = 0$ as soon as there is a path in $B_n$ from $A_n^0$ to $A_n^1$ all of whose edges have zero resistance. But the probability that such a connection exists in $[0,n]\times[0,n]\times\{i(3)\}\times\dots\times\{i(d)\}$ equals the sponge-crossing probability $S_{p(0)}(n,n)$ of Seymour and Welsh (1978). By their results (see pp.233, 234) for $p(0) \ge \frac{1}{2}$

$$S_{p(0)}(n,n) \ge S_{1/2}(n,n) \ge S_{1/2}(n,n+1) = \frac{1}{2}^{1)}.$$

Since crossings in $[0,n]\times[0,n]\times\{i(3)\}\times\dots\times\{i(d)\}$ for different $i(3),\dots,i(d)$ are independent, it follows that

1) Here we merely need that $S_{1/2}(n,n)$ is bounded away from zero. By going over to site-percolation we can also obtain this from Theorem 5.1. However, the proof of Seymour and Welsh (1978) is much simpler in the special case of bond-percolation on $\mathbb{Z}^2$.

$$P\{R_n = 0\} \geq 1-2^{-(n+1)^{d-2}} \quad \text{if} \quad p(0) \geq \frac{1}{2}.$$

(11.19) thus follows from the Borel-Cantelli lemma.

Also (11.20) is easy. By Theorem 5.1, (5.16) and the end of the proof of Lemma 5.4 (see (5.55)) one has for $1-p(\infty) < p_{S,d}$

$$P\{\exists \text{ conducting path in } B_n \text{ from } A_n^0 \text{ to } A_n^1\}$$

$$\leq \sum_{v\in A_n^0} P\{\text{number of edges reachable by a conducting path from } v \text{ is at least } n\}$$

$$\leq (n+1)^{d-1} C_1 e^{-C_2 n} .$$

Again, it follows from the Borel-Cantelli lemma that with probability one for all large $n$ there does not exist a conducting path in $B_n$ from $A_n^0$ to $A_n^1$. In view of (11.59) this implies (11.20).

We finally turn to (11.21). Its proof rests on Lemma 11.2. First we replace the resistance of each edge $e$ which does not have each endpoint in $\mathcal{C}_1$ by $\infty$. Here $\mathcal{C}_1$ is as in Lemma 11.2 with $\mathcal{G}$ = restriction of $\mathbb{Z}^d$ to $B_n$. This replacement does not change $R_n$. Denote the midpoint of $e$ by $m(e) = (m_1(e),\dots,m_d(e))$ and set

$J_M(e) = 0$ if there exists a conducting path in the full network $\mathbb{Z}^d$ from one of the endpoints of $e$ to one of the two hyperplanes $x(1) = m_1(e)\pm M$,

and $J_M(e) = 1$ otherwise. Then for $M < m_1(e) < n-M$, $J_M(e) = 1$ implies that both endpoints of $e$ are outisde $\mathcal{C}_1$, since they are not connected to $A_n^0 \cup A_n^1$ by a conducting path in $\mathbb{Z}^d \cap B_n$. Therefore the modified resistance for such edges is at least $R(e) + J_M(e)\cdot\infty$. Thus by Lemma 11. $R_n$ is at least as large as the resistance between $A_n^0$ and $A_n^1$ when $R(e)+J_M(e)\cdot\infty$ is used instead of $R(e)$ for the resistance of each edge $e$ with $M < m_1(e) < n-M$. We next reduce to zero the resistances of all "vertical" edges between two neighbors $(i(1),\dots,i(d))$ and $(i(1),i(2),\dots,i'(s),\dots,i(d))$ with $2 \leq s \leq d$, $|i'(s)-i(s)| = 1$. By Lemma 11.4 once more this does not increase $R_n$. Set

$$\tilde{R}(e) = \begin{cases} R(e)+J_M(e)\cdot\infty & \text{if } e \text{ is a "horizontal" edge and} \\ & \quad M < m_1(e) < n-M \\ R(e) & \text{if } e \text{ is a "horizontal" edge with} \\ & \quad 0 \leq m_1(e) \leq M \text{ or } n-M \leq m_1(e) \leq n \\ 0 & \text{if } e \text{ is a "vertical" edge.} \end{cases}$$

A "vertical" edge was defined above, and a horizontal edge is an edge from $(i(1),\dots,i(d))$ to $(i(1)+1,i(2),\dots,i(d))$ for some $0 \le i(1) < n$, $0 \le i(2),\dots,i(d) \le n$. Denote by $\tilde{R}_n$ the resistance between $A_n^0$ and $A_n^1$ in $B_n$, when $\tilde{R}(e)$ is the resistance of the generic edge $e$. Then, by the above $R_n \ge \tilde{R}_n$. However, $\tilde{R}_n$ is easy to calculate. As discussed in Sect. 11.3 all vertices in a "vertical plate" $\{i(1)\} \times [0,n]^{d-1}$ will have the same potential since they are connected by zero resistances. We may therefore identify these vertices to one vertex. If we do this for each $i(1) \in [0,n]$, then we obtain a graph $\mathcal{K}_n$ whose vertices we denote by $\hat{0},\dots,\hat{n}$, with $\hat{i}$ corresponding to the plate $\{i\} \times [0,n]^{d-1}$ in $\mathbb{Z}^d \cap B_n$. There are $(n+1)^{d-1}$ edges between $\hat{i}$ and $(\widehat{i+1})$ with resistances $\tilde{R}(e_{ij})$, where $j$ runs through the $(n+1)^{d-1}$ possible values for $(i(2),\dots,i(d))$ and $e_{ij}$ denotes the edge from $(i,j)$ to $(i+1,j)$ (see Fig. 11.4). These resistances are

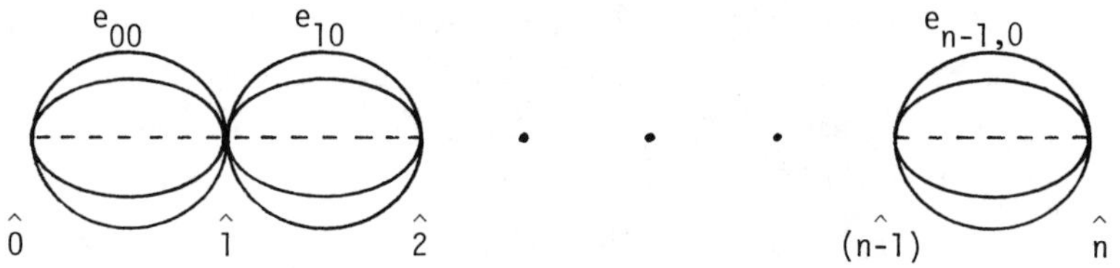


Figure 11.4. The graph $\mathcal{K}_n$ obtained by identifying vertices on "vertical plates".

in parallel, and equivalent to a single resistance of size

$$\{\sum_j (\tilde{R}(e_{ij}))^{-1}\}^{-1}$$

between $\hat{i}$ and $(\widehat{i+1})$. The resistances between $\hat{i}$ and $(\widehat{i+1})$ for $i = 0,1,\dots,n-1$ are in series so that

$$\tilde{R}_n = \sum_{i=0}^{n-1} \{\sum_j (\tilde{R}(e_{ij}))^{-1}\}^{-1} \ge \sum_{i=M}^{n-M} \{\sum_j (\tilde{R}(e_{ij}))^{-1}\}^{-1}$$

$$\ge (n-M+1)^2 \{\sum_{i=M}^{n-M} \sum_j (\tilde{R}(e_{ij}))^{-1}\}^{-1} .$$

The last inequality again results from the fact that the arithmetic mean is at least as large as the harmonic mean. Consequently, by the ergodic theorem (Tempel'man (1972), Theorem 6.1, Cor. 6.2 or Dunford and Schwartz (1958), Theorem VIII.6.9).

$$\begin{aligned}\liminf n^{d-2}R_n &\geq \liminf n^{d-2}\tilde{R}_n \geq \lim n^d \{\sum_{i=M}^{n-M} \sum_j (\tilde{R}(e_{ij}))^{-1}\}^{-1} \\ &= (E\{(\tilde{R}(e_0))^{-1}\})^{-1} \\ &= (P\{J_M(e_0) = 0\})^{-1}\{\int \frac{1}{x}\, dF(x)\}^{-1} ,\end{aligned}$$

for any fixed $M$, and any fixed edge $e$. Finally, as $M \to \infty$, $P\{J_M(e_0) = 0\}$ converges to

$$\begin{aligned}&P\{\text{the cluster of all edges connected to } e_0 \text{ by a conducting path is unbounded} \mid R(e_0) < \infty\} \\ &= \frac{\theta_d(1-p(\infty))}{1-p(\infty)} .\end{aligned}$$

This proves (11.21). □

<u>Remark.</u>

(i) To prove the lower bound in (11.11) without using Straley's duality lemma (Lemma 11.3) one can proceed along the lines of the above proof of (11.21). First we replace $R(e)$ by $\tilde{R}(e)$. However, we do not form $\mathcal{K}_n$ by identifying the vertices in each segment $\{i\} \times [0,n]$ now. Instead, consider disjoint vertical crossings $r^{j*}$, $1 \leq j \leq k$, of $[\frac{1}{2}, n - \frac{1}{2}] \times [-\frac{1}{2}, n + \frac{1}{2}]$ on $(\mathbb{Z}^2)_d$ such that all edges in each $r_i^*$ intersect an edge of $\mathbb{Z}^2$ with strictly positive resistance. If $r^{j*}$ contains the edges $e_i^{j*}$, and $e_i^j$ is the edge of $\mathbb{Z}^2$ which intersects $e_i^{j*}$, then we form a vertex of $\mathcal{K}_n$ by identifying the endpoints of the $e_i^j$, $i = 1,2,\ldots$ which are immediately to the left of $r^{j*}$. Another vertex of $\mathcal{K}_n$ is formed by identifying the endpoints of the $e_i^j$, $i = 1,2,\ldots$ immediately to the right of $r^{j*}$. By choice of $r^{j*}$, $R(e_i^j) > 0$. After constructing $\mathcal{K}_n$ by making these identifications for each $j$, $1 \leq j \leq k$ we can essentially copy the rest of the proof of (11.21). All we need is a lower bound for the number $k$ of disjoint vertical crossings $r^{j*}$ of the above type. A lower bound of order $\frac{1}{2} C_1(\frac{1}{2} - p(0))^{\delta_1} n$ can be obtained from Theorem 11.1 in the same way as in the estimate for $k(n,M)$ in the proof of the upper bound in (11.11).

## 12. UNSOLVED PROBLEMS.

We shall list here some problems which seem of interest to us, in the order of the chapters to which they refer. It appears that the most significant problem is problem 8. We know little about how the problems compare in difficulty, but some of the problems are only of technical interest.

To Chapter 3.

Problem 1. Prove that for bond-percolation on the triangular lattice with three parameters, as discussed in Application 3.4 (iii) the critical surface is

(12.1) $$p(1) + p(2) + p(3) - p(1)\,p(2)\,p(3) = 1 .$$ ///

Sykes and Essam (1964) conjectured that (12.1) gives the critical surface for this bond-percolation problem, and we mentioned several strong indications for the truth of this in Application 3.4 (iii). We also mentioned without proof that we can prove that for this problem

(12.2) $$\theta(p) = 0 , \quad \text{whenever} \quad p >> 0 \quad \text{and} \quad p(1) + p(2) + p(3) - p(1)\,p(2)\,p(3) \leq 1.$$

The proof of this fact is based on the following theorem.

Theorem 12.1. Let $(\mathcal{G},\mathcal{G}^*)$ be a matching pair of periodic graphs in in $\mathbb{R}^2$ and let $P_p$ be a $\lambda$-parameter periodic probability measure on the occupancy configurations of $\mathcal{G}$ based on the partition $\mathcal{V}_1,\dots\mathcal{V}_\lambda$ of the vertices of $\mathcal{G}$ (cf. Sect. 3.2). Assume that

$$P_p\{v \text{ is occupied}\} > 0 \quad \text{for all} \quad v.$$

Assume also that at least one of the following two symmetry conditions holds:

(i) the first or second coordinate axis is an axis of symmetry for $\mathcal{G}$ as well as for the partition $\mathcal{V}_1,\dots,\mathcal{V}_\lambda$ (cf. Def. 3.4),

(ii) $\mathcal{G}$ and $P_p$ are symmetric with respect to the origin, i.e., if v(e) is a vertex (edge) of $\mathcal{G}$, then so is -v (-e) and

$$P_p\{v \text{ is occupied}\} = P_p\{-v \text{ is occupied}\}.$$

(Of course $-v = (-v(1),-v(2))$ if $v = (v(1),v(2))$ and similarly for -e).

If

$$\theta(p) > 0,$$

then for every rectangle B

(12.3) $$P_p\{\exists \text{ an occupied circuit on } \mathcal{G} \text{ surrounding } B\} = 1.$$

We do not prove this theorem. We merely give the easy deduction of (12.2) for the three-parameter bond-percolation problem on the triangular lattice from this theorem. Let $p_0 = (p_0(1),p_0(2),p_0(3)) >> 0$ satisfy (12.1). Assume that $\theta(p_0) > 0$. We derive a contradiction from this as follows. The three parameter bond-problem on the triangular lattice has the symmetry property (ii) above.

Thus, if $p_0 >> 0$ and $\theta(p_0) > 0$ then (12.3) holds for $p = p_0$ on $\mathcal{G}$, the covering graph of the triangular lattice. However, the proof of Condition A for Application 3.4(iii), or more precisely, the proof of (3.79), shows that then also

(12.4) $$P_{p_0}\{\exists \text{ vacant circuit on } \mathcal{G}^* \text{ surrounding } B\} = 1,$$

for each rectangle B. As we saw in the proof of Theorem 3.1(i) this implies $\theta(p_0) = 0$ (see the lines following (7.34)). It follows from this contradiction that $\theta(p_0) = 0$ for all $p_0 >> 0$ which satisfy (12.1), and a fortiori for all $p_0 >> 0$ with

$$p_0(1)+p_0(2)+p_0(3)-p_0(1)p_0(2)p_0(3) \le 1.$$

Thus (12.2) holds.

To settle Problem 1 we would have to prove $\theta(p) > 0$ for any $0 << p << 1$ which satisfies

$$p(1)+p(2)+p(3)-p(1)p(2)p(3) > 1.$$

The present proof of Theorem 3.1 relies on Theorem 6.1, which we have been unable to prove so far without the symmetry condition (i) of Theorem 12.1. This leads as directly to the next question, which is more general than Problem 1.

Problem 2. Prove a version of Theorem 3.1 which does not require the symmetry property (i) of Theorem 12.1. ///

Perhaps even more disturbing than the symmetry restrictions in Theorems 3.1 and 3.2 is the fact that these results apply only to special graphs imbedded in the plane. No results seem to be known in dimension greater than two. This gives rise to the following questions.

Problem 3. Prove that

$$p_T = p_H$$

for a percolation problem on a periodic graph $\mathcal{G}$ imbedded in $\mathbb{R}^d$ with $d > 2$. ///

This problem is not even settled for $\mathcal{G} = \mathbb{Z}^3$.

Problem 4. Is it true that there can be at most one infinite occupied cluster on a periodic graph $\mathcal{G}$? ///

Newman and Schulman (1981) proved that if there can be more than one infinite occupied cluster under $P_p$, then

(12.5) $\qquad P_p\{\exists$ infinitely many infinite occupied clusters$\} = 1$.

It seems likely that if $\mathcal{G}$ is imbedded in $\mathbb{R}^2$, then (12.5) cannot occur. In fact we know this to be the case whenever Theorem 3.1 or 3.2 apply. However, if $\mathcal{G}$ is imbedded in $\mathbb{R}^d$ with $d > 2$ then very little is known about the impossibility of (12.5). For the site- or bond-percolation on $\mathbb{Z}^d$, $d \geq 2$, we can prove that

(12.6) $\qquad P_p\{\exists$ a unique infinite occupied cluster$\} = 1$

whenever $p > p_H^\infty$. Here $p_H^\infty$ is the decreasing limit of $p_H^k$, $k \to \infty$, and $p_H^k = p_H(\mathcal{G}^k)$ is the critical probability for site-, respectively bond-percolation on the graph $\mathcal{G}^k := \mathbb{Z}^2 \times \{0,1,\dots,k\}$. $\mathcal{G}^k$ is the restriction of $\mathbb{Z}^3$ to $(k+1)$ copies of $\mathbb{Z}^2$ on top of each other; $\mathcal{G}^0$ is isomorphic to $\mathbb{Z}^2$. From Ex. 10.2(iii) we know that $p_H^\infty < p_H(\mathbb{Z}^2)$, and in particular for the bond-problem $p_H^\infty < \frac{1}{2}$. We conjecture (but have no proof) that

$$p_H^\infty = p_H(\mathbb{Z}^3),$$

both for site- and bond-percolation.

To Chapter 5.

The uniqueness of infinite clusters (see Problem 4) is related to continuity of the percolation probability $\theta(p)$. The relationship between the two problems was mainly one of similarity in methods of attack in the case of graphs imbedded in the plane. For both problems one tries to show that if $\theta(p) > 0$, then crossing probabilities of certain large rectangles are close to one and consequently arbitrarily large circuits exist. (cf. Russo (1981), Prop. 1 and the proof of Theorem 3.1 in Ch.7). However, recently M. Keane and J. van der Berg (private communication) have made the relationship between the problems far more explicit. They prove that in a one-parameter problem, if $p > p_H$ and (12.6) holds, then $\theta(\cdot)$ is continuous at $p$. Perhaps the converse also holds. In any case, the continuity properties of $\theta(\cdot)$ are of interest. Partial results about these are given in the Remark following Theorem 5.4, but in general the following question remains.

Problem 5. Is $\theta(p)$ a continuous function of $p$ in every one-parameter percolation problem? In particular, is always

$$\theta(p_H) = 0? \qquad ///$$

One may also want to investigate further smoothness properties of $\theta(p,v)$, as a function of $p$, especially in one-parameter problems. For $\mathcal{G}$ one of a pair of matching graphs we already pointed out in Remark 5.2(iii) that under some symmetry condition $\theta(p,v)$ is infinitely differentiable for $p > p_H$.

Problem 6. Is $\theta(p,v)$ an analytic function of $p$ for $p > p_H$? ///

For a directed site-percolation problem on the plane and $p$ close to one Problem 6 was answered affirmatively by Vasil'ev (1970) (see Griffeath (1981), especially Sect. 9, for the relation between Vasil'ev's result and directed percolation).

To Chapter 6.

We already pointed out that Problem 1 would be solved if we could prove the Russo-Seymour-Welsh Theorem without symmetry assumptions. The same holds for Problems 2, and in dimension two also for Problems 4 and 5. Thus, one possible attack on these problems is to try and settle the following more specific problem.

Problem 7. Can one prove Theorem 6.1 without symmetry assumption? ///

To Chapter 8.

Problem 8. Prove any of the power laws (8.1)-(8.3) and get good estimates (or the precise values) of $\beta$ and $\gamma_{\pm}$. ///

It is believed that (8.1) holds for a $0 < \beta < 1$. We do not even know for any graph whether

$$\frac{d}{dp}\theta(p) \to \infty \quad \text{as} \quad p \downarrow p_H . \tag{12.7}$$

Grimmett (private communication) suggested that Russo's formula (Prop. 4.2) might be helpful, since $\theta(p,v_0)$ is the $P_p$-probability of the increasing event $\{\#W(v_0) = \infty\}$. It does seem very difficult though to estimate the number of pivotal sites for this event.

To Chapter 9.

Problem 9. Does the function $p \to \Delta(p,\mathcal{G})$ introduced in Ch. 9 (cf. (9.12)) have a singularity at $p_H(\mathcal{G})$ for suitable $\mathcal{G}$? If yes, is there a power law of the form

$$\Delta(p,\mathcal{G}) \sim C_0|p-p_H|^{\nu\pm} \quad \text{as} \quad p \downarrow p_H$$
$$\text{or} \quad p \uparrow p_H, \text{ respectively?}$$ ///

The first part of the above problem is of historical interest, because Sykes and Essam (1964) wanted to base their arguments on $\Delta(p,\mathcal{G})$ having a unique singularity at $p = p_H$, at least for certain nice $\mathcal{G}$. Theorem 9.3 shows that for "nice" $\mathcal{G}$ $\Delta(p,\mathcal{G})$ can only have a singularity at $p = p_H$, but we could not establish that there really is a singularity at $p_H$ (see also Remark 9.3 (iv)).

To Chapter 10.

Problem 10. Prove that $p_H(\mathcal{H}) > p_H(\mathcal{G})$ in cases where $\mathcal{H}$ is a subgraph of $\mathcal{G}$ formed by removing edges of $\mathcal{G}$ (see Remark 10.2(ii)).

Problem 11. Find a quantitative estimate for $p_H(\mathcal{H})-p_H(\mathcal{G})$ in the cases where this quantity is known to be strictly positive by Theorem 10.3.

To Chapter 11.

As in Chapter 11, let $R_n$ be the resistance of the restriction of $\mathbb{Z}^d$ to $[0,n]^d$ between the faces $A_n^0 := \{0\} \times [0,n]^{d-1}$ and $A_n^1 := \{n\} \times [0,n]^{d-1}$, when the resistances of the individual edges are independent random variables.

Problem 12. Does

$$\lim_{n\to\infty} n^{d-2}R_n$$

exist in probability or with probability one? (See also Remark 11.1(vi).)

Problem 13. If the distribution of the individual resistances $R(e)$ are given by (11.6)-(11.8), is

$$\limsup_{n\to\infty} n^{d-2} R_n < \infty$$

whenever $1-p(\infty) = P\{R(e) < \infty\} >$ critical probability for bond-percolation on $\mathbb{Z}^d$? ///

Of course Theorem 11.2 answers Problem 13 affirmatively for $d = 2$.

We only discussed in Ch. 11 the resistance between two opposite faces of a cube. It is also interesting to look at the resistance, $r_n$ say, between the origin and the boundary of the cube $[-n,n]^d$. If all edges of $\mathbb{Z}^d$ have resistance 1 ohm, then $r_n$ is bounded as $n \to \infty$ for $d \geq 3$.

Problem 14. If $d \geq 3$, $P\{R(e) = 1\} = p$, $P\{R(e) = \infty\} = q = 1-p$ and $p >$ percolation probability for bond-percolation on $\mathbb{Z}^d$, does it follow that

$$P_p\{\limsup r_n < \infty \mid \text{the origin is connected to infinity by a conducting path}\} = 1?$$

# APPENDIX. SOME RESULTS FOR PLANAR GRAPHS.

In this appendix we prove several graph theoretical, or point-set topological results, in particular Propositions 2.1-2.3 and Corollary 2.2 which were already stated in Ch.2. The proofs require somewhat messy arguments, even though most of these results are quite intuitive. We base most of our proofs on the Jordan curve theorem (Newman,(1951), Theorem V. 10.2). Some more direct and more combinatorial proofs can very likely be given; see the approach of Whitney (1932, 1933). Especially Whitney (1933), Theorem 4, is closely related to Cor. 2.2., Prop. 2.2 and Prop. A.1, and has been used repeatedly in percolation theory.

Throughout this appendix $\mathcal{M}$ is a mosaic, $\mathcal{F}$ a subset of the collection of faces of $\mathcal{M}$ and $(\mathcal{G},\mathcal{G}^*)$ a matching pair based on $(\mathcal{M},\mathcal{F})$. These terms were defined in Sect. 2.2. $\mathcal{G}_{p\ell},\mathcal{G}^*_{p\ell}$ and $\mathcal{M}_{p\ell}$ will be the planar modifications as defined in Sect. 2.3. We fix an occupancy configuration $\omega$ on $\mathcal{M}$ and extend it as in (2.15), (2.16). $W(v)$ and $W_{p\ell}(v)$ are the occupied cluster of $v$ on $\mathcal{G}$ and $\mathcal{M}_{p\ell}$ (or $\mathcal{G}_{p\ell}$), respectively, in the configuration $\omega$. $\partial W$, the boundary of $W$, is defined in Def. 2.8; $v \, \mathcal{G} \, w$ means that $v$ and $w$ are adjacent vertices on $\mathcal{G}$.

Proposition 2.1. Let $\partial W_{p\ell}(v)$ be the boundary of $W_{p\ell}(v)$ on $\mathcal{M}_{p\ell}$. If $W_{p\ell}(v)$ is non-empty and bounded and (2.3)-(2.5) hold with $\mathcal{G}$ replaced by $\mathcal{M}$, then there exists a vacant circuit $J_{p\ell}$ on $\mathcal{M}_{p\ell}$ surrounding $W_{p\ell}(v)$, and such that all vertices of $\mathcal{M}_{p\ell}$ on $J_{p\ell}$ belong to $\partial W_{p\ell}(v)$.

We owe the idea of the proof to follow to R. Durrett. We shall write $W_{p\ell}$ and $\partial W_{p\ell}$ instead of $W_{p\ell}(v)$ and $\partial W_{p\ell}(v)$. On various occasions we shall use the symbol for a path to denote the set of points which belong to some edge in the path. Thus in (A.2), the left hand side is the set of points which belong to $\pi$ and to $W \cup \partial W_{p\ell}$. In (A.5) $\text{int}(J) \setminus \tilde{\pi}$ is the set of points in $\text{int}(J)$ which do not lie on $\tilde{\pi}$ . This abuse of notation is not likely to lead to confusion.

We shall actually prove the slightly stronger statement that the vertices of $\mathcal{M}_{p\ell}$ on $J_{p\ell}$ belong to $\partial_{ext} W_{p\ell}$ , the "exterior boundary of $W_{p\ell}$", where

(A.1) $$\partial_{ext} W_{p\ell} := \{u \in \partial W_{p\ell} : \exists \text{ path } \pi \text{ from } u \text{ to } \infty \text{ on } \mathcal{M}_{p\ell} \text{ such that } u \text{ is the only point of } \pi \text{ in } W_{p\ell} \cup \partial W_{p\ell}\} .$$

The crucial property of $\partial_{ext} W_{p\ell}$ is given in the following lemma.

Lemma A.1. Assume that (2.3)-(2.5) hold with $\mathcal{G}$ replaced by $\mathcal{M}$. If $W_{p\ell}$ is non-empty and bounded, then $\partial_{ext} W_{p\ell} \neq \emptyset$ . Let $u \in \partial_{ext} W_{p\ell}$ , $w \in W_{p\ell}$ and $\pi$ a path from $u$ to $\infty$ on $\mathcal{M}_{p\ell}$ such that

$$u \sim_{\mathcal{M}_{p\ell}} w$$

and[1])

(A.2) $$\pi \cap \{W \cup \partial W_{p\ell}\} = \{u\} .$$

Let $e$ be an edge of $\mathcal{M}_{p\ell}$ from $w$ to $u$ and $\tilde{\pi}$ the simple path consisting of $e$ followed by $\pi$ . Then there exists a Jordan curve $J$ in $\mathbb{R}^2$ such that

(A.3) $$u \in \text{int}(J) ,$$

(A.4) $J$ intersects each edge of $\mathcal{M}_{p\ell}$ incident to $u$ exactly once, but all edges of $\mathcal{M}_{p\ell}$ not incident to $u$ belong to ext(J),

(A.5) $\text{int}(J)\backslash\tilde{\pi}$ has exactly two components, K' and K" say. Any edge between $u$ and a vertex $\tilde{u} \in \partial_{ext} W_{p\ell}$ intersects exactly one of the components K' and K". There exists a vertex $u' \in \partial_{ext} W_{p\ell}$ and an edge $e'$ of $\mathcal{M}_{p\ell}$ between $u$ and $u'$ which intersects only K'. There also exists a vertex $u'' \in \partial_{ext} W_{p\ell}$ and an edge $e''$ of $\mathcal{M}_{p\ell}$ between $u$ and $u''$ which intersects only K" ($u' = u''$ is possible!).

(Fig. A.1 gives a schematic illustration of the situation.)

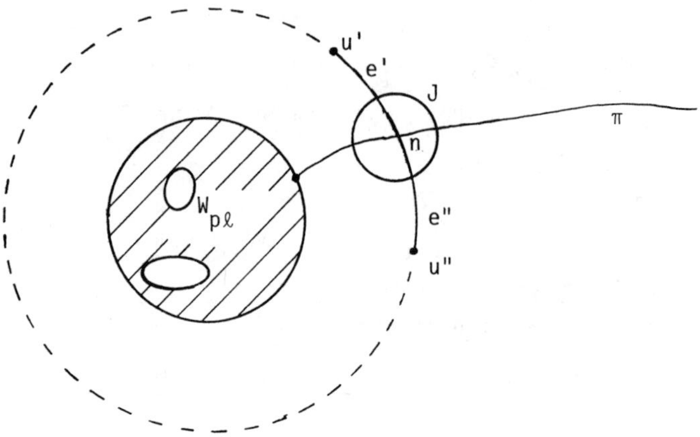


Figure A.1. $W_{p\ell}$ is the hatched region. The vertices of $\partial_{ext}W$ are on the dashed curve. J is the small circle surrounding u.

Proof: If $W_{p\ell}$ is non-empty and bounded, then any path from $\infty$ to $W_{p\ell}$ must intersect $\partial W_{p\ell}$ a first time. This intersection belongs to $\partial_{ext} W_{p\ell}$. Thus $\partial_{ext} W_{p\ell} \neq \emptyset$ in this situation.

Now take $u \in \partial_{ext} W_{p\ell}$. By definition there exists a simple path $\pi$ from u to $\infty$ on $\mathcal{M}_{p\ell}$ satisfying (A.2) and a $w \in W_{p\ell}$ which is adjacent to u. The self-avoiding path $\pi$ cannot intersect e in its interior (because $\mathcal{M}_{p\ell}$ is planar), nor in the point w (by (A.2)), and goes through the point u only once (at its beginning). Thus $\tilde{\pi}$ has no double points. Now let D be a small open disc around u such that $\overline{D}$ does not intersect any edge of $\mathcal{M}_{p\ell}$ not incident to u. (Use (2.4) to find such a disc). If all edges incident to u are piecewise linear, then the perimeter of D will satisfy (A.3) and (A.4) provided D is sufficiently small. The general situation can be reduced to this simple case by means of a homeomorphism of $\mathbb{R}^2$ onto itself which takes pieces of the edges of $\mathcal{M}_{p\ell}$ incident to u onto straight line segments radiating from the origin (see Newman (1951), exercise VI. 18.3 for the existence of such a homeomorphism). We may therefore assume that we have a Jordan curve $J$ satisfying (A.3) and (A.4).

Note that $e$, as well as the unique edge of $\pi$ incident to $u$ (the first edge of $\pi$) each intersect $J$ exactly once (by (A.4)) so that $\tilde{\pi}$ intersects $J$ exactly twice, and $\text{int}(J)\backslash\tilde{\pi}$ has indeed two components - which we call $K'$ and $K''$ (see Newman (1951), Theorem V. 11.7). Let $e_0 = e$, and let $e_1, e_2, \ldots, e_{\nu-1}, e_\nu = e_0$ be the edges of $\mathcal{M}_{p\ell}$ incident to $u$, listed in the order in which they intersect $J$ as we traverse $J$ in one direction from $e_0 \cap J$; there are only finitely many of these by (2.4). Write $u_i$ for the endpoint of $e_i$ different from $u$, and $x_i$ for the intersection of $e_i$ and

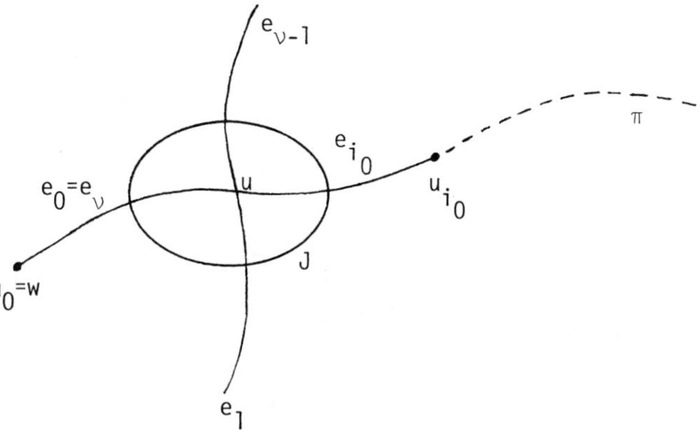


Figure A.2.

$J$. Thus $u_0 = w$. The first edge of $\pi$ is one of the $e_i$, say $e_{i_0}$. For $i \neq 0, i_0, \nu$, $e_i$ runs from $u$ to $x_i$ inside one component $K'$ or $K''$, and then from $x_i$ to $u_i$ it is in $\text{ext}(J)$ by (A.4) (note $u_i \in \text{ext}(J)$, also by (A.4)). Thus, each of these edges intersect exactly one of $K'$ and $K''$. Since each of the two arcs of $J$ from $x_0$ to $x_{i_0}$ form part of the boundary of one the components $K'$ and $K''$ (Newman (1951), Theorem V.11.8), it follows that $e_i$, $1 \leq i < i_0$, intersect the same component, $K'$ say, while $e_i$, $i_0 < i < \nu$ intersect the other, which will be $K''$. This proves the first statement in (A.5) (since $u_0 = u_\nu \in W$ and hence not in $\partial W_{p\ell}$

and also $u_{i_0} \varepsilon \pi$ does not belong to $\partial W_{p\ell}$).

We write $A_i$ for the arc of $J$ from $x_i$ to $x_{i+1}$, $0 \leq i \leq \nu-1$. Then $A_i \backslash \{x_i, x_{i+1}\}$ does not intersect any edge and therefore lies entirely in one face of $\mathcal{M}_{p\ell}$. Since all faces of $\mathcal{M}_{p\ell}$ are triangles (Comment 2.3(vi)), this implies that $e_i$ and $e_{i+1}$ lie in the boundary of a triangle, and $u_i \mathcal{M}_{p\ell} u_{i+1}$, $u_0 = w \varepsilon W_{p\ell}$, while $u_{i_0} \varepsilon \pi$ is not in $W_{p\ell}$. Hence the index

$$i_1 = \max \{j : 0 \leq j \leq i_0, u_j \varepsilon W_{p\ell}\}$$

is well defined. As observed above, $u_{i_1+1}$ is a neighbor of $u_{i_1} \varepsilon W_{p\ell}$, but by definition of $i$, $u_{i_1+1} \notin W_{p\ell}$. Therefore, $u_{i_1+1} \varepsilon \partial W_{p\ell}$. Also, $u_{i_0} \varepsilon \pi$ does not belong to $\partial W_{p\ell}$ by (A.2). Thus $i_1+1 < i_0$ and we can define $i_2$ by

$$i_2 = \max \{j : i_1 < j < i_0, u_j \varepsilon \partial W_{p\ell}\} .$$

We can connect $u_{i_2}$ to $\infty$ by a path consisting of edges from $u_j$ to $u_{j+1}$, $i_2 \leq j < i_0$, followed by the piece of $\pi$ from $u_{i_0}$ to $\infty$. The vertices $u_{i_2+1}, \ldots, u_{i_0}$ do not belong to $W_{p\ell} \cup \partial W_{p\ell}$ by choice of $i_1$, $i_2$, so that $u_{i_2} \varepsilon \partial_{ext} W_{p\ell}$ with $0 < i_2 < i_0$. Finally we define

$$i' = \min\{0 < j \leq i_2 : u_j \varepsilon \partial_{ext} W_{p\ell}\} .$$

By the above $i'$ is well defined, and $u' := u_{i'}$ is connected to $u$ by an the edge $e_{i'}$ which intersects $K'$, but does not intersect $K''$. Similarly we can define

$$i'' = \max\{i_0 < j < \nu : u_j \varepsilon \partial_{ext} W_{p\ell}\}$$

and $u'' = u_{i''} . e_{i''}$ only intersects $K''$. This proves the existence of the desired $u'$, $e'$, $u''$ and $e''$ for A.5. □

<u>Proof of Proposition 2.1:</u> For a non-empty and bounded $W_{p\ell}$ pick any $u_0 \varepsilon \partial_{ext} W_{p\ell}$ and apply Lemma 1 with $u_0$ for $u$. Let $u_1$ be one of the vertices $u'$, $u'' \varepsilon \partial_{ext} W_{p\ell}$ adjacent to $u_0$ whose existence is guaranteed by Lemma A.1. Say we picked $u'$ for $u$. Let $e_1$

be an edge between $u_0 = u$ and $u_1 = u'$ which intersects only $K'$ as in Lemma A.1. Assume we have already constructed $u_0, e_1, u_1, \dots, e_i$, $u_i$ with $u_i \in \partial_{ext} \mathcal{M}_{p\ell}$ and $e_j$ an edge of $\mathcal{M}_{p\ell}$ between $u_{j-1}$ and $u_j, e_{j-1} \neq e_j$, $1 \leq j \leq i$. We then apply Lemma A.1 to $u_i$. Associated with $u_i$ are two components $K'$ and $K''$. Assume $e_i$ intersects $K'$. Then by (A.5) we can find an edge $e_{i+1}$ from $u_i$ to some $u_{i+1} \in \partial_{ext} W_{p\ell}$, such that $e_{i+1}$ intersects only $K''$ and not $K'$, and hence with $e_{i+1} \neq e_i$. We continue in this way until the first time we obtain a double point, i.e., to the smallest index $\nu$ for which there exists a $\rho < \nu$ with $u_\rho = u_\nu$. $\nu < \infty$ because $W_{p\ell}$ is bounded, and therefore $\partial_{ext} W_{p\ell} \subset \partial W_{p\ell}$ finite (see (2.3), (2.4)). $\rho$ will be unique by the minimality of $\nu$. Since $\mathcal{M}_{p\ell}$ is planar, $J_{p\ell} = (u_\rho, e_\rho, \dots, e_\nu, v_\nu)$ - or more precisely the curve made up from $e_\rho, e_{\rho+1}, \dots, e_\nu$ - is a Jordan curve. We now show that it has the required properties. The vertices on $J_{p\ell}$ belong to $\partial_{ext} W_{p\ell} \subset \partial W_{p\ell}$ by choice of the $u_i$, and since each vertex of $\partial W_{p\ell}$ has to be vacant, $J_{p\ell}$ is vacant. To show that $W_{p\ell} \subset \text{int}(J_{p\ell})$ observe first that all vertices of $J_{p\ell}$ belong to $\partial W_{p\ell}$ and therefore not to $W_{p\ell}$. Thus $W_{p\ell} \cap J_{p\ell} = \emptyset$ and the connected set $W_{p\ell}$ lies entirely in one component of $\mathbb{R}^2 \setminus J_{p\ell}$. Now write $u$ for $u_{\rho+1}$ and let $\pi$ be a path on $\mathcal{M}_{p\ell}$ from $u$ to $\infty$ satisfying (A.2), and $e$ an edge of $\mathcal{M}_{p\ell}$ from $u$ to some $w \in W_{p\ell}$. We apply Lemma A.1 once more with this choice of $u$, $\pi$, $w$ and $e$. With $\tilde{\pi}$ and $J$ as in Lemma A.1 we may assume (by virtue of the construction of $J_{p\ell}$) that the two edges $e_\rho$ and $e_{\rho+1}$ incident to $u$ intersect different components of $\text{int}(J) \setminus \tilde{\pi}$. We shall prove now that this implies

(A.6) $\tilde{\pi}$ crosses $J_{p\ell}$ from $\text{ext}(J_{p\ell})$ to $\text{int}(J_{p\ell})$ at $u$.

This will suffice, since the part $\pi \setminus \{u\}$ of $\tilde{\pi}$ clearly lies in $\text{ext}(J_{p\ell})$, so that (A.6) will imply that $e \setminus \{u\}$ belongs to $\text{int}(J_{p\ell})$. In particular $w$ will belong to $\text{int}(J_{p\ell})$. Hence $W_{p\ell} \subset \text{int}(J_{p\ell})$ and $J_{p\ell}$ surrounds $W_{p\ell}$.

To prove (A.6) note that the Jordan curve $J$ surrounding $u$, constructed in Lemma A.1 intersects $J_{p\ell}$ in two points only, say $x'$ on $e_\rho$ and $x''$ on $e_{\rho+1}$ (by (A.4)). The two open arcs of $J$ between $x'$ and $x''$ must lie in different components of $\mathbb{R}^2 \setminus J_{p\ell}$, one in $\text{int}(J_{p\ell})$ and the other in $\text{ext}(J_{p\ell})$. Indeed each of these arcs lies entirely in one component of $\mathbb{R}^2 \setminus J_{p\ell}$, and they cannot both lie in the same component, because $u \in J_{p\ell}$ lies on the boundary of $\text{int}(J_{p\ell})$ as well as the boundary of $\text{ext}(J_{p\ell})$. Thus, there exists continuous curves from $J$ to points in its interior near $u$ which lie in $\text{int}(J_{p\ell})$, and there also are such curves in $\text{ext}(J_{p\ell})$. Now we have by (A.4) (or more directly by its proof) that $\pi$ intersects $J$ exactly once, in $y'$ say, and $e$ also intersects $J$ exactly once, in $y''$ say (see Fig. A.3).

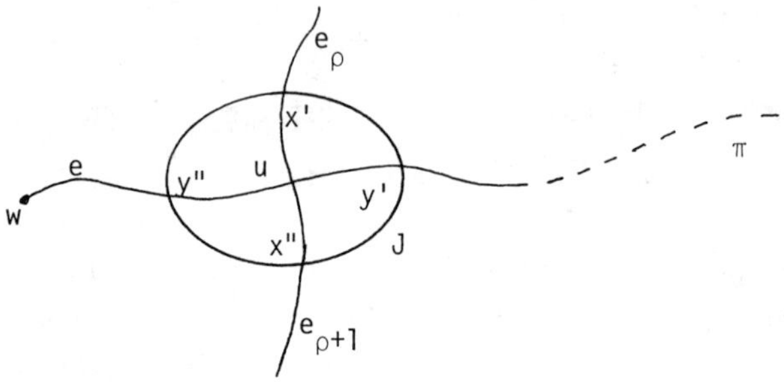


Figure A.3

$x'$ and $x''$ cannot lie on the same arc of $J$ between $y'$ and $y''$ because $x'$ and $x''$ are the endpoints of the pieces of $e_\rho \cap \text{int}(J)$ and $e_{\rho+1} \cap \text{int}(J)$, respectively, while by construction $e_\rho \cap \text{int}(J)$ and $e_{\rho+1} \cap \text{int}(J)$ belong to different components of $\text{int}(J) \setminus \tilde{\pi}$. These two different components, $K'$ and $K''$, each have one of the arcs of $J$ from $y'$ to $y''$ in their boundary, so that $x'$ has to lie in the arc bounding $K'$ and $x''$ in the other arc, bounding $K''$. But this means that $y'$ and $y''$ separate $x'$ and $x''$ on $J$. Therefore, $y'$ and $y''$ do not lie on the same arc of $J$ between $x'$ and $x''$. Since we saw above that one of these open arcs was in $\text{int}(J_{p\ell})$ and the other in $\text{ext}(J_{p\ell})$ it follows that one of the points $y'$ is in $\text{int}(J_{p\ell})$ and the other in $\text{ext}(J_{p\ell})$. (A.6) now follows. □

<u>Corollary 2.2. If $W(v)$ is non-empty and bounded and (2.3)-(2.5) hold, then there exists a vacant circuit $J^*$ on $\mathcal{G}^*$ surrounding</u> $W(v)$.

<u>Proof</u>: By Cor. 2.1 $W \subset W_{p\ell}$ and by Prop. 2.1 there exists a vacant circuit $J_{p\ell}$ on $\mathcal{M}_{p\ell}$ surrounding $W_{p\ell}$, and therefore also $W$. Note that $J_{p\ell}$ cannot contain any central vertex of $\mathcal{G}$ since these are all occupied (cf. (2.15)). Thus, $J_{p\ell}$ is actually a circuit on $\mathcal{G}^*_{p\ell}$. Assume it is made up from the edges $e^*_1,\dots,e^*_\nu$ of $\mathcal{G}^*_{p\ell}$, and that the endpoints of $e^*_i$ are $v^*_{i-1}$ and $v^*_i$. Then $r^* = (v^*_0,e^*_1,\dots,e^*_\nu,v^*_\nu)$ is a path on $\mathcal{G}^*_{p\ell}$ with one double point, to wit $v^*_0 = v^*_\nu$. We now apply the procedure of the proof of Lemma 2.1a, with $\mathcal{G}^*$ instead of $\mathcal{G}$, to remove the central vertices from $v^*$. Let $0 \le i_0 < i,\dots, < i_\rho \le \nu$ be the indices for which $v^*_{i_j}$ is not a central vertex of $\mathcal{G}^*_{p\ell}$. Then, as in Lemma 2.1a $i_0 \le 1$, $i_\rho \ge \nu-1$, and $i_{j+1} - i_j \le 2$. If $i_{j+1} = i_j+1$ so that $v^*_{i_j}$ and $v^*_{i_{j+1}}$ are adjacent on $\mathcal{G}^*$, and $e^*_{j+1}$ is an edge of $\mathcal{G}^*$, then we do not change $e^*_{j+1}$. If $i_{j+1} = i_j+2$, then $v^*_{i_{j+1}}$ is the central vertex on $\mathcal{G}^*$ of some face $F$ which is close-packed in $\mathcal{G}^*$. We then replace the piece $e^*_{i_j+1}$, $v^*_{i_j+1}$, $e^*_{i_j+2}$ of $r^*$ by the single edge of $\mathcal{G}^*$ through $F$, with endpoints $v^*_{i_j}$ and $v^*_{i_j+2}$. We write $\tilde{v}^*_j$ for $v^*_{i_j}$ and $\tilde{e}^*_{j+1}$ for the edge from $\tilde{v}^*_j$ to $\tilde{v}^*_{j+1}$. We make these replacements successively. Assume for the sake of argument that $i_0 = 0$ (this can always be achieved by numbering the vertices of $r^*$ such that it starts with a non-central vertex). Assume also that we already made all replacements between $v^*_{i_0} = v^*_0$ and $v^*_{i_k}$. We then have the sequence $\tilde{v}^*_0$, $\tilde{e}^*_0,\dots,\tilde{e}^*_k,\tilde{v}^*_k$, $e^*_{i_k+1},\dots,v^* = \tilde{v}^*_0$, and can form the curve $J_k$ made up from $\tilde{e}^*_0,\dots,\tilde{e}^*_k$, $e^*_{i_k+1}$, $e^*_{i_k+2},\dots,e^*_\nu$ (even though this is neither a curve on $\mathcal{G}^*_{p\ell}$ nor on $\mathcal{G}^*$). Assume that $J_k$ is a Jordan curve which contains $W$ in its interior. We shall now show that then $J_{k+1}$, is also a Jordan curve which contains $W$ in its interior. This will prove the corollary, since $J_0 = J_{p\ell}$ has these properties and $J_\rho$ or $J_{\rho+1}$ will be a curve on $\mathcal{G}$ with the properties required of $J^*$. If $\tilde{e}^*_{k+1} = e^*_{i_k+1}$, then there is nothing to prove. Assume therefore $i_{k+1} = i_{k+2}$ and that $\tilde{e}^*_{k+1}$ is the edge in the closed face

$\overline{F}$ of $\mathcal{M}$ from $\tilde{v}^*_k = v^*_{i_k}$ to $\tilde{v}^*_{k+1} = v^*_{i_k+2}$, while $v^*_{i_k+1}$ is the central vertex of F. By Comment 2.3(i) the three edges $e^*_{i_{k+1}}$, $e^*_{i_{k+2}}$ and $\tilde{e}^*_{k+1}$ then form the topological boundary of a closed "triangle", T say. $J_{k+1}$ is again a Jordan curve, because it contains only vertices of $J_k$, and $e^*_j$ with $i+2 < j \leq \nu$ cannot intersect the interior of the edge $\tilde{e}^*_{k+1}$ of $\mathcal{G}$. The latter statement results from Comment 2.3(i) and the fact that $e^*_j$ does not contain the central vertex $v^*_{i_k+1}$ of F, because $J_k$ is self-avoiding. From the facts that W consists of vertices and edges of $\mathcal{G}$ and $W \subset \text{int}(J_k)$ and from Comment 2.3(i) it follows that W cannot intersect Fr(T). Since $\mathring{T}$ contains no vertices of $\mathcal{G}$, $W \subset \mathring{T}$ is also impossible so that $W \cap T = \emptyset$. But this implies $W \subset \text{int}(J_{k+1})$ because $\text{int}(J_k) \setminus \text{int}(J_{k+1}) \subset T$, and $W \subset \text{int}(J_k)$. □

In the proof of Prop. 2.2 we shall use the next lemma, which follows from Alexander's separation lemma (Newman (1951), Ch.V.9). Actually one can deduce Prop. 2.2 from Prop. 2.1 without this lemma, but it is needed a few times later on anyway. Lemma A.2 is essentially the same as Lemma 3 in Kesten (1980a).

Lemma A.2. Let $J_1$ be a Jordan curve in $\mathbb{R}^2$ which consists of four closed arcs $A_1, A_2, A_3, A_4$ with disjoint interiors, which occur in this order when $J_1$ is traversed in one direction. (Some of these arcs may reduce to a single point.) Further, let $J_2$ be a Jordan curve in $\mathbb{R}^2$ with

$$A_1 \subset \text{int}(J_2) \text{ but } A_3 \subset \text{ext}(J_2). \tag{A.7}$$

Then $J_2$ contains an arc B with one endpoint each on $\mathring{A}_2$ and $\mathring{A}_4$ and such that the interior of B is contained in $\text{int}(J_1)$.

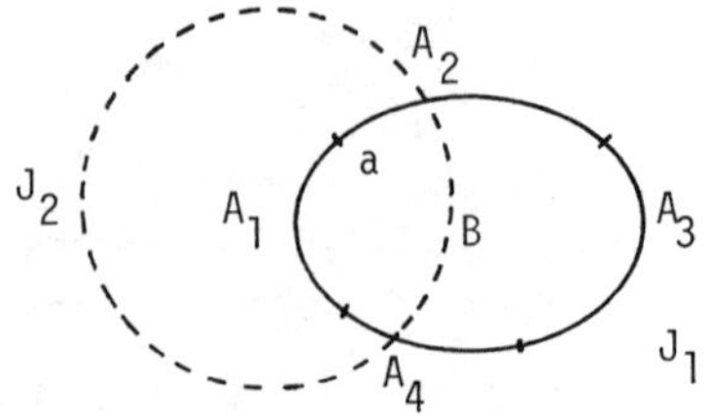


Figure A.4 $J_1$ is the solidly drawn curve. $J_2$ is dashed.

Proof: We write $\bar{J}_1$ for $J_1 \cup \text{int}(J_1)$. Also for $x,y \in J_2$ and $[x,y]$ one of the closed arcs of $J_2$ from $x$ to $y$, we shall write $(x,y]$ for $[x,y]\setminus\{x\}$ and $(x,y)$ for $[x,y]\setminus\{x,y\}$. $(x,y)$ is the interior of $[x,y]$. For $r = 2,4$ we define

(A.8) $$G_r = \{x \in J_2 \cap \bar{J}_1 : \text{there exists a point } y \in J_2 \cap A_r \text{ such that the interior } (x,y) \text{ of one of the arcs of } J_2 \text{ from } x \text{ to } y \text{ is contained in } \text{int}(J_1)\}.$$

The first task is to show that $G_r$ is closed. First we observe that $J_2$ is closed so that

(A.9) $$\bar{G}_r \subset \text{closure of } J_2 = J_2 .$$

Now if $z \in \bar{G}_r \cap \text{int}(J_1)$, then $z \in J_2 \cap \text{int}(J_1)$ and it is easy to see that $z \in G_r$ in this case. We therefore restrict ourselves to showing that any $z \in \bar{G}_r \cap J_1$ lies in $G_r$ itself. This is true by definition if $z \in J_2 \cap A_r$, since

(A.10) $$J_2 \cap A_r \subset G_r$$

(take $y = x$ in (A.8) for $x \in J_2 \cap A_r$; in this case one of the arcs from $x$ to $y$ has an empty interior). In addition, by virtue of (A.7),

(A.11) $$J_2 \cap (A_1 \cup A_3) = \emptyset .$$

Thus we only have to consider $z \in \bar{G}_r \cap A_4$ if $r = 2$ and $z \in \bar{G}_r \cap A_2$ if $r = 4$. For the sake of definiteness take $r = 2$, $z \in \bar{G}_2 \cap A_4$. Let $x_n \in G_2$, $x_n \to z$. There is nothing to prove if $x_n = z$ for some $n$, so that we may assume $x_n \neq z$. Without loss of generality we may also assume that $x_n \in J_2$ approaches $z$ from one side, i.e., that we can choose the arcs $[z,x_n]$ of $J_2$ such that

(A.12) $$[z,x_n] \downarrow [z,z] = \{z\} , \quad x_n \neq z.$$

Furthermore, there exist $y_n \in J_2 \cap A_2$ and choices of the arcs $[x_n,y_n]$ on $J_2$ from $x_n$ to $y_n$ such that

(A.13) $$(x_n,y_n) \subset \text{int}(J_1) .$$

Since $A_2$ and $A_4$ are separated on $J_1$ by $A_1$ and $A_3$ we must have $A_2 \cap A_4 \subset A_1 \cup A_3$ and

$$J_2 \cap A_2 \cup A_4 \subset J_2 \cap (A_1 \cup A_3) = \emptyset \quad (\text{by (A.11)}).$$

Therefore $y_n \in J_2 \cap A_2$ is bounded away from $z \in J_2 \cap A_4$. In addition, from (A.12) and (A.13) the arc $[x_n, y_n]$ does not contain the point $z \in A_4 \subset J_1$. It follows that from some $n_0$ on the arcs $[z, x_n]$ and

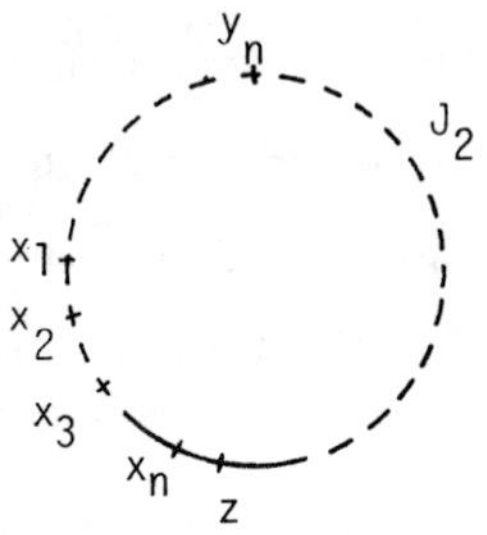


Figure A.5. The location of some points on $J_2$. $y_n$ cannot lie in the solidly drawn segment.

$[x_n, y_n]$ only have the point $x_n$ in common, and $x_{n_0} \in (x_n, y_n)$. But then, by virtue of (A.12)

$$(z, x_{n_0}] = \bigcup_{n \geq n_0} (x_n, x_{n_0}] \subset \bigcup_{n \geq n_0} (x_n, y_n) \subset \mathrm{int}(J_1) .$$

Consequently also

$$(z, y_{n_0}) = (z, x_{n_0}] \cup (x_{n_0}, y_{n_0}) \subset \mathrm{int}(J_1)$$

so that $z \in G_2$. This proves that $G_2$ is closed and the same proof works for $G_4$.

Next we take for $A_r'$, $r = 2,4$, a closed subarc of $A_r$ which contains the common endpoint of $A_r$ and $A_1$, but not the common endpoint of $A_r$ and $A_3$, and which is such that

$$J_2 \cap A_r \subset A_r' . \tag{A.14}$$

Such $A_r'$ exist since $J_2 \cap A_3 = \emptyset$ (by (A.7)). Note that by (A.7) also $J_2 \cap A_1 = \emptyset$ so that $A_2$ and $A_4$ must have nonempty interiors. We can and shall therefore also take the interiors of $A_2'$ and $A_4'$ nonempty. Now define

$$F_2 = G_2 \cup A_2' ,$$

$$F_4 = G_4 \cup A_4' \cup A_1 .$$

Since $A_1$, $A_2'$ and $A_4'$ and $G_r$ are closed, $F_2$ and $F_4$ are closed.

First we assume

(A.15) $$G_2 \cap G_4 \neq \emptyset .$$

We can then find an $x_0 \in G_2 \cap G_4 \subset J_2 \cap \bar{J}_1$ and points $y_r \in J_2 \cap A_r$ and arcs $[x_0,y_r]$ of $J_2$ from $x_0$ to $y_r$ such that $(x_0,y_r) \subset \text{int } J_1$, $r = 2,4$. Note that automatically $y_r \in \mathring{A}_r$ since by (A.7)

$$J_2 \cap A_r \subset \mathring{A}_r \text{ , } r = 2,4.$$

If $x_0 \in A_2$, then the arc $[x_0,y_4]$ satisfies all requirements for $B$ and we are done. Similary if $x_0 \in A_4$. $x_0 \in J_2 \cap (A_1 \cup A_3)$ is impossible, by virtue of (A.11). Since $J_1 = A_1 \cup A_2 \cup A_3 \cup A_4$ this takes care of $x_0 \in J_1$, and leaves us with $x_0 \in J_2 \cap \text{int}(J_1)$. In this case, the arc $[x_0,y_r]$ hits $J_1$ first in $J_2 \cap A_r$ (at $y_r$), and neither of the arcs $[x_0,y_2]$ and $[x_0,y_4]$ can be a subarc of the other. Thus $[x_0,y_2]$ and $[x_0,y_4]$ only have the point $x_0$ in common and we can take $B = [x_0,y_2] \cup [x_0,y_4]$. This is the arc of $J_2$ from $y_2$ to $y_4$ through $x_0$, with

$$\mathring{B} = (x_0,y_2) \cup (x_0,y_4) \cup \{x_0\} \subset \text{int}(J_1).$$

Thus, in this case the lemma is again true, and we have found $B$ whenever (A.15) holds.

Now assume that

(A.16) $$G_2 \cap G_4 = \emptyset .$$

We shall complete the proof by showing that (A.16) leads to a contradiction. Denote by $a$ the common endpoint of $A_1$ and $A_2$ (see Fig. A.4). If (A.16) holds, then

(A.17) $$G_2 \cap (A'_4 \cup A_1) = \emptyset \text{ ,}$$

since $G_2 \subset J_2$ implies

$$G_2 \cap A_1 \subset J_2 \cap A_1 = \emptyset \quad \text{(by (A.7)),}$$

$$G_2 \cap A'_4 \subset G_2 \cap J_2 \cap A_4 \subset G_2 \cap G_4 = \emptyset \quad \text{(by (A.10)).}$$

Similary $G_4 \cap A'_2 = \emptyset$ so that

(A.18) $$F_2 \cap F_4 = A'_2 \cap (A'_4 \cup A_1) = \{a\} .$$

Next we choose a point $b \in \text{int}(J_1) \cap \text{int}(J_2)$ sufficiently close to $a$, so that we may connect $b$ to $A'_2 \setminus \{a\}$ and to $A_1 \cup A'_4 \setminus \{a\}$ by continuous paths $\phi_2$ and $\phi_4$, respectively, which are contained in $\text{int}(J_1) \cap \text{int}(J_2)$ except for the final point of $\phi_2$ which lies on $A_2'$ and the final point of $\phi_4$ which lies on $A_1 \cup A_4'$. This can be done because $a \in A_1 \subset \text{int}(J_2) \cap J_1$, and by exercise VI.18.3 in Newman (1951) we may assume that $A_2'$ and $A_1 \cup A_4'$ are segments radiating from $a \in J_1 \cap \text{int}(J_2)$; note that $A_2'$ and $A_4'$ have nonempty interiors by construction. Finally, let $c \in A_3$. We can then connect b to c by the following curve $\pi_2$: Go from b to $A_2'$ along $\phi_2$ and then continue along $A_2 \cup A_3 \setminus \{a\}$ to c. This path is disjoint from $F_4$ because $A_2 \cup A_3 \setminus \{a\}$ and $A_4' \cup A_1$ are disjoint, while $\phi_2$ minus its final point lies in $\text{int}(J_1) \cap \text{int}(J_2)$ which is disjoint from $F_4 \subset J_1 \cup J_2$, and finally

$$(A_2 \cup A_3 \setminus \{a\}) \cap G_4 \subset (A_2 \cap J_2 \cap G_4) \cup (A_3 \cap J_2) \subset G_2 \cap G_4 = \emptyset$$

(compare proof of (A.17).

In the same way we can connect b with c by a path which moves along $\phi_4$, and $A_1 \cup A_4 \cup A_3 \setminus \{a\}$, and which does not intersect $F_2$. Since $F_2 \cap F_4$ is connected (see (A.18)), Alexander's lemma (Newman (1951), Theorem V.9.2) implies that b is connected to c by a continuous curve $\psi$ disjoint from $F_2 \cup F_4$. This, however, is impossible as we now show. $\psi$ begins at $b \in \text{int}(J_1) \cap \text{int}(J_2)$ and ends at $c \in A_3 \subset \text{ext}(J_2) \cap J_1$. Let d be the first point of $\psi$ in $J_1$. Then, since $\psi$ is disjoint from $F_2 \cup F_4$, we must have

$$d \in A_3 \cup (A_2 \setminus A_2') \cup (A_4 \setminus A_4'). \tag{A.19}$$

The right hand side of (A.19) lies in $\text{ext}(J_2)$ by (A.7) and the fact that $A_r \setminus A_r'$ is (by (A.14)) disjoint from $J_2$ and contains the common endpoint of $A_r$ and $A_3$ in $\text{ext}(J_2)$. Therefore, in going from $b \in \text{int}(J_1) \cap \text{int}(J_2)$ to d along $\psi$ we must hit $J_2$ in a point $e \in J_2 \cap \bar{J}_1$ (because d is the first point of $\psi$ on $J_1$). But any such point e must lie in $F_2 \cup F_4$ since we can go from e along some arc of $J_2$ to $\text{ext}(J_1)$ ($J_2 \subset \bar{J}_1$ is impossible by (A.7)). If this arc hits $A_2$ before $A_4$ then $e \in G_2$, and if it hits $A_4$ before $A_2$ then $e \in G_4$. Thus $\psi$ must intersect $F_2 \cup F_4$ and we have deduced a contradiction from (A.16). □

Proposition 2.2. Let J be a Jordan curve on $\mathcal{M}$ (and hence also on $\mathcal{G}$ and on $\mathcal{G}^*$) which consists of four closed arcs $A_1, A_2, A_3, A_4$ with disjoint interiors, and such that $A_1$ and $A_3$ each contain at least one vertex of $\mathcal{M}$. Assume that one meets these arcs in the order $A_1$, $A_2, A_3, A_4$ as one traverses $J$ in one direction. Then there exists a path $r$ on $\mathcal{G}$ inside $\bar{J} = J \cup \text{int}(J_1)$ from a vertex on $A_1$ to a vertex on $A_3$, and with all vertices of $r$ in $\bar{J} \setminus A_1 \cup A_3$ occupied, if and only if there does not exist a vacant path $r^*$ on $\mathcal{G}^*$ inside $\bar{J} \setminus A_1 \cup A_3$ from a vertex of $\mathring{A}_2$ to a vertex of $\mathring{A}_4$.

Proof: First assume that there exists a vacant path $r^*$ on $\mathcal{G}^*$ inside $\bar{J} \setminus A_1 \cup A_3$ from $y_2 \in \mathring{A}_2$ to $y_4 \in \mathring{A}_4$. Since $A_2$ and $A_4$ separate $A_1$ and $A_3$ on $J$ any path $r$ inside $\bar{J}$ from a vertex on $A_1$ to a vertex on $A_3$ must intersect $r^*$ (e.g. by Newman (1951) Theorem V.11.8). If $r$ is on $\mathcal{G}$ and $r^*$ on $\mathcal{G}^*$, then they must intersect in a vertex of $\mathcal{M}$ (and of $\mathcal{G}$ and $\mathcal{G}^*$) by Comment 2.2(vii). This vertex would lie in $\bar{J} \setminus A_1 \cup A_3$ and be vacant, as a vertex of $r^*$. Thus any path on $\mathcal{G}$ in $\bar{J}$ connecting a vertex on $A_1$ with a vertex of $A_3$ would have to contain a vacant vertex in $\bar{J} \setminus A_1 \cup A_3$. Consequently, no path $r$ as required in the lemma exists. This proves one direction of the proposition.

Now for the converse. Without loss of generality we may assume that the plane has been mapped homeomorphically onto itself such that $J$ is now the unit circle, that $A_1$ $(A_3)$ intersects the line segment

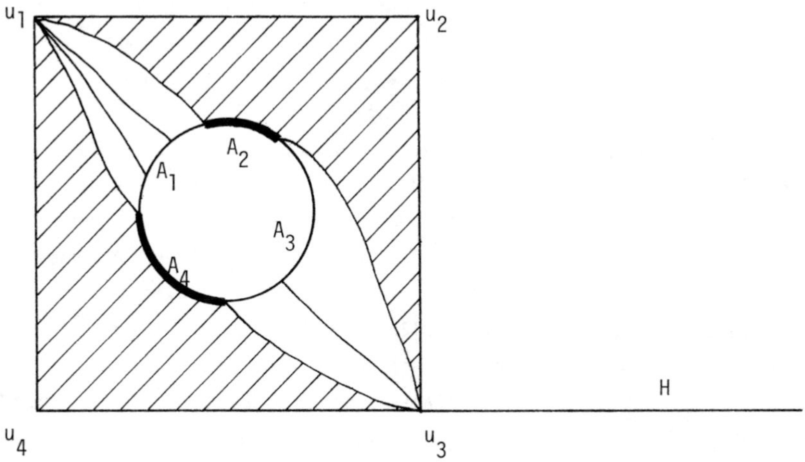


Figure A.6. $J$ is the circle in the center. $A_2$ and $A_4$ are the boldly drawn arcs. The two hatched regions are two faces of $\mathcal{M}_1$.

from the origin to $(-2,+2)$ (to $(2,-2)$), while $A_2$ ($A_4$) lies between $A_1$ and $A_3$ ($A_3$ and $A_1$) as we go around $J$ clockwise. We next modify the graphs outside $\bar{J}$, as well as the occupancy configuration outside $\text{int}(J)$. We shall then apply Cor.2.2 to the modified graph and configuration. The mosaic $\mathcal{M}$ is modified to a mosaic $\mathcal{M}_1$ as follows. The vertices of $\mathcal{M}_1$ are the vertices of $\mathcal{M}$ in $\bar{J}$ plus all points of the form $(2i_1,2i_2)$, $i_1,i_2 \in \mathbb{Z}$. As for edges, there is an edge of $\mathcal{M}_1$ between $(2i_1,2i_2)$ and the four points $(2i_1 \pm 2, 2i_2 \pm 2)$. The edges of $\mathcal{M}$ in $\bar{J}$ are also edges of $\mathcal{M}_1$. Finally, we write

$$u_1 = (-2,2),\ u_2 = (2,2),\ u_3 = (2,-2),\ u_4 = (-2,-2)$$

and we give $\mathcal{M}_1$ an edge between $u_r$ and any vertex on $A_r$, $r = 1$ or 3 (see Fig. A.6). $\mathcal{M}_1$ has no further edges. We insert the edges from $A_r$ to $u_r$ in such a way that they lie in $\text{int}(S_1) \setminus \bar{J}$, except for their endpoints, where $S_1$ is the square

$$S_1 = \{(x_1,x_2) : |x_1| \le 2, |x_2| \le 2\}\ .$$

Moreover, we choose these edges such that an edge from $A_1$ to $u_1$ and an edge from $A_3$ to $u_3$ do not intersect, while the edges from $A_r$ to $u_r$ intersect in $u_r$ only (see Fig. A.6). Thus $\mathcal{M}_1$ contains a copy of the mosaic $\mathcal{M}$ of Ex. 2.2(i) (multiplied by a factor two). In $\bar{J}$ $\mathcal{M}_1$ coincides with the original $\mathcal{M}$, while there are no edges in $S_1 \setminus \text{int}(J)$ which have interior intersections. The faces of $\mathcal{M}_1$ are the open squares into which the plane is divided by the lines $x_1 = 2i_1$, $x_2 = 2i_2$, $i_1,i_2 \in \mathbb{Z}$ - with the exclusion of $\mathring{S}_1$ - as well as the faces of $\mathcal{M}$ inside $J$, plus certain faces in $\mathring{S}_1 \setminus \bar{J}$. The last kind of faces are either "triangular" bounded by two edges from $u_r$ to $A_r$ and an edge of $\mathcal{M}$ in $A_r$, or a face bounded by the two edges on the perimeter of $S_1$ incident to $u_s$, $s = 2,4$, one edge from $u_1$ to $A_1$ and one from $u_3$ to $A_3$ plus an arc of $J$ containing $A_s$ (these are the hatched faces in Fig. A.6). It is clear that $\mathcal{M}_1$ is a mosaic.

We next take for $\mathcal{F}_1$ the collection of faces of $\mathcal{M}$ in $\bar{J}$ which belong to $\mathcal{F}$. In other words, a face $F$ of $\mathcal{M}_1$ belongs to $\mathcal{F}_1$ iff $F \subset \text{int}(J)$ (in which case $F$ is also a face of $\mathcal{M}$) and $F \in \mathcal{F}$. Note that since $J$ is a Jordan curve made up from edges of $\mathcal{M}$, which are also edges of $\mathcal{M}_1$, each face of $\mathcal{M}$ and of $\mathcal{M}_1$ lies either entirely in $\text{int}(J)$ or in $\text{ext}(J)$. We take $(\mathcal{G}_1,\mathcal{G}_1^*)$ as the matching pair based on $(\mathcal{M}_1,\mathcal{F}_1)$. Clearly $\mathcal{G}_1$ and $\mathcal{G}_1^*$ coincide with $\mathcal{G}$ and $\mathcal{G}^*$, respectively, in $\bar{J}$.

Finally we define the modified occupancy configuration on $\mathcal{M}_1$. Let $\omega$ be the original occupancy configuration on $\mathcal{M}$. Let $H$ be the half line from $u_3$ parallel to the first coordinate axis: $H = \{(x_1,x_2): x_1 \geq 2, x_2 = -2\}$. Then we take

$$\text{(A.20)} \qquad \begin{aligned} \omega_1(v) &= \omega(v) \quad \text{if} \quad v \in \bar{J} \setminus A_1 \cup A_3 , \\ \omega_1(v) &= +1 \quad \text{if} \quad v \in A_1 \cup A_3 \cup H , \\ \omega_1(v) &= -1 \quad \text{if} \quad v \notin \bar{J} \text{ and } v \notin H. \end{aligned}$$

We choose a vertex $v$ in $A_1$ and take

$W_1 = W_1(v,\omega_1)$ = occupied component of $v$ on $\mathcal{G}_1$ in the configuration $\omega_1$.

Now assume that there does not exist any path $r$ on $\mathcal{G}$ in $\bar{J}$ from a vertex on $A_1$ to a vertex on $A_3$ with all vertices on $r$ and in $\bar{J} \setminus A_1 \cup A_3$ occupied. In this case $W_1$ cannot contain any point on $A_3$. For if there would be an occupied path $r_1$ on $\mathcal{G}_1$ from $v$ to a vertex of $A_3$, then either $r_1$ is contained in $\bar{J}$ or it leaves $\bar{J}$ before it reaches $A_3$. The first case cannot arise, for if $r_1$ stays in $\bar{J}$, then $r_1$ is also a path on $\mathcal{G}$ and the vertices on $r_1$ in $\bar{J} \setminus A_1 \cup A_3$ would also have to be occupied in $\omega$ ($\omega(v) = \omega_1(v)$ for all such vertices; see (A.20)). Thus, the piece of $r_1$ from its last vertex on $A_1$ to its first vertex on $A_3$ would be a path $r$ of the kind which we just assumed not to exist. Also the second case is impossible, because the only way to leave $\bar{J}$ on $\mathcal{G}_1$ without hitting $A_3$ is via $u_1$ and $u_1$ is vacant in $\omega_1$ by (A.20). Thus no occupied path $r_1$ can go through $u_1$. It follows that indeed $W_1 \cap A_3 = \emptyset$. Since all vertices of $A_3 \cup H$ are occupied in $\omega_1$, and can therefore be connected by occupied paths on $\mathcal{G}_1$ in $\omega_1$, it follows that they belong to one component, and

$$\text{(A.21)} \qquad W_1 \cap (A_3 \cup H) = \emptyset.$$

Since all vertices outside $\bar{J}$ and not on $H$ are vacant we obtain also $W_1 \subset \bar{J}$.

We are now ready to apply Cor. 2.2. This Corollary, applied to the cluster $W_1$ on $\mathcal{G}_1$ shows that there exists a vacant circuit $J^*$ on $\mathcal{G}_1^*$ surrounding $W_1$. Now all vertices on $A_1$ are occupied in $\omega_1$ (see (A.20)) and hence belong to $W_1$ (since $v \in A_1$). Thus

(A.22) $$A_1 \subset W_1 \subset \text{int}(J^*).$$

Also, $J^*$ being vacant cannot intersect $A_3 \cup H$, since it would then have to intersect this set in a vertex (see Comment 2.2(vii)) and all vertices on $A_3 \cup H$ are occupied in $\omega_1$. But since $H$ goes out to $\infty$ and $A_3 \cup H$ together with the edges from $A_3$ to $u_3$ form a connected set, this means that

(A.23) $$A_3 \cup H \subset \text{ext}(J^*).$$

We can now apply Lemma A.2 with $J_1 = J$, $J_2 = J^*$ - (A.22) and (A.23) correspond to (A.7). $J^*$ therefore must contain an arc $B$ such that $\mathring{B} \subset \text{int}(J) \subset \bar{J} \setminus A_1 \cup A_3$ and one endpoint on each of $\mathring{A}_2$ and $\mathring{A}_4$. The arc $B$ therefore lies in $\bar{J} \setminus A_1 \cup A_3$ and in this region $\mathcal{G}_1^*$ coincides with $\mathcal{G}^*$ and $\omega_1$ with $\omega$. Thus all vertices of $\mathcal{G}^*$ on $B$ are vacant. Also, all points of $B$ belong to edges of $\mathcal{G}^*$ in $\bar{J} \setminus A_1 \cup A_3$, because $J^*$ is a circuit on $\mathcal{G}^*$. The endpoints of $B$ belong to $J^* \subset \mathcal{G}^*$, as well as to $J \subset \mathcal{G}$ (since $\mathring{A}_2 \cup \mathring{A}_4 \subset J$), hence are necessarily vertices of $\mathcal{G}^*$ (see Comment 2.2(vii)). It follows that $B$ is made up of the complete edges of a vacant path $r^*$ on $\mathcal{G}^*$ inside $\bar{J} \setminus A_1 \cup A_3$, and runs from a vertex on $\mathring{A}_2$ to a vertex $\mathring{A}_4$. The existence of such an $r^*$ was just what we wanted to prove. □

We remind the reader of the set up for Proposition 2.3. $J$ is a Jordan curve consisting of four nonempty closed arcs $B_1, A, B_2, C$ with $A$ and $C$ separating $B_1$ and $B_2$ on $J_i$. $L_i: x(1) = a_i$, $i = 1,2, a_1 < a_2$, are two axes of symmetry for $\mathcal{G}_{p\ell}$, and for $i = 1,2$

(A.24) $B_i$ is a curve made up from edges of $\mathcal{M}_{p\ell}$, or $B_i$ lies on $L_i$ and $J$ lies in the halfplane $(-1)^i(x(1)-a_i) \leq 0$.

The proposition deals with paths $r = (v_0, e_1, \dots, e_\nu, v_\nu)$ on $\mathcal{G}_{p\ell}$

(A.25) $v_1, e_2, \dots, e_{\nu-1}, v_{\nu-1} \subset \text{int}(J)$,

(A.26) $e_1$ has exactly one point in common with $J$. This lies in $B_1$ and is either $v_0$, or in case $B_1 \subset L_1$ it may be the midpoint of $e_1$,

and

(A.27) $e_\nu$ has exactly one point in common with $J$. This lies in $B_2$ and is either $v_\nu$, or in case $B_2 \subset L_2$, it may be the midpoint of $e_\nu$.

$J^-(r)$ and $J^+(r)$ are the components of $\mathrm{int}(J)\setminus r$ with $A$ and $C$ in their boundary, respectively. $r_1 \prec r_2$ means $J^-(r_1) \subset J_2^-(r_2)$ (see Def. 2.11 and 2.12). For a path $r$ and a subset $S$ of $\mathbb{R}^2$ $r \subset S$ means that all edges and vertices of $r$ lie in $S$. We only consider sets $S$ for which

(A.28) $$B_1 \cap B_2 \cap S = \emptyset .$$

Proposition 2.3. Assume that (2.3)-(2.5) hold with $\mathcal{G}$ replaced by $\mathcal{M}$ and that $L_i : x(1) = a_i$, $i = 1,2$, are axes of symmetry for $\mathcal{G}_{p\ell}$, with $a_1 < a_2$. Let $J$ be a Jordan curve consisting of four closed nonempty arcs $B_1$ $A$, $B_2$ and $C$ as above satisfying (A.24). Let $S$ be any subset of $\mathbb{R}^2$ such that (A.28) holds. Denote by $\mathfrak{R} = \mathfrak{R}(S,\omega)$ the collection of all occupied paths $r$ on $\mathcal{G}_{p\ell}$ which satisfy (A.25) -(A.27) and $r \subset S$. If $\mathfrak{R} \neq \emptyset$, then it has a unique element $R = R(S,\omega)$ which precedes all others. Any occupied path $r$ on $\mathcal{G}_{p\ell}$ which satisfies (A.25)-(A.27) and $r \subset S$ also satisfies

(A.29) $$r \cap \bar{J} \subset \bar{J}^+(R) \quad \text{and} \quad R \cap \bar{J} \subset \bar{J}^-(r).$$

Finally, let $r_0$ be a fixed path on $\mathcal{G}_{p\ell}$ satisfying (A.25)-(A.27) and $r_0 \subset S$ (no reference to its occupancy is made here). Then, whether $R = r_0$ or not depends only on the occupancies of the vertices of $\mathcal{G}_{p\ell}$ in the set

(A.30) $$(\bar{J}^-(r_0) \cup V_1 \cup V_2) \cap S,$$

where $V_i = \emptyset$ if $B_i$ is made up from edges of $\mathcal{M}_{p\ell}$, while

$V_i = \{v : v$ a vertex of $\mathcal{G}_{p\ell}$ such that its reflection $\tilde{v}$ in $L_i$ belongs to $\bar{J}^-(r_0)$ and such that $e \cap \bar{J} \subset \bar{J}^-(r_0) \cap S$ for some edge $e$ of $\mathcal{G}_{p\ell}$ between $v$ and $\tilde{v}\}$, $i = 1,2$,

in case $B_i$ lies in $L_i$, but is not made up from edges of $\mathcal{M}_{p\ell}$.

Proof: Assume $\mathfrak{R} \neq \emptyset$ and $r_1, r_2 \in \mathfrak{R}$. We shall first construct a path $r$ on $\mathcal{G}_{p\ell}$ satisfying (A.25)-(A.27) as well as

(A.31) each edge of $\mathcal{G}_{p\ell}$ which appears in $r$ also appears in $r_1$ or in $r_2$,

and

(A.32) $$r \prec r_1 \text{ and } r \prec r_2 .$$

Since the vertices on $r$ are endpoints of the edges appearing in $r$, each vertex on $r$ also lies on $r_1$ or $r_2$. In particular since $r_1, r_2 \subset S$ (A.31) will imply $r \subset S$. Moreover all vertices on $r$ will be occupied since this holds for $r_1, r_2 \in \mathcal{R}$. Thus $r$ will be an element of $\mathcal{R}$ which precedes $r_1$ and $r_2$. By carrying out this process repeatedly we obtain paths $r \in \mathcal{R}$ which occur earlier and earlier in the partial order. After a finite number of steps we shall arive at the minimal crossing $R$.

Now for the details. Let $r_1 = (v_0, e_1, \dots, e_\nu, v_\nu)$ and $r_2 = (w_0, f_1, \dots, f_\tau, w_\tau)$. Both of these paths are self-avoiding, so that the curve $C_1$ made up from $e_1, \dots, e_\nu$ is a simple arc with endpoints $v_0$ and $v_\nu$. $C_1$ intersects $J$ in exactly two points, $m_0 \in B_1$ and $m_\nu \in B_2$. $m_0$ equals $v_0$ or the midpoint of $e_1$, and $m_\nu$ equals $v_\nu$ or the midpoint of $e_\nu$. The open arc of $C_1$ between $m_0$ and $m_\nu$ lies in $\text{int}(J)$. Similar comments apply to the curve $C_2$ made up from the edges of $r_2 : f_1, \dots, f_\tau$.

If $C_2$ contains no point in $J^-(r_1)$ then we take $r = r_1$. We shall see below (after (A.44)) that this implies (A.32). ((A.25)-(A.27) and (A.31) are obvious in this case). Let us therefore assume that $C_2$ contains a point $x \in J^-(r_1)$. Then $x$ belongs to some edge of $r_2$, say $x \in f_\alpha$. We note that all edges of $r_1$ and $r_2$ are edges of the planar graph $\mathcal{G}_{p\ell}$. Two such edges, if they do not coincide, can intersect only in a vertex of $\mathcal{G}_{p\ell}$, which is a common endpoint of these edges. Thus an edge $f$ of $r_2$ which contains a point of $J^-(r_1)$ cannot leave $J^-(r_1)$ by crossing $r_1$. If it crosses $\text{Fr}(J^-(r_1)) \setminus r_1$ then it crosses $J$ and $f$ must be $f_1$ or $f_\tau$, and $f$ intersects $J$ only once, in the midpoint of $f$. In this case one half of $f$ lies in $\text{ext}(J) \cup J$ while the interior of the other half - which contains a point of $J^-(r_1)$ - must lie entirely in $J^-(r_1)$ (cf. Comment 2.4(ii)). Thus for any edge $f$ of $r_2$ we must have

(A.33) $$\text{either } \mathring{f} \cap \text{int}(J) \subset J^-(r_1) \text{ or } f \cap \text{int}(J) \subset \overline{J}^+(r_1).$$

In particular

(A.34) $$\mathring{f}_\alpha \cap \text{int}(J) \subset J^-(r_1).$$

Also, if we move along the arc $C_2$ from $x$ to $w_0$, then the first intersection with $C_1$, if any, must be a vertex of $\mathcal{G}_{p\ell}$ which is a common endpoint of an edge of $r_2$ and an edge of $r_1$. In particular it must equal $v_\beta$ for some $0 \le \beta \le \nu$. If such an intersection exists we take $b$ equal to this intersection; if no such intersection exists we take $b = w_0$, the initial point of $r_2$. Similarly, if moving along $C_2$ from $x$ to $w_\tau$ there is an intersection with $C_1$ then we take $c$ equal to the first such intersection; otherwise we take $c = w_\tau$, the final point of $r_2$. In all cases $b$ and $c$ are vertices of $r_2$, and if $c$ is on $r_1$, then $c = v_\gamma$ for some $0 \le \gamma \le \nu$. We write $\rho$ for the piece of $r_2$ between $b$ and $c$. I.e., if $b = w_\delta$, $c = w_\varepsilon$ with $\delta < \varepsilon$ then $\rho = (w_\delta, e_{\delta+1}, \dots, e_\varepsilon, w_\varepsilon)$, and $\delta$ and $\varepsilon$ are interchanged when $\delta > \varepsilon$. The same argument used above for showing (A.33) shows that $\rho$ - which contains the point $x \in J^-(r_1)$ - cannot leave $J^-(r_1)$ through $r_1$, and that if $\rho$ crosses $J$, then $\rho$ contains a half edge in $\mathrm{ext}(J) \cup J$, the other half being in $J^-(r_1)$. Thus

(A.35) $$\mathring{\rho} \cap \mathrm{int}(J) = (\rho \setminus \{b,c\}) \cap \mathrm{int}(J) \subset J^-(r_1).$$

In the sequel we restrict ourselves to the case where $b = w_\delta$ and $c = w_\varepsilon$ with $1 \le \delta < \varepsilon \le \tau - 1$. This means that (A.35) simplifies to

(A.36) $$\mathring{\rho} = \rho \setminus \{b,c\} \subset J^-(r_1).$$

We leave it to the reader to make the simple changes which are necessary when $b = w_0$ and/or $c = w_\tau$. We define a new path $\tilde{r}_1$ by replacing the piece of $r_1$ between $b$ and $c$ by $\rho$. Note that we may have $b = v_\beta = w_\delta$, $c = v_\gamma = w_\varepsilon$ with $\gamma < \beta$. We then have to reverse $\rho$ and in this case $\tilde{r}_1$ becomes

$$\tilde{r}_1 = (v_0, e_1, \dots, e_\gamma, v_\gamma = w_\varepsilon, f_\varepsilon, w_{\varepsilon-1}, \dots, f_{\delta+1}, w_\delta = v_\beta, e_{\beta+1}, \dots, e_\nu, v_\nu).$$

(In the simpler case $\beta < \gamma$ $\rho$ is inserted in its natural order.) We show that $\tilde{r}_1$ is a path satisfying (A.25)-(A.27). $\tilde{r}_1$ consists of one or two pieces of $r_1$ and $\rho$. Each of these pieces is a piece of a self-avoiding path, hence self-avoiding. Also, $\mathring{\rho}$ does not intersect $r_1$, and if $\tilde{r}_1$ contains two pieces of $r_1$ then they are disjoint (because $b$ and $c$ are distinct, being two points of the simple arc $C_2$, one strictly before and one strictly after $x$ on $C_2$). Therefore $\tilde{r}_1$ is self-avoiding. Let $\tilde{r}_1 = (\tilde{v}_0, \tilde{e}_1, \dots, \tilde{e}_\xi, \tilde{v}_\xi)$. Then by construction each of the edges $\tilde{e}_i$, $2 \le i \le \xi - 1$, is one of the edges

$e_2,\ldots,e_{\nu-1},f_2,\ldots f_{\tau-1}$, and similarly

$$\{\tilde{v}_1,\ldots,\tilde{v}_{\xi-1}\} \subset \{v_1,\ldots,v_{\nu-1},w_1,\ldots,w_{\tau-1}\}.$$

Thus $\tilde{r}_1$ satisfies (A.25), because $r_1$ and $r_2$ do. Also (A.26) and (A.27) hold, because $\tilde{e}_1 = e_1$, $\tilde{e}_\xi = e_\nu$ when $1 \le \delta < \varepsilon \le \tau-1$. (But even when $b = w_0$ (A.26) is easy for then $\tilde{e}_1 = f_1$; similarly for (A.27).)

For brevity denote by $E(r)$ the collection of edges of $\mathcal{G}_{p\ell}$ appearing in $r$. Then it is clear from the construction that

(A.37) $$E(\tilde{r}_1) \subset E(r_1) \cup E(r_2).$$

(A.37) says that (A.31) holds for $\tilde{r}_1$ instead of $r$. Since $r_1 \subset \overline{J}^-(r_1)$ by definition, it is also immediate from the construction and (A.35) that

(A.38) $$\tilde{r}_1 \cap \overline{J} \subset \overline{J}^-(r_1).$$

We show that (A.38) implies

(A.39) $$r_1 \cap \overline{J} \subset \overline{J}^+(r_1) \subset \overline{J}^+(\tilde{r}_1)$$

and

(A.40) $$J^-(\tilde{r}_1) \subset J^-(r_1).$$

To see this, observe first that the arc, $J_1$ say, of $J$ between the points of intersection of $r_1$ and $J$, and containing $A$, is the only part of $\overline{J}^-(r_1)$ on $J$. By (A.38) the points of intersection of $\tilde{r}_1$ and $J$ must lie on $J_1$. Consequently the arc of $J$ between these intersection points containing $C$ also contains that arc of $J$ between the intersection points of $J$ and $r_1$ containing $C$. The latter arc is just $J \setminus J_1$. Any interior point $z_0$ of $J \setminus J_1$ lies therefore in $Fr(J^+(r_1)) \cap Fr(J^+(\tilde{r}_1))$. Such interior points exist since the endpoints of $J \setminus J_1$ are the intersections of $r_1$ with $J$; these lie on $B_1 \cap S$ and $B_2 \cap S$, respectively, and cannot coincide by virtue of (A.28). Pick a point $z_0$ in the interior of $J \setminus J_1$. Any point $z_1 \in int(J)$ sufficiently close to $z_0$ belongs to $J^+(r_1) \cap J^+(\tilde{r}_1)$. Choose such a $z_1$ and let $y$ be an arbitrary point of $J^+(r_1)$. There then exists a continuous curve $\psi$ from $y$ to $z_1$ in $J^+(r_1)$. By (A.38) $\psi$ cannot hit $\tilde{r}_1$, and since $\psi$ lies in $J^+(r_1)$ it cannot hit $J$ either. Thus $\psi$ does not hit $Fr(J^+(\tilde{r}_1))$ and ends at $z_1 \in J^+(\tilde{r}_1)$. Thus all of $\psi$ lies in $J^+(\tilde{r}_1)$ and in particular $y \in J^+(\tilde{r}_1)$. Since

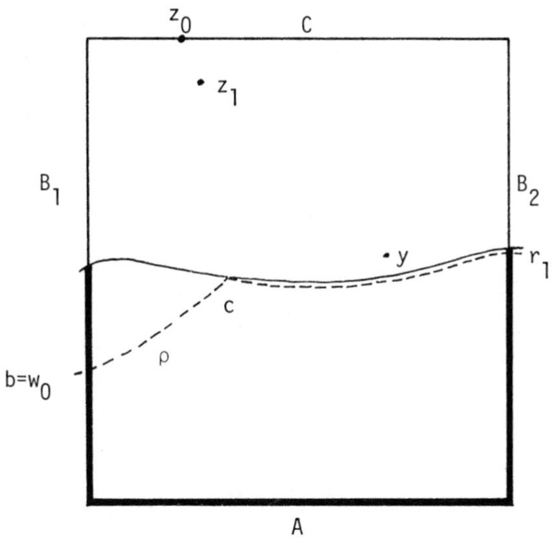


Figure A.7. Schematic diagram giving relative locations J is the perimeter of the rectangle. $J_1$ is the boldly drawn part of J. $r_1$ is drawn solidly and $\tilde{r}_1$ is dashed. $\tilde{r}_1$ coincides with $\tilde{r}$ in the part drawn as $\overline{\overline{---}}$ . The figure illustrates a case with $b=w_0$ .

y was an arbitrary point of $J^+(r_1)$ we proved

(A.41) $$J^+(r_1) \subset J^+(\tilde{r}_1).$$

The second inclusion in (A.39) follows immediately from this, while the first inclusion in (A.39) is immediate from the definition of $J^+$. (A.40) follows from (A.39) since $J^-(r) = \text{int}(J)\setminus\overline{J}^+(r)$.

(A.40) implies that if an edge f of $r_2$ satisfies $\mathring{f} \cap \text{int}(J) \subset J^-(\tilde{r}_1)$, then also $\mathring{f} \cap \text{int}(J) \subset J^-(r_1)$. By virtue of (A.33) the other edges f of $r_2$ satisfy $f \cap \text{int}(J) \subset \overline{J}^+(r_1)$ . $f_\alpha$ is not one of these, by (A.34). However, $f_\alpha$ is part of ρ , and hence of $\tilde{r}_1$ so that $f_\alpha \cap \text{int}(J) \subset \overline{J}^+(\tilde{r}_1)$. Therefore, if we write N(r) for the number of edges f or $r_2$ with $\mathring{f} \cap \text{int}(J) \subset J^-(r)$, then $f_\alpha$ is counted in $N(r_1)$ but not in $N(\tilde{r}_1)$. Moreover, by the preceding observation, any f counted in $N(\tilde{r}_1)$ must also be counted in $N(r_1)$. Thus

(A.42) $$N(\tilde{r}_1) < N(r_1).$$

We now replace $r_1$ by $\tilde{r}_1$ and repeat the procedure, if necessary. If $C_2$ still contains a point in $J^-(\tilde{r}_1)$ then we form $\tilde{r}_2$ such that

$$E(\tilde{r}_2) \subset E(\tilde{r}_1) \cup E(r_2) \subset E(r_1) \cup E(r_2), \quad \text{(cf. (A.37))},$$

$$J^-(\tilde{r}_2) \subset J^-(\tilde{r}_1) \subset J^-(r_1) \qquad \text{(cf. (A.40))},$$

and

$$N(\tilde{r}_2) < N(\tilde{r}_1) < N(r_1) \qquad \text{(cf. (A.42))}.$$

Since $r_2$ has finitely many edges $N(r_1) < \infty$, and $N$ decreases with each step. Thus, after a finite number of steps, say $\lambda$ steps, we arrive at a path $\tilde{r}_\lambda$ satisfying (A.25)-(A.27) and

(A.43) $$E(\tilde{r}_\lambda) \subset E(\tilde{r}_{\lambda-1}) \cup E(r_2) \ldots \subset E(r_1) \cup E(r_2),$$

(A.44) $$J^-(\tilde{r}_\lambda) \subset J^-(\tilde{r}_{\lambda-1}) \subset \ldots \subset J^-(r_1),$$

and such that $C_2$ contains no more points in $J^-(\tilde{r}_\lambda)$, or equivalently

(A.45) $$r_2 \cap \overline{J} \subset \overline{J}^+(\tilde{r}_\lambda).$$

The case where $C_2$ contains no points in $J^-(r_1)$ mentioned in the beginning of the proof is subsumed under this, if we take $\tilde{r}_\lambda = r_1$ for this case. We now take $r = \tilde{r}_\lambda$ . (A.43) gives us (A.31) while (A.44) and (A.45) give us (A.32). Indeed (A.45) implies $J^-(\tilde{r}_\lambda) = J^-(r) \subset J^-(r_2)$ just as (A.38) implies (A.41) (merely interchange + and -). This completes the construction of $r$.

Now that we have constructed $r$ from $r_1$, $r_2$ the remainder of the proof is easy. Denote the elements of $\mathfrak{R}$ in some order by $r_1, r_2, \ldots, r_\sigma$. If $\mathfrak{R} = \emptyset$ we don't have to prove the existence of $R$, and when $R$ has only one element, $r_1$, then $R = r_1$. In general $\mathfrak{R}$ is finite by virtue of (2.3), (2.4). For $\sigma \geq 2$ let $r$ be the path constructed above from $r_1$ and $r_2$. For $\sigma = 2$ take $R = r$. For $\sigma \geq 3$ go through the above construction with $r_1$ and $r_2$ replaced by $r$ and $r_3$, respectively. The resulting path, $\overline{r}$ say, is again in $\mathfrak{R}$ and satisfies

$$E(\overline{r}) \subset E(r) \cup E(r_3) \subset E(r_1) \cup E(r_2) \cup E(r_3) \quad \text{(cf. (A.31))}$$

and

$$\overline{r} \prec r_3 \text{ and } \overline{r} \prec r, \text{ hence } \overline{r} \prec r_i,\ 1 \leq i \leq 3 \quad \text{(cf. (A.32))}.$$

After a finite number of such constructions we obtain a path $R \in \mathcal{R}$ which satisfies

$$E(R) \subset \bigcup_{i=1}^{\sigma} E(r_i),$$

(A.46) $$R \prec r_i,\ 1 \le i \le \sigma .$$

This $R$ precedes all elements of $\mathcal{R}$. (A.46) implies

$$R \cap \bar{J} \subset \bar{J}^-(R) \subset \bar{J}^-(r_i),\quad 1 \le i \le \sigma ,$$

and hence $r_i \cap \bar{J} \subset \bar{J}^+(R)$ (just as (A.38) implied (A.39)). Thus (A.29) holds. The uniqueness of $R$ is immediate for if $R' \in \mathcal{R}$ also precedes all elements of $\mathcal{R}$, then $R \prec R'$ and $R' \prec R$. Then (A.29) holds for $R$ as well as $R'$ so that

$$R \cap \bar{J} \subset \bar{J}^-(R'),\quad R \cap \bar{J} \subset \bar{J}^+(R'),$$

whence

$$R \cap \bar{J} \subset \bar{J}^-(R') \cap \bar{J}^+(R') = R' \cap \bar{J}.$$

Interchanging $R$ and $R'$ yields $R \cap \bar{J} = R' \cap \bar{J}$, which together with (A.26) and (A.27) leads to $R = R'$.

Finally, if $r_0$ is a path on $\mathcal{G}_{p\ell}$ satisfying (A.25)-(A.27) and $r_0 \subset S$, then $R = r_0$ if and only if $r_0 \in \mathcal{R}$ but $r_0$ is not preceded by any other element of $\mathcal{R}$. Thus $R = r_0$ is equivalent to

(A.47) $r_0$ is occupied, but any path $r$ on $\mathcal{G}_{p\ell}$ satisfying (A.25)-(A.27) with $r \subset S$ with $r \prec r_0$, $r \ne r_0$ cannot be occupied.

Clearly, (A.47) only depends on the occupancies of sites on $r_0$ or on paths $r \prec r_0$ with $r \subset S$. But all such sites belong to $\bar{J}^-(r_0) \cap S$ or are an initial or final point in $\text{ext}(J)$ of a path $r \prec r_0$ with $r \subset S$. Since $r$ has to satisfy (A.26) and (A.27) one easily sees that all these sites belong to the set (A.30)(cf. Comment 2.4(ii)). □

We next prove a purely graph-theoretical proposition, which is needed only in Ch. 9. It was first proved by Sykes and Essam (1964). We find it somewhat simpler to prove the version below which refers to $\mathcal{G}_{p\ell}$ and $\mathcal{G}^*_{p\ell}$ rather than $\mathcal{G}$ and $\mathcal{G}^*$. We remind the reader of the definition of $\mathcal{G}_{p\ell}$ ($\omega$; occupied) for an occupancy configuration $\omega$ on $\mathcal{M}_{p\ell}$ satisfying (2.15) and (2.16). $\mathcal{G}_{p\ell}$ ($\omega$; occupied) is the graph with vertex set the set of occupied vertices of $\mathcal{G}_{p\ell}$ and edge set the set of edges of $\mathcal{G}_{p\ell}$ both of whose endpoints are occupied. $\mathcal{G}^*_{p\ell}$ ($\omega$;vacant) is defined similarly; see the proof of Theorem 9.2.

Proposition A.1. Let $\omega$ be a fixed occupancy configuration on $\mathcal{M}_{p\ell}$, satisfying (2.15) and (2.16). Two vacant vertices of $\mathcal{G}^*_{p\ell}$ $v_1$ and $v_2$ lie in the same component of $\mathcal{G}^*_{p\ell}$ ($\omega$; vacant) if and only if $v_1$ and $v_2$ lie in the same face of $\mathcal{G}_{p\ell}$ ($\omega$; occupied).

Proof: $v_1$ and $v_2$ lie in the same component of $\mathcal{G}^*_{p\ell}$ ($\omega$; vacant) iff there exists a vacant path on $\mathcal{G}^*_{p\ell}$ from $v_1$ to $v_2$. If such a path exists, then it cannot intersect any edge of $\mathcal{G}_{p\ell}$ ($\omega$; occupied) (by virtue of Comment 2.3(v)) so that the path lies entirely in ine face of $\mathcal{G}_{p\ell}$ ($\omega$; occupied). Thus in one direction the proposition is trivial.

For the converse, assume $v_1, v_2 \in \mathcal{G}^*_{p\ell}$ are vacant and lie in the same face of $\mathcal{G}_{p\ell}$ ($\omega$;occupied). By definition of such a face as a component of $\mathbb{R}^2\backslash\mathcal{G}_{p\ell}$ ($\omega$;occupied) this means that there exists a continuous curve $\psi$ in $\mathbb{R}^2\backslash\mathcal{G}_{p\ell}$ ($\omega$;occupied) from $v_1$ to $v_2$. In order to complete the proof we show how one can modify $\psi$ so that it becomes a path on $\mathcal{G}^*_{p\ell}$ ($\omega$; vacant). To make this modification we recall that all faces of $\mathcal{M}_{p\ell}$ are "triangles" (Comment 2.3(vi)). Assume that $\psi$ intersects such a face, say the open triangle $F$ with distinct vertices $w_1, w_2, w_3$ and edges $e_1$ between $w_2$ and $w_3$, $e_2$ between $w_3$ and $w_1$, and $e_3$ between $w_1$ and $w_2$. Moving from $v_1$ to $v_2$ along $\psi$ let $x_1$ ($x_2$) be the first (last) intersection with $\bar{F}$. The $x_i$ are necessarily on the perimeter of $F$, since both endpoints of $\psi$ are vertices of $\mathcal{G}^*_{p\ell}$, hence not in any of the open triangular faces of $\mathcal{M}_{p\ell}$. If $x_i \in e$, then at least one endpoint of $e$ must be vacant, for otherwise $e$ belongs to $\mathcal{G}_{p\ell}$ ($\omega$; occupied), while $\psi$ is disjoint from this graph. This implies that $x_1$ can be connected to $x_2$ by a simple arc along the perimeter of $F$, which still does not intersect $\mathcal{G}_{p\ell}$ ($\omega$; occupied). For example, let $x_1 \in e_1$, $x_2 \in e_2$. If the common endpoint $w_3$ of $e_1$ and $e_2$ is vacant, then move from $x_1$ to $w_3$ along $e_1$ and from $w_3$ to $x_2$ along $e_2$. If $w_3$ is occupied, then $w_1$ and $w_2$ must be vacant, and one can go from $x_1$ to $w_2$ along $e_1$, from $w_2$ to $w_1$ along $e_3$, and from $w_1$ to $x_2$ along $e_2$. These connections from $x_1$ to $x_2$ do not intersect $\mathcal{G}_{p\ell}$ ($\omega$; occupied), because if an edge $e$ does not belong to $\mathcal{G}_{p\ell}$ ($\omega$; occupied), then no interior point of $e$ can belong to $\mathcal{G}_{p\ell}$ ($\omega$; occupied). $\psi$ intersects only finitely many faces, say $F_1,\dots,F_\nu$. We can successively replace the piece of $\psi$ between the first and last intersection of $\bar{F}_i$ with a simple arc along the perimeter of $F_i$. Making such a replacement cannot introduce a new face whose interior is entered by $\psi$. On the contrary, each such replacement diminishes the number of such faces. Consequently, after a finite number of steps we obtain a continuous curve, $\phi$ say, from $v_1$ to $v_2$, disjoint from $\mathcal{G}_{p\ell}$ ($\omega$; occupied), and which is contained in the union of the edges of $\mathcal{M}_{p\ell}$. $\phi$ may not be a path on $\mathcal{G}^*_{p\ell}$. For instance it can contain only part of an edge $e$, rather than the whole edge $e$, and $\phi$ is not necessarily simple. Note, however, that $\phi$ begins at the vertex $v_1$ of $\mathcal{G}^*_{p\ell}$, and ends at $v_2$ which we may take different from $v_1$ (there is nothing to prove if $v_1 = v_2$). Let $w_1$ be the first vertex of $\mathcal{M}_{p\ell}$ different from $v_1$ through which $\phi$ passes. Set

$$t_0 = \max\{t \in [0,1]: \phi(t) = v_1\},$$

$$t_1 = \min\{t \in [0,1]: \phi(t) = w_1\}.$$

We can then discard the piece of $\phi$ from $t = 0$ to $t = t_0$; the restriction of $\phi$ to $[t_0,1]$ is still a path from $v_1$ to $v_2$. Also for $t_0 < t < t$, $\phi(t)$ cannot equal any vertex of $\mathcal{M}_{p\ell}$ and therefore is contained in the union of the interiors of the edges of $\mathcal{M}_{p\ell}$. Since the continuous path $\phi$ cannot go from the interior of one edge to the interior of another edge without passing through a vertex, this means that $\phi(t)$ for $t_0 < t < t_1$ is contained in the interior of a single edge $e_1$ from $v_1$ to $w_1$. Also by connectedness $\phi$ passes through all points of $e_1$. We can therefore replace the piece of $\phi$ from $t = 0$ to $t = t_1$ by the simple arc $e_1$. After this replacement $\phi$ still is a continuous path in $\mathbb{R}^2 \setminus \mathcal{G}_{p\ell}$ ($\omega$; occupied). We repeat this process with $w_1$ in place of $v_1$. After a finite number of replacements we obtain a path $\rho$ on $\mathcal{M}_{p\ell} \setminus \mathcal{G}_{p\ell}$ ($\omega$; occupied), with possible double points, from $v_1$ to $v_2$. Since $\rho$ does not intersect $\mathcal{G}_{p\ell}$ ($\omega$; occupied) it contains only vacant vertices, and in particular no central vertices of $\mathcal{G}_{p\ell}$ (see (2.15)). Thus $\rho$ is a path with possible double points on $\mathcal{G}^*_{p\ell}$ ($\omega$; vacant). Loop-removal (see Sect. 2.1) from $\rho$ finally yields the required self-avoiding path on $\mathcal{G}^*_{p\ell}$ ($\omega$; vacant) from $v_1$ to $v_2$. □

Finally we prove a simple lemma which is used repeatedly, and which guarantees the existence of "periodic paths" resembling straight lines on periodic graphs.

Lemma A.3. Let $\mathcal{G}$ be a periodic graph imbedded in $\mathbb{R}^d$. Then for each $1 \leq i \leq d$ there exists a vertex $v_0 = (v_0(1),\dots,v_0(d))$ of $\mathcal{G}$ and a path $r_0 = (v_0,e_1,v_1,\dots,e_\sigma,v_\sigma)$ on $\mathcal{G}$ such that

(A.48) $$0 \leq v(j) < 1,\ 1 \leq j \leq d,$$

(A.49) $$v_\sigma = v_0+\alpha\xi_i \quad \text{for some integer } \alpha \geq 1$$

and

(A.50) for all $n \geq 1$ the path on $\mathcal{G}$ obtained by successively traversing $r_0+k\alpha\xi_i$, $k = 0,1,\dots,n$ is a self-avoiding path on $\mathcal{G}$ connecting $v_0$ with $v_0+(n+1)\alpha\xi_i$.

Proof: Let $w_0$ be any vertex of $\mathcal{G}$ and $r$ a path on $\mathcal{G}$ connecting $w_0$ with $w_0+\xi_i$. Then the path on $\mathcal{G}$ obtained by successively traversing $r+k\xi_i$, $k = 0,\dots,n$ connects $w_0$ with $w_0+(n+1)\xi_i$, but it may have double points. To get rid of the double points we choose $w_1$, $w_2$ on $r$ as follows. First let $\alpha$ be the maximal integer for which there exist vertices $w_1$, $w_2$ on $r$ with

(A.51) $$w_2 = w_1+\alpha\xi_i .$$

Since the endpoint of $r$, $w_0+\xi_i$, differs from the initial point of $r$ by $\xi_i$ we see that $\alpha \geq 1$. We now select a pair $w_1$, $w_2$ satisfying (A.51) and lying "as close together as possible", in the sense that there does not exist any pair of vertices $(w_3,w_4) \neq (w_1,w_2)$ on the segment of $r$ from $w_1$ to $w_2$ with $w_4 = w_3+\alpha\xi_i$. Denote the segment of $r$ from $w_1$ to $w_2$ by $s$. Let $\ell_1,\dots,\ell_d$ be the unique integers for which $w_0+\sum_1^d \ell_j\xi_j$ lies in the unit cube $[0,1)^d$. We claim that we can take $v_0 = w_0 + \sum_1^d \ell_j\xi_j$ and $r_0 = s + \sum_1^d \ell_j\xi_j$. Since $r$ is self-avoiding so is $s$ and by virtue of periodicity we only have to show that for any $k > 1$ $s$ and $s + k\alpha\xi_i$ cannot intersect, and that the only common point of $s$ and $s + \xi_i$ is $w_2 = w_1 + \alpha\xi_i$, the endpoint of $s$ and initial point of $s + \xi_i$. To see that this is indeed the case consider a vertex $w_4$ of $\mathcal{G}$ which lies on $s$ as well as on $s + k\alpha\xi_i$. Then $w_3:=w_4-k\alpha\xi_i$ also lies on $s$. By our definition of $\alpha$, this is possible only if $k = 1$. Moreover, if $k = 1$, by our choice of $(w_1,w_2)$ this is possible only if $w_3 = w_1$ and $w_4 = w_2$, as claimed. □

## REFERENCES

Aizenman, M. (1982) Geometric analysis of $\phi^4$ fields and Ising models, part III, to appear.

Aizenman, M., Delyon, F., and Souillard, B. (1980) Lower bounds on the cluster size distributions, J. Stat. Phys. 23, 267-280.

Aizenman, M. and Fröhlich, J. (1982) to appear.

Batty, C.J.K. and Bollman, H.W. (1980) Generalized Holley-Preston inequalities on measure spaces and their products, Z. Wahrsch. verw. Geb. 53, 157-173.

Bollobás, B. (1979) Graph theory. An introductory course, Springer Verlag.

Brånvall, G. (1980) A note on limit theorems in percolation, Z. Wahrsch. verw. Geb. 53, 317-328.

Breiman, L. (1968) Probability, Addison-Wesley Publ. Co.

Broadbent, S.R. (1954) In discussion of Symposium on Monte Carlo methods, J. Roy. Stat. Soc. (B) 16, 68.

Broadbent, S.R., and Hammersley, J.M. (1957) Percolation processes, Proc. Cambr. Phil. Soc. 53, 629-641 and 642-645.

Cox, J.T., and Grimmett, G. (1981) Central limit theorems for percolation models, J. Stat. Phys. 25, 237-251.

Delyon, F. (1980) Taille, forme et nombre des amas dans les problèmes de percolation, Thèse de 3$^{me}$ cycle, Université Pierre et Marie Curie, Paris.

Doyle, P., and Snell, J.L. (1982) Random walk and electric networks; Dartmouth College preprint.

Dunford, N. and Schwartz, J.T. (1958) Linear Operators, vol. I., Interscience Publishers.

Durrett, R. and Griffeath, D. (1983) Supercritical contact processes on $\mathbb{Z}$, Ann. Prob. 11.

Essam, J.W. (1972) Percolation and cluster size, pp. 197-270 in Phase transitions and critical phenomena, Vol. II, Domb, C. and Green, M.S. eds, Academic Press.

Essam, J.W. (1980) Percolation theory, Reports on Progress in Physics, 43, 833-912.

Feynman, R.P., Leighton, R.B., and Sands, M. (1963) The Feynman lectures on Physics, Vol. I-III, Addison-Wesley Publ. Co.

Fisher, M.E. (1961) Critical probabilities for cluster size and percolation problems, J. Math. Phys. 2, 620-627.

Fisher, M.E. and Essam, J.W. (1961) Some cluster size and percolation problems, J. Math. Phys. 2, 609-619.

Fortuin, C.M., Kasteleyn, P.W., and Ginibre, J. (1971) Correlation inequalities on some partially ordered sets, Comm. Math. Phys. 22, 89-103.

Freedman, D. (1973) Another note on the Borel-Cantelli lemma and the strong law, with the Poisson approximation as a by-product, Ann. Prob. 1, 910-925.

Frisch, H.L. and Hammersley, J.M. (1963) Percolation processes and related topics, J. Soc. Ind. Appl. Math. 11, 894-918.

Golden, K. and Papanicolaou, G. (1982) Bounds for effective parameters of heterogeneous media by analytic continuation, to appear in Comm. Pure. Appl. Math.

Griffeath, D. (1981) The basic contact processes, Stochastic Process. Appl. 11, 151-185.

Griffeath, D. and Liggett, T.M. (1983) Critical phenomena for Spitzer's reversible nearest particle systems, Ann. Prob. 11.

Grimmett, G.R. (1976) On the number of clusters in the percolation model, J. London Math. Soc. (2) 13, 346-350.

Grimmett, G.R. (1981) On the differentiablility of the number of clusters per vertex in the percolation model, J. London Math. Soc. (2) 23, 372-384.

Grimmett, G.R. and Kesten, H. (1982) First-passage percolation, network flows and electrical resistances, to appear.

Hammersley, J.M. (1957) Percolation processes. Lower bounds for the critical probability Ann. Math. Statist. 28, 790-795.

Hammersley, J.M. (1959) Bornes supérieures de la probabilité critique dans un processus de filtration, pp. 17-37 in Le calcul des probabilites et ses applications, CNRS, Paris.

Hammersley, J.M. (1961) Comparison of atom and bond percolation, J. Math. Phys. 2, 728-733.

Hammersley, J.M. (1980) A generalization of McDiarmid's theorem for mixed Bernoulli percolation, Proc. Cambr. Phil. Soc. 88, 167-170.

Hammersley, J.M. and Welsh, D.J.A. (1980) Percolation theory and its ramifications, Contemp. Phys. 21, 593-605.

Harris, T.E. (1960) A lower bound for the critical probability in a certain percolation process, Proc. Cambr. Phil. Soc. 56, 13-20.

Helms, L.L. (1969) Introduction to potential theory, Wiley-Interscience

Higuchi, Y. (1982) Coexistence of the infinite (*) clusters; a remark on the square lattice site percolation, Z. Wahrsch. verw. Geb.

Hille, E. (1959) Analytic function theory, Vol. I., Ginn and Co.

Hille, E. (1962) Analytic function theory, Vol. II., Ginn and Co.

Kasteleyn, P.W. and Fortuin, C.M. (1969) Phase transition in lattice systems with random local properties, Proc. Intern. Conf. Stat. Mech. Kyoto, 1968 = J. Phys. Soc. Japan 26, Supplement, 11-14.

Kesten, H. (1980a) The critical probability of bond percolation on the square lattice equals $\frac{1}{2}$, Comm. Math. Phys. 74, 41-59.

Kesten, H. (1980b) On the time constant and path length of first passage percolation, Adv. Appl. Prob. 12, 848-863.

Kesten, H. (1981) Analyticity properties and power law estimates of functions in percolation theory, 25, 717-756.

Kirkpatrick, S. (1978) Models of disordered materials, Course 5 in La matière mal condensée/Ill condensed matter, Les Houches, Session XXXI, R. Balian et al. eds. North Holland Publ. Co., 1979.

Kunz, H. and Souillard, B. (1978) Essential singularity in percolation problems and asymptotic behavior of cluster size distribution, J. Stat. Phys. 19, 77-106.

McDiarmid, C. (1980) Clutter percolation and random graphs, Math. Progr. Study 13, 17-25.

Milton, G.W. (1981) Bounds on the complex permittivity of a two-component composite material, J. Appl. Phys. 52, 5286-5293 (see also pp. 5294-5304).

Nerode, A. and Shank, H. (1961) An algebraic proof of Kirchhoff's network theorem, Amer. Math. Monthly 68, 244-247.

Newman, C.M. (1980) Normal fluctuations and the FKG inequalities, Comm. Math. Phys. 74, 119-128.

Newman, C.M., and Schulman, L.S. (1981) Infinite clusters in percolation models, J. Stat. Phys. 26, 613-628 (see also J. Phys. A: Math. Gen. 14 (1981) 1735-1743).

Newman, C.M. and Wright, A.L. (1981) An invariance principle for certain dependent sequences, Ann. Prob. 9, 671-675.

Newman, M.H.A. (1951) Elements of the topology of plane sets of points, 2nd ed., Cambridge Univ. Press.

Oxley, J.G. and Welsh, D.J.A. (1979) On some percolation results of J.M. Hammersley, J. Appl. Prob. 16, 526-540.

Papanicolaou, G.C. and Varadhan, S.R.S. (1979) Boundary value problems with rapidly oscillating random coefficients, pp. 835-873 in Colloquia Math. Soc. János Bolyai 27. Random fields, Esztergom (Hungary) North-Holland Publ. Co.

Renyi, A. (1970) Probability theory, North Holland/American Elsevier.

Rudin, W. (1966) Real and complex analysis, McGraw-Hill Book Co.

Russo, L.(1978) A note on percolation, Z. Wahrsch. verw. Geb. 43, 39-48.

Russo, L. (1981) On the critical percolation probabilities, Z. Wahrsch. verw. Geb. 56, 229-237.

Russo, L. (1982) An approximate zero-one law, Z. Wahrsch. verw. Geb.

Seymour, P.D. and Welsh, D.J.A. (1978) Peroclation probabilities on the square lattice, Ann. Discrete Math. 3, 227-245.

Slepian, P. (1968) Mathematical foundations of network analysis, Springer-Verlag.

Smythe, R.T. and Wierman, J.C. (1978) First-passage percolation on the square lattice, Lecture notes in Mathematics, Vol. 671, Springer-Verlag.

Stauffer, D. (1979) Scaling theory of percolation clusters, Phys. Reports 54, No. 1, 1-74.

Straley, J.P. (1977) Critical exponents for the conductivity of random resistor lattice,s Phys. Rev. B 15, 5733-5737.

Sykes, M.F. and Essam, J.W. (1964) Exact critical percolation probabilities for site and bond problems in two dimensions, J. Math. Phys. 5, 1117-1127.

Tempel'man, A.A. (1972) Ergodic theorems for general dynamical systems, Trans. Moscow. Math. Soc. 26, 94-132.

Van der Berg, J. (1981) Percolation theory on pairs of matching lattices, J. Math. Phys. 22, 152-157.

Vasil'ev, N.B. (1970) Correlation equations for the stationary measure of a Markov chain, Theory Probab. Appl. 15, 521-525.

Walters, P. (1982) An introduction to ergodic theory, Springer-Verlag.

Whitney, H. (1932) Non-separable and planar graphs, Trans. Amer. Math. Soc. 34, 339-362.

Whitney, H. (1933) Planar graphs, Fund. Math. 21, 73-84.

Wierman, J.C. (1978) On critical probabilities in percolation theory, J. Math. Phys. 19, 1979-1982.

Wierman, J.C. (1981) Bond percolation on honeycomb and triangular lattices, Adv. Appl. Prob. 13, 293-313.

Wierman, J.C. (1982a) Percolation theory, Ann. Prob. 10 , 509-524.

Wierman, J.C. (1982b) Duality in mixed percolation models, Abstract 180-27 in Bull. Inst. Math. Statist. 11, 149.

AUTHOR INDEX

SUBJECT INDEX

# INDEX OF SYMBOLS

## General notation.

| | |
|---|---|
| $A := B$ | means that $A$ is defined by $B$ |
| $\mathring{A}$ | interior of $A$. When $A$ is a subset of $\mathbb{R}^d$ this has the usual meaning. When $A$ is an edge of a graph or an arc in $\mathbb{R}^d$ we also use $\mathring{A}$ to denote $A$ minuts its endpoints. |
| $\mathrm{Fr}(A)$ | Topological boundary of $A$ |
| $\overline{A}$ | closure of $A$. If $A$ is a Jordan curve in the plane we also use $\overline{A}$ to denote $A \cup \mathrm{int}(A)$. |
| $\partial A$ | boundary on a graph of a set $A$ in the graph (see p.29). |
| $\partial_{ext} A$ | exterior boundary on a graph of a set $A$ in the graph (see p.387). |
| $\#A$ | number of vertices in $A$ (on rare occasions $\#A$ denotes the number of edges in $A$). |
| $A \setminus B$ | the set of points in $A$ but outside $B$. |
| $\xi_i$ | i-th coordinate vector |
| $\overline{0}$ | zero vector |
| $\overline{1}$ | vector of all ones |
| $p_1 >> p_2$ | $p_1(i) > p_2(i)$, $1 \le i \le d$, for two d-vectors $p_1$ and $p_2$. |
| $[a(1),b(1)]\times\dots\times[a(d),b(d)] = \Pi[a(i),b(i)]$ | Cartesian product of the intervals $[a(i),b(i)]$, i.e., $\{x \in \mathbb{R}^d : a(i) \le x(i) \le b(i),\ 1 \le i \le d\}$ . |
| $\{a\} \times [b(1),b(2)]$ | the vertical line segment $\{x \in \mathbb{R}^2 : x(1) = a,\ b(1) \le x(2) \le b(2)\}$. $[b(1),b(2)] \times \{a\}$ denotes a horizontal line segment. |
| $a \wedge b$ | $\min(a,b)$ for real numbers $a$, $b$ |
| $a \vee b$ | $\max(a,b)$ for real numbers $a$, $b$ |
| $\lfloor a \rfloor$ | largest integer $\le a$ |
| $\lceil a \rceil$ | smallest integer $\ge a$ |
| $v \mathcal{G} w$ | $v$ and $w$ are adjacent vertices on $\mathcal{G}$ |
| /// | denotes the end of a Comment, Remark, or Problem. |

## Probability notation.

| | |
|---|---|
| $I[E]$ | indicator function of the event $E$ |
| $P\{E\}$ | probability of $E$ |

| | |
|---|---|
| $P\{E\|F\}$ | conditional probability of E, given F (for an event F) |
| $P\{E\|\mathfrak{F}\}$ | conditional probability of E, given $\mathfrak{F}$ (for a $\sigma$-field $\mathfrak{F}$). |
| $E\{X\}$ | expectation of the random variable X with respect to P (subscripts on E correspond to the same subscripts on P). |
| $E\{X;F\}$ | $E\{XI[F]\}$ = integral of X over F with respect to the probability measure |
| $E\{X\|F\}$ | conditional expectation of X given F (for an event F) |
| $E\{X\|\mathfrak{F}\}$ | conditional expectation of X given $\mathfrak{F}$ (for a $\sigma$-field $\mathfrak{F}$). |

Special symbols.

We list here the numbers of the pages where some symbols which are used in the same meaning throughout the book are defined.